COMPLETE GUIDE TO
SECURITY AND
PRIVACY METRICS

COMPLETE GUIDE TO SECURITY AND PRIVACY METRICS

Measuring Regulatory Compliance,
Operational Resilience, and ROI

Debra S. Herrmann

Auerbach Publications
Taylor & Francis Group
Boca Raton   New York

Auerbach Publications is an imprint of the
Taylor & Francis Group, an informa business

Disclosure: The views and opinions expressed are those of the author and not necessarily those of her employers.

Auerbach Publications
Taylor & Francis Group
6000 Broken Sound Parkway NW, Suite 300
Boca Raton, FL 33487-2742

© 2007 by Taylor & Francis Group, LLC
Auerbach is an imprint of Taylor & Francis Group, an Informa business

No claim to original U.S. Government works
Printed in the United States of America on acid-free paper
10 9 8 7 6 5 4 3 2 1

International Standard Book Number-10: 0-8493-5402-1 (Hardcover)
International Standard Book Number-13: 978-0-8493-5402-1 (Hardcover)

Library of Congress Cataloging-in-Publication Data

Herrmann, Debra S.
   Complete guide to security and privacy metrics / Debra S. Herrmann.
     p. cm.
   Includes bibliographical references and index.
   ISBN 0-8493-5402-1 (alk. paper)
   1. Telecommunication--Security measures--Evaluation. 2. Computer security--Evaluation. 3. Public records--Access control--Evaluation. 4. Computer crimes--Prevention--Measurement. I. Title.

TK5102.85.H4685 2007
005.8--dc22
                                          2006048710

Visit the Taylor & Francis Web site at
http://www.taylorandfrancis.com

and the Auerbach Web site at
http://www.auerbach-publications.com

Dedication

To Lilac, Slate, and Tzvi

Debra S. Herrmann

Contents

List of Tables

List of Figures

Other Books by the Author

Using the Common Criteria for IT Security Evaluation, Auerbach Publications (2003)

A Practical Guide to Security Engineering and Information Assurance, Auerbach Publications (2001)

Software Safety and Reliability: Techniques, Approaches and Standards of Key Industrial Sectors, IEEE Computer Society Press (1999)

About the Author

Debra Herrmann has more than 20 years of experience in software safety, software reliability, and security engineering in industry and the defense/intelligence community, beginning before the *Orange Book* was issued. Currently she is the Technical Advisor for Information Security and Software Safety for the U.S. Federal Aviation Administration. In this capacity she leads research initiatives to identify engineering best practices to reduce the time and cost to certify and deploy systems, while at the same time increasing confidence in the security and integrity of those systems. Previously she was the ITT Manager of Security Engineering for the $1.78B FAA Telecommunications Infrastructure Program, one of the first programs to apply the Common Criteria for IT Security Evaluation to a nationwide safety-critical WAN. She has published several articles and three other books, each the first full-length book to be published on that topic. Debra has been active in the international standards community for many years, serving as the U.S. Government representative to International Electrotechnical Commission (IEC) software safety standards committees, Chair of the Society of Aerospace Engineers (SAE) subcommittee that issued the JA 1002 software reliability engineering standard, and member of the IEEE Software Engineering Standards balloting pool. She teaches graduate and undergraduate computer science courses and is a frequent invited guest speaker at conferences.

Chapter 1

Introduction

> It is an undisputed statement that measurement is crucial to the progress of all societies.
>
> —S.H. Kan[174]

1.1 Background

Until the late 1970s, a student attending a university could not even obtain a copy of his own transcript. A student could request that a copy of his official transcript be sent to another university, but that was all. Credit cards were hardly used. Instead, each retailer maintained separate accounts for each customer. Merchandise for which cash was not paid was taken out "on approval" or "put on lay away." Medical records were typed on manual typewriters (or if the typist was fortunate, an electric typewriter) and manually filed. Medical records rarely left the building or office in which they were created. Ironically, social security numbers were used for collecting social security taxes, federal income taxes, and state income taxes. There was not anything equivalent to nationwide credit reporting services that anyone could access. Instead, local banks and businesses "knew" who paid their bills on time and who did not; local bill collectors were sent out to motivate the latter. Direct deposit meant a person took his paycheck directly to the bank on payday. Identity theft meant someone's checkbook had been stolen. Computers were a monstrosity of spinning tape drives and card readers that took up the entire basement of a building — they were too heavy to put anywhere else. Networks connected dumb terminals in the same building or nearby to the computer in the basement. For special operations there were remote job entry (RJE) stations where punch cards could be read in from a distance at the lightning speed of 2400 or maybe 4800 baud if one was lucky. Telephone conversations were carried over analog lines; when the receiver was hung up, that was the end of it. Voice mail did not exist, and telephone messages were recorded on paper. Desktop telephones did not keep lists of calls received, calls placed, and the duration of each. Conversations were not recorded by employers or other busybodies — unless a person was on the FBI's ten most wanted list and then special permits had to be obtained beforehand. Friends did not anonymously tape record conversations with "friends" or surreptitiously snap photographs of "friends" or total strangers from their cell phones. Car phones did not appear until the 1980s. Data networks were separate from voice networks — it did not make any sense to combine them — and satellites were just beginning to become commercially viable. While large IBM clusters supported an interactive "talk" capability within an organization, e-mail as we know it was a long ways off. Information security and privacy issues were simple. All that was needed was good physical security controls and perhaps a little link layer bulk encryption here and there.

Despite this state of affairs, two organizations had the foresight to see (1) the forthcoming information security and privacy pandemic, and (2) the need for an epidemiological approach (looking across the entire population of systems and networks) versus a pathological approach (looking at a single system or network) to, if not solve, at least stay on top of the information security and privacy pandemic. These two organizations were the Organization for Economic Cooperation and Development (OECD), to which 29 countries belong, including the United States, and the U.S. Department of Health, Education and Welfare (HEW).

The OECD had the foresight to see the need for security and privacy regulations almost two decades before most organizations or individuals were aware of the dark side of the digital age. The OECD Privacy Guidelines (issued September 23, 1980) apply to any personal data that is in the public or private sector for which manual or automated processing or the nature of the intended use presents a potential "danger to the privacy of individual liberties."[69] It is assumed that diverse protection mechanisms, both technical and operational, will be needed, depending on the different types of personal data; the various processing, storage, collection, and dissemination methods; and the assorted usage scenarios. The Guidelines are presented in eight principles and make it clear that the principles presented are considered the minimum acceptable standard of protection:

- *Collection Limitation Principle.* The volume and type of personal information collected is limited to the minimum needed for the stated purpose.
- *Data Quality Principle.* Organizations that collect and disseminate information are responsible for ensuring that the information is current, complete, and accurate.
- *Purpose Specification Principle.* Individuals must be informed beforehand of the uses to which the personal information being collected will be put.
- *Use Limitation Principle.* Personal information can only be used for the stated purpose given at the time the information was collected; individuals must be informed and give their consent before personal information can be used for any new purpose.

- *Security Safeguards Principle.* Organizations are responsible for employing appropriate physical, personnel, IT, and operational security controls to protect personal information.
- *Openness Principle.* Organizations are responsible for keeping individuals informed about what personal information they hold and their rights to view the information.
- *Individual Participation Principle.* Individuals have the right to challenge the accuracy of personal information held by an organization and insist that inaccuracies be corrected
- *Accountability Principle.* Organizations holding personal information are held accountable for complying with these principles and must designate an official as the senior accountable official within their organization.

Two events that occurred almost a decade before the passage of the Privacy Act in 1974 marked the beginning of interest in privacy matters in the United States. The House of Representatives held a series of hearings on issues related to the invasion of personal privacy. At the same time the Department of Health, Education and Welfare* (HEW) issued a report entitled "Records, Computers, and the Rights of Citizens." This report recommended a "Code of Fair Information Practices" that consisted of five key principles[125]:

1. There must be no data record-keeping systems whose very existence is secret.
2. There must be a way for an individual to find out what information about him is kept in a record and how it is used.
3. There must be a way for an individual to prevent information about him obtained for one purpose from being used or made available for other purposes without his consent.
4. There must be a way for an individual to correct or amend a record of identifiable information about him.
5. Any organization creating, maintaining, using, or disseminating records of identifiable personal data must assure the reliability of the data for their intended use and must take reasonable precautions to prevent misuse of the data.

So what prompted the concern about the privacy of electronic data? The answer lies with the agency that issued the report — HEW. During the 1960s, HEW became responsible for implementing a series of legislation related to social security benefits, food stamps, welfare, aid to dependent children, loans for college students, etc. To do so, they needed to collect, validate, and compare a lot of personal information, such as name, social security number, date of birth, place of birth, address, marital status, number of children, employment, income, and the like — information that most people would

---

* HEW was later split into three cabinet level agencies: the Department of Health and Human Services (HHS), the Department of Education (ED), and the Social Security Administration (SSA).

consider private. HEW felt an obligation to keep this information under wraps. At the same time they were responsible for preventing fraud — welfare payments to people above the minimum income level, social security payments to deceased individuals, food stamps to college students who just did not feel like working, defaulting on student loans that could have been paid, etc. Different organizations within HEW collected the information for the various entitlement programs and stored it on separate computer systems. Before long, HEW began what is referred to as "matching programs"; they compared data collected for one entitlement program with the data supplied for another to discern any discrepancies that might indicate fraud. Soon, personal information was shared across multiple federal agencies, not just within HEW, and all sorts of "matching programs" were under way, especially for law enforcement and so-called "historical research." The fear expressed in the 1930s that social security numbers would become social surveillance numbers was becoming real. Fortunately, a few people had the foresight to see what a Pandora's box had been opened in relation to the privacy of personal data, and there was a push to create some protections at the federal level. Hence the HEW report and the Congressional hearings.

Times have changed. Since then, the world has become a pantheon of dynamically connected, wired and wireless, computers and networks. As a result, the predictions, insights, and goals espoused by these two visionary organizations have become all the more urgent, serious, and crucial with each passing year.

1.2 Purpose

Contrary to popular lore, security engineering is not new. Physical and personnel security have been around in various forms for centuries. IT and operational security have been practiced since the beginning of the computer age in the 1940s. However, what is difficult to understand is how IT and operational security could have existed for so many decades without metrics. Yes, there were metrics to estimate the strength of the blast it would take to blow the concrete door off the entrance to the computer center and metrics to estimate how long it would take to crack an encryption algorithm, but that was about it.

It is a well-known fact that it is nearly impossible to manage, monitor, control, or improve anything without measuring it.[57, 137, 138, 174] If a company does not continually measure its profits and losses, and revenue and expenditures, it will go out of business. Delivery services are measured by their ability to deliver packages on time and intact. Airlines are measured by their safety record and their rate of on-time arrivals and on-time departures. Statistical process control is used to measure the productivity of manufacturing plants (the people, processes, and equipment) and find areas that can be improved. The reliability and performance of all sorts of mechanical, electromechanical, and electronic equipment is measured to see if it is performing according to specification, what the maximum and minimum tolerances are, and whether it needs to be calibrated, repaired, or replaced. The performance of telecommunications networks is continually monitored in terms of throughput, capacity, and availability. Why should it be any different for security engineering?

During the 1970s, most computer science majors were required to take a course titled "Computers and Society." People then were not as into "touchy-feely" things as they are today. Still, among a few enlightened souls, there was a nagging feeling that perhaps there was a down side to collecting vast amounts of information, storing the information on permanent media, and freely exchanging the information with others. They were right. We now live in an age that is spiraling toward the potential for total electronic surveillance, which causes some to question whether privacy should be added to the endangered species list. Automated teller machine (ATM) cards, credit cards, and debit cards leave an electronic trail of where a person was at a specific time and what they purchased. Cell phone usage can be tracked through the use of global positioning system (GPS) satellites. Automobile anti-theft devices can be used to track the location of a vehicle, as can the "easy passes" used to automatically pay highway tolls. Recently, a suggestion was made in the Washington, D.C. area to automatically distribute information about major traffic congestion and alternate routes to drivers in the vicinity via their cell phones. How could that be accomplished unless the sender knew where the person, his vehicle, and cell phone were at any given moment? Radio frequency identification (RFID) tags are being embedded in passports, drivers' licenses, subway smart-cards, and employee badges. Frequently, way more personal information than necessary to accomplish the stated purpose is being embedded in the RFID tags, which can be read at any time with or without the owner's knowledge or consent. RFID tags can also be used to capture a complete chronology of where the holder was at any point in time. E-mail and Internet usage privacy are as nonexistent as the privacy of telephone conversations and voice mail. In the spring of 2006, the news media was abuzz with stories of cell phone companies selling subscriber calling records and Internet service providers being subpoenaed to provide the names of subscribers who accessed pornographic Web sites and the frequency with which they were accessed. Electronic information about financial transactions (what was purchased, where it was purchased, when it was purchased, deposits and withdrawals from accounts, etc.) is everywhere — not to mention pervasive video surveillance by retailers and law enforcement. In short, it is nearly possible to know, 24/7, where a person is or was, what he is or was doing, and what he is saying or has said. "1984" has arrived but "Big Brother" is not watching. Instead, a host of overlapping, competing, and sometimes warring "Big Brothers" are watching and listening.

The arrival of the age of total electronic surveillance coincides with a geometric increase in identity theft and other cyber crime. Weekly, if not daily, new announcements are made in the news media of yet another break-in, a "misplaced" tape or laptop, or the theft of thousands of individuals' personal information in a single heist. The individuals responsible for the heist may or may not be prosecuted. The organization whose negligence allowed the attack to succeed is fined by the appropriate regulatory authority and subjected to negative publicity, and the thousands of victims are left to fend for themselves. In January 2006, ChoicePoint, Inc. was fined $10 million by the Federal Trade Commission as the result of one of the first high-profile identity theft cases in which the personal information of 160,000 people was stolen. In addition, ChoicePoint, Inc. agreed to submit to independent security audits for the next 20 years. Sometimes the victims are notified immediately; other times they do not find out until after severe damage has been done. On average, it has been reported that it takes each person approximately six months and $6000 to recover from identity theft, not accounting for the sheer frustration, aggravation, and inconvenience. Some cases are not recoverable. Suppose wrong information gets out into cyberspace, such as inaccurate medical, employment, or legal records, which can lead to employment and other forms of discrimination. Such information can be extremely damaging and follow a person around for years. The corporate world agrees. In the summer of 2006 twelve companies, including Google, eBay, Hewlett-Packard, Microsoft, Intel, Eastman Kodak, Eli Lilly, and Procter & Gamble, formed the Consumer Privacy Legislative Forum to lobby for stronger federal regulations to protect consumer privacy.[313]

Attempts have been made to create so-called "safe harbor" legislation to absolve companies of any liability for the negligence that allowed personal information to be stolen. The underlying premise seems to be that security engineering is some opaque mystical force against which companies are helpless. In fact, this perception could not be further from the truth. All of the recent major heists have used very low-tech methods — something a security engineering 101 graduate should have been able to prevent. Several of the high-publicity incidents involved insider collusion. Instead of absolution, rigorous enforcement of the security and privacy regulations discussed in Chapter 3 is needed, along with a requirement to submit security and privacy metrics as evidence of due diligence. It all goes back to the fact that it is not possible to manage, monitor, control, or improve security engineering unless the effectiveness of these features, functions, policies, procedures, and practices is continually measured.

There has been a fair amount of discussion and debate about the cost of compliance with security and privacy regulations, in particular the Sarbanes-Oxley Act. However, looking at the numbers, it is difficult to empathize with this weeping, wailing, and gnashing of teeth. In a survey of 217 companies with average annual revenues of $5 billion, the average one-time start-up cost of compliance was $4.26 million,[171, 244] or 0.0852 percent of the annual revenue. The annual cost to maintain compliance was less. This is a small price to pay to protect employees, pensioners, shareholders, and creditors, not to mention the company's reputation. Furthermore, $4.26 million is peanuts compared to the losses incurred when a corporation such as Enron, WorldCom, or Tyco crashes. The WorldCom fraud was estimated to be $11 billion. It is difficult to come up with a valid reason why a corporate board would not want to make such a small investment to ensure that its financial house is in order. Thousands of people lost their jobs, pensions, and investments due to the lack of robust security regulations such as the Sarbanes-Oxley Act. Taxpayers pick up the cost of investigating and prosecuting cases of corporate fraud. The corporations and their business partners (or what is left of them) had to pay rather stiff fines. Tyco settled for $134 million in restitution and $105 million in fines. The Enron settlement was a record $6.1 billion.[263]

Security engineering is the gold rush of the 21st century. As with any gold rush, there are the usual con men, shysters, and imposters scattered among the honest folk who are just trying to do their jobs. No other engineering discipline has been so equally duped. It is difficult to imagine reliability engineers and safety engineers falling into the trap of always buying the latest and greatest black box, without any engineering metrics to substantiate advertising claims, simply because a salesman told them to do so. The situation is analogous to a very competitive digital fashion fad, except that most of the fads are little more than digital placebos when it comes to security. How did security engineering get into this state of affairs? Part of the answer has to do with competence, which by the way is a personnel security issue. (See Chapter 4, Section 4.3.) Many people have inherited, almost overnight, significant security responsibilities without having the necessary knowledge, skills, or experience. They are very conscientious and trying very hard but are caught in a perpetual game of catch-up and on-the-job training, which is fertile ground for unscrupulous salesmen. However, the larger part of the problem centers around funding. Wherever there is a significant challenge to overcome, the instant solution seems to be to throw a lot of money at it. That approach is certainly easier than doing the in-depth engineering analysis needed to solve the problem, but it is hardly productive. Following 9/11, grants and loans were available from the federal government to rebuild businesses that had been impacted. An audit three years later found that more than half the funds had been given to businesses outside the state of New York. Following the devastation of Hurricane Katrina, federal money flowed into New Orleans. An audit conducted weeks later showed that, instead of being used to rebuild the city's infrastructure or homes, the funds were spent on housing disaster workers on expensive cruise ships. The Department of Homeland Security, created in a flurry of activity following 9/11, has been in the news frequently for one contracting fraud after another where millions of dollars were spent with nothing to show for it. Throwing money at problems does not solve them and in the end usually about 90 percent of the money is wasted. More money does not make IT infrastructures more secure; good security engineering, backed up by metrics, does. If an organization is in search of practical, workable IT and operational security solutions, it should cut the budget in half. That will force some creative problem solving, and the staff will actually get a chance to do some real security engineering for a change.

Many diverse organizations, from opponents of outsourcing to the U.S. National Security Agency (NSA), have called for the use of security metrics as a means to enforce the quality of protection provided, similar to service level agreements, which are a standard part of telecommunications contracts. The need for a comprehensive set of security and privacy metrics is well understood and has been acknowledged in several high-level publications over the past five years, including:

- "Federal Plan for Cyber Security and Information Assurance Research and Development," issued by the National Science and Technology Council of the Executive Office of the President, April 2006, stated that security metrics are needed to: (a) determine the effectiveness of security processes, products, and solutions, (b) improve security accountability, and (c) make well informed risk-based IT security investments.
- The Committee on National Security Systems (CNSS) 2006 Annual Conference identified the need for an effective definition of what success looks like regarding security and a meaningful way to measure it. The CNSS stated further that efforts to monitor compliance and enforce policies become more meaningful because they measure how far along departments and agencies are in achieving success.
- The INFOSEC Research Council Hard Problem List (November 2005) identified "enterprise-level security metrics" as being among the top-eight security research priorities.
- Cyber Security: A Crisis of Prioritization, President's IT Advisory Committee (February 2005), identified security metrics as being among the top-ten security research priorities.
- IT for Counterterrorism: Immediate Actions, Future Possibilities (National Research Council, 2003) identified the need to develop meaningful security metrics.
- Making the Nation Safer: The Role of Science and Technology in Countering Terrorism (National Research Council, 2002) highlighted the need for security metrics to evaluate the effectiveness of IT security measures.

At this point the need for security and privacy metrics is widely acknowledged. What is needed now is for organizations to start using metrics. To paraphrase a major retailer, "Security metrics — just use them!"

While extremely important, the definition of security and privacy metrics is not an intractable problem — nor is it a problem that requires millions of research and development dollars to solve. (If it did, this book would not be selling for around $100!) Instead, what is needed is the ability to "think outside of the box" and a willingness to learn from the experiences of parallel disciplines, such as safety engineering, reliability engineering, and software engineering. These three disciplines have made extensive use of metrics, in some cases for decades. It is difficult to measure the distance to another planet or galaxy but we do that without using a tape measure. How is the resilience of anything measured? Some positive measurements are taken (indicating the presence of resilience), some negative measurements are taken (indicating the absence of resilience), a confidence level is applied to the two sets of measurements, and they are correlated to derive the resilience. The process is no different for security and privacy metrics.

The high-tech industry has been wandering in the wilderness for years when it comes to IT security metrics. Some false prophets have declared that return on investment (ROI) metrics represent the true manifestation of IT security metrics. Other equally misguided oracles have latched onto statistics emanating from intrusion detection system (IDS) logs as the divine truth. A third group seeks an epiphany from monolithic high-level process metrics, while the remainder await divine revelation from the latest and greatest whiz-bang gizmo their anointed salesman guided them (like sheep) to buy. Jelen describes this situation quite aptly[169]:

You have to know what "it" is before you can measure it!

The problem is that many people, in all types of organizations and at all levels within an organization, have a vague, distorted, incomplete, fragmented, or microscopic understanding of IT security. Compounding the problem is the fact that most of these people are unaware of their knowledge gap, due to the barrage of misinformation from the general media and overzealous salesmen. Hence the difficulty the industry has had in developing useful IT security metrics. In essence, the right questions must be asked, and the correct security attributes must be measured.[169] That is why, instead of just jumping into a list of metrics, Chapters 3 through 5 start with a discussion of each topic and the particular security and privacy issues involved. Afterward, items are identified that should be measured and an explanation is provided of how to measure them.

One factor that contributed to the delay in the development of security metrics is the confidentiality, integrity, and availability (CIA) model. To be blunt, this model is overly simplistic. It ignores the extensive interaction among all four security engineering domains: physical security, personnel security, IT security, and operational security. This model also ignores several topics that are crucial in achieving and sustaining a robust security posture enterprisewide. In contrast, this book approaches metrics from a holistic view that encompasses all four security engineering domains. Furthermore, IT security is viewed from the perspective of an IT security control system and an IT security protection system, which together are composed of sixteen elements, not just the three in the CIA model. This broader perspective is essential because attackers will find and exploit the weakest link, whether it is physical security, personnel security, IT security, or operational security, such as inadequate resource management.

Security and privacy metrics should not be thought of as four or five magic numbers that will convey everything an organization needs to know about the robustness of its IT infrastructure. There are no such magic metrics and there never will be. Rather, metrics should be thought of in terms of medical tests. During an annual physical, a series of standardized tests is performed. A physician does not just take someone's blood pressure or weight to determine if she is healthy. Instead, tests are conducted to evaluate the performance of all organs, systems, and structures. Should a particular test show abnormalities, more in-depth metrics are collected in that area. Then an overall assessment is made. A similar process is followed during the use and interpretation of security and privacy metrics because ultimately what counts is that the enterprise is secure, not just a single router or server.

A word of caution is in order about the collection and use of metrics. It is essential to understand up front what a metric does and does not measure. Unwarranted enthusiasm or short-sightedness can lead to drawing the wrong conclusion from metric results. To illustrate, it is a reasonably established fact that 25 percent of aviation accidents occur during take-off. Another 25 percent of aviation accidents occur during landing. One could conclude that 50 percent of aviation accidents would be eliminated by suspending take-offs and land-ings! (Actually, 100 percent of aviation accidents would be eliminated because no one would by flying...)

1.3 Scope

Note that the title of this book is *Complete Guide to Security and Privacy Metrics: Measuring Regulatory Compliance, Operational Resilience, and ROI.* Rather than being limited to just IT security, this book covers all four security engineering domains: physical security, personnel security, IT security, and operational security. The simple truth is that IT security cannot be accom-plished in a vacuum, because there are a multitude of dependencies and interactions among all four security engineering domains. Security engineering terms are frequently misused. Just to make sure everyone has a clear under-standing of what these four domains are, let us quickly review their definitions. *Physical security* refers to the protection of hardware, software, and data against physical threats, to reduce or prevent disruptions to operations and services and loss of assets.[156] *Personnel security* is a variety of ongoing measures undertaken to reduce the likelihood and severity of accidental and intentional alteration, destruction, misappropriation, misuse, misconfiguration, unauthorized distribution, and unavailability of an organization's logical and physical assets, as the result of action or inaction by insiders and known outsiders, such as business partners. *IT security* is the inherent technical features and functions that collectively contribute to an IT infrastructure achieving and sustaining confidentiality, integrity, availability, accountability, authenticity, and reliability. *Operational security* involves the implementation of standard operational security procedures that define the nature and fre-quency of the interaction between users, systems, and system resources, the purpose of which is to (1) achieve and sustain a known secure system state at all times, and (2) prevent accidental or intentional theft, release, destruction, alteration, misuse, or sabotage of system resources.[156]

This book also focuses on privacy, a topic that is not well understood. Privacy is a precursor to freedom. Where there is no privacy, there can be no freedom. Identity theft is perhaps the most well-known and well-publicized example of a violation of privacy. Privacy is a legal right, not an engineering discipline. That is why organizations have privacy officers — not privacy engineers. Security engineering is the discipline used to ensure that privacy rights are protected to the extent specified by law and organizational policy. Privacy is not an automatic outcome of security engineering. Like any other security feature or function, privacy requirements must be specified, designed, implemented, and verified to the integrity level needed. There are several legal aspects to privacy rights. People living in the United States and other countries have a basic legal right to privacy. That means that their personal life and how they live it remains a private, not public, matter. The right to privacy is protected by privacy laws. Although the exact provisions of privacy laws in each country differ, the common ground is restricting access to private residences and property, personnel information, and personal communications. The intent is to prevent harassment and unwarranted publicity. The laws provide legal remedies should privacy rights be violated. A person's privacy is considered to have been invaded when his persona is exploited or private matters are made public without his consent. Usually this is done with the intent of causing personal, professional, or financial harm. Whenever a breach of privacy or invasion of privacy occurs, the victim has the right to pursue a legal remedy based on the contents of the applicable privacy laws and regulations. Both the individuals and the organization(s) responsible for the privacy violation can be prosecuted. A variety of laws and regulations have been enacted to protect privacy rights in the digital age, as discussed in Chapter 3. Privacy rights extend to personal data, which is understood to mean *any* information relating to an identified or identifiable individual.[69] Personal data includes financial, medical, scholastic, employment, demographic, and other information, such as purchasing habits, calling records, e-mail, and phone conversations, whether it is in the public or private sector. The mere fact that this information is available in electronic form presents a potential danger to the privacy of individual liberties.[69] This is true due to the potential for malicious misuse of the information, which could have a serious negative economic or social impact to the individuals involved. Hence the genesis of the enactment and enforcement of robust privacy legislation worldwide.

The essence of security engineering is anticipating what can go wrong, then taking appropriate steps to prevent or preempt such occurrences. If it is 10°F outside, most people can tell from the thermometer that they need to wear a hat, coat, and gloves. They do not wait until their "IDS" tells them they have pneumonia to decide if it would have been a good idea to wear a hat, coat, and gloves. Metrics provide the information an organization needs to be prepared to prevent cyber crime by establishing a quantitative basis for measuring security. Note also that this book uses the term "IT security" rather than cyber security. That is done deliberately. IT security is a much broader topic than cyber security. Conversely, cyber security is a subset of IT security. Information must be handled securely at all times, not just when it is traversing the public Internet. Systems and networks must be protected from all types and sources of attacks, not just those originating from the public Internet.

While others have limited their scope to attack data and IDS logs, this book encompasses the full spectrum of security and privacy metrics. IDS logs and attack data tell what *other* people have been doing. An organization needs to know how well *it* has implemented security controls to protect the IT infrastructure. The metrics presented in this book are technology and platform independent; they cover the entire security engineering life cycle from the initial concept through decommissioning. The metrics are appropriate for any application domain and industrial sector. The metrics are applicable to a single product, system, or network *and* an entire facility, region, or enterprise. The metrics provide useful insights for first-level technical support staff and all the way up to the Chief Information Officer (CIO), Chief Security Officer (CSO), Chief Information Security Officer (CISO), and corporate suite. Auditors and regulatory affairs specialists will feel right at home with these metrics also. Individual metrics can be used stand-alone, or several different metrics can be combined to obtain a comprehensive view or investigate a cross-cutting issue.

Three major categories of metrics are defined:

1. *Compliance metrics:* metrics that measure compliance with current security and privacy regulations and standards, such as the Health Information Portability and Accountability Act (HIPAA), Sarbanes-Oxley (SOX), Graham-Leach-Bliley (GLB), Federal Information Security Management Act (FISMA), the Privacy Act, and the OECD Security and Privacy Guidelines.
2. *Resilience metrics:* metrics that measure the resilience of physical security controls, personnel security controls, IT security controls, and operational security controls before and after a product, system, or network is deployed.
3. *Return on investment (ROI) metrics:* metrics that measure the ROI in physical security controls, personnel security controls, IT security controls, and operational security controls to guide IT capital investments.

1.4 How to Get the Most Out of This Book

For the first time, this book collects over 900 security and privacy metrics in one place. Just as you do not use every word in a natural language dictionary when writing a sentence, paragraph, or report, only the metrics needed to answer a particular question are used at any given time. No organization should attempt or even could implement all of these metrics and still accomplish its mission or return a profit. Rather, this collection should be considered like a menu from which to pick and choose metrics that will be meaningful to your organization; most likely, the metrics considered useful will change over time due to a variety of factors. Often, there are subtle differences in the way the data is analyzed and presented from one metric to the next in the same category. It is up to you to decide which are the appetizers, entrees, and desserts, and whether you want the low-salt or spicy version. An inventory of the security and privacy metrics presented in this book is given in Table 1.1. Special effort was expended to ensure that these metrics would be accessible and usable by the largest population possible. The intent was to avoid the limitations associated with many software engineering reliability metrics that require a Ph.D. in math to use the metric or understand the results. The metrics in this book have been collected from a variety of sources and converted into a uniform format to facilitate comparison, selection, and ease of use. When a subcategory was identified for which no standard metrics could be found, the author filled in the gap. Table 1.2 itemizes the metrics and the original source that published them.

This book is organized into three major divisions, as shown in Figure 1.1. An introduction to the topic of metrics (Chapter 2) is first, followed by an explanation of the issues, what needs to be measured, and how to measure it (Chapters 3 through 5).

Chapter 2 sets the stage for the rest of the book by illuminating the fundamental concepts, historical notes, philosophic underpinnings, and application

Table 1.1 Inventory of Security and Privacy Metrics

1 Measuring Compliance with Security and Privacy Regulations and Standards		
Sub-category	*Regulations and Standards*	*Number of Metrics*
Financial	1.1 Gramm-Leach-Bliley — U.S.	7
	1.2 Sarbanes-Oxley Act — U.S.	13
Healthcare	1.3 HIPAA — U.S.	13
	1.4 Personal Health Information Act — Canada	30
Personal Privacy	1.5 OECD Security and Privacy Guidelines	29
	1.6 Data Protection Directive 95/46/EC	16
	1.7 Data Protection Act — U.K.	11
	1.8 PIPEDA — Canada	44
	1.9 Privacy Act — U.S.	33
Homeland Security	1.10 FISMA — U.S.	78
	1.11 Homeland Security Presidential Directives — U.S.	14
	1.12 NERC Cyber Security Standards	9
	1.13 Patriot Act — U.S.	55
Total		352

Table 1.1 Inventory of Security and Privacy Metrics (continued)

2 Measuring Resilience of Physical, Personnel, IT, and Operational Security Controls

Sub-category	Sub-element	Number of Metrics
2.1 Physical Security	2.1.1 Facility Protection	68
	2.1.2 Asset Protection	61
	2.1.3 Mission Protection	10
2.2 Personnel Security	2.2.1 Accountability	12
	2.2.2 Background Investigations	9
	2.2.3 Competence	8
	2.2.4 Separation of Duties	9
	2.2.5 Workforce Analysis	16
2.3 IT Security		
IT security control system	2.3.1 Logical Access Control	21
	2.3.2 Data Authentication, Non-Repudiation	7
	2.3.3 Encryption, Cryptographic Support	17
	2.3.4 Flow Control (operational and data)	9
	2.3.5 Identification and Authentication	20
	2.3.6 Maintainability, Supportability	11
	2.3.7 Privacy	12
	2.3.8 Residual Information Protection	5
	2.3.9 Security Management	23

Table 1.1 Inventory of Security and Privacy Metrics (continued)

2 Measuring Resilience of Physical, Personnel, IT, and Operational Security Controls

IT security protection system	2.3.10 Audit Trail, Alarm Generation	14
	2.3.11 Availability	18
	2.3.12 Error, Exception, Incident Handling	15
	2.3.13 Fail Safe, Fail Secure, Fail Operational	11
	2.3.14 Integrity	21
	2.3.15 Domain Separation	13
	2.3.16 Resource Management	12
2.4 Operational Security		
Security engineering life-cycle activities	2.4.1 Concept Formulation	8
	2.4.2 Security Requirements Analysis and Specification	12
	2.4.3 Security Architecture and Design	14
	2.4.4 Development and Implementation	16
	2.4.5 Security Test & Evaluation, Certification & Accreditation, Validation & Verification	13
	2.4.6 Delivery, Installation, and Deployment	4
	2.4.7 Operations and Maintenance	12
	2.4.8 Decommissioning	11
Ongoing security risk management activities	2.4.9 Vulnerability Assessment	18
	2.4.10 Security Policy Management	18
	2.4.11 Security Audits and Reviews	10
	2.4.12 Security Impact Analysis, Privacy Impact Analysis, Configuration Management, Patch Management	23
	2.4.13 Security Awareness and Training, Guidance Documents	11
	2.4.14 Stakeholder, Strategic Partner, Supplier Relationships	9
Total		601

Table 1.1 Inventory of Security and Privacy Metrics (continued)

3 Measuring Return on Investment (ROI) in Physical, Personnel, IT, and Operational Security Controls	
Sub-category	Number of Metrics
3.1 Problem Identification and Characterization	*
3.2 Total Cost of Security Control	1
3.3 Depreciation Period	1
3.4 Tangible Benefits	1
3.5 Intangible Benefits	3
3.6 Payback Period	3
3.7 Comparative Analysis	3
3.8 Assumptions	*
3.9 ROI Summary	7
Total	19
Grand Total	**972**

* Only primitives are defined.

Table 1.2 Metric Sources

Source	Number of Metrics
Corporate Information Security Working Group[105]	90
Herrmann — the author	734
IEEE Std. 982.[8] and IEEE Std. 982.2[9]	6
OMB FISMA Guidance[72c]	43
Garigue and Stefaniu[143]	14
Information Security Governance[163]	13
NIST SP 800-55[57]	35
O'Connor[197]	2
Asset Protection and Security Management Handbook[116]	1
Jelen[169]	12
Bayuk[117]	17
ISO/IEC 15408[19–21]	4
Soo Hoo[214]	1
Total	972

context of security and privacy metrics. Chapter 2 introduces key metrics principles and how they relate to security and privacy. A quick refresher course on measurement basics is presented first. Then topics such as data collection and validation, measurement boundaries, and the uses and limits of metrics are explored. Best practices to implement, as well as snares to sidestep, are highlighted along the way. Similarities and differences between security and privacy metrics and other metrics, such as reliability engineering, safety engineering, and software engineering metrics are examined. They are all first cousins of security and privacy metrics, and there are significant lessons to be learned.

Chapters 3 through 5 define security and privacy metrics, many for the first time, using the following paradigm. First the relevant topics under each category are discussed. Next the pertinent security and privacy issues associated with each topic are identified. Then what needs to be measured for each issue and how to measure it are defined.

As any competent engineer knows, one hallmark of a good requirement is that it is testable. Likewise, one property of a good regulation is that compliance can be measured easily and objectively through the use of metrics. Chapter 3 navigates the galaxy of compliance metrics and the security and privacy regulations to which they apply. A brief discussion of the global regulatory environment starts the chapter. Particular attention is paid to the legal ramifications of privacy. Then 13 current national and international security and privacy regulations are examined in detail, along with the role of metrics in demonstrating compliance. The strengths and weaknesses of each regulation are discussed from a security engineering perspective, a

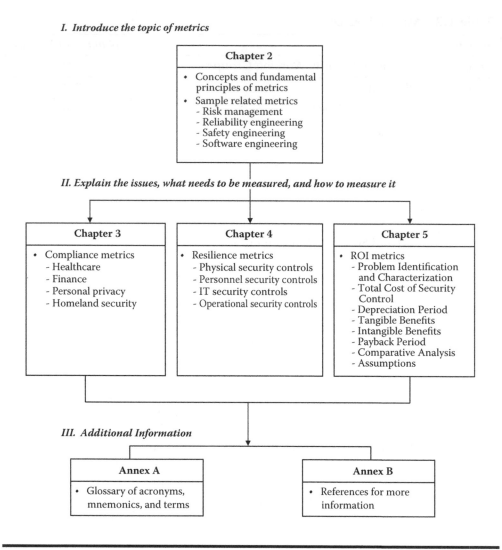

I. Introduce the topic of metrics

Chapter 2

- Concepts and fundamental
  principles of metrics
- Sample related metrics
  - Risk management
  - Reliability engineering
  - Safety engineering
  - Software engineering

II. Explain the issues, what needs to be measured, and how to measure it

Chapter 3

- Compliance metrics
  - Healthcare
  - Finance
  - Personal privacy
  - Homeland security

Chapter 4

- Resilience metrics
  - Physical security controls
  - Personnel security controls
  - IT security controls
  - Operational security controls

Chapter 5

- ROI metrics
  - Problem Identification
    and Characterization
  - Total Cost of Security
    Control
  - Depreciation Period
  - Tangible Benefits
  - Intangible Benefits
  - Payback Period
  - Comparative Analysis
  - Assumptions

III. Additional Information

Annex A

- Glossary of acronyms,
  mnemonics, and terms

Annex B

- References for more
  information

Figure 1.1   Organization and flow of the book.

vantage point that is all too often neglected during the development of regulations. These 13 regulations are discussed on their technical merits alone: what makes sense, what does not make sense, and what should be in the regulation and is not. Then metrics are presented that measure how well an organization is complying with each regulation and whether it is doing so in an efficient manner. Compliance with each security and privacy provision in the regulations is measured both in terms of complying with the "letter of the law" as well as the "spirit of the law." Similarities and differences between the regulations are highlighted, and not-so-subtle hints are dropped on how the regulations could (should?) be improved from a security engineering point of view. The discussion of whether or not a particular policy is a good policy or legal is left to the political science majors and attorneys.

The security solutions an organization deploys, whether physical, personnel, IT, or operational security, are or should be in response to specific threats. Countermeasures are or should be proportional to the likelihood of a specific threat or combination of threats being instantiated and the worst-case consequences, should this occur. Nearly all the standards and regulations discussed in Chapter 3 state the requirement to deploy security controls that are commensurate with the risk. There are standardized methods by which to assess risk. But unless the resilience of the security controls is measured first, there is no factual basis on which to make the claim that the security controls are indeed commensurate with risk. Likewise, it is not possible to determine the return on investment (ROI) in physical, personnel, IT, and operational security controls unless their resilience has been measured against the risk. Hence the importance of the resilience metrics defined in Chapter 4. Chapter 4 examines each of the four security engineering domains in detail. Individual metrics are presented that measure a particular aspect of the resilience of a given security control and an organization's approach to achieving and sustaining that control. Then sample reports are generated that explain how to combine multiple different metrics to evaluate cross-cutting issues. The extensive interdependence and interaction among the four security engineering domains is emphasized throughout the chapter.

Chapter 5 defines metrics that measure the ROI in physical, personnel, IT, and operational security controls. In particular, a new comprehensive security ROI model is presented that:

- Is appropriate for all four types of security controls (physical, personnel, IT, and operational)
- Can be used at any point in the security engineering life cycle
- Can be used to evaluate individual security controls or collections of security controls
- Acknowledges different asset values and different threat environments
- Builds upon the foundation already established for compliance and resilience metrics

This information provides essential inputs to IT capital planning decisions by answering the perennial question, "Where should limited security funds be invested to gain the most benefit?" Security and privacy ROI metrics are tied to asset value, as expected; but more importantly, they are tied to asset criticality. The intent is to ensure that assets are neither over-protected nor under-protected.

Additional information is provided in Annexes A and B. Annex A contains a glossary of security and privacy acronyms, mnemonics, and terms. Given the frequency with which IT and security terms are reused and misused and the fact that the meaning of many security engineering terms is not the same as in everyday conversation, it is a good idea to consult Annex A every now and then. Annex B is a reference to the sources cited in this book as well as publications of interest for further reading.

1.5 Acknowledgments

Research is like a relay race. One person or project moves the state of knowledge and understanding from point A to point B. The next person or project moves the concept from point B to point C, and so forth. That is why it is called (re)search. Accordingly, I would like to acknowledge the people who and projects that took the first steps in the field of security and privacy metrics. While this list is not as long as the thank-you list during an Oscar acceptance speech, it is a noteworthy list. To date there have been three significant security and privacy metrics publications. This book builds upon the foundation established by these pioneering efforts:

- Corporate Information Security Working Group (CISWG), "Report of the Best Practices and Metrics Teams" (January 10, 2005)
- Information Security Governance (ISG), "Corporate Governance Task Force Report" (April 2004)
- NIST SP 800-55, "Security Metrics Guide for Information Technology Systems" (July 2003)

In addition, certain people must be acknowledged for giving the need for security and privacy metrics the high-level visibility and attention they deserve, in particular as related to preventing identity theft. This list, while not exhaustive, includes Representative Tom Davis (Virginia); Gregg Dvorak of the Office of Science and Technology Policy (OSTP); Karen Evans of the Office of Management and Budget (OMB); Senator Diane Feinstein (California); Clay Johnson of the OMB; Dr. Douglas Maughan of the Department of Homeland Security; Marshall Potter, Chief Scientist for IT, U.S. Federal Aviation Administration; Mark Powell, Chief Technology Officer, U.S. Federal Aviation Administration; Dr. Arthur Pyster of SAIC; Representative Adam Putnam (Florida); Orson Swindle of the Federal Trade Commission; Gregory Wilshusin of the General Accountability Office (GAO); Tim Young of the OMB; and Marc Rotenberg of the Electronic Privacy Information Center.

Chapter 2

The Whats and Whys of Metrics

Security reporting remains a half-science, half-art skill. The challenge is to move on the fast track from art to science by selecting a security reporting framework that is aligned with business objectives and organizational culture. Identifying and reporting on a set of credible and relevant metrics provides the basis for prudent decision making and continuous improvement of the security posture of the organization.

—R. Garigue and M. Stefaniu[143]

2.1 Introduction

This chapter sets the stage for the remainder of the book by illuminating the fundamental concepts, historical notes, philosophic underpinnings, and application context of security and privacy metrics. This chapter introduces key metrics concepts and how they relate to security and privacy. A quick refresher course on measurement basics is presented first. Then topics such as data collection and validation, measurement boundaries, and the uses and limits of metrics are explored. Best practices to implement, as well as snares to sidestep, are highlighted along the way. Similarities and differences between security and privacy metrics and other metrics, such as reliability engineering, safety engineering, and software engineering metrics, are examined. They are all first cousins of security and privacy metrics and there are lessons to be learned. Finally, the universe of security and privacy metrics is revealed, and it is probably considerably more expansive than you may have imagined.

Basili, a pioneer in the field of software engineering metrics, created the Goal Question Metric (GQM) paradigm. The idea was straightforward — metrics should be tied to a goal your organization is trying to accomplish.

The goal is defined first. To determine if progress is being made toward achieving or sustaining that goal, a series of questions is formulated. Finally, specific metrics are defined, collected, and analyzed to answer those questions. There may be multiple questions that correspond to a single goal and multiple metrics that correspond to a single question in this paradigm. For example:

Goal: Increase software reliability.
Question1:   What is the current fault removal rate compared to earlier releases of this product?
Metric 1a: Current percent and number of faults removed by life-cycle phase and fault severity for this release
Metric 1b: Previous percent and number of faults removed by life-cycle phase and fault severity for earlier releases

This book adapts the GQM paradigm by defining a question that indicates the purpose of each chapter and the questions it intends to answer. A GQM box is contained at the beginning of each chapter. To illustrate, see the GQM for Chapter 2 below.

GQM for Chapter 2

What are security and privacy metrics and why do I need them?

Metrology is the science of measurement, while *metrics* are a standard of measurement. As the quote at the beginning of this chapter indicates, metrics are a technique by which to move the practice of security and privacy engineering forward, in industry in general and in your organization in particular. Metrics are a tool with which to pursue security and privacy engineering as a disciplined science, rather than an ad hoc art. They allow you to bridge the gap in your organization between the state of the art and the state of the practice of security and privacy engineering.[174] Metrics permit you to move from guessing about your true security and privacy status and capability to confronting reality. The judicious use of metrics promotes visibility, informed decision making, predictability, and proactive planning and preparedness, thus averting surprises and always being caught in a reactive mode when it comes to security and privacy. Figure 2.1 summarizes the life cycle of metrics.

The initial reaction of some organizations or individuals may be fear — fear of implementing a metrics program because of the perhaps unpleasant facts that metrics may bring to light; that is, the proverbial "emperor has no clothes" syndrome. This response is to be expected, at first anyway; however, this view is very short sighted in the long run. It is always preferable for an organization to have a firm grasp of its true security and privacy situation that is based on facts, no matter how stable or shaky that situation may be. How else can you assign resources, determine priorities, or take preventive, adaptive, or corrective

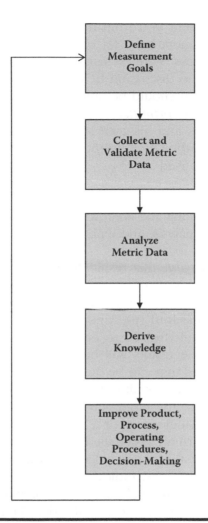

Figure 2.1 Metrics life cycle.

action? To view this scenario from a different perspective, would you prefer to have a competitor, adversary, or federal regulatory body discover the weaknesses in your security and privacy programs for you? No, I did not think so.

In summary, to paraphrase DeMarco, Kan, Fenton, and Pfleeger, you cannot manage, monitor, understand, control, or improve something you cannot measure. Accordingly, if you want to manage, monitor, understand, control, or improve security and privacy in your organization, you need to employ security and privacy metrics like those presented in this book.

2.2 Measurement Basics

Before proceeding, it is essential to understand the basic terms and concepts associated with metrology, or the what, why, how, and when of metrics. These basic principles are applicable to all metrics, not just security and privacy metrics. This awareness will help you avoid misusing metrics. In particular, this knowledge will prevent you from making mistakes common to metrics newcomers — that of generating a lot of illegitimate and useless metrics as a result of overzealousness. Further insights on how to avert this common pitfall are contained in the discussion below. Now on to terminology.

The first terms that you should be able to understand and distinguish are *metric, measurement,* and *primitive.* It seems as if everyone has his own definitions of these terms and his own ideas about which is a subset of the other. To clarify this situation (within the context of this book at least), the following definitions are used.

> **Metric:** a proposed measure or unit of measure that is designed to facilitate decision making and improve performance and accountability through collection, analysis, and reporting of relevant data.[57, 138]

That is, a metric is a *value* that results from measuring something. Metrics provide a numeric description of a certain characteristic of the items being investigated. The metric defines both what is being measured (the attribute) and how it is being measured (the unit of measure). The unit of measure must be clarified and standardized to ensure uniform measurements across populations, otherwise the results will be meaningless. The unit of measure can include most anything that can be quantified, such as counts, percentage, proportions, rate, ratio, length, width, weight, memory usage, frequency, time interval, monetary unit or any other standardized unit of measure. A metric can be generated for a single item or a group of items. The results can be compared against the current, previous, or future populations, or some pre-defined benchmark or goal. Acknowledge up front any conditions or limitations for using the metric results. Indicate whether the metric should be used on an ongoing basis for continual assessment or whether it is limited to a particular life-cycle phase. Note also that the definition refers to the analysis and reporting of *relevant* data.

Two special instances of metrics are *predictive* metrics and *situational* metrics. Predictive metrics are compared against a numerical target related to a factor to be met during system design and development. Predictive metrics provide an early indication of whether or not a product, process, or project goal will be met.[12] Predictive metrics are useful when measuring resilience or return on investment (ROI). Situational metrics refer to the appropriate collection of measures to control a project, given its characteristics.[138] Situational metrics are useful for measuring compliance with regulatory requirements. Metrics promote informed decision making in support of product improvement, process improvement, or rework.[210] Put another way, if there is no legitimate use for a metric, there is no point in collecting and analyzing the data.[8, 9]

> **Measurement:** the process by which numbers or symbols are assigned to entities in the real world in such a way as to describe them according to clearly defined rules.[137, 138] The comparison of a property of an object to a similar property of a standard reference.[8, 9]

In simple terms, measurement is the *process* of collecting metrics. Measurement can be performed for assessment or prediction purposes, as we will see later in Chapters 3 through 5. A distinction should be made here between measurement and calculation. Measurement is considered a "direct quantification," while a calculation is an "indirect quantification"; that is, measurements are combined in some manner to produce a quantified item.[137] Estimates are an example of a calculation — a calculation is performed to estimate what a value is or will be. In contrast, measurement yields the actual value. The measurement process details everything associated with capturing the metric data; nothing is left ambiguous that could be subject to different interpretations. That is, the measurement process delineates the constraints or controls under which the metrics will be collected. To illustrate, suppose you are assigned to measure air temperature. The measurement process should define: (1) when the temperature readings should be taken — the exact time(s) during the day; (2) the exact altitude(s) at which the readings should be made; (3) the temperature scale that should be used (e.g., Fahrenheit, Celsius, or Kelvin); (4) the degree of precision needed in the temperature readings — the number of decimal points to which the temperature should be recorded; (5) the instrument to use to measure the temperature and its accuracy; and (6) the conditions under which the measurements should be made (such as standing still, moving at 500 mph, in the sunshine, in the shade, etc.).

The measurement process also provides rules for interpreting the results. There is no need to develop an elaborate or convoluted measurement process; this is certainly not the way to gain management or stakeholder buy-in. Rather, a measurement process that is straightforward, complete, and logical is less error prone and more likely to be accepted and successful in the long run. A note of caution: when comparing metrics, be sure to verify that they were collected according to the same exact measurement process.

> **Primitive:** data relating to the development or use of software that is used in developing measures of quantitative descriptions of software. Primitives are directly measurable or countable, or may be given a constant value or condition for a specific measure. Examples include error, fault, failure, time, time interval, date, and number of an item.[8, 9]

Sometimes, but not always, metrics are composed of sub-elements; they are referred to as primitives. Consider percentages. The metric may be a percentage, but the numerator and denominator are primitives. Primitives are a numeric description of a certain feature of the sub-elements being explored. Primitives correspond to the specified unit of measure. The same issues that arise with metrics are equally applicable to primitives as well. Any constraints or controls related to collecting the primitives are defined in the measurement process. Again, the unit of measure can include most anything that can be quantified. In general, it is not useful to perform comparisons at the primitive level; instead, comparisons ought to take place among metrics. Figure 2.2 illustrates the interaction between primitives and metrics.

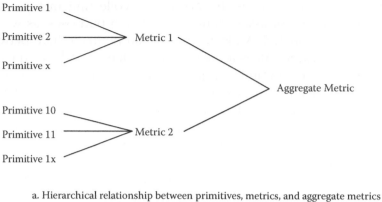

a. Hierarchical relationship between primitives, metrics, and aggregate metrics

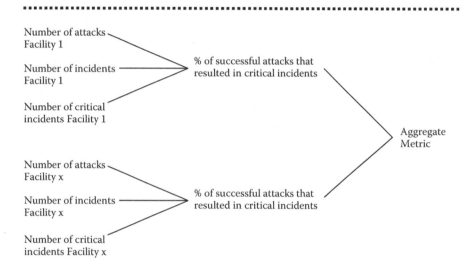

b. Sample primitive, metric, and aggregate metric hierarchy

Figure 2.2   Interaction between primitives and metrics.

When working with primitives, it is important to be aware of the potential dependencies among them, real or induced. Primitives can be dependent or independent. As the name implies, the value of dependent primitives is affected by changes in one or more independent primitives.[137] In contrast, independent primitives are factors that can characterize a product, process, or project and influence evaluation results; they can be manipulated to affect the outcome.[137] Independent primitives are also referred to as *state primitives*. Suppose we want to assign a difficulty level of 1 (lowest) to 10 (highest) for the difficulty in cracking passwords. The difficulty level is a function of password length, the rules for permissible passwords (such as use of special characters and numbers), how often passwords are changed, how often passwords can be reused, how well the passwords are protected, etc. The difficulty level is a dependent primitive because it will vary in response to changes in independent primitives, such as password length.

Metrics are collected about specific attributes of particular entities. An attribute is a feature or property of an entity.[137] Attributes depict some distinct aspect or trait of an entity that can be measured and compared to a reference point, other entities, or a previous measurement of the same entity. An *entity* is an object or an event in the real world.[137] An entity can be logical or physical. To illustrate, software is a logical entity, yet software is stored or captured on physical media. A cyber attack is a logical entity, but manifests itself through physical media, such as electrons. An attacker, or human being, is physical. It is debatable whether a human being's actions can be considered logical; certainly that it not a true statement for all human beings. Anyway, remember when defining metrics that it is important to clearly distinguish between entities and attributes. To illustrate, an encryption device is an entity while the speed of performing encryption and key length are attributes.

An entity may have one or multiple attributes. It is not necessary for the entities being compared to have all the same attributes. Consider your personal library. You may want to know the average page length of the books in your library. All books have covers, pages, and chapters; these are standard attributes of the entity "book." Average page length is a metric. The number of books and the total number of pages, which are used to calculate average page length, are primitives. The measurement process defines how pages are counted — whether or not total pages are counted or just the numbered pages in the body of the book. Biographical, historical, and professional books usually contain an index; fiction and poetry do not. You can measure the average page length of all the books in your library because all books have the attribute of page length. However, you can only determine the average number of entries in an index from those books that have an index, which is a subset of all the books in your library.

This analogy illustrates another fact about the relationship between attributes and entities. Speaking in a hierarchical sense, entities possess attributes. In some, but not all cases, an attribute may reflect a sub-entity. We just determined the average page length of the books in your library. "Page" is a sub-entity of the entity "book." A page also possesses attributes, such as the number of words, paragraphs, or sentences per page. Because of this relationship it is important to clearly define the entities you are comparing and the attributes you are measuring to ensure that you end up with meaningful and valid results. That is, you need to avoid trying to compare an entity with a sub-entity.

Attributes can be internal or external. *Internal attributes* can be measured purely in terms of the product, process, or resource itself, separate from its execution or behavior.[137, 138] Examples of internal attributes include number of functions performed, number of modules, extent of redundancy, extent of diversity, percent syntactic correctness on first compile, and number of calculations performed. *Internal attributes* are also referred to as internally valid measures, that is, a measure that provides a numerical characterization of some intuitively understood attribute.[209] In comparison, external attributes can be measured only with respect to how the product, process, or resource reacts or performs in a given environment, not the entity itself.[137, 138] Examples of

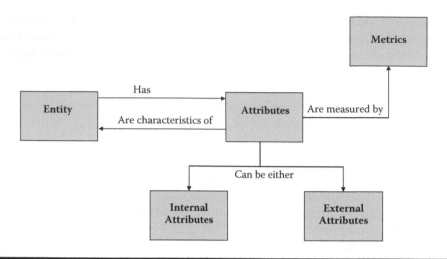

Figure 2.3   Relationship between entities and attributes.

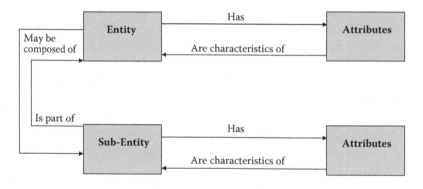

Figure 2.4   Relationship between entities and sub-entities.

external attributes include installation time, execution efficiency, throughput, and capacity. External attributes are also referred to as externally valid measures, that is, a measure that can be shown to be an important component or predictor of some behavioral attribute of interest.[209] Sometimes internal attributes can be used as a predictor of external attributes.[137] This highlights the need to have a good understanding of the attributes for the entity you wish to evaluate before defining or selecting any metrics. Figures 2.3 and 2.4 depict the relationship between entities, attributes, and sub-entities.

Metrics must exhibit four key characteristics to be meaningful and usable:

1. Accuracy
2. Precision
3. Validity
4. Correctness

The conclusions drawn from or actions taken as a result of metrics will be severely misguided if the metrics are not accurate, precise, valid, and correct.

Unfortunately, the importance of these four aspects of metrics are often overlooked.

In day-to-day conversation, these four terms are often used interchangeably. However, within the context of metrics, they have very distinct meanings. *Accuracy* is the degree of agreement of individual or average measurements with an accepted reference value or level.[204] Accuracy infers that the measurement of an attribute was true or exact according to the standard unit of measure specified by the measurement process. An important feature of accuracy is that accurate measurements can easily be authenticated by another party. Simply put, accuracy means that if you measure an entity to be 12 inches long, it is indeed 12 inches long and not 11.85 or 12.12 inches long.

Precision is the degree of mutual agreement among individual measurements made under prescribed conditions, or simply, how well identically performed measurements agree with each other.[204] Precision captures the notion of the repeatability of accurate measurements under similar conditions. Precision accounts for drift in test equipment and other sources of variability during measurement, such as human error, inattention to detail, or fatigue. Accordingly, this concept is applied to a set of measurements, not a single measurement.[204] Precision implies that if you measured ten entities to be 12 inches long, each would indeed be considered 12 inches long, given the known or stated precision of the measuring instrument, which is often referred to as the degree of precision or, conversely, the margin of error. Perhaps one entity was actually 12.0001 inches long, but the measurement equipment you were using could not measure to less than a tenth of an inch.

Validity brings in another aspect of metrics, that is, whether or not the metric really measures what it was intended to measure.[174] Expressed formally, validity is the extent to which an empirical measure adequately reflects the real meaning of the concept under consideration.[174] The validity of a metric depends a lot on the completeness and coherence of the measurement process. Suppose you want to measure the number of severe network security incidents during the previous 30 days. To do so, several items must be detailed in the measurement process. First, does the 30 days refer to business days or calendar days? Second, for which network do you want to count the number of severe security incidents: a particular corporate LAN, the corporate intranet, the corporate WAN, all corporate networks? If for a WAN or LAN only, you need to clearly delineate where one network "stops" and the other "starts." Third, you need to clearly define a severe security incident, as opposed to a serious or moderate incident. Fourth, a clear distinction must be made between attacks (attempts) and incidents (successful attacks that had some negative impact). Fifth, a decision must be made about exactly how to count incidents. For example, is a cascading or multipoint attack counted as one attack, or is each facility or asset impacted considered a separate attack? And so on. Metric results cannot be normalized without this level of detail in the description of the metric and measurement process. To put it in the vernacular, you will have a mixture of apples, broccoli, and sunflower seeds rather than valid metrics. Continuing the earlier example, validity implies that you actually measured the length of each entity and not the width or some other attribute.

Finally, *correctness* infers that the data was collected according to the exact rules defined in the metric.[137] Correctness reflects the degree of formality that was adhered to during the measurement process. This is an important but often overlooked facet of metrics, because the conditions under which measurements are made can have a significant impact on the results. As an example, consider the percentage of popcorn kernels that popped. Three bags of popcorn are prepared. The first one is left in the microwave oven for two minutes. The second one is cooked for three minutes. The third bag remains in the microwave oven for four minutes. You can determine which time setting yielded the higher percentage of popped popcorn kernels. However, do not try to compute an average percentage of popped kernels because the measurements were made under different conditions. If two or more measurements are made under different conditions, the metrics do not meet the correctness test and cannot be legitimately compared. To close out the earlier example, if the metric specified that the measurement was to be made at exactly 7 a.m. or exactly when the entity had reached a temperature of 50°F, that is indeed when each 12-inch measurement was recorded.

If we examine the relationship between these four characteristics of metrics, the following truths are noted. First and foremost we note that our metrics need to have all four characteristics: accuracy, precision, validity, and correctness; otherwise we are wasting our time as well as that of the system owners, end users, stakeholders, and management. Second, if a group of metrics is determined to be precise, then the individual metrics in that group are most likely also accurate. Third, just because a metric is determined to be accurate does not mean it is valid or correct. In fact, a metric can be valid and not be accurate, precise, or correct. There is no linkage between correctness and validity. If a metric is correct, it may also be accurate — but this is not always the case. This brings us back to the first point: good metrics are accurate, precise, valid, *and* correct. Consequently, subjective assessments do not meet the criteria for good metrics.

Four standard measurement scales are generally recognized. They are listed below from lowest to highest in terms of mathematical utility. When defining or comparing metrics, you should be aware of these different types of scales, as well as their uses and limitations:

- Nominal scale
- Ordinal scale
- Interval scale
- Ratio scale

The lowest measurement scale is known as a nominal scale. A nominal scale represents a classification scheme in which categories are mutually exclusive and jointly exhaustive of all possible categories of an attribute.[174] Furthermore, the names and sequence of the categories do not reflect assumptions about relationships between or among categories.[174] Nominal scales are useful for sorting or organizing things. There may or may not be sub-categories within categories. As an analogy, a nominal scale can be applied to the world of books. There are two main categories of books: fiction and non-fiction. Fiction can be divided into many sub-categories: mystery, science fiction, poetry, cook books, novels, etc. Likewise, non-fiction can be divided into many sub-categories: history, biography, current events, math, science, technical reference, and law. You can count how many books have been published in each category and sub-category and determine percentages and proportions. However, you cannot multiply "history" by "mystery" or say that "biography" is inherently more than "poetry."

An ordinal scale permits limited measurement operations through which items can be arranged in order; however, there is no precise information on the magnitude of the differences between items.[174] Ordinal scales are useful for arranging items in sequence, such as identifying greater than and less than relationships when it is not necessary to know the exact delta between items. As a result, arithmetic functions, such as addition, subtraction, multiplication, and division, cannot be performed on items measured by an ordinal scale. Bookstores often display the top-ten best sellers of the week in both the fiction and non-fiction categories. As a consumer, you only know that a given book is in first place on the best-seller list. You do not know or need to know the difference in the volume of sales between first place and second place.

A frequent misuse of ordinal scales common in the IT industry and elsewhere is the customer satisfaction survey. Customer satisfaction surveys attempt to quantify satisfaction using a numeric scale of: very satisfied (9–10 points), satisfied (7–8 points), neutral (5–6 points), unsatisfied (3–4 points), and very unsatisfied (1–2 points). This approach appears to be scientific and is, in fact, endorsed by some quality organizations. In practice, many statistics are generated from these surveys to prove or disprove all sorts of things. The verbal categories are alright; however, the assigning of numerical points to the categories is flawed. Determining whether one is "satisfied" versus "very satisfied," not to mention the reason for such a rating, is totally subjective and varies from individual to individual. Anything beyond counting the responses in each category and calculating proportions or percentages is mathematically unsound. Consequently, it is preferable to use a color-coded scheme, where the colors represent a continuum of ranges, rather than assigning discrete numerical values. A well-known example is the color-coded scale used to monitor the national threat level.

A common misuse of nominal scales is the pass/fail scenario: how many people passed the CISSP exam the first time they took the exam versus how many failed; how many systems passed security certification and accreditation during the first assessment versus how many failed. Usually, all sorts of percentages are calculated and hypotheses are generated to explain the results. Unfortunately, pass/fail scores by themselves are not very meaningful because you do not know how far above or below the pass/fail threshold each entry was. For example, how many people passed the CISSP exam by only one point? How many people failed the exam by only one point? How many systems barely passed certification and accreditation, such that the approval authority had to hold their nose when they signed off? Trying to extrapolate anything more than the number of passes and fails, or the proportion or percentage of each, belongs under the category of fiction.

Entity = apple
Attribute = color or type of apple

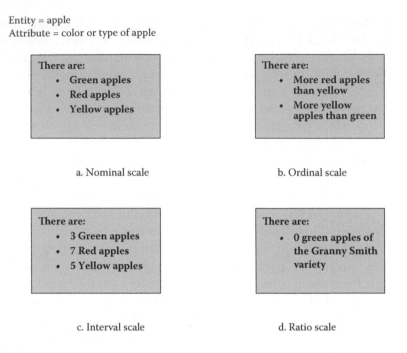

Figure 2.5   **Standard measurement scales.**

Nominal and ordinal scales are instances of qualitative metrics. Interval and ratio scales, discussed below, are instances of quantitative metrics. The scenarios discussed above highlight some of the limitations of and differences between qualitative and quantitative metrics, which should be kept in mind when setting up a metrics program.

An interval scale takes the idea of an ordinal scale one step further by indicating the exact differences between measurement points.[174] To do so, an interval scale requires a well-defined standardized unit of measure, like standardized measurements for weight, volume, or temperature. For example, you know (1) that 72° Fahrenheit is exactly 2° warmer than 70°, and (2) the meaning of a degree for the Fahrenheit scale. Because of this feature, all basic arithmetic operations can be performed on measurements taken according to an interval scale.

Finally, a ratio scale improves upon the idea of an interval scale by adding an absolute or non-arbitrary zero point.[174] This features allows positive and negative values to be captured in relation to the zero point. The four types of standard measurement scales are shown in Figure 2.5.

There are four basic types of measurements, as listed below. The first three are considered static because, if the exact same population is measured repeatedly, the value will remain the same. The fourth type of measurement is considered dynamic because it changes over time:

1. Ratio
2. Proportion
3. Percentage
4. Rate

A *ratio* results from dividing one quantity by another. The numerator and denominator are from two distinct populations and are mutually exclusive.[174] Because a book cannot be both fiction and non-fiction, we could calculate the ratio of fiction to non-fiction books in a book store, and then compare that ratio among several different stores.

A *proportion* results from dividing one quantity by another, where the numerator is part of the denominator. Proportions are best used to describe multiple categories within one group, rather than comparing groups.[174] For example, we could determine the proportion of books in each fiction sub-category in the bookstore, such as one third of the books in the fiction area are mysteries.

Percentage simply converts a proportion to terms of per-hundred units.[174] Instead of saying that one third of the books in the fiction area are mysteries, we say that 33 percent of the books are mysteries. Percentages are popular on business briefing slides, such as the common pie charts and bar charts. As a result, many of the metrics in this book are defined in terms of percentages.

Rate reflects the dynamic rate of change of the phenomena of interest over time.[174] For example, weather reports cite the temperature several times throughout the day. These are static measures. The delta between one temperature reading and the next, or all readings taken during a 24-hour period, represents the rate of change. The degree to which the temperature warmed up during the day and cooled off during the night represents the rate of change. Examples of the four types of measurements are highlighted in Figure 2.6.

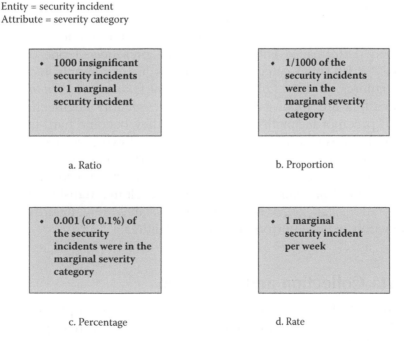

Entity = security incident
Attribute = severity category

- 1000 insignificant security incidents to 1 marginal security incident

a. Ratio

- 1/1000 of the security incidents were in the marginal severity category

b. Proportion

- 0.001 (or 0.1%) of the security incidents were in the marginal severity category

c. Percentage

- 1 marginal security incident per week

d. Rate

Figure 2.6   Types of measurements.

A few more concepts and ideas should be clarified before beginning to define, select, or compare metrics. In particular, you need to understand the distinction between the definitions of and relationships among:

- Error
- Fault
- Failure

Strictly speaking, errors are the difference between a computed, observed, or measured value or condition and the true specified, or theoretically correct, value or condition.[8–12] Humans introduce errors into products, processes, and operational systems in two ways: through (1) errors of omission and (2) errors of commission. An error of omission is an error that results from something that was not done.[125] An error of omission is something that was left undone during a life-cycle process or activity. An error of omission can be accidental or intentional. In contrast, an error of commission is an error that results from making a mistake or doing something wrong.[125] An error of commission can also be accidental or intentional. The consequences of an error of omission or an error of commission are independent of whether it was introduced accidentally or intentionally.

The manifestation of an error is referred to as a fault. A fault is a defect that results in an incorrect step, process, data value, or mode/state.[125] Faults may be introduced into a product or system during any life-cycle phase. Faults that are present in the deployed product or system are often called latent defects.

Should an execution or transaction path exercise a fault, a failure results; a fault remains dormant until exercised. A failure refers to the failing or inability of a system, entity, or component to perform its required function(s), according to specified performance criteria, due to the presence of one or more fault conditions.[8–12, 197] Three categories of failures are commonly recognized: (1) incipient failures, (2) hard failures, and (3) soft failures.[8–12, 97] *Incipient* failures are failures that are about to occur. Proactive security engineering measures attempt to preempt incipient failures before they become hard failures. *Hard* failures are failures that result in a complete shutdown of a product or system. Reactive security engineering measures respond to hard failures as they are occurring or after they occur, and attempt recovery to a known predefined soft failure state. *Soft* failures are failures that result in a transition to degraded-mode operations, fail soft, or a fail operational status.[8–12, 197] Figure 2.7 illustrates the interaction between errors, faults, and failures.

2.3 Data Collection and Validation

As shown in Table 2.1, there are seven steps involved in planning for metric data collection and validation. The purpose of all seven steps is to ensure that the fruit of your labors yields accurate, precise, valid, correct, complete, usable, and useful metrics. These seven steps do not necessarily have to be

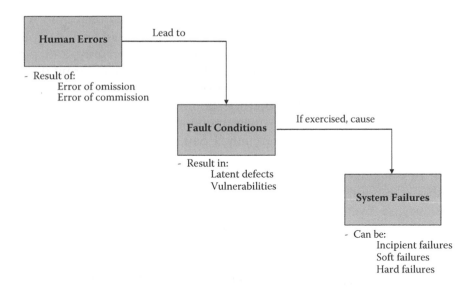

Figure 2.7   Errors, faults, failures.

Table 2.1   Planning for Data Collection and Validation

Step 1: WHAT?

Define what information is going to be collected.

Step 2: WHY?

Define why this information is being collected and how it will be used.

Step 3: HOW?

Define how the information will be collected, the constraints and controls on the collection process.

Step 4: WHEN?

Define the time interval and frequency with which the information is to be collected.

Step 5: WHERE?

Identify the source(s) from which the information will be collected.

Step 6: ENSURE DATA INTEGRITY

Define how the information collected will be preserved to prevent accidental or intentional alteration, deletion, addition, other tampering, or loss.

Step 7: DERIVE TRUE MEANING

Define how the information will be analyzed and interpreted.

performed sequentially or by the same person or organizational unit. A well-designed metric data collection and validation process should be accomplished as a collateral duty. The collection and validation of security and privacy metrics should not be an adjunct process, whereby a red team army descends upon a project saying, "Give me your data or else!" Rather, the collection and validation of security and privacy metrics should be embedded in the security engineering life cycle and tied to measurement goals and decision making. Security and privacy metrics are certainly a part of the configuration management or change control process.

When first setting up a data collection and validation process, an organization should carefully consider the cost of collection and analysis and avoid the tendency of over-collection and under-analysis, and vice versa.[174] IEEE Standards 982.1 and 982.2 sum up this situation quite accurately[8, 9]:

> Patient, accurate data collection and recording is the key to producing accurate measurements. If not well organized, data collection can become very expensive. To contain these costs, the information gathering should be integrated with verification and validation activities.

The first step is to define exactly what information is going to be collected. This sounds like a simple step. However, after considering the differences between and relationships among attributes, sub-entities, entities, primitives, and metrics, you gain a realization that this step, while straightforward, is not necessarily simple and must be given careful consideration. That is, the "what" needs to be defined clearly, concisely, and unambiguously to ensure that the exact information needed is collected — no more and no less.

The second step is to define why this information is being collected and how it is going to be used. (If you cannot answer these questions, go back to step 1.) Step 2 is where the GQM paradigm comes into play. At this point, you make sure that there is a legitimate reason for collecting this particular information; if not, there is no point in proceeding. In addition, you verify that this particular information will contribute to answering the *question* stated in the GQM and provide insight into how well the organization is achieving or sustaining the *goal* stated in the GQM. An important factor to consider is whether the results will be used to improve a product, process, or the metrics program itself. Or, are the metrics being used to provide visibility into a development process, the effectiveness of an operation, establish a performance baseline, or plan, monitor, or control a project?[138]

Step 3 defines how the information will be collected, in particular, the constraints and controls on the collection and measurement process. The purpose of this step is to ensure measurement integrity, which will produce data accuracy and precision. To avoid any confusion (or wasted time), the measurement instructions must be as detailed and specific as possible; any assumptions are stated up front. Several questions must be answered, such as what standardized unit of measure is being used? What measurement instrument is being used? What degree of precision is needed? Is visual observation necessary? Do the measurements have to be verified by an independent third party at the time of measurement? Do you need to demonstrate that the measurements are repeatable? Where are the measurements to be performed: in the field, at headquarters, in a controlled laboratory environment? How are the measurements to be recorded: by bar code scanner, by hand, on a laptop, automatically by the test equipment? What degree of control is needed over dependent and independent primitives? Another consideration is whether metric data will be collected from a sample or an entire population. If sampling is used, you need to determine how a representative sample will be selected. Finally, the process for verifying adherence to the specified measurement controls and constraints is defined to ensure consistency.

Step 4 defines when the information is to be collected, in other words, the exact time interval and frequency of collection. Do not overlook the importance of this step. If you want to know how many of a certain event happened in a week, you need to define exactly what you mean by week: the five-day work week, the seven-day calendar week, a seven-day interval starting on the first day of the month? When does one day stop and another start: at one minute past midnight? At the beginning of the first shift at 7 a.m.? Also, is the data collection to take place actually at the end of the "week" or can it occur some time later? Often, the cost of collecting data after the fact can be prohibitive.[8, 9] Is this measurement to be performed every week, or are weeks that contain holidays skipped? During what life-cycle phase(s) should the data be collected? As you can see, many details need to be explained about the time interval and frequency of metric data collection. Likewise, the process for verifying adherence to the specified data collection interval and frequency must be defined.

The fifth step is to identify where the metric data will come from. The purpose of this step is to ensure data validity. The source(s) from which metric data can (or cannot) be collected must be specified. For example, should only original sources of raw data be used, or can summary, historical, draft/preliminary, or second-hand data be referenced? There are a variety of potential information sources that are a normal part of the security engineering life cycle: security requirements specifications, security architecture specifications, detailed designs, vulnerability assessments, security audits and inspections (physical, personnel, and IT), system security audit trails, security fault analysis (SFA), security test and evaluation (ST&E) plans, ST&E results, stress testing, trouble reports, and operational procedures. Consider these information sources first to avoid having to fabricate data that does not already exist, which can be time consuming and expensive. Defining a verification process to ensure that the data was indeed collected from a valid source is also a must.

The sixth step is to determine how the integrity of the data will be preserved throughout the collection and analysis process. The purpose of this step is to ensure data correctness. The need for accurate data collection and validation cannot be overemphasized.[137] It is essential to prevent accidental or intentional alternation, deletion, addition, other tampering, or loss of some or all of the data during the collection and analysis process. Procedures for ensuring data integrity (i.e., the accuracy, precision, validity, and correctness) during actual measurement, storage, and analysis must be explained. Define chain of custody rules, along with rules for controlling access to the data. Determine how the data will be stored and how long it needs to be kept, prior to collecting any data. Also consider the need for independent verification of data integrity during collection or analysis; this may be appropriate for a some metrics, but not all.

The seventh step is to define the rules for analyzing metric data and interpreting the results. Just as the metric data itself needs to be valid, so does the way in which the metrics are analyzed and interpreted. The purpose of data analysis is to describe the statistical distribution of the attribute values examined and the relationships between and among them.[137] That is, the data analysis tries to answer the questions about the goal specified in the GQM paradigm. The analysis process will vary depending on a variety of parameters, such as the population or sample size, the distribution of values, the analysis of variance, and type of metric data collected. The results can be presented in a variety of ways, from simple comparisons of percentages to box plots, scatter plots, correlation of analysis, measures of association, linear regression, and multi-variate regression. It all depends on what you are trying to discern.

Rules for analyzing and interpreting the metric results are specified to ensure as much objectivity as possible. They must meet the test of a controlled experiment — the experiment can be independently repeated and the results can be independently reproduced. A variety of different types of controls and constraints can be levied on the analysis and interpretation process, as shown in Table 2.2. The exact nature and scope of these controls is a function of what you are trying to learn from the metrics.

Metric data will metamorphose over time, from raw data to extracted data, refined data, validated data, and finally analyzed data.[137, 138] It is essential to ensure integrity throughout each of these transformations by defining the correct procedures and rules for handling the data during each of these stages. Raw data is the initial set of measurement data, as collected. Extracted data is a subset of the raw data. During the extraction process, data that was not collected correctly, collected from an invalid source, collected outside the specified time interval, etc. is removed. The extracted data is then subjected to a refinement process to remove, to the extent possible, any remnants of variability in the measurement process. To illustrate, assume the measuring equipment was calibrated following each measurement cycle and on the third cycle it was noted that the readings were 0.001 too high. The extracted data from the third cycle would be decreased by 0.001; data from all other measurement cycles would not be changed. The integrity of the collected data is verified at each stage, as explained above in Step 6. Likewise, the integrity of the measurement and collection process is verified at each stage, as explained in Steps 3 through 5 above. The combination of verifying the integrity of the data collected and the integrity of the measurement process yields valid data for analysis. Beware of the temptation to jump directly from raw data to analyzed data, unless you plan to be out of town during your next performance appraisal. Because the analyzed data will not even come close to passing the accuracy, precision, validity, or correctness test.

Table 2.2   Examples of Issues to Consider When Specifying Analysis and Interpretation Rules

---

Performing the Analysis:

Types of analysis that are legitimate to perform on the primitives or metrics

Types of analysis that are not legitimate to perform on the primitives or metrics, because they will yield invalid or misleading results

Exactly how the analysis should be performed

What data should be included or excluded, any normalization needed

Exact formula for the calculation

Whether or not different metrics will be combined to perform an aggregate measurement

Interpreting the Results:

Limitations on the use and interpretation of individual or aggregate measurements

Expected normal and abnormal ranges for the results, including the goal or target value; for example, 40–50 is minimally acceptable, 51–60 is acceptable, 61–70 is ideal, less than 40 or over 70 indicate serious problems because…

Potential factors that could influence the results, positively or negatively, and yield invalid results

How the results should be labeled (units, color coding, etc.)

How the results should be compared to previous results or a predefined benchmark

Whether the results will be used for improving a product, process, or the metrics program itself

How the results will be reported, when, and to whom

2.4 Defining Measurement Boundaries

Measurement boundaries provide a framework for classifying the entities to be examined and focusing measurement activities on those areas needing the most visibility, understanding, and improvement.[137] Once you have decided what you are going to measure, why you are going to measure it, and how the measurement will be performed, the next question to be answered concerns the measurement scope or boundaries — specifically, what entities are to be included or excluded from the measurement process. Examples of items to consider when defining measurement boundaries include:

- Are you interested in only one security domain, a combination, or all four (physical, personnel, IT, and operational security)?
- What system risk, information sensitivity, or asset criticality categories should be included or excluded?
- What time interval is of interest?

- How does the metric consumer influence the scope of the measurement boundaries?
- Do you need to account for constraints in the operational environment?
- Should a single system or a single type of system be examined?
- Is the whole system being investigated or just the security features and functions?
- Is data examined separately from software, hardware, and telecommunications equipment?
- Are documentation and operational procedures considered part of the system?
- What about the network or other external interfaces the system is connected to?
- Perhaps it would be better to examine all the systems connected to a single network.
- Then again, maybe the enterprise security architecture needs investigating.

Think of the definition of measurement boundaries as a zoom in/zoom out function that focuses your metric lens on the right objects, and with the relevant level of detail visible. These same issues must be addressed when defining security test and evaluation (ST&E) and certification and accreditation (C&A) boundaries. For this reason the first step in the U.K. Central Computing Telecommunications Agency (CCTA) Risk Analysis and Management Methodology (CRAMM), developed in 1991, and its successors BS 7799 and ISO/IEC 17799 (2000-12), is to define assessment boundaries.

Appropriate measurement boundaries are essential to producing metric results that are valid and useful. If the measurement boundaries are too broad or too narrow to answer the specific GQM, the results will be misleading. Suppose the state of Maryland increased funding to public high schools last year and the governor wants to know how that affected student achievement. One approach would be to compare this year's scores, on the standardized test all students must pass to graduate from high school in Maryland, with the scores from previous years. This approach is an example of measurement boundaries that are too broad. Unless the measurement boundaries are defined to (1) normalize the data across counties to reflect concurrent county funding increases or decreases for public high school education, and (2) exclude test scores from private high schools and home-schooled students, this approach is flawed. An example of measurement boundaries that are too narrow would be to compare the old and new test scores from public high schools in only one county in the state. In summary, you need to proceed with caution when defining measurement boundaries.

In the high-tech world, it is common to think of systems as consisting of only hardware, software, and telecommunications equipment. A broader view, adding items such as people, operational procedures, and the supporting infrastructure, is necessary to end up with complete and comprehensive security and privacy metrics. When doing so, entities can take on a variety of forms, such as logical, physical, animate, inanimate, primary, support, dynamic, and static. The following are examples of each type of entity:

- *Logical.* Software is a logical entity.
- *Physical.* Software executes and is stored on physical entities such as computers, hard drives, floppy drives, PROMs, PLCs, and ASICs.
- *Animate.* Human users, system administrators, trainers, and maintenance staff are the animate entities within a system.
- *Inanimate.* Most other entities are inanimate; for example, archives or locks on equipment cabinets.
- *Primary.* Primary entities are those that contribute directly to accomplishing an organization's mission.
- *Support.* The electric power grid and the telecommunications backbone are examples of support entities, as are most infrastructure systems. They are essential but contribute indirectly to mission accomplishment.
- *Dynamic.* System configurations and operational procedures are dynamic entities. Both tend to evolve or be modified frequently over the life of a system, due to enhancements, maintenance, and changes in technology.
- *Static.* The entities that are static will vary from organization to organization. In one case, a maintenance schedule may be static; in another, the electromechanical components may be static.

Note that an entity can take on more than one form. For example, an entity could be logical, primary, and dynamic. Only the pairs are mutually exclusive: logical/physical, animate/inanimate, primary/support, and dynamic/static. When defining measurement boundaries, it is important to consider which entity forms will provide meaningful metric data.

In the IT domain, systems are often used as measurement boundaries. Everyone knows what a system is, right? Wrong. "System," as the term is normally used, has little to do with the true engineering definition of a system. Not to mention what you call a system, the next person calls a sub-system or a system of systems. Rather, "systems" as they are usually referred to are really procurement boundaries. An organization could afford to specify, design, develop, and deploy a certain amount of functionality at a given point in time; this functionality became known as a "system." The remaining functionality, for which the specification changed over time, was added later, probably in more than one increment, each of which was given a different "system" name because it runs on newer hardware or software. The old "system" became too expensive to convert, so it was left alone as a legacy stovepipe. During the middle of this "system" evolution business process, reengineering was attempted but abandoned because the Web became too tangled. Does this scenario sound familiar? Then you understand the necessity for being very careful about using "system" as a measurement boundary.

A similar conundrum is encountered in physical security when trying to define a facility. Is a facility a building, a few floors in a building, a computer center, a campus, or what? Does the facility include the underground parking, the parking lot, landscaped courtyard, or sidewalk? Facilities tend to grow or shrink in size over time. Likewise, the number of people and the number and type of equipment and assets they house change accordingly. So what is a facility? Be sure you define it explicitly when using "facility" as a measurement boundary.

This situation is somewhat simpler in the world of personnel security — a person is a person. Personnel security measures cannot be applied to fractional people. However, be careful when using definitions such as employee, customer, stakeholder, and supplier. These are dynamic populations. For example, does "employee" include current and former employees, or current employees only? How many years back do you go when talking about former employees? Does "current employee" include only full-time company employees or consultants, sub-contractors, part-time, and temporary employees as well? What about new employees who are still in a probationary period, or individuals who have accepted an employment offer but have not started to work yet?

Once the measurement boundaries have been defined precisely and the dynamic nature of certain entities has been taken into account, verify the validity of both; an independent verification is preferable. That is, will this set of information provide valid and correct metrics in response to the question being answered. In some instances it may be useful to compare metrics from different levels of abstraction to spot trends or identify sources of weaknesses. Metrics can be compared and aggregated from a component, product, sub-system, system, and collection of systems to the entire enterprise. The results of this hierarchical analysis are often quite enlightening and can be used to confirm or refute isolated findings for a single level of abstraction. NIST SP 800-55 was the first major security metrics publication to report this observation.[57]

The definition of valid measurement boundaries can also contribute to determining the scope of ST&E regression testing needed after an upgrade or other maintenance activity. Security impact analysis metrics, such as those discussed in Chapter 4, can be used to demonstrate that the boundaries for regression testing were selected correctly and prove that the scope and depth of regression testing was appropriate. Furthermore, security metrics can augment proof that the ST&E was successful.

Measurement boundaries can be influenced by entity attributes such as risk, sensitivity, severity, likelihood, or asset criticality. To ensure uniform assignment of entities to measurement boundaries across people and organizational units, standardized definitions must be used for each of these items. That way your use of "occasional" and "catastrophic" is the same as the next person's. Please refer to Tables 2.3 through 2.7 for the standardized definitions.

Risk is the level of impact on an organization's operations (including mission, functions, image, or reputation), assets, or individuals resulting from the operation of an information system given the potential impact of a threat and the probability of that threat occurring.[50, 51] Sensitivity assesses the relative degree of confidentiality and privacy protection(s) needed for a given information asset to prevent unauthorized disclosure. In the government sector, low sensitivity equates to For Official Use Only (FOUO), moderate sensitivity equates to Sensitive Security Information and Secret, while high sensitivity equates to Top Secret and above. The categories for risk and sensitivity are the same. However, risk applies to systems while sensitivity applies to information assets. Risk and sensitivity are generally referred to in the three categories defined in Table 2.3.

Table 2.3   Risk and Sensitivity Categories

Category	Definition[a]
Low	The loss of confidentiality, integrity, or availability could be expected to have a *limited* adverse effect on organizational operations, organizational assets, or individuals. Adverse effects on individuals may include, but are not limited to, loss of privacy to which individuals are entitled under law. A limited adverse effect means that, for example, the loss of confidentiality, integrity, or availability might (1) cause a degradation in mission capability to an extent and duration that the organization is able to perform its primary functions, but the effectiveness of the functions is noticeably reduced; (2) result in minor damage to organizational assets; (3) result in minor financial loss; or (4) result in minor harm to individuals.
Moderate	The loss of confidentiality, integrity, or availability could be expected to have a *serious* adverse effect on organizational operations, organizational assets, or individuals. Adverse effects on individuals may include, but are not limited to, loss of privacy to which individuals are entitled under law. A serious adverse effect means that, for example, the loss of confidentiality, integrity, or availability might (1) cause a significant degradation in mission capability to an extent and duration that the organization is able to perform its primary functions, but the effectiveness of the functions is significantly reduced; (2) result in significant damage to organizational assets; (3) result in significant financial loss; or (4) result in significant harm to individuals that does not involve loss of life or serious life threatening injuries.
High	The loss of confidentiality, integrity, or availability could be expected to have a *severe or catastrophic* adverse effect on organizational operations, organizational assets, or individuals. Adverse effects on individuals may include, but are not limited to, loss of privacy to which individuals are entitled under law. A severe or catastrophic adverse effect means that, for example, the loss of confidentiality, integrity, or availability might (1) cause a severe degradation in or loss of mission capability to an extent and duration that the organization is not able to perform one or more of its primary functions; (2) result in major damage to organizational assets; (3) result in major financial loss; or (4) result in severe or catastrophic harm to individuals involving loss of life or serious life threatening injuries.

[a] Adapted from NIST FIPS 199, Standard for Security Categorization of Federal Information and Information Systems, December 2003.

Risk levels are also determined as a function of the likelihood of threat instantiation and the potential worst-case severity of the consequences. Ratings are assigned to likelihood and severity categories. The product of the likelihood and severity ratings is compared to determine the risk level. As shown in Table 2.4, a product of 40 to 100 equates to a high risk rating. A product of 11 to 39 equates to a moderate risk level, and a product of 1 to 10 equates to a low risk level. (Severity and likelihood categories are defined below in Tables 2.5 and 2.6.)

Table 2.4   Risk Level Determination[a]

Threat Likelihood	Severity of Consequences			
	Insignificant (10)	*Marginal (40)*	*Critical (70)*	*Catastrophic (100)*
Incredible (0.1)	10 × 0.1 = 1.0	40 × 0.1 = 4.0	70 × 0.1 = 7.0	100 × 0.1 = 10.0
Improbable (0.20)	10 × 0.2 = 2.0	40 × 0.2 = 8.0	70 × 0.2 = 14.0	100 × 0.2 = 20.0
Remote (0.40)	10 × 0.4 = 4.0	40 × 0.4 = 16.0	70 × 0.4 = 28.0	100 × 0.4 = 40.0
Occasional (0.60)	10 × 0.6 = 6.0	40 × 0.6 = 24.0	70 × 0.6 = 42.0	100 × 0.6 = 60.0
Probable (0.80)	10 × 0.8 = 8.0	40 × 0.8 = 32.0	70 × 0.8 = 56.0	100 × 0.8 = 80.0
Frequent	10 × 1 = 10	40 × 1 = 40	70 × 1 = 70.0	100 × 1 = 100

Note: Risk scale: High = 40 to 100, Moderate = 11 to 39, Low = 1 to 10.

[a] Adapted from NIST SP 800-30, Risk Management Guide for Information Technology Systems, October 2001.

Table 2.5   Severity Categories

Category	Definition[a]
Insignificant	Could result in loss, injury, or illness not resulting in a lost workday, property loss (including information assets) exceeding $2K but less than $10K, or minimal environmental damage
Marginal	Could result in loss, injury, or occupational illness resulting in a lost workday, property loss (including information assets) exceeding $10K but less than $200K, or mitigable environmental damage
Critical	Could result in loss, permanent partial disability, injuries, or occupational illness that may result in hospitalization of at least three personnel, property loss (including information assets) exceeding $200K but less than $1M, or reversible environmental damage
Catastrophic	Could result in loss, death, permanent total disability, property loss (including information assets) exceeding $1M, or irreversible environmental damage

[a] Adapted from MIL-STD 882D, Mishap Risk Management, U.S. Department of Defense Standard Practice, October 1998.

Severity is the worst-case consequences should a potential hazard occur.[125] Most international standards define four levels of hazard severity, as shown in Table 2.5. Note that the severity categories take into account all the possible consequences of threat instantiation, whether they are cyber, financial, physical, or environmental. Financial loss can be the cost of downtime, lost revenue, damaged equipment, or fines from being noncompliant with federal regulations.

Likelihood is the qualitative or quantitative probability that a potential hazard will occur or a potential threat will be instantiated.[125] Most international

Table 2.6 Likelihood Categories

Category	Definition[a]
Incredible	Unlikely to occur in the life of an item, with a probability of occurrence less than 10^{-7}
Improbable	So unlikely, it can be assumed occurrence may not be experienced, with a probability of occurrence less than 10^{-6}
Remote	Unlikely, but possible to occur in the life of an item, with a probability of occurrence of less than 10^{-3} but greater than 10^{-6}
Occasional	Likely to occur sometime in the life of an item, with a probability of occurrence of less than 10^{-2} but greater than 10^{-3}
Probable	Will occur several times in the life of an item, with a probability of occurrence of less than 10^{-1} but greater than 10^{-2}
Frequent	Likely to occur often in the life of an item, with a probability of occurrence greater than 10^{-1}

[a] Adapted from MIL-STD 882D, Mishap Risk Management, U.S. Department of Defense Standard Practice, October 1998.

Table 2.7 Asset Criticality Categories

Category	Definition[a]
Routine	Systems, functions, services, or information that if lost, would *not significantly degrade* the capability to perform the organization's mission and achieve the organization's business goals
Essential	Systems, functions, services, or information that if lost, would reduce the capability to perform the organization's mission and achieve the organization's business goals
Critical	Systems, functions, services, and information that if lost, would *prevent* the capability to perform the organization's mission and achieve the organization's business goals

[a] Adapted from FAA NAS-SR-1000, National Airspace System (NAS) System Requirements Specification, April 2002.

standards define six levels of likelihood as shown in Table 2.6. Note that the likelihood categories are defined both quantitatively and qualitatively. Most people are intuitively more comfortable with quantitative measures. The common perception is that quantitative measures are more objective, the result of a more thorough and disciplined assessment, and repeatable.[199] Quantitative measures can be misleading if the accuracy, precision, validity, and correctness test is not met; so, do not trust a metric just because it is quantitative. Qualitative measures are needed in addition to quantitative measures because in some situations the sample population cannot be measured with an interval or ratio scale. That is where nominal and ordinal scales come into play, like the continuum represented by the Capabilities Maturity Model (CMM) levels.

Qualitative measures can be subjective if the measurement rules are not defined precisely, so proceed carefully.

Criticality identifies the relative importance of an asset in performing or achieving an organization's mission. Criticality differs from risk in that an asset may be extremely critical to accomplishing an organization's mission and at the same time be low risk. That is, risk and criticality are independent characteristics. Most organizations assign asset criticality to one of the three categories as shown in Table 2.7.

2.5 Whose Metrics?

The nature and scope of security and privacy metrics that are deemed useful are also a function of the:

- Particular life-cycle phase the product, process, or project being examined is in
- Role or function of the metric consumers within the organization
- Level of the metric consumers within the organization
- Organization's mission and business values

In short, you need to have a good understanding of who are the metric consumers. These different perspectives are often referred to as views.

In the ideal world, the end users would formulate the **G**oal and **Q**uestions, while the security engineering staff would develop the **M**etrics. It is essential to take the time to find out what these people want to know, or conversely are not interested in, before deluging them with metrics. To be blunt, you are wasting your time and money if you do not include the metric consumers during the definition of the metrics program, and the results will be as popular as systems and applications that are designed and developed without first ascertaining the end users' requirements and preferences.

View the metrics requirements gathering process as an ongoing dialog, as the metric consumers refine their view of the information they want and you improve your understanding of their needs. This process is very similar to an IT requirements gathering process. Do not expect the end users to tell you the exact calculations to perform. Instead, they will speak in general terms of a vision, especially at first when you are establishing the metrics program. Over time, as the metric consumers become familiar with the metrics program and the types of insight metrics can provide, this vision will become more focused. A variety of formats can be used to capture metric consumers' requirements: interviews, surveys, case studies, focus groups, etc. The more creative and interesting you make it for the metric consumers, the better participation you will get in return. The important thing is to do your homework first.

Another important fact must be stated at this time. Raw metric data can often be used for multiple purposes. That is, raw metric data can be "sliced and diced" to support many different analyses and answer several GQMs for various levels and functions throughout the organization. Be sure to keep this fact in mind when designing your metric data collection and analysis process; it will keep you from (1) collecting multiple overlapping sets of metric data, and (2) annoying the groups from which the data is being collected. Think REUSE — a well-designed metric can save a lot of time.

A key factor influencing what metrics are deemed useful is the particular life-cycle phase in which the product, process, or project being examined is. This is only logical; different issues, concerns, and challenges arise at different points in the system engineering life cycle. These issues, concerns, and challenges affect not just IT security and privacy, but also physical, personnel, and operational security. Why are life-cycle phases being discussed in a section titled "Whose Metrics?" The answer is simple — different people with different skill sets perform the requirements, design, development, verification and validation, operations, and maintenance engineering functions. (Metrics associated with different phases of the security engineering life cycle are explored in detail in Section 4.4 of Chapter 4.) This factor is often referred to *as situational metrics.* As Schulenklopper notes[138]:

> Measurement activities are an essential part of management. When the management approach is tuned to a specific situation, different control information needs may arise.

Next we look at how the role or function of metric consumers within an organization influences what metrics they consider useful. A person's role in an organization determines what information is important or valuable to them; other information may be interesting but it will not help them perform their primary job function. As a result, the metrics needed vary by position and role. The type of metrics needed will also vary as the security controls mature.[57] It has been noted that, in general, the private sector tends to be more interested in technical or operational metrics while the government sector tends to be more interested in process metrics.[223] These different needs can be referred to as *lateral views of metrics.*

To demonstrate this point, consider the following goal:

> **G**: Ensure the security and privacy of customer and corporate data, in accordance with its sensitivity category, during transmission across our WAN.

A set of questions and metrics are spawned from this single goal that are consistent with diverse lateral views. Given space considerations, only one question and metric are shown per lateral view; in reality, there would be many. As shown, all the questions and metrics tie back to the same goal, yet at the same time they are tailored for the specific lateral view. Eight lateral views, common to most organizations, are explored: (1) security engineer, (2) telecommunications engineer, (3) privacy officer, (4) end users or stakeholders, (5) quality assurance, (6) legal, (7) finance, and (8) marketing or public relations.

1. Security engineer:

   Q: How thoroughly was the robustness of the security and privacy controls evaluated during ST&E?

   M: Percentage of as-built system security and privacy controls that has been verified to perform correctly during stress testing and under other abnormal conditions.

2. Telecommunications engineer:

   Q: Do the IT and operational security controls ensure data integrity during transmission without interfering with throughput, capacity, and latency?

   M: Ratio of security overhead to data traffic.

3. Privacy officer:

   Q: Will the controls implemented ensure data security and privacy in accordance with federal regulations?

   M: Number and distribution of problems encountered during validation and verification, by life-cycle phase and severity category.

4. End users or stakeholders:

   Q: Is my data secure and private across the network?

   M: Distribution of problem reports, open and closed, generated during ST&E, by life-cycle phase and severity category.

5. Quality assurance:

   Q: Do the security controls comply with corporate security and privacy policies and industry standards?

   M: Degree to which the as-built system complies with corporate security and privacy policies, using an interval scale of 1 (low) to 10 (completely).

6. Legal:

   Q: Do the security controls comply with federal regulations and meet the test of due diligence?

   M: Degree to which the as-built system meets or exceeds federal security and privacy regulations, using an ordinal scale of does not meet (red), meets most but not all provisions of the regulations (yellow), meets all provisions (green), and meets or exceeds all provisions of the regulations, especially in the area of due diligence (blue).

7. Finance:

   Q: Did we spend funds smartly on the right security controls to achieve the requisite data security and privacy?

   M: Distribution of IT capital investment by major security functional area, such as access control, authentication, encryption, etc., and its correlation to achieving data security and privacy requirements.

8. Marketing or public relations:

> **Q:** To what extent can I market the security and privacy features of our WAN without overdoing it?
>
> **M:** Comparison of the robustness of the security and privacy controls to information asset sensitivity categories, using a nominal scale of high, moderate, and low.

Finally, we examine how the level of metric consumers within an organization determines what metrics they consider useful. A person's level in an organization governs what information is important or valuable to him. People might be performing the same function (security engineering) but have different information needs because of their level within an organization. The range of information needs generally reflects a difference in the span of control, authority, and responsibility, which translates into the need for distinct levels of abstraction and measurement boundaries. Information may be too detailed or too summarized to be useful, depending on the position level; this is especially true in large organizations. As a result, metric needs vary by level. These contrasting needs can be referred to as *hierarchical views of metrics.* The Corporate Information Security Working Group (CISWG) provided the first major security metrics publication to acknowledge hierarchical views of metrics.[105]

To illustrate this point, consider the following goal:

> **G:** Ensure the confidentiality of corporate data, in accordance with its sensitivity category, while the data is in electronic form and resident on desktops, servers, the corporate LAN, and in online, offline, and off-site archives.

Again, a set of questions and metrics are spawned from this single goal that are consistent with diverse hierarchical views. Likewise, given space considerations, only one question and metric are shown per lateral view; in reality, there would be many. As shown, all the questions and metrics tie back to the same goal, yet at the same time they are tailored for the specific hierarchical view. Four hierarchical views, common to most organizations, are explored: (1) Chief Executive Officer (CEO), (2) Chief Security Officer (CSO), (3) Information System Security Manager (ISSM), and (4) Information System Security Officer (ISSO).

1. Chief Executive Officer (CEO):

> **Q:** What is the corporate risk of sensitive electronic data being inadvertently exposed?
>
> **M:** Probability of physical, personnel, IT, and operational security controls failing individually or in combination, such that a leak results.

2. Chief Security Officer (CSO):

> **Q:** Are the appropriate physical, personnel, IT, and operational security controls in place, and have they been verified?
>
> **M:** Percentage of physical, personnel, IT, and operational security controls that have been tailored by information sensitivity category and independently verified.

3. Information Systems Security Manager (ISSM):

    Q: Are the access control and encryption functions sufficiently robust for all the systems and LANs in my department?

    M: Percentage of access control rights and privileges, cryptographic operation and operational procedures, and encryption algorithms for systems and LANs in my department that have been independently verified to perform as specified during normal operations, stress testing, and under abnormal conditions.

4. Information System Security Officer (ISSO):

    Q: Are the access control and encryption functions sufficiently robust for the system (or LAN) that I manage?

    M: Percentage of access control rights and privileges, cryptographic operation and operational procedures, and encryption algorithms for my system (or LAN) that have been independently verified to perform as specified during normal operations, stress testing, and under abnormal conditions.

The nature and scope of security and privacy metrics that are deemed useful are also a function of an organization's size, mission, and business values.[105] This aspect of metrics is explored in Section 2.12 below.

2.6 Uses and Limits of Metrics

Security and privacy metrics are a tool that can be used by engineers, auditors, and management. Employed correctly, they can help plan or control a project or process; improve the security and privacy of operational procedures, an end product, or system; provide visibility into a current situation or predict future scenarios and outcomes; and track performance trends.[12, 137, 174, 204] Metrics furnish the requisite factual foundation upon which to base critical decisions about security and privacy, the absence of which increases an organization's cost, schedule, and technical risk, and possibly liability concerns.

Metrics must possess certain characteristics in order to yield these benefits to an institution. Table 2.8 lists the attributes of what are referred to as "good metrics." The goodness of a given metric is a function of the resultant metric value as well as the metric definition, collection, and analysis process that produced it. A good metric value exhibits certain intrinsic properties, such as accuracy, precision, validity, and correctness, which were discussed previously. Good metric values are consistent with metrics that measure similar attributes. Consider the following three metrics:

1. Percentage of systems for which approved configuration settings have been implemented as required by policy
2. Percentage of systems with configurations that do not deviate from approved standards
3. Percentage of systems that are continuously monitored for configuration policy compliance with out-of-date compliance alarms or reports, by system risk category

Table 2.8　Characteristics of Good Metrics[57, 137, 174, 204, 223]

The Metric Value:
Accurate
Precise
Valid
Correct
Consistent
Current or time stamped
Can be replicated
Can be compared to previous measurements, target values, or benchmarks
Can stand on its own
The Metric Definition, Collection, and Analysis Process:
Objective calculations and measurement rules
Availability or ease of collecting primitive data
Uncertainty and variability in the measurement process have been removed
Tied to specific business goal or GQM
Results are meaningful and useful for decision makers, provide value-added to organization
Results are understandable and easy to interpret

The results from these three metrics should be consistent; in particular, the first two should be extremely consistent. Inconsistencies in the results from similar metrics are indications of serious flaws in the data collection and analysis process. Sloppy data collection can wreak havoc on the goodness of metrics.[169] For example, is a failure really a result of a security incident or slipshod patch management? Good metrics are tied to a fixed time interval or reference point. The time interval can be expressed as a range (last 30 calendar days) or a fixed point (2 p.m. on Tuesday, May 5, 2005). All raw data that is collected must conform to the specified time interval for the results to be valid. Discard any data that is outside the specified time interval during the extraction process. A popular litmus test to ascertain the goodness of a metric is whether or not the results can be replicated. Does the exact data collection and analysis process yield the same results? In particular, can an independent third party reproduce the results when following the same measurement rules? The answer should be a resounding yes. If not, there is some ambiguity in the metric definition or variability in the collection and analysis process that must be alleviated before proceeding. A good metric value can be compared to previous measurements, target values, or benchmarks. The repetition of uniform measurements at different points in time provides useful information to track behavior patterns or performance trends. If the measurements are not uniform, the comparisons cannot be made. A target value or range should be specified for each metric. This value ties back to the goal the organization is trying to accomplish. To determine if progress is being made toward achieving or sustaining that goal, you must be able to compare the metric results to that target value or range. Finally, a good metric value is able to stand on its own. Consider the following two examples:

1. Twelve security incidents were experienced.
2. A total of twelve marginal IT security incidents were experienced at all facilities during the past six calendar months, beginning January 1, 2005.

The first example is not a good metric; it is incomplete; several crucial facts are missing. Incomplete metrics are prone to misuse and misinterpretation because end users erroneously fill in the details themselves. The second is an example of a complete metric that is able to stand on its own.

The second aspect of good metrics is the metric definition, collection, and analysis process that was used to produce the metric values. As Fenton and Pfleeger point out, metrics are only as good as the data collected, validated, and analyzed.[137] If this process is askew, so will be the metric values. First and foremost, good metrics are based on objective calculations and measurement rules. *Objective* calculations and measurement rules produce values that are valid, correct, and consistent, and they can be replicated. *Subjective* calculations and measurement rules do not. Metrics are intended to provide value-added to an organization. The time and cost to collect primitive data should not outweigh the benefits. A well-designed metrics program is folded into the system engineering life cycle and takes advantage of existing artifacts. Precision is based on the absence of uncertainty and variability in the measurement process. Given that this is not possible in all situations, data is refined or normalized to account for known or potential variability. Hence, it is important to ensure that the refinement process is not neglected. Good metrics are defined in response to a business objective or goal, not the other way around. The GQM paradigm epitomizes this fact. The business objective can be a technical, financial, management, marketing, or regulatory goal. Good metrics are designed to answer questions related to these goals and objectives. They provide valuable insights to an organization that are both meaningful and useful. Think of the metrics program as providing a service to key decision makers — they have questions, you have answers. For information to be useful, it must also be understandable and easy to interpret. This does not mean everyone walking down the street will understand the metric values; rather, tailor the presentation of the metric values to the specific consumer. Metric values can be presented in a variety of formats: graphs, charts, tables of numbers, bulleted text, etc. Find out what format the metric consumer wants beforehand and pay special attention to the units in which they expect the measurements to be. One other word of caution: just answer the question; skip the fluff and get to the point the metric consumer wants to know. The following two examples illustrate this concept; hopefully I do not have to tell you which is which....

1. Sometime last winter, Harry misconfigured sixteen firewalls at five locations that caused the 12th bit in the dumb-dumb register to overflow on nine servers containing mostly miscellaneous data. Sam thinks this resulted in about twelve security incidents, but we are checking on it.

2. A total of twelve marginal IT security incidents were experienced at all facilities during the past six calendar months, beginning January 1, 2005. The total loss from these twelve marginal security incidents, including downtime, lost productivity, and rework, is estimated to be $7.5K. No customers or outside stakeholders were affected.

Capability Maturity Models (CMMs) are very popular in the software and system engineering domains. These models assess the maturity of organizational processes and projects. The maturity ratings are referred to as levels on an ordinal scale, with 1 being the lowest and 5 the highest. The use of metrics is required to move from level 4 to level 5; the goal is to use metrics to provide valuable feedback to improve and control processes and projects. The benefits of using metrics are referred to as *predictability* and *repeatability*.

The judicious use of security and privacy metrics can provide these benefits as well. As Jelen notes, product metrics can be used to indicate the extent to which a given security attribute is implemented and functioning correctly in terms of its operational effectiveness and security efficiency.[169] Product metrics can be used to measure or predict the effectiveness of security controls, individually or collectively. Product metrics can be used to track the performance of particular security appliances or the resilience of the enterprise security architecture. Product metrics can be used to highlight strengths or weaknesses in configurations and the need to reassign resources. Product metrics can also be used to determine if a system is ready to deploy.

A common use of product metrics is to measure actual performance against contractual service level agreements (SLAs). This has been practiced in the telecommunications sector for years. It is imperative to invoke SLAs and rigorous security metrics when outsourcing responsibility for all or part of corporate security functions. SLAs can also be used between one corporate division and another. This concept is referred to as the use of security metrics to enforce the quality of protection provided. The customer defines the SLAs and the metrics. The vendor is responsible for providing the metrics to prove that the SLAs were met. Contractual fines and penalties are imposed when SLAs are not met, proportional to the customer's business losses. The following are examples of security metrics tied to SLAs. The actual metrics and SLAs will vary, of course, by the system risk, information sensitivity, and asset criticality.

- Maximum allowable number of outages of 10 minutes or less due to catastrophic security incidents throughout the duration of the contract: 0
- Maximum allowable number of outages of 20 minutes or less due to critical security incidents throughout the duration of the contract: 2
- Maximum percentage of all marginal security incidents per month that result in an outage of more than 30 minutes: 5 percent
- Maximum time a marginal security incident can remain open without progress toward resolution: 15 minutes
- Maximum time allowed to submit an initial security incident report to the customer: 5 minutes

- Maximum time allowed to submit an interim security incident report to the customer: 24 hours
- Maximum time allowed to issue a security credential after it is authorized: 5 business days
- Maximum time allowed to revoke a security credential after notification to do so: 10 minutes

Process metrics can be used to measure the policies and processes that were established to produce a desired outcome.[105] Process metrics can be used to measure how fully a process has been implemented or is being followed.[105] Process metrics can be used to measure the maturity and effectiveness of corporate security and privacy policies and procedures. The results from each process step can be analyzed to track project performance and highlight problem areas. Process metrics can also be used to identify organizational strengths and weaknesses related to security and privacy and any new skills needed. Statistical process control is commonly used in the manufacturing sector. Statistical process control, a collection of techniques for use in the improvement of any process, involves the systematic collection of data related to a process and graphical summaries of that data for visibility.[204] Its use is becoming more prevalent in the software engineering domain as well; methodologies such as the Six Sigma are particularly popular. Pareto analysis, identifying the vital few problem areas that offer the greatest opportunity for improvement by prioritizing their frequency, cost, or importance, is also widespread [204] Pareto analysis is often referred to as the 80-20 rule: 80 percent of the defects are found in 20 percent of the system entities. Statistical process control, Six Sigma, and Pareto analysis are all possible because of well-defined metrics. There is no reason why these techniques cannot be applied to security and privacy engineering — not today perhaps, but in the near future.

Security and privacy metrics are neither a panacea unto themselves, nor do they make a system or network secure or information private on their own. Metrics are a tool that, if used correctly, can help you achieve those goals. However, you need to be aware of their limitations. All metrics have certain limitations that you need to be aware of to avoid over- or mis-using them. It is important to understand the context in which the metric is intended to be used and the purpose for which it was designed. Likewise, it is essential to comprehend the rules by which the metric data was collected and analyzed and how the results were interpreted. Metric consumers have the responsibility to ask some probing questions to discern the accuracy, precision, validity, and correctness of metrics that are presented to them. We are talking about security and privacy metrics after all; there is no room for "trust me's" here!

As pointed out previously, the types of analysis that can be legitimately performed on metrics are limited by the measurement type and scale. If subjectivity in the metric definition and data collection process is not removed, the results belong in the bit bucket. Potential sources of error in the measurement process, whether random or systematic, need to be identified, acknowledged, and mitigated.[137] This information must be passed on to the metric consumers. Be sure not to confuse primitives with metrics or non-metrics with metrics. A common misuse of metrics is confusing product and process metrics, or relying on only one or the other. Another frequent error is to look only at IT security metrics, to the neglect of physical, personnel, and operational security metrics. A well-designed metrics program includes a balance of product and process metrics from all four security domains.

Product metrics are generally tied to a specific configuration, operational environment, release, and so forth. That is, they were true at a certain point in time for a given installation. Be careful not to read more than that into them. Process metrics do not necessarily measure the appropriateness of the process for a given situation or the skill level of the personnel implementing it. An organization may have a wonderful process but if it is inappropriate for the situation to which it is being applied, all bets are off. Likewise, an organization may have a wonderful process, but if you are relying on personnel who do not have the right skill set to implement it, the results will be haphazard. Unfortunately, process metrics do not capture either of these situations. Likewise, process metrics may fail to take into account externally imposed constraints.[223]

The following two examples illustrate the pitfalls of using faulty metrics. They highlight common practices, such as trying to develop metrics for incomplete questions and confusing primitives with metrics; avoid these mistakes at all cost. Also, keep in mind that when faulty metrics get out, they are difficult to retrieve.

Go to any conference in the Washington, D.C. area that is remotely connected to security and privacy, and someone in the audience will inevitably ask, "How much should I be spending on security?" Without hesitation, the speaker answers, "4 percent." The audience nods their heads in approval and the session moves on to the next question. This mantra has been repeated in government circles since at least 2000, to the extent that the number has become sacrosanct. In reality, this number is a prime example of a faulty metric or, to be more exact, a non-metric. Think about it for a minute: do you really think that NSA and the Fish and Wildlife Service should spend the same percentage of their budgets on security? Both the question and the answer are flawed. Let us look at each in detail to see why.

"How much should I be spending on security?" This is an example of an incomplete question and one that is not tied back to a goal. As a result, the "metrics" derived from it are meaningless. To illustrate, the question "how much should I be spending on security?" cannot be answered unless you know a lot more facts. The following are just a few of the facts that are needed before you can even begin to answer the question:

- What type of security are you talking about: physical, personnel, IT, or operational security? A combination of domains? All of the above?
- What is the risk of the system or network you are trying to protect?
- What is the sensitivity of the information you are trying to protect?
- What is the criticality of the asset(s) you are trying to protect?
- Where are you in the system engineering life cycle?

- What is the volume and type of information entered, processed, stored online and offline, and transmitted?
- What is the geographical distribution of system resources?
- How many operational and backup sites are there?
- How many internal and external users are there? What is the trust level and trust type for each?
- How many high-level and low-level security requirements are there? To what level of integrity must the requirements be verified?
- What is the nature of the operational environment?

"4 percent of your budget." Not surprisingly, this answer is as incomplete and imprecise as the question. The answer neglects to state what budget this 4 percent comes from. The IT capital budget? The IT operations and maintenance budget? The budget for software and hardware licenses? The budget for contractors? The payroll? The facilities management budget? The organization's entire budget? The answer neglects to state what time interval to which the 4 percent applies. Only during system development? Only during operations and maintenance? The entire life of the system? Forever? Also, how could the 4 percent be a constant when everything else in the budget is changing, not to mention inflation and other escalation factors?

Another sacred number in Washington, D.C. circles, especially among the Federal Information Security Management Act (FISMA) crowd, is the number of systems for which the security certification and accreditation (C&A) process has been completed. Agencies like to brag about this number, as if it were some embellished fishing story: "We have completed C&A on 5317 systems, while you have only completed 399." This is another example of a metric gone awry or, to be more precise, a primitive that has become confused with a metric. Let us look at this number in detail and see why.

Standard practice is to report the number of systems that have been through the security C&A process, the number remaining, and the number awaiting recertification. (As we will see in Chapter 3, FISMA requires federal agencies to conduct security C&A on their systems every three years or following a major system upgrade.) The number of systems that have been through the security C&A process by itself does not tell us much, if anything. As mentioned above, this number is a primitive; it should be combined with other primitives to derive any meaningful information. For example, this number does not tell you anything about:

- The quality or thoroughness of the security C&A process that was performed
- The skill level of the C&A team
- The duration of the C&A effort
- Whether the C&A results were independently verified
- The number of problems found during C&A
- The severity of problems found during C&A
- The number of problems that were fixed prior to approval and those that remain to be fixed

- The system risk, information sensitivity, or asset criticality categories
- Whether the system is new, operational, or a legacy system
- The number of waivers that have been signed, by risk, sensitivity, and criticality categories
- The number of interim approvals to operate that have been granted, by risk, sensitivity, and criticality categories

The difficulties in defining what constitutes a system versus a sub-system or system or systems were discussed previously. Perhaps the number includes a mixture of systems and sub-systems, rendering it misleading. Also, because a pass/fail scale is used, there is no indication of whether the system barely passed the threshold for C&A or sailed through with flying colors. Would you trust your bank account to a system that barely squeaked by? Furthermore, there is no evidence to indicate whether or not the primitives have been verified. Consequently, they may not meet the accuracy, precision, validity, and correctness standards.

2.7 Avoiding the Temptation to Bury Your Organization in Metrics

Why does a book promoting the use of security and privacy metrics contain a section entitled "Avoiding the Temptation to Bury Your Organization in Metrics"? Because this is the most common mistake made by metrics programs, especially when the metrics program is new and the staff a bit overzealous. The temptation to deliver hundreds of "interesting" metrics that consumers have not asked for, and cannot use, is sometimes irresistible but deadly. Here is some advice on how to avoid this frequent blunder (refer to Table 2.9).

The first maxim comes from IEEE Std. 982[8, 9]:

> If there are no prestated objectives on how the results will be used, there should be no measurements.

A good metrics program operates top-down, using the GQM paradigm. The metric consumer establishes the measurement **G**oal. The metric consumer and security metrics engineer work together to derive **Q**uestions from the **G**oal.

Table 2.9   How to Avoid Burying Your Organization in Metrics

If there are no prestated objectives on how the results will be used, there should be no measurements.[8, 9]
Establish pragmatic goals for the metrics program from the outset.
Distinguish between what can be measured and what needs to be measured.
Balance providing value-added to metric consumers with the overhead of the metrics program.
Use common sense.

Then the security metrics engineer identifies **M**etrics that can be used to answer each **Q**uestion. As mentioned previously, you have to know what you are measuring and why before you can even begin to identify and define metrics. You have to know the question before you can supply the answer. Do not start with a metric (or primitive) and try to fabricate a goal and question the metric can be used to support. Metrics and primitives can be recycled to answer different questions; they cannot be retrofitted to nonexistent goals and questions. Beware of prospectors who want to go digging for metrics in the hills of your IDS logs... "There must be some metrics in here somewhere... perhaps if we do some Markov modeling..." They may line their pockets with gold, but you will be none the wiser.

The second maxim is to establish pragmatic goals for the metrics program from the outset. It is difficult for an organization or individual to recover from a failed metrics program. The best approach is to start small and grow slowly, according to the needs of a particular project, program, or organization, while building on successes.[137] At the same time, manage metric consumers' expectations. Be realistic — avoid overselling the program and the benefits it can provide. A few people will grasp the potential benefits of security and privacy metrics immediately. For others, enthusiasm and support will follow the demonstrated accomplishments.

The third maxim is to distinguish between what can be measured and what needs to be measured. It is better to select a handful of well-designed and concise metrics that will comprehensively answer the **Q**uestion, than to deliver 200 irrelevant metrics. Do not measure something just because it can be measured or because it is an intellectually interesting pursuit. Avoid the excesses of the quality bubble in the 1990s — having process for process sake and measuring anything and everything just because it could be done. This is another example of zealots at work. Likewise, avoid the theater of the absurd and the syndrome of measuring the "number of gnats on a head of pin." Ask yourself: "Who will care about these results and how can they be used?" There is no magic number of what constitutes too many, too few, or the right number of metrics for a particular situation. This number will vary, depending on what is being measured, why, and how often. Higher risk, sensitivity, and criticality categories generally infer more security requirements, more intense security assurance activities, and more in-depth security certification and accreditation (C&A) and ST&E activities. However, they do not necessarily mean more metrics are needed. It is the job of the security metrics engineer to zero in on what is and is not meaningful for a particular GQM. As we have seen from the previous sections, there are several parameters to consider, such as the measurement boundaries, life-cycle phase, and the role and level of the metric consumer. Keep the attributes of a good metric, as listed in Table 2.8, in mind as you proceed.

The fourth maxim is to balance providing value-added to metric consumers with the overhead of the metrics program. A well-designed metrics program is embedded in standard business practices and the system engineering life cycle. Artifacts from which primitives are gleaned are part of standard business practices and the system engineering life cycle; they should not have to be fabricated after the fact. All stakeholders are part of and have a vested interest in a good metrics program. Do not waste time looking for the ultimate metric, because such does not exist. Instead, a set of metrics will always be needed to examine any topic thoroughly and answer the question authoritatively. Do the best you can with the information that is available today, and then improve upon it tomorrow. This brings up a topic most people shy away from — do not be afraid of augmenting or updating metrics after they have been released. For example, suppose you reported in January that the answer to question x was 12. In March, new information was discovered and the answer to question x is now calculated as 10.5. By all means, report this observation. All you have to say is that the January number was based on the best information available at the time. Now new information is available and you have a more definitive answer. Metric consumers will appreciate your honesty, not to mention having the correct answer. A good metrics program is designed to be flexible; this is essential in order to adapt to changing situations and priorities. Metric consumers' goals are likely to be very dynamic. A good metrics program can adjust just as quickly. A new metrics program is bound to take a few missteps in the beginning. The best thing to do is to own up to these mistakes. Instead of trying to hide mistakes, learn from them to improve the metrics program.

The fifth maxim is obvious: use common sense. Do not think that people will be more impressed if you inundate them with mounds of metrics. On the contrary, they will think that either you are (1) an incompetent, not to mention unorganized, fool and do not know what you are doing, or (2) that you are trying to hide something in the midst of the mounds. Instead of impressing people, this will trigger an extra level of scrutiny. Consider the case below.

Once I was asked to review a security C&A package for a legacy system, as an independent observer. The system was low risk and the information it contained was of moderate sensitivity. However, the asset criticality was critical. The security C&A package filled two 3.5-inch binders. There were unlabeled tab dividers, but no table of contents. The fact that I was asked to review the package was the first red light; this is not part of my normal duties. The condition of the C&A package was the second red light. The third red light was the insistence by the system owner that I hurry, that everything was ok and he needed to get it signed (approved) this week. The prose was perfect and the charts were stylish, but for the most part the information was irrelevant. Hidden in the middle of the second notebook was a two-page table that told me everything I needed to know. The table was a bulleted list of the problems that were found during the security audit; they were only alluded to vaguely in the request for a waiver. The "problems" included items such as the fact that the system had no identification and authentication function, no access control functions, no audit trail, no backup or recovery procedures, etc. In short, the system had no security functionality whatsoever. But a waiver would make everything alright!

Focus on what the metric consumers *really* need to know. It is preferable to deliver the message in 20 to 30 metrics, rather than 200. Pay close attention

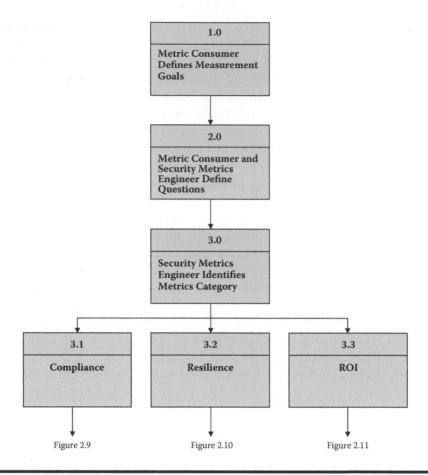

Figure 2.8   **How to identify and select the right metrics.**

to the presentation of the metric results. Know when to aggregate data or when to let it stand on its own. You should be able to tell the metrics story in a variety of different formats and lengths. Plan on having a ten-minute version, a thirty-minute version, and a two-hour version ready. Yes, have back-up data available to answer any questions that might arise. But there is something wrong if you can only do a two-(or more) hour version of the presentation.

So how do you find the right set of metrics to use, given that there are more than 900 metrics defined in this book? The place to start is with the GQM, as shown in Figure 2.8. The first step is to define the measurement **G**oal; this is the responsibility of the metric consumers. Next, the metric consumers and security metrics engineer work together to define the **Q**uestion(s) that can be asked to measure progress toward achieving or sustaining that goal. Then the security metrics engineer begins to identify the right set of **M**etrics to use to answer each **Q**uestion completely, no more and no less. The first decision is to determine whether (1) compliance with security and privacy regulations and standards; (2) the resilience of physical, personnel, IT, and operational security controls; or (3) the return on investment in physical, personnel, IT, and operational security controls is being measured.

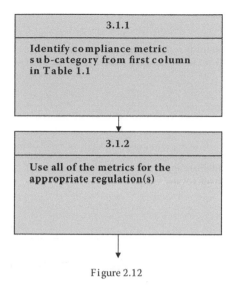

Figure 2.12

Figure 2.9   How to identify and select the right metrics (continued).

The metric selection process is relatively straightforward, if compliance is being measured. (See Figure 2.9.) First, the corresponding compliance metric sub-category (financial, healthcare, personal privacy, or homeland security) in the first column of Table 1.1 is located. Metrics for each of the 13 current security and privacy regulations are assigned to one of these sub-categories; they are discussed at length in Chapter 3. To demonstrate compliance with the security and privacy provisions of a particular regulation, all the metrics listed for that regulation are used. The exception is FISMA metrics. Metrics 1.10.1 through 1.10.35 are optional, while metrics 1.10.36 through 1.10.78 are required. The set of candidate metrics is then tailored, if needed, to reflect the specific measurement boundaries, system risk, information sensitivity, asset criticality, and role and level of the metric consumer. To save time during the analysis phase, identify what primitives can be reused for multiple metrics. Keep in mind that there may be multiple consumers of compliance metrics, because compliance metrics can be generated for internal consumption as well as for regulatory bodies. Finally, a decision is made about how the metric results will be presented. Issues such as the need for metric aggregation are explored at this time.

If resilience is being measured, a few more decisions must be made. (See Figure 2.10.) The first action is to identify the appropriate resilience sub-category from the first column in Table 1.1. For what security domain are you measuring resilience: physical, personnel, IT, or operational? Are metrics from more than one sub-category needed? In general, it is best to consider all four domains, especially if you think you are "only" looking at IT security. Next, the applicable metric sub-element(s) are identified from the second column in Table 1.1. Each resilience metric sub-category is broken into sub-elements. Decide which of these are applicable to the Question being answered. If the metrics are for a new system, the sub-elements for life-cycle phases may be more appropriate. If the metrics are for an operational or legacy system, other

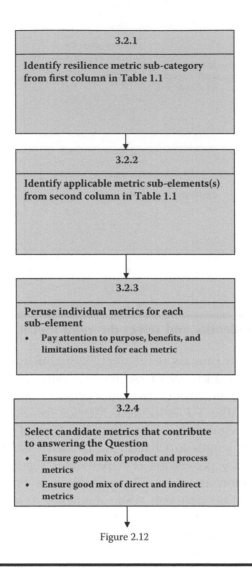

Figure 2.12

Figure 2.10   How to identify and select the right metrics (continued).

sub-elements may be more appropriate. Then peruse the individual metrics listed for each sub-element. Select candidate metrics that contribute to answering the **Q**uestion. Some of the metrics answer the **Q**uestion directly, while others answer it indirectly. Most likely you will want to use a combination of direct and indirect metrics. Strive to have a combination of product and process metrics. Notice that some of the metrics are very different, while there are subtle differences in the others. Pay particular attention to the stated purpose, benefits, and limitations for each metric. Pick the ones that correspond precisely to the **Q**uestion being answered. The other metrics may look interesting, but leave them for now; they will come in handy another time. Repeat this step for each sub-category. Now examine the set of candidate metrics you have selected. Do they make a complete, comprehensive, and cohesive whole? If not, get rid of any duplicate, overlapping, or out-of-scope metrics. Verify that each metric makes a valid and unique contribution to answering the **Q**uestion. Then tailor the metrics, if needed,

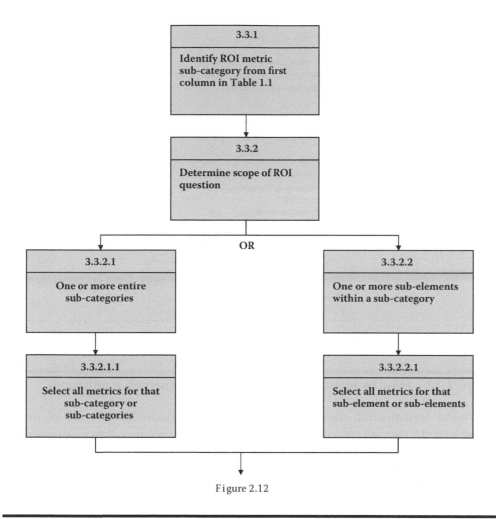

Figure 2.12

Figure 2.11   How to identify and select the right metrics (continued).

to reflect the specific measurement boundaries, system risk, information sensitivity, asset criticality, and the role and level of the metric consumers. To save time during the analysis phase, identify what primitives can be reused for multiple metrics. Finally, decide how the metric results will be presented. Issues such as metric aggregation are explored at this point.

Figure 2.11 and Figure 2.12 illustrate the selection process for ROI metrics. The first step is to identify the appropriate ROI metric sub-category from the first column in Table 1.1. The appropriate sub-category is determined by what security ROI is being measured: physical security, personnel security, IT security, or operational security. Perhaps a combination of security domains is being examined. Next, the scope of the ROI Question is clarified. Does the scope cover one or more entire sub-categories? Or does the scope include one or more sub-elements within a single sub-category? The scope depends on what the ROI Question seeks to answer. If one or more entire sub-categories are being studied, then all the metrics for that sub-category or sub-categories are selected. If one or more entire sub-elements within a single sub-category

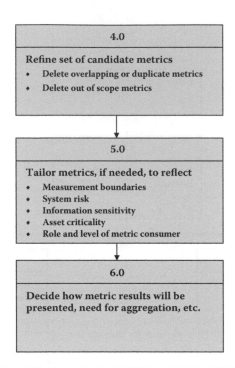

Figure 2.12   How to identify and select the right metrics (continued).

are being investigated, then all metrics for that sub-element or sub-elements are selected. The set of candidate metrics is then refined. Overlapping and duplicate metrics are deleted, as are out-of-scope metrics. Next, the metrics are tailored, if needed, to reflect the exact measurement boundaries, system risk, information sensitivity, and asset criticality specified in the **Q**uestion. The metrics are also tailored to be appropriate for the role and level of the metric consumers. Also, to save time during the analysis phase, primitives that can be reused for multiple metrics are identified. Finally, decisions are made about how the results of the metrics will be presented. Issues such as the need for metric aggregation are explored at this time.

The following example portrays the metric identification and selection process for resilience metrics.

The ABC organization has a long-standing goal:

> **G**: Ensure sensitive corporate data is adequately protected from unau-
> thorized access, that is, reading, copying, viewing, editing, altering,
> inserting, deleting, misappropriating, printing, storing, or releasing
> to unauthorized people or others who do not have a need-to-know.

Recently there have been several sensational items on the evening news about corporate data being stolen and the senior executives at ABC organization are nervous. They (the metric consumers) come to you (the security metrics engineer) and say, "We have a lot summer interns and guest researchers coming onboard in the next few months. Protocol and time prevent us from doing extensive background checks on these people. How do we know that they cannot get to our most sensitive corporate R&D data?" You work together to formulate several specific questions to measure sustainment of that goal. This highlights the fact that goals tend to be static, while questions tend to be dynamic. One such question might be:

Q: How robust are the access controls on our sensitive R&D data?

As the security metrics engineer, you turn to Table 1.1. Under the resilience category you notice the physical and personnel security sub-categories. Maybe…. No, that will not help much, these people will be insiders. On to the IT security sub-category. Hey, there is a whole sub-element titled logical access control. Let us take a look at those. Several of the access control metrics are right on target. Two will identify the potential for misusing old and inactive accounts. One will highlight the likelihood of unauthorized users tailgating on a session that was inadvertently left open, while the "real" user stepped away or went to lunch or a sudden meeting. Others will provide confidence that the summer interns and guest researchers' access rights and privileges are narrowed to only those resources to which they need access to perform their job. And so, you continue through the access control metrics, picking out ones that will help answer the executive's **Q**uestion and ignoring the rest. Knowing that logical access control mechanisms depend on a strong identi-fication and authentication front end, you start browsing through that sub-element. You find some gems here as well. One will let you know the likelihood of an active user ID being used by more than one person. Another will verify that the systems the student interns and guest researchers are accessing enforce password policies to the extent specified in policy. Just to double-check that number, a second metric captures the number of successful system accesses by unauthorized users. Others ensure that the passwords given to the student interns and guest researchers will expire the minute they are off duty. One will let you know whether or not sensitive corporate R&D data is protected by strong identification and authentication mechanisms, not just the traditional user ID and password. Students are pretty smart these days. Another metric provides assurance that they cannot take advantage of default or vendor-supplied accounts and passwords. To be on the safe side, company policy requires accounts that attempt unauthorized accesses be locked. A final one will let you know how thoroughly this policy is being enforced. And so you continue through the metrics listed in the identification and authentication sub-category. Then you look back at Table 1.1 to see if any other resilience sub-elements might be of use.

After you have finished selecting a set of candidate metrics, you refine them. Perhaps you got carried away a bit and need to get rid of some duplicate, overlapping, and out-of-scope metrics. Next you tailor the metrics so that they reflect the **Q**uestion's focus on critical corporate R&D information assets. To save time during the analysis phase, you also identify primitives that can be used for multiple metrics. Given that the results are being presented to senior executives, you decide which metric results will be aggregated in the presentation so that you can get the answer across in 15 minutes. And you are on your way.

Metrics permit you to answer the senior executives' questions authoritatively. The alternative, of course, is to say, "Sure boss, everything's fine," and then keep your fingers crossed.

Using metrics to manage, monitor, understand, control, or improve products, processes, and projects is not a new concept. Unlike security engineering, other disciplines, such as safety engineering and reliability engineering, have been using metrics for several decades. The field of software engineering metrics began in the 1980s. These disciplines are closely related to security engineering. So we look at each of these topics next to discern lessons that can be applied to the practice of security and privacy metrics.

2.8 Relation to Risk Management

A discussion of the relationship between risk management and security engineering is a good place to begin a comparison of security and privacy metrics with those already in use by the reliability, safety, and software engineering communities. We live in a world filled with risk. This is not something to be afraid of; it is just a fact of life. There is risk in breathing (air pollution); there is risk in not breathing (asphyxiation). There is risk in commuting to work (train wrecks, car wrecks, bridge collapses); there is risk in not commuting to work (getting fired). There is risk in investing (stock market loss); there is risk in not investing (your money is stolen or depreciates in value). There is always a trade-off between the risk of taking one particular action or another and the risk of doing nothing. The important thing is to be aware of these risks, plan, prepare for, and manage them. Civilizations, societies, and organizations that do not take managed risks eventually collapse of their own inertia.

There are many different types of risk, such as business risk, medical risk, financial risk, legal risk, and career risk. Within the engineering domain, three categories of risks are generally acknowledged: (1) technical risk, (2) schedule risk, and (3) cost risk. Technical risks are a common concern when designing or building first-of-a-kind systems or systems that are quite different from that with which an organization is familiar. Technical risks can take on many forms. They may include failing to deliver the complete or correct functionality and services as specified — the system does not work right. There may be performance problems — the system is too slow, data is not kept long enough, the system cannot handle the specified number of concurrent users, etc. Inadequate safety, reliability, and security features may pose technical risks as well. The safety design fails to take into account constraints in the operational environment. The reliability features only work under one operational profile, not all possible operational scenarios. The security design forgot about remote access by one business partner or new federal privacy regulations. Maintainability can also raise a variety of technical risks. Suppose one of the technology vendors goes out of business or stops supporting a product. Perhaps there is an 18-month backlog on orders for spare parts that you need today.

Schedule risk is the risk of not meeting a promised schedule to deliver a system, product, service, or information. Schedule risk sounds simple but, in fact, it is not. Realistic and comprehensive planning is essential but the key to controlling schedule risk, like other types of risk, is managing uncertainty. On any given project there are things you have control over and many more that you do not. A new intrusion prevention device is more complex than you estimated and will take twice as long to implement. The database conversion scheme is not quite right and you end up with duplicate fields; more time is needed to study the problem. The application layer security is incompatible with timing constraints for the new LAN infrastructure; time is needed to contact the vendors of both products. Then there are always the common delays due to power outages, sick personnel, shipping delays, problems with suppliers, etc. Managing uncertainty involves acknowledging these possibilities up front and having one or more contingency plans ready to go so that you can continue to make progress and stay on schedule.

Cost risk also sounds simple, but avoiding unplanned expenses is not always that easy. Again there is a combination of factors that you do and do not have control over, such as inflation and currency fluctuations on the international monetary markets. Cost risk can be a direct outcome of uncontrolled technical and schedule risks or independent of them. Technical failings of any sort result in rework, ordering new parts, financial penalties for defaulting on contracts, and other activities that drive up costs. Schedule slippage increases costs because labor and facility costs increase while revenues are delayed. This book is primarily concerned with managing or, more precisely, measuring technical risk as it pertains to security and privacy; however, the interaction among all three types of risk will be seen throughout, particularly in Chapter 5, which deals with ROI.

Terminology related to risk is often misused and misunderstood. Terms such as risk, threat, and vulnerability are frequently used interchangeably in everyday conversation, when in fact they have very distinct meanings. Let us clarify these terms and their meanings, especially within the context of security engineering. An in-depth understanding of these terms and concepts is a prerequisite to producing security and privacy metrics that meet the accuracy, precision, validity, and correctness test. If you are confused about these concepts and terms, your security and privacy metrics will be equally as confused. Standard definitions for these terms are presented to avoid adding to the confusion. The best place to start is with the definition of risk itself.

> **Risk:** possibility that a particular threat will adversely impact an information system by exploiting a particular vulnerability.[100] The level of impact on agency operations (including mission, functions, image, or reputation), agency assets, or individuals resulting from the operation of an information system given the potential impact of a threat and probability of that threat occurring.[50, 51] The possibility of harm or loss to any software, information, hardware, administrative, physical, communications, or personnel resource within an automated information system or activity.[49]

Here we see three definitions of risk that are closely intertwined; the first is from *the National Information Assurance Glossary,* and the last two are from NIST publications. Each definition incorporates the notion of threat, the likelihood of the threat being instantiated, and the magnitude of the corresponding loss. Risk is expressed in terms of the likelihood of occurrence, which can be described quantitatively or qualitatively using the standard categories defined in Table 2.6, and the worst-case severity of the consequences, using the standard severity categories defined in Table 2.5. These three definitions were developed especially for risk related to using IT systems. Yet note that the potential repercussions go way beyond the technology itself and include items such as a negative impact on an organization's image, reputation, assets, physical resources, and people. We looked at risk categories and risk levels in Tables 2.3 and 2.4; that information is not repeated here.

> **IT-related risk:** the net mission impact considering (1) the probability that a particular threat-source will exercise (accidentally trigger or intentionally exploit) a particular information system vulnerability, and (2) the resulting impact if this should occur. IT-related risks arise from legal liability or mission loss due to[50]:
>
> - Unauthorized (malicious or accidental) disclosure, modification, or destruction of information
> - Unintentional errors and omissions
> - IT disruptions due to natural or man-made disasters
> - Failure to exercise due care and diligence in the implementation and operation of the IT system

This definition, also from a NIST publication, zeroes in on the business impact and potential legal liability of the risk associated with using IT systems. This definition is more complete because it acknowledges that threats can be triggered accidentally or intentionally; it also cites four possible causes of threat instantiation. Notice the mention of errors of omission and errors of commission, as well as management failures — lack of due care and diligence. The latter is often a result of schedule or budget crunches.

> **Community risk:** probability that a particular vulnerability will be exploited within an interacting population and adversely impact some members of that population.[100]

Risk resulting from the interaction among multiple systems and networks is referred to as community risk. The level of community risk fluctuates among the community members according to the level of trust placed in the various business partners and other third parties with which common IT systems and networks interact. Some risks are easier to contain than others, depending on the technology used, interfaces, operational procedures, geographical distribution of system resources, etc. Risk is rarely limited to a single IT system or network. There are a minuscule number of stand-alone systems still in existence. Unfortunately, most risk assessments performed today ignore that fact.

If risk were limited only to a single system or network, viruses and worms would not spread around the world in seconds.

The prime directive of security engineering is to manage risk. There are two components to risk management. The first half concerns analyzing and assessing risks. The second half involves controlling and mitigating risks.

> **Risk analysis:** a series of analyses conducted to identify and determine the cause(s), consequences, likelihood, and severity of hazards. Note that a single hazard may have multiple causes.[156] Examination of information to identify the risks to an information system.[100]

> **Risk assessment:** process of analyzing threats to and vulnerabilities of an information system, and the potential impact resulting from the loss of information or capabilities of a system. This analysis is used as a basis for identifying appropriate and cost-effective security countermeasures.[100] The process of identifying risks to agency operations (including mission, functions, image, or reputation), agency assets, or individuals by determining the probability of occurrence, the resulting impact, and additional security controls that would mitigate this impact. Part of risk management, synonymous with risk analysis, and incorporates threat and vulnerability analyses.[50, 51]

Risk analysis and risk assessment are synonymous. The safety and reliability engineering communities tend to use the term "risk analysis," while the security engineering community uses the term "risk assessment." The difference in terminology is probably due to the fact that, to date, the safety and reliability engineering communities have been much more scientific in their approach to analyzing risk than the security engineering community. We are about to change that. A variety of static analysis techniques are used to perform a risk assessment. The intent is to methodically identify and thoroughly characterize the potential vulnerabilities and threats associated with using an IT system in terms of their root cause, the severity of consequences, and the likelihood of occurrence. In short, a risk assessment tells you what is likely to go wrong, how often, and how bad the consequences will be. This information is the primary input to the risk control and mitigation half of the risk management equation. Risk assessments should not be performed in cookie-cutter fashion, where you check all systems and networks to see if they have the same dozen or so predefined vulnerabilities and threats, and if not report that they are good to go. Rather, a risk assessment should be completely tailored for each unique system and network, and focus on the specific functionality provided, operational environment and constraints, configuration, user community, interconnectivity, etc. Risk assessments are part of due diligence and should be incorporated into standard business practices.[199]

> **Risk control:** techniques that are employed to eliminate, reduce, or mitigate risk, such as inherent safe and secure (re)design techniques or features, alerts, warnings, operational procedures, instructions for use, training, and contingencies plans.[156]

Risk mitigation: the selection and implementation of security controls to reduce risk to a level acceptable to management, within applicable constraints.[60]

The terms "risk control" and "risk mitigation" are also synonymous. The safety and reliability engineering communities tend to use the term "risk control," while the security engineering community uses the term "risk mitigation." The goal is to determine how to prevent, control, and reduce the threat frequency and severity in a technically feasible and cost-effective manner. As Hecht states[153]:

... failures cannot be prevented in an absolute sense, but must be controlled to be within the limits dictated by consumer demands, government regulation, ... and economic considerations.

The results of a risk assessment are used to prioritize risk mitigation activities. Threats considered to be in a low severity category or a low likelihood category receive less attention than those in higher categories. Risk mitigation budgets and resources are allocated accordingly. Note that the risk mitigation solution does not have to rely on technology alone; instead, it may include alerts, warnings, operational procedures, instructions for use, training, and contingency plans.[156] Risk mitigation techniques are tailored to the specific threat scenario and the exact circumstances that caused the threat; they correspond directly to the risk assessment. An important consideration is to know where the system is in the risk cycle.[199] Some vulnerabilities are exposed continually, while others are tied to a periodic event, such as Y2K or end-of-month processing. Risk mitigation activities should take this fact into account. As Peltier points out, competent risk mitigation allows you to implement *only* those controls as safeguards that are actually needed and effective.[199] Contrary to a lot of advertising you may read, there is not a one-size-fits-all security risk mitigation solution. This fact highlights the fallacy of deploying a risk mitigation solution before conducting a thorough risk assessment; a point that becomes loud and clear when ROI is discussed in Chapter 5.

Risk management: systematic application of risk analysis and risk control management policies, procedures, and practices.[156] The process of managing risks to agency operations (including mission, functions, image, or reputation), agency assets, or individuals resulting from the operation of an information systems. It includes risk assessment; cost-benefit analysis; the selection, implementation, and assessment of security controls; and the formal authorization to operate the system. This process considers effectiveness, efficiency, and constraints due to laws, directives, polices, or regulations.[50, 51] The ongoing process of assessing the risk to automated information system resources and information, as part of a risk-based approach used to determine adequate security for a system by analyzing the threats and vulnerabilities and selecting appropriate cost-effective controls that achieve and maintain an acceptable level of risk.[49]

These last three definitions are a mouthful, but they bring up some important points about risk management that are often overlooked. The goal of risk management is predictable system behavior and performance under normal and abnormal situations so that there are no surprises. Accordingly, risk management, risk assessment, and risk mitigation are ongoing activities throughout the life of a system, from concept through decommissioning. The first consideration is cost-benefit analysis. In most instances, there is more than one way to mitigate a given risk; be sure to take the time to find out which is most cost-effective in the long term. Second, risk mitigation activities must also take legal and regulatory constraints into account. Perhaps one mitigation solution is cheaper than another but does not quite conform to regulatory requirements. (The fines will make up the difference.) Finally, the notion of "adequate security" is introduced. We touch on that next, from both legal and technical perspectives.

To summarize the concepts and terms discussed thus far:

- Risk is a function of (likelihood of occurrence + the worst-case severity of consequences).
- Risk assessments yield a list of specific potential threats, their individual likelihood and severity.
- Risk mitigation implements security controls (technical and management) to reduce the likelihood or severity of each identified threat that is above a certain threshold.
- Risk management is the systematic combination and coordination of risk assessment and risk mitigation activities from the big-picture point of view.

The notion of "adequate security" brings up four more terms: (1) residual risk, (2) acceptable risk, (3) ALARP, and (4) assumption of risk. Adequate security infers that an IT system or network is neither over- nor under-protected. The security requirements, and the integrity level to which the implementation of these requirements has been verified, are commensurate with the level of risk. If so, the ROI will be high; if not, the ROI will be low or negative.

> **Residual risk:** portion of risk remaining after security measures have been applied.[100] The risk that remains after risk control measures have been employed. Before a system can be certified and accredited, a determination must be made about the acceptability of residual risk.[156]

> **Acceptable risk:** a concern that is acceptable to responsible management, due to the cost and magnitude of implementing countermeasures.[49]

> **ALARP:** As Low As Reasonably Practical; a method of correlating the likelihood of a hazard and the severity of its consequences to determine risk exposure acceptability or the need for further risk reduction.[156]

In normal situations, risk is almost never reduced to zero. Risk mitigation activities may have reduced the likelihood from occasional to remote and reduced the severity from catastrophic to marginal. However, some risk remains. This is referred to as *residual risk*. On a case-by-case basis, a decision must be made about the acceptability of residual risk. A variety of factors influence this decision, such as the organization's mission, applicable laws and regulations, technical hurdles that need to be overcome to reduce the risk any further, schedule constraints that must be met, the cost of reducing the risk any more, and stakeholders' perceptions of what constitutes acceptable risk. One approach to determine the acceptability of residual risk is known by the acronym ALARP, which stands for "as low as reasonably practical." Likelihood is plotted on the vertical axis, while severity is captured on the horizontal axis. Then three risk regions are identified that correlate with the likelihood and severity of a threat being instantiated. The lower region represents risks that are broadly acceptable. The middle region represents risks that have been reduced as low as reasonably practical, given technical, cost, schedule, and legal constraints. The upper region represents risks that are intolerable. The shape of these regions is determined on a case-by-case basis, as a function of the influential factors cited above. The regions can be applied to an individual threat scenario or multiple threats, as appropriate. Keep in mind that what you consider an acceptable risk, other stakeholders may not; all viewpoints should be reflected in the final decision. There is a direct link between residual risk and resilience, and this idea is explored in Chapter 4. The legal definitions are reprinted from *Black's Law Dictionary*® (H. Black, J. Nolan, and J. Nolan-Haley, 6th edition, 1991. With permission of Thomson West). The legal definitions are applicable to the legal system of the United States.

> **Assumption of risk:** a plaintiff may not recover for an injury to which he assents; that is, that a person may not recover for an injury received when he voluntarily exposes himself to a known and appreciated danger. The requirements for the defense … are that (1) the plaintiff has knowledge of facts constituting a dangerous condition, (2) he knows that the condition is dangerous, (3) he appreciates the nature or extent of the danger, and (4) he voluntarily exposes himself to the danger. Secondary assumption of risk occurs when an individual voluntarily encounters known, appreciated risk without an intended manifestation by that individual that he consents to relieve another of his duty. (*Black's Law Dictionary*®)

A final issue concerns the legal nature of risk assumption. Be sure to read this definition carefully to keep you and your organization out of court. For an employee, customer, business partner, or other stakeholder to have legally assumed the responsibility for any security or privacy risks, he must be fully informed about the nature and extent of the risk *and* consent to it beforehand. Putting up a sentence or two about a privacy policy on a Web site does not meet this legal test. Using a Web site for E-commerce does not mean that customers have assumed the risk of identify theft. Forcing employees to use a Web site for travel arrangements does not mean they have consented to the risk of credit card fraud. If risk has not been legally assumed, your organization is liable for the consequences. This is another instance where full disclosure is the best policy. As one discount retailer says in its ads, "An informed consumer is our best customer."

The terms "threat" and "vulnerability" crept into some of the definitions above. It is time to sort out these concepts as well.

> **Threat:** any circumstance or event with the potential to adversely impact an information system through unauthorized access, destruction, disclosure, modification of data, or denial of service.[51, 100] The potential for a threat source to exercise (accidentally trigger or intentionally exploit) a specific vulnerability.[50]

> **Threat analysis:** examination of information to identify the elements comprising a threat.[100] Examination of threat-sources against system vulnerabilities to determine the threats for a particular system in a particular operational environment.[50]

> **Threat assessment:** formal description and evaluation of threats to an information system.[51, 100]

That is, a threat is the potential for a vulnerability to be exploited. This potential is a function of the opportunity, motive, expertise, and resources needed and available to exploit a given vulnerability. As the definitions above note, vulnerabilities can be exploited accidentally or intentionally. Some vulnerabilities may be continually exploited, while others go untouched. Another interesting point is that a single vulnerability may be subject to exploitation by a variety of different threats; these different exploitation paths are often called *threat vectors*. The process of identifying and characterizing threats is referred to as either *threat analysis* or *threat assessment*; these terms are synonymous. A threat assessment must be tailored to a specific operational environment, usage profile, installation, configuration, O&M procedures, release, etc.

> **Vulnerability:** weakness in an information system, system security procedure, internal control, or implementation that could be exploited or triggered by a threat source.[51, 100] A flaw or weakness in the design or implementation of an information system (including the security procedures and security controls associated with the system) that could be intentionally or unintentionally exploited to adversely affect an organization's operations or assets through a loss of confidentiality, integrity, or availability.[60] A flaw or weakness in system security procedures, design, implementation, or internal controls that could be exercised (accidentally triggered or intentionally exploited) and result in a security breach or a violation of the system's security policy.[50]

> **Vulnerability analysis:** examination of information to identify the elements comprising a vulnerability.[100]

> **Vulnerability assessment:** formal description and evaluation of vulnerabilities of an information system.[51, 100]

These three definitions of vulnerability are all very similar. They highlight the fact that a vulnerability is a weakness that can be exploited. Weaknesses are the result of human error, either accidental or intentional. Weaknesses can be introduced into the security requirements, system design, implementation, installation, operational procedures, configuration, and concurrent physical and personnel security controls. A vulnerability exists independent of whether or not it is ever exploited. The identification and characterization of vulnerabilities can be referred to as either vulnerability analysis or vulnerability assessment; the terms are synonymous. Like a threat assessment, vulnerability assessments are tailored to a specific operational environment, usage profile, installation, configuration, O&M procedures, release, etc. Humans also have vulnerabilities. That aspect of a vulnerability assessment is discussed in Chapter 4, under "Personnel Security."

Let us put all the pieces together now:

- A vulnerability is an inherent weaknesses in a system, its design, implementation, operation, or operational environment, including physical and personnel security controls.
- A threat is the potential for a vulnerability to be exploited. Threat is a function of the opportunity, motive, expertise, and resources needed and available to effect the exploitation.
- Risk is a function of the likelihood of a vulnerability being exploited and a threat instantiated, plus the worst-case severity of the consequences.
- Risk assessments are used to prioritize risk mitigation activities.
- Vulnerability assessments and threat assessments are prerequisites for conducting a risk assessment.

A simple analogy will highlight these concepts. Suppose you park your car and leave the doors unlocked. The unlocked doors are a vulnerability. The threat is for someone other than you to enter the car. Anyone who walks by your car and notices that the doors are unlocked has the opportunity. A small percentage of people are thieves, so in most cases motive is lacking. The expertise required to exploit this vulnerability is minimal — knowing how to open a car door. The resources required are also minimal, about three seconds and a little energy. The likelihood of occurrence is a function of where you parked your car. If you parked it downtown in a major metropolitan area, the likelihood is much higher than if you parked it in the country. The severity of the consequences could range from minor theft, like stealing your CDs, to vandalism, slashing your leather seats, to total theft of your vehicle. Another worst-case scenario would be that a child takes your car joy riding and crashes it. Here we see the same opportunity, expertise, and resources but a different motive at work. The vulnerability assessment identifies the unlocked doors. The threat assessment identifies the vandals, car thieves, joy riders, and the likelihood of them being in the neighborhood. The risk assessment identifies the probability of you coming back to find your car stolen or destroyed, the financial consequences, and your ability to find your way home using another mode of transportation. The risk assessment also considers the regulatory aspect of this scenario, whether or not your car insurance company will reimburse you for damages, because leaving car doors unlocked might be considered negligence. After going through all these scenarios in your head, you decide to implement some risk mitigation by going back and locking your car doors, assuming it is not too late. Just a reminder that preliminary risk assessments should be done before systems are deployed.

Previously in Section 2.2 and Figure 2.7 we talked about errors, faults, and failures and the following observations were made. Human error, either an error of omission or an error of commission, leads to fault conditions that result in latent defects or vulnerabilities. If a fault condition is exercised, it can cause a system failure. The result of a fault condition is a vulnerability. The potential to exercise a fault condition is a threat. The likelihood of a system failing and the severity of the consequences, should it do so, is the risk. It is important to understand these relationships to be able to use two of the most prevalent tools for analyzing vulnerabilities, threats, and risk. These tools are (1) failure mode effects criticality analysis (FMECA) and (2) fault tree analysis (FTA).

The FMECA identifies the ways in which a system could fail accidentally or be made to fail intentionally.[156] The objective of conducting an FMECA is to evaluate the magnitude of risk relative to system entities or process activities and help prioritize risk control efforts.[120] All stakeholders are involved in an FMECA to ensure that all aspects of a failure are adequately evaluated. FMECAs are conducted and refined iteratively throughout the life of a system. There are four conventional types of FMECA: (1) functional FMECA, (2) design FMECA, (3) process FMECA, and (4) interface FMECA.[7] A design FMECA identifies potential system failures during the design phase, so that appropriate mitigation activities can be employed. A functional FMECA assesses the as-built or operational system. A process FMECA evaluates opportunities for process activities to produce wrong results, such as the introduction of a fault. An interface FMECA focuses exclusively on internal and external system interfaces, hardware, software, and telecommunications. Pay special attention to the interface FMECA because failures at hardware/software interface boundaries are difficult to diagnose.[197] Design, functional, and interface FMECAs are used to assess resilience, while a process FMECA is used to appraise compliance with policies and regulations. An FMECA can and should be conducted at the entity level (hardware, software, telecommunications, human factors) and at the system level. FMECAs can be used to help optimize designs, operational procedures, and risk mitigation activities, uncover new operational constraints, and verify system resilience or the need for additional corrective action.[7, 120, 156, 158]

The procedure for conducting an FMECA is straightforward. The system or sub-system under consideration is broken into logical components, such as functions or services. Potential worst-case failure modes are predicted for each component, through a bottom-up analysis. The cause(s) of these failure modes and their effect on system behavior is postulated. Finally, the severity and likelihood of each failure mode are determined. In general, *quantitative* likelihoods are used to estimate random failures, while *qualitative* likelihoods are used to estimate systematic failures.[7]

The effect of each failure mode is evaluated at several levels in the system security architecture and the organization's IT infrastructure, in particular the impact on its mission. The effect of failure is examined at different levels to optimize fault containment or quarantine strategies and identify whether or not a failure at this level creates the conditions or opportunity for a parallel attack, compromise, or failure elsewhere. The principal data elements collected, analyzed, and reported for each failure mode include:

- System, entity, and function
- Operational mission, profile, and environment
- Assumptions and accuracy concerns
- Failure mode
- Likelihood of the failure occurring
- Severity of the consequences of the failure
- Responsible component, event, or action
- Current compensating provisions
- Recommended additional mitigation

FTA is used to identify potential root causes of undesired top-level system events (accidental and intentional) so that risk mitigation features can be incorporated into the design and operational procedures.[120, 158] FTA aids in the analysis of events and combinations or sequences of events that may lead to a security violation. The analysis is carried out backward along the path of precursor events and conditions that triggered the incident in a top-down fashion, starting at the top event that is the immediate cause of a security incident. Together these difference paths depict the fault tree. Combinations of events are described with logical operators (AND, OR, IOR, EOR).[7] Intermediate causes are analyzed in the same manner back to the root cause.[7] The different fault paths are ranked in terms of their significance in contributing to the top event risk. This, in turn, determines the risk mitigation priority. FTA should be conducted iteratively throughout the life of a system and in conjunction with an FMECA.[156] The application of FTA to security engineering is sometimes referred to as security fault analysis (or SFA).

The following example demonstrates how to use FMECA and FTA and the interaction between the two techniques. In particular, this example highlights how these analytical techniques can be applied to security engineering.

Assume you have just deployed a new AES encryption device enterprise-wide and things do not seem to be quite right. The boss asks you to find out why. You start by performing a functional FMECA, like the one shown in Table 2.10. This example only shows four potential failure modes; in reality, there are many more.

The FMECA is split into two parts. The first part captures information about current known or potential failure modes, as this is a functional FMECA. A failure mode is the way a device or process fails to perform its intended function.[120] In this example, one failure mode is decomposed into four possible failure mechanisms or root causes of the failure.[120] State tables and diagrams that capture transitions under normal conditions and abnormal conditions, like peak loading and attack scenarios, can be very helpful in locating failure modes.[153] The effects of each of these failure modes are examined, along with existing controls, if any. Then a risk ranking is determined for the current situation. Before that can be done, a value is assigned to the likelihood of the failure occurring (P), the severity of the consequences (S), and the potential damage to the organization (D), using an interval scale of 1 (lowest) to 10 (highest). The standard severity and likelihood categories from Tables 2.5 and 2.6 are spread along the 10-point scale, as shown below:

Insignificant:	1–2	Incredible:	1
Marginal:	3–4	Improbable:	2
Critical:	5–7	Remote:	3–4
Catastrophic:	8–10	Occasional:	5–6
		Probable:	7–8
		Frequent:	9–10

The risk ranking is the product of multiplying P × S × D. Part 2 evaluates the effectiveness of mitigation activities. Recommendations for further corrective action are given for each failure cause. The status of the corrective action is tracked to closure, along with the responsible organizational unit and person. Then a final risk ranking is calculated. These examples show quite a spread of current risk rankings, from 1000 (the maximum) to 180. The final risk rankings range from 180 to 90. Each organization establishes a threshold below which no further action will be taken to mitigate risks. Perhaps no further action was needed in the case of the 180 current ranking. These examples show how risk rankings can be lowered by reducing the likelihood of occurrence. Risk rankings can also be reduced by decreasing the severity of the consequences, which in turn will reduce the damage to the organization.

The FMECA example above illustrates bottom-up analysis. FTA is top-down, as shown in the following example.

> **Top Event**: Unauthorized or Unintended Release of Sensitive Information Assets

The first level in the fault tree would consist of the following four items:

> **Level 1:** Failure of personnel security controls OR
> Failure of physical security controls OR
> Failure of IT security controls OR
> Failure of operational security controls

Then each of these four items is decomposed, level by level, in a top-down fashion until all possible events that could contribute to the risk of the top event are identified. All the possible paths are put together to form the fault tree. Then the likelihood of each unique path occurring is estimated. This

Table 2.10   Sample Functional FMECA: Encryption Device

System: Enterprise Telecommunications Network

Sub-system: Network Security Architecture

Function: Data Confidentiality

Configuration Control/Version Number: 1A

Implementation Date: 13 February 2005

Part 1: Evaluate Current Failure Modes and Controls

Failure Mode	Failure Mechanism/Cause	Failure Effect	Current Controls	Risk Ranking			
				P	S	D	R
1. Cleartext data is exposed	1.1 Data is encrypted/decrypted at each node in transmission path (bad design).	Loss of data confidentiality, possible unauthorized disclosure	Only trusted partners have access to telecom equipment and nodes	10	10	10	1000
	1.2 Encryption device fails to open.	Some data is transmitted in the clear before switching to a hot standby	Switch to hot standby encryption device upon detecting a fail open state	4	10	9	360
	1.3 Encryption process fails, leaving cleartext and ciphertext on hard drive of server.	"Leftover" data can be retrieved by anyone with access to the server	Restart encryption if alarm is generated	2	10	9	180
	1.4 Access control mechanisms fail, attacker gains access to data before it is encrypted.	Loss of data confidentiality, possible unauthorized disclosure, attacker knows what type of encryption is used	None	3	10	9	270

Part 2: Evaluate Mitigation Activities

Recommended Corrective Action	Action Taken to Date	Final Risk Ranking				Responsible Organization/Person
		P	S	D	R	
1.1 Implement end-to-end encryption, with only one encrypt/decrypt cycle.	Implemented and tested, 04/10/05	1	10	10	100	NS-1000 J. Smith
1.2 Reconfigure encryption device to cease transmitting immediately upon detection of any fault condition. Do not commence transmission until redundant device is fully operational.	Awaiting final ST&E results, 05/01/05	2	10	9	180	NS-1020 S. Keith
1.3 Install processor to monitor encryption. If process is aborted or fails, delete all temporary files immediately.	Under development, 04/29/05	1	10	9	90	NS-1052 S. Robertson
1.4 Implement multiple independent access control mechanisms for information assets that are sensitive enough to be encrypted.	Completed ST&E, awaiting C&A approval to operate, 06/15/05	1	10	9	90	NS-1017 T. Hale

information is used to prioritize risk mitigation activities. The four failure mechanisms listed in Table 2.10 would eventually be identified when decomposing the different paths for "Failure of IT security controls." That is why FMECA is an input to FTA, and FTA is used to cross-check FMECA.

In summary, the P, S, and D values in an FMECA report are primitives, while the risk ranking (or R) is a metric. The risk ranking can be used in a variety of ways to analyze individual (a single metric) or composite (an aggregate metric) risks and the effectiveness of risk mitigation strategies. Be creative. The FMECA report can be presented or used as backup data. The risk rankings for an entire sub-system, system, network, or enterprise can be displayed on a scatter plot or histogram or overlaid on an ALARP graph to obtain a consolidated picture of the robustness of the security architecture and pinpoint problem areas. A "before and after" graph, showing the initial and final risk rankings, will underscore the value of security engineering and provide constructive input for ROI calculations. Risk management tools and techniques are a ready source of primitives and metrics to analyze security risks. Security and privacy metrics should not be pulled from thin air. Rather, they should be based on a solid analytical foundation, such as that provided by FMECA and FTA.

2.9 Examples from Reliability Engineering

The purpose of reliability engineering is to ensure that a system and all of its components exhibit accurate, consistent, repeatable, and predictable performance under specified conditions. A variety of analysis, design, and verification techniques are employed throughout the life of a system to accomplish this goal. Current and thorough technical documentation is an important part of this process because it will explain the correct operation of a system, applications for which the system should and should not be used, and procedures for preventive, adaptive, and corrective maintenance.

System reliability is the composite of hardware and software reliability predictions or estimations for a specified operational environment. *Hardware reliability* is defined as[156]:

> *The ability of an item to correctly perform a required function under certain conditions in a specified operational environment for a stated period of time*

Software reliability is defined as[158]:

> *A measure of confidence that the software produces accurate and consistent results that are repeatable, under low, normal, and peak loads, in the intended operational environment*

Hardware is primarily subject to random failures, failures that result from physical degradation over time, and variability introduced during the manufacturing process. Hardware reliability is generally measured quantitatively. Software is subject to systematic failures, failures that result from an error of omission, an error of commission, or an operational error during a life-cycle activity.[158] Software reliability is measured both quantitatively and qualitatively. To illustrate, a failure due to a design error in a memory chip is a systematic failure. If the same chip failed because it was old and worn out, that would be considered a random failure. A software failure due to a design or specification error is a systematic failure. A server failure due to a security incident is a systematic failure. A security incident that is precipitated by a hardware failure is a random failure. As a result, system reliability measurements combine quantitative and qualitative product and process assessments. Another aspect to reliability is data reliability — ensuring that data is processed on time, and not too late or too early.[197] This is a variation on the theme of data integrity that concerns security engineers.

Reliability engineering emerged as an engineering discipline in earnest following World War II. The defense and aerospace industries led this development; other industries such as the automotive, telecommunications, and consumer electronics became involved shortly thereafter. Initial efforts focused on electronic and electromechanical components, then sub-systems and systems. A variety of statistical techniques were developed to predict and estimate system reliability. Failure data was collected, analyzed, and shared over the years so that reliability techniques could be improved, through the use of failure reporting corrective systems (FRACASs). The concept of software reliability did not begin until the late 1970s.

Early software reliability models tried to emulate hardware reliability models. They applied statistical techniques to the number of errors found during testing and the time it took to find them to predict the number of errors remaining in the software, as well as the time that would be required to find them. Given the difference in hardware and software failures, the usefulness of these models was mixed. The limitations of early software reliability models can be summarized as follows[158]:

1. They do not distinguish between the type of errors found or predicted to be remaining in the software (functional, performance, safety, reliability, or security).
2. They do not distinguish between the severity of the consequences of errors found or predicted to be remaining in the software.
3. They do not take into account errors found by techniques other than testing, such as static analysis techniques such as FMECA and FTA, or errors found before the testing phase.

These limitations led to the development of new software reliability models and the joint use of qualitative and quantitative assessments.

Reliability requirements are specified at the system level, then allocated to system components such as software. A series of analyses, feasibility studies, and trade-off studies are performed to determine the optimum system architecture that will meet the reliability requirements. A determination is made about how a system should prevent, detect, respond to, contain, and recover from errors, including provisions for degraded mode operations. Progress toward meeting reliability goals is monitored during each life-cycle phase through the use of reliability metrics.

There are several parallels between reliability engineering and security engineering. The goal of both disciplines is to prevent, detect, contain, and recover from erroneous system states and conditions. However, reliability engineering does not place as much emphasis on intentional malicious actions as security engineering.

Dependability is a special instance of reliability. Dependability infers that confidence can be placed in a system and the level of service it delivers, and that one can rely on the system to be free from failures during operation.[112] Dependability is the outcome of[112]:

- **Fault prevention:** preventing the introduction or occurrence of faults during system life-cycle activities.
- **Fault removal:** reducing the presence, number, and seriousness of faults.
- **Fault forecasting:** estimating the present number, future incidence, and consequences of faults.
- **Fault tolerance:** ensuring a service is able to fulfill the system's mission in the presence of faults.
- **Fault isolation:** containing the impact of exercised faults.

If you remember our earlier discussion about fault conditions creating vulnerabilities, then you can begin to see the importance of reliability engineering, in particular dependability, to security engineering and metrics. Notice the emphasis on proactive activities to prevent faults from being in the deployed system. Let us now see how this dependability model can be applied to security engineering.

- **Fault prevention:** preventing the introduction or exploitation of vulnerabilities during system life-cycle activities through the use of static analysis techniques. It is not possible to prevent the introduction of all vulnerabilities, but the opportunity to exploit them can be reduced drastically. Static analysis is the most cost-effective means of failure prevention; it is cheaper than modeling and much cheaper than testing.[153]
- **Fault removal:** reducing the presence, number, and seriousness of vulnerabilities. This is accomplished through risk mitigation activities, after thorough vulnerability and threat analyses are completed.
- **Fault forecasting:** estimating the present number, future incidence, and consequences of vulnerabilities. Again, static analysis techniques such as FMECA and FTA can help achieve this.
- **Fault tolerance:** ensuring a service is able to fulfill the system's mission in the presence of vulnerabilities. Reliability engineering techniques such as redundancy, diversity, and searching for common cause failures, discussed below, can be applied to security engineering as well. The judicious use of IT security and operational security metrics, especially early in the life cycle, can help achieve resilience.
- **Fault isolation:** containing the impact of exercised vulnerabilities. This is similar to a network or server isolation or quarantine capability. The astute use of IT security metrics early in the life cycle can help identify the optimum strategy for deploying an isolation or quarantine capability.

Of late there have been discussions in the reliability engineering community that security incidents are nothing more than a special class of failures or, on the more extreme end, that security engineering is a subset of reliability engineering. (The proponents of this position believe that safety engineering is also a subset of reliability engineering.) There is some merit to this discussion. However, others contend that this position is more a reflection of professional pride and the current availability of research funds. A more apt way to express this relationship is to say that safety, reliability, and security engineering are closely related concurrent engineering disciplines that use similar tools and techniques to prevent and examine distinct classes of potential failures, failure modes, and failure consequences from unique perspectives. A case in point: why, if a telecommunications switch has been designed and sold as having a reliability rating of .999999, can a clever attacker take the switch and its redundant spare down in a manner of minutes? Furthermore, security failures do not always conform to the traditional sense of failure. This position does not account for situations where sessions or systems are hijacked or spoofed. The session or system functions 100 percent normally, but not for the intended users or owners. Regardless, as Randall points out, terminology does remain a problem[112]:

> *In particular, it is my perception that a number of dependability concepts are being re-invented, or at least renamed, in the numerous overlapping communities that are worrying about deliberately-induced failures in computer systems — e.g., the survivability, critical infrastructure, information warfare, and intrusion detection communities. The most recent example is the National Research Council report titled "Trust in Cyber Space" (1998), which uses the term trustworthiness in exactly the broad sense of dependability.*

The fact remains that a system can be reliable but not secure, safe but not reliable, secure but neither safe nor reliable, etc. These three systems states are independent and each is the outcome of specialized engineering activities. Table 2.11 accentuates this situation.

Table 2.11   Possible System States Related to Reliability, Safety, and Security

Alternate States	Safe	Reliable	Secure
1	No	No	No
2	Yes	No	No
3	No	Yes	No
4	No	No	Yes
5	Yes	Yes	No
6	No	Yes	Yes
7	Yes	No	Yes
8	Yes	Yes	Yes

A key consideration of reliability engineering is maintainability, or the ability of an item, under stated conditions of use, to be retained in, or restored to, a state in which it can perform its required functions, when maintenance is performed under stated conditions and using prescribed procedures and resources.[197] Hardware, software, and networks all must be maintained in a state of operational readiness. Let us face it, some systems, networks, and products are much easier to maintain than others. The longer an item is in service, that fact becomes more apparent. Maintenance activities fall into three general categories: (1) corrective, (2) preventive, and (3) adaptive. *Corrective maintenance* is the most familiar to end users: something does not work, so you call the help desk to come fix it. The problem can range anywhere from simple to complex. Corrective maintenance represents the actions performed, as a result of a failure, to restore an item to a specified condition.[197] Corrective maintenance is reactive. While everyone knows that corrective maintenance will be needed, it is an unscheduled activity because the date, time, and place the failures will manifest themselves or the nature of the failures is unknown until after the fact. Corrective maintenance can rarely be performed without taking down the system, network, or some portion thereof; in the case of a hard failure, it is already down.

In contrast, *preventive maintenance* is proactive. Preventive maintenance activities are preplanned and scheduled in an attempt to retain an item in a specified condition by providing systematic inspection, detection, and prevention of incipient failures.[197] Some preventive maintenance actions can be performed without impacting uptime, others require the system or network to be taken down temporarily.

Adaptive maintenance refers to the gradual process of updating or enhancing functionality or performance to adapt to new requirements or operational constraints. Perhaps a problem report was generated, when what the user is really asking for is a new feature. The line between when adaptive maintenance is really maintenance and when it is new development is very gray. Often, new development is done under a maintenance contract, and called adaptive maintenance, because it is easier to use an existing contractual vehicle than to go through the competitive process for a new development contract. Adaptive maintenance can only take you so far, and it has the potential to wreak havoc on a system and its security if strict configuration control and security impact analysis procedures are not followed. Adaptive maintenance should be avoided whenever possible.

Maintainability is a key concern for security engineering. If a security architecture or appliance cannot be retained in, or restored to, a state in which it can perform its required functions, any hope of maintaining a robust operational security posture is nil because there is a direct correlation between maintainability and availability and operational resilience. Maintenance actions themselves raise security concerns, even when rigorous configuration control and security impact analysis procedures are followed. Are new vulnerabilities created while the maintenance activity is being performed? If the maintenance activity requires downtime, how does that impact the enterprise security architecture? Do the maintenance engineers meet the trustworthiness requirements for the information sensitivity and asset criticality categories? How does remote maintenance impact risk exposure? Do end users need further security training as a result of the maintenance action?

As O'Connor points out, it is important to understand how a product works, how it will be used, and how humans will interact with it (if at all) before determining potential failure modes.[197] One basic distinction is the mode in which the product or device will operate. Some appliances operate in continuous mode, 24/7, while others operate in demand mode, that is, they are called upon to function on demand or periodically. This observation is similar to calculating failure rates per calendar time versus operating time. Failure rates for devices that operate in continuous mode are calculated in calendar time because they operate continuously. By comparison, failure rates for devices that operate in demand mode are calculated in operating time. An IDS (intrusion detection system) operates in continuous mode. However, it may be configured to send a shun or blocking message to the neighborhood router if a particular signature is encountered. The router's block or shun response is an example of demand mode operation. This type of information is captured in an operational profile through formal scenario analysis and greatly influences reliability design and measurement.

Common cause failures (CCFs) and common mode failures (CMFs) are sought out during the requirements analysis and design phases, through the use of static analysis techniques. Both can have a major negative impact on reliability. CCFs are the outcome of the failure of multiple independent system components occurring from a single cause that is common to all of them. CMFs are the result of the failure of multiple independent system components that fail in the identical mode. CCFs are particularly deadly because they can lead to the failure of all paths in a homogenous configuration. To illustrate, if all network appliances run the same operating system, release, and version, they all have the same inherent vulnerabilities. If that vulnerability is exploited on one or more network appliances, the potential exists for a cascading incident that will cause all network devices to fail. Use static analysis techniques to locate and remove potential CCFs and CMFs in the security architecture, preferably during the design phase. Pay particular attention to the failure of non-security components or sub-systems that can have a security impact.

Two design techniques are frequently employed by reliability engineers to enhance system reliability: (1) redundancy and (2) diversity. Redundancy can take several forms: hardware redundancy, software redundancy, hot stand-by, and cold stand-by. Software redundancy by itself does not provide any value. Because software failures are systematic, all copies of a given version and release of software contain the same faults. Hot stand-by offers near instantaneous transition, while cold stand-by does not. The useful life span of a hot stand-by is the same as the device it supports. Because the cold stand-by has been in a state of hibernation, its useful life span is longer than the device it supports. On occasion, transition to a cold stand-by fails because its configuration has not been kept current. Evaluate stand-by options carefully. Diversity can also take several forms: hardware diversity, software diversity, and path diversity in the telecommunications domain. Software diversity can be implemented at several levels, depending on the degree of reliability needed. Different algorithms can be used to implement the same functionality. Different languages or compilers can be used to implement the same functionality. The applications software can be run on different operating systems, and so forth. Diversity increases maintenance costs, so it is generally only used in high-reliability scenarios.

Hardware redundancy can be implemented in a serial, parallel, or complex serial/parallel manner, each of which delivers a different reliability rating, as shown below.[120, 153, 197] In short, parallel redundancy offers the highest reliability, complex serial/parallel the next highest, and serial redundancy the lowest; but it is still considerably higher than installing a single device. If the parallel redundancy is triple instead of dual, the reliability rating is even higher.

a.   **Serial redundancy**

$$R_t = R(A) \times R(B)$$

b.   **Parallel redundancy (dual)**

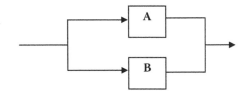

$$R_t = 1 - [\{1 - R(A)\}\{1 - R(B)\}]$$

c.   **Complex serial/parallel mode**

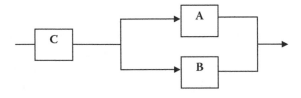

$$R_t = R(C) \times 1 - [\{1 - R(A)\}\{1 - R(B)\}]$$

The different redundancy scenarios and their reliability ratings can be applied to security engineering scenarios. The following example illustrates how security defense in depth can be implemented using reliability metrics. Suppose you need to protect a critical server that is connected to the Internet. Common sense tells you that a single firewall is not enough. You have several other options. You could install two different types of firewalls, a packet filtering and an application layer firewall, in a serial manner, using a combination of redundancy and diversity. You could install two identical firewalls, either packet-filtering or application layer, in a parallel manner, but configure them differently. Network traffic could be duplicated so that it must traverse both firewalls. Only if both firewalls permit the traffic, would it be allowed to reach the server. A third option is to implement complex serial/parallel redundancy, whereby a circuit level or proxy firewall is installed in conjunction with the parallel configuration described above. A fourth option is to implement a triple parallel, configuration. The reliability rating of firewall X may not be able to be calculated to five decimal points. But it is a fact that a serial, dual parallel, triple parallel, or complex serial/parallel firewall configuration is more reliable and offers greater protection than a single firewall.

Availability, a key component of the Confidentiality, Integrity, and Availability (or CIA) security model, is actually an outcome of reliability engineering. Availability is an objective measurement indicating the rate at which systems, data, and other resources are operational and accessible when needed, despite accidental and intentional sub-system outages and environmental disruptions.[156] Availability is a security goal that generates the requirement for protection against (1) intentional or accidental attempts to perform unauthorized deletion of data or otherwise cause a denial of service or data, and (2) unauthorized use of system resources.[50] Availability is usually defined as[153]:

$$A_i = MTBF/(MTBF + MTTR)$$

where
MTBF = Mean time between failures
MTTR = Mean time to repair

A point of clarification needs to be made here. Some system components can be repaired and others cannot. Non-repairable items are replaced. MTBF is used for repairable items, while MTTF (mean time to failure) is used for non-repairable items. MTBF is the ratio of the mean value of the length of time between consecutive failures, computed as the ratio of the cumulative observed time to the number of failures under stated conditions, for a stated period in the life of an item.[197] MTBF is expressed as[197]:

$$MTBF = Total\ time/Number\ of\ failures$$

In contrast, MTTF is the ratio of the cumulative time for a sample to the total number of failures in the sample during the period under stated conditions, for a stated period in the life of an item.[197] MTTR, on the other hand, is the total maintenance time divided by the total number of corrective maintenance actions during a given period of time.[197]

There are three variations of the availability calculation — known as inherent availability, operational availability, and achieved availability — that take into account different life-cycle phases and the information that is accessible. *Inherent availability* is the estimated availability, while a system or sub-system is still in the development phase.[197] The same calculation cited above is used, but it is a prediction rather than an actual measurement. Inherent availability is also referred to as potential availability.

Operational availability is the observed availability following initial system deployment.[197] Operational availability is expressed as[197]:

$$A_o = MTBMA/(MTBMA + MDT)$$

where
MTBMA = Mean time between maintenance actions (preventive and corrective)
MDT   = Mean downtime

Operational availability is also referred to as actual availability.

Achieved availability is the observed availability once a system has reached a steady state operationally.[197] Achieved availability is expressed as[197]:

$$A_a = MTBMA/(MTBMA + MMT)$$

where
MTBMA = Mean time between maintenance actions, both preventive and corrective
MMT   = Mean maintenance action time
         ((Number of corrective maintenance actions per 1000 hours ×
            MTTR for corrective maintenance) +
         (Number of preventive maintenance actions per 1000 hours ×
            MTTR for preventive maintenance))/
         (Number of corrective maintenance actions +
            Number of preventive maintenance actions)

Achieved availability is also referred to as final availability. In summary, the three availability calculations measure availability differently because the measurements are taken at discrete points during the life of a system using diverse primitives.

With minor modifications, the operational and achieved availability calculations can be used to measure the operational resilience of a single security appliance or an information system security architecture for a single system or network, a facility or campus, or the entire enterprise.

Operational Security Availability

$$A_o = MTBMA/(MTBMA + MDT)$$

where
MTBMA = Mean time between security maintenance actions
             (preventive and corrective)
MDT   = Mean downtime due to security failures

Achieved Security Availability

$$A_a = MTBMA/(MTBMA + MMT)$$

where

MTBMA = Mean time between security maintenance actions, both preventive and corrective

MMT = Mean security maintenance action time

((Number of corrective security maintenance actions per 1000 hours × MTTR for corrective security maintenance) +

(Number of preventive security maintenance actions per 1000 hours × MTTR for preventive security maintenance))/

(Number of corrective security maintenance actions + Number of preventive security maintenance actions)

In Sections 2.2 and 2.8 we talked about errors, faults, and failures and their relationship to vulnerabilities, threats, and risk. Specifically, (1) the result of a fault condition is a vulnerability, (2) the potential to exercise a fault condition is the threat, and (3) the likelihood of a system failing, and the severity of the consequences should it do so, is the risk. Several reliability metrics focus on the time spans between when the fault (or vulnerability) was created, detected, and corrected. The shorter the time frame between creation, detection, and correction, the better; these measures indicate the effectiveness of the reliability engineering program. Root cause analysis is performed to determine the date and activity that created the fault. This and other information is captured in the failure reporting analysis and corrective action system or FRACAS, a mainstay of reliability engineering, as listed below.[197] This permits failure data to be shared across many projects and organizations so that the lessons learned can be imparted on a wider basis.

- Failure symptoms, effects
- Immediate repair action
- Equipment operating at the time
- Operating conditions
- Date and time of failure
- Failure classification
- Failure investigation (root cause analysis)
- Recommended corrective action
- Actual remediation

Compare this situation with how security incidents are analyzed or the mounds of data produced by sensors. A security incident report usually says something like "Code Red took down 12 servers in 5 minutes." That report tells you about the effectiveness of Code Red, nothing more. Would it not be nice to know what vulnerability in your security architecture or operational procedures allowed Code Red to be successful? Or why it only took down those particular 12 servers? A better approach would be to create a FRACAS for security incidents containing the data elements above. With this information, in particular the root cause analysis, a variety of security metrics can be generated that will provide information about the resilience of your security architecture and operational procedures and what needs to be done to make them resistant to this and similar attacks in the future. This topic is explored further in Chapter 4.

Care needs to be taken when classifying failures — security incidents or otherwise. When performing root cause analysis, be sure to make a distinction between symptoms and causes, and between failures due to product faults and failures due to user error. Avoid assuming that the root cause of all failures is technical; other potential causes should also be considered, including[8, 9]:

- Poor or out-of-date user documentation
- Overly complex GUI
- Lack of end-user training
- Lack of help desk support
- End user has insufficient relevant education or experience
- End user is unaware of the prescribed operational procedures and constraints imposed by the operational environment
- Inconsistencies between product specification and end user's application environment
- Equipment misconfiguration

IEEE Std. 982 presents 39 software reliability engineering metrics that can be used to predict or measure different aspects of software reliability at various points in the system life cycle. There is a combination of product and process metrics. The product metrics focus on the following items: errors, faults, and failures, failure rates, MTBF, MTTR, and MTTF, reliability growth and projection, remaining product faults or fault freeness, completeness and consistency, and complexity. The process metrics focus on items related to the appropriateness and completeness of life-cycle activities, such as test coverage, the extent and effectiveness of management controls, and cost-benefit trade-off analyses. Next we examine a few of these metrics.

Four product metrics that are of interest include the following. First we look at the metric as it is defined in IEEE Std. 982; and then we see how it can be adapted for use in security engineering.

1. Requirements compliance
2. Cumulative failure profile
3. Defect density
4. Defect indices

Requirements Compliance

Three requirements compliance metrics are defined[8, 9]:

- Percent (%) inconsistent requirements

    $$= N1/(N1 + N2 + N3) \times 100$$

- Percent (%) incomplete requirements

    $$= N2/(N1 + N2 + N3) \times 100$$

- Percent (%) misinterpreted requirements

    $$= N3/(N1 + N2 + N3) \times 100$$

where
$N1$ = Number of errors due to inconsistent requirements
$N2$ = Number of errors due to incomplete requirements
$N3$ = Number of errors due to misinterpreted requirements

This measurement is applied throughout the life cycle to measure the correctness of software requirements, in particular the correctness of their implementation in the design and as-built system.

This metric can easily be applied to security requirements, and three additional types of requirements errors can be captured that are of interest to security engineers:

- Percent (%) inconsistent security requirements

    $$= N1/(N1 + N2 + N3 + N4 + N5 + N6) \times 100$$

- Percent (%) incomplete security requirements

    $$= N2/(N1 + N2 + N3 + N4 + N5 + N6) \times 100$$

- Percent (%) misinterpreted security requirements

    $$= N3/(N1 + N2 + N3 + N4 + N5 + N6) \times 100$$

- Percent (%) missing security requirements

    $$= N4/(N1 + N2 + N3 + N4 + N5 + N6) \times 100$$

- Percent (%) nonexistent security requirements

    $$= N5/(N1 + N2 + N3 + N4 + N5 + N6) \times 100$$

- Percent (%) security requirements with unresolved dependencies

    $$= N6/(N1 + N2 + N3 + N4 + N5 + N6) \times 100$$

where
$N1$ = Number of errors due to inconsistent security requirements
$N2$ = Number of errors due to incomplete security requirements
$N3$ = Number of errors due to misinterpreted security requirements
$N4$ = Number of errors due to missing requirements that are not implemented

N5 = Number of errors due to unintended features and functionality that are not specified in the security requirements

N6 = Number of errors due to the lack of resolving dependencies between security requirements

This metric could be further refined to capture errors by security requirements domain or security functional area, like the following examples. Then graphs could be developed to show the distribution of requirements errors by life-cycle phase, type of requirement error, security domain the error occurred in, etc. The root cause of most vulnerabilities is a requirements error, so this metric should be taken seriously.

Nx_f — physical security

Nx_p — personnel security

Nx_i — IT security

Nx_o — operational security

Nx_a — access control

Nx_e — encryption

Nx_i — incident handling

Cumulative Failure Profile

The cumulative failure profile metric is used to produce a graphical depiction of the cumulative number of unique failures during the life-cycle phases[158] and is defined as[8, 9]:

$$f_i = \text{Total number of failures found during life-cycle phase i}$$

This metric can easily be adapted for use in security engineering. If the definition were modified to mean security-related "errors, faults and failures found," the metric could be applied to all life-cycle phases.[158] The metric definition could also be expanded to reflect the severity category of the errors, faults, and failures and the security domain to which they apply:

$$f_{isd} = \text{Total number of failures found in life-cycle phase i}$$
$$\text{of severity s in security domain d}$$

Defect Density

The defect density (DD) metric calculates the ratio of software defects per lines of code or lines of design.[8, 9] The source lines of design can include formal design specifications such as VDM, pseudo code, and the like; this measurement should not be applied to a design specification written in a natural language (i.e., English).

$$DD = \sum_{i=1}^{I} D_{iy} \Big/ \text{KSLOC (or KSLOD)}$$

where

D_{iy} = Number of unique defects found during the i-th inspection process of a life-cycle phase y

I = Total number of inspections

KSLOC = During the development phase and beyond, the number of executable source code statements plus data declarations, in the thousands

KSLOD = During the design phase, the number of source lines of design statements, in the thousands

The defect density metric can easily be adapted for use in security engineering. Instead of measuring the defect density in application software, the defect density in the security architecture for a system, facility, or enterprise could be measured with a few simple modifications to the calculation. Assume the term "defect" has been expanded to include any type of security error, fault, or failure.

$$DD = \sum_{i=1}^{I} D_{iy} \Big/ \text{SA (or SF)}$$

where

D_{iy} = Number of unique security defects found during the i-th security audit of a life-cycle phase y

I = Total number of security audits (including ST&E and C&A activities)

SA = During the development phase and beyond, the number of security appliances (hardware or software) installed

SF = During the design phase, the number of major security features and functions

The number of security appliances installed includes the number of different types of appliances (firewall, encryption, access control, etc.) and the number of each. SA can be presented at different levels of granularity to provide more visibility into where the defects are being found (e.g., SA_{fw}, SA_{en}, SA_{ac}).

Defect Indices

The defect indices (DI) metric calculates a relative index of software correctness throughout the different life-cycle phases[8, 9]:

$$DI = \sum (i \times PI_i) / PS$$

$$PI = (W1 \times (S_i/D_i)) + (W2 \times (M_i/D_i)) + (W3 \times (T_i/D_i))$$

where
D_i = Total number of defects detected during the i-th phase
S_i = Total number of serious defects detected during the i-th phase
M_i = Total number of medium defects detected during the i-th phase
T_i = Total number of trivial defects detected during the i-th phase
W1 = Weighting factor for serious defects, default is 10
W2 = Weighting factor for medium defects, default is 3
W3 = Weighting factor for trivial defects, default is 1
PS = Product size at i-th phase

Product size is measured in KSLOC or KSLOD, as calculated at the end of each phase, and is weighted by phase, such that i = 1, ..., 7.

The defect indices metric can easily be adapted for use in security engineering by substituting the four standard severity categories for the three provided and adjusting the weighting factors and product size accordingly.

$$DI = \sum (i \times PI_i) / PS$$

$$PI = (W1 \times (CAT_i/D_i)) + (W2 \times (CR_i/D_i))$$
$$+ (W3 \times (MAR_i/D_i) + (W4 \times (INi/D_i))$$

where
D_i = Total number of defects detected during the i-th phase
CAT_i = Total number of catastrophic defects detected during the i-th phase
CR_i = Total number of critical defects detected during the i-th phase
MAR_i = Total number of marginal defects detected during the i-th phase
IN_i = Total number of insignificant defects detected during the i-th phase
W1   = Weighting factor for catastrophic defects, default is 10
W2   = Weighting factor for critical defects, default is 8
W3   = Weighting factor for marginal defects, default is 4
W4   = Weighting factor for insignificant defects, default is 1
PS   = Product size at i-th phase

Again, product size can be calculated as the number of security appliances (hardware or software) installed, during the development phase and beyond, or the number of major security features and function, during the design phase. The number of security appliances installed includes the number of different types of appliances (firewall, encryption, access control, etc.) and the number of each. PS can be presented at different levels of granularity to provide more visibility into where the defects are being found (e.g., PS_{fw}, PS_{en}, PS_{ac}).

Three process metrics that are of interest include the following:

1. Functional test coverage
2. Fault days
3. Staff hours per defect detected

First we look at the metric as it is defined in IEEE Std. 982; and then we see how it can be adapted for use in security engineering.

Functional Test Coverage

The functional test coverage (FTC) metric expresses the ratio between the number of software functions tested and the total number of functions in an application system[8, 9]:

$$FTC = FE/FT$$

where
FE = Number of software functional requirements for which all test cases have been satisfactorily completed
FT = Total number of software functional requirements

Notice that the definition of FE states "for which **all** test cases" have been completed. This infers that each function has been tested exhaustively, not on a sampling or superficial basis. Functional testing includes verifying that the function performs correctly under normal and abnormal conditions, such as peak loading. It is possible to due exhaustive functional (black box) testing; it is not possible to do exhaustive logical or structural (white box) testing.

The functional test coverage metric can easily be used in security engineering by altering the definitions of FE and FT to indicate how thoroughly security functions have been tested:

$$FTC = FE/FT$$

where
FE = Number of security functional requirements for which all test cases have been satisfactorily completed
FT = Total number of security functional requirements

Be sure to count the number of security functional requirements consistently to have a valid metric. That is, do not mix the count of high-level and low-level requirements. In the Common Criteria methodology, this distinction is very clear. There are security functional requirement classes, families, components, and elements. The logical place to count low-level requirements is at the component level. The logical place to count high-level requirements is at the family level.

Fault Days

The fault days (FD) metric evaluates the number of days between the time an error is introduced into a system and when the fault is detected and removed[8, 9]:

$$FD = \sum_{i=1}^{I} FD_i$$

where
FD_i = Fault days for the i-th fault
    = $f_{out} - f_{in}$ (or $ph_{out} - ph_{in}$)
f_{in} = Date error was introduced into the system
f_{det} = Date fault was detected
f_{out} = Date fault was removed from the system
ph_{in} = Phase error was introduced into the system
ph_{det} = Phase fault was detected
ph_{out} = Phase fault was removed from the system
I   = Total number of faults found to date

If the exact date an event took place is not known, it is assumed to have occurred during the middle of the corresponding life-cycle phase.

This metric and collection of primitives can be used in a variety of ways to improve the security engineering process. The metric can be used as-is to track security fault days. Fault days can be calculated by severity categories. Intermediate values can be calculated to evaluate the time span between error introduction and fault detection, and likewise the time span between fault detection and fault removal to pinpoint weaknesses in fault prevention strategies. It is also informative to look at the minimum and maximum security fault days, by severity category, in addition to the average. The measurement boundaries for the security fault days can be a single system or network, an entire facility or campus, or enterprisewide.

Staff Hours per Defect Detected

The staff hours (SH) per nontrivial defect detected metric measures the efficiency of verification activities[8, 9]:

$$SH = \sum_{i=1}^{I} (T_1 + T_2)_i \left/ \sum_{i=1}^{I} S_i \right.$$

where
T_1 = Preparation time expended by the verification team for verification activity i
T_2 = Time expended by the verification team to conduct verification activity i
S_i = Number of nontrivial defects detected during verification activity i
I = Total number of verification activities conducted to date

The SH will be lower during early life-cycle phases, when most defects are detected. The SH will be higher during the operations and maintenance phase, after a steady state has been reached.

This process metric can be easily modified for use in security engineering. S, the number of defects, could be limited to security defects and further broken down by severity category or major security functional area. SH could be calculated for the security architecture of a single system or network, a facility or campus, or the entire enterprise. SH could be calculated by organization or shift, and whether in-house or independent third-party staff performed the verification activity. Remember that this metric only captures defects found by verification activities; it does not record successful security incidents.

Finally, there is more to reliability engineering than just technology, such as human factors engineering and cultural considerations. These items can be monitored through the use of appropriate personnel security and operational security metrics. Hecht identifies several organizational causes of failure that should receive special attention; they were gleaned from recent high-profile system failures[153]:

- Stifling dissenting views or questions
- Rigid adherence to schedule, such that problems get "brushed under the rug"
- Financial incentives for meeting the schedule
- Safety, reliability, and security engineers are expected to be "team players"
- Lack of engineering checks and balances
- Inadequate preparation for contingencies
- Ineffective anomaly reporting, tracking, and analysis
- Incomplete system test
- Inadequate training and warnings about consequences of not following prescribed safety and security engineering procedures

2.10 Examples from Safety Engineering

Safety engineering is quite similar to security engineering. There are parallels in all four domains: (1) physical safety/physical security, (2) personnel safety/personnel security, (3) IT safety/IT security, and (4) operational safety/operational security. In addition, safety engineering, unlike reliability engineering, is concerned about accidental and malicious intentional actions. The purpose of safety engineering is to manage risks that could negatively impact humans, equipment and other property, and the environment. This is accomplished through a combination of analysis, design, and verification activities, as well as operational procedures. A series of hazard analyses are performed throughout the life cycle to identify risks, their causes, the severity of the consequences should they occur, and the likelihood of them occurring. Risks are then eliminated or controlled through inherent safe (re)design features, risk mitigation or protective functions, system alarms and warnings, and comprehensive instructions for use and training that explain safety features, safety procedures, and the residual risk.

MIL-STD 882D defines system safety as:

> *The application of engineering and management principles, criteria, and techniques to achieve acceptable mishap risk, within the constraints of operational effectiveness, time, and cost throughout all phases of the system life cycle.*

The term "mishap risk" is used to distinguish between the type of risk of concern to system safety and that of schedule or cost risk. MIL-STD 882D defines mishap risk as:

> *An expression of the possibility and impact of an unplanned event or series of events resulting in death, injury, occupational illness, damage to or loss of equipment or property (physical or cyber), or damage to the environment in terms of potential severity and probability of occurrence.*

Software, whether operating systems, applications software, or firmware, is of utmost concern to security engineers, and there are several parallels to software safety. Software safety is defined as[158]:

> *Design features and operational procedures which ensure that a product performs predictably under normal and abnormal conditions and the likelihood of an unplanned event occurring is minimized and its consequences controlled and contained; thereby preventing accidental injury or death, environmental or property damage, whether intentional or accidental.*

The discipline of system safety originated in the defense and aerospace industries, then spread to the nuclear industry and others. The practice of software safety has spread as rapidly as analog hardware and discrete logic is replaced by PROMs, PLCs, and ASICs. The railway, automotive, power generation, commercial aircraft, air traffic control, process control, and bio-medical industries are all active players in the field of software safety today. MIL-STD 882 has been the foundation of the system safety program for the U.S. military since the original version of the standard was issued in 1969.

To achieve system or software safety, safety requirements must be specified — both functional safety requirements and safety integrity requirements. Safety integrity requirements explain the level of integrity to which the functional safety requirements must be verified. These requirements explain how a system should prevent, detect, respond to, contain, and recover from faults so that the system remains in a known safe state at all times. This includes specifying must work functions (MWFs) and must not work functions (MNWFs), and under what conditions a system should fail safe or fail operational. An MWF is a safety-critical function that must function correctly for the system to remain in a known safe state at all times. An MNWF is an illegal function or operational state that the system must never be allowed to perform or reach, or system safety will be seriously compromised.

IEC 61508 is the current international standard for system safety; it consists of seven parts.[1-7] It recommends or highly recommends a series of design features and engineering techniques to use throughout the system life cycle to achieve and sustain system safety. These features and techniques fall into three categories:

1. Controlling random hardware failures
2. Avoiding systematic failures
3. Achieving software safety integrity

Table 2.12   Design Features and Engineering Techniques to Avoid Systematic Failures[7]

Design Features:
Hardware diversity
Partitioning
Safety/security kernels
Engineering Techniques:
Computer-aided specification tools
Computer-aided design tools
Design for maintainability
Dynamic analysis: black box testing, boundary value testing, equivalence class partitioning, fault injection, interface testing, statistical-based testing, stress testing, white box testing
Formal inspections, reviews, walk-throughs
Formal methods
Human factors engineering
Protection against sabotage
Semi-formal methods
Simulation and modeling
Static analysis: audits, CCF/CMF analysis, cause consequence analysis, event trees, finite state machine, FMECA, FTA, HAZOP studies, Petri nets, root cause analysis, sneak circuit analysis, state transition diagrams, truth tables, worst-case analysis

The features and techniques for controlling random hardware failures were discussed above under reliability engineering in Section 2.8. The other two categories — avoiding systematic failures and achieving software safety integrity — are directly applicable to security engineering and will be explored in detail.

Table 2.12 lists the design features and engineering techniques IEC 61508 recommends or highly recommends for avoiding systematic failures. The specified safety integrity level determines whether a feature or technique is recommended or highly recommended.

Table 2.13 lists the design features and engineering techniques that IEC 61508 recommends or highly recommends for achieving software safety integrity. Again, the specified safety integrity level determines whether a feature or technique is recommended or highly recommended.

IEC 61508 requires the specification of safety functional requirements and safety integrity requirements. Safety integrity requirements stipulate the level to which functional safety requirements are verified. These levels are referred to as safety integrity levels (or SILs). As noted above, specific design features and engineering techniques to be performed during life-cycle phases are either recommended or highly recommended in accordance with the SIL. An SIL is defined as[4]:

Table 2.13   Design Features and Engineering Techniques to Achieve Software Safety Integrity[7]

Design Features:
Defensive programming
Design for degraded mode operations, graceful degradation
Dynamic reconfiguration
Error and exception handling
Information hiding, encapsulation
Limited use of interrupts, recursion, pointers
Partitioning
Recovery blocks: forward, backward, retry
Safety/security kernels
Software diversity
Engineering Techniques:
Dynamic analysis: black box testing, boundary value testing, equivalence class partitioning, fault injection, interface testing, statistical-based testing, stress testing, white box testing
Formal methods: B, VDM, Z
Static analysis: audits, CCF/CMF analysis, cause consequence analysis, event trees, finite state machine, FMECA, FTA, HAZOP studies, Petri nets, root cause analysis, sneak circuit analysis, state transition diagrams, truth tables, worst-case analysis
Use of certified compilers, specification and design tools

> *A level of how far safety is to be pursued in a given context, assessed by reference to an acceptable risk, based on the current values of society.*

Note the reference to acceptable risk, as discussed in Section 2.8. IEC 61508 acknowledges five SILs, as shown below. These levels are comparable to the Common Criteria evaluation assurance levels (EALs). EALs 0 to 3 map to SILs 0 to 2, EAL 4 corresponds to SIL 3, while EALs 5 to 7 compare to SIL 4.

> SIL 0 — None
> SIL 1 — Low
> SIL 2 — Medium
> SIL 3 — High
> SIL 4 — Very high

Several factors are taken into account when determining the appropriate SIL: severity of injury, number of people exposed to the danger, frequency at which a person or people are exposed to the danger, duration of the exposure, public perceptions, views of those exposed to the hazard, regulatory guidelines, industry standards, international agreements, expert advice, and legal considerations.[5] SILs are specified in terms of risk levels, so that it is clear about what is and is not deemed acceptable risk in terms of likelihood and severity categories.

Safety integrity is defined as[5]:

> *The probability of a safety-related system satisfactorily performing the required safety functions under all stated conditions within a stated period of time. Safety integrity relates to the performance of the safety-related systems in carrying out the specified safety requirements.*

Safety integrity is composed of two elements: (1) hardware safety integrity, which is a function of avoiding random failures; and (2) systematic safety integrity, which is a function of avoiding systematic failures in safety-critical or safety-related hardware and software. The level of safety integrity achieved is a combination of all safety controls: physical, personnel, IT, and operational safety; risk mitigation activities are apportioned accordingly.[5] The SIL of each safety-related system component must be greater than or equal to the SIL specified for the system as a whole. When specifying an SIL or apportioning risk mitigation activities, IEC 61508 distinguishes between safety control systems and safety protection systems, and between systems that operate in continuous mode and those that operate in demand mode. As an analogy, a security control system controls the execution of a major security function, like encryption or access control. A security protection system is a system that prevents or contains the damage following a failure, such as a network isolation or server quarantine capability. In general, safety control systems operate in continuous mode, while safety protection systems operate in demand mode.

Now let us look at a few of the design features and engineering techniques recommended or highly recommended by IEC 61508 and how they could be applied to security engineering. Both are a ready source of IT resilience metrics, which are explored further in Chapter 4. These metrics are used to determine how well and how thoroughly specific design features were implemented or engineering techniques were applied to enhance the integrity of system security. A design feature could be implemented incorrectly and have no or a negative impact on security integrity; or a design feature could be implemented appropriately and enhance security integrity. Likewise, an engineering technique could be applied minimally or incorrectly and have no or a negative impact on security integrity; or an engineering technique could be used appropriately and enhance security integrity. Just because a design technique was employed or an engineering technique was used does not automatically mean that the level of security integrity has increased. Metrics reveal whether these features and techniques have been employed effectively and the benefits derived from doing so.

Five design features are particularly applicable to security engineering:

1. Block recovery
2. Boundary value analysis
3. Defensive programming
4. Information hiding
5. Partitioning

Block Recovery

Block recovery is a design technique that provides correct functional operation in the presence of one or more errors.[7] For each critical module, a primary and secondary module (employing diversity) are developed. After the primary module executes, but before it performs any critical transactions, an acceptance test is run. This test checks for possible error conditions, exceptions, and out-of-range variables. If no error is detected, normal execution continues. If an error is detected, control is switched to the corresponding secondary module and another more stringent acceptance test is run. If no error is detected, normal execution resumes. However, if an error is detected, the system is reset either to a previous (backward block recovery) or future (forward block recovery) known safe and secure state. In backward block recovery, if an error is detected, the system is reset to an earlier known safe state. In forward block recovery, if an error is detected, the current state of the system is manipulated or forced into a future known safe state. This method is useful for real-time systems with small amounts of data and fast-changing internal states.[7] Block recovery is recommended for SILs 1 to –4.[7]

This design feature can easily be applied to security engineering. From the definition it is clear that block recovery is a design technique that can be used to enhance the operational resilience of IT systems. The acceptance tests, both primary and secondary, could be designed to monitor error conditions typical of security incident precursor events. Resetting the system state backward or forward to a known secure state would allow suspicious sessions and transactions to be safely and securely preempted and dropped. Block recovery could be implemented at the network level or application system level. Several security metrics could be used to evaluate the effectiveness of block recovery, including:

- Number of places in the enterprise security architecture where block recovery is implemented
- Number of places in the network security architecture where block recovery is implemented
- Number of places in the application software system security architecture where block recovery is implemented
- Number of parameters evaluated during primary acceptance test
- Number of parameters evaluated in secondary acceptance test
- Number of options for forward block recovery
- Number of options for backward block recovery
- Percent (%) increase in operational and achieved availability due to block recovery

Boundary Value Analysis

Boundary value analysis identifies software errors that occur in safety-critical and safety-related functions and entities when processing at or beyond specified parameter limits. During boundary value analysis, test cases are designed that exercise the software's parameter processing algorithms. The system's response to specific input and output classes is evaluated, such as:

- Parameter below minimum specified threshold
- Parameter at minimum specified threshold
- Parameter at maximum specified threshold
- Parameter over maximum specified threshold
- Parameter within specified minimum/maximum range

Zero or null parameters tend to be error-prone. Specific tests are warranted for the following conditions as well[7]:

- Zero divisor
- Blank ASCII characters
- Empty stack or list
- Full matrix
- Zero entry table

Boundary value analysis is used to verify processing of parameters that control safety-critical and safety-related functions. Boundary value analysis complements plausibility checks. The intent is to verify that the software responds to all parameters correctly, so that the system remains in a known safe state at all times. Error and exception handling routines are triggered if a parameter is out of the specified range or normal processing continues if a parameter is within the specified range. Boundary value analysis can also be used to verify that the correct data type is being used: alphabetic, numeric, integer, real, signed, pointer, etc. Boundary value analysis enhances data integrity by ensuring that data is within the specified valid range before acting upon it. Boundary value analysis is highly recommended for SILs 1 to 4.[7]

This design feature can easily be applied to enhance security integrity. Bad data, whether accidental or intentional, is frequently a cause of security incidents. Couple that with the fact that commercial off the shelf (COTS) software products are designed and developed to be function-rich, not necessarily secure, and the need for boundary value analysis in the safety and security engineering communities is clear. Boundary value analysis could be implemented in the scripts and middleware that envelop COTS software to prevent many common incidents, such as buffer overflows. Several security metrics could be used to evaluate the effectiveness of boundary value analysis, such as:

- Number and percentage of security appliances, functions, control systems, and protection systems that implement boundary value analysis, by system risk and asset criticality categories
- Percent (%) of boundary value analysis routines that check for parameter values that are below or at the minimum threshold, before acting upon them
- Percent (%) of boundary value analysis routines that check for parameter values that are above or at the maximum threshold, before acting upon them

- Percent (%) of boundary value analysis routines that check for zero or null data fields, before acting upon them
- Percent (%) of boundary value analysis routines that check for correct data types, before acting upon them
- Percent (%) of different types of error conditions identified by boundary value analysis routines for which there is a corresponding error or exception handling routine
- Percent (%) decrease in security incidents due to the implementation of boundary value analysis, by incident severity

Defensive Programming

Defensive programming prevents system failures or compromises by detecting errors in control flow, data flow, and data during execution and reacting in a predetermined and acceptable manner.[7] Defensive programming is a set of design techniques in which critical system parameters and requests to transition system states are verified before acting upon them. The intent is to develop software that correctly accommodates design or operational shortcomings. This involves incorporating a degree of fault tolerance using software diversity and stringent checking of I/O, data, and commands. Defensive programming is recommended for SILs 1 to 2 and highly recommended for SILs 3 to 4.[7] Defensive programming techniques include[7]:

- Plausibility and range checks on inputs and intermediate variables that affect physical parameters of the system
- Plausibility and range checks on output variables
- Monitoring system state changes
- Checking the type, dimension, and range of parameters at procedure entry
- Regular automatic checking of the system and software configuration to verify that it is correct and complete

This design feature can easily be applied to security engineering to prevent system failures or compromises due to security incidents by detecting errors in control flow, data flow, and data during execution and preempting the event. Plausibility and range checks could be performed on inputs and intermediate variables related to security-critical and security-related functions, especially those for security control and protection systems. Likewise, plausibility and range checks could be performed on output variables of security control and protection systems to detect any accidental or intentionally induced processing errors. An independent monitoring function could be established specifically to monitor state changes in security-related MWFs and NMWFs. The type, dimension, and range of security parameters could be validated at procedure entry and appropriate action taken if errors are detected. Finally, the configuration of all security appliances could be verified automatically on a regular basis and alarms generated if any misconfigurations are detected. Several security metrics could be used to evaluate the effectiveness of defensive programming, including:

- Percent (%) of security control systems that implement plausibility and range checks on inputs
- Percent (%) of security control systems that implement plausibility and range checks on outputs
- Percent (%) of security protection systems that implement plausibility and range checks on inputs
- Percent (%) of security protection systems that implement plausibility and range checks on outputs
- Percent (%) of MWFs for which state transitions are monitored
- Percent (%) of MNWFs for which state transitions are monitored
- Percent (%) of security parameters for which type, state, and range are validated at procedure entry, before any action is taken
- Percent (%) of security appliances whose configuration is automatically monitored on a continual basis

Information Hiding

Information hiding is a design feature that is incorporated to (1) prevent accidental access to and corruption of software and data, (2) minimize introduction of errors during maintenance and enhancements, (3) reduce the likelihood of CCFs, and (4) minimize fault propagation. Dr. David Parnas developed the information hiding design technique to minimize the interdependency or coupling of modules and maximize their independence and cohesion.[158] System functions, sets of data, and operations on that data are localized within a module. That is, the module's internal processing is "hidden." This is accomplished by making the logic of each module and the data it utilizes as self-contained as possible.[158] In this way, if later on it is necessary to change the functions internal to one module, the resulting propagation of changes to other modules is minimized, as are CCFs. Information hiding is recommended for SILs 1 and 2 and highly recommended for SILs 3 and 4.[7]

This design feature could be easily adapted for use in security engineering, particularly security-related CCFs. Modules that perform security-related functions, such as identification and authentication or access control, could be hidden from modules that are strictly functional. The "need-to-know" rule could be applied to the sharing of parameters across software interfaces, such that the minimum amount of data is shared or its presence revealed. Security management functions and security management information could be encapsulated. Several security metrics could be used to evaluate the effectiveness of information hiding, including:

- Number and percentage (%) of security management information parameters that are shared with or accessible by non-security-related functions
- Number and percentage (%) of security management functions that interface directly with non-security-related functions
- Number and percentage (%) of security management functions that are implemented in security kernels

- Percentage (%) increase in the integrity of security management information due to the use of information hiding principles
- Percentage (%) decrease in CCFs due to the use of information hiding principles

Partitioning

Partitioning enhances integrity by preventing non-safety-related functions and entities from accidentally or intentionally corrupting safety-critical functions and entities. Partitioning is a design feature that can be implemented in hardware or software, or both. In the case of software, partitioning can be logical or physical. Safety-critical and safety-related functions and entities are isolated from non-safety-related functions and entities. Both design and functionality are partitioned to prevent accidental and intentional interference, compromise, and corruption originating from non-safety-related functions and entities. Well-partitioned systems are easier to understand, verify, and maintain. Partitioning facilitates fault isolation and minimizes the potential for fault propagation. Furthermore, partitioning helps identify the most critical system components so that resources can be more effectively concentrated on them. Partitioning is recommended for SILs 1 and 2 and highly recommended for SILs 3 and 4.[7]

This design feature can easily be adapted for use by security engineering. Partitioning could be implemented in a variety of ways in the security architecture. Security functions could be partitioned from non-security functions. Security functions could be partitioned from each other according to risk and criticality. Security control systems could be partitioned from security protection systems. Security management information could be partitioned from all other data, such as network management data, system management data, and end-user data. Several security metrics could be used to evaluate the effectiveness of partitioning, including:

- Percentage (%) of enterprise security architecture that implements partitioning, by system risk category and asset criticality
- Percentage (%) of enterprise security architecture that implements physical partitioning
- Percentage (%) of enterprise security architecture that implements logical partitioning
- Number and percentage (%) of security control systems that are not partitioned from non-security-related functions
- Number and percentage (%) of security protection systems that are not partitioned from non-security-related functions
- Increase in maintainability of security appliances, functions, and systems due to implementing partitioning, using an ordinal scale of 0 (none) to 10 (very high)

Four engineering techniques recommended or highly recommended by IEC 61508 are particularly applicable to security engineering:

1. Equivalence class partitioning
2. HAZOP studies
3. Root cause analysis
4. Safety audits, reviews, and inspections

Equivalence Class Partitioning

Equivalence class partitioning is performed to identify the minimum set of test cases and test data that will adequately test each input domain. During equivalence class partitioning, the set of all possible test cases is examined to determine which test cases and data are unique or redundant, in that they test the same functionality or logic path. The intent is to obtain the highest possible test coverage with the least possible number of test cases. Input partitions can be derived from the requirements and the internal structure of a program.[7] At least one test case should be taken from each equivalence class for all safety-critical and safety-related functions and entities. Testing activities are much more efficient when equivalence class partitioning is employed. Equivalence class partitioning is highly recommended for SILs 1 to 4.[7]

This engineering technique could be easily applied to security engineering to enhance the thoroughness of ST&E activities. Often, ST&E activities are driven by schedules and budgets, rather than by security engineering needs. Few projects have unlimited ST&E budgets. Equivalence class partitioning can help focus and maximize ST&E activities, within schedule and budget constraints. Several security metrics could be used to evaluate the effectiveness of equivalence class partitioning, including:

- Percentage (%) increase in ST&E coverage, due to implementing equivalence class partitioning
- Percentage (%) decrease in time and resources required to perform ST&E, due to implementing equivalence class partitioning
- Percentage (%) increase in errors found during ST&E, due to implementing equivalence class partitioning, by severity category
- Number and percentage (%) of security appliances, functions, control systems, and protection systems for which equivalence class partitioning was applied during ST&E, by system risk and asset criticality categories

HAZOP Studies

A hazard and operability (HAZOP) study is conducted to prevent potential hazards by capturing domain knowledge about the operational environment, parameters, models and states, etc. so that this information can be incorporated into the requirements, design, as-built system, and operational procedures. A HAZOP study is a method of discovering hazards in a proposed or existing system, their possible causes and consequences, and recommending solutions to minimize the likelihood of occurrence.[7] The hazards can be physical or cyber in nature and result from accidental or malicious intentional action.

Design and operational aspects of the system are analyzed by an interdisciplinary team. A neutral facilitator guides the group through a discussion of how a system is or should be used. Particular attention is paid to usability issues, operator actions (correct and incorrect, under normal and abnormal conditions), and capturing domain knowledge. A series of guide words is used to determine correct design values for system components, interconnections, and dependencies between components, and the attributes of the components. This is one of the few techniques to focus on (1) hazards arising from the operational environment and usability issues, and (2) capturing domain knowledge from multiple stakeholders.[7] HAZOP studies are recommended for SILs 1 and 2 and highly recommended for SILs 3 and 4.[7]

This engineering technique can easily be utilized by security engineering to prevent the introduction of security faults into an as-built system and the associated operational procedures. Instead of focusing on safety-related hazards, the emphasis would be on security-related vulnerabilities. (A VULOP study?) Domain experts and operational staff are particularly adept at identifying MWFs and MNWFs, illegal system states, prohibited parameter values, and timing and other constraints in the operational environment. They are also the preferred stakeholders to validate human factors engineering issues, a frequent source of accidental induced or invited security errors. Several security metrics could be used to evaluate the effectiveness of HAZOP (or VULOP) studies, such as:

- Number of MWFs identified during the HAZOP study
- Number of MNWFs identified during the HAZOP study
- Number of illegal system states, prohibited parameter values, and operational constraints identified during the HAZOP study
- Number of errors in proposed operational procedures identified during the HAZOP study, by severity category
- Number of errors in the human computer interface identified during the HAZOP study, by severity category
- Total number of faults prevented, by severity category, as a result of conducting the HAZOP study
- Number and percentage (%) of stakeholder groups that were represented during the HAZOP study

Root Cause Analysis

Root cause analysis identifies the underlying cause(s), events, conditions, or actions that individually, or in combination, led to an incident and determines why the defect was not detected earlier. Root cause analysis is an investigative technique used to determine how, when, and why a defect was introduced and why it escaped detection in earlier phases. Root cause analysis is conducted by examining a defect, then tracing back, step by step, through the design, decisions, and assumptions that supported the design to the source of the defect. Root cause analysis facilitates defect prevention, continuous process improvement, and incident investigation. The process of conducting root cause analysis may uncover defects in other areas as well. Root cause analysis is recommended for SILs 1 and 2 and highly recommended for SILs 3 and 4.[7]

This engineering analysis technique could easily be adapted to improve the security engineering process. The root cause of security incidents is rarely, if ever, investigated. Instead, a simple explanation is given (e.g., syn flood, buffer overflow, etc.); usually this explanation is not a cause at all, but rather the type of attack. The root cause of security incidents should be investigated to determine how, when, and why a vulnerability was introduced that allowed a specific attack to become successful. Just as important, root cause analysis should be conducted to determine why this vulnerability was not detected previously, or if it was, why the risk mitigation activities failed. The scope of root cause analysis includes all four security domains: physical, personnel, IT, and operational security. Root cause analysis enhances resilience by preventing the same or similar attacks from becoming successful in the future. If the root cause of a security incident is not investigated, its repetition cannot be prevented. During the investigation, other errors are usually uncovered and corrected as well. Several security metrics could be used to evaluate the effectiveness of root cause analysis, such as:

- Percentage (%) of security incidents for which root cause analysis was conducted, by severity category
- Percentage (%) of security incidents, by severity category, whose root cause was due to the failure of a physical security control
- Percentage (%) of security incidents, by severity category, whose root cause was due to the failure of a personnel security control
- Percentage (%) of security incidents, by severity category, whose root cause was due to the failure of an IT security control
- Percentage (%) of security incidents, by severity category, whose root cause was due to the failure of an operational security control
- Percentage (%) of security incidents, by severity category, whose root cause was due to the failure of a control in more than one security domain
- Distribution of the root causes of security incidents, of severity categories marginal or higher, that were due to a failure of physical security controls
- Distribution of the root causes of security incidents, of severity categories marginal or higher, that were due to a failure of personnel security controls
- Distribution of the root causes of security incidents, of severity categories marginal or higher, that were due to a failure of IT security controls
- Distribution of the root causes of security incidents, of severity categories marginal or higher, that were due to a failure of operational security controls
- Number of other errors discovered, by severity category and security domain, that were uncovered while performing root cause analysis

Audits, Reviews, and Inspections

Safety audits, reviews, and inspections are conducted throughout the life of a system to uncover errors that could affect integrity. These safety audits, reviews, and inspections comprise a static analysis technique that is used to find errors of commission and errors of omission. Requirements, designs, implementations, test cases, test results, and operational systems can be subjected to safety audits. Unlike other audits and reviews, these focus solely on issues that impact safety; for example, verifying that fault tolerance has been implemented correctly, test coverage was adequate, operational safety procedures are being followed, etc. Any open issues or discrepancies are assigned a severity category and tracked through resolution. Safety audits complement requirements traceability activities. Communication among all stakeholders is facilitated through safety audits, reviews, and inspections. More and different types of errors are detected, due to the involvement of multiple stakeholders.[156] Safety audits, reviews, and inspections are highly recommended for SILs 1 to 4.[7]

Security audits are not new; however, to date, their use has been primarily to enforce compliance with federal regulations and company security and privacy policies. The use of security audits can be expanded to reduce the introduction of errors of omission and errors of commission in all life-cycle phases. Conduct security audits regularly using in-house staff. Security audits conducted by independent third parties can be used to augment and confirm the findings of internal audits. The audits can be focused very narrowly, on a single security feature or issue; very broadly, on all four security domains; or somewhere in between. The important thing is to define the scope of the audit beforehand. Security audits can be active (interactive design reviews, interviews, etc.) or passive in nature (documentation reviews). Several security metrics can be used to evaluate the effectiveness of security audits, reviews, and inspections, to include:

- Number and percentage of security appliances, functions, control systems, and protection systems for which security audits were conducted this reporting period, by risk and criticality categories
- Number of errors found by security domain and severity category, as a result of conducting all security audits
- Number of errors found by security domain and severity category, as a result of conducting internal security audits
- Number of errors found by security domain and severity category, as a result of conducting independent third-party security audits
- Number of errors found by life-cycle phase and severity category, as a result of conducting all security audits
- Number of errors found by life-cycle phase and severity category, as a result of conducting internal security audits
- Number of errors found by life-cycle phase and severity category, as a result of conducting independent third-party security audits
- Number of errors, by severity category, that were prevented from reaching the as-built system and the operational procedures, as a result of conducting security audits
- Number of errors, by severity category, that were detected and corrected in the same life-cycle phase, as a result of conducting security audits

These examples illustrate how (1) specialized design features and engineering techniques can be used throughout the life cycle to prevent and remove vulnerabilities, especially before they reach the as-built system; and (2) how security metrics can be used to measure the effectiveness of these practices. Now let us put all the pieces together. Consider an access control function for a safety-critical system, such as an air traffic control system. The air traffic control system has been specified to have an SIL of 3, while the security functions for this system have been specified to have an EAL of 4. The project is near the completion of the design phase. The customer has asked for some proof, not the usual verbal assurances or back-slapping, that the SIL and EAL will indeed be met. Meeting the EAL also implies that the ST&E and C&A activities will be completed successfully with no major setbacks or surprises. What do you do?

To start, you prepare a metrics worksheet similar to that shown in Table 2.14. First you list the design features and engineering techniques that are recommended or highly recommended for the specified safety and security integrity levels. (This example only uses nine features and techniques; in reality, there could be more.) Then you determine whether or not these design features were incorporated and the engineering activities performed — and if not, why not. If they were not incorporated or performed due to an error of omission, some rework is necessary. This information is recorded in Part 1 of the worksheet. Part 2 of the worksheet captures metrics for the individual design features and engineering techniques that are applicable to the customer's request. These metrics are derived from the standard metrics listed above for each feature and technique. Not all the standard metrics listed are used, only the ones that directly contribute to answering the request. The metrics are tailored for the stated life-cycle phase (in this case, design) and the scope of measurement. In this example, we are only looking at the access control function, not an entire system or enterprise; hence, several of the metrics are modified to reflect that fact. Part 3 of the worksheet aggregates the individual metrics into a handful of metrics for the design features as a whole, and the engineering techniques as a whole. In this example, 23 individual design feature metrics were aggregated into 7 metrics, while 18 individual engineering technique metrics were aggregated into 6 metrics. Finally, you prepare the presentation of the security metrics results. Depending on the customer's preferences, the information from Part 3 can be presented, with the information in Part 2 as backup data; or the information in Part 2 can be presented, with the information in Part 3 listed last as a summary.

2.11 Examples from Software Engineering

Although not recognized as such, software engineering is also a first cousin of security engineering. IT security appliances, whether for networks, servers, or desktops, are software based; the one exception being hardware-based bulk encryptors. Physical security surveillance, monitoring, and access control equipment are software based. Personnel security information and assessments rely on software-based systems for information storage and retrieval, not to mention controlling access to that information. Human factors engineering, in

Table 2.14   Sample Metrics Worksheet for Integrity Levels

System: Air Traffic Control
Sub-system: IT Security
Function: Access Control
Integrity Level: Safety = 3, Security = 4

Part 1: Assessment of Design Features and Engineering Techniques

Feature/Technique	R	HR	Notes
1. Design Features			
Block recovery	x		Incorporated
Boundary value analysis		x	Incorporated
Defensive programming		x	Incorporated
Information hiding		x	Not used; design is partitioned into safety and security kernels
Partitioning		x	Incorporated
2. Engineering Techniques			
Equivalence class partitioning		x	Performed during ST&E planning
HAZOP (VULOP) study		x	Conducted
Root cause analysis		x	Conducted
Safety/security audits		x	Conducted

Part 2: Identify Applicable Individual Metrics

Feature/Technique	Individual Metrics Selected
1. Design Features	
Block recovery	Number of places in the access control sub-system where block recovery is implemented
	Number of parameters evaluated during primary acceptance test
	Number of parameters evaluated in secondary acceptance test
	Number of options for forward block recovery
	Number of options for backward block recovery
	Expected percentage (%) increase in inherent availability due to block recovery

Table 2.14   Sample Metrics Worksheet for Integrity Levels (continued)

Feature/Technique	Individual Metrics Selected
Boundary value analysis	Number and percentage of access control functions that implement boundary value analysis, by risk and criticality categories
	Percentage (%) of boundary value analysis routines that check for parameter values that are below or at the minimum threshold, before acting upon them
	Percentage (%) of boundary value analysis routines that check for parameter values that are above or at the maximum threshold, before acting upon them
	Percentage (%) of boundary value analysis routines that check for zero or null data fields, before acting upon them
	Percentage (%) of boundary value analysis routines that check for correct data types, before acting upon them
	Percentage (%) of different types of error conditions identified by boundary value analysis routines for which there is a corresponding error/exception handling routine
	Expected percentage (%) decrease in security incidents due to the implementation of boundary value analysis, by incident severity
Defensive programming	Percentage (%) of access control functions that implement plausibility and range checks on inputs
	Percentage (%) of access control functions that implement plausibility and range checks on outputs
	Percentage (%) of access control MWFs for which state transitions are monitored
	Percentage (%) of access control MNWFs for which state transitions are monitored
	Percentage (%) of access control parameters for which type, state, and range are validated at procedure entry, before any action is taken
Information hiding	N/A
Partitioning	Percentage (%) of access control functions that implement partitioning, by risk category
	Percentage (%) of access control functions that implement physical partitioning
	Percentage (%) of access control functions that implement logical partitioning

Table 2.14   Sample Metrics Worksheet for Integrity Levels (continued)

Feature/Technique	Individual Metrics Selected
Partitioning (cont.)	Number and percentage (%) of access control functions that are not partitioned from non-security-related functions
	Expected increase in maintainability of access control functions, due to implementing partitioning, using an ordinal scale of 0 (none) to 10 (very high)
2. Engineering Techniques	
Equivalence class partitioning	Percentage (%) increase in ST&E coverage, due to implementing equivalence class partitioning
	Percentage (%) decrease in time and resources required to perform ST&E, due to implementing equivalence class partitioning
	Percentage (%) increase in errors found during ST&E, due to implementing equivalence class partitioning, by severity category
	Number and percentage (%) of access control functions for which equivalence class partitioning was applied during ST&E, by risk and criticality categories
HAZOP (VULOP) study	Number of MWFs identified during the HAZOP study
	Number of MNWFs identified during the HAZOP study
	Number of illegal system states, prohibited parameter values, and operational constraints identified during the HAZOP study
	Number of errors in proposed operational procedures identified during the HAZOP study, by severity category
	Number of errors in the human computer interface identified during the HAZOP study, by severity category
	Total number of faults prevented, by severity category, as a result of conducting the HAZOP study
Root cause analysis	Percentage (%) of errors in the design for the access control function for which root cause analysis was conducted, by severity category
	Distribution of the root causes of errors in the design for the access control function, of severity categories marginal or higher
	Number of other errors discovered, by severity category and security domain, that were uncovered while performing root cause analysis of errors in the design of the access control function

Table 2.14 Sample Metrics Worksheet for Integrity Levels (continued)

Feature/Technique	Individual Metrics Selected
Safety/security audits	Number and percentage of access control functions for which security audits were conducted, by risk category
	Distribution of errors found by internal and independent third-party audits
	Number of errors found by life-cycle phase and severity category, as a result of conducting security audits
	Number of errors, by severity category, that were prevented from reaching the as-built system and the operational procedures, as a result of conducting security audits
	Number of errors, by severity category, that were detected and corrected in the same life-cycle phase, as a result of conducting security audits

Part 3: Identify Appropriate Aggregate Metrics

Category	Aggregate Metrics
Design features	Percentage (%) of the highly recommended design features that were incorporated
	Percentage (%) of the recommended design features that were incorporated
	Percentage (%) of access control functions that incorporate all highly recommended design features
	Percentage (%) of access control functions that incorporate 75% or more of the highly recommended design features
	Expected percentage (%) increase in inherent availability, due to incorporating these design features
	Expected percentage (%) decrease in security incidents, due to incorporating these design features
	Expected increase in maintainability, due to incorporating these design features, using an ordinal scale of 0 (none) to 10 (very high)
Engineering techniques	Percentage (%) of the highly recommended engineering techniques that were performed
	Percentage (%) of the recommended engineering techniques that were performed
	Number of faults that were prevented, by severity category, by performing these engineering techniques
	Number of errors that were detected, by security domain and life-cycle phase, by performing these engineering techniques
	Number and percentage of stakeholder groups that were represented while these engineering techniques were performed
	Distribution of engineering activities that were performed by in-house staff, independent third parties, and both

particular preventing induced and invited human error, is equally important to software and security engineering. As a result, it is important to understand software engineering metrics and what they mean to security engineering.

Computer programming, in various forms, has been around since the 1940s. Originally, one person was responsible for programming and operating the computer. By the 1960s the need for two separate skill sets — computer programmers and computer operators — was recognized. By the 1970s, a third skill set was identified, that of systems analyst. In the 1980s, systems analysts were gradually replaced by software engineers. This evolution in skill sets reflected the concurrent evolution of computer hardware and software, but more importantly the need for a broader range of specialized skills. This evolution was similar to the recognition today that telecommunications engineers, network operations staff, software developers, and security engineers have different specialized skills.

The paradigm shift from programming to software engineering was significant. Software engineering brought more discipline and rigor to the process of software development and introduced a seven-phase life-cycle methodology: (1) concept, (2) requirements analysis and specification, (3) design, (4) development, (5) validation and verification, (6) operations and maintenance, and (7) decommissioning. Over time, software engineers began to specialize in certain life-cycle phases, such as requirements analysis and specification or validation and verification. The old notion of "programming" became one of the seven software engineering phases — development. At the same time, software engineering became one of the eight standard components of a computer science curriculum.

The scope of software engineering today is much broader than the "programming" of old. In the 1960s and 1970s, programmers were limited to a large mainframe computer and dumb terminals that were in the same building, if not the same floor. User involvement was limited to receiving hardcopy printouts. Today the world of software engineering includes application software, middleware, operating systems, real-time (R/T) software applications, firmware, application-specific integrated circuits (ASICs), programmable logic controllers (PLCs), and erasable programmable read-only memory (EPROM) chips, and this trend will only continue.

The first international consensus software engineering standard was issued by The Institute of Electrical and Electronic Engineers (IEEE) in 1980; since then more than 40 new standards have been developed by the IEEE that cover topics such as:

- Configuration management
- Software quality assurance
- Software requirements specifications
- Software validation and verification
- Software design descriptions
- Software reviews and audits
- Software project management plans
- Software user documentation

In parallel, an internationally recognized standard body of knowledge (or SWEBOK) has been identified for software engineers and a certification program initiated under the joint auspices of IEEE and The Association for Computing Machinery (ACM). The intent is to promote a consistent definition of software engineering worldwide, clarify the role and boundaries of software engineering with respect to other academic disciplines and professions, and provide a uniform foundation for curriculum development.[158] The SWEBOK consists of the following ten components, which cover the software engineering life cycle and the associated tools and techniques. As you can see, the field has come a long way since the days of the one-person computer operator/ programmer.

1. Software configuration management
2. Software construction
3. Software design
4. Software engineering infrastructure
5. Software engineering management
6. Software engineering process
7. Software evolution and maintenance
8. Software quality analysis
9. Software requirements analysis
10. Software testing

Software engineering metrics generally fall into three categories: (1) product metrics, (2) process metrics, and (3) project metrics. *Process metrics* measure the implementation of, adherence to, and effectiveness of software engineering processes. The GQM paradigm introduced earlier in this chapter was developed within the context of software engineering, the central idea being that software engineering processes need feedback, in the form of metrics, to evaluate their effectiveness, improve them, and tie them back to business goals.[138] *Product metrics* measure some attribute of the software itself (internal attributes) or its execution (external attributes). Software engineering product metrics are analogous to security engineering IT resilience metrics. *Project metrics* measure various aspects of the management of a software engineering project, such as schedules, budgets, or staffing.

The three most prevalent software engineering process measurement frameworks are ISO 9000 Compendium,[13] the software engineering Capability Maturity Model (SW-CMM), and ISO/IEC 15504 (Parts 1–5) known as the Software Process Improvement and Capability Determination or SPICE.[23–27] The SW-CMM and SPICE are limited to process measurement, while the ISO 9000 Compendium is not. Both the SW-CMM and SPICE use an ordinal scale to measure software engineering process maturity; neither standard evaluates products. The levels represent a continuum from none (or very low) to high software engineering process maturity. Both standards define a series of processes and key process activities to be performed during specific life-cycle phases or throughout a project. Assessments determine the extent to which each process and key process activity has been institutionalized by an organization and assign a maturity rating based on the predefined levels. The goal of both assessments is to identify software suppliers whose performance is predictable and repeatable so that cost, schedule, and end-product quality can be controlled. The SW-CMM was developed under contract to the U.S. Department of Defense, while SPICE is an international consensus standard. Recently, a specialized version of the CMM was developed for security engineering (i.e., SSE-CMM®). This version of the CMM was spearheaded by the Information Systems Security Engineering Association (ISSEA) and issued as ISO/IEC 21827, Systems Security Engineering — Capability Maturity Model (SSE-CMM®) in 2002.

The first edition of ISO 9000, "Quality Management and Quality Assurance Standards — Guidelines for Selection and Use," was published in 1987. This standard provided a foundation for a series of international standards that became known as the ISO 9000 Quality Management framework. The ISO 9000 family of standards is applied to multiple industrial sectors, not just software engineering. (I have even seen the ISO 9000 certification logo on a restaurant menu!) The two standards of most importance to software engineering are (1) ISO 9000-3, "Quality Management and Quality Assurance Standards — Part 3: Guidelines for the Application of ISO 9001 to the Development, Supply and Maintenance of Software"; and (2) ISO 9001, "Quality Systems — Model for Quality Assurance in Design/Development, Production, Installation and Servicing." The ISO 9000 model consists of two-axis, life-cycle activities and supporting activities that are not life-cycle dependent (e.g., configuration management). ISO 9000 was one of the first standards to go beyond the scope of a "self-contained" project and include external entities such as suppliers (and their processes), customers (and their requirements and expectations), and personnel assigned to the project. ISO 9000 assessments use a nominal pass/fail scale. Since their advent, there has been some confusion about the scope of ISO 9000 certifications. Be sure to read the certification document carefully to determine whether it applies to a single project, process, department, or the entire company. ISO 9000 also endorsed the use of product and process metrics.

The use of product metrics that are relevant to the particular software product is mandated to manage the development and delivery process.[13] Suppliers of software products are required to collect and act on quantitative software quality measures. In particular, the following practices are called out[13]:

- Collecting data and reporting metric values on a regular basis
- Identifying the current level of performance on each metric
- Taking remedial action if metric levels grow worse or exceed established target levels
- Establishing specific improvement goals in terms of the metrics

Process metrics are intended to support process control and improvement. The standard does not specify what metrics are to be used, only that they "fit the process being used and have a direct impact on the quality of the delivered software."[13] Software suppliers are required to use quantitative measures to monitor the quality of the development and delivery process; specifically,[13]

- How well the development process is being carried out in terms of milestones and in-process quality objectives being met on schedule
- How effective the development process is at reducing the probability that faults are introduced or that any faults introduced go undetected

Notice that both the product and process metrics are tied to specific goals, similar to performance levels and fault prevention.

ISO 9000 emphasizes a comprehensive approach to corrective action, without which process control and improvement goals will not be met. Assignment of responsibilities for corrective action, evaluation of the significance or impact of the defect, cause/consequence analysis, root cause analysis, and new process controls are required to close out the problem and prevent its recurrence.

People are very much a part of the ISO 9000 quality equation. Specialized training is required by position function, level, risk, and criticality. Staff members must possess *bona fide* credentials for the positions they occupy. Employee motivation and awareness of their contribution to overall product quality are monitored. Likewise, communication skills and paths receive special attention. This is only logical; as discussed previously, people commit errors of omission or errors of commission, which create the fault conditions that cause system failures.

During the early days of software engineering metrics, there was some "irrational exuberance," to paraphrase Alan Greenspan. The newness of software engineering as a discipline, combined with the even more newness of software engineering metrics, led to an attempt to measure anything and everything remotely connected to software, whether or not the metric yielded any value. Fortunately, V. Basili, the creator of the GQM paradigm, and others recognized the situation and cooler heads soon prevailed. Given the newness of security and privacy metrics, it is worthwhile to look at one of these early excesses to learn some lessons so that the same mistakes will not be made. A prime example is lines of code.

Lines of code (LOC) were singled out in an early attempt estimate the cost of software development projects. The assumption was that there was a direct correlation between software size and development cost. The idea of estimating and measuring LOC sounded logical, at first at least. However, LOC is a primitive, not a metric, and it does not meet the precision or validity tests discussed previously. The closest analogy to LOC in security engineering would be wading through mounds of IDS sensor data searching for metrics. Here are some of the problems associated with LOC[158]:

- There are several inconsistent definitions concerning what constitutes an LOC. Does it measure source code or object code? Does it measure executable statements only, or does it include data statements and comments? Does it measure logical lines or physical lines?
- Source code statements in different languages (C++, ADA, Java, Visual Basic, and etc.) yield a different number of object code statements; they are not equivalent.

- Some software engineers are more skilled and efficient than others. Software engineer A may only take 3 LOC to implement the same function that software engineer B takes 50 LOC to implement.
- The use of automated tools affects the LOC that software engineers produce, both in terms of quantity and quality.

Now let us look at some software engineering metrics that passed the accuracy, precision, validity, and correctness test. In particular, some of the product metrics can be used as an indicator of operational resilience and maintainability. The software development methodology, automated tools, and languages used, as well as the function(s) the software is intended to perform, will determine the exact metrics that are useful for a given project. Here are six metrics that can be easily adapted for use by security engineering:

1. Cyclomatic or static complexity
2. Data or information flow complexity
3. Design integrity
4. Design structure complexity
5. Performance measures
6. Software maturity index

Cyclomatic or Static Complexity

The cyclomatic or static complexity (SC) metric is used to determine the structural complexity of a software module[8, 9]:

$$SC = E - N + 1$$

$$\approx RG$$

$$\approx SN + 1$$

where
N = Number of nodes or sequential groups of statements
E = Number of edges or flows between nodes
SN = Number of splitting nodes or nodes with more than one edge emanating from it
RG = Number of regions or areas bounded by edges with no edges crossing

An automated tool is used to analyze the software to identify nodes, edges, splitting nodes, entry and exit points, and the control flow between them.[158] A value of 10 is considered the maximum acceptable value. Higher values indicate modules that are good candidates for redesign.

This metric can be used to analyze the complexity of custom-developed software applications that implement security functions. Several commercial tools are on the market that perform this analysis. Complexity metrics are a predicator of the security of a system once deployed. Complexity complicates maintainability and verification activities, and as such it is a potential source of vulnerabilities.

Data or Information Flow Complexity

The data or information flow complexity (IFC) metric measures inter-module complexity[8, 9]:

$$IFC = (\text{Fan-in} \times \text{Fan-out})^2$$

$$WIFC = \text{Weighted IFC}$$

$$= IFC \times \text{Length}$$

where
Fan-in = lfi + Data-in
Fan-out = lfo + Data-out
lfi = Local flows into a procedure
Data-in = Number of data structures from which the procedure receives data
lfo = Local flows out of (from) a procedure
Data-out = Number of data structures that the procedure updates
Length = source LOC or source lines of design

This metric can be applied during the design, development, and operations and maintenance phases to check for overly complex inter-module interactions, which hint at a lack of functional clarity.[158]

Like the cyclomatic complexity metric above, which measured intra-module complexity, this metric can be used to analyze the inter-module complexity of custom-developed software applications that implement security functions. As mentioned previously, complexity complicates maintainability and verification activities; hence, complexity metrics are a predicator of the security of a system once it is deployed.

Design Integrity

The design integrity metric, introduced in 1998, measures how well the software design has incorporated features to minimize the occurrence of fault propagation and the consequences of potential failures.[159] The presence or absence of several specific design features is measured.[159] Weighting factors can be assigned to those design features that are the most important to a given product or project.[158] Additional design features can be added to the metric or deleted from the list, depending on the unique needs of each project. Design integrity (DI) is defined as[158]:

$$DI = \sum_{i=1}^{10} df_i$$

where
df_1 = 0 if block recovery is not implemented
= 1 if block recovery is implemented
df_2 = 0 software diversity is not implemented
= 1 if software diversity is implemented
df_3 = 0 if information hiding or encapsulation is not implemented
= 1 if information hiding or encapsulation is implemented
df_4 = 0 if partitioning is not implemented
= 1 if partitioning is implemented
df_5 = 0 if defensive programming is not implemented
= 1 if defensive programming is implemented
df_6 = 0 if software fault tolerance is not implemented
= 1 if software fault tolerance is implemented
df_7 = 0 if dynamic reconfiguration is not implemented
= 1 if dynamic reconfiguration is implemented
df_8 = 0 if error detection and recovery is not implemented
= 1 if error detection and recovery is implemented
df_9 = 0 if the system is not designed to fail safe/secure
= 1 if the system is designed to fail safe/secure
df_{10} = 0 if there is not a provision for degraded mode operations
= 1 if there is a provision for degraded mode operations

This metric can easily be applied to measure the design integrity of custom developed software applications that perform security functions. The metric can be used as defined or tailored to reflect the specific needs of a project or product. Design integrity is a predictor of how resilient a given software application or sub-system will be in the operational environment.

Design Structure Complexity

The design structure complexity metric (DSM) measures the complexity of a detailed software design, including data elements, by appraising several parameters[8, 9]:

$$DSM = \sum_{i=1}^{6} W_i D_i$$

where
D_1 = 0 if top-down design
= 1 if not top-down design
D_2 = module dependence
= P_2/P_1
D_3 = module dependence on prior processing
= P_3/P_1
D_4 = database size
= P_5/P_4
D_5 = database compartmentalization
= P_6/P_4
D_6 = module single entrance, single exit
= P_7/P_1

and

P_1 = Total number of modules in program
P_2 = Number of modules dependent on the input or output
P_3 = Number of modules dependent on prior processing states
P_4 = Number of database elements
P_5 = Number of nonunique database elements
P_6 = Number of database segments
P_7 = Number of modules not single entrance, single exit

D_1 assumes that a top-down design is preferred; if not, substitute the preferred software engineering methodology.[158] W_i is the weighting factor assigned to each derivative D_i based on the priority of that attribute, such that $0 < W_i < 1$.[158] DSM will vary such that $0 < DSM < 1$, with the lower values indicating less complexity.[158] Additional derivatives can be defined and weighted according to project priorities and needs.

This metric combines features from the cyclomatic complexity and information flow complexity metrics with some new attributes, like database parameters. It can easily be applied to custom-developed application software that performs security functions. As mentioned previously, complexity complicates maintainability and verification activities, and hence the need to measure complexity and, if need be, reduce it during the design phase. This metric helps isolate overly complex parts of a system or sub-system design.

Performance Measures

The performance measures metric (PM), introduced in 1998, measures, or estimates, depending on the life-cycle phase, success in meeting stated performance criteria: the "how many, how fast" type of requirements.[159] The performance measures metric is defined as[8, 9]:

$$PM = \sum_{i=1}^{8} P_i$$

where
P_1 = 0 if accuracy goals not met
     = 1 if accuracy goals are met
     = 2 if accuracy goals are exceeded
P_2 = 0 if precision goals not met
     = 1 if precision goals are met
     = 2 if precision goals are exceeded
P_3 = 0 if response time goals not met
     = 1 if response time goals are met
     = 2 if response time goals are exceeded (less than specified)
P_4 = 0 if memory utilization goals not met
     = 1 if memory utilization goals are met
     = 2 if memory utilization goals are exceeded (less than specified)

P_5 = 0 if storage goals not met
   = 1 if storage goals met
   = 2 if storage goals exceeded (less than specified)
P_6 = 0 if transaction processing rates not met under low loading conditions
   = 1 if transaction processing rates met under low loading conditions
   = 2 if transaction processing rates exceeded under low loading conditions (faster than specified)
P_7 = 0 if transaction processing rates not met under normal loading conditions
   = 1 if transaction processing rates met under normal loading conditions
   = 2 if transaction processing rates exceeded under normal loading conditions (faster than specified)
P_8 = 0 if transaction processing rates not met under peak loading conditions
   = 1 if transaction processing rates met under peak loading conditions
   = 2 if transaction processing rates exceeded under peak loading conditions (faster than specified)

Reliable and predictable system performance is necessary to maintain a system in a known secure state at all times. In contrast, erratic system performance creates potential vulnerabilities. Hence, this metric should be used to estimate system performance during the design phase and measure actual system performance during the development and operations and maintenance phases. Different performance parameters can be used in addition to or instead of those shown. For example, the speed at which the identification and authentication function is performed could be a parameter.

Software Maturity Index

The software maturity index (SMI) metric evaluates the effect of changes from one baseline to the next to determine the stability and readiness of the software.[158] The software maturity index can be calculated two different ways[8, 9]:

$$SMI = (M_t - (F_a + F_c + F_{del}))/M_t$$
$$= (M_t - F_c)/M_t$$

where
M_t = Number of software functions or modules in current baseline
F_c = Number of software functions or modules in current baseline that include internal changes from the previous baseline
F_a = Number of software functions or modules in current baseline that have been added to previous baseline
F_{del} = Number of software functions or modules not in current baseline that have been deleted from previous baseline

Software maturity is an indication of the extent to which faults have been identified and removed; hence, this metric is directly applicable to security engineering. Software that is constantly changing is not mature, lacks functional clarity, and most likely contains many undiscovered faults. This metric should be used to evaluate custom-developed software applications that perform security functions during the design, development, and operations and maintenance phases.

Other common software engineering metrics include measuring items such as:

- Number of valid problem reports by severity category and fix time[174]
- Number of delinquent problem reports by severity category and age[174]
- Effective use of national and international consensus software engineering standards[158]
- Efficiency: execution time and resource utilization[12]
- Functionality: completeness, correctness, compatibility, interoperability, consistency[12]
- Portability: hardware independence, software independence, installability, scalability, reusability[12]
- Usability: understandability, ease of learning[12]

The following example illustrates how to use software engineering metrics in the security engineering domain. Assume you are responsible for developing a role-based access control sub-system that will run as a front-end processor on the server (or servers) containing sensitive corporate financial data. You could not find a COTS product that performed this function and was compatible with your existing IT infrastructure. So, the sub-system is primarily custom developed. Your development team is about to finish the design and start software development. Everything you have seen and heard so far sounds OK but you want to make sure; so you decide to use some metrics. In particular, you want to know if the design (1) is mature enough to proceed to software development, and (2) will meet stated performance goals. As a result, you select the design integrity, design structure complexity, performance measures, and software maturity index metrics to obtain a composite picture. Next you tailor the metrics so that they will answer the questions for your specific situation.

Design Integrity (Tailored)

$$DI = \sum_{i=1}^{9} df_i$$

where
df_1 = 0 if block recovery is not implemented
    = 1 if block recovery is implemented
df_2 = 0 software diversity is not implemented
    = 2 if software diversity is implemented
df_3 = 0 if information hiding or encapsulation is not implemented
    = 1 if information hiding or encapsulation is implemented

df_4 = 0 if partitioning is not implemented
    = 1 if partitioning is implemented
df_5 = 0 if defensive programming is not implemented
    = 1 if defensive programming is implemented
df_6 = 0 if software fault tolerance is not implemented
    = 2 if software fault tolerance is implemented
df_7 = 0 if error detection and recovery is not implemented
    = 1 if error detection and recovery is implemented
df_8 = 0 if the system is not designed to fail safe/secure
    = 2 if the system is designed to fail safe/secure
df_9 = 0 if there is not a provision for degraded mode operations
    = 2 if there is a provision for degraded mode operations

The primitive for dynamic reconfiguration was deleted because it was not applicable to the role-based access control sub-system. The fail safe/secure, provision for degraded mode operations, implementation of software fault tolerance, and software diversity primitives were double weighted due to the concern for correct functioning of the role-based access control sub-system under normal and abnormal conditions. The tailored design integrity metric has nine primitives with a total maximum value of 26.

Design Structure Complexity (Tailored)

$$DSM = \sum_{i=1}^{6} W_i D_i$$

where
D_1 = 0 if object-oriented design
    = 1 if not object-oriented design
      Weighting (W_1 = 0.2)
D_2 = Module dependence
    = P_2/P_1
      Weighting (W_2 = 0.15)
D_3 = Module dependence on prior processing
    = P_3/P_1
      Weighting (W_3 = 0.15)
D_4 = Database size
    = P_5/P_4
      Weighting (W_4 = 0.15)
D_5 = Database compartmentalization
    = P_6/P_4
      Weighting (W_5 = 0.2)
D_6 = Object single entrance, single exit
    = P_7/P_1
      Weighting (W_6 = 0.15)

and

P_1 = Total number of modules in role-based access control sub-system
P_2 = Number of modules dependent on the input or output
P_3 = Number of modules dependent on prior processing states
P_4 = Number of role-based access control database elements
P_5 = Number of non-unique role-based access control database elements
P_6 = Number of role-based access control database segments
P_7 = Number of modules not single entrance, single exit

The D_1 primitive is tailored to reflect a preference for object-oriented design. The other primitives are used "as-is"; however, the measurement boundaries are limited to the role-based access control sub-system, instead of the whole financial application system. D_1 (use of object-oriented design methodology) and D_5 (database compartmentalization) are weighted more than the other primitives. The value for DSM is such that $0 < DSM < 1$, with lower values indicating lower complexity.

Performance Measures (Tailored)

$$PM = \sum_{i=1}^{6} P_i$$

where
P_1 = 0 if accuracy goals not met
    = 1 if accuracy goals are met
P_2 = 0 if response time goals not met
    = 1 if response time goals are met
P_3 = 0 if memory utilization goals not met
    = 1 if memory utilization goals are met
P_4 = 0 if transaction processing rates not met under low loading conditions
    = 1 if transaction processing rates met under low loading conditions
P_5 = 0 if transaction processing rates not met under normal loading conditions
    = 1 if transaction processing rates met under normal loading conditions
P_6 = 0 if transaction processing rates not met under peak loading conditions
    = 1 if transaction processing rates met under peak loading conditions

Two primitives are deleted — storage utilization and precision — because they are not applicable to role-based access control. Instead, the focus shifts to primitives that are important to the role-based access control sub-system: accuracy in mediating access control rights and privileges, and the speed with which the sub-system performs this function. All primitives have only two possible values, 0 or 1. Because this is the design phase, static analysis techniques can be used to determine whether or not these performance goals will be met. However, it is not possible to determine with certainty if the role-based access control sub-system will perform faster than specified. That evaluation cannot take place until the development phase. The maximum value for the tailored version of this metric is 6.

Software Maturity Index (Tailored)

$$SMI = (M_t - (F_a + F_c + F_{del}))/M_t$$

$$= (M_t - F_c)/M_t$$

where

M_t = Number of software functions or modules in current baseline

F_c = Number of software functions or modules in current baseline that include internal changes from the previous baseline

F_a = Number of software functions or modules in current baseline that have been added to previous baseline

F_{del} = Number of software functions or modules not in current baseline that have been deleted from previous baseline

This metric can be used "as-is," except that the measurement boundary is the role-based access control sub-system, not the entire financial system. You elect to use the second equation to calculate software maturity.

You establish target values for all four metrics and a goal for the overall assessment of the role-based access control sub-system design, as shown in the worksheet below. The design integrity and performance measures metrics are weighted double, while the other two metrics receive a single weight. The actual value for each individual metric is compared to the target value, to highlight potential problem areas. Then the total value is compared to the overall goal.

As shown, the overall rating is 94 out of a possible 100 points. The performance measures metric only received 27 out of a possible 33 points. The other three metrics received 100 percent of the possible points. The passing threshold for the overall design assessment was 90 points, and so the design passed. It is decided that the deficiency noted in the performance measures metric can be remedied during the development phase, so you give your approval for the team to proceed. Is it not nice to have some facts (metrics) upon which to base this decision?

Metric	Max. Value	Target Value	Actual Value	Weighting	Subtotal
Design Integrity	26	23	24	33	33
Design Structure Complexity	1	.5	.43	17	17
Performance Measures	6	6	5	33	27
Software Maturity Index	100	.85	86.6	17	17
Total		90		100	94

This worksheet is based on the following assumptions. See if you can calculate the same metric values.

- Block recovery, software diversity, partitioning, software fault tolerance, error detection, fail safe/secure design, and provision for degraded mode operations incorporated in the design
- Encapsulation and defensive programming are not incorporated in the design
- Number of modules (P_1, MT) = 15
- Number of modules dependents on input/output = 5
- Number of modules dependent on prior processing states = 10
- Number of data elements = 10
- Number of non-unique data elements = 0
- Number of database segments = 3
- Number of modules not single entry/exit = 2
- Accuracy, response time, and memory utilization goals are met
- Transaction processing times are met for low and normal loading conditions, but not peak loads
- Number of modules changed from previous baseline = 2
- Number of added modules = 1
- Number of deleted modules = 1

Now that the first cousins have been introduced, it is time to meet the family of security and privacy metrics proper.

2.12 The Universe of Security and Privacy Metrics

To date, there have been four pioneering initiatives related to security and privacy metrics, three of which have resulted in a significant publication:

1. NIST SP 800-55, "Security Metrics Guide for Information Technology Systems" (July 2003)
2. Security Metrics Consortium (or secmet.org) (February 24, 2004)
3. "Information Security Governance," Corporate Governance Task Force Report (April 2004)
4. Corporate Information Security Working Group, "Report of the Best Practices and Metrics Teams" (January 10, 2005)

Each of these is discussed in detail below. At the time of writing, there were no national or international consensus standards under development in the area of privacy metrics.

NIST SP 800-55

NIST SP 800-55, "Security Metrics Guide for Information Technology Systems," issued July 2003 by the U.S. National Institute of Standards and Technology

(NIST), was the first major security metrics publication. NIST SP 800-55 was the first publication to (1) identify the need for security metrics to be aligned with business objectives and organizational culture, (2) identify the need for aggregate metrics to accommodate different hierarchical views within an organization, and (3) present the idea of weighting some metrics over others in an overall assessment. These three observations were significant because, prior to this publication, security metrics had been viewed as a one-size-fits-all proposition.

NIST is tasked with the responsibility of developing computer security standards and guidelines, either as special publications (known as SPs) or federal information processing standard publications (known as FIPS PUBs) for the U.S. federal government. Several of these documents are voluntarily used by industry and outside the United States. NIST SP 800-55 focuses on information security management process metrics that can be used to demonstrate compliance with the Federal Information Security Management Act (FISMA) to which federal agencies must adhere. (FISMA is discussed at length in Chapter 3.)

The NIST SP 800-55 metrics primarily examine security policy and process issues associated with operational systems. The emphasis is on measuring the implementation of security policies and processes, their efficiency, effectiveness, and business impact. The front part of the document discusses how to set up a metrics program, while the metrics themselves are contained in an appendix. The metrics fall into the 17 categories, as listed below; they align with the five management control topics, nine operational control topics, and three technical control topics identified in NIST 800-26, "Security Self Assessment Guide for Information Technology Systems."[57] The metric is defined, along with the recommended measurement frequency and target value. The standard only contains security metrics; it does not contain any privacy metrics.

- Risk management (2)
- Security controls (2)
- System development life cycle (2)
- Certification and accreditation (2)
- System security plan (2)
- Personnel security (2)
- Physical and environment protection (3)
- Production, input/output controls (2)
- Contingency planning (3)
- Hardware and systems software maintenance (3)
- Data integrity (2)
- Documentation (2)
- Security awareness, training, and education (1)
- Incident response capability (2)
- Identification and authentication (2)
- Logical access controls (3)
- Audit trails (1)

The metrics presented in NIST 800-55 are general in nature, in that they do not take into account system risk, information sensitivity, or asset criticality categories. The enhanced definition of these metrics in this book adds this capability. Enhancements like these help an organization prioritize and focus resources on the most critical security issues. To illustrate, the NIST version and the enhanced version of the same metric are:

NIST SP 800-55 version: percentage (%) of systems with the latest approved patches installed[57]

Enhanced version: percentage (%) of systems with the latest approved patches installed, by system risk category and severity category of the vulnerability the patch claims to mitigate

Several of the security metrics only measure the presence or absence of a technical control, without assessing the appropriateness or resilience of that control within the context of the security architecture or operational environment. The value of such metrics is limited. For example, one metric measures the percentage of laptops that have an encryption capability. Encryption for encryption's sake is not necessarily good. This metric gives no indication of whether (1) the encryption algorithm is too weak or overly robust; (2) the encryption software is installed and configured correctly so that additional vulnerabilities are not introduced; (3) end users are required to use the encryption tool or they can bypass it; etc.

NIST SP 800-55 covers 17 categories of security metrics. However, there are only one to three metrics per category. As a result, no category is covered comprehensively.

Because NIST SP 800-55 was the first major security metrics publication, it does not reference any other metrics publications. However, subsequent publications do reference NIST SP 800-55.

Security Metrics Consortium (secmet.org)

The formation of the Security Metrics Consortium, a non-vendor forum, was announced at the February 2004 RSA Conference. The mission of this group is "to define standardized quantitative security risk metrics for industry, corporate, and vendor adoption."[219] William Boni, one of the founders, elaborated on the need for security metrics[219]:

> *CFOs use a profit and loss statement to share the health of the company with board members, executives, and shareholders; yet CSOs and CISOs have no such structure or standard to demonstrate organizational health from a security standpoint. Network security experts cannot measure their success without security metrics and what can not be measured cannot be effectively managed.*

The group has a clear mission statement and a definite understanding of the need for security metrics. However, as of the time of writing, no further news has been released from the consortium or posted on its Web site. It is unclear if the consortium is still in existence.

Information Security Governance

The Corporate Governance Task Force issued the Information Security Governance (ISG): A Call to Action report in April 2004. The all-industry group, composed of vendors, resellers, and consumers of IT security products, began work in December 2003. The group's starting point was the statement that "information security governance reporting must be closely aligned to the organization's information security management framework."[143] According to *Webster's Dictionary*, "governance" and "management" are synonymous. Perhaps the term "governance" was chosen because it sounds more profound or noble than management. Then again, perhaps the term "governance" was chosen on purpose because some organizations have not been too effective at managing security, and the name was changed to protect the innocent. Anyway, another buzz word has been added to the IT security lexicon although most people are unaware that it is not new, but just a synonym.

The ISG report added some new ideas to the concept of security metrics. First, security metrics should be aligned with the system development and operational life cycle. Prior to this, most, if not all, effort was placed on the operations and maintenance phase. Second, the security metrics framework should be scalable. Again, this was an attempt to move away from the notion of a one-size-fits-all set of security metrics. Third, the report promoted the idea that security is an enterprise and corporate responsibility, and not the sole responsibility of the IT staff. Accordingly, security metrics need to reflect that corporate responsibility. Finally, the report emphasizes that security metrics must consider people and processes, not just technology.

The ISG framework consists of 70 questions or primitives that are organized into four categories or metrics, as shown below. All relate to security; none relate to privacy.

1. Business dependency on IT (15)
2. Risk management (9)
3. People (12)
4. Processes (34)

Each of the 70 primitives is framed as a question about how thoroughly something has been done. The answer is given using an ordinal scale of: 0 — not implemented, 1 — planning, 2 — partially, 3 — close to completion, and 4 — fully implemented. The values for business dependency are totaled and compared against a rating scale. The values for the other three areas — risk management, people, and processes — are totaled and cross-referenced to the business dependency rating. A maximum of 220 points are possible: 36 in risk management, 48 for people, and 136 for processes. Three overall assessments are given: poor, needs improvement, and good. The point value assigned to each rating varies, depending on the business dependency on IT.

For example, if the business dependency is very high, the ranges are 0–139 poor, 140–179 needs improvement, and 180–220 good. In contrast, if the business dependency is low, the ranges are 0–84 poor, 85–134 needs improvement, and 135–220 good. Rating scales are not provided for the three individual categories.

There are some disadvantages to this approach. The uneven distribution of points among the three categories leads to a greater emphasis on process than the other two categories combined. The overall assessment does not indicate which area or sub-area needs improvement. And as discussed in Section 2.2, ordinal scales have limited use.

Although ISG was issued ten months after NIST SP 800-55, the NIST standard is not listed in the bibliography or referenced. Twenty-one of the primitives have been reworded or enhanced as stand-alone metrics in this book.

Corporate Information Security Working Group

The Corporate Information Security Working Group (CISWG) was convened by Rep. Adam Putnam (R-Florida) of the Subcommittee on Technology, Information Policy, Intergovernmental Relations and the Census, Government Reform Committee, of the U.S. House of Representatives. Phase 1 of the Working Group began in November 2003, with the charter to examine best practices and information security program elements "essential for comprehensive enterprise management of information security."[105] Phase 2 began in June 2004 with the goal of identifying a "comprehensive structure of principles, policies, processes, controls, and performance metrics to support the people, processes, and technical aspects of information security."[105] The initial CISWG report was issued 17 November 2004; the revised edition was released 10 January 2005. The CISWG report acknowledges the prior work published by NIST SP 800-55, the ISG report, and its predecessor, the Corporate Information Security Evaluation for CEOs developed by TechNet. All Working Group members were from industry or industry associations; a few of the adjunct members were from the federal government.

The CISWG report promotes the use of security metrics to (1) identify risks and establish acceptable performance thresholds for technology and security-related processes, and (2) measure the implementation strategies, policies, and controls to mitigate those risks.[188] Information protection is viewed as a fiduciary responsibility. The CISWG report is the first to note the need for different metrics depending on the size of an organization. As a result, the metrics in the report are recommended as either baseline metrics, for small and medium organizations, or for large organizations. The CISWG report confirmed the NIST SP 800-55 observation concerning the need for different metrics, depending on the level within the organization. Accordingly, different sets of metrics are recommended for the board of directors or trustees, management, and technical staff. Eleven categories of metrics are spelled out in the report, as listed below. Five categories are similar to NIST SP 800-55; the rest are new or aggregate categories. None of the metrics pertain to privacy.

1. Identification and authentication
2. User account management and privileges (access control)
3. Configuration management
4. Event and activity logging and tracking (audit trail)
5. Communications, e-mail, and remote access
6. Malicious code protection
7. Software configuration management
8. Firewalls
9. Data encryption
10. Backup and recovery
11. Incident and vulnerability detection and response

A total of 99 metrics are distributed among the 11 categories. Because the CISWG drew upon NIST SP 800-55, not all 99 metrics are new; there is some overlap. They are assigned as follows:

Organization Level	*Organization Size*
Board of directors/trustees – 12	Baseline metrics – 40
Management – 42	Small and medium – 65
Technical – 45	Large or all metrics – 99

Unlike the ISG report, these metrics do not consider the development life cycle, but rather only the operations and maintenance phase. The metric alone is supplied, not the measurement frequency, target value, or goal. Only one of the 99 metrics addresses regulatory compliance and in a general sense. None evaluate security return on investment (ROI). The CISWG report acknowledges the need for different security metrics at varied hierarchical layers within an organization, but not the need for different security metrics for different lateral roles, as discussed in Section 2.5. Organization size is only one parameter in determining appropriate security metrics. It is difficult, if not impossible, to say what security metrics an organization needs without knowing its mission, industry, what life-cycle phase the system or project is in, or the criticality of the assets (internally to the organization and externally to the general public). For example, a small or medium-sized organization may be responsible for a safety-critical power distribution plant, while a large organization may be a clothing retailer. The CISWG developed security engineering process areas, then assigned security metrics to each process. It is curious that the CISWG did not use or reference the System Security Engineering Capability Maturity Model (SSE-CMM®). This international standard, ISO/IEC 21827, issued in October 2002, defines system security engineering processes and key process activities for five levels of maturity, similar to other CMMs.[29] All the metrics are contained in this book; however, some of the metrics have been enhanced to distinguish system risk, information sensitivity, and asset criticality categories, like the example below. Again, these enhancements help an organization prioritize and focus resources on the most critical security issues.

> *CISWG version*: percentage (%) of system and network components for which security-related configuration settings are documented[105]
>
> *Enhanced version*: percentage (%) of system and network components for which security-related configuration settings are documented, by system risk category

The Universe of Security and Privacy Metrics

Some common themes emerge from these three pioneering publications. First and foremost is the universally acknowledged pervasive need for security metrics in order to plan, control, monitor, manage, and improve the ongoing operational security posture of an organization. Second is the recognition that security is an organization-wide responsibility. All three publications agree that there is no "one-size-fits-all" set of 20 to 30 metrics that is appropriate for every organization and situation. It is an accepted fact that security metrics must be scalable to the organization's business goals, objectives, and size. All agree that security metrics should not just focus on technology, but also evaluate process and people issues. NIST SP 800-55 and the ISG report noted the necessity of being able to aggregate metrics to obtain an overall assessment. NIST SP 800-55 added the idea of weighting individual metrics within an aggregate metric. The ISG report pointed out the need to tie metrics to the development *and* operations and maintenance phases of the system engineering life cycle. None of the three presented any privacy metrics. Ironically, most recent short courses, conferences, and magazine articles equate security metrics with return on cyber security investment (or ROI), yet none of the three publications contained a single security ROI metric.

The NIST, ISG, and CISWG publications provided a good security metrics foundation; however, some things are missing. Let us look at the gaps and why they need to be filled.

Most of the metrics proposed to date focus on process issues. Process issues are important, but not an end unto themselves. It is possible to have a high score on security process metrics and still not have private or secure data, systems, or networks. Safety and reliability are not evaluated on process alone. Would you want to fly in an airplane that had only undergone a process assessment? Of course not! That is why process, design, and interface FMECAs are conducted, along with other static and dynamic analysis techniques. Processes exist for the purpose of producing a product that has certain characteristics. Hence, a good balance of product and process metrics, one that covers all aspects of security engineering and privacy, from all four security domains is needed.

Metrology is the science of measurement. At the highest level there are three things that security and privacy metrics can measure:

1. Compliance with national and international security and privacy regulations
2. Resilience of the composite security posture of an enterprise or a subset of it, including physical, personnel, IT, and operational security controls
3. The return on investment for physical, personnel, IT, and operational security controls

That is why the title of this book is *Complete Guide to Security and Privacy Metrics* and not *Complete Guide to IT Security Metrics* or *Complete Guide to Security ROI Metrics*. Everything that can be asked about an organization's security and privacy architecture, infrastructure, controls, processes, procedures, and funding falls within these three categories. All aggregate and individual security and privacy metrics fall into one of these three classes. Consequently, this book presents a model of the universe of security and privacy metrics that consists of three galaxies, as shown in Figure 2.13. These three galaxies capture the core concerns of security and privacy metrics. More solar systems and planets may be discovered in the future, but there are only three galaxies. Each galaxy can be summarized in a separate GQM:

1. Compliance:

   G: Ensure compliance with applicable national and international security and privacy regulations

   Q: How well are we complying with the requirements in each applicable security and privacy regulation?

   M: Chapter 3

2. Resilience:

   G: Ensure our IT infrastructure, including physical, personnel, and operational security controls, can maintain essential services and protect critical assets while pre-empting and repelling attacks and minimizing the extent of corruption and compromise.

   Q: How can we monitor and predict the operational resilience of our IT infrastructure, including physical, personnel, and operational security controls?

   M: Chapter 4

3. ROI:

   G: Ensure we invest wisely in security controls for all four security domains, both in the long term and short term.

   Q: Given limited budgets, where should we spend our funds to achieve the greatest security ROI?

   M: Chapter 5

Compliance metrics measure compliance with national or international security and privacy regulations. The Compliance galaxy contains multiple regulatory compliance solar systems. Planets within each solar system orbit around a unique critical asset sun. Four suns are shown in the figure: (1) critical financial assets, (2) critical healthcare assets, (3) personal privacy assets, and (4) critical homeland security assets. Several planets orbit each sun; they represent current security and privacy regulations related to that type of critical asset. These are the 13 security and privacy regulations and the associated metrics discussed in Chapter 3. For the most part, each country has issued its own financial, healthcare, personal privacy, and homeland security regulations. Most corporations are global these days. Perhaps there is an opportunity to

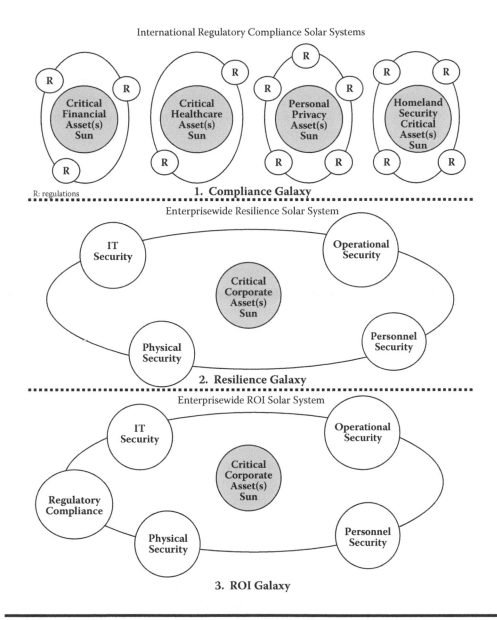

Figure 2.13   The universe of security and privacy metrics.

harmonize these regulations via international standards so that (1) the best practices of each can be adopted, and (2) there is only one set of rules for everyone to follow. More on that thought in Chapter 3. The metrics presented in Chapter 3 measure compliance with each of the 13 security and privacy regulations. As you can see, the scope of compliance metrics is rather broad.

Resilience is the capability of an IT infrastructure, including physical, personnel, and operational security controls, to maintain essential services and protect critical assets while preempting and repelling attacks and minimizing the extent of corruption and compromise. Resilience metrics measure the extent of that capability in each of the four security domains. The Resilience galaxy contains multiple enterprisewide resilience solar systems. The diagram depicts one solar system, that for critical corporate assets. The twin to this solar system, which is not shown in the diagram, is critical infrastructure assets. Some critical corporate assets are also critical infrastructure assets; for example, an electric power distribution facility. In this case, a single planet is part of two solar systems. Four planets orbit the critical corporate assets sun: (1) IT security, (2) physical security, (3) operational security, and (4) personnel security. These four planets represent the four domains of enterprisewide security. Chapter 4 presents metrics that measure the resilience of each of the four security domains. When aggregated, these metrics measure the resilience of the enterprise. Note that the term "IT security" is used and not "cyber security." That is on purpose because IT security encompasses a lot more than Internet access. Likewise, there is a lot more to IT security metrics than just the operations and maintenance phase. In fact, 16 sub-elements have been identified for IT security metrics, as shown in Table 1.1. Notice also that there are four planets, and not just IT security. That is because security engineering encompasses a lot more than IT security; there is a significant amount of synergy between the four security domains, particularly at the enterprise level. If you are relying on just IT security or, even worse, just cyber security measures to secure your critical corporate assets, you have some gaping holes to fill in your security posture. You may have the world's best IT security controls but if you ignore personnel security, you are in for trouble. Over the past decade, insiders, or insiders colluding with outsiders, have accounted for more than 80 percent of all serious security incidents. Personnel security metrics assess items such as trustworthiness, accountability, and competence and can highlight potential problem areas. Some question the value of physical security in the age of the global information grid. True, physical security does not provide the same protection it did in the days when the "computer" and "network" were all in one building. However, do not forget about the value of physical security for protecting backup operational centers, archives, and controlling physical access to other critical assets. IT security can be great but it is ineffective if it is not combined with effective and appropriate operational security procedures. Operational security metrics examine the interaction between people, technology, and the operational environment. Simple things such as when and how security credentials are issued, revoked, and stored, or practicing contingency and disaster recovery procedures, are essential to securing the IT infrastructure. In summary, if you want to know the resilience of your IT infrastructure, you must measure all four security domains. An attacker will find the weakest link in the enterprise, be it physical, personnel, operational, or IT security. Should you not use metrics to find the weakest link before they do? Consequently, there are five sub-categories of security resilience metrics, one for each of the four planets (or security domains), plus enterprisewide security, which is an aggregate of the other four. Resilience metrics are discussed in Chapter 4.

The ROI galaxy contains multiple enterprisewide ROI solar systems. Critical corporate assets are the sun around which the planets orbit. Each solar system in this galaxy has five planets: (1) IT security, (2) physical security, (3) operational security, (4) personnel security, and (5) regulatory compliance.

The ROI of each of the four security domains (IT security, physical security, operational security, and personnel security) can be measured individually and then aggregated at the enterprise level to obtain a composite picture. At the other level of abstraction, the ROI of a sub-element of one of the four security domains can also be measured, such as encryption. Very few organizations are not subject to one or more of the security and privacy regulations discussed in Chapter 3. As a result, the cost of complying with regulations must be considered when calculating ROI. For example, did compliance require enhanced resilience or additional security features? Complying with regulations avoids the cost of penalties, other fines, and lost revenue or customers. Chapter 5 presents ROI metrics.

The universe of security and privacy metrics is probably considerably more expansive than you might have imagined or any publication has acknowledged to date. NIST SP 800-55 provides information security management process metrics. The 21 ISG metrics and 99 CISWG metrics focus on process issues related to IT and operational security. They are weak on product metrics and barely address physical security and personnel security, if at all; neither do they contain any privacy metrics. These earlier publications focus on one or two planets in one solar system in one galaxy. In contrast, this book covers all the planets in all the solar systems in all three galaxies. Chapters 3 through 5 define over 900 security and privacy metrics, allocated as shown in Table 1.1 by category, sub-category, and sub-element. Hence, this book has filled in the gaps by:

- Discovering new galaxies, solar systems, and planets that comprise the universe of security and privacy metrics
- Replacing the old paradigm of product, process, and people metrics with the new paradigm of physical, personnel, IT, and operational security and privacy metrics
- Recognizing the interaction between compliance, resilience, and ROI metrics
- Drawing the connection between security and privacy metrics and their first cousins — safety, reliability, and software engineering metrics

Most organizations will need to do some intergalactic travel between metric solar systems over time, as priorities and focus change from compliance to resilience to ROI and back again, similar to the discussion earlier in Section 2.5 about situational metrics. So, welcome to the universe of security and privacy metrics. Now that you have completed basic training and know what galaxies and solar systems you need to visit, travel at light speed is permitted.

2.13 Summary

Chapter 2 set the stage for the rest of the book by illuminating the fundamental concepts, historical notes, philosophical underpinnings, and application context of security and privacy metrics. Metrics are a tool with which to pursue security and privacy engineering as a disciplined science, rather than an ad hoc art. Metrics permit you to move from guessing about your true security and privacy status and capability to confronting reality. The judicious use of metrics promotes visibility, informed decision making, predictability, and proactive planning and preparedness, thus averting surprises and always being caught in a reactive mode when it comes to security and privacy. Metrics provide a numeric description of a certain characteristic of the items being investigated. A metric defines both what is being measured (the attribute) and how it is being measured (the unit of measure). Metrics are composed of sub-elements referred to as primitives. Metrics are collected about specific attributes of particular entities. Metrics must exhibit four key characteristics to be meaningful and usable: (1) accuracy, (2) precision, (3) validity, and (4) correctness.[137, 138]

Measurement, the process of collecting metrics, can be performed for assessment or prediction purposes. Four standard measurement scales are generally recognized: (1) nominal scale, (2) ordinal scale, (3) interval scale, and (4) ratio scale. When defining or comparing metrics, be aware of these different types of scales, and their uses and limitations. There are four basic types of measurements: (1) ratio, (2) proportion, (3) percentage, and (4) rate. The first three are static, while the fourth is dynamic because it changes over time.

Errors are the difference between a computed, observed, or measured value or condition and the true specified, or theoretically correct value or condition.[8–12] Humans introduce errors into products, processes, and operational systems in two ways, through (1) errors of omission and (2) errors of commission. The manifestation of an error is referred to as a fault. A fault is a defect that results in an incorrect step, process, data value, or mode/state.[125] Should an execution or transaction path exercise a fault, a failure results; a fault remains dormant until exercised. Three categories of failures are commonly recognized: (1) incipient failures, (2) hard failures, and (3) soft failures.[8–12, 197]

The metric data collection and validation process consists of seven steps:

1. Defining what information is going to be collected
2. Defining why this information is being collected and how it will be used
3. Defining how the information will be collected, and the constraints and controls on the collection process
4. Defining the time interval and frequency with which the information is to be collected
5. Identifying the source(s) from which the information will be collected
6. Defining how the information collected will be preserved to prevent accidental or intentional alteration, deletion, addition, other tampering or loss
7. Defining how the information will be analyzed and interpreted

The measurement scope or boundaries define what entities are to be included or excluded from the measurement process. Appropriate measurement boundaries are essential to producing metric results that are valid and useful. If the measurement boundaries are too broad or too narrow to answer the specific GQM, the results will be misleading. Measurement boundaries may be influenced by entity characteristics such as risk, sensitivity, severity, likelihood, or criticality.

To ensure uniform assignment of entities to measurement boundaries across people and organizational units, standardized definitions must be used for each of these items.

The nature and scope of security and privacy metrics that are deemed useful are a function of (1) the particular life-cycle phase the product, process, or project being examined is in; (2) the role or function of the metric consumers within the organization; (3) the level of the metric consumers within the organization; and (4) the organization's mission and business values.

In short, you should have a good understanding of who the metric consumers are. These different perspectives are often referred to as *views*.

Security and privacy metrics are a tool that can be used by engineers, auditors, and management. Employed correctly, they can help plan or control a project or process; improve the security and privacy of operational procedures, an end product, or system; provide visibility into a current situation or predict future scenarios and outcomes; and track performance trends.[12, 137, 174, 204] Metrics furnish the requisite factual foundation upon which to base critical decisions about security and privacy, the absence of which increases an organization's cost, schedule, and technical risk, and possibly liability concerns. Security and privacy metrics are not a panacea unto themselves, nor do they make a system or network secure or information private on their own. Metrics are a tool that, if used correctly, can help you achieve those goals. All metrics have certain limitations that you need to be aware of to avoid over- or mis-using them. It is important to understand the context in which the metric is intended to be used and the purpose for which it was designed. Likewise, it is essential to comprehend the rules by which the metric data was collected and analyzed and how the results were interpreted. Metric consumers have the responsibility to ask some probing questions to discern the accuracy, precision, validity, and correctness of metrics that are presented to them.

The most common mistake made by metrics programs, especially when the metrics program is new and the staff a bit overzealous, is to deluge their organization with metrics. The temptation to deliver hundreds of interesting metrics that consumers have not asked for, and cannot use, is sometimes irresistible but deadly. Five guidelines will help you to avoid this temptation: (1) do not collect metrics if there are no pre-stated objectives on how the results will be used[8, 9]; (2) establish pragmatic goals for the metrics program from the onset; (3) distinguish between what can be measured and what needs to be measured; (4) balance providing value-added to metric consumers with the overhead of the metrics program; and last but not least, (5) use common sense.

A *vulnerability* is an inherent weaknesses in a system, its design, implementation, operation, or operational environment, including physical and personnel security controls. A *threat* is the potential for a vulnerability to be exploited. Threat is a function of the opportunity, motive, expertise, and resources needed and available to effect the exploitation. *Risk* is a function of the likelihood of a vulnerability being exploited and a threat instantiated, plus the worst-case severity of the consequences. Risk assessments are used to prioritize risk mitigation activities. Vulnerability assessments and threat assessments are prerequisites for conducting a risk assessment. Risk management tools and techniques are a ready source of primitives and metrics to analyze security risks. Security and privacy metrics should not be pulled from thin air. Rather, they should be based on a solid analytical foundation, such as that provided by FMECA and FTA.

There are several parallels between reliability engineering and security engineering. The goal of both disciplines is to prevent, detect, contain, and recover from erroneous system states and conditions. However, reliability engineering does not place as much emphasis on intentional malicious actions as security engineering. Dependability, a special instance of reliability, is an outcome of fault prevention, fault removal, fault forecasting, fault tolerance, and fault isolation. Two design techniques are frequently employed by reliability engineers to enhance system reliability: (1) redundancy and (2) diversity. Hardware redundancy can be implemented in a serial, parallel, or complex serial/parallel manner, each of which delivers a different reliability rating. Diversity can take several forms as well: hardware diversity, software diversity, and path diversity in the telecommunications domain. Availability, a key component of the Confidentiality, Integrity, and Availability (CIA) security model, is actually an outcome of reliability engineering. Availability is an objective measurement indicating the rate at which systems, data, and other resources are operational and accessible when needed, despite accidental and intentional sub-system outages and environmental disruptions.[156] There are three variations of the availability calculation, known as inherent availability, operational availability, and achieved availability, that take into account different life-cycle phases and the information that is accessible.

Safety engineering is quite similar to security engineering. There are parallels in all four domains: physical safety/physical security, personnel safety/personnel security, IT safety/IT security, and operational safety/operational security. In addition, safety engineering, unlike reliability engineering, is concerned about accidental and malicious intentional actions. IEC 61508, the current international standard for system safety, recommends or highly recommends a series of design features and engineering techniques to use throughout the system life cycle to achieve and sustain system safety. These features and techniques fall into three categories: (1) controlling random hardware failures, (2) avoiding systematic failures, and (3) achieving software safety integrity. IEC 61508 requires the specification of safety functional requirements and safety integrity requirements. Safety integrity requirements stipulate the level to which functional safety requirements are verified. These levels are referred to as safety integrity levels, or SILs. Specific design features and engineering techniques performed during life-cycle phases are either recommended or highly recommended in accordance with the SIL. Several factors are taken into account when determining the appropriate SIL: severity of injury, number of people exposed to the danger, frequency with which a person or people are exposed to the danger, duration of the exposure, public perceptions, views of those exposed to the hazard, regulatory guidelines, industry standards, international agreements, expert advice, and legal consid-erations.[5] SILs are specified in terms of risk levels, so that it is clear about what is and is not deemed acceptable risk in terms of likelihood and severity categories. Metrics provide the evidence needed to confirm that a given SIL has been achieved.

Although not recognized as such, software engineering is also a first cousin of security engineering. IT security appliances, whether for networks, servers, or desktops, are software based, the one exception being hardware-based bulk encryptors. Physical security surveillance, monitoring, and access control equipment is software based. Personnel security information and assessments rely on software-based systems for information storage and retrieval, not to mention controlling access to that information. Human factors engineering — in particular, preventing induced and invited human error — is equally important to software and security engineering. As a result, it is important to understand software engineering metrics and what they mean to security engineering.

To date there have been three significant security and privacy metrics publications:

1. NIST SP 800-55, "Security Metrics Guide for Information Technology Sys-tems" (July 2003)
2. Information Security Governance (ISG), "Corporate Governance Task Force Report" (April 2004)
3. Corporate Information Security Working Group (CISWG), "Report of the Best Practices and Metrics Teams" (January 10, 2005)

Some common themes emerge from these three pioneering publications. First and foremost is the universally acknowledged pervasive need for security metrics in order to plan, control, monitor, manage, and improve the ongoing operational security posture of an organization. Second is the recognition that security is an organization-wide responsibility. All three publications agree that there is no "one-size-fits-all" set of 20 to 30 metrics that is appropriate for every organization and situation. It is an accepted fact that security metrics must be scalable to the organization's business goals, objectives, and size. All agree that security metrics should not just focus on technology, but also evaluate process and people issues. NIST SP 800-55 and the ISG report noted the necessity to be able to aggregate metrics to obtain an overall assessment. NIST SP 800-55 added the idea of weighting individual metrics within an aggregate metric. The ISG report pointed out the need for metrics to be tied to the development *and* operations and maintenance phases of the system engineering life cycle. None of the three presented any privacy metrics. Ironically, most recent short courses, conferences, and magazine articles equate security metrics with return on cyber security investment (or ROI). However, none of these three publications contain a single security ROI metric. The NIST, ISG, and CISWG publications provided a good security metrics founda-tion; however, some things are missing.

Metrology is the science of measurement. At the highest level, there are three things that security and privacy metrics can measure:

1. Compliance with national and international security and privacy regulations
2. Resilience of the composite security posture of an enterprise or a subset of it, including physical, personnel, IT, and operational security controls
3. The return on investment for physical, personnel, IT, and operational security controls

Everything that can be asked about an organization's security and privacy architecture, infrastructure, controls, processes, procedures, and funding falls within these three categories. All aggregate and individual security and privacy metrics fall into one of these three classes. Consequently, this book presents a model of the universe of security and privacy metrics that consists of three galaxies, as shown in Figure 2.13. These three galaxies capture the core concerns of security and privacy metrics. More solar systems and planets may be discovered in the future, but there are only three galaxies.

Unlike the previous three publications, this book covers all the planets in all the solar systems in all three galaxies. Chapters 3 through 5 define over 900 security and privacy metrics. Hence, this book fills in the gaps by:

- Identifying the galaxies, solar systems, and planets that comprise the universe of security and privacy metrics
- Replacing the old paradigm of product, process, and people metrics with the new paradigm of physical, personnel, IT, and operational security and privacy metrics
- Recognizing the interaction between compliance, resilience, and ROI metrics
- Drawing the connection between security and privacy metrics and their first cousins — safety, reliability, and software engineering metrics

In Chapter 3 we travel to the galaxy of international and national security and privacy regulations and the metrics that can be used to demonstrate compliance with these regulations.

2.14 Discussion Problems

1. What are security and privacy metrics? How can they benefit your organization? Give specific examples.
2. Cite an example of an attribute that could be confused with an entity.
3. Cite an example of a primitive that could be confused with an entity.
4. Give an example of the problems that can arise when attempting to compare attributes from sub-entities with those of entities.
5. Can a primitive be a sub-entity? Why or why not?
6. Describe everyday uses of nominal, ordinal, interval, and ratio scales in your organization.

7. Describe the relationship between (1) incipient failures and latent defects, (b) accidental errors of omission and intentional errors of commission, and (c) vulnerabilities and soft failures.
8. What is the most important step in the data collection and validation process? Why?
9. Give examples of how primitives or metrics could be analyzed incorrectly.
10. Give examples of how metric results could be misinterpreted.
11. What is more important when defining measurement boundaries, the metric consumer's role or their level? Why?
12. Which of the sample metrics could be used for (a) ST&E evidence, or (b) C&A evidence?
13. Give examples of what security and privacy metrics cannot be used for. Explain why.
14. What is the key ingredient to a successful metrics program?
15. What is a good ratio of (a) questions to goals, and (b) metrics to questions?
16. How can static analysis techniques be applied to security engineering? Give a specific example.
17. When should qualitative measures be used? When should quantitative measures be used? Which is better?
18. Give an example of (a) an entity that is low risk and essential criticality, and (b) high sensitivity and routine criticality.
19. Prepare an interface FMECA for a Web server.
20. Calculate the achieved availability of your corporate e-mail system for the previous calendar month.
21. How could partitioning be applied to enhance the security of your corporate WAN?
22. How big is the universe of security and privacy metrics? Is it expanding or contracting? Why?
23. Within the universe of security and privacy metrics, what do the moons represent?

Chapter 3

Measuring Compliance with Security and Privacy Regulations and Standards

---

Protecting information involves implementing information security principles, policies, processes, and controls, and generally includes establishing performance standards and compliance metrics to ... monitor whether or not information security is being effectively managed.

—Corporate Information Security Working Group[105]

3.1 Introduction

As any competent engineer knows, one hallmark of a good requirement is that it is testable. Likewise, one property of a good regulation is that compliance can be measured easily and objectively through the use of metrics. Chapter 3 navigates the galaxy of compliance metrics and the security and privacy regulations to which they apply. A brief discussion of the global regulatory environment starts the chapter. Particular attention is paid to the legal ramifications of privacy. Then, 13 current security and privacy regulations are examined in detail, along with the role of metrics in demonstrating compliance. Compliance with internal corporate security and privacy policies is discussed in Chapter 4, under Section 4.5, "Operational Security."

Following the pattern set up in Chapter 2, the GQM for Chapter 3 is to measure compliance with national and international security and privacy regulations through the use of metrics. Appropriate metrics are defined for each regulation in the corresponding sections below.

GQM for Chapter 3

G: Ensure compliance with applicable national and international security and privacy regulations.

Q: How well are we complying with the requirements in each applicable security and privacy regulation?

M: See metrics defined in Chapter 3.

Security and privacy regulations have been issued at a dizzying pace around the world in the past few years in an attempt to bring laws and regulations in line with state-of-the-art technology and in recognition of the rapid advent of cyber crime. In essence, these regulations are intended to prevent mishandling, misuse, and misappropriation of sensitive information, whether financial, personal, healthcare, or related to critical infrastructure protection. Given the delta between the speed at which regulations are passed and the speed with which technology changes, this effort is almost a "mission impossible."

Technology and regulations are quite an odd couple. How did security and privacy come to garner so much attention in national and international laws and regulations? Whenever the private sector does not do a good job of regulating itself, the federal government has a responsibility to step in and balance the equation. Sometimes a proactive response is necessary when the forthcoming abuses are obvious. If governments do not perform this function, no one else will. If governments do not perform this function, what is the point of having a government?

Most organizations, whether in the public or private sector, are subject to one or more security and privacy regulations. By definition, the "regulated" cannot ever claim to like regulations; that would be taboo. There must always be some weeping, wailing, and gnashing of teeth and complaints about how federal regulations are impeding progress, economic growth, exports, or whatever is in vogue at the moment. Let us face it, the public and private sectors have been regulated by national governments, regardless of the form of government, throughout the course of human history because they have been unable to regulate themselves. Why else would the following biblical injunction have been written 3200 years ago?

> *You shall not falsify measures of length, weight, or capacity. You shall have an honest balance, honest weights, an honest ephah, and an honest hin.*
>
> **—Leviticus 19:35–36**

People have not changed much since then; they still have weaknesses. Corporations established for the purpose of making a profit have occasional ethical lapses. This is human nature at work and humans are not perfect; hence the need for friendly reminders or incentives in the form of regulations. This situation is particularly true in the disciplines of safety, reliability, and security engineering. For some inexplicable reason, whenever a project or organization is facing a budget crunch, the first place costs are cut is in the areas of safety, reliability, or security. Talk about shooting yourself in the foot! If you want to end the "regulatory burden," improve human nature. In the meantime, this chapter provides some metrics to shorten your journey through the regulatory maze.

There are four solar systems in the regulatory compliance galaxy:

1. Financial
2. Healthcare
3. Personal privacy
4. Homeland security

as depicted in Chapter 2, Figure 2.13. Each solar system has a number of regulations (or planets) assigned to it. Table 3.1 lists 13 current security and privacy regulations, the issuing organization, and date of publication. To date there are two major financial regulations in the United States (U.S.) that pertain to security and privacy: (1) the Gramm-Leach-Bliley Act and (2) the Sarbanes-Oxley Act. Two regulations relating to the security and privacy of healthcare information have been issued in North America to date: (1) the Health Insurance Portability and Accountability Act (HIPAA), issued in the United States, and (2) the Personal Health Information Act, issued in Canada. Five regulations have been issued that specifically target protecting personal privacy in the digital age:

1. The Privacy, Cryptography, and Security Guidelines, issued by the Organization for Economic Cooperation and Development (OECD)
2. The Data Protection Directive, issued by the European Parliament and Council (E.C.)
3. The Data Protection Act, issued by the United Kingdom (U.K.)
4. The Personal Information Protection and Electronic Documents Act (PIPEDA), issued by Canada
5. The Privacy Act, issued by the United States

Four regulations focus on security and privacy issues in connection with homeland security. The Federal Information Security Management Act (FISMA) was issued in the United States in 2002. A series of 12 Homeland Security Presidential Directives (HSPDs) were issued between 2001 and 2004 in the United States. The most well known of the U.S. regulations, the Patriot Act, was issued in 2001. The North American Electric Reliability Council's (NERC) cyber security standards were also finalized in 2006. Except for the U.S. Privacy Act, all the security and privacy regulations were issued in the last decade; two thirds of the regulations were issued in the last five years. Similar standards have been issued in other countries around the world.

Each of these regulations is discussed in detail in Sections 3.2 through 3.14 that follow, using the following format. The regulations are grouped in the same sequence as presented in Table 3.1.

Table 3.1   Thirteen Current Security and Privacy Regulations

Regulation	Issuing Country or Organization	Date Issued	Page Count
I. Financial			
Gramm-Leach-Bliley Act, Title V	U.S.	1999	36[a]
Sarbanes-Oxley Act	U.S.	2002	66[a]
II. Healthcare			
Health Insurance Portability and Accountability Act (HIPAA)	U.S.	1996	16[a]
Personal Health Information Act	Canada	1997	29
III. Personal Privacy			
Privacy Guidelines Cryptography Guidelines Security Guidelines	OECD	1980 1997 2002	116
Data Protection Directive	E.C.	1995	42
Data Protection Act	U.K.	1998	137
Personal Information Protection and Electronic Documents Act (PIPEDA)	Canada	2000	55
Privacy Act	U.S.	1974	26
IV. Homeland Security			
Federal Information Security Management Act (FISMA), plus Office of Management and Budget guidance	U.S.	2002	50[b]
Homeland Security Presidential Directives (HSPDs) 1–12	U.S.	2001– 2004	61[b]
Cyber Security Standards, plus Reliability Functional Model	NERC	2005	109
Patriot Act	U.S.	2001	142
Total			885

Key: NERC = North America Electric Reliability Council; OECD = Organization for Economic Cooperation and Development.

[a] Not including page count from implementation in Code of Federal Regulations (CFR).

[b] Not including page count from NIST standards used to implement the policy.

- Title and purpose of the regulation
- Issuing organization or country, and date
- Scope of the regulation: what organizations, industrial sectors, and individuals the regulations apply to
- Relation to other laws and regulations, if any
- Summary of the security and privacy provisions in the regulation
- Metrics that can be used to demonstrate compliance with the security and privacy provisions

At present, the normal approach to regulation goes something like this:

- A legislative body writes regulations telling individuals or organizations to do x.
- The regulated organization writes notebooks full of documentation to prove that they did x; the documentation is signed off by senior management.
- Regulators send in auditors to review the documentation to determine if the organization really did x.
- Regulators write an audit report, sometimes lengthy, stating that the organization: (1) passed, (2) is granted a waiver and has some corrective action to perform, (3) failed and has some corrective action to perform, or (4) failed and fines or other penalties are imposed.
- The regulated organization performs the corrective action and updates the documentation.
- The auditors return in six to twelve months to verify that the corrective action has taken place and the process is repeated.

For the most part, the documentation produced is not part of standard business processes and is generated solely for the purposes of the upcoming audit. That is, the documentation is an adjunct artifact.

This process has all the earmarks of the excesses of the quality bubble of the 1990s — producing reams of documentation just to make auditors happy. In this case, the documentation described all sorts of business processes that no one in the company knew about or followed. A few people may have been primed just before the audit, but other than that no one knew the documentation or processes existed. The writers of the documentation were detached from the project about which they were writing. In effect, the notebooks looked nice but sat on a shelf unused. This is not an efficient or effective way to determine the true state of affairs of any organization.

Another common problem in the regulatory environment is the dichotomy of complying with the "letter of the law" versus complying with the "spirit of the law." Some organizations and auditors take a minimalist approach to compliance, while others take a broader view by determining what needs to be done not only to comply with regulations, but also to ensure safety, security, and reliability. Some organizations and auditors just want to check off the boxes, while others focus on the big picture and how the public at large will perceive the safety, reliability, and security of their product or service. The latter views compliance as an opportunity to increase an organization's performance and efficiency.[205] So the state of measuring regulatory compliance, at present, does not meet the test of a repeatable or consistent process.

Compliance should be methodical and logical, not painful or superfluous. Metrics provide the objective evidence needed to ensure big-picture regulatory compliance. Metrics, drawn from artifacts produced as part of standard business practices, present factual insights into the true state of affairs. Auditors and management of the regulated organization can use the same metrics to get a clear understanding about the product, process, or project of interest. Well-chosen metrics give a coherent and concise view of the situation, including strengths and weaknesses. Instead of requiring reams of paper with signatures from people with fancy titles, auditors should require a 15- to 25-page report of metrics that demonstrate and prove compliance. This would be considerably more schedule and cost efficient for both parties and provide much greater insight into reality. If you agree, call your lobbyist, write your Senators and Congressional Representatives. Of course the metrics must meet the criteria of "good metrics," as discussed in Chapter 2, have appropriate measurement boundaries, etc. This chapter provides metrics that do exactly this for each of the 13 security and privacy regulations cited above.

Privacy has been mentioned several times so far, but not yet defined. Most people have their own ideas about what privacy means, especially to themselves. Some even question the possibility of privacy in the age of the global information grid. A clear understanding of privacy and what it does and does not entail is necessary before delving into regulations.

Privacy is a legal right, not an engineering discipline. That is why organizations have privacy officers, not privacy engineers. Security engineering is the discipline used to ensure that privacy rights are protected to the extent specified by law and company or organizational policy. Privacy is not an automatic outcome of security engineering. Like any other security feature or function, privacy requirements must be specified, designed, implemented, and verified to the integrity level needed.

There are several legal aspects to privacy rights; let us look at those definitions now. All legal definitions are reprinted from *Black's Law Dictionary®*, 6th edition, by H. Black, J. Nolan, and J. Nolan-Haley, 1991, with the permission of Thomson West. The legal definitions are applicable to the legal system of the United States.

> **Privacy — right of:** *Black's Law Dictionary®* — right to be left alone; right of a person to be free from unwarranted publicity; and right to live without unwarranted interference by the public in matters with which the public is not necessarily concerned. There are four general categories of tort actions related to invasion of privacy: (a) appropriation, (b) intrusion, (c) public disclosure of private facts, and (d) false light privacy.

People living in the United States and other countries have a basic legal right to privacy. That means that their personal life and how they live it remains a private, not public, matter.

Privacy laws: *Black's Law Dictionary®* — those federal and state statutes, which prohibit an invasion of a person's right to be left alone (e.g., to not be photographed in private), and also restrict access to personal information (e.g., income tax returns, credit reports) and over-hearing of private conversations (e.g., electronic surveillance).

The right to privacy is protected by privacy laws. Although exact provisions of privacy laws in each country differ, the common ground is restricting access to private residences and property, personal information, and personal communications. The intent is to prevent harassment and unwarranted publicity. The laws provide legal remedies should privacy rights be violated.

Privacy — invasion of: *Black's Law Dictionary®* — unwarranted appropriation or exploitation of one's personality, publicizing one's private affairs with which the public has no legitimate concern, or wrongful intrusion into one's private activities, in such a manner as to cause mental suffering, shame, or humiliation to a person of ordinary sensibilities.

A person's privacy is considered to have been invaded when their persona is exploited or private matters are made public without their consent. Usually this is done with the intent of causing personal, professional, or financial harm.

Privacy — breach of: *Black's Law Dictionary®* — knowingly and without lawful authority: (a) intercepting, without consent of the sender or receiver, a message by telephone, telegraph, letter, or other means of private communications; (b) divulging, without consent of the sender or receiver, the existence or contents of such message if such person knows that the message was illegally intercepted, or if he illegally learned of the message in the course of employment with an agency transmitting it.

A person or organization commits a breach of privacy whenever they knowingly and without legal authority or consent from the individuals involved obtain, release, or disseminate the contents of private communications, regardless of the means of communications. Whenever a breach of privacy or invasion of privacy occurs, the victim has the right to pursue a legal remedy based on the contents of the applicable privacy laws and regulations. Both the individuals and the organization(s) responsible for the privacy violation can be prosecuted.

Privacy impact: an analysis of how information is handled: (a) to ensure handling conforms to applicable legal, regulatory, and policy requirements regarding privacy; (b) to determine the risks and effects of collecting, maintaining, and disseminating information in identifiable form in an electronic information system; and (c) to examine and evaluate protections and alternative processes for handling information to mitigate potential privacy risks.[52]

To avoid ending up on the wrong side of a privacy lawsuit, organizations conduct privacy impact analyses to identify best practices and those needing immediate improvement.

The digital age has brought many advantages. In terms of privacy, however, it has opened up a virtual Pandora's box. To help ameliorate this situation, the regulations that follow tackle the issue of privacy and electronic records that contain personally identifiable information. Privacy is not just another regulatory issue. Identity theft is the most spectacular example of a violation of privacy rights. We all have a lot at stake here, both as individuals and organizations; these regulations and the metrics that support them deserve your apt attention.

Now we are going to look at 13 current security and privacy regulations and the metrics that can be used to demonstrate compliance with them. They represent a total of 885 pages of regulations, plus an equivalent amount of supplemental documents. If you are a real policy enthusiast, you may want to read the actual regulations yourself. If you are not into a barrage of whereas's, heretofore's, and notwithstanding's, and the flowery superfluous repetitive circuitous language of clause 12, section 3.2.c, and paragraph (a)(2)(iii)(C)(2), you may want to stick to the technical abstracts below. Just be glad these people write regulations and not software. It would take a supercomputer to calculate the cyclomatic complexity of some of these regulations. Perhaps someone should author the book entitled *A Guide to Writing Object-Oriented Legislation*. In the meantime, two security and privacy regulations from the financial sector are up next. One word of caution: regulations by their very nature do not make for the most exciting reading.

FINANCIAL INDUSTRY

3.2 Gramm-Leach-Bliley (GLB) Act — United States

The Financial Services Modernization Act, known as the Gramm-Leach-Bliley Act (GLB), was enacted 12 November 1999. The late 1990s was a time when the stock market was soaring, the economy was booming, and Congress was debating how to spend the budget surplus or the so-called peace dividend from the end of the Cold War. The GLB Act, passed during this rosy economic climate, "modernized" the financial services industry by eliminating the barriers between banks, brokerage firms, and insurance companies that were erected in response to the Great Depression of the 1920s and 1930s.[141] The economic situation has changed since then and time will tell whether this was a wise decision. The good news is that now these other types of financial institutions have to adhere to the same security and privacy regulations as banks.[183]

The GLB Act consists of seven titles; most deal with financial issues. Title V is of interest to us because it specifies privacy requirements for personal financial information. Financial services is an information-based industry.[141] Almost all information that is processed or generated in the financial services industry is potentially sensitive or private, and there is a potential for significant monetary loss due to the lack of keeping this information private.[141]

Section 501 of Title V starts off with a declaration that[75]:

> *... each financial institution has ... a continuing obligation to respect the privacy of its customers and to protect the security and confidentiality of those customers' nonpublic personal information.*

Federal financial regulatory agencies are then assigned the responsibility to develop robust regulations to enforce the administrative, technical, and physical safeguards essential for protecting that information, specifically[75]:

- To ensure the security and confidentiality of customer records and information
- To protect against any anticipated threats or hazards to the security and integrity of such records
- To protect against unauthorized access to or use of such records or information that could result in substantial harm or inconvenience to any customer

The intent is for financial institutions to think about security and privacy of customers' nonpublic personal information as a standard part of their broader business practices and regulatory compliance process, instead of just as an afterthought.[141] Notice that the bill says "to any customer"; the threshold is set at one customer being harmed or inconvenienced, not thousands of customers. Note also that "substantial harm" is not defined in terms of dollars, presumably because what constitutes "substantial harm" is different for someone living on $60,000 a year than for someone else living on $50 million a year.

Section 502 of Title V delves into the privacy of nonpublic personal information with both feet. Nonpublic information is defined as[75]:

> *personally identifiable financial information: (i) provided by a consumer to a financial institution; (ii) resulting from any transaction with the consumer or any service performed for the consumer; or (iii) otherwise obtained by the financial institution.*

Examples of nonpublic information include information a consumer submits on an application for a financial service, account numbers, payment histories, loan or deposit account balances, credit or debit card purchases, and information obtained about an individual from court records, consumer reports, or other sources.[75f] Lists of individuals with whom a financial institution has a consumer relationship is also considered nonpublic information; a list, database, or other collection of information is considered nonpublic information if it contains any nonpublic information elements.[97, 179]

Per Section 502, a financial institution may not disclose nonpublic personal information to a third party without notifying a customer beforehand and gaining their consent. The customer must be notified in writing (or electronically if they agree to it) and given an opportunity to opt out or say no to the proposed disclosure. There are a few exceptions, of course, such as disclosure to third parties who are under contract to perform a service to the financial institution and are bound by that contract to protect the confidentiality of the information, or disclosures necessary to perform a transaction on behalf of the customer or other legal obligations. Section 502 places additional limits on the disclosure of nonpublic personal information. Third parties cannot disclose or reuse information they receive as part of their contractual relationship with a financial institution. Financial institutions cannot disclose nonpublic personal information to direct marketing firms.

Furthermore, financial institutions must inform customers of their privacy policies and procedures, per Section 503. This information must be shared with customers at the time an account is opened or financial relationship established. If an ongoing relationship is established, customers must be re-advised of this policy and any changes to it at least annually. Specifically, customers are to be told[75]:

- What types of disclosures of nonpublic personal information are made to third parties and the categories of information disclosed about current and former customers
- What policies and procedures are in place to protect the confidentiality and security of nonpublic personal information
- The categories of information that the institution collects from other sources about its current and former customers
- Customer rights and procedures for opting out of these disclosures

This requirement puts customers in the driver's seat: they can: (1) shop around for a privacy policy they like, and (2) opt out of any disclosures they do not like.[179] Opt out directions from customers remain in effect permanently, unless canceled in writing by the customer, or electronically if the customer agrees to this mode.[75f] If a customer establishes a new relationship with the same financial institution, the privacy notices and opt out opportunity must be given anew.[75f] Even if a customer returns an opt out direction late, a financial institution must honor it as quickly as reasonable.[179]

Sections 504 through 507 take care of logistical matters. For example, federal agencies are to coordinate the individual regulations they each promulgate through the Code of Federal Regulations, so that the regulations are "essentially similar," taking into account the different types of financial institutions regulated. Enforcement responsibilities are clarified as being the institutions over which each regulatory agency has jurisdiction. Insurance companies are the exception because they are state regulated.

Section 508, the last section in Subtitle A of Title V, is a curious section. It looks like an attempt to water down some of the GLB Act's provisions in the future and was probably included as a result of a compromise vote. Anyway, Section 508 required the Secretary of the Treasury, the Federal Trade Commission, and the other federal financial regulatory agencies to conduct a study of information sharing practices among financial institutions. Nine specific topics were to be addressed[75]:

1. Purpose(s) for sharing confidential customer information
2. Extent and adequacy of security protections for confidential customer information
3. Potential risks to customer privacy
4. Benefits to financial institutions
5. Potential benefits to customers
6. Adequacy of existing laws to protect customer privacy
7. Adequacy of financial institutions' privacy policies
8. Feasibility of different approaches for customers to opt out
9. Feasibility of restricting the sharing of information only for specific purposes as directed by the customer

The wording of these topics is especially curious: "*potential* risks to customer privacy," "*potential* benefits to customers," but just "benefits to financial institutions" — no potential included. It is easy to see which direction the section's drafters were headed. This report was due to Congress in 2002. Because the GLB Act had not been amended by 2005, nor have the regulations issued by each agency, it is fair to assume that the report had no impact.

Subtitle B of Title V attacks fraudulent access to financial information. Section 521 makes it illegal to obtain, attempt to obtain, or cause to be disclosed nonpublic personal information of any customer of a financial institution. It does not matter how this nonpublic personal information was fraudulently obtained; the bill gives several examples: false, fictitious, fraudulent statements to financial institutions or other customers, forged or counterfeit documents, verbal or written solicitation of information. Included, of course, are the fraudulent e-mails that continually float around asking for information about your bank accounts. Criminal penalties are imposed by Section 523 (both fines and jail time of up to five years). Repeat offenders within a 12-month period can receive double the fines and jail time of up to ten years. Given that the fraudulent e-mail requests for financial information surface weekly, it would appear that the criminal penalties for such activity are not serving as much of a deterrent. Such enforcement activities are to be documented in an annual report to Congress by each financial regulatory agency.

Federal financial regulatory agencies include the Federal Trade Commission (FTC), the Federal Reserve Bank, the Office of Thrift Supervision, the Office of the Comptroller of the Currency, the National Credit Union Association, the Securities and Exchange Commission, the Commodities and Futures Traders Commission, and the state insurance authorities. Each federal regulatory agency was tasked to issue federal regulations, via the Code of Federal Regulations or CFR, for the financial institutions over which they have jurisdiction. Two separate rules were to be issued, one addressing the standards for safeguarding customer information and one addressing the privacy of consumer financial information. As noted previously, the federal agencies were tasked to coordinate their regulations and the enforcement of them. No regulations were issued regarding fraudulent access to financial data; that is not a regulatory function, but rather a law enforcement activity for the

Department of Justice to investigate and prosecute. We will now look at the two rules issued by the Federal Trade Commission as an example of how the GLB Act was codified. The rules issued by the federal regulatory agencies mirror those stated in the GLB Act. However, they provide more specifics and several illustrations to ensure that the rules are interpreted correctly.

The FTC issued the final rule for the Privacy of Consumer Financial Information on 24 May 2000, which became 16 CFR 313. The purpose of this rule is to "govern the treatment of nonpublic personal information about consumers by the financial institutions" over which the FTC has jurisdiction.[75b] The examples given include mortgage lenders, finance companies, check cashers, wire transferors, travel agencies operated in conjunction with financial services, collection agencies, credit counselors, tax preparation services, investment advisors, leasing of personal property, and third parties who receive information from these organizations. The scope of the rule is limited to personal and family finances; the finances of corporations and non-profits is not covered. And the statement is made that this rule does not interfere with or supersede any provision in the Health Information Portability and Accountability Act (HIPAA), discussed below in Section 3.4 of this chapter.

Section 313.4 requires an initial notice of the institution's privacy policy immediately whenever an individual initiates a customer-type relationship. This notice must also be made to consumers before disclosing nonpublic personal information to a third party. Some exceptions are cited, such as transferring loans. Here we see a distinction being made between customers and consumers. A customer is someone who has a long-term, ongoing relationship with a financial institution. In contrast, a consumer is someone who conducts a one-time transaction with a financial institution, such as cashing a check or wiring funds.[97] A former customer reverts to being a consumer when he no longer has an active ongoing relationship.[97] Likewise, someone who submitted an application for a financial service but was rejected is considered a consumer, not a customer.[179]

Section 313.5 reiterates the requirement for customers to receive an annual notice of the financial institution's privacy policy and practices, and any changes that have been made since the previous notice. The terms "clear and conspicuous" are used to describe the notice. In essence, this means that the notice must be legible, readable, and easily understandable by the public at large — no six-point fonts or obtuse language. Section 313.6 follows suit by defining the required content of the privacy notice. Eight specific items are to be included:

1. Categories of nonpublic personal information collected (from the customer or elsewhere)
2. Categories of nonpublic personal information disclosed
3. Who the nonpublic personal information is disclosed to
4. Categories of nonpublic information disclosed about former customers and to whom
5. Categories of third parties the financial institution contracts with
6. Customers' rights to opt out of any disclosure

7. Disclosures made under the Fair Credit Reporting Act
8. Company policies and procedures to protect nonpublic personal information, such as who has access to the information and why

The procedures for opt out notices are discussed in Section 313.7. Each customer must receive one. The notices are required to clearly state what nonpublic information may be disclosed, and that the customer has a right to say no to this disclosure and opt out. The method customers are to follow to opt out must be simple and be explained. Often, customers have the choice of calling an 800-number or faxing or mailing in a form showing their opt out selections. Whenever privacy policies are revised, Section 313.8 requires that customers be notified, sent the new policy, and given another opportunity to opt out. Opt out notices should be delivered to each customer annually in writing; they may be delivered electronically only if the customer agrees to this beforehand, per Section 313.9

Section 313.10 clarifies the limitations on disclosing nonpublic personal information. In short, nonpublic personal information may be disclosed only if (1) a notice is sent to the customer about the proposed disclosure beforehand, (2) the customer has a reasonable amount of time to say no and opt out of the disclosure, and (3) the customer does not opt out. The same process applies to consumers. Section 313.11 attempts to place limits on other types of disclosure and reuse, such as those among affiliates. Information can be re-disclosed to an institution it was received from or to an affiliate, if they could have legally received it from the same institution. There is a problem with this clause. If an institution already possesses nonpublic personal information it should not have, there is nothing to prevent it from disclosing or reusing it. Section 313.12 prohibits the disclosure of nonpublic account information to direct marketing firms. This provision sounds good on paper, but direct marketing firms still seem to be getting the information somehow. Why else would people be receiving offers for new credit cards or insurance in the mail almost weekly? Sections 313.13 and 313.14 repeat the exceptions to the limits on disclosure that are stated in the GLB Act. Information can be disclosed (1) to third parties who are under contract to the financial institution to perform some service, (2) to perform a service at the customer's request, (c) if the customer has consented to the disclosure beforehand and has not revoked his consent, and (4) to prevent fraudulent activities.

The FTC issued a final rule for the Safeguarding of Customer Information on 23 May 2002, which became 16 CFR 314. The purpose of this rule was to implement the safeguard provisions of Sections 501 and 502 of the GLB Act. In particular, this rule sets standards for developing, implementing, and maintaining reasonable administrative, technical, and physical safeguards to protect the security, confidentiality, and integrity of customers' nonpublic personal information. This rule applies to all financial institutions under the jurisdiction of the FTC, like the examples listed above for the Privacy Rule. In addition, the scope of the rule is all nonpublic personal information that the financial institution possesses about customers and consumers, whether they are the originator or receiver of such information.

It is important to clarify some terminology before looking at the individual sections in this rule.

Customer information: any record containing nonpublic personal information about a customer of a financial institution, whether in paper, electronic, or other form, that is handled or maintained by or on behalf of the institution or its affiliates.[75e]

Information security program: the administrative, technical, and physical safeguards used to access, collect, distribute, process, protect, store, use, transmit, dispose of, or otherwise handle customer information.[75e]

Service provider: any person or entity that receives, maintains, processes or otherwise is permitted access to customer information through its provision of services directly to a financial institution that is subject to this rule.[75e]

Customer information is all inclusive of the types and formats of information a financial institution might have about its current or former customers, whether or not that institution originated the information. Examples include faxes and voice mail records from outside sources. As we will see shortly, this rule requires financial institutions to establish an information security program to protect customer information. The terms "administrative," "technical," and "physical safeguards" correspond to physical, personnel, IT, and operational security; that is, this information security program is expected to cover all types of security engineering activities. In addition, this program is to control all manners in which customer information is handled and used. Finally, this rule uses the term "service provider" to clarify the role of third parties in relation to financial institutions.

Sections 314.3 and 314.4 spell out in detail the requirements financial institutions' information security programs must meet. Financial institutions are responsible for developing, implementing, and maintaining a comprehensive information security program. The details of this program are to be written down and regularly communicated to employees and contractors. The specific administrative, technical, and physical safeguards employed are to be appropriate for the size, complexity, nature, and scope of the financial institution's activities and the sensitivity of the customer's information. A financial institution's information security program is to be designed to ensure the security and confidentiality of customer information by protecting against (1) anticipated threats or hazards to the security and integrity of such information, and (2) unauthorized access to or use of that information that could result in substantial harm or inconvenience to a customer. To do so, financial institutions are expected to designate an individual who is accountable for ensuring the success of the information security program. A key part of this information security program is a comprehensive ongoing risk assessment and mitigation effort that evaluates the potential for unauthorized access, misuse, disclosure, alteration, destruction, or other compromise of customer information. The adequacy of current administrative, technical, and physical safeguards is to be tested and verified regularly, preferably through an independent assessment. Robust incident prevention, detection, and containment capabilities and procedures are expected to be in place. Employees and contractors are to be regularly trained in all aspects of the information security program. Responsibilities for adhering to the information security program should be passed on to service providers through contractual means; this is considered part of the financial institution's due diligence responsibilities.[179] Financial institutions were expected to have their information security programs in place within one year after the FTC issued the rule.[179] What does all this mean to an organization that handles sensitive nonpublic personal information as a part of doing business? It is plain and simple. If they employ inadequate administrative, technical, or physical safeguards and an identity theft ring decides to raid their data, they are liable and subject to an enforcement action by federal regulators. In addition, regulatory agencies, law enforcement officials, and customers must be notified about any compromise or misappropriation of sensitive information that could be misused.[264] Furthermore, the identity theft ring is subject to the criminal penalties of the GLB Act.

The FTC has taken these rules and its role in enforcing them seriously. For example, the FTC charged Petco with deceptive claims about the security that Petco provided for consumers' personal information submitted to their Web site. The FTC alleged "that contrary to Petco's claims, it did not take reasonable or appropriate measures to prevent commonly known attacks by hackers." The flaws allowed a hacker to access consumer records, including credit card numbers.[201] The suit was settled 17 November 2004. The settlement required that Petco implement a comprehensive information security program for its Web site designed to protect the security, confidentiality, and integrity of personal information collected about or from consumers. In addition, they are required to have independent security audits conducted biennially and retain records so that the FTC can monitor their compliance with the GLB Act.

Petco was not alone. On 16 November 2004, the FTC charged Nationwide Mortgage and Sunbelt Lending Services with violations of the safeguards rule of the GLB Act. Both failed to protect customers' names, social security numbers, credit histories, bank account numbers, income tax returns, and other sensitive information, per the basic requirements of the rule.[140] In addition, Nationwide Mortgage failed to train its employees on information security issues, oversee loan officers' handling of customer information, and monitor its network for vulnerabilities.[140] Sunbelt also failed to oversee security practices of its third-party service providers and of its loan officers working from remote locations throughout the state of Florida.[140] Neither company provided customers with the required privacy notices.[140] The consent agreement reached with Sunbelt Lending Services requires, among other things, that they have an independent security audit conducted to measure compliance every year for the next ten years.

The GLB Act, while including Title V that addresses security and privacy issues, actually increases the risk to customers' nonpublic personal information; that is because of the provisions in the other six titles in the bill. They have[141]:

- Increased the number of agents involved in financial transactions
- Fostered large conglomerates that have large distributed IT infrastructures
- Resulted in a large number of customer service and back office workers, such as call center representatives, who have broad access to sensitive customer data
- Led to extensive outsourcing to third-party service providers, often offshore, who have lower incentives to preserve customer privacy

The last bullet is not an idle concern. A new outsourcing scandal in India was reported in the *Washington Post* on 24 June 2005[250]:

> "... *a reporter posing as a businessman purchased the bank account details of 1,000 Britons — including customers of some of Britain's best known banks — for $5.50 each. The worker who allegedly sold the information bragged to the undercover reporter that he could 'sell as many as 200,000 account details a month'.*"

The worker provided the reporter with the names, account passwords, addresses, phone numbers, credit card numbers, passports numbers, and driver's license numbers.[250] This episode followed an earlier report of another outsourcing scandal in India in which $426,000 was stolen from New York-based customers of Citibank.[250] And because outsourcing firms rarely work for just one company, they are in an ideal position to collect and aggregate sensitive personal data from multiple sources.[256]

Robust enforcement of the GLB Act provisions is seriously needed. As Fuldner reports from a study conducted by IBM and Watchfire[141]:

- 66 percent of the financial institutions surveyed had one or more Web forms that collected personally identifiable information but did not use SSL encryption.
- 91 percent of these institutions used weak forms of SSL encryption, such as 40-bit RSA, rather than the 128-bit encryption recommended by federal bank regulators.

In the meantime, Fuldner also proposes some technical and operational solutions to the increased risks to customers' nonpublic personal information[141]:

- Develop an alternative for using social security numbers and one's mother's maiden name to authenticate customers.
- Develop a secure method for authenticating a financial institution's Web site to customers to prevent e-mail scams and other fraudulent electronic access to financial information.
- Employ need-to-know access control mechanisms and audit trails, rather than allowing all customer services representatives to see everything.
- Use strong legal enforcement of third-party service providers responsibilities to prevent situations such as those just described.

One industrial sector has taken the proverbial bull by the horns in response to the GLB Act. The payment card industry quickly realized that, due to the near-complete, intertwined nature of their business, *all* organizations had to play by the same rules if any *one* organization's data was to be secure. As a result, the Payment Card Industry Data Security Standard was developed. It represents a merger of the best practices from previous security standards used by Visa and MasterCard. The standard, which took effect 30 June 2005, applies to organizations and equipment across the board[266]:

> *Requirements apply to all Members, merchants, and service providers that store, process, or transmit cardholder data. Additionally, these security requirements apply to all "system components" which is defined as any network component, server, or application included in, or connected to, the cardholder data environment. Network components include, but are not limited to, firewalls, switches, routers, wireless access points, network appliances, and other security appliances. Servers include, but are not limited to, Web, database, authentication, DNS, mail, proxy, and NTP. Applications include all purchased and custom applications, including internal and external (Web) applications.*

The standard is organized around six goals or principles. Each goal is further decomposed into three tiers of specific requirements, as shown in Table 3.2. The standard states the security goal; this is followed by a concise rationale explaining why the goal is needed. Next, high-level, mid-level, and low-level requirements are derived. The requirements are specific and to the point. The requirements address physical security, personnel security, operational security, and IT security, including threats from insiders and outsiders. The Data Security Standard supports the Open Web Application Security Project Guidelines. The standard does not address privacy.

Table 3.2   Organization of Payment Card Industry Data Security Standard

Goals/Principles	No. of High-Level Requirements	No. of Mid-Level Requirements	No. of Low-Level Requirements
Build and maintain a secure network	2	8	29
Protect cardholder data	2	8	16
Maintain a vulnerability management program	2	7	22
Implement strong access control measures	3	17	27
Regularly monitor and test networks	2	12	18
Maintain an information security policy	1	9	31
Total	12	61	143

Compliance with the standard is required by all participants. The requirement for independent validation of compliance is based on the annual volume of transactions. The one exception is merchants that have suffered a cyber attack that resulted in the compromise of account data; they are required to have an independent validation of compliance, regardless of their transaction volume. Participants are divided into service providers and merchants. All service providers had to demonstrate independent validation of compliance by 30 June 2005. Level 1 merchants, those that process over 6 million transactions annually, had to demonstrate independent validation of compliance by 30 September 2004. Level 2 merchants, those that process between 150,000 and 6 million transactions annually, had to demonstrate independent validation compliance by 30 June 2005, as did Level 3 merchants that process between 20,000 and 150,000 transactions annually. Level 4 merchants, those that process less than 20,000 transactions annually, are required to comply with the standard and strongly encouraged to seek independent validation of compliance.

The Payment Card Industry Data Security Standard is an excellent, logical, and practical standard. Its 12 pages contain a more common-sense, while at the same time thorough, approach to cyber security than many other much longer standards. I highly recommend reading this standard, even if you are not in the payment card industry.

The following metrics can be used by Congress, oversight agencies, public interest groups, federal financial regulatory agencies, and financial institutions to measure the effectiveness of the provisions of the GLB Act and the enforcement of them. Because identity theft represents a severe violation of the GLB security and privacy safeguards, not to mention the prohibition against fraudulent access to financial information, everyone should pay close attention to these metrics. They fall into five categories, corresponding to the sections in Title V of the bill:

1. Safeguarding Customer Information
2. Privacy Policies
3. Disclosure of Nonpublic Personal Information
4. Regulatory Enforcement Actions
5. Fraudulent Access to Financial Information

Safeguarding Customer Information

Number and percentage of financial institutions audited and found to be in compliance with provisions of the rule for safeguarding customer information, by fiscal year and regulatory agency: 1.1.1

a. They have a written information security program that is communicated regularly to employees and contractors
b. Their administrative, technical, and physical safeguards are appropriate for the size, complexity, nature, and scope of their activities and the sensitivity of their customers' information
c. They have designated a coordinator who is accountable for the information security program

d. They perform regular risk assessments of their operations, safeguards, technology base, and procedures

e. They have robust incident prevention, response, and containment procedures in place

f. Requirements for safeguarding customer information are passed on to service providers through contractual means

Privacy Policies

Number and percentage of financial institutions audited and found to be in compliance with provisions of the privacy rule for customers' financial information, by fiscal year and regulatory agency: 1.1.2

a. They informed customers of their privacy policy at the time a relationship was established

b. They notified customers at least annually about their privacy policy or when any change was made to it

c. Their privacy policy notices contained all required information

Disclosure of Nonpublic Personal Information

Number and percentage of financial institutions audited and found to be in compliance with the limits on disclosure of nonpublic personal information, by fiscal year and regulatory agency: 1.1.3

a. Disclosures were only made with prior customer consent or consistent with a valid exception to the rule

b. They informed customers of their right to opt out prior to a disclosure being made

c. The method for customers to opt out was simple and straightforward

Regulatory Enforcement Actions

Number of enforcement actions taken against financial institutions or their service providers, by fiscal year and regulatory agency, for: 1.1.4

a. Failure to ensure confidentiality and integrity of customer records and information

b. Failure to protect against anticipated threats or hazards to the security and integrity of customer records and information

c. Failure to protect against unauthorized access to or use of such records or information which resulted or could have resulted in substantial harm or inconvenience to a customer

Number of enforcement actions taken against financial institutions or their service providers, by fiscal year and regulatory agency, for: 1.1.5

a. Disclosing nonpublic personal information without notifying a customer

b. Disclosing nonpublic personal information without giving the customer the opportunity to opt out beforehand

    c. Disclosing nonpublic personal information without the customer's consent

    d. Disclosing nonpublic personal information for reasons other than a valid exception to the rule

Number of enforcement actions taken against financial institutions or their service providers, by fiscal year and regulatory agency: 1.1.6

    a. Failure to disclose their privacy policy and procedures

    b. Failure to inform customers and consumers of their right to opt out

    c. Failure to inform customers and consumers of the method to use to opt out

Fraudulent Access to Financial Information

Number of criminal penalties imposed for fraudulent access to financial information, by fiscal year: 1.1.7

    a. For making false, fictitious, or fraudulent statements to financial institutions or their customers

    b. For using forged or counterfeit documents to obtain the information

    c. Through e-mail scams

    d. For repeat offenders

3.3 Sarbanes-Oxley Act — United States

The Corporate and Auditing Accountability, Responsibility, and Transparency Act, known as the Sarbanes-Oxley Act, was enacted 23 January 2002. This Act was in response to the stream of corporate meltdowns that resulted from extremely creative accounting practices at places such as Enron, WorldCom, and Tyco, just to name a few. Financial reporting had ceased to be a disciplined science and had become instead a competitive race to see who could manufacture the biggest piece of fiction. Massive debts disappeared overnight or were used to capitalize new offshore subsidiaries. Optimistic sales projections became *bona fide* revenue. Customers and orders were fabricated out of thin air. A year or so before this parade of collapsing dominoes, Alan Greenspan, Chairman of the Federal Reserve, spawned the phrase "irrational exuberance" to describe the state of the economy in general and the stock market in particular. In his mind, the numbers did not add up. His assessment was correct; however, the exuberance was not due to misplaced optimism, but rather widespread mythical corporate financial reports. This shell game epidemic was not limited to the United States; instead, it spanned most industrialized nations. In the aftermath, other countries also passed bills similar to the Sarbanes-Oxley Act, such as Bill C-13: An Act to Amend the Criminal Code (Capital Markets Fraud and Evidence-Gathering) in Canada.

    The very people who were sold this bill of goods were the ones to suffer the consequences: company employees who became unemployed overnight and saw their 401K accounts vaporize, company pensioners who suddenly had no pension checks, shareholders left holding worthless stock, and creditors with uncollectible debts. They were the ones left holding the worthless monopoly money when the facts came to light. After yet another example of industry (or human nature) being unable to regulate itself, Congress stepped in and passed the Sarbanes-Oxley Act to[96]:

> *... protect investors by improving the accuracy and reliability of corporate disclosures made pursuant to the securities laws ... to protect the interests of investors and further the public interest in the preparation of informative, accurate, and independent audit reports for companies the securities of which are sold to, and held by and for, public investors.*

or, as some have described it, to prevent further "corporate chicanery."[244] The Sarbanes-Oxley Act has been likened to the "most significant law affecting public companies and public accounting firms since the passage of the Securities and Exchange Commission Act of 1934,"[151] which was enacted in response to the stock market crash that precipitated the worldwide Great Depression of 1929–1934. There was some "irrational exuberance" at work then too and Congress stepped in.

Undoubtedly, Enron, WorldCom, and Tyco were not the only ones cooking their books; they just happened to tumble first and got caught. The heightened publicity gave other corporations time to do some spring cleaning and quietly report a quarterly loss due to "accounting adjustments." To convince corporate boards that they were serious, Congress dramatically increased the fines and penalties for fraudulent corporate financial reports. Depending on the exact nature of the fraudulent act, corporate officers who certify fraudulent reports as being accurate can be fined from $1 million to $5 million and jailed from 10 to 20 years.

The Sarbanes-Oxley Act took effect in 2003. The Securities and Exchange Commission was tasked with the responsibility of codifying the Act in the Code of Federal Regulations, similar to the process used to codify the Gramm-Leach-Bliley Act. The provisions of the Act apply to any public corporation or organization that is required to file annual reports to the U.S. Securities and Exchange Commission. This includes subsidiaries that are located and do business in the United States, although corporate headquarters are in another country. The Act does not apply to privately held companies or non-profit organizations that are not listed on the stock exchange. If a privately held company is about to issue an initial public offering (IPO), it would be a good idea to become familiar with the provisions of the Sarbanes-Oxley Act beforehand.

There has been a fair amount of discussion and debate about the cost of compliance with the provisions of the Sarbanes-Oxley Act versus the benefits. However, when looking at the numbers, it is difficult to empathize with this weeping, wailing, and gnashing of teeth. In a survey of 217 companies with average annual revenues of $5 billion, the average one-time start-up cost of compliance was $4.26 million[171, 244] — or 0.0852 percent of the annual revenue. The annual cost to maintain compliance was considerably less. This is a small price to pay to protect employees, pensioners, shareholders, and creditors, not to mention the company's reputation. Furthermore, $4.26 million is peanuts compared to the losses incurred when a corporation such as Enron, WorldCom, or Tyco crashes. The WorldCom fraud was estimated at $11 billion. It is difficult to come up with a valid reason why a corporate board would not want to make such a small investment to ensure that its financial house is in order. This gets back to our prior discussion about complying with "the letter of the law" versus "the spirit of the law." Several companies are taking a broader view of compliance and acknowledge that resources being spent on compliance will prove to be money well spent.[167] They realize that while the short-term costs of compliance may have been high, companies will benefit in the long term by having a better understanding of their business practices and an opportunity to refine them.[244] In fact, the April 2005 edition of *CIO Decisions* reported a case study of how Pacer Global Logistics successfully implemented provisions of the Sarbanes-Oxley Act and enhanced the way it conducts business.[171] In summary, a holistic approach was taken toward replacing, improving, and creating new process flows and controls across the enterprise, organizational dynamics were improved, and the new processes are being institutionalized as a way of life for the good of the company.[171] Or as Rasch states[260]:

> *... SOX provides an incentive to companies to do that which they reasonably should be doing anyway. ... The better reason to have controls over IT and IT security, however, is not because it will make you SOX compliant — but because it will make your business more efficient, enable you to better utilize the data, and allow you to trust ALL the data, not just financial reporting data.*

The Sarbanes-Oxley Act does not mention, not even once, the terms IT, computer, information security, or privacy. The phrase "information system" is only mentioned once and that in a prohibition. So why has this Act received so much attention in the IT community? There are two reasons. First, the phrases certifying the accuracy and attesting to the reliability of financial reports are scattered throughout the bill. Second, the Act mandates adequate internal controls to ensure the accuracy and reliability of the IT systems and operational procedures used to generate financial reports. While the Act does not dictate specifics, a goodly portion of these internal controls is expected to relate to the design, development, operation, and interaction with information systems. In IT speak, this means ensuring data, information, systems, and network integrity.

Most articles about the Sarbanes-Oxley Act jump to Section 404 and discuss it exclusively. While this is an important section, there are other sections that IT professionals should be aware of also, such as the following sections, which are discussed below:

- Section 104 — Inspections of registered public accounting firms
- Section 105 — Investigations and disciplinary proceedings

- Section 201 — Services outside scope of practice of auditors
- Section 302 — Corporate responsibility for financial reports
- Section 401 — Disclosures in periodic reports
- Section 404 — Management assessment of internal controls
- Section 802 — Criminal penalties for altering documents
- Section 805 — Review of federal sentencing guidelines for obstruction of justice and extensive criminal fraud
- Section 906 — Corporate responsibility for financial reports
- Section 1102 — Tampering with a record or otherwise impeding an official proceeding

Section 104 assigns inspection responsibilities to the Public Company Accounting Oversight Board (PCAOB). For our purposes, what is important to note is that the PCAOB is tasked to evaluate the sufficiency of a company's quality control system, specifically the documentation, communication, and procedures of that system. Undoubtedly, that quality control system is intended to encompass financial information systems and the reports they produce.

Section 105 defines what type of information the PCAOB may request a company to produce during testimony or in response to a subpoena. First, it should be noted that the PCAOB can request the testimony of "any person associated with a registered public accounting firm," including clients. This person may be asked to provide any working papers, documents, records, testimony, or other information that the PCAOB requests and has decided to inspect to verify the accuracy. "Any person" includes the IT staff, and "records and other information" includes any information stored in any format as part of an information system.

Section 201 prohibits registered public accounting firms from engaging in non-audit services and explicitly lists "financial information systems design and implementation" as an example. This provision is intended to maintain auditor independence — auditors, it is felt, cannot maintain their independence and objectivity if they are auditing a system that their company designed and developed. This provision is a direct result of the WorldCom scandal; the same accounting firm designed and developed WorldCom's creative accounting systems and then certified their accuracy. If you are employed by a registered public accounting firm as a member of the IT staff and the company starts to sell your services out to clients, you should immediately raise some red flags and point to Section 201 of the Sarbanes-Oxley Act. If that does not correct the situation, find a new job fast!

Section 302 contains the first mention of corporate accountability and internal controls. Section 302 mandates that corporate officers certify each annual and quarterly report filed with the Securities and Exchange Commission. This certification is to explicitly state that (1) each signing officer has reviewed the report, (2) the report does not contain any untrue statement, does not omit any material fact, and is not misleading, (3) the report fairly presents all information related to the financial condition and operations of the issuer for the reporting period, and (4) the signing officers are responsible for establishing and maintaining the company's internal controls. Several specific stipulations are made about the internal controls. Internal controls are to be designed to ensure that all material information related to the company and its subsidiaries is captured and made known to the signing officers. That is, the internal controls are to prevent disappearing debts and phantom revenue. The signing officers are required to attest to the fact that the effectiveness of the internal controls was evaluated within 90 days prior to the report being issued. For quarterly reports, this implies that the internal controls are evaluated quarterly. For annual reports, this implies that the internal controls are evaluated within the three-month period during which the report was issued. Furthermore, the signing officers are to document in the report all conclusions about the effectiveness of the internal controls resulting from the evaluation. In particular, three items have to be disclosed: (1) all deficiencies in the design or operation of internal controls that could adversely affect the ability to record, process, summarize, and report financial data; (2) any fraud committed by management or other employees who have a significant role in the internal controls; and (3) any significant changes to the internal controls or other factors that could significantly affect internal controls and thus the accuracy of the financial reports after the assessment.[96] Suppose a financial report is in the process of being prepared concurrent with the assessment of the internal controls. The assessment finds several material weaknesses in the internal controls. This fact is documented in the financial report so that the readers know not to take the numbers too seriously. By the next reporting period, however, it will be expected that the internal controls have been brought up to par and the financial numbers are real.

Section 401 reiterates and expands the requirements for accurate financial reports, this time related to assumptions that are known as *pro forma* figures. Public disclosures and press or other releases are included, not just reports to the Securities and Exchange Commission. Again, the requirement is for the information reported to not contain any untrue statement, not omit any material fact, and not be misleading, related to the financial condition and operations of the issuer for the reporting period.

More details about the assessment of internal controls are provided in Section 404. This section repeats the requirements for all annual financial reports to include an internal control report that makes two primary statements: (1) the corporate officers' responsibility for establishing and maintaining adequate internal controls, and (2) the most recent assessment of the effectiveness of the internal control structure and procedures. Then comes the kicker. The registered public accounting firm that audits the company is required to attest to the accuracy and completeness of the assessment of internal controls. The review of the internal controls assessment by the auditing firm is in addition to that performed by the PCAOB of a company's quality control system and internal audits. This is a polite way of saying "Thou shalt not falsify your internal control assessment either." Auditing firms want repeat business from the companies they audit. So usually there is a lot of back-and-forth about what is wrong with the internal controls and what is needed to fix them. However, as mentioned under Section 201, the auditing firm is prohibited from implementing the fixes; the company must do that.

Section 802 specifies criminal penalties for destruction, alteration, or falsification of records. The scope is rather broad[96]:

> *Whoever knowingly alters, destroys, mutilates, conceals, covers up, falsifies, or makes a false entry in any records, document of tangible object with the intent to impede, obstruct, or influence the investigation, or proper administration of any matter within the jurisdiction of any department or agency of the United States....*

That is, any physical or electronic record that any agency of the federal government has jurisdiction over is included. The penalty is significant fines and up to 20 years in jail. Section 1101 repeats the prohibition against tampering and the subsequent criminal penalties. So the next time someone bypasses the normal procedures and comes directly to you with an "emergency favor, just this once" to load, enter, edit, or delete some files, the answer should be a resounding NO! This theme is repeated again in Section 805, which sets the context[96]:

> *... the offense involved abuse of a special skill or a position of trust.*

"Abuse of a special skill" sounds a lot like in-depth knowledge of a company's information systems and networks, while "a position of trust" could certainly be interpreted to mean the IT staff who have access to these systems and networks.

Section 806 provides a little relief for the IT staff and others with a conscience. This is the whistleblower protection clause. Any public company that is required to file with the Securities and Exchange Commission is prohibited from "discharging, demoting, suspending, threatening, harassing, or discriminating" against an employee because of a lawful action they took, such as providing accurate information during an investigation.[96] An employee who was mistreated has the right to file a complaint with the Secretary of Labor or a district court of the United States. The complaint must be filed within 90 days of the ill treatment. Compensatory damages include reinstatement with the same seniority status, back pay with interest, and compensation for any special damages sustained as a result of the discrimination, including litigation costs, expert witness fees, and reasonable attorney fees.

Section 906 repeats the requirement for corporate officers to certify the accuracy of financial reports and imposes stiff penalties — $1 million to $5 million and 10 to 20 years in jail — for certifying reports they know have been falsified.

Why is there so much interest in internal controls? Congress wants to ensure that the annual financial reports submitted by publicly traded companies are accurate and complete; hence, the Sarbanes-Oxley Act mandates (1) robust internal controls and (2) stiff penalties when they are not followed. Internal controls are a mechanism to implement and enforce honest and transparent financial reporting. This is another way of telling corporations that they are expected to practice due diligence in regard to information integrity. Some postulate that if internal controls, like those required by the Sarbanes-Oxley Act, had been in place earlier, they may have detected and prevented, or at least minimized, the Bearings Bank/Nick Leeson fraud and the Allied Irish Bank/Allfirst fraud.[260] A lot of different types of people and organizations make important business and investment decisions based on these financial reports, such as employees, creditors, customers, business associates, suppliers, investors, etc. They have a right to expect that these reports are accurate and complete. Also, you would hope that the board of directors of a company would want accurate numbers on which to make long-term strategic plans and short-term tactical decisions. Not to mention that if the "cooking the books" scandal had been allowed to continue unabated, it would have led to an economic meltdown of the industrialized nations.

Concerns about information integrity are not limited to annual financial reports. Information fuels each country's national economy, security, and stability. Decision makers at all levels of society need to have confidence in the integrity of information upon which they make decisions. In the absence of information integrity, intelligent, correct, and timely decisions cannot be made at any level in an organization, and eventually the organization is unable to perform its mission. In simple terms, information integrity implies that the information is "fit" for its intended use. There are several aspects to information integrity, which encompasses the characteristics of data integrity, information systems integrity, communications integrity, and the integrity of the operational procedures used to capture, enter, manipulate, store, and report information. In summary, information integrity is the condition that exists when data is unchanged from its source, it is accurate, complete, consistent, and has not been subject to accidental or malicious unauthorized addition, deletion, modification, or destruction.[71, 100, 156]

For annual financial reports (and other information) to be accurate, reliable, and complete, the appropriate checks and balances must be in place to guarantee the integrity of the data, information systems, communications networks, and operational procedures that are used to produce them. All of the raw, processed, generated, and stored data must be correct and complete — no duplicate, erroneous, bogus, or out-of-date data. Likewise, data cannot be corrupted when transmitted from one location to another. All the steps taken to produce a report, including all calculations and operations performed on the data, must be correct and complete. Data from one division cannot be ignored by a software program simply because it shows a loss. Data from another division cannot be counted twice simply because it shows a profit. Assets cannot be reported as showing a 10 percent increase in value when the actual increase was 1 percent. These are the internal controls referred to in the Sarbanes-Oxley Act; they are to prevent accidental and intentional errors from being introduced at any time, whether from internal or external sources, in the data, information systems, networks, and operational procedures.

A variety of formal methodologies exist that define a set of internal controls and how to assess compliance with them. Some of these methodologies or frameworks address the broader concept of enterprise risk management, as discussed in the Basel II Accords[63, 66, 66a, 67] and the Committee of the Sponsoring

Organizations of the Treadway Commission or COSO Guidelines, issued by the American Institute of Certified Public Accountants. Others focus more directly on internal controls related to the design, development, implementation and operation of IT systems, such as:

- Control Objectives for Information and Related Technologies (COBIT), issued by the IT Governance Institute and the Information Systems Audit and Control Association (ISACA)
- ISO/IEC 17799 (2000-12) — Information Technology — Code of practice for information security management
- IT Control Objectives for Sarbanes-Oxley, issued by the IT Governance Institute, April 2004
- ISO 9000 Compendium

To its credit, the Sarbanes-Oxley Act does not mandate a particular internal control methodology. The message to corporations is that they are responsible for selecting a methodology, implementing it, justifying why that particular methodology was selected, and proving that it was and is being followed. The main thing is to use common sense. A corporation knows its business, company, people, procedures, standards, strengths, and weaknesses better than anyone else. As a result, a corporation is in the strongest position to select the methodology that is best for it. Perhaps it is one of the methodologies listed above; then again, maybe a methodology developed in-house will work better.

A series of integrity control points can be identified if we look at the timeline or chronology of financial data. (The timeline and integrity control points are applicable to other types of data as well.) As shown in Table 3.3, there are four major phases in the financial data timeline: (1) data capture, (2) data aggregation and manipulation, (3) data reporting, and (4) data storage, archiving, and destruction. These phases are repeated numerous times before the data is permanently archived and eventually destroyed. A set of discrete integrity control points is associated with each phase. A control objective should be defined for each integrity control point that includes both proactive control activities that will prevent internal controls from being violated and reactive control activities that will detect attempted or actual violations of internal controls.[240] When documenting control objectives, control activities, and verification techniques, keep in mind that they need to be written so that they are understandable by external auditors.[240]

The first integrity control point occurs when raw data enters an information system. This can occur in a variety of ways at diverse locations. To illustrate, consider a corporate checking account. Raw data for the account can be generated through direct deposits, deposits made in person at a bank branch, checks written against the account, automatic bill payment debits, ATM withdrawals, use of a debit card, and interest credited to the account. Some of these sources are trustworthy; others are more prone to errors and misuse. Some of the raw data only exists in electronic form and is transmitted across multiple systems and networks before it reaches the host bank; the rest

Table 3.3　Integrity Control Points throughout the Financial Data Timeline

Phase	Integrity Control Points	Issues
Data capture	Raw data entered into information system Raw data validated against (hardcopy) source information Corrections are made, if needed Validated data is stored online	Integrity of the source of the raw data Accuracy of raw data Who is authorized to enter, edit, view, store, and validate data Need audit trail of all access to data Internal quality control procedures
Data aggregation and manipulation	Operations are performed on the data or it is combined with other stored data New information is generated	Many different data streams may feed into a single operation Many operations may take place on the data before a report is generated Need for audit trail, sanity checks of new results, and roll-back capability Internal quality control procedures
Data reporting	Select data results are printed or output electronically for periodic reports Internal review of reports Distribution of reports to stakeholders	Correctness of the software functions Correctness of the IT security features and operational security procedures Completeness and effectiveness of configuration management practices Internal quality control procedures
Data storage, archiving, and destruction	Data is maintained in online storage Current data is stored in backup offsite archives Old data is stored in permanent archives for the required time period Data no longer needed is destroyed	Access controls to online storage Access controls to archives Integrity of backup media and procedures Proper data retention, no premature data destruction Internal quality control procedures

originated as paper and is read or keyed in somewhere along the line. Regardless, all the raw data needs to be validated before it is posted to the corporate account; this is the second integrity control point. Most banks have procedures in place whereby all transactions are triple-verified before they are accepted as legitimate. They also perform sanity checks on transactions and compare them against what is considered to be normal activity for an account. For example, if a $50 million direct deposit suddenly shows up in an account and the largest previous direct deposit was $1 million, most likely some alarms will be triggered. If any errors are detected, such as duplicate entries or transposed digits, they are corrected before the data is accepted as valid. Separation of duties is a major part of the internal controls for data capture. Separation of duties involves not only limiting access, but also creating separate user roles for who can enter, edit, view, store, validate, and delete data before and after it is posted to an account. A robust multi-thread audit trail function complements this effort to ensure that internal controls are not being bypassed or tampered with.

Integrity control points are also necessary when data is being aggregated and manipulated. The accuracy of the calculations and operations performed on the data must be verified regularly. Debits and credits need to be posted only once and only during the valid reporting period. Debits and credits need to be posted in the order that they occurred and to the correct account. Interest and other calculations need to be performed correctly. In essence, what we are talking about here is software reliability. This is no small challenge for a large distributed corporation with multiple divisions, groups, and subsidiaries who are all capturing and reporting data at different levels of aggregation, at different times, and on different systems and networks. The more systems and networks the data traverses, the greater the chance that the data has been corrupted, accidentally or intentionally by insiders or outsiders. This creates the need for robust access controls, audit trails, and confidentiality mechanisms. Regular sanity checks of the data should be required by operational procedures at various points in time. In addition, a rollback capability needs to be available in case significant errors are detected.

Reporting data creates the need for further integrity control points. Certain data is selected to be reported and other data is not. Basically, the report provides a snapshot in time because most financial data is extremely dynamic. There must be a check to verify that this is the correct data to report and that the data and report are complete and accurate. This involves, among other things, verifying that the data is what it is claimed to be in the report and not a subset or other variation of the data. Again, software reliability is an issue, but so are the operational procedures by which the data was selected, generated, and reported. Configuration management and patch management have a definite role to play in maintaining system integrity. All reports should undergo an internal quality control review to verify their accuracy, completeness, and currency before they are released to the public.

Active data is stored online and in off-site backups. Old data is archived and eventually destroyed when by law it no longer needs to be retained. During all of these phases, the integrity of the data, backup media, backup procedures, and restoral procedures must be ensured. This involves (1) controlling electronic and physical access to the data, (2) controlling what authorized users can and cannot do to and with the data, and (3) verifying the integrity of the backup media and procedures regularly. There are legal requirements for how long financial records must be kept. Consequently, operational procedures need to ensure that data is retained as long as required, but not necessarily any longer.

The above are examples of generic integrity control points. Internal control objectives and activities need to be defined for each integrity control point. In addition, be sure to define techniques that can be used by internal and external auditors to verify that the internal controls are working — techniques that demonstrate that attempts to disable or bypass internal controls are detected and prevented.

The following metrics can be used by corporations, internal auditors, external auditors, public interest groups, and others to measure the extent of compliance with the Sarbanes-Oxley Act.

Section 104

Evaluation of a company's quality control procedures, using the following scale: 1.2.1

0 – procedures do not exist or are not documented
1 – procedures are under development
2 – procedures are missing one or more key elements and/or they are out of date, they do not reflect the current system
3 – procedures are current, but are missing some minor information or contain minor errors
4 – procedures are complete, correct, comprehensive, and current

Frequency of training and other activities related to communicating the company's quality control procedures, by fiscal year: 1.2.2

a. Date of most recent activity
b. Percentage of target population reached by these activities

Section 201

Number of times a public accounting firm attempted to or actually did engage in non-audit services for a client, by fiscal year: 1.2.3

a. Dollar amount per event (actual or potential)
b. Distribution of total events per client

Sections 302 and 906

Number of times since 2002 a company submitted a financial report: 1.2.4

a. That was not certified by the appropriate corporate officers
b. That was later found to contain false, misleading, or incomplete information
c. That failed to a contain a current assessment of the company's internal controls

Number of times since 2002 a company: 1.2.5

a. Failed to assess their internal controls within 90 days of preparing a financial report
b. Did not report known deficiencies in their internal controls

    c. Did not report changes made to their internal controls that may have affected the accuracy of financial reports

Number of fraudulent activities committed during the reporting period: 1.2.6
    a. By employees
    b. By consultants, contractors, suppliers, or external maintenance staff
    c. By other outsiders
    d. Distribution by type of fraudulent activity

Section 401

Number of public disclosures of financial figures that were later found to be inaccurate, misleading, or incomplete by fiscal year: 1.2.7
    a. Distribution by company

Section 404

Number of times, by fiscal year, a company's financial report: 1.2.8
    a. Failed to acknowledge the corporate officers' responsibility for internal controls
    b. Failed to include an independent auditor's attestation that the current assessment of the company's internal controls is accurate and complete

Number of deficiencies found during current assessment of internal controls:
                                                  1.2.9
    a. Date of assessment
    b. Distribution of deficiencies by severity
    c. Distribution of deficiencies by type and control objective
    d. Percentage of deficiencies corrected prior to generating current financial report
    e. Average time to correct deficiencies

Number and percentage of control objectives for which: 1.2.10
    a. No proactive preventive control activities are defined, or those defined are erroneous
    b. No reactive detective control activities are defined, or those defined are erroneous
    c. No verification techniques are defined, or those defined are erroneous
    d. No evidence was generated as proof the internal control is being followed and works

Number and percentage of companies whose internal controls failed to, and distribution by company: 1.2.11
    a. Prevent duplicate data from being entered
    b. Prevent data from any internal or external source from being accepted by an information system without first being validated

    c. Prevent out-of-date data from being included in a report
    d. Enforce access controls to systems, networks, data, archives, and hard-copy information
    e. Maintain complete multi-thread audit trails
    f. Maintain data confidentiality while sensitive financial data was entered, processed, stored online, stored offline, or transmitted
    g. Verify the reliability and security of the software used to produce financial reports
    h. Verify the reliability and security of the corporate telecommunications infrastructure used to produce financial reports
    i. Enforce configuration and patch management procedures
    j. Enforce operational security procedures
    k. Enforce data retention requirements
    l. Trigger alarms when non-normal activity occurred
    m. Perform sanity checks on data before including them in a calculation
    n. Provide a rollback capability, in case significant data or operational errors are detected
    o. Verify that all relevant data is included in the calculations and other operations used to produce financial reports
    p. Verify backup data, backup media, backup procedures, and restoral procedures
    q. Verify physical security controls
    r. Verify personnel security controls
    s. Verify operational security controls

Sections 802 and 1101

Number of times, by fiscal year, that fines and jail sentences were imposed for altering, destroying, mutilating, concealing, or falsifying financial records:

1.2.12

    a. Distribution by company
    b. Distribution by single offense versus multiple offenses per event

Section 806

Number of complaints filed with the Secretary of Labor and/or U.S. District Courts by employees against companies for ill treatment as a result of lawfully cooperating with an investigation into the company's finances, by fiscal year:

1.2.13

    a. Distribution by company
    b. Percentage of complaints that were upheld

HEALTHCARE

Two regulations have been issued in North America to date to protect the security and privacy of healthcare information; they are examined next.

3.4 Health Insurance Portability and Accountability Act (HIPAA) — United States

The Health Insurance Portability and Accountability Act, known as HIPAA, was passed by Congress in August 1996. Healthcare reform was a major goal of the Clinton administration and this is one of the outcomes. There were concerns about an individual having the right to transfer medical insurance from one employer to another and continue medical insurance after ending employment with a given employer, while at the same time protecting the privacy of medical records as they were being transferred among physicians, hospitals, clinics, pharmacies, and insurance companies. Concurrently, due to spiraling costs, there was a recognized need to make the whole healthcare industry more efficient. For example, one provision of the bill concerns the use of standardized data elements for medical procedures, diagnosis, tests, prescriptions, invoicing, payment, etc. Some see this as a first step to the federal government's broader vision of E-prescriptions, accessible E-health records, E-invoicing, and E-payments.[206] Specifically, as the preamble to the bill states, Congress felt it necessary to[80]:

> ... *improve the portability and continuity of health insurance coverage in the group and individual markets, to combat waste, fraud, and abuse in health insurance and healthcare delivery, to promote medical savings accounts, to improve access to long-term care services and coverage, and to simplify the administration of health insurance.*

HIPAA was codified by the Department of Health and Human Services (HHS) by amending 45 CFR Parts 160, 162, and 164. Two separate rules were issued, the Security Standards Final Rule[81] and the Standards for the Privacy of Individually Identifiable Health Information Final Rule.[82] The healthcare industry had plenty of time, almost a decade, to prepare for implementing the requirements of these rules. Compliance with the Privacy Rule was required not later than April 2004, while compliance with the Security Rule was required by April 2005 for medium and large organizations and by April 2006 for small organizations. This ten-year ramp-up time may explain in part why there has been less vocal opposition to HIPAA than other security and privacy regulations. Another likely reason is the fact that HIPAA provisions represent mostly common-sense best practices that the healthcare industry should be doing already.[206] Or as De Brino states, HIPAA is "an important jolt to move healthcare IT into the 21st century."[130] HIPAA applies to the healthcare industry across the board[81]:

- Medical health plans
- Healthcare providers (physicians, clinics, hospitals, pharmacies)
- Healthcare clearinghouses (organizations that process and maintain medical records)

HIPAA defines some clear-cut terminology in regard to security and privacy requirements and their implementation. Let us take a moment to understand these terms.

Protected health information: individually identifiable health information that is transmitted by electronic media, maintained by electronic media, or created, received, maintained, or transmitted in any other form or medium.[81]

The definition of protected health information is very broad and includes any type or any format of record that contains medical information that can be associated with a certain individual. The only such records that are excluded are those maintained by an employer, such as a pre-employment physical, and those maintained by an educational institution, such as proof of vaccinations.

Access: the ability or the means necessary to read, write, modify, or communicate data/information or otherwise use any system resource.[81]

Disclosure: release, transfer, provision of, access to, or divulging in any other manner of information outside the healthcare care entity holding the information.[81]

Use: sharing, employment, application, utilization, examination, or analysis of information within a healthcare entity that maintains such information.[81]

As we will see, HIPAA restricts access, disclosure, and use of personal health information. The definition of access is not limited to viewing a record. Instead, the definition includes any method of interaction with personal health information or the supporting IT infrastructure. The definition of disclosure deserves close attention as well. Note that it refers to divulging personal health information in any manner by any entity that holds the information. This includes the verbal release of information, such as reading from a report or database over the telephone. The definition refers to any entity that holds the information, not just the one that originated it. This is an important distinction because it assigns responsibility to all holders of the information. The definition of use implies any type of activity that can be performed on or with personal health information. Again, the responsibility for monitoring and controlling use of such information remains with the entity that holds it, not the source who originated it. That is, HIPAA does not allow for any passing of the buck when it comes to responsibility for implementing security and privacy requirements.

Administrative safeguards: administrative actions, and policies and procedures, to manage the selection, development, implementation, and maintenance of security measures to protect electronic protected health information and to manage the conduct of the healthcare entity's workforce in relation to the protection of that information.[81]

Several publications speak of administrative controls or safeguards, but the HIPAA Security Rule is the first to really define this term. "Administrative safeguards" is a synonym for operational security. Every procedure related to the specification, design, development, deployment, operation, and maintenance of an information system or network is included. Note that the definition covers all system life-cycle phases and all people processes and interaction with the system.

Now we will look at the provisions of the final Security Rule.

Security Rule

Before getting into specifics, HIPAA states some ground rules concerning responsibility for the security requirements in the bill. In summary, healthcare entities are to[81]:

- Ensure the confidentiality, integrity, and availability of all electronic protected health information they create, receive, maintain, or transmit
- Protect against anticipated threats or hazards to the security or integrity of such information
- Protect against anticipated uses or disclosures of such information that are not permitted or required
- Ensure compliance by its workforce with all provisions in the bill

HIPAA does not mandate specific technical solutions; rather, the bill states implementation independent requirements and lets the healthcare entity design the solution. It is expected that the implementation of HIPAA security requirements will be tailored based on the[81]:

- Size, complexity, and capabilities of the healthcare entity
- Healthcare entity's technical infrastructure, hardware, and software security capabilities
- Likelihood and severity of potential risks to electronic protected health information
- Cost of security measures

In the final rule, security requirements are designated as being "required" or "addressable." Healthcare entities must implement required security requirements. HIPAA gives healthcare entities some flexibility in regard to addressable requirements. In effect, the rule is saying that we think you should do this. However, if after a healthcare entity analyzes the requirement, they devise an alternate approach that accomplishes the same goal or determine that the requirement is not applicable to their situation, they do not have to implement it. The healthcare entity does have to document the rationale and justification for whatever action they take in response to addressable requirements.

Requirements in the final security rule are grouped into three categories: (1) administrative safeguards (operational security controls), which are specified in § 164.308; (2) physical safeguards (physical security controls), which are specified in § 164.310; and (3) technical safeguards (IT security controls), which are specified in § 164.312. No personnel security controls are stated. HIPAA requires healthcare entities to maintain documentary evidence that they have performed the activities stated in the security rule. For example, all policies and procedures required by the administrative, physical, and technical safeguards are to be documented and made available to all personnel who are responsible for implementing them. Policies and procedures are to be reviewed and updated on a regular schedule. All activities required by the administrative, physical, and technical safeguards, such as assessments, are to be documented by the healthcare entity. All documentation is to be maintained for six years from the date of creation or the date last in effect, whichever is later. Documentation can be maintained in hardcopy or electronic form.

Table 3.4 lists the HIPAA administrative security safeguards. Administrative safeguards are specified as an overall statement or goal. Most, but not all, administrative safeguards are described in further detail through a series of subtasks, which are either required or addressable. When a safeguard is specified without any accompanying subtasks, the safeguard is required. The HIPAA Security Rule contains a total of nine safeguards and twenty-one subtasks for administrative security controls.

Table 3.4   HIPAA Administrative Security Safeguards

Safeguard and Subtasks	Implementation Specification	Required (R) or Addressable (A)
Security Management: implement policies and procedures to prevent, detect, contain, and correct security violations		
Risk analysis	Conduct an accurate and thorough assessment of the potential risks and vulnerabilities to the confidentiality, integrity, and availability of electronic protected health information held by the healthcare entity	R
Risk management	Implement sufficient security measures to reduce risks and vulnerabilities to a reasonable and appropriate level	R
Sanction	Apply appropriate sanctions against workforce members who fail to comply with the security policies and procedures of the covered entity	R
Information system activity review	Implement procedures to regularly review records of information system activity, such as audit logs, access reports, and security incident tracking reports	R
Assigned Security Responsibility: identify the security official for the healthcare entity who is responsible for the development and implementation of the required policies and procedures		
Workforce Security: implement policies and procedures to ensure that all members of the workforce have appropriate access to electronic protected health information and prevent those workforce members who do not have access from obtaining access to electronic protected health information		

Table 3.4   HIPAA Administrative Security Safeguards (continued)

Safeguard and Subtasks	Implementation Specification	Required (R) or Addressable (A)
Authorization and supervision	Implement procedures for the authorization and supervision of workforce members who work with electronic protected health information or in locations where it might be accessed	A
Workforce clearance procedure	Implement procedures to determine that the access of a workforce member to electronic protected health information is appropriate	A
Termination procedures	Implement procedures for terminating access to electronic protected health information when the employment of a workforce member ends or is no longer needed	A
Information Access Management: implement policies and procedures for authorizing access to electronic protected health information		
Isolating healthcare clearinghouse functions	If a healthcare clearinghouse is part of a larger organization, the clearinghouse must implement policies and procedures that protect the electronic protected health information of the clearinghouse from unauthorized access by the larger organization	R
Access authorization	Implement policies and procedures for granting access to electronic protected health information, for example, through access to a workstation, transaction, program, process, or other mechanism	A
Access establishment and modification	Implement policies and procedures to establish, document, review, and modify a user's right of access to a workstation, transaction, program, or process	A
Security Awareness and Training: implement a security awareness and training program for all members of the workforce, including management		
Security reminders	Periodic security updates, such as e-mail, posters, and all-hands meetings	A
Protection from malicious software	Procedures for guarding against, detecting, and reporting malicious software	A
Log-in monitoring	Procedures for monitoring log-in attempts and reporting discrepancies	A
Password management	Procedures for creating, changing, and safeguarding passwords	A

Table 3.4   HIPAA Administrative Security Safeguards (continued)

Safeguard and Subtasks	Implementation Specification	Required (R) or Addressable (A)
Security Incident Procedures: implement policies and procedures to address preventing and handling security incidents		
Response and reporting	Identify and respond to suspected or known security incidents; mitigate, to the extent practicable, harmful effects of security incidents that are known, and document security incidents and their outcomes	R
Contingency Plan: establish and implement as needed policies and procedures for responding to an emergency or other occurrence, for example, fire, vandalism, system failure, and natural disaster, that damages systems that contain electronic protected health information		
Data backup plan	Establish and implement procedures to create and maintain retrievable exact copies of electronic protected health information	R
Disaster recovery plan	Establish and implement procedures to restore loss of data	R
Emergency mode operation plan	Establish and implement procedures to enable continuation of critical business processes for protection of the security of electronic protected health information while operating in emergency mode	R
Testing and revision	Implement procedures for periodic testing and revision of contingency plans	A
Applications and data criticality analysis	Assess the relative criticality of specific applications and data in support of other contingency plan components	A
Evaluation: perform periodic technical and nontechnical evaluations that establish the extent to which an entity's security policies and procedures are compliant with the Act		
Business Associate Contracts and Other Arrangements: a healthcare entity may permit a business associate to create, receive, maintain, or transmit electronic protected health information on their behalf only if satisfactory assurances are obtained that the business associate will appropriately safeguard this information		
Written contract or other arrangement	Document the satisfactory assurances required through a written contract or other arrangement with the business associate	R

Security management is the first administrative safeguard mentioned. Activities that contribute to preventing, detecting, containing, and correcting security violations fall into this category. All four subtasks associated with security management are required; given the importance of security management functions, this is to be expected. The healthcare entity is to conduct regular risk analyses to identify potential risks to the confidentiality, integrity, and availability of the electronic protected health information it holds. These risks are not limited to technology; they can be operational, environmental, physical, contractual, organizational, or technical in nature. The results from the risk analyses are used to guide the selection and implementation of appropriate risk mitigation measures. The effectiveness of these measures is monitored and evaluated by ongoing reviews of system audit trails, activity logs, and security incident reports. If need be, risk mitigation measures are modified based on observations from this information. Finally, the security management safeguard addresses people issues. If members of the workforce do not follow established security policies and procedures, they are to be sanctioned. The term "workforce" refers to employees, consultants, contractors, vendors, and external maintenance engineers.

The second administrative safeguard, *assigned security responsibility,* does not have any subtasks associated with it. This safeguard requires that the healthcare entity designate an individual as its overall security official. Nothing is said about the rank of this official or where he fits into the organization's hierarchy. The security official is ultimately responsible and accountable for developing and implementing the security policies and procedures required by HIPAA.

The third administrative safeguard is *workforce security.* This safeguard is designed to ensure the definition and implementation of appropriate access control rights and privileges relative to protected health information. The three subtasks associated with workforce security are addressable, probably because the size and geographic distribution of an organization have a major influence on the implementation of these requirements. Access to protected health information by members of the workforce is to be supervised and monitored. Each type of access to protected health information by individuals must be specifically authorized, as well as the types of actions they can perform once that access is given. Healthcare entities must implement procedures to determine and periodically verify that access control rights and privileges are appropriate for each individual — their rights are neither too broad nor too narrow for their assigned job responsibilities. No mention is made of a requirement for separation of duties. Likewise, procedures are to be implemented to ensure that access control rights and privileges are terminated when an individual no longer needs access or has left the organization. The security rule does not establish a fixed time frame for terminating access control rights and privileges; however, to be consistent with the risk control subtask in the security management safeguard, it is fair to assume that this must be done quickly.

The fourth administrative safeguard is *information access management.* The workforce security safeguard above dealt with the people side of controlling access to protected health information. In contrast, this safeguard addresses the technical and operational aspects of access control. The first subtask of this safeguard is required. Occasionally, healthcare entities are part of a large diverse corporation that may or may not share a common IT infrastructure. In that instance, the healthcare entity is required to ensure and demonstrate that other parts of the corporation cannot access any personal health information held by the healthcare entity. This separation or isolation of information can be accomplished through a combination of logical and physical access control mechanisms. The other two subtasks for this safeguard are addressable. The healthcare entity is responsible for implementing mechanisms to control access to workstations, servers, networks, transactions, programs, processes, data records, archives, etc. Again, a combination of logical and physical access control mechanisms can be implemented to accomplish this objective. In addition, documented procedures are to be in place that define (1) how access control rights and privileges are determined for an individual or other system resource, (2) how often access control rights and privileges are reviewed and validated and by whom, and (3) how access control rights and privileges are changed or updated and who has the authority to authorize this.

The fifth administrative safeguard is *security awareness and training*. This safeguard applies to all members of the workforce, including management. Members of the workforce are to receive regular reminders of the importance of following security policies, procedures, and practices and their responsibility for doing so. These reminders may take the form of friendly e-mail reminders, motivational posters, and all-hands meetings. The security awareness and training safeguard also extends into operational practices. For example, the healthcare entity is responsible for implementing measures to protect against malicious software and its spread, including a capability to detect and report instances of malware. Attempts to log on to the healthcare entity's systems and networks are to be monitored for normal and abnormal events. Suspicious activity, such as repeated failed log-on attempts are to trigger special reports. To help prevent invalid access to protected health information, policies and procedures should be in place that explain what constitutes a valid password, how often passwords have to be changed, and how the password file itself is to be protected. All four of these subtasks are addressable.

Continuing in the same vein, the next safeguard concerns *security incident prevention and handling procedures* that are required. The healthcare entity is responsible for preventing attacks from becoming successful security incidents by implementing effective mitigation measures. These mitigation measures may include a combination of operational, environmental, physical, and technical security controls. Healthcare entities must identify and respond to known or suspected security incidents. In addition, they are to document all security incidents, their response, and the resultant consequences. Unfortunately, the Security Rule is silent on the matter of notifying HHS or, more importantly, the individuals involved of any potential compromises of protected health information; this is a major oversight. Also, it would probably be a good idea to notify business associates when systems, networks, or data are compromised.

The *contingency planning* safeguard is next. In short, a healthcare entity is responsible for planning and preparing for any natural or man-made contingency or disaster situation that could affect systems and networks that process or maintain protected health information. This safeguard consists of five subtasks; the first three are required, while the last two are addressable. Healthcare entities are to have plans and procedures in place for creating and maintaining regular data backups. They are also responsible for verifying the data recovery procedures and that the backup data is accurate. Healthcare entities are to have contingency and disaster recovery plans and procedures in place to prevent the loss of any data. No specific time frames are specified regarding how quickly system resources and data need to be restored; this is left for each healthcare entity to determine for itself. Emergency operation plans are to be developed as well, to ensure that the healthcare entity can continue to operate critical business functions and protect personal health information during emergency situations. The goal is to maintain continuity of operations, albeit on a smaller scale perhaps, during a major crisis until full system functionality can be restored. Depending on the size of an organization, this may involve switching to geographically dispersed backup sites. While preparing data backup plans, contingency and disaster recovery plans, and emergency operations plans, healthcare entities are to take the time to determine the relative criticality of specific applications and data to their operations. Not all data, systems, and networks are as critical to an organization's operations. As such, assets should be classified as critical, essential, or routine in order prioritize restoral, recovery, and backup activities. Data backup plans, contingency and disaster recovery plans, and emergency operation plans are not to just sit on the bookshelf. It is expected that the healthcare entity will regularly practice and update these plans.

The eighth administrative safeguard concerns *evaluations*. This safeguard does not have any subtasks associated with it. A healthcare entity is expected to conduct regular assessments to evaluate the extent of its compliance with the provisions of the Security Rule. These assessments may be done by internal auditors, external auditors, or a combination of both. The results of the audits are to be documented, along with any corrective action taken to resolve outstanding issues.

The last administrative safeguard addresses relationships between a healthcare entity and its business associates. This is not surprising because, if you recall, the terms defined above referred to entities that held, not originated, protected health information. This provision is quite clear — that the healthcare entity is responsible for passing along to all business associates the complete set of provisions in the Security Rule, preferably through written contractual means. If both parties are government agencies, this arrangement can be formalized through a memorandum of agreement (MOA) instead. Once this arrangement is in place, the healthcare entity may permit a business associate to create, receive, maintain, or transmit protected health information on its behalf. The healthcare entity retains responsibility for monitoring its business associate's compliance with these provisions. The business associate is responsible for reporting all security incidents to the healthcare entity. If any violations of the Security Rule are discovered, the healthcare entity must immediately take steps to remedy the situation. If a material breach or pattern of noncompliant activity occurs, the healthcare entity is expected to terminate the business relationship. If for some reason the relationship cannot be terminated in a timely manner, the healthcare entity must notify the Secretary of HHS promptly.

Table 3.5 lists the HIPAA physical security safeguards. Like administrative safeguards, physical safeguards are specified as an overall statement or goal.

Table 3.5   HIPAA Physical Security Safeguards

Safeguard and Subtasks	Implementation Specifications	Required (R) or Addressable (A)
Facility Access Controls: implement policies and procedures to limit physical access to electronic protected health information systems and the facility or facilities in which they are housed, while ensuring that properly authorized access is allowed		
Contingency operations	Establish and implement procedures that allow facility access in support of restoration of lost data under the disaster recovery plan and emergency mode operations plan in the event of an emergency	A
Facility security plan	Implement policies and procedures to safeguard the facility and the equipment therein from unauthorized physical access, tampering, and theft	A
Access control and validation	Implement procedures to control and validate a person's access to facilities based on their role or function, including visitor control, and control of access to software programs for testing and revision	A
Maintenance records	Implement policies and procedures to document repairs and modifications to the physical components of a facility which are related to security, for example, hardware, walls, doors, and locks	A
Workstation Use: implement policies and procedures that specify the proper functions to be performed, the manner in which those functions are to be performed, and the physical attributes of the surroundings of a specific workstation or class of workstation that can access electronic protected health information		
Workstation Security: implement physical safeguards for all workstations that access electronic protected health information, to restrict access to authorized users		
Device and Media Controls: implement policies and procedures that govern the receipt and removal of hardware and electronic media that contain electronic protected health information into and out of a facility, and the movement of these items within the facility		
Disposal	Implement policies and procedures to address the final disposition of electronic protected health information, and/or the hardware or electronic media on which it is stored	R
Media reuse	Implement procedures for removal of electronic protected health information from electronic media before the media are made available for re-use	R

Table 3.5   HIPAA Physical Security Safeguards (continued)

Safeguard and Subtasks	Implementation Specifications	Required (R) or Addressable (A)
Accountability	Maintain a record of the movements of hardware and electronic media and the person responsible for the movement	A
Data backup and storage	Create a retrievable, exact copy of electronic protected health information, when needed, before movement of equipment	A

Two physical safeguards are described in further detail through a series of subtasks, which are either required or addressable. Safeguards that are specified without any accompanying subtasks are required. The HIPAA Security Rule contains a total of four safeguards and eight subtasks for physical security controls.

As expected, the first physical security safeguard concerns *controlling access to facilities*. Healthcare entities are to implement policies and procedures to limit physical access to systems and networks that contain electronic protected health information, as well as the facility or facilities that house them. These policies and procedures are to be spelled out in a facility security plan. Document procedures for validating an individual's physical access to a facility, equipment room, and specific IT equipment in the facility security plan. Also describe how these practices differ for employees, contractors, vendors, business associates, and other categories of visitors and how tampering and theft of equipment will be prevented. Likewise, devise a method to determine what physical access rights an individual should have based on his role, function, and relationship to the healthcare entity. These rights may change over time, so they must be revalidated periodically. To illustrate, as an employee, John Smith may have one set of physical access rights. Assume that he leaves the healthcare entity and accepts employment with a vendor who performs preventive and corrective maintenance on hardware hosting protected health information. At this point, he would have different physical access rights and may even need an escort. This situation occasionally causes problems; some people may not know that John has ended his employment with the healthcare entity and assume he still has his former physical access rights. Hence, the need for (1) keeping physical access rights current, and (2) consistent verification and enforcement of physical access rights. It is also important to keep track of components that establish physical security perimeters, such as video monitoring, turnstiles, barrier walls, doors, equipment cabinets, and locks. Repairs and modifications to these components could disrupt a physical security perimeter, accidentally or intentionally. As a result, it is a good idea to keep track of what repairs and modifications were made, who made them, and by whom and when the repairs and modifications were verified. Otherwise, the organization might be in for some surprises. Contingency planning is all about being prepared for the unexpected. As part of this planning effort, consider how different emergency scenarios might alter what physical access rights are needed and how physical access rights will be verified and enforced. There is never much time to think about these things when a disaster strikes, so take the time to do so beforehand when everyone is still calm and collected.

The second physical security safeguard relates to *workstation use.* A healthcare entity is responsible for defining and implementing a comprehensive program to ensure that workstations that have access to protected health information are used properly. To start with, identify which workstations are and are not allowed to access protected health information. Do not forget to include laptops and other mobile devices in this discussion. Next, delineate what functions may and may not be performed on such workstations, and the circumstances under which they may be executed. Then clarify the physical configuration of these workstations relative to other system assets, interfaces, etc. For example, do these workstations have removable hard drives? Are users allowed to copy information to floppy disks, CDs, or memory sticks? If not, are these interfaces disabled? Do these workstations contain wireless interfaces or modems in addition to LAN interfaces? How is use of wireless interfaces and modems controlled? Is information displayed on a user's screen readable from a distance? Do the workstations have their own printers, or are shared printers used? What limits are placed on the production of hardcopies? Can the workstation be disconnected from the LAN and operated in stand-alone mode, bypassing network security? These are just some of the issues to evaluate when developing physical security measures for workstations.

Concurrently, a healthcare entity is responsible for controlling physical access to workstations by members of the workforce and others. This includes peripherals that may be connected to a workstation, such as printers, scanners, and external drives. For example, are workstations in a controlled access room? Are keyboards locked when workstations are not in use? Are network interfaces and cables secured? How easy is it to remove a workstation from a controlled space? Is an equipment inventory maintained? Is it kept current? How quickly is the fact that equipment is missing identified? What physical security measures are in place to prevent unauthorized IT equipment from being brought into a facility? What physical security measures are in place to detect attempted unauthorized physical access to a workstation or other IT equipment? How quickly are such attempts reported? What controls are in place to detect and prevent unauthorized personnel from gaining access to internal workstation hardware components? A variety of aspects of physical security must be considered when developing procedures to control access to workstations.

The final physical security safeguard concerns *protecting portable devices and media.* A healthcare entity is responsible for ensuring that robust policies and procedures are in place to account for all portable devices and media that enter and leave its premises. The intent, of course, is to make sure that no protected health information leaves the facility in an unauthorized manner, such as a hidden or personal CD or memory stick. This would imply that a healthcare entity is also responsible for monitoring the presence and use of portable recording devices on its premises. The motion picture industry is having a major problem in this area; let us hope that the healthcare industry is more successful. A good starting point is to maintain a record of all portable equipment and media, their current whereabouts and use (e.g., what buildings, rooms, and meetings they were taken to), and who had possession of them at the time. This practice should be applied to portable equipment and media the healthcare entity owns, as well as that brought in by vendors, business associates, and others. Some government agencies require visitors to deposit all portable electronic equipment and media in a safe at the entrance to the building, to prevent unauthorized recording of information. In some circumstances, it may make sense to add automatic detection of the presence of this type of equipment and media in high-sensitivity areas. When equipment is being relocated for legitimate business purposes, it may be advisable to make a copy of all protected health information, so that it can be restored quickly if necessary. Procedures should be in place to track all such copies and the ultimate destruction of fixed and portable storage media that contained protected health information, once it is no longer needed. Media and equipment that can be reused one or more times, prior to destruction, must be sanitized prior to each reuse. There are different levels and methods of sanitization, each of which yields a different probability that information can or cannot be recovered after sanitization and the amount of time required to do so. And the techniques vary, depending on the equipment and media being sanitized. The Security Rule does not specify a particular sanitization technique or level of confidence. It is fair to assume, however, that while NSA-level sanitization is probably not needed, something akin to that used by the financial industry would be appropriate. No, sending a file to the recycle bin does not even begin to address this requirement — deletion does not equal sanitization.

Table 3.6 summarizes the HIPAA technical security safeguards. Like physical safeguards, technical safeguards are specified as an overall statement or goal. Three technical safeguards are described in further detail through a series of subtasks, which are either required or addressable. When a safeguard is specified without any accompanying subtasks, the safeguard is required. The HIPAA Security Rule contains a total of five safeguards and seven subtasks for IT security controls.

The first technical safeguard concerns *access controls*. A healthcare entity is responsible for implementing technical solutions and operational procedures that ensure access to protected health information is limited to authorized individuals and software processes. Each user and process is to be assigned a unique user name or identification number that can be used to monitor and control their activities. Access controls must also be designed to permit authorized access to protected health information during emergency operational conditions. These requirements are required. There are also two addressable requirements: (1) terminating user accounts and sessions after a predefined interval of inactivity, and (2) encrypting protected health information.

Healthcare entities are responsible for employing a *robust and comprehensive audit capability* for all assets related to protected health information, such as systems, workstations, and networks. Information about specific resources accessed and activities performed is to be recorded and analyzed, in comparison

Table 3.6   HIPAA Technical Security Safeguards

Safeguard and Subtasks	Implementation Specifics	Required (R) or Addressable (A)
Access Control: implement technical policies and procedures for electronic information systems that maintain electronic protected health information to allow access only to those persons or software programs that have been granted access rights		
Unique user identification	Assign a unique name or number for identifying and tracking user identity	R
Emergency access procedure	Establish and implement procedures for obtaining electronic protected health information during an emergency	R
Automatic logoff	Implement electronic procedures that terminate an electronic session after a predetermined time of inactivity	A
Encryption and decryption	Implement a mechanism to encrypt and decrypt electronic protected health information	A
Audit Controls: implement hardware, software, or procedural mechanisms that record and examine activity in information systems that contain or use electronic protected health information		
Integrity: implement policies and procedures to protect electronic protected health information from improper alteration or destruction		
Mechanism to authenticate electronic protected health information	Implement electronic mechanisms to corroborate that electronic protected health information has not been altered or destroyed in an unauthorized manner	A
Person or Entity Authentication: implement procedures to verify that a person or entity seeking access to electronic protected health information is the one claimed		
Transmission Security: implement technical security measures to guard against unauthorized access to electronic protected health information that is being transmitted over an electronic communications network		
Integrity controls	Implement security measures to ensure that electronically transmitted electronic protected health information is not improperly modified without detection until disposed of	A
Encryption	Implement a mechanism to encrypt electronic protected health information whenever deemed appropriate	A

to access control rights and privileges and user roles. Audit logs fall under the category of information that must be maintained by a healthcare entity for six years.

Likewise, *rigorous technical solutions and operational procedures* are to be implemented by healthcare entities to protect and ensure the integrity of protected healthcare information. This is not an idle task. Suppose information in a medical record has been altered, accidentally or intentionally, prior to surgery or having a prescription filled. The results from a loss of data integrity in medical records could be catastrophic. Mechanisms are to be implemented that continually verify the integrity of protected health information from creation through destruction, ensuring that the information has not been accidentally or intentionally modified.

Reliable identification and authentication mechanisms are required to be implemented as well. Access control rights and privileges are ineffective unless preceded by reliable identification and authentication mechanisms. This requirement applies to software processes, internal and external systems, and human users that attempt to access protected health information.

The fifth technical safeguard concerns *transmission security*. Healthcare entities are required to implement technical solutions and operational procedures to protect health information from unauthorized access, modification, use, misappropriation, and destruction while it is transmitted over a network. This includes LANs, WANs, corporate intranets, and the Internet, whether through wired or wireless connections. Both prevention and detection capabilities are to be provided. To further this goal, healthcare entities are to consider encrypting protected healthcare information.

Now we will look at the provisions of the final HIPAA Privacy Rule.

Privacy Rule

The HIPAA Privacy Rule is not written with the same degree of clarity and specificity as the Security Rule. As a result, it is not easy to discern the exact privacy requirements. The discussion centers around uses and disclosures of protected health information: what is allowed, which uses and disclosures require authorization, and when an individual must be given an opportunity to agree or object. The Privacy Rule states what is allowed in general terms for different scenarios, similar to use cases but without the precision. Many circular references are included in this discussion. No distinction is made about disclosure mechanisms or media: verbal, hardcopy, fax, e-mail, Internet, intranet, microfilm, photography, sound recordings, etc. One is left to assume that the Privacy Rule applies to all disclosure mechanisms and media. The rule does not explicitly state what uses and disclosures are not allowed. In the end it is not clear whether the Privacy Rule is a "firewall" in which the rule set is to (1) allow all traffic (use and disclosure) that is not explicitly disallowed, or (2) disallow all traffic (use or disclosure) that is not explicitly allowed.

The Privacy Rule does not address penalties and enforcement issues. No mention is made of what is to be done to employees of a healthcare entity who violate the rule. What happens to a clinic that does not comply with the Privacy Rule? Are they subject to fines and prosecution? Is their license revoked?

Does someone go to jail? What rights do individuals whose privacy has been violated have? How do they exercise these rights? HIPAA fails to assign anyone the responsibility for educating the public about their rights under the bill. Instead, what usually happens is that an individual walks into a clinic or pharmacy only to be handed a stack of papers to sign with no explanation. The Department of Health and Human Services (HHS) is not a regulatory agency. The Food and Drug Administration (FDA), a component of HHS, has a regulatory responsibility for the safety and efficacy of pharmaceuticals, medical devices, the blood supply, processed food, etc. However, personal health information maintained by hospitals, clinics, labs, and insurance companies is not within their jurisdiction.

From personal experience it seems as if healthcare entities are complying with the requirement to make customers sign that they have received the entity's privacy practices. However, it is unclear that they are actually adhering to these practices. A while back I took a pet bird to the veterinarian for a respiratory infection. The veterinarian wrote a prescription for antibiotics. Because the clinic was new, the pharmacy was not open yet. I was instructed to dissolve one tablet in a gallon of water, to dilute it to the right strength, and make a new batch each day. So far, so good. Then I went to the (human) pharmacy. First I had to convince the pharmacist (a non-native English speaker) that my first name was not parakeet. Next he asked me how old my "child" was. I said four years. In horror he told me that this type of antibiotic is not for use by children under 12 years of age. In vain I tried to convince him the prescription was not for a child. Then he returned to the discussion about my first name being parakeet. Finally I suggested he call the doctor whose name was on the prescription. After that he shut up and gave me the five tablets, but only after I signed the privacy statement. Undoubtedly there is a record of forbidden antibiotics being sold to Parakeet Herrmann, age 4, floating around somewhere in cyberspace. Good thing the pharmacist did not ask me the "child's" weight — one half ounce!

The Privacy Rule expands the scope of HIPAA to include employer medical insurance plans. This is a much-needed provision, because many employers are rather cavalier about sending social security numbers and other personal information to medical insurance companies and others. Shortly after HIPAA was passed, most employers and insurance companies ceased to use social security numbers to identify individuals. The Privacy Rule also takes the time to define what constitutes individually identifiable health information[82]:

> *Information that is a subset of health information, including demographic information collected from an individual, and (1) is created or received by a health care provider, health plan, employer, or health care clearinghouse, and (2) relates to the past, present, or future physical or mental health, or condition of an individual; the provision of health care to an individual, or the past, present, or future payment for the provision of health care to an individual, and (a) that identifies the individual, or (b) with respect to which there is reasonable basis to believe the information can be used to identify the individual.*

This is a rather complete definition. However, I have not figured out how a record could contain information about an individual's *future* physical or mental condition, *future* treatment, or *future* payment. Planned future treatment perhaps, but not actual future treatment. Yes, I have read articles about tele-medicine, but it was not my understanding that tele-medicine extended into the future.

The HIPAA Privacy Rule starts with a general statement that a healthcare entity is permitted to use or disclose protected health information for treatment, payment, or healthcare operations, incident to a use or disclosure otherwise permitted or required, or to the individual, parent, or guardian. Disclosures are limited to the minimum amount of information necessary and, of course, this use or disclosure must not conflict with any other provisions of the rule. A discussion of organizational responsibilities follows. A healthcare plan or clearinghouse is prohibited from using or disclosing protected health information it creates or receives on behalf of another healthcare entity, or it violates the rule. Healthcare entities are responsible for designating and documenting organizational components that they exchange information with in order to conduct business. Healthcare entities are also responsible for ensuring that the proposed recipients of protected healthcare information, such as HMOs and group health plans, have sufficient policies and procedures in place to comply with the Privacy Rule. A healthcare entity may disclose protected health information for treatment activities of a healthcare provider, for payment, or if the individual already has a relationship with the second entity. Individual consent may be obtained by a healthcare entity before using or disclosing protected health information. Individual consent, however, does not override provisions of the rule that restrict use and disclosure. Healthcare entities are responsible for implementing reasonable safeguards to protect health information from accidental or intentional unauthorized use or disclosure.

In some situations, a healthcare entity must obtain consent from an individual prior to using or disclosing protected health information. A healthcare entity may not use or disclose protected health information without an authorization that is valid and the subsequent disclosure must be consistent with the authorization. An authorization is required for any use or disclosure of psychotherapy notes. An exception is allowed to carry out treatment, payment, or healthcare operations, for the training of psychotherapy professionals, or in response to legal action. An authorization is also required if the use or disclosure is for marketing purposes; if the healthcare entity receives any remuneration, that must be stated in the authorization. A healthcare entity cannot (1) withhold treatment if an individual refuses to sign an authorization, or (2) create compound authorizations from separate pieces of information for new or additional use or disclosure scenarios. An individual may revoke an authorization at any time, as long as it is in writing. Healthcare entities must retain copies of all signed authorizations. A valid authorization must contain the following information[82]:

- A description of the information to be used or disclosed
- Identification of the people authorized to make the disclosures or uses

- Statement of purpose of the use or disclosure
- An expiration date for the authorization
- Signature of the individual, parent, or guardian
- Statement of the individual's right to revoke the authorization and procedures for doing so
- Statement that the healthcare entity cannot withhold treatment for failing to sign an authorization
- The consequences of not signing an authorization
- Potential redisclosure of the information by the recipient

The individual must be given a copy of the signed authorization. An authorization is invalid if the expiration date has passed, it is not filled out completely, it has been revoked by the individual, or it contains false information.

A healthcare entity may use or disclose protected health information, provided that the individual is informed in advance of the use or disclosure and has the opportunity to agree to or prohibit or restrict the use or disclosure. In certain circumstances, it is not necessary to give the individual the opportunity to agree or object; for example, to report adverse events that are under the regulatory jurisdiction of the FDA, track FDA-regulated products, enable product recalls, repairs, or replacement, conduct post-marketing surveillance, or in research scenarios where the risk to an individual's privacy is minimal. However, the research organization is required to have an adequate plan in place to protect the information, destroy the unique identifiers at the earliest opportunity, and ensure that the information will not be redisclosed.

The Privacy Rule talks about permitted disclosures in terms of limited data sets. A limited data set may not contain[82]:

- Names
- Addresses
- Telephone numbers
- Fax numbers
- E-mail addresses
- Social security numbers
- Medical record numbers
- Health plan numbers
- Account numbers
- Vehicle license plate or serial numbers
- Medical device identifier or serial numbers
- URL
- IP address
- Biometric identifiers
- Photographic images

A healthcare entity may use or disclose a limited data set for the purposes of research, public health, or healthcare operations. A healthcare entity may use or disclose a limited data set only if formal assurance is received from the recipient limiting the use and disclosure of the information. This written assurance must document the permitted uses and disclosures, who is permitted to use and disclose the information, the required security and privacy safeguards, requirements to report any unauthorized use or disclosure, extending the agreement to subcontractors and vendors, and requirements not to identify individuals. Healthcare entities that establish or maintain relationships with another entity that has a record of violating the Privacy Rule are considered to be noncompliant.

Healthcare entities are required to furnish individuals with a copy of their privacy policies no later than the first date of service delivery and obtain an acknowledgment that they were received. Under emergency situations, privacy policies are to be delivered as soon as reasonable. Copies of such notices and acknowledgments must be retained by the healthcare entity, even in the case of electronic notices, such as online pharmacies.

Healthcare entities are required to keep records of the disclosures of protected health information that state the purpose of the disclosure, the type of information disclosed, the date or period of time in which the disclosure occurred, the name and address of the entity to whom the information was disclosed, and a statement of whether or not the disclosure was related to a research activity.

The following metrics can be used by organizations, public interest groups, and regulatory authorities to measure the extent of compliance with the HIPAA Security and Privacy Rules.

Security Rule

General

Number and percentage of healthcare entities, by calendar year, that: 1.3.1
  a. Did not implement all required security requirements
  b. Average number of required security requirements that were not implemented
  c. Did not implement, or provide a rationale for not implementing, all addressable requirements
  d. Did not tailor the security requirements appropriately
  e. Did not create or maintain current documentary evidence
  f. Did not retain documentary evidence for 6 years as required

Administrative Safeguards

Number and percentage of health entities, by calendar year, that: 1.3.2
  a. Have a complete and current risk assessment
  b. Have implemented appropriate risk mitigation measures
  c. Regularly review audit trails and security incident information
  d. Sanction employees for violations of the Security Rule
  e. Have designated a security official who is accountable for compliance with the Security Rule

Number and percentage of healthcare entity workforce members, by calendar year: 1.3.3
   a. Who are authorized beforehand to work with protected health information
   b. Who are supervised while working with protected health information
   c. Whose rights and privileges to access protected health information are validated regularly
   d. Whose rights and privileges to access protected health information were terminated this reporting period

Distribution of healthcare clearinghouses that have, by calendar year, separated their functions from the larger organization: 1.3.4
   a. Completely, there is no physical or electronic communications link
   b. Partially through the use of internal firewalls or DMZs
   c. Partially through the use of private servers
   d. Partially at the application system or by encrypting the data (on the public servers)
   e. Not at all

Number and percentage of healthcare entities, by calendar year, that: 1.3.5
   a. Implement policies and technical procedures to control electronic access to protected health information
   b. Implement policies and procedures to determine, document, review, and modify a user's right to access protected health information

Number and percentage of healthcare entities, by calendar year, that: 1.3.6
   a. Issue periodic security reminders, such as e-mail updates, posters, and all-hands meetings
   b. Have technical procedures for detecting, preventing, and reporting malicious software
   c. Have technical procedures for monitoring unauthorized log-in attempts
   d. Have technical procedures for creating, changing, and safeguarding passwords
   e. Have policies and technical procedures in place for preventing, detecting, reporting, and responding to security incidents

Number and percentage of healthcare entities, by calendar year, that: 1.3.7
   a. Have implemented procedures to create data backups and retrieve protected health information from them
   b. Have implemented procedures to restore lost data
   c. Have implemented procedures to enable business continuity and data security during emergency operations
   d. Periodically test their contingency and disaster recovery plans
   e. Have assigned criticality categories to assets in order to prioritize their recovery and restoral during contingencies

Number and percentage of healthcare entities that regularly evaluate whether their ongoing security practices are compliant with the provisions of the Security Rule.   1.3.8

Number and percentage of healthcare entities that have written contractual arrangements with business associates concerning their responsibility for implementing the HIPAA security safeguards. 1.3.9

Physical Security Safeguards

Number and percentage of healthcare entities, by calendar year, that: 1.3.10

    a. Have current facility security plans to prevent unauthorized access, tampering, and theft of protected health information and associated IT equipment and media

    b. Control physical access to facilities and IT equipment and media that host protected health information

    c. Maintain current records about maintenance, repairs, and modifications to physical security controls

    d. Have established procedures for physical access controls and rights during emergency operations

Number and percentage of workstations that can access protected health information, by calendar year: 1.3.11

    a. To which physical access is controlled

    b. For which the operational environment is controlled

    c. For which they functions that can be performed and the manner in which they can be executed is controlled

Number and percentage of healthcare entities, by calendar year, that: 1.3.12

    a. Maintain current records about the (re)location of hardware and electronic media that is used to process protected health information

    b. Have implemented procedures for sanitizing reusable media that contained protected health information, prior to its reuse

    c. Back up protected health information before reconfiguring and relocating IT equipment

    d. Have implemented policies and technical procedures to destroy protected health information after it is no longer needed

Technical Security Safeguards

Number and percentage of healthcare entities that have implemented robust access control mechanisms, by calendar year, that: 1.3.13

    a. Assign a unique ID to each user or process and use that identifier for identification and authentication purposes and to track system activity

    b. Automatically terminate inactive sessions after a predetermined idle period

    c. Encrypt protected health information

    d. Have established policies and technical procedures that govern access controls during emergency operations

Number and percentage of healthcare entities, by calendar year, that: 1.3.14

  a. Have implemented a multi-thread audit trail capability
  b. Regularly review audit trail data for anomalies
  c. Have implemented policies and technical procedures to protect health information from unauthorized alteration, addition, deletion, and destruction
  d. Have implemented mechanisms to verify data integrity

Privacy Rule

General

Number of healthcare entities who used or disclosed protected health information in violation of the Privacy Rule, by calendar year: 1.3.15

  a. Average number of individuals whose records were involved per violation

Number and percentage of healthcare entities who failed to document relationships with internal and external business associates, by calendar year.
                                                                    1.3.16

Number and percentage of healthcare entities who failed to ensure and monitor their internal and external business associates compliance with the Privacy Rule.   1.3.17

Uses and Disclosures

Number of times a healthcare entity used or disclosed protected health information, by calendar year, that was not for treatment, payment, or healthcare operations purposes: 1.3.18

  a. Distribution by type of unauthorized use or disclosure

Number of times a healthcare entity used or disclosed more than the minimum amount of protected health information that was necessary, by calendar year:
                                                                    1.3.19

  a. Number of individuals whose protected health information was involved

Number of times a healthcare entity used or disclosed a limited data set that contained a prohibited data element, by calendar year: 1.3.20

  a. Distribution by type of prohibited data element
  b. Number of individuals whose protected health information was involved

Number of times a healthcare entity used or disclosed a limited data set, by calendar year, without first obtaining assurances from the recipient that they would comply with the Privacy Rule: 1.3.21

  a. Number of individuals whose protected health information was involved

Number of times a healthcare entity used or disclosed a limited data set, by calendar year, even though the assurance document was missing: 1.3.22

    a. Distribution by type of missing field

    b. Number of individuals whose protected health information was involved

Number and percentage of healthcare entities that established and maintained relationships with other entities even though they had a history of violating the Privacy Rule, by calendar year: 1.3.23

    a. Number of noncompliant relationships established or maintained

    b. Number of individuals whose protected health information was involved

Authorizations

Number of times a healthcare entity used or disclosed protected health information without a valid authorization, by healthcare entity and calendar year:
           1.3.24

    a. Percentage of uses or disclosures that related to psychotherapy records

    b. Percentage of uses or disclosures that related to marketing purposes

    c. Percentage of uses or disclosures that related to marketing purposes for which the healthcare entity received remuneration

    d. Number of individuals whose protected health information was involved

Number of times a healthcare entity used or disclosed protected health information based on a defective authorization, by healthcare entity and calendar year: 1.3.25

    a. Number of individuals whose protected health information was involved

    b. Distribution by type of defect

Individuals Rights

Number and percentage of times an individual was given the opportunity to approve or object to their protected health information being used or disclosed, by healthcare entity and calendar year: 1.3.26

    a. Percentage of individuals that agreed

    b. Percentage of individuals that objected

Number and percentage of times protected health information was used or disclosed without giving an individual the opportunity to agree or object, by healthcare entity and calendar year: 1.3.27

    a. Distribution by type of use or disclosure

Number of times an individual revoked their authorization to use or disclose their protected health information: 1.3.28

    a. Distribution of times individuals were and were not told of their rights to revoke an authorization

Percentage of times individuals were not given a copy of their signed authorizations.   1.3.29

Number of instances where treatment was withheld or threatened to be
withheld if an individual did not sign an authorization.   1.3.30

3.5 Personal Health Information Act (PHIA) — Canada

The Personal Health Information Act became part of the statutes of Canada
on 28 June 1997. Each provincial legislature subsequently passed the bill and
it took effect at the end of 1997. The preamble to the Personal Health
Information Act is quite clear in explaining the need and rationale for the bill[61]:

- Health information is personal and sensitive and its confidentiality must
  be protected so that individuals are not afraid to seek healthcare or to
  disclose sensitive information to health professionals.
- Individuals need access to their own health information as a matter of
  fairness, to enable them to make informed decisions about health care
  and to correct inaccurate or incomplete information about themselves.
- A consistent approach to personal health information is necessary because
  many persons other than health professionals now obtain, use, and disclose
  personal health information in different contexts and for different purposes.
- Clear and certain rules for the collection, use, and disclosure of personal
  health information are an essential support for electronic health information
  systems that can improve both the quality of patient care and the management of healthcare resources.

Digitizing medical records and sharing them electronically has created a
virtual Pandora's box. Bills such as this are an attempt to put the genie, or
at least part of it, back in the bottle and for good reason. No one wants
personal health information floating around in cyberspace, broadcast on the
local radio or television station, or splashed all over the newspaper. There is
not much information that is more personal than health information. If people
have sufficient doubts about how their information will be used or protected,
they can elect not to seek medical help. Already, many people are avoiding
certain medical tests because they fear employment discrimination. The days
of the omnipotent shaman are over. Most people are sufficiently well informed
to read their own medical reports, seek second or third opinions, and make
their own decisions. Likewise, they have every right in the world to review
their own records and insist that inaccurate, incomplete, or out-of-date information be corrected. Not that long ago, medical records were stored on paper
in a file cabinet at your physician's office and nowhere else; your doctor and
his or her assistants were the only ones who had access to the information.
People used to buy their own medical insurance, just like they buy car
insurance today, at a quarterly rate that was less than what most people pay
biweekly today. Then employers began paying for medical insurance and
naturally the premiums went up — employers could afford higher rates. In
the mid-1980s, employers started passing part of the bill back to the employees.
Because the insurance companies could bill both the employer and the

employee, rates, of course, continued to climb. Soon there were all sorts of organizations that felt they needed access to your medical information and it began being transferred all over the place. By the mid-1990s, most federal and state governments realized the need to put some controls on this situation to protect individual privacy and prevent fraud. Hence, the Personal Health Information Act.

Six specific purposes or objectives are stated for the Act[61]:

1. To provide individuals with a right to examine and receive a copy of personal health information about themselves maintained by a trustee, *subject* to the limited and specific exceptions set out in this Act
2. To provide individuals with a right to request corrections to personal health information about themselves maintained by a trustee
3. To control the manner in which trustees may collect personal health information
4. To protect individuals against the unauthorized use, disclosure or destruction of personal health information by trustees
5. To control the collection, use and disclosure of an individual's personal health identification number
6. To provide for an independent review of the decisions of trustees under this Act

Here we see three different roles, responsibilities, and rights being distinguished, each of which will be elaborated on later. First is the individual to whom the health information pertains. Second is the trustee or health professional, healthcare facility, public body, or health services agency that collects or maintains personal health information.[61] Trustees may have a contractual relationship with information managers to provide IT services and process, store, or destroy personal health information.[61] Third is the independent reviewer, who is known as the ombudsman. In some instances, the role of the ombudsman may be supplemented by the courts.

The scope of the Personal Health Information Act encompasses almost anything related to biological or mental health, such as diagnostic, preventive, and therapeutic care, services, or procedures, including prescription drugs, devices, and equipment. Non-prescription items are not included. Personal health information includes any recorded information about an individual's health, healthcare history, genetic information, healthcare services provided, or payment method and history. Conversations between a healthcare provider and an individual are not included, unless they were recorded. Information recorded in any format (electronic, handwritten, graphical, mechanical, photographic image, etc.) is covered by the Act. The Personal Health Information Act does not apply to anonymous information that does not contain any personally identifiable information and is intended solely for statistical research.

Rules of precedence have been established that define how this Act relates to existing and possible future legislation. The Mental Health Act takes precedence over this Act, should there be any conflict in the provisions of the two Acts. Part 3 of this Act, which defines the privacy provisions, takes precedence over other Acts, unless another Act has more stringent privacy requirements. Finally, a trustee may refuse to comply with the provisions in Part 2 of this Act that define rights to access health information, if another Act prohibits or restricts such access.

The Personal Health Information Act is organized in seven parts. The first part contains introductory material, such as definitions. The last part states when the Act takes effect and the requirements for reviewing the effectiveness of the provisions. The middle five parts elaborate on the roles, responsibilities, and rights of individuals, trustees, and the ombudsman:

- Part 2 — Access to Personal Health Information
- Part 3 — Protection of Privacy
- Part 4 — Powers and Duties of the Ombudsman
- Part 5 — Complaints
- Part 6 — General Provisions

Each of these parts is discussed in order below.

After reading Part 2, it becomes apparent that the drafters of the legislation were familiar with the OECD Privacy Guidelines (discussed in Section 3.6 of this chapter) and the Data Protection Directive (discussed in Section 3.7 of this chapter), both of which were published previously. Many of the concepts of and approaches to controlling access and protecting the privacy of personal health information are similar.

An individual has the right to examine and request a copy of any personal health information held by a trustee. The requests must be made in writing and submitted to the trustee. If need be, an individual can ask for help from the trustee in preparing the request.

Trustees are expected to assist individuals in preparing requests for information, when needed. In addition, if they are not the correct source of the information, trustees are required to refer individuals to the correct source within seven days of receipt. Trustees must respond to a request within 30 days and provide accurate and complete information or state that the requested information does not exist or cannot be found. Any terms, codes, and abbreviations used in the information are to be explained. Furthermore, the information is to be provided in a format and media that the individual can easily use. Before releasing any information, trustees are responsible for verifying the identity of the person requesting the information and ensuring that only that person will receive the information. Trustees are allowed to charge a "reasonable" fee for these services.

So far this all sounds fine. However, trustees can also take another course of action, that of refusing to supply the information "in whole or in part." In this case, the trustee must also (1) supply a reason for refusing to comply with the request, and (2) inform the individual of their right to file a complaint with the ombudsman. Nine valid reasons are cited for refusing to give individuals access to their own medical records; some of these reasons appear reasonable, while others are difficult to justify[61]:

- Knowledge of the information could reasonably be expected to endanger the health or safety of the individual or another person.
- Disclosure of the information would reveal personal health information about another person who has not consented to the disclosure.
- Disclosure of the information could reasonably be expected to identify a third party, other than another trustee, who supplied the information in confidence under circumstances in which confidentiality was reasonably expected.
- The information was compiled and is used solely for the purpose of (a) peer review by health professionals, (b) review by a standards committee established to study or evaluate healthcare practice in a healthcare facility or health services agency, (c) a body with statutory responsibility for the discipline of health professionals or for the quality of standards of professional services provided by health professionals, or (d) risk management assessment.
- The information was compiled principally in anticipation of, or for use in, a civil, criminal, or quasi-judicial proceeding.

The first two bullets are particularly difficult to account for. How could knowing what is in your own medical records endanger your health and safety or that of another person? Assuming you are not criminally insane, in which case you would probably not ask for a copy of the records in the first place. This one is a real stretch, as is the second bullet. How could knowing what is in your own medical records reveal information about another person and why should they be able to veto the release of your medical records to you? I fail to see the logic in this. Then we get to the third bullet, where some anonymous source who is not a legitimate trustee has provided uncorroborated information that has ended up in your medical records, except that you are not allowed to see it? At this point I began wondering why I should bother reading the rest of the Act. There is over a half a page of reasons why information can be withheld from an individual and only two lines stating that they have a right to access it. The anonymous sources seem to have more rights than the individual about whom the records are being maintained. Even the fourth bullet is questionable. Yes, these activities need to be conducted, but there is no reason why a person's name, identification number, or contact information could not be deleted from the information first. Only the fifth bullet seems to have any merit.

Assuming an individual actually receives any personal health information from a trustee, that person has the right to request that any inaccurate, incomplete, or out-of-date information be corrected. This request must also be in writing.

A trustee has 30 days to respond to a correction request. A trustee may take four possible courses of action; he can (1) simply correct the information and make sure that the correction is associated with the proper record, (2) claim that the information no longer exists or cannot be found, (3) forward the correction request to the appropriate source of the information, for them to handle, or (4) refuse to make the correction, for any reason. If a trustee refuses to make a correction, he must inform the individual of (1) the reason for the refusal, (2) their right to file a statement disagreeing with the record, and (3) their right to file a complaint with the ombudsman. The trustee must maintain the statement of disagreement as part of the record in question. Finally, trustees are responsible for notifying any other trustees with whom they shared information in the past year of all corrections and statements of disagreements. Trustees who receive this information are required to update their files accordingly. No fees may be charged for processing corrections or statements of disagreement.

The last three courses of action are troublesome. An individual requests information from a trustee, receives it, and notices some errors. The individual then writes back to request that the errors be corrected — only to have the trustee state that the information no longer exists or cannot be found. It is difficult to believe that the information could disappear that quickly. This is an improbable situation, as is the third option. This time, instead of saying he cannot find the information, the trustee responds that he is not the right organization to contact. He just sent the individual the information and now he is washing his hands of the affair. The refusal option is even more difficult to explain — a trustee can refuse to make a correction for *any* reason he so chooses. What a loophole! Why bother to include a correction clause in the bill at all? Why should an ethical organization incur the time and expense to make corrections if an unethical organization can simply refuse to make corrections and both will be considered in compliance with the Act? There is no business incentive to comply with correction requests, except perhaps public opinion.

No roles or responsibilities are assigned to the ombudsman under Part 2.

Part 3, Protection of Privacy, levies additional responsibilities on trustees and their information managers. Personal health information cannot be collected about an individual unless the information is needed and collected for a lawful purpose on the part of the trustee; collection of unrelated information is not allowed under the Act. Information is to be collected directly from the individual whenever possible. Prior to collecting any information, a trustee is required to inform the individual of the purpose for which the information is being collected and who to contact if any questions arise. Again, there are exceptions to these provisions; if collecting the information directly from the individual might (1) endanger their health or safety or that of another person, (2) result in inaccurate information being collected, or (3) take too long, then the information can be collected through another method or source. Likewise, if the individual has previously consented to an alternate form of collection or an alternate form of collection has been approved by legal means, then it is permissible. However, before using or acting upon any personal health information, trustees are expected to verify that the information is accurate, current, and complete. Requirements are also established for retention and destruction of personal health information. Trustees are responsible for instituting a written policy about the retention and destruction of personal health information that states how long information is to be kept and how it is to be destroyed. Trustees are required to ensure that personal privacy is protected during the destruction process. In addition, trustees are required to keep records of what information was destroyed, when it was destroyed, how it was destroyed, and who supervised the destruction activities.

The second division of Part 2 defines mandatory security safeguards. Trustees are required to implement "reasonable" administrative, technical, and physical security safeguards to protect personal health information. In addition, the safeguards are to be in proportion to the sensitivity of the information being protected. The bill does not define reasonable safeguards, but gives some examples, such as limiting access to personal information maintained by a trustee to authorized users, limiting use of personal health information to valid uses and authenticated users, preventing unauthorized electronic interception of personal health information, and validating requests for information before acting on them. In essence, the bill is instructing trustees to practice due care and due diligence in regard to all personal health information they and their information manager maintain, without getting into technical specifics.

The next five pages of the Act are devoted to restrictions on the use and disclosure of personal health information. The first three statements have merit. Trustees cannot disclose information except as authorized by the bill. The minimum amount of personal health information is to be used or disclosed in every situation. Only employees and contractors the trustee has confidence in are allowed to handle the information and only to perform authorized transactions related to the purpose for which the information was collected in the first place. This is followed by a list of eight exceptions. Some of the exceptions are reasonable; for example, a new use is directly related to the original use, the individual has given his consent, or to prevent a serious immediate threat to the health of the individual. Other exceptions are questionable, such as to monitor or evaluate the healthcare services provided at a facility, or research and planning related to healthcare or payment for services. Why, in this situation, could the information not be rendered anonymous first? There is no need for personally identifiable information to be included in these latter two situations. The bill then goes on to state that personal health information is not to be disclosed unless the individual or their representative has given their consent beforehand. This statement is followed by a list of 30 exceptions. Again, a few of the exceptions are understandable. However, the majority are not and represent situations in which the information could easily be rendered anonymous prior to disclosure and still accomplish the stated goal, such as research, monitoring healthcare services, etc. Even more troubling is the fact that it is difficult to come up with a scenario that does not fall into one of these 30 exceptions. The positions have become reversed. The trustee makes all the decisions about when and how information is used and disclosed — not the individual. Also, the expression "disclosure" is used in general terms; it is not limited to releasing electronic records. Nothing limits or controls the verbal release of information, in person or over the telephone. An employee of the trustee or information manager could go scanning through a database and find out that Senator

Smith's wife had a tummy tuck, tell someone who tells someone else, and the next morning this information is on the front page of the newspaper.

If trustees contract with information managers to provide IT services, they are required to include contractual clauses that enforce the security provisions of the bill. Requirements to protect the information from risks such as unauthorized access, use, disclosure, destruction, etc. must be stated explicitly. Today IT services are often outsourced offshore; as a result, it is unclear how well security requirements could be enforced or damages collected in the event of a dispute. The only real leverage a trustee has is to cancel the contract. Also, although the trustee has passed on security and privacy requirements to an information manager, he (the trustee) remains ultimately liable for any violations.

Part 4 defines the duties and responsibilities of the ombudsman. The ombudsman serves in an independent oversight role to ensure that (1) trustees are living up to their duties and responsibilities, as defined in the Act; and (2) individuals are aware of their rights and afforded an opportunity to exercise them. The ombudsman is to monitor compliance with the Act through investigations and audits. In doing so, the ombudsman may request that the trustee turn over any requested records or other information; the trustee has 14 days to comply. The ombudsman can conduct on-site audits during regular business hours and interview any person or contractor employed by the trustee. The ombudsman is required to notify the Minister of Justice and Attorney General of any suspected violations of this or any other Act uncovered during an investigation or audit. Less serious matters can be handled through recommendations submitted directly to the trustee in question. In addition, the ombudsman is to submit an annual report to the legislature describing the complaints received, audits and investigations conducted, the status of recommendations being implemented by trustees, and any other relevant matters. The ombudsman can also issue an ad hoc report if a serious matter arises. Furthermore, the legislature can ask the ombudsman to comment on proposed new legislation and other issues related to the privacy of personal health information and the use of IT.

At the same time, the ombudsman is responsible for informing the public about their rights under the Personal Health Information Act and responding to their correspondence. In particular, the ombudsman is responsible for acknowledging and investigating complaints. Individuals have a right to file a complaint about any action or inaction on the part of a trustee, such as (1) failure to grant them access to their personal health information; (2) refusal to correct inaccurate personal health information; (3) taking an unreasonable amount of time to process an individual's request; (4) charging unreasonable fees for supplying information; (5) collecting, using, or disclosing personal health information in violation of the Act; and (6) failing to implement appropriate administrative, technical, or physical security safeguards. Individuals must submit their complaints in writing to the ombudsman and supply all necessary backup material. The ombudsman is required to investigate and resolve all complaints, unless (1) the complaint is considered frivolous, (2) too much time has passed since the event occurred, or (3) the internal complaint process has not been tried at the facility in question. The ombudsman is to act as a neutral party and hear information from both the complainant and the trustee before rendering a decision in the matter. Outside experts may also be consulted. Access complaints must be resolved within 45 days, and privacy complaints must be resolved within 90 days. The ombudsman's final report and recommendations to remedy the situation are sent to both the complainant and the trustee. A trustee has 14 days to respond to the ombudsman's report. If the trustee accepts the recommendations, he has an additional 15 days to implement them. If the trustee rejects the recommendations or the ombudsman did not rule in the complainant's favor, the individual has the right to take the matter to court. The suit must be filed within 30 days of receiving the ombudsman's final report.

Part 6 defines a series of miscellaneous provisions related to the Act. To start with, each healthcare facility is expected to appoint a Privacy Officer to ensure compliance with the Act and that all employees and contractors receive appropriate training in this regard. A Health Information Privacy Committee is also established to monitor requests for access to personal health information for research projects. Specific violations of the Act and the accompanying penalties are defined[61]:

- Making a false statement to, misleading, or attempting to mislead the ombudsman
- Obstructing the ombudsman
- Destroying or erasing personal health information to evade an individual's request for information
- Obtaining another person's health information by false representation
- Producing, collecting, or using another person's health identification number under false pretenses
- Disclosing personal health information in violation of the Act
- Collecting, using, or selling personal health information in violation of the Act
- Failing to practice due care and due diligence when protecting personal health information
- Disclosing personal health information, in violation of this Act, with the intent of obtaining a monetary benefit

No distinction is made as to who commits the offense. The penalty is $50,000. If an offense lasts longer than one day, each 24-hour period is treated as a separate offense.

Finally, the bill is to be reviewed periodically to evaluate its effectiveness and make recommendations on how it could be improved.

The following metrics can be used by regulatory authorities, individuals, public interest groups, and healthcare facilities themselves to measure the extent to which the provisions of the Personal Health Information Act are being adhered to and enforced.

Part 2

Number of individuals who requested access to their personal health information, by calendar year: 1.4.1

   a. Percentage of requests that were granted
   b. Percentage of requests that were referred to another source
   c. Percentage of requests that were denied because the information no longer existed or could not be found
   d. Percentage of requests that were denied for another reason

Distribution by healthcare trustee and calendar year: 1.4.2

   a. Percentage of requests for access to personal health information that were granted
   b. Percentage of requests for access to personal health information that were referred to another source
   c. Percentage of requests for access to personal health information that were denied because the information no longer existed or could not be found
   d. Percentage of requests for access to personal health information that were denied for another reason

Number and percentage of requests for access to personal health information that were not responded to within 30 days, by healthcare trustee and calendar year: 1.4.3

   a. Distribution by reason

Number of individuals who requested that corrections be made to their personal health information, by calendar year.:   1.4.4

   a. Percentage of correction requests that were acted upon
   b. Percentage of correction requests that were referred to another source
   c. Percentage of correction requests that were not acted upon because the information no longer existed or could not be found
   d. Percentage of correction requests that were refused

Distribution by healthcare trustee and calendar year: 1.4.5

   a. Percentage of correction requests that were acted upon
   b. Percentage of correction requests that were referred to another source
   c. Percentage of correction requests that were not acted upon because the information no longer existed or could not be found
   d. Percentage of correction requests that were refused

Number and percentage of correction requests that were not responded to within 30 days, by healthcare trustee and calendar year: 1.4.6

   a. Distribution by reason

Number and percentage of trustees who failed to properly file statements of disagreement with personal health information: 1.4.7

    a. Distribution by healthcare trustee
    b. Number of such cases by trustee

Part 3

Percentage and number of healthcare trustees found not to be in compliance with the Act during an audit or investigation by the ombudsman: 1.4.8

    a. More personal health information was collected than needed for the stated purpose
    b. Personal health information was collected without informing the individual of the purpose for which the information was collected or how it would be used
    c. Personal health information was not collected directly from an individual when it could have been
    d. For failure to establish policies for the retention and destruction of personal health information
    e. For failure to keep records about what personal health information was destroyed, when it was destroyed, and who supervised the destruction

Number and percentage of trustees who failed to implement reasonable administrative, technical, and physical security safeguards to protect personal health information: 1.4.9

    a. Number and percentage of trustees who failed to contractually pass this requirement on to their information manager(s)
    b. Number and percentage of trustees who had inadequate administrative security safeguards
    c. Number and percentage of trustees who had inadequate technical security safeguards
    d. Number and percentage of trustees who had inadequate physical security safeguards

Part 4

Ombudsman activities by calendar year: 1.4.10

    a. Number of bona fide complaints received
    b. Number of audits conducted
    c. Number of investigations conducted
    d. Number of final reports issued
    e. Number of complaints resolved through recommendations to the trustee
    f. Number of annual reports submitted to the legislature on time
    g. Number of special ad hoc reports issued

Part 5

Number of complaints that were pursued through the courts, by calendar year:
    1.4.11

    a. Percentage that were resolved in the complainant's favor
    b. Percentage that upheld the ombudsman's report

Part 6

Number and distribution of offenses that were prosecuted and resulted in fines, by calendar year: 1.4.12

    a. Making a false statement to, misleading, or attempting to mislead the ombudsman
    b. Obstructing the ombudsman
    c. Destroying or erasing personal health information to evade an individual's request for information
    d. Obtaining another person's health information by false representation
    e. Producing, collecting, or using another person's health identification number under false pretenses
    f. Disclosing personal health information in violation of the Act
    g. Collecting, using, or selling personal health information in violation of the Act
    h. Failing to practice due care and due diligence when protecting personal health information
    i. Disclosing personal health information, in violation of this Act, with the intent of obtaining a monetary benefit

Distribution of offenses that were prosecuted and resulted in fines, by health-care trustee and calendar year.   1.4.13

PERSONAL PRIVACY

Five current regulations focus on the security and privacy of personally identifiable information. These regulations and the metrics that can be used to demonstrate compliance to them, are discussed next.

3.6 Organization for Economic Cooperation and Development (OECD) Privacy, Cryptography, and Security Guidelines

The Organization for Economic Cooperation and Development (OECD) is an independent international organization with voluntary membership that was founded in 1960. The stated purpose and mission of the OECD is to[68]:

■ Achieve the highest sustainable economic growth and employment and a rising standard of living in Member States, while maintaining financial stability, and thus to contribute to the development of the world economy

■ Contribute to sound economic expansion in Member as well as non-member States in the process of economic development

■ Contribute to the expansion of world trade on a multilateral, non-discriminatory basis in accordance with international obligations

Currently there are 29 Member States: Australia, Austria, Belgium, Canada, the Czech Republic, Denmark, Finland, France, Germany, Greece, Hungary, Iceland, Ireland, Italy, Korea, Luxembourg, Mexico, the Netherlands, New Zealand, Norway, Poland, Portugal, the Slovak Republic, Spain, Sweden, Switzerland, Turkey, the United Kingdom, and the United States. In addition, the Commission of the European Communities participates in OECD forums.

The OECD is actively involved in the area of science and technology and fosters the development and promulgation of consensus standards, policies, and regulations that are mutually beneficial to all Member States and their citizens. The OECD had the foresight to see the need for security and privacy regulations almost two decades before most organizations or individuals were aware of the dark side of the digital age. Three pioneering sets of guidelines, and supporting documentation, issued by the OECD laid the groundwork in this area:

1. OECD Guidelines on the Protection of Privacy and Trans-border Flows of Personal Data, 23 September 1980
2. OECD Guidelines for Cryptography Policy, 1997
3. OECD Guidelines for the Security of Information Systems and Networks: Towards a Culture of Security, 25 July 2002

The three guidelines, and the associated supporting documentation, form a cohesive whole and are meant to be used in conjunction with each other. The privacy and security of personal information are closely intertwined, as is shown in the discussion below. Cryptography is one technical control that, if used correctly, can help achieve the security and privacy of personal information.

The regulations discussed in Sections 3.7 through 3.10 of this chapter are from three Member States of the OECD and the European Commission, which coordinates with the OECD. The common source these regulations evolved from will become apparent. As a result, our discussion of privacy regulations begins with the OECD Privacy Guidelines.

The OECD established a panel of experts in 1978 to investigate "transborder data barriers and privacy protections." Their findings and recommendations were issued in 1980 as the OECD Guidelines on the Protection of Privacy and Trans-Border Flows of Personal Data. The stated purpose of the guidelines is to[69]:

- Prevent unlawful storage of personal data, storage of inaccurate personal data, abuse or unauthorized disclosure of such data
- Prevent economic disruption if information flows are curtailed
- Represent a consensus on basic principles that can be built into national laws and regulations
- Help harmonize national privacy legislation adopted by Member States

The OECD Privacy Guidelines are organized into a Preface (or rationale) and an Annex. The Annex contains five parts that specify what should be done to ensure the privacy of personal data and an explanatory memo that provides supplementary informative material. The OECD Privacy Guidelines have been in effect for 25 years. In 1998, the OECD released a Ministerial Declaration reaffirming the importance of the Privacy Guidelines and encouraged Member States to make progress within two years on protecting personal information on global networks.[71c] Two terms are key to understanding the content and context of the Guidelines:

> **Data controller:** a party who, according to domestic law, is competent to decide about the contents and use of personal data regardless of whether or not such data are collected, stored, processed or disseminated by that party or by an agent on its behalf.[69]

> **Personal data:** any information relating to an identified or identifiable individual (data subject).[69]

The data controller is the person who has ultimate authority to decide about how personal data is collected, processed, stored, released, and used. The data controller may have several subordinate people or organizations reporting to him, either directly or through contractual vehicles. Personal data is any personally identifiable data, regardless of the format or content, that can be tied to a unique individual, who is referred to as the data subject.

The OECD Privacy Guidelines apply to any personal data that is in the public or private sectors for which manual or automated processing or the nature of the intended use presents a potential "danger to the privacy of individual liberties."[69] It is assumed that diverse protection mechanisms, both technical and operational, will be needed, depending on the different types of personal data; the various processing, storage, collection, and dissemination methods; and the assorted usage scenarios. The Guidelines make it clear that the principles presented are considered the minimum acceptable standard of protection. Personal data for which collection, processing, and dissemination do not pose a risk is not covered by the Guidelines. Presumably innocuous items such as eye color or preferred type of coffee or tea fall into this category. The Guidelines also exempt personal data that is needed for national security reasons or public safety and welfare; however, there is a caveat that these exemptions should be used "as few times as possible and made known to the public."[69] The intent is to prevent misuse and overuse of this clause. Member States are encouraged to implement the Guidelines through domestic legislation to ensure that the rights of individuals are protected, that they are not discriminated against for asserting these rights, and that appropriate legal remedies are available whenever these rights are violated. Member States are also encouraged to cooperate with each other, share information about implementation of the Guidelines, and promote mutual recognition of legislation.

The Guidelines are presented in eight principles. (Eight seems to be a popular number with the OECD. The cryptography guidelines also consist of eight principles.) The principles are logical, practical, and straightforward.

Together they form a cohesive whole. The eight principles reinforce and amplify each other. As is appropriate for Guidelines, the principles explain what needs to be done to protect the privacy of individuals' personal data, without saying how this is to be accomplished. Rather, the "how" is left to be defined in the regulations passed by each Member State.

Some common themes emerge from a review of the eight principles in the OECD Privacy Guidelines. For example, there is a fundamental conflict between the free flow of information necessary for an open society and economy and an individual's universal right to privacy. As a result, it is necessary to regulate how this is accomplished, from the initial collection of personal data, through processing of that data, and on to its final erasure or destruction. At the same time, it is necessary to set limits on what information can be collected, how it is collected, and how it can be used. As the Guidelines point out, there may be times when it is difficult to distinguish what does or does not constitute personal data. A case in point is that of a sole proprietor where the business and the person are one and the same.[69] Regardless, individuals have the right to know what personal information has been collected about them, to view that information, and insist that errors be corrected. Finally, individuals have the right to know the identity of the person responsible for ensuring compliance with privacy regulations. Now let us look at each of the eight principles.

Collection Limitation Principle

The first principle, referred to as the Collection Limitation Principle, sets limits on what personal data can be collected and how it can be collected. The Guidelines insist that the minimum amount of data necessary to perform the prestated purpose be collected and no more. That is, fishing trips and social engineering are not allowed. Furthermore, the data must be collected in a legal manner and with the individual's full knowledge and consent beforehand. Deceptive or hidden data collection methods are prohibited. As the Guidelines point out, certain types of data controllers may be subject to more stringent limits imposed by their Member State, such as additional regulations for health-care professionals.

Data Quality Principle

The second principle, referred to as the Data Quality Principle, emphasizes that the data controller and any organizations working for him who collect and process personal data have a responsibility to ensure that the data is accurate, complete, and current. The concern is that if the data does not meet these quality standards, the individual may suffer unwarranted harm as a result of the data being processed or disseminated. Reinforcing the first principle, the Data Quality Principle requires personal data to be consistent with the prestated purpose for which it was collected. Ad hoc usage scenarios are not allowed.

Purpose Specification Principle

The third principle is known as the Purpose Specification Principle. It is intended to keep the data controller and organizations collecting and processing personal data for him out of trouble. This principle reminds everyone that individuals must be told, before any data is collected, explicitly why the data is being collected, how it will be used, to whom it will be disseminated, and how long it will be retained. Any subsequent use of the data must be consistent with the original stated purpose. Should the data controller want to use the data for any other purpose, the individual must be notified again and give consent beforehand. And to prevent any future unauthorized homesteading among the data, this principle insists that all personal data be erased, destroyed, or rendered anonymous at the end of the specified period of use.

Use Limitation Principle

The fourth principle is known as the Use Limitation Principle. Just to make sure everyone understands, this principle reiterates in stand-alone form that personal data cannot be disclosed or used for any other purposes than those stated at the time of collection. Deviation from the original stated purpose, whether processing or dissemination, is not permitted unless the individual is notified and gives prior consent. Only one exception to this principle is allowed — if a government authority directs the data controller to do so for the sake of national security or public safety or welfare.

Security Safeguards Principle

The fifth principle is known as the Security Safeguards Principle. The Guidelines remind data collectors and organizations that collect, process, and disseminate personal data that they are responsible for providing adequate safeguards to protect against unauthorized access, alteration, use, release, and destruction of this data. Furthermore, the Guidelines point out that to have adequate safeguards, a combination of technical (IT security) and organizational (physical, personnel, and operational security) controls is needed. These controls should be proportionate to the risk of unauthorized access or processing, whether by manual or automated means. This, of course, implies that thorough risk assessments are performed regularly.

Openness Principle

Openness is the sixth principle in the OECD Privacy Guidelines. At first, this may seem like a contradiction of terms — requiring openness in a privacy regulation. However, in this instance, openness refers to open communication with the individuals from whom personal data has been collected. Data controllers are required to be frank with these individuals. They must receive regular communication from data controllers holding their personal data.

Specifically, individuals must be told (1) what information the organization has; (2) the procedures followed for collecting, processing, storing, and releasing the information; (3) that they have a right to view the information; and (4) the contact information for the data controller. The Guidelines assume that this will be an ongoing dialog as long as the data is kept and used, and not a one-time event.

Individual Participation Principle

The seventh principle, Individual Participation, continues the openness theme. The Openness Principle levied communication obligations on data controllers. The other side of the coin is to spell out individuals' rights with regard to these organizations, which the Individual Participation Principle does. These rights are very clear-cut. Individuals have the right to easily and quickly obtain information about the type and extent of personal data a data controller has about them. Individuals have a right to receive a copy of that data for a reasonable fee. Furthermore, they can challenge any data that is withheld or inaccurate.

Accountability Principle

The OECD Privacy Guidelines saved accountability for last. What can be more important in a regulatory framework than accountability? Without an explicit definition of who is accountable for what, there will be no compliance. If there is no compliance, there is no point in wasting the taxpayers' money passing regulations. The Guidelines make it clear that ultimate responsibility for protecting the privacy of personal data rests with the data controller. Others may also be held accountable for their actions following a violation, but the data controller bears the ultimate responsibility. The Guidelines do not define the specific penalties for a lack of accountability, keeping true to the nature of Guidelines; that is left to each Member State.

In addition, the OECD Privacy Guidelines include what could be called a ninth principle, although it is not referred to as such — basic principles that should guide implementation of the eight privacy principles by Member States. These basic principles apply to activities within and among Member States. Member States are encouraged to implement reasonable regulations, in response to the eight privacy principles, that will promote uninterrupted and secure data flows.[69] The implications of both domestic processing and (re)exporting of personal data are to be considered when Member States develop these regulations. The Guidelines note that the privacy principles apply even to data that transits a country, even if that country is not the final destination. Member States are free to restrict data flows when there is a significant difference in privacy regulations; in fact, they are encouraged to avoid processing personal data in Member States whose regulations are not up to par yet or are not being enforced.

The OECD Cryptography Guidelines were issued in 1997, some 17 years after the Privacy Guidelines. If you remember, at that time all sorts of debates were raging within the United States and elsewhere about whether or not cryptography equipment should be allowed in the private sector and, if so, how. Some contended that cryptographic equipment and even algorithms were the exclusive domain of national governments. The advent of public key cryptographic and inexpensive mechanisms severely weakened that argument. At first, attempts were made to control the export of cryptographic material, but that proved unenforceable. Then some sort of deal was struck between industry and government, whereby law enforcement officials and designated others would receive a copy of all encryption-related materials. So, if they happened to intercept some encrypted electronic communications (telephone conversations, e-mail, e-mail attachment, etc.), they would be able to decrypt it. And of course there were the Clipper chip wars and others. In the midst of all this turmoil, the OECD had the calmness and singleness of purpose to issue the Cryptography Guidelines.

The stated purpose of the Cryptography Guidelines was to[71]:

- Promote the use of cryptography to enhance confidence in global telecommunications networks and information systems
- Enhance the security and privacy of sensitive personal data
- Facilitate interoperability among cryptographic systems and their effective use among Member States
- Foster cooperation internationally among the business, research and development, and government communities

In March 1997, the Council issued recommendations and an endorsement of the Cryptography Guidelines. Member States were encouraged to develop national regulations to implement the Guidelines, particularly in the areas of electronic commerce and protection of intellectual property rights. The Guidelines are applicable to both the public and private sectors, except in situations where national security is a concern. The Guidelines define 20 terms related to cryptography, all of which are contained in Annex A. It is especially important to understand how two of these terms are used in the Guidelines:

Confidentiality: the property that data or information is not made available or disclosed to unauthorized individuals, entities, or processes.[71]

Cryptography: the discipline which embodies principles, means, and methods for the transformation of data in order to hide its information content, establish its authenticity, prevent its undetected modification, prevent its repudiation, and/or prevent its unauthorized use.[71]

This definition of confidentiality is broader than most because it includes unauthorized entities and processes. The use of confidential data by unauthorized processes is almost always overlooked, despite the prevalent use of middleware and temporary files and disk swapping by common operating systems. The definition of cryptography is also much broader than most. Note first that it is not limited to IT. Then notice that in addition to preventing undetected modification (the usual definition), preventing repudiation and unauthorized use is part of the definition.

Like the Privacy Guidelines, the Cryptography Guidelines are organized around eight principles, which form an interdependent set. There is no priority or order of importance associated with the presentation of the eight principles.

Trust in Cryptographic Methods

The first principle is referred to as Trust in Cryptographic Methods. The Guidelines promote the use of cryptography as a means of gaining public confidence in the security and privacy of nationwide and global information systems and telecommunications networks, both in the public and private sectors. The OECD understood that if people did not trust the ability of these systems and networks to protect their sensitive personal data, they would not use them despite the convenience factor. The concern about the ability to protect sensitive personal data, particularly financial information, was real when online shopping and electronic banking began. At first, the number of people participating was low. Over time, as customer confidence grew, more and more people started to participate in E-commerce and even electronic filing of their income taxes. The end result is the use of more robust and standardized cryptographic methods that benefit everyone.

Choice of Cryptographic Methods

The second OECD cryptography principle is known as Choice of Cryptographic Methods. Having a realistic grasp of the situation, the OECD appreciated the fact that a variety of different cryptographic methods were necessary to satisfy the diverse data security requirements of different organizations.[71] When you think of the number of different types of organizations and different types of information they process, and the different reasons and ways they process it, you can see the wisdom of this decision. As a result, the Guidelines endorse the principle of choice — because of their different needs, organizations need the ability to choose what cryptographic method to employ. Data controllers and data processors are responsible for ensuring adequate security and privacy of personal data. As a result, it is only logical that they have the right to determine what constitutes an appropriate cryptographic method for them to employ. The OECD Guidelines take the position that the governments of Member States should not limit or otherwise interfere with an organization's choice of cryptographic method.[71] At the same time, it is acknowledged that the governments of Member States may require government agencies to use a particular cryptographic method to protect personal data, similar to the requirement that civilian agencies in the United States use the Advanced Encryption Standard (AES) encryption algorithm.

Market-Driven Development of Cryptographic Methods

The third principle is referred to as Market-Driven Development of Cryptographic Methods. The OECD Guidelines believe in the free market approach to cryptographic methods — that the development cryptographic algorithms, techniques, and methods should be driven by the private-sector marketplace, not the governments of Member States. That is, let the creative and collective energy of the marketplace devise cost-effective and technically efficient solutions. This is only common sense. Organizations in the private sector have a greater and more in-depth understanding of their own needs than any government agency. They also have more at stake: loss of revenue, loss of customers, and liability lawsuits. This principle reinforces (1) the statement above that the governments of Member States should not limit or interfere with an organization's choice of cryptographic methods,[71] and (2) the earlier statement that the Guidelines do not apply to national security applications.

Standards for Cryptographic Methods

The fourth principle is known as Standards for Cryptographic Methods. An excellent way to promote market-driven development of cryptographic methods is through international consensus standards. The development and promulgation of international consensus standards captures the collective knowledge and experience from multiple organizations, projects, and countries.[158] The OECD Cryptography Guidelines encourage the generation and use of international standards as a way to achieve interoperability, portability, and mobility of cryptographic methods.[71] Because all parties involved in an encrypted transaction have to use the same cryptographic method, proprietary or one-country solutions are of limited use. In response, more than 30 international consensus standards have been released jointly through the International Organization for Standardization (ISO) and the International Electrotechnical Commission (IEC). These standards cover everything from hash functions, to digital signatures, digital certificates, non-repudiation, and key management.

The Guidelines also encourage initiation of a program of mutually recognized accredited labs to evaluate conformance to these standards. The United States and Canada already have such an arrangement through their joint cryptographic module validation program (CMVP), which certifies products that conform to Federal Information Processing Standards (FIPS) encryption standards, such as AES. At the September 2004 CMVP meeting, it was announced that other labs outside the United States and Canada would soon be accredited. While FIPS are not international consensus standards per se, anyone can comment on the standards during their development and any organization or country is free to use them.

Protection of Privacy and Personal Data

Protection of Privacy and Personal Data is the fifth principle. The OECD Guidelines promote the use of cryptographic methods as one means of protecting an individual's right to privacy and sensitive personal data. Encryption by itself does not guarantee the security or privacy of personal data. Appropriate cryptographic methods must be employed and they must be employed smartly. Encryption devices that are installed, configured, and operated incorrectly provide no protection whatsoever. Several issues must be dealt with on a case-by-case basis:

- What cryptographic method(s) to deploy
- Whether message headers, payloads, or both need to be encrypted
- Key length, generation, distribution, management, and revocation
- The strength of the encryption algorithm that is needed
- Whether data on the corporate intranet needs to be encrypted or just that traversing the Internet
- Which files and directories on corporate servers need to be encrypted
- Which files and directories on individual desktops need to be encrypted
- The extent of encryption needed for online and offline archives
- How hardcopy printouts from encrypted files are handled
- Controls placed on copying and accessing encrypted files

These and other issues are left to individual organizations, consistent with the second Cryptography Principle.

Lawful Access

The sixth principle refers to lawful access to encrypted data by authorized government officials. The OECD Guidelines acknowledge that there will be times, hopefully few in number, when law enforcement representatives will need to read or interpret encrypted electronic files. Supposedly this capability will be limited to scenarios such as drug trafficking, money laundering, and other criminal investigations.[71] The fear was that the "bad guys" would be able to send and receive encrypted messages, leading to further criminal activity, that the "good guys" would not be able to understand even though they could intercept them. Herein lies the problem with this principle. On the surface this principle seems innocuous enough. In reality, it permits the infamous "Big Brother is watching" syndrome. What constitutes lawful access is not defined. Who decides what is lawful access is not defined. Who appropriate government officials are is not defined. And so on. Basically this principle is a big loophole for electronic surveillance by the government of any Member State whenever they feel like it. There is nothing to prevent electronic snooping to see if an individual's online shopping patterns are consistent with the income reported on his tax forms. There is nothing to prevent decryption of a message sent to a business partner congratulating them on winning a $20M contract from triggering an audit of corporate tax records. Just because a permit was obtained to read Greedo, the drug kingpin's encrypted e-mail does not mean other so-called suspicious e-mail that is stumbled upon will not be investigated. Basically, the OECD Guidelines blew it on this principle. This principle is based on the faulty assumption that the "bad guys" will only use commercially available encryption equipment. Why in the world would they do that when they can afford to develop their own proprietary methods? In reality, there is no need for this principle because situations affecting national security are exempt from the Guidelines. Most likely, some Member States, which shall remain nameless, refused to concur with the Guidelines unless this principle was included.

Liability

The seventh principle, Liability, starts to hit home. The OECD Guidelines call out three different parties and their different roles with respect to liability:

1. Companies that sell cryptographic products
2. Organizations that use cryptographic products, including their subcontractors and business partners
3. Companies that provide security services, such as certificate authorities

The intent is provide a serious form of accountability in regard to how cryptographic methods are used. This principle delivers a significant incentive for employing appropriate cryptographic methods correctly and efficiently. This principle eliminates sloppy encryption as the scapegoat when the private financial information for 25,000 people is stolen in an identity theft raid. The excuse that "golly gee, we encrypted the data, what else could we do?" will not work anymore.

Companies that sell cryptographic products are expected to be up-front about their product's features, functions, strengths, weaknesses, limitations, and correct mode and environment of operation. Misleading or incomplete information in this regard creates a liability for damages or harm suffered by their customers.

Organizations that deploy cryptographic methods are responsible for using them appropriately. Organizations are accountable for selecting cryptographic methods that are robust enough for the given application and operational environment. They are responsible for ensuring that cryptographic methods are installed, configured, and operated correctly, along with all necessary associated technical and organizational controls. Ignorance is no excuse — organizations are liable for any negligent or misuse scenarios. If a company is smart, it will extend this liability to its business partners and subcontractors through enforceable contractual mechanisms.

Companies that provide managed security services or perform functions such as being a certificate authority are equally liable for any damages or harm resulting from their actions, lack of action, or negligence, according to the Guidelines. What the Guidelines are saying in effect is that outsourcing security may solve one headache, but it creates several more. State this liability, and any additional penalties being imposed by the organization, quite clearly in the contract with the security services provider.

International Cooperation

The eighth and last principle concerns International Cooperation. This principle ties back to the stated purpose of the Guidelines — to promote the use of cryptography to enhance the public's confidence in global telecommunications networks and information systems.[71] International cooperation is seen as the key to making the first five principles work. Trust in cryptographic methods, having a choice about what cryptographic methods to use, letting free market forces drive the development of cryptographic methods, fostering international cryptographic consensus standards, and widespread use of encryption to protect the privacy of sensitive personal data can only be achieved through international cooperation. Accordingly, the OECD Guidelines strongly encourage Member States to collaborate and cooperate in the broad areas of cryptographic methods and polices.

The OECD Guidelines for the Security of Information Systems and Networks were issued 25 July 2002. The Guidelines, subtitled "Toward a Culture of Security," replaced the 1992 OECD Guidelines for the Security of Information Systems. The introduction explained the reason for the new Guidelines[68]:

> *As a result of increasing interconnectivity, information systems and networks are now exposed to a growing number and wider variety of threats and vulnerabilities. Consequently, the nature, volume, and sensitivity of information that is exchanged has expanded substantially.*

In short, the Guidelines needed to be updated to reflect the significant advances in IT in the past decade.

The Security Guidelines form the third part in the OECD Security and Privacy trilogy that began in 1980 with the issuance of the Privacy Guidelines. The purpose of the Security Guidelines is to promote proactive, preventive security measures, versus reactive ones. The Guidelines emphasize the importance of security engineering activities early in the system engineering life cycle. In particular, attention focuses on specifying security requirements and the design and development of secure systems and networks. This is an intentional shift from the old way of viewing information security as an afterthought during the operational phase. In addition, the intent of the Guidelines is to raise awareness about the multitude of options organizations have when selecting what technical and organizational security controls to deploy.

The OECD Security Guidelines make the statement that they apply to "all participants in the new information society."[68] The Guidelines apply to all levels of government, industry, non-profit organizations, and individuals.[68] At the same time, the Guidelines acknowledge that different participants have different security roles and responsibilities, such as those discussed in Chapter 2[68]:

> *The Security Guidelines apply to all participants, but differently, depending on their roles in relation to information systems and networks. Each participant is an important actor in the process of ensuring security.*

Because they are guidelines, the OECD Security Guidelines fall under the category of voluntary recommendations. However, Member States are strongly encouraged to update their national policies and regulations to reflect and promote the new OECD Security Guidelines and collaborate at the international level in regard to implementation. Furthermore, given the rapid evolution of IT, the OECD has tasked itself to review and update the Guidelines every five years. The next review is scheduled for July 2007. Perhaps we can encourage the Member States to (1) include metrics, like those discussed below, in the next version of the Guidelines, and (2) report metrics in response to future surveys about the status of how Member States have implemented the Guidelines.

Two other documents supplement the OECD Security Guidelines and are subordinate to them. An Implementation Plan for the OECD Security Guidelines was issued 2 July 2003 that reinforced the guiding philosophy behind the Guidelines and the need for them.[68a] The Implementation Plan notes that the Security Guidelines were the "basis for Resolution A/RES/57/239 adopted by the 57th Session of the United National General Assembly."[68a] Some time after the Implementation Plan was issued, a survey was conducted to assess the progress Member States were making toward full implementation. The responses were summarized and issued in a separate report.[68b]

The OECD Security Guidelines are presented as a complementary set of nine principles that address the technical, policy, and operational aspects of information security. Each of the principles is discussed below. Again, there is no priority or order of importance associated with the sequence in which the principles are presented.

Awareness

The first principle of the OECD Security Guidelines is Awareness. This principle zeroes in on the fact that organizations and individuals must be fully aware of the need for security before there can be any hope of achieving it, especially on a global scale. The Guidelines are not talking about a one day a year, general-purpose security awareness event. Rather, an in-depth understanding of all four security domains — physical, personnel, IT, and operational security — is envisaged, along with an appreciation of how the four domains interact to ensure enterprisewide security. Fluency in the various tools and techniques that can be used to optimize security in each of the four domains is a key part of this awareness.[68] Likewise, it is expected that individuals and organizations will have a thorough understanding of the potential worst-case consequences that could result from not adhering to the OECD Security Guidelines. In short, individuals and organizations should be fully aware of what needs to be done to ensure the security of global information systems and networks, why it needs to be done, how it needs to be done, and what will happen if it is not done.

Responsibility

The second principle of the OECD Security Guidelines is Responsibility. As noted earlier, the Guidelines consider that all participants have responsibilities related to security that are tied to their roles and interaction with information systems and networks.[68a] Organizations are responsible for the secure design and operation of information systems and networks. Individuals are responsible for the secure handling of sensitive information and adherence to corporate security policies and operational procedures. Together, organizations and individuals are responsible for regularly reassessing the resilience of their operational security posture and remedying any deficiencies in a timely manner. Vendors also have responsibilities. According to the Guidelines, vendors are responsible for keeping customers informed on a regular basis about the current features, functionality, weaknesses, limitations, and updates for their products.[68] These responsibilities translate into accountability for all participants. Responsibilities not fully assumed give rise to liability concerns, similar to those discussed under the OECD Cryptography Guidelines.

Response

The third principle of the OECD Security Guidelines is Response, or perhaps *responsiveness* would be more accurate. The idea is that an organization should not deploy its security architecture and declare victory — "Whew, that is done, now we can move on to more important things." Rather, security engineering is viewed as a full life-cycle undertaking that does not stop until after a system or network is decommissioned. Individuals and organizations are expected to be responsive or agile enough to adapt to continually changing threat scenarios and operational security constraints. Proactive, preventive measures that can preempt security incidents are preferred. The Guidelines encourage cooperation and collaboration among Member States to achieve the greatest agility and responsiveness, similar to the various Computer Emergency Response Teams (CERTs) that have been established in the past five years. This is a noble goal, but perhaps a bit impractical. Sharing of security incident prevention and response information is a good idea in theory. But who decides who the information is or is not shared with? Who decides how this information is distributed and to whom? If the information is posted on public Web sites for all to see, would-be attackers know your prevention strategies and will find a workaround. So, what have you really accomplished? Not much. This is not an idle concern in the days of state-sponsored cyber terrorism. It is also somewhat counterproductive to post "newly discovered" vulnerabilities in COTS products on the Web. All that this really accomplishes is to give second-string would-be attackers a chance at notoriety before some organizations that are slow learners get around to patching them.

Ethics

The fourth principle of the OECD Security Guidelines concerns Ethics, in particular the ethical basis for protecting the rights and freedoms of individuals. Individuals have an inherent right to privacy and the right to expect that their sensitive personal information will be adequately protected by all public and private organizations that handle it, regardless of their geographical location.

This right translates into an ethical responsibility on the part of all data controllers, data processors, and their subcontractors involved in any transaction. Basic business ethics dictate that organizations have a duty to take their security responsibilities seriously, not cut corners or budgets, and exercise due care and due diligence. Furthermore, this implies that an organization hires staff who are qualified and competent to perform these duties, not the neighbor kid next door because he needs a summer job. Organizations are responsible for the ethical behavior of all their employees; awareness and personnel security controls have a role to play here. On the other hand, the consequences of not taking these ethical duties seriously include, but are not limited to, fines, other penalties, lost revenue, lost customers, damage to an organization's reputation, liability lawsuits, and other similar unpleasant experiences. Some contend that the whole notion of business ethics is dead in the wake of the Enron, WorldCom, and other recent scandals. That may or may not be true. What is for certain is that financial and legal penalties for a lapse in business ethics are alive and well.

Democracy

Democracy is the fifth principle in the OECD Security Guidelines. This principle embodies the concept that the security of sensitive personal information is consistent with the values of a democratic society.[68] Open societies encourage the free exchange of ideas, but at the same time respect an individual's right to privacy. Democratic countries understand the value of the free flow of information, but recognize the need to protect certain classes of information, like intellectual property rights. That is, there are times when information can be circulated openly and there are other times when access should be restricted. Organizations need to know which category the data they process falls into and handle it accordingly.

Risk Assessment

The sixth principle of the OECD Security Guidelines concerns Risk Assessments. Consistent with the stated purpose of the Guidelines — to promote a proactive, preventive approach to security — organizations are encouraged to perform frequent and thorough risk assessments throughout the life cycle of a system or network. Risk assessments are seen as the cornerstone to protecting sensitive personal information. The scope of the risk assessments is expected to encompass all four security domains (physical, personnel, IT, and operational security) and all parties involved (employees, subcontractors, business partners, and other third parties). The risk assessments are to be conducted in a methodical and comprehensive manner, not superficially, and identify all potential risks associated with collecting, processing, storing, and releasing sensitive personal information. Risk acceptability is determined from the point of view of the individual, not the organization, and the potential worst-case consequences of the harm they might experience.[68] Technical and organizational controls employed to mitigate risks must correspond to the information sensitivity and system risk.

Security Design and Implementation

The seventh principle of the OECD Security Guidelines is Security Design and Implementation. This principle reflects the shift in emphasis toward viewing security engineering as a concurrent engineering activity that is executed during all life-cycle phases, instead of a reactive afterthought during the operations and maintenance phase. Organizations are encouraged to integrate security engineering into their standard business practices and operational procedures. The previous principle required that risk assessments be performed throughout the life of an information system or telecommunications network. The preliminary risk assessment is used to identify potential generic vulnerabilities inherent in the collection, processing, storage, and dissemination of sensitive personal information and those that are unique to the specific application and operational environment. Security requirements, derived from the identified vulnerabilities, define the necessary security features and functions and how they work, along with the level of resilience required for each feature and function. Security requirements form the foundation of the security design or architecture for the system or network. The development process proceeds from the security design to ensure the secure implementation of the system or network. The preliminary risk assessment identifies the need for both technical and operational controls. As a result, security requirements are also used to define operational procedures to ensure the secure operation of a system or network. The preliminary risk assessment is repeated, updated, and refined during the design, implementation, and operational phases. In short, the sixth and seventh principles work in tandem. For a system or network to be secure, it must first be designed and built to be secure. Grafting on appliances after the fact does not work. The OECD Guidelines have made this point quite clear through the use of the sixth and seventh principles.

Security Management

The eighth principle of the OECD Security Guidelines concerns Security Management. The Guidelines are clear that to be effective, security management must be comprehensive, dynamic, and active throughout the life of a system or network.[68] Security management activities must also encompass all four security domains (physical, personnel, IT, and operational security). To get an appreciation of the depth and variety of issues involved, let us take a closer look at IT security management.

IT security management functions are performed by a group of authorized users with distinct roles and responsibilities, per the separation of duties principle. Through IT security management functions, these authorized users initialize, control, and maintain a system or network in a known secure state. IT security management functions include, but are not limited to[20]:

- Configuring and managing security features and functions, such as access control, authentication, encryption, and audit trails
- Configuring and managing security attributes associated with users, user roles, and other assets and resources
- Creating and managing security data, such as audit information, system, device, and network configuration parameters, and system clock information
- Defining and monitoring the expiration of security attributes
- Revoking security credentials, such as passwords, PINs, and digital certificates
- Defining and maintaining security management roles

Reassessment

A risk assessment was completed. The system or network passed the security certification and accreditation (C&A) process and has been deployed. You are all finished, right? Not hardly.

Systems and networks are constantly being upgraded or modified to address new requirements or constraints. The environment in which these systems and networks operate is ever-changing. The variety and complexity of internal and external systems and networks to which connectivity must be provided are a dynamic mix. The internal and external user populations are in a constant state of flux. Last, but not least, is the ever-changing threat scenario.

So what is a good security engineer to do? The ninth and final principle of the OECD Security Guidelines is Reassessment, Reassessment, Reassessment. The security posture, operational security procedures, and operational resilience of a system or network should be reassessed continually; otherwise, you are flying blind. A variety of methods can be used: operational risk assessments, security test and evaluation (ST&E), red teams, verifying the validity and currency of operational procedures, practicing contingency and disaster recovery procedures, conducting independent security audits, using the static analysis techniques discussed in Chapter 2, etc. Configuration management tools and techniques, especially performing security impact analysis on all proposed changes, upgrades, and patches, can be extremely insightful. The important thing is to do the reassessments regularly and in all four security domains.

A total of 25 principles are presented in the OECD Privacy, Cryptography, and Security Guidelines. The three Guidelines are intended to be used as a complementary set of principles and best practices to protect the security and privacy of sensitive personal data, especially as it traverses global information systems and networks. Member States are to use the three Guidelines and the principles they promote as the starting point for defining national data security and privacy policies and regulations. If we look at these 25 principles as a set, they can be grouped into four broad categories:

1. Limitations on data controllers and data processors
2. Individuals' rights and expectations
3. Roles and responsibilities of public and private sector organizations
4. Use and implementation of technical and organizational security controls

Table 3.7   Summary of OECD Privacy, Cryptography, and Security Principles

OECD Privacy Principles	OECD Cryptography Principles	OECD Security Principles
1. Limitations on Data Controllers and Data Processors		
Collection Limitation Data Quality Purpose Specification Use Limitation Accountability	Liability	Responsibility
2. Individuals' Rights and Expectations		
Openness Individual Participation	Trust in Cryptographic Methods	Democracy
3. Roles and Responsibilities of Public and Private Sector Organizations		

	Choice of Cryptographic
	  Methods
	Market Driven Development
	  of Cryptographic Methods
	Standards for Cryptographic
	  Methods
	Lawful Access
	International Cooperation
		Awareness
		Response
		Ethics

4. Use and Implementation of Technical and Organizational Security Controls		

Security Safeguards	Protection of Privacy and
	  Personal Data
		Risk Assessment
		Security Design and
		  Implementation
		Security Management
		Reassessment

Table 3.7 arranges the 25 principles into these four categories. Metrics that measure compliance with the principles in each of the four groups are discussed below. These metrics can be used by data controllers, internal and external auditors, Member States, third parties wishing to do business with Member States, public interest groups, and oversight authorities to demonstrate compliance with the OECD Guidelines.

Limitations on Data Controllers and Data Processors

The Guidelines place limits on what data controllers and data processors can and cannot do in regard to the collection, processing, storage, analysis, and dissemination of sensitive personal data. These ten metrics measure compliance with specific provisions in the Principles. For example, is data being collected illegally or through deceptive methods? How often is more data being collected than necessary for stated purposes? Are individuals being told why the data is really being collected and given an opportunity to review and correct inaccurate data? Is data being disposed of correctly afterward? Is consent sought from individuals before putting the data to a new use? Data controllers and data processors are not free to collect and use sensitive personal data at any time or for any purpose they dream up. The results from these metrics are a good indication of whether or not they take their accountability, responsibility, and liability seriously.

Number of data collection activities where more data was collected than necessary for the stated purpose and number of data subjects affected. 1.5.1

Distribution and number of data records obtained legally, with the data subject's consent, and illegally, without the data subject's consent.   1.5.2

Number of instances in which deceptive or hidden data collection methods were used, including the number of data subjects involved and the number of court actions that resulted.   1.5.3

Number of times data controllers were requested to correct incomplete, inaccurate, or old data.   1.5.4

Number and percentage of data controllers and data processors found not to have procedures in place to ensure the completeness, accuracy, and currency of the data they hold.   1.5.5

Distribution and number of data controllers who did and did not inform data subjects of the real reason for collecting the data beforehand.   1.5.6

Distribution and number of data controllers who did and did not erase, destroy, or render anonymous the data in their possession at the end of its stated use.   1.5.7

Distribution and number of data controllers who did and did not notify data subjects and receive their consent prior to using existing data for a new purpose.   1.5.8

Number and percentage of data controllers involved in liability lawsuits due to negligent handling of sensitive personal data.   1.5.9

Number and percentage of data controllers and data processors who have codes of conduct for accountability and responsibility related to handling of sensitive personal data built into employee performance appraisals.   1.5.10

Individuals Rights and Expectations

Individuals, or data subjects, are active participants in regard to the security and privacy of their personal data. The OECD Guidelines acknowledge their rights and expectations that the Principles will be followed. These two metrics measure whether or not (1) data controllers are fulfilling their communication obligations to data subjects, and (2) data subjects are actively asserting their rights.

Distribution of data controllers who did and did not inform data subjects:

1.5.11

a. Of the contact information for the data controller
b. That they had their personal data
c. That they had a right to access, receive, review, and correct that data

Number of individuals who: 1.5.12

a. Requested a copy of their personal data
b. Filed complaints for not receiving a copy of their personal data in a timely manner
c. Challenged the accuracy of their personal data
d. Filed complaints because their personal data was not being adequately protected and the number of these complaints that resulted in court actions
e. Refused to supply certain data due to a lack of confidence in either the technical controls, operational controls, or both

Roles and Responsibilities of Public and Private Sector Organizations

The OECD Guidelines expect the free marketplace to drive the development and implementation of cryptographic methods, along with other technical security controls. Participation in international forums, such as the development and promulgation of international consensus standards related to security and privacy technology, is promoted by the Guidelines. Sharing information and experiences fosters an awareness of the need for security and privacy and the tools and techniques to achieve it. Furthermore, the Guidelines encourage Member States not to interfere in this process. These ten metrics measure the extent to which these principles are being adhered to.

Number and names of Member States that limit the data controller's choice of cryptographic methods. 1.5.13

Number and names of third parties who are not Member States that limit the data processor's choice of cryptographic methods. 1.5.14

Number and names of Member States who are involved in the development and promulgation of international consensus standards for cryptographic methods. 1.5.15

Number and names of Member States who participate in collaborative forums related to the interoperability, portability, and mobility of cryptographic methods, such as conformance assessment. 1.5.16

Distribution and names of Member States who do and do not limit access to encrypted private information and communications by government officials. 1.5.17

Number and percentage of data controllers and data processors who have *bona fide* credentials and policies in place to ensure an understanding of the need for physical, personnel, IT, and operational security and the tools and techniques for achieving this. 1.5.18

Number and percentage of data controllers and data processors who have been cited for violations or involved in court actions related to deficiencies in technical or organizational security controls.   1.5.19

Number and percentage of data controllers who have a proven track record for: 1.5.20

  a. Proactive action to preempt and contain the damage from and spread of a security incident
  b. Quickly notifying all affected data subjects
  c. Coordinating responses with business partners and other third parties

Number and percentage of data controllers who failed to: 1.5.21

  a. Take appropriate action to preempt or contain a security incident
  b. Notify affected data subjects in a timely manner
  c. Coordinate or communicate with business partners and other third parties during a security incident

Use and Implementation of Technical and Organizational Security Controls

The OECD Guidelines expect Member States to ensure that appropriate safe-guards are employed to guarantee the security and privacy of sensitive personal data. This includes a combination of technical and organizational controls in all four security domains. Cryptographic methods are cited as one example of a technical control. Likewise, the Guidelines promote security engineering as a full life-cycle endeavor, with special emphasis given to security requirements, security design, and continual risk assessments. Data controllers and data processors are expected to employ comprehensive, robust, and agile security management tools and techniques. These eight metrics will measure whether or not they got the message.

Number and percentage of data controllers and data processors found to have appropriate technical and organizational security controls in place to prevent unauthorized loss, destruction, use, modification, and disclosure of sensitive personal data.   1.5.22

Number and percentage of data controllers and data processors found to have employed appropriate cryptographic methods and deployed them correctly to protect sensitive personal data.   1.5.23

Number and percentage of data controllers and data processors that regularly perform risk assessments throughout the life of an information system and telecommunications network.   1.5.24

Number and percentage of data controllers and data processors that require their subcontractors to perform regular risk assessments throughout the life of an information system or telecommunications network.   1.5.25

Number and percentage of data controllers that use the results of risk assessments to define their security requirements.   1.5.26

Number and percentage of data controllers and data processors who use security requirements to design their security architecture and guide the implementation of their information system or telecommunications network. 1.5.27

Number and percentage of data controllers and data processors who use security requirements to guide the development of operational security procedures and controls.   1.5.28

Number and percentage of data controllers and data processors found to have robust and current security management policies, procedures, and practices in the area of: 1.5.29

   a. Physical security
   b. Personnel security
   c. IT security
   d. Operational security

Now we will look at four regulations that evolved from the OECD Guidelines.

3.7 Data Protection Directive — E.C.

Directive 95/46/EC, known as the Data Protection Directive, was issued 24 October 1995 by the European Parliament and Council. The Directive consists of seven chapters and 34 articles and was amended in 2003.

The purpose of the Directive is to protect individuals' personal data and the processing and free movement of this data necessary for economic integration and the flow of goods and services among Member States. A lengthy rationale is given for the Directive, relating to the role of technology in society and limits that must be imposed to prevent potential abuses. Information systems are required to be designed and operated so that they respect the fundamental rights and freedoms of individuals, particularly their right to privacy. The Directive notes that the rapid evolution of information technology and telecommunication networks have made the exchange of personal data easier, and hence the need for placing limits on how, when, and under what conditions that data may be collected and exchanged. Prior to the Directive, Member States had different levels of protection for the rights and freedoms of individuals, notably their right to privacy. As a result, the need for a consistent level of protection was identified to protect individuals and promote economic integration. At the same time, a uniform provision for judicial remedies, damage compensation, and sanctions was created, should individual privacy rights be violated. The Directive established the position of a Supervisory Authority per Member State to monitor the implementation of the Directive and derivative national laws. The Supervisory Authority was granted the power to investigate, intervene, and take legal action to preempt or halt privacy violations. The Directive also established a Working Party, consisting of the Supervisory Authorities, or their representatives, from each Member State. The Working Party has the authority to give opinions and interpretations concerning the Directive and its application in national laws.

The Working Party is charged with submitting an annual report to the European Parliament documenting compliance with the Directive's provisions.

The Data Protection Directive is the outgrowth of two preceding pieces of legislation. The Data Protection Directive is an extension of the Right to Privacy contained in Article 8 of the European Convention for the Protection of Human Rights and Fundamental Freedoms. The Data Protection Directive also amplifies provisions in the Council of Europe Convention of 28 January 1981 for the Protection of Individuals with regard to Automatic Processing of Personal Data. The Directive is not intended to have an adverse effect on trade secrets, intellectual property rights, or copyrighted material.

The scope of the Data Protection Directive is rather broad. It is defined as applying to[65]:

> *...processing of personal data wholly or partly by automatic means, and to the processing otherwise than by automatic means of personal data which form part of a filing system or are intended to form part of a filing system.*

That is, the Directive applies to data that is in electronic form online, offline in electromagnetic archives, or in hardcopy form in filing cabinets. Textual, sound, and image data are included within the scope of the Directive if they contain any personally identifiable data. The protections of the Directive apply to individuals residing in any of the Member States. The provisions of the Directive apply to any organization residing within a Member State that collects and processes personal data, not just government agencies. This includes divisions of corporations residing within a Member State, although the corporate headquarters are elsewhere and the company is foreign owned. The provisions of the Directive extend to third parties with whom the organization that collected data has a contractual relationship regarding processing of that data. The Directive does not apply to communication between individuals or personal records, such as address books. The Directive also does not apply in cases of criminal investigations, public safety or security, or national defense. The originator of the information is considered the owner of the data, not the organization collecting, processing, storing, or transmitting it — unlike the current situation in the United States. Member States were granted three years from the date of issuance (1995) to pass derivative national laws and apply the Directive to automated systems. Member States were granted 12 years from the date of issuance to bring manual filing systems up to par. New Member States have three years from the time they joined the European Commission to issue derivative national laws and begin applying them.

Several terms are defined that are used throughout the Directive and are instrumental to understanding its provisions.

> **Personal data:** any information relating to an identified or identifiable natural person ("data subject"); an identifiable person is one who can be identified, directly or indirectly, in particular by reference to an identification number or to one or more factors specific to his physical, physiological, mental, economic, cultural, or social identity.[65]

> **Personal data filing system**: any structured set of personal data which are accessible according to specific criteria, whether centralized, decentralized, or dispersed on a functional or geographic basis.[65]

Personal data is any textual, image, or sound data that can be traced to or associated with an individual and characteristics of their identity, such as race, religion, age, height, health, income, etc. The definition of what constitutes a personal data filing system is all encompassing: any collection of personal information, regardless of its form or locations, from which any personally identifiable data can be extracted. This definition goes well beyond what most people ascribe to the idea of an information system.

> **Processing of personal data:** any operation or set of operations which is performed upon personal data, whether or not by automatic means, such as collection, recording, organization, storage, adaptation or alteration, retrieval, consultation, use, disclosure by transmission, dissemination or otherwise making available, alignment or combination, blocking, erasure, or destruction.[65]

The definition of processing of personal data is equally broad. Note that it includes any operation on personal data, from collection, to alteration, disclosure, blocking, and destruction, whether by manual or automated means.

> **The data subject's consent:** any freely given and specific and informed indication of his wishes by which the data subject signifies his agreement to personal data relating to him being processed.[65]

The focus of the Directive is to protect the rights and freedoms of individuals, which are referred to as data subjects. The data subject's unambiguous consent must be obtained before any personal data is collected or processed.

> **Controller:** natural or legal person, public authority, agency, or any other body which alone or jointly with others determines the purposes and means of the processing of personal data; where the purposes and means of processing are determined by national or Community laws and regulations, the controller or specific criteria for his nomination may be designated by national or Community law.[65]

> **Processor:** a natural or legal person, public authority, agency, or any other body which processes personal data on behalf of the controller.[65]

Two key roles spelled out in the Directive are that of the controller and that of the processor. The controller is responsible for determining how and why personal data will be processed, unless that is already specified in national laws. The processor is responsible for the actual processing of personal data and acts under the direction of the controller.

Third party: any natural or legal person, public authority, agency, or any other body other than the data subject, the controller, the processor, and the persons who, under the direct authority of the controller or processor, are authorized to process the data.[65]

Recipient: natural or legal person, public authority, agency, or any other body to whom data are disclosed, whether a third party or not; however, authorities which may receive data in the framework of a particular inquiry shall not be regarded as recipients.[65]

Under specified conditions, personal data may be released to two classes of outsiders: third parties and recipients. Third parties are individuals or organizations with whom the controller or processor has established a contractual relationship to perform some aspect of processing personal data. The Directive requires that (1) all privacy provisions and safeguards be invoked in contracts with third parties, and (2) third parties be held accountable for compliance. Recipients are individuals or organizations that are legally entitled to receive processed personal data.

The Directive establishes several security and privacy rules to which Member States must comply. Member States are permitted to invoke more-detailed rules, but not less stringent measures. The first set of rules pertains to the integrity of the data collected. The data is required to be processed fairly and lawfully. The data must be collected and used only for a prestated specific and legitimate purpose; it cannot be used later for other purposes, such as data mining. The data must be complete but not excessive and relevant for the purpose for which it was collected. The organization collecting and retaining the data has the responsibility to ensure that the data is accurate and current; inaccurate or incomplete data must be deleted or corrected. Finally, the data cannot be kept for any longer than needed to perform the prestated processing purposes.

The second rule relates to what is referred to as legitimate processing of personal data. Prior to processing personal data, the organization is required to obtain unambiguous consent from the data subject. A few exceptions are given, such as situations where the organization is under contract to provide some service for the individual or perform some task that is in the public interest, or has received official approval from the controller.

Other rules define special cases where the processing of personal data is or is not allowed. For example, personal data that reveals information about an individual's race, ethnic origin, political opinions, religious or philosophical beliefs, trade-union membership, health status, or sex life is prohibited. Some exceptions to this prohibition are noted, such as the individual has given his consent, instances where it is medically necessary to aid the data subject, information is collected by a non-profit organization to which the data subject belongs, and data made public during court proceedings. Another prohibition concerns the right not to be the subject of an automated decision about work performance, creditworthiness, reliability, or personal conduct that has legal or employment ramifications. This is another example of a provision that is currently lacking in the United States legal system.

Other provisions explain the extent of information that must be given to data subjects beforehand. In all cases, data subjects must be notified about the purpose of collecting the data, how the data will be processed, and how long the data will be retained. Data subjects must be told whether supplying the data is mandatory or voluntary. Of course, employment or other application forms can still bypass this provision by invoking the phrase "supplying this information is strictly voluntary; however, without this information we cannot process your application." Data subjects must be informed about who will receive the data and under what circumstances. The "who" may be listed as classes of recipients rather than exact names. Data subjects must also be given the identity and contact information of the controller and told that they have the right to access, verify, and correct the data. Data subjects must be given the same information when data about them is collected from other sources and not directly from themselves.

The Directive stipulates special data processing confidentiality and security rules. A processor cannot process personal data unless directed to do so by the controller or national law. The processor is responsible for ensuring that appropriate technical and organizational controls have been implemented to prevent accidental or intentional unlawful destruction, loss, alteration, disclosure, or access to personal data. A risk assessment is required to be performed to determine potential risks to individuals' rights and freedoms as a result of processing personal data. It is imperative that the risk control measures implemented by the processor are proportional to the identified level of risk. The transfer of personal data to a non-Member State is allowed only when the third country can guarantee that adequate safeguards and equivalent laws are in force. The processor and controller must notify the Commission immediately of any violations of the Directive by third countries, to help prevent other Member States from transferring personal data to that non-Member State.

As mentioned previously, the Working Party, composed of Supervisory Authorities, is tasked with preparing an annual report to the Commission, outlining compliance with the Data Protection Directive across the Member States. This implies that they have to gather information related to compliance. Security and privacy metrics, such as those presented below, are a concise, objective, and factual way to collect, analyze, and report the status of compliance with provisions in the Directive. Processors could report these metrics to controllers on a quarterly or semi-annual basis. Controllers, in turn, could submit the metrics to the Supervisory Authority for their Member State. Each Supervisory Authority would aggregate the metrics for the Member State they represent. The Supervisory Authorities, as members of the Working Party, would then aggregate the metrics to prepare their annual report to the Commission. Metrics provide greater insight than textual discussion alone, facilitate comparing compliance results from year to year and from Member State to Member State, and highlight specific areas needing improvement.

Three categories of security and privacy metrics can be used to demonstrate compliance with the Data Protection Directive; together they provide a comprehensive picture of the current situation.

1. Metrics that measure of the integrity of the personal data
2. Metrics that measure compliance with the consent, notification, and legitimate processing provisions
3. Metrics that measure the extent of prohibited processing, inadequate safeguards, and other violations

Data Integrity

The collection and processing of personal data diminishes personal privacy, whether or not the data subject has given their consent. What could be worse than for some of this information to be wrong? Suppose wrong information is disseminated and decisions are made based on the wrong data. It is very time consuming and expensive for an individual to recover from this situation. That is why the Directive has provisions for: (1) ensuring the accuracy of this information, (2) giving the data subject the opportunity to review and correct any invalid data, and (3) judicial remedies and damage compensation for any harm suffered by the data subject as a result of mishandling of personal data. Likewise, the Directive does not allow personal information to be collected as part of a massive snooping expedition, used for any purpose that may come to mind before or after the data is collected, or kept as long as the processor wants. The following three metrics measure compliance with the data integrity provisions of the Directive. They determine whether or not the data subject records are accurate and have been collected, processed, stored, and kept in an appropriate manner. These metrics could be applied on a per-organization basis, and then aggregated at the Member State level.

Percentage (%) and number of data subject records collected, processed, and stored that are lawful, fair, adequate, relevant, and not excessive.   1.6.1

Percentage (%) and number of data subject records that have not been kept for longer than needed for stated processing purposes.   1.6.2

Percentage (%) and number of data subject records verified to be accurate and current.   1.6.3

Consent, Notification, and Legitimate Processing

The first category of metrics dealt with the personal data itself. This category examines how the data was obtained and processed. The Directive is very clear that personal data can only be collected with the data subject's unambiguous consent. If the data was obtained from a third party without the data subject's consent, the data subject must be notified. Not only do data subjects have to give their consent prior to collecting any personal data, but they must be told the purpose for which the data is being collected, how the data will be stored, and for what period of time. They must also be given the identity and contact information for the controller who authorized collecting and processing the personal data. Finally, to give data subjects visibility into this situation, the processor is required to let data subjects know that they have a right to access their personal data. The following five metrics measure compliance with the consent, notification, and legitimate processing provisions of the Directive. The first measures the extent to which consent was obtained prior to collecting any personal data. The second determines whether or not data subjects are being told when personal data is obtained from a third party without their knowledge or consent. The third and fourth metrics evaluate compliance with the requirements to explain to data subjects how the data will be used and handled, along with their access rights. Just to make sure people are really being told about their access rights, the fifth metric ascertains how many people have actually requested to access their records. If this number is extremely low or zero, it is questionable whether they are really being told about their rights.

Percentage (%) of data subject records for which the data subject's consent was obtained prior to collection. 1.6.4

Percentage (%) and number of data subjects notified that data was obtained from a third party. 1.6.5

Percentage (%) of data subjects who were notified in advance of how the data would be used, how it would be stored, and how long it would be kept. 1.6.6

Percentage (%) of data subjects notified of their right to access and correct their data records. 1.6.7

Number of data subjects who requested access to their records. 1.6.8

Prohibited Processing, Inadequate Safeguards, and Other Violations

One hundred percent compliance with any regulation is rarely achieved in any country or jurisdiction. As a result, it is important to know where the problems are occurring and the cause of noncompliance. The final eight metrics zero in on the type and extent of violations. The transfer of personal data to third countries is of particular concern. The controller and Supervisory Authority need to know whether or not the third countries to which personal data was transferred have a proven track record of providing and enforcing appropriate safeguards. The first metric answers this question. Time frames were established for bringing both automated and manual filing systems into compliance with the Directive. The next two metrics measure the level of compliance that has been achieved to date. To take remedial and, if necessary, legal action, controllers and Supervisory Authorities need to know how many violations have occurred, how many data subject records were affected per violation, and the type of violation. The fourth metric will indicate the extent and distribution of violations. Perhaps the majority of the violations are occurring in one area and the reason needs to be investigated. It is important to know whether violations are a result of accidental or intentional action. Intentional violations will of course be prosecuted differently than accidental ones, unless gross negligence is the root cause. The Directive requires implementation of adequate technical (IT security) and organizational (physical, personnel, and operational security) controls. The fifth and sixth metrics evaluate the distribution of violations by source (accidental or intentional), cause (failure of technical or organizational controls), and type. Failure to perform a thorough risk assessment before collecting and processing personal data is the likely cause of inadequate technical or organizational controls. How else can an organization know what specific risk control measures are needed or the level of integrity required for those measures? The seventh metric assesses the prevalence of this oversight. A concrete measure of the number and severity of violations is the number of data subjects that sought judicial remedies and damage compensation, as a result of these violations. The eighth metric captures this information. Also, look for inconsistencies between the results of the different metrics. For example, if more data subjects sought judicial remedies (1.6.16) than violations were reported (1.6.12, 1.6.13, 1.6.14), other problems need to be investigated as well.

Number of data subject records transferred to third countries, by third country:
1.6.9

    a. Percentage (%) of these third countries who have known and proven safeguards and laws in force
    b. Percentage (%) of these third countries who do not have known and proven safeguards and laws in force

Percentage (%) and number of automated personal information systems that comply with the Directive and the number of data subject records in each, by processor, controller, Supervisory Authority, and Member State.   1.6.10

Percentage (%) and number of automated personal information systems that do not comply with the Directive and the number of data subject records in each, by processor, controller, Supervisory Authority, and Member State.
1.6.10

Percentage (%) and number of manual personal information systems that comply with the Directive and the number of data subject records in each, by processor, controller, Supervisory Authority, and Member State.   1.6.11

Percentage (%) and number of manual personal information systems that do not comply with the Directive and the number of data subject records in each, by processor, controller, Supervisory Authority, and Member State.   1.6.11

Number and distribution of violations by prohibited processing category, and how many data subject records were affected per violation: 1.6.12
    a. Race or ethnic origin
    b. Political opinions
    c. Religious or philosophical beliefs
    d. Trade-union membership
    e. Health records
    f. Sex life
    g. Work performance
    h. Creditworthiness

      i. Reliability
      j. Personal conduct
      k. Processing without the approval of the controller
      l. Processing without the approval of the Supervisory Authority

Number and distribution of accidental violations due to (1) inadequate technical or (2) inadequate organizational safeguards, by type: 1.6.13
      a. Unauthorized destruction of personal data
      b. Unauthorized loss of personal data
      c. Unauthorized alteration of personal data
      d. Unauthorized disclosure of personal data
      e. Unauthorized access to personal data

Number and distribution of intentional unlawful violations due to inadequate technical or organizational safeguards, by type: 1.6.14
      a. Unauthorized destruction of personal data
      b. Unauthorized loss of personal data
      c. Unauthorized alteration of personal data
      d. Unauthorized disclosure of personal data
      e. Unauthorized access to personal data

Number of organizations that failed to adequately evaluate the potential risks to data subjects' rights and freedoms before initializing a personal data filing system.   1.6.15

Number of data subjects who sought judicial remedies and damage compensation for violations of their privacy rights under the Directive and national laws.   1.6.16

3.8 Data Protection Act — United Kingdom

The Data Protection Act is an example of a national law that was derived from the Data Protection Directive. The Data Protection Act was enacted by the U.K. Parliament on 24 July 1998 and took effect 24 October 1998, meeting the three-year deadline specified in the Directive for Member States to comply. The Data Protection Act consists of six parts and 16 schedules. Two transition periods are specified for implementation. The first period, from 24 October 1998 through 23 October 2001, allowed time for automated personal data processing systems to be brought into compliance with the Act. The second period, from 24 October 2001 through 23 October 2007, allows time for manual personal data filing systems to be brought into compliance, consistent with the 12-year period specified in the Directive.

    The purpose of the Act is to "make new provision for the regulation of the processing of information relating to individuals, including the obtaining, holding, use or disclosure of such information."[64] Unlike the Directive, the Data Protection Act does not mention any economic reasons for enactment. The Act gives the role of Supervisory Authority, as defined in the Directive, the title of Data Protection Commissioner. The Commissioner is responsible for (1) promoting and enforcing compliance to the provisions in the Act by data controllers, and (2) keeping the public informed about the provisions of the Act and the status of its implementation. The Commissioner is tasked with submitting an annual activity report to both Houses of Parliament. A Data Protection Tribunal assists the Commissioner in rendering decisions and inter-pretations and hearing complaints. The Tribunal is staffed to equally represent the interests of data subjects and data controllers.

The scope of the Data Protection Act is equivalent to that of the Directive. The Data Protection Act applies to any personally identifiable data that is in electronic form online, offline in electromagnetic archives, or in hardcopy form in filing cabinets, including textual, sound, and image data. The protec-tions of the Act apply to individuals "ordinarily resident" in the United Kingdom.[64] No distinction is made between citizens and non-citizens or different age groups. It is unclear how long a temporary resident or foreign student would have to reside in the United Kingdom before he is protected by the Act as well. The provisions of the Act apply to any organization residing within the United Kingdom that collects and processes personal data, not just government agencies. This includes divisions of corporations residing within the United Kingdom, although the corporate headquarters are elsewhere and the company is foreign owned. The Act requires that its provisions be extended to third parties with whom the organization that collected data has a contractual relationship regarding the processing of that data. The Act does not apply to communication between individuals or personal records, such as address books. Like the Directive, the Act does not apply in cases of criminal inves-tigations, public safety or security, or national defense. The Act adds additional categories of exemptions, such as tax investigations and educational records. Again, the originator of the information is considered the owner of the data, not the organization collecting, processing, storing, or transmitting it. The Act notes that its provisions only apply to living persons; exemptions are cited for the purposes of historical research. That seems rather strange. The deceased should be entitled to as much privacy, if not more so, than the living. The deceased are not in a position to defend themselves from charges of character assassination. Why should the remaining family members have to deal with such an invasion of privacy along with their loss? This also raises questions about obtaining consent from the next of kin, processing data after the fact for purposes other than for which it was originally collected, and the length of time the data can be retained.

The Data Protection Act of 1998 repeals two earlier pieces of legislation: (1) The Data Protection Act of 1984 and (2) The Access to Personal Files Act of 1987. The Act also replaces various sections in other Acts, such as The Data Protection Registration Fee Order of 1991.

The terminology of the Data Protection Act is consistent with the Directive from which it was derived. The Data Protection Act uses the terms "data controller" versus "controller" and "data processor" versus "processor" similar to the OECD Guidelines. The Data Protection Act defines two additional terms that are noteworthy:

Data subject: an individual who is the subject of personal data.[64]

Sensitive personal data: personal information consisting of information as to:

a. Racial or ethnic origin of the data subject
b. His political opinions
c. His religious beliefs or other beliefs of a similar nature
d. Whether he is a member of a trade union
e. His physical or mental health or condition
f. His sexual life
g. Commission or alleged commission by him of any offence
h. Any proceedings for any offence committed or alleged to be have been committed by him, the disposal of such proceedings or the sentence of any court in such proceedings[64]

Because the data subject is the primary reason the Act exists, it is only logical to clearly define this term. Likewise, it is necessary to state explicitly what constitutes sensitive personal data. This definition is an expansion and special instance of the definition of personal data contained in the Data Protection Directive. Note that this list does not include date of birth, place of birth, financial records, or the equivalent of a social security number, items that are considered sensitive in the United States.

The Data Protection Act fills in certain details, such the role of courts in enforcement actions, required time frames to perform certain tasks, and when fees are applicable. These types of items were left out of the Directive because they are unique to each Member State's legal system. A fair amount of detail is provided about the rights of data subjects. Data subjects must be informed by the data controllers that they possess personal data, how that data will be used, who the likely recipients of the data are, and the source of the data if it was not collected from the data source directly.[64] However, the notification process is not automatic. The data subject must request this information in writing from the data controller. This, of course, assumes that the data subject knows all the potential data controllers who have or are likely to obtain personal data about them. That is, this responsibility has been shifted from the data controller to the data subject. On the other hand, data controllers are expected to go to some length to authenticate the data subject and their request before replying to it, to prevent release of information to unauthorized people. Unlike the Directive, the Act permits data controllers to withhold information if releasing it would reveal the source, and supposedly invade the privacy of the source. This provision is rather contradictory — an act that is supposed to protect the privacy and integrity of personal information allows unnamed sources to supply potentially damaging misinformation that the data subject has no right to see or validate. Surely the drafters of the Act have heard of gossipy neighbors, jealous co-workers, and people who just do not like someone because of their race, ethnicity, religion, economic status, etc.

An interesting twist to the Act is the provision that states there must be "reasonable intervals" between requests. Supposedly this is to prevent data subjects from submitting weekly requests to data controllers, just to see if anything new has popped up. Perhaps this has happened in the past, and hence the statement. Another new aspect is the right of data subjects to, in effect, send the data controller a cease and desist order if the data subject feels that the release of such personal data will or has caused them unwarranted harm, damage, or distress. The data controller has 21 days to respond to the cease and desist order or face a court order. The data subject may also give a cease and desist order to direct marketing associations, who likewise must comply or face a court order. That provision is sorely needed in the United States.

The Data Protection Act assigns several specific responsibilities to data controllers and the Commissioner. Data controllers are the party responsible for paying damages to data subjects, not data processors, for any violations under the Act. This deviates from the Directive, which cites certain cases under which controllers are exempt from such liability. Notifications to data subjects must include the name and address of the data controller. Data controllers cannot authorize processing of personal data unless they have (1) registered with the Commissioner, and (2) received prior permission from the Commissioner. The Commissioner is responsible for (1) making all registrations available to the public, and (2) determining if the processing of personal data is likely to cause harm to the data subject, and if so, ordering its cessation. The Commissioner has the authority to issue enforcement notices to data controllers if they suspect that any provisions of the Act have been contravened. In addition, the data subject can request that the Commissioner investigate suspected violations.

The Schedules restate and amplify the data protection principles contained in the Directive to clarify what does and does not constitute compliance. For example, the Act states that it is illegal to use deceptive practices when explaining why personal data is being collected or how it will be used. The risk assessment must factor in the magnitude of harm the data subject could experience, should the technical and/or organizational controls prove inadequate. The Act specifically calls out the need for the data controller to employ "reliable" personnel. The Act also points out that it is illegal to sell personal data that was obtained without the data subject's consent.

Table 3.8 notes the unique provisions of The U.K. Data Protection Act, compared to Directive 95/46/EC. Three classes of metrics were developed for the Data Protection Directive, discussed above: (1) data integrity; (2) consent, notification, and legitimate processing; and (3) prohibited processing, inadequate safeguards, and other violations. These three categories and the metrics defined for them are equally applicable to the U.K. Data Protection Act. Given the unique provisions of the Act, as noted in Table 3.8, some additional metrics are warranted as well.

Data Integrity

No additional metrics are needed.

Table 3.8   Unique Provisions of the U.K. Data Protection Act

Differences from Directive 95/46/EC

Does not tie rationale for the Act to economic reasons
Does not exempt the data controller from liability considerations
Shifts responsibility for notification to the data subject — they have to request the information
Allows data controllers to withhold some information if revealing it could violate the privacy of the source of that information

Additional Detailed Provisions

Adds the role of the Tribunal to assist the Data Protection Commissioner
Adds the role of the courts in enforcement actions
Tasks the Data Protection Commissioner with keeping the public informed
Adds the responsibility for the data controller to authenticate requests for personal information
Defines maximum time intervals for certain items to be completed
Gives data subjects the right to issue "cease and desist" orders to data controllers if they believe release of information would cause unwarranted harm, damage, or distress
Gives data subjects the right to request the Data Protection Commissioner to investigate potential violations or situations that they believe may cause them harm
States that it is illegal to sell personal data if it was not obtained by consent

Consent, Notification, and Legitimate Processing

One more metric is needed under the category of legitimate processing due to the additional provisions in the U.K. Data Protection Act. This metric concerns the frequency with which information is being withheld from data subjects. If this metric indicates that this is a prevalent practice, there may be deceptive or other illegal collection activities going on, or misinformation is purposely being disseminated. Either situation warrants further investigation.

Number of requests for information received from data subjects: 1.7.1

   a. Percentage (%) for which data controller withheld information to protect privacy of sources
   b. Percentage (%) for which data controller did not withhold information to protect privacy of sources

Prohibited Processing, Inadequate Safeguards, and Other Violations

Three additional metrics are needed under the category that monitors violations. The U.K. Data Protection Act requires that data controllers authenticate requests before releasing personal information. This provision protects data subjects by ensuring that their personal information is not released to others without their authorization. If a large percentage of requests fail the authentication test, some attempted fraud may be under way, such as identity theft. The first metric will bring this situation to light.

The last two metrics focus on illegal activities by data processors and data controllers. Serious violations go beyond "cease and desist" orders and result in the payment of fines. The number of times data controllers had to pay fines, and any upward or downward trends in these numbers, are a good indication of whether or not compliance is taken seriously by controllers and processors. It can also be enlightening to see if the same data controllers are repeat offenders.

With cases of identity theft being rampant, a crucial number to watch is the number of attempted or actual illegal sales of personal information. Identity theft, especially where thousands of people are involved, usually involves insiders (data processors) colluding with outsiders. Pay close attention to the number of attempts and the number of data subjects involved. Some patterns may begin to emerge. Identity thieves rarely target a single individual. This metric surfaces an issue that the Data Protection Act does not address — notifying data subjects that their personal information may or has been illegally released. Data subjects deserve notification so that they can take action to preempt or contain the damage. Failure to notify data subjects of a breach in a timely manner would seem to represent negligence, or dereliction of duty at a minimum, on the part of the data controller.

Distribution and number of requests for personal information from data subjects that passed and did not pass the authentication test.   1.7.2

Number of cases in which the data controller had to pay damages.   1.7.3

Number of cases involving the illegal sale of personal information and the number of data subject records involved.   1.7.4

Action Taken in the Public Interest

As noted in Table 3.8, new and more detailed roles and responsibilities are defined in the Act. Consequently, a new category of metrics is needed, Action Taken in the Public Interest. These are the types of metrics the public and public interest groups will want to know. These metrics bring to life the facts that paragraphs of bland text never will. Used properly, these metrics can increase the public's confidence in the effectiveness of the regulatory process.

The Act established a new role, that of the Tribunal, to assist the Data Protection Commissioner. To find out if the Tribunal is being used, why not measure the number of cases in which it became involved. How about the Commissioner? Is he taking his job seriously or just giving it lip service? One answer to this question comes from the number of cases in which he took proactive action to prevent violations and harm to data subjects. Another answer comes from the number and type of activities through which the Commissioner has attempted to keep the public informed. Are the provisions of the Act being enforced? The number of court orders that were issued to enforce compliance is one indication. Do data subjects really feel that they have rights under this Act? One method to find out is to measure the number of times and ways they have attempted to exercise these rights. For example, how many "cease and desist" requests did data subjects submit? How many times did data subjects ask the Data Protection Commissioner to undertake an investigation? How frequently do data subjects request to view public registers? If these numbers are low or show a downward trend, the public has lost confidence in the regulatory process.

Number of cases in which the Tribunal became involved. 1.7.5

Number of cases in which the Data Protection Commissioner took proactive action to prevent violations and harm to data subjects. 1.7.6

Number of cases in which specified time intervals were exceeded and court orders were necessary. 1.7.7

Number of "cease and desist" requests sent by data subjects: 1.7.8
  a. To data controllers to prevent unwarranted harm, damage, or distress
  b. To direct marketing associations

Number of investigations data subjects requested the Data Protection Commissioner to undertake. 1.7.9

Number and type of activities undertaken by the Data Protection Commissioner to keep the public informed. 1.7.10

Average number of requests per month by data subjects to view public registers and the number of data subject records accessed. 1.7.11

3.9 Personal Information Protection and Electronic Documents Act (PIPEDA) — Canada

Bill C-6, the Personal Information Protection and Electronic Documents Act (PIPEDA), was issued by the Canadian Parliament on 13 April 2000. The stated purpose of the Act is twofold[62]:

1. To support and promote electronic commerce by protecting personal information that is collected, used, or disclosed
2. To provide rules to govern the collection, use, and disclosure of personal information in a manner that recognizes the right of privacy of individuals with respect to their personal information and the need of organizations to collect, use, and disclose personal information for purposes that a reasonable person would consider appropriate in the circumstances

That is, the Act is intended to protect individuals while at the same time promoting E-commerce. Note that the PIPEDA assigns everything that can be done to or with personal information to three categories of activities: (1) collection, (2) use, and (3) disclosure. This grouping is logical and it simplifies provisions in the Act. The phrase "that a reasonable person would consider appropriate in the circumstances" is a metaphor for saying "in a non-negligent manner."

PIPEDA consists of five parts, one schedule, and ten principles. Part 1 establishes the rights for protection of personal information, while Schedule 1 states the actual privacy principles. Part 2 defines when digital signatures can be used and when documents, testimony, and payments can be submitted electronically. Parts 3 through 5 amend existing legislation. Consequently, Parts 2 through 5 are beyond the scope of this book. Instead, we concentrate on Part 1 and Schedule 1. The Canadian Parliament is serious about implementing the privacy provisions of the Act. The Act states that Part 1 of the PIPEDA takes precedence over any Act or provision that is enacted afterward, unless there is an explicit declaration in the subsequent legislation to the contrary. Furthermore, Provincial legislatures were given three years from the date of enactment (13 April 2000) to implement the Act within their provinces. Health-care professionals and organizations were given less time — one year from the date of enactment. The PIPEDA also established the federal office of Privacy Commissioner, who is tasked with receiving, investigating, and resolving reports of noncompliance. Parliament has given itself the responsibility of reviewing Part 1 of the PIPEDA every five years and reaffirming or updating it within a year. The intent is to keep the Act in synch with the rapid evolution of technology and society norms.

It is important to understand two terms and how they are used within the Act:

> **Personal information:** information about an identifiable individual, but does not include the name, title, or business address or telephone number of an employee of an organization.[62]

> **Record:** any correspondence, memorandum, book, plan, map, drawing, diagram, pictorial or graphic work, photograph, film, microfilm, sound recording, videotape, machine-readable record, and any other documentary material, regardless of physical form or characteristics, and any copy of any of those things.[62]

Under the Act, personal information is any information that can be associated with an individual, except their contact information at work. This exclusion seems a bit odd and no explanation is provided. No distinction is made between personal information and sensitive personal information. The definition of record is extremely broad and includes anything that has been recorded, regardless of the format or media.

The PIPEDA applies to any organization that collects, uses, or discloses personal information, whether for a commercial activity, government-related work, or for employment purposes within the legal boundaries of Canada. Personal information that is used by individuals or government agencies covered by the Privacy Act are excluded. Exemptions are also made for journalistic, artistic, or literary purposes; however, it seems that it would be easy to misuse this exemption for malicious purposes. Specific exemptions are also cited for each of the three types of transactions — collection, use, and dissemination. These exemptions are discussed under the applicable principle below.

The PIPEDA rearranged the OECD privacy principles in order of priority and dependency. The PIPEDA also expanded the eight principles from the OECD Privacy Guidelines into ten principles and augmented them. The OECD Use Limitation principle was expanded to include disclosure and retention and renamed accordingly. Obtaining consent from individuals, before collecting, using, or disclosing their personal information, was broken out as a separate principle to emphasize the importance of this activity. Likewise, the right of individuals to challenge an organization's compliance with any provision of the PIPEDA was made into a new principle, separate from their right of access, to reinforce the fact that individuals are active participants in this process. Each principle is discussed below in the sequence presented in Schedule 1.

Accountability

The first principle is accountability. What better place to start privacy provisions than to spell out who is accountable The Act makes it quite clear that an organization that collects, uses, and discloses personal information is ultimately responsible for protecting its privacy. In fact, the discussion on accountability incorporates many features found in the OECD Security Guidelines Responsibility principle, although the PIPEDA was issued first. Without strong accountability language up-front, the rest of the principles and provisions would be moot. Just to make sure they understand, organizations are expected to designate an individual who is to be held personally accountable for compliance with all the provisions in Part 1 and Schedule 1 of the PIPEDA. This eliminates any chance of pleading ignorance following a violation. The contact information for this person is to be made available to the public, upon request. A major responsibility of this office is to document the organization's privacy policies and procedures specifically as they relate to handling of personal information. This documentation is to be kept up-to-date and communicated to employees on a regular basis. In addition, frequent specialized training about privacy practices and procedures is to be held. Complaints and inquiries from individuals must also be responded to by this office and in a reasonable time frame. Furthermore, organizations are responsible for the actions of any third parties to whom they may give personal information. As such, organizations are encouraged to include robust accountability clauses in contracts with these third parties. The Privacy Commissioner is accountable for ensuring that organizations comply with the PIPEDA. To underscore the importance of the privacy principles and accountability for adhering to them, the Privacy Commissioner may audit an organization at any time if a potential or actual violation is expected. The Privacy Commissioner may conduct interviews, take testimony, and subpoena records as part of an audit.

The following metrics can be used by organizations, internal and external auditors, and public interest groups to demonstrate compliance with the Accountability principle. These metrics can also be aggregated to measure the extent of compliance and highlight problem areas at the Provincial and federal levels.

Distribution of organizations that do and do not have a designated official who is accountable for compliance with the privacy provisions of the PIPEDA.
                                                                                    1.8.1

Date designated accountability official was appointed: 1.8.2

  a. Date position was created
  b. Tenure in the position

Number of requests received for contact information of the designated accountability official: 1.8.3

  a. Number and percentage responded to

Distribution of organizations who: 1.8.4

  a. Have documented their policies and procedures for handling personal information
  b. Conduct regular training for employees about their policies and procedures for handling personal information

Date an organization's policies and procedures for handling personal information were written: 1.8.5

  a. Frequency with which the polices and procedures are reviewed and updated
  b. Frequency with which employees receive training about the policies and procedures

Average time for an organization to respond to a request made by an individual.
                                                                                    1.8.6

Number and percentage of contracts with third parties that contain accountability clauses for the handling of personal information.   1.8.7

Number of audits conducted by the Privacy Commissioner that were not in response to a complaint.   1.8.8

Identifying Purposes

The first privacy principle clarifies who is accountable. The second through eighth principles explain what they are being held accountable for doing. The ninth and tenth principles amplify individuals rights.

   Under the second principle, organizations are expected to first document the reason personal information is being collected and how it will be used This document is then to be used as the basis for determining exactly what information does or does not need to be collected, so that no unnecessary or additional information is gathered. That is, organizations are supposed to proceed methodically, not haphazardly, when planning for and dealing with personal information. Organizations have an obligation to tell individuals precisely why they are collecting personal information and how it will be used and disclosed at or before the time of collection. This explanation can be done orally or in writing. The stated purpose is static; it cannot grow new arms and legs later, without the active participation of the individual. The individual must be notified in detail of any proposed new use of personal information that has already been collected and give consent before the proposed new use is acted upon.

The following metrics can be used by organizations, internal and external auditors, and public interest groups to demonstrate compliance with the Identifying Purposes principle. These metrics can also be aggregated to measure the extent of compliance and highlight problem areas at the Provincial and federal levels.

Number and percentage of categories of personal information for which the reason for collecting and using it is documented.   1.8.9

Number of reviews conducted to ensure that no unnecessary or additional information is being collected.   1.8.10

Distribution of times individuals were and were not told the precise: 1.8.11

    a. Reason for collecting personal information
    b. Use of the personal information
    c. Recipients of the personal information

Distribution and number of times individuals were and were not informed:
                    1.8.12

    a. Prior to the collection of personal information
    b. Prior to the use of personal information
    c. Prior to the disclosure of personal information
    d. Prior to putting the personal information to a new use

Consent

An organization must obtain and have evidence of the full knowledge and consent of individuals before any personal information is collected, used, or disclosed. The PIPEDA is quite clear about this point. An organization is expected to clearly define the purpose for which the personal information will be used, so that the individual has a complete and concise understanding of this. Scenarios similar to radio and television commercials where the announcer explains the terms and conditions while talking at 100 mph are not acceptable and the so-called consent obtained in these situations is void. Likewise, subjecting an individual to coercion, deception, intimidation, or misleading information to obtain consent is unacceptable and invalidates the individual's response. Requiring an individual to provide personal information before providing a product or service is prohibited.[62] The Act distinguishes between express and implied consent and notes that either is acceptable as long as it is appropriate for the given situation. Express consent is active, direct, and unequivocal and can be given verbally or in writing. Implied consent is more passive in nature and is generally inferred rather than being a result of direct action. For example, giving the telephone company your name and address to start service is an act of express consent to deliver service and bill you at that address. It does not necessarily imply that you consent to having your phone number given out to telemarketers or others. Finally, unlike other privacy acts, the PIPEDA allows individuals to withdraw their consent after the fact. This is a significant feature. Oftentimes, the consent process is legal and above board but the individual is under duress. This provision puts individuals back in the driver's seat, where they belong.

The consent provision does not apply in three instances: (1) it is in the individual's best interest and consent cannot be obtained in a timely manner, such as medical emergencies; (2) consent would impair the availability or accuracy of the information collected during a criminal investigation; and (3) the information is already in the public domain.[62] An exception is also made in the case of scholarly research when obtaining consent is not practical.[62] In this case, the organization must notify the Privacy Commissioner and obtain permission beforehand.

The following metrics can be used by organizations, internal and external auditors, and public interest groups to demonstrate compliance with the Consent principle. These metrics can also be aggregated to measure the extent of compliance and highlight problem areas at the Provincial and federal levels.

Distribution of times an organization did and did not obtain consent from individuals before their personal information was: 1.8.13
   a. Collected
   b. Used
   c. Disclosed

Number and percentage of times an individual's consent was obtained: 1.8.14
   a. Through coercion
   b. Through deception
   c. Through misleading information
   d. By intimidation
   e. Under duress

Number and percentage of times individuals withdrew their consent after the fact.   1.8.15

Limiting Collection

If the privacy of personal information is to be protected and its use and disclosure controlled, it stands to reason that limits must first be placed on collection. We have already discussed the requirements for obtaining consent and fully informing the individual of the purpose for which the information is being collected and used. The next step is to place limits on (1) what information can be collected, (2) the methods used to collect the information, and (3) the volume of information collected, and the PIPDEA does just that. The process of collecting personal information must be fair, open, and legal. Deceptive, coercive, or misleading collection practices are not permitted.

Organizations are limited to collecting only the personal information they need for their pre-stated purpose, and no more. They cannot collect personal information randomly for some potential future, as yet undefined application. The volume of personal information that can be collected is also limited — there must be a legitimate reason why an individual is approached. Either that individual is a customer or a potential customer versus contacting every person in a city or province.

The following metrics can be used by organizations, internal and external auditors, and public interest groups to demonstrate compliance with the Limiting Collection principle. These metrics can also be aggregated to measure the extent of compliance and highlight problem areas at the Provincial and federal levels.

Number and percentage of times personal information was collected through:
1.8.16

   a. Coercion
   b. Deceptive means
   c. Misleading information
   d. Intimidation
   e. Under duress

Number and percentage of times more personal information was collected than was necessary for the pre-stated purpose:
1.8.17
   a. Number of individuals involved

Number and percentage of times personal information was collected from more individuals than needed for the pre-stated purpose.
1.8.18

Number and percentage of times personal information was collected for no or a vaguely stated purpose:
1.8.19
   a. Number of individuals involved

Limiting Use, Disclosure, and Retention

As noted previously, the PIPEDA expands the OECD privacy principle of Use Limitation to include disclosure and retention. This is only logical. Retaining data is quite different from using it and may accidentally or intentionally lead to uses beyond the original authorized scope. Disclosure is not using the data; it facilitates others' use of the data. It is conceivable that disclosure could represent a form of unauthorized collection on the part of the receiver. As such, disclosure and retention also should be limited. The fifth principle gets right to the point in this regard. An organization may not use, disclose, or retain personal information after the time period or for purposes other than for which the individual originally gave consent. Personal information must be erased, destroyed, or rendered anonymous once that date has been reached. To ensure compliance with this principle, organizations are strongly encouraged to develop policies and procedures to explain and enforce these provisions among their employees and business partners. An exception is made to this disclosure provision in the case of ongoing legal actions, such as debt collection, subpoenas, warrants, or court orders.[62]

The following metrics can be used by organizations, internal and external auditors, and public interest groups to demonstrate compliance with the Limiting Use, Disclosure, and Retention principle. These metrics can also be aggregated to measure the extent of compliance and highlight problem areas at the Provincial and federal levels.

Number and percentage of times an organization: 1.8.20

    a. Used
    b. Disclosed
    c. Retained

personal information for other than the prestated purpose.

Number and percentage of times an organization: 1.8.21

    a. Used
    b. Disclosed
    c. Retained

personal information after the pre-stated time period.

Number and percentage of times an organization failed to destroy, erase, or render anonymous personal information after the end of the prestated use and time frame of use.   1.8.22

Distribution of organizations that do and do not have current written policies and procedures in place that explain limits on using, disclosing, and retaining personal information.   1.8.23

Accuracy

The sixth principle is accuracy; it corresponds to the Data Quality principle in the OECD Privacy Guidelines. What can be more important than for personal information that is about to be used by and disclosed to total strangers to be accurate? Once inaccurate data gets out, it is difficult if not impossible to retrieve. Consider the ramifications of inaccurate information being used or disclosed. Your application for a mortgage on a new home is rejected because of erroneous information on your credit report. Your application to law school is turned down because of erroneous information about your conduct while an undergraduate student. Your application for a security clearance is denied because of inaccurate information in your medical records. And so on. None of these decisions is subject to an appeal process. The decisions are final because the institutions involved have no concept of inaccurate electronic data — computers do not make mistakes.

The PIPEDA is quite clear that organizations are accountable for ensuring that all personal information they collect, use, or disclose is accurate. That information must be accurate, complete, and current for the stated purpose for which it was collected.[62] If it is not and it is released, the accountability and liability provisions take effect. Furthermore, organizations are warned not to willy-nilly attempt to update any information they possess themselves. Think about the repercussions of an organization updating your personal information for a moment. Where did the information come from? Because sources are not held accountable for the accuracy of the information they supply, there is a lot of potential for damage to be done to an individual — hence the prohibition from updating information. This raises the question of why any information that was accurate when collected and is being used only for the stated purpose would ever need to be updated. The ninth and tenth principles explain the correct way to update personal information.

The following metrics can be used by organizations, internal and external auditors, and public interest groups to demonstrate compliance with the Accuracy principle. These metrics can also be aggregated to measure the extent of compliance and highlight problem areas at the Provincial and federal levels.

Number of times personal information was found to be inaccurate, incomplete, or out of date: 1.8.24

    a. Number of individuals affected
    b. Number of records affected

Number of times inaccurate, incomplete, or out-of-date information was:
                                                            1.8.25

    a. Transferred to third parties
    b. Disclosed

Average length of time personal information remained inaccurate before an organization corrected it.   1.8.26

Number of times inaccuracies in personal information were due to an organization attempting to update the information themselves.   1.8.27

Safeguards

The seventh principle describes (1) the types of safeguards that must be employed to ensure the privacy of personal information, and (2) the issues to consider when selecting and deploying these safeguards. Because an organization is accountable for employing appropriate safeguards, these decisions are not to be taken lightly. Safeguards are required to protect personal information from unauthorized access, disclosure, copying, use, and modification, as well as theft and accidental or intentional loss.[62] The protection provisions also apply when personal information is being destroyed, erased, or rendered anonymous, to prevent the unauthorized activities described above. Protective measures are expected to be proportional to the sensitivity of the information and the harm that could result from misuse. A combination of physical, personnel, IT, and operational security controls are to be used. This principle mentions the use of encryption to protect the privacy of personal information, consistent with the principle in the OECD Cryptography Guidelines.

Finally, employees need to receive regular training about the correct (1) procedures for handling personal information, and (2) operation, use, and interaction with all technical controls.

The following metrics can be used by organizations, internal and external auditors, and public interest groups to demonstrate compliance with the Safeguards principle. These metrics can also be aggregated to measure the extent of compliance and highlight problem areas at the Provincial and federal levels.

Number of times safeguards failed to protect personal information from:
1.8.28

    a. Unauthorized access
    b. Unauthorized disclosure
    c. Unauthorized copying
    d. Unauthorized use
    e. Unauthorized modification
    f. Loss
    g. Theft and the number of individuals affected in each case

Percentage of failures of safeguards that were due to inadequate: 1.8.29
    a. Physical security controls
    b. Personnel security controls
    c. IT security controls
    d. Operational security controls
    e. A combination of security controls

Frequency with which an organization's employees receive training about:
1.8.30

    a. Proper procedures for handling personal information
    b. Correct operation and use of IT and operational security controls

Openness

It is impossible to achieve accountability behind closed doors. As a result, the eighth principle concerns openness, or the transparency with which an organization must conduct its activities in relation to the individuals whose personal information they collect, use, and disclose. This transparency, it is felt, will (1) enhance the privacy of personal information, and (2) by default encourage compliance. Openness is also a requirement of a free democratic society. The openness requirements fall squarely on the shoulders of the organization, not the individuals. Organizations are responsible for providing the contact information of the individual who is accountable for compliance with the Act, when so requested. Organizations are responsible for informing individuals about what personal information they hold and how they can obtain copies of it. Organizations are also responsible for disclosing the policies and procedures they use to protect personal information. That last item provides a pretty good incentive for having robust policies and procedures in place.

The following metrics can be used by organizations, internal and external auditors, and public interest groups to demonstrate compliance with the Openness principle. These metrics can also be aggregated to measure the extent of compliance and highlight problem areas at the Provincial and federal levels.

Number of requests received for contact information of the designated accountability official: 1.8.31

    a. Number and percentage responded to

Number of times an organization informed individuals about: 1.8.32

    a. What personal information they hold
    b. How they can obtain a copy of it
    c. Their policies and procedures for protecting personal information

Individual Access

The ninth and tenth principles amplify individuals' rights in regard to the collection, use, and disclosure of personal information. In particular, the ninth principle explains an individual's right to access his personal information and what action he can take once he has accessed it. An individual can submit a request to an organization to document his possession of any personal information, how this information has been used, and to whom it has been disclosed. An individual can request access to that information at the same time. Individuals must submit their requests in writing, directly to the organization holding the information. An organization has a maximum of 30 days to respond. Extensions are possible under limited circumstances, but the individual must be notified of when he can expect to receive a response. If an organization refuses to respond, it must inform the individual and the Privacy Commissioner of the reason for the refusal and inform the individual of his right to file a complaint.[62] Ignoring the request or stone silence is not an option. Information must be provided to the individual at minimal or no cost; the individual has to agree to the cost beforehand. An organization must provide the information in a form and format that is understandable. A hexadecimal data dump is not acceptable. In special circumstances, the organization is required to make the information available in alternative formats for individuals with sensory disabilities.[62] The organization must indicate the source of the information, the use it has been put to, and the parties to whom it has been disclosed.[62] An organization can withhold information to protect a source, unless the source gives its consent, or on the grounds that national security, law enforcement, or intelligence-gathering activities would be compromised. In this instance, the burden of proof is on the organization. Finally, an individual has the right to challenge the accuracy and completeness of any personal information and demand that it be corrected quickly. This right extends to all third parties to whom the organization has given the information. The organization bears the full cost of correction. All unresolved challenges to the accuracy of any information must be documented and submitted to both the individual and the Privacy Commissioner.

The following metrics can be used by organizations, internal and external auditors, and public interest groups to demonstrate compliance with the Individual Access principle. These metrics can also be aggregated to measure the extent of compliance and highlight problem areas at the Provincial and federal levels.

Number of requests submitted by individuals asking: 1.8.33

   a. Organizations to acknowledge that they hold personal information
   b. The uses to which this information has been put
   c. To whom the information has been disclosed

Number and percentage of requests submitted by individuals that were:
                                                                  1.8.34

   a. Responded to
   b. Refused
   c. Responded to within the required 30-day period
   d. Not responded to within the required 30-day period (an extension was needed)

Number and percentage of requests submitted by individuals in which the response was provided in an alternative format.   1.8.35

Number and percentage of requests submitted by individuals in which: 1.8.36

   a. The source of the information was supplied
   b. The source of the information was withheld
   c. The uses of the information were supplied
   d. The uses of the information were not supplied
   e. The parties to whom the information was disclosed were revealed
   f. The parties to whom the information was disclosed were not revealed

Number and percentage of times information was withheld: 1.8.37

   a. And the organization gave no reason
   b. To protect the source
   c. On grounds that national security would be compromised
   d. On grounds that law enforcement activities would be compromised
   e. On grounds that intelligence gathering activities would be compromised

Number of times individuals requested inaccurate information to be corrected.
                                                               1.8.38

Distribution of the times requests to correct inaccurate personal information were and were not accommodated.   1.8.39

Challenging Compliance

The tenth principle was elevated to a separate principle to emphasize the right of individuals to challenge an organization's compliance with the provisions of the PIPEDA. An individual can challenge whether an organization is complying with one or more provisions of the Act. A three-tiered process is followed when filing challenges or complaints. First, an individual files a complaint directly with the responsible organization, in particular the individual designated accountable for compliance. The intent is to give the individual and organization the opportunity to remedy the situation themselves. Organizations are required to investigate all complaints and report back to the individual. If the individual is not satisfied that the issue is resolved, he can proceed to the second tier — filing a complaint with the Privacy Commissioner. If this avenue proves unsatisfactory, an individual can proceed to the third tier — the courts.

An individual has the right to file a complaint with the Privacy Commissioner if he is unsatisfied with the way an organization responded to his challenge. An individual must file a complaint with the Privacy Commissioner within six months after an organization responded to the challenge. The individual filing the complaint can request anonymity. An organization is notified by the office of the Privacy Commissioner whenever a complaint is received. During an investigation, the Privacy Commissioner can interview employees of the organization, take testimony, review records, and conduct on-site visits. Organizations are prohibited from retaliating against employees who cooperate with the Commissioner during an investigation. Furthermore, they can be fined $10,000 to $100,000 for obstructing an investigation. Within one year of receiving the complaint, the Privacy Commissioner must file a report of their findings, recommendations, any settlement that was reached, and any remedial action remaining. A copy of the report is sent to the individual and the organization. The Commissioner has two other duties. He is responsible for submitting an annual report to Parliament on the status of implementing the PIPEDA throughout Canada, investigations, and court actions. The Commissioner is also responsible for educating the public about the provisions of the PIPEDA and their rights.

If the individual is unhappy with the Privacy Commissioner's report, he can request a court hearing. This request must be filed within 45 days of receiving the Commissioner's report. The courts have the authority to order compliance by the organization and award damages to the individual.

The following metrics can be used by organizations, internal and external auditors, and public interest groups to demonstrate compliance with the Challenging Compliance principle. These metrics can also be aggregated to measure the extent of compliance and highlight problem areas at the Provincial and federal levels.

Number and distribution of complaints filed by individuals to: 1.8.40

    a. Organizations
    b. The Privacy Commissioner
    c. The courts

Number and distribution of complaints filed by individuals that were investigated by: 1.8.41

    a. The organization's designated accountability official
    b. The Privacy Commissioner
    c. The courts

Table 3.9   Unique Provisions of the Canadian PIPEDA

Individuals can withdraw their consent at a later time.
Consent cannot be forced as a condition of supplying a product or service.
Individuals have a right to know the source that supplied the information, the uses to which it has been put, and to whom it has been disclosed.
Individuals filing a complaint with the Privacy Commissioner can request anonymity.
Information supplied to individuals by organizations in response to a request must be in a form and format that is readily understandable. Organizations must make the information available in an alternative format for individuals with a sensory disability.
Academic records are not excluded from protection.
A time limit is placed on disclosure prohibitions; the earlier of: (a) twenty years after the death of the individual whose personal information is held, or (b) one hundred years after the record of the individual's personal information was created.
The Privacy Commissioner can audit an organization at any time, not just in response to a complaint, if potential or actual violations are expected.
Organizations are prohibited from retaliating against an employee who cooperates with the Privacy Commissioner during an investigation.
Organizations are prohibited from updating personal information themselves.

Distribution of complaints that were resolved to the satisfaction of the individual at each level: 1.8.42

    a. By agreement between the individual and the organization
    b. By the Privacy Commissioner
    c. By court order
    d. By court order and an award of damages

Number of cases in which organizations were fined for obstructing the Privacy Commissioner's investigation.   1.8.43

Number of cases in which an organization retaliated against employees for cooperating with the Privacy Commissioner.   1.8.44

The PIPEDA contains some unique provisions that other OECD Member States would do well to consider, as shown in Table 3.9. The first three provisions are particularly noteworthy.

3.10 Privacy Act — United States

The Privacy Act was originally issued in 1974 as Public Law 93-579 and codified in the United States Code at 5 U.S.C. 552a. The Act was passed in late December 1974, after reconciliation and signed by President Ford; it amended Chapter 5 Title 5 of the U.S.C., which dealt with administrative procedures, by inserting a new Section 552a after Section 552.

Background

Two events that occurred almost a decade earlier marked the beginning of interest in privacy matters. The House of Representatives held a series of hearings on issues related to the invasion of personal privacy. At the same time the Department of Health, Education and Welfare* (HEW) issued a report titled: "Records, Computers, and the Rights of Citizens." This report recommended a "Code of Fair Information Practices" that consisted of five key principles[125]:

- There must be no data record-keeping systems whose very existence is secret.
- There must be a way for an individual to find out what information about him is kept in a record and how it is used.
- There must be a way for an individual to prevent information about him obtained for one purpose from being used or made available for other purposes without his consent.
- There must be a way for an individual to correct or amend a record of identifiable information about him.
- Any organization creating, maintaining, using or disseminating records of identifiable personal data must assure the reliability of the data for their intended use and must take reasonable precautions to prevent misuse of the data.

Remember that we are talking about the late 1960s and early 1970s. The computers in use at that time were large mainframes with magnetic tapes, disc packs, and punch cards for data entry. The computers were in one building and users were given hardcopy 11×14-inch green and white striped printouts. Occasionally there were remote job entry (RJE) stations where punch cards could be read in from a distance on a 2400- to 4800-baud modem line. You would think that it would have been much easier to maintain data security and privacy at that time, than with the computer and networking equipment in use today. So what prompted the concern about the privacy of electronic data? The answer lies with the agency that issued the report — HEW. During the 1960s, HEW became responsible for implementing a series of legislation related to social security benefits, food stamps, welfare, aid to dependent children, loans for college students, etc. To do so, they needed to collect, validate, and compare a lot of personal information, such as name, social security number, date of birth, place of birth, address, marital status, number of children, employment, income, and the like; information that most people would consider private. HEW felt an obligation to keep this information under wraps. At the same time they were responsible for preventing fraud — welfare payments to people above the minimum income level, social security payments to deceased individuals, food stamps to college students who just did not feel like working, defaulting on student loans that could have been paid, etc. Different organizations within HEW collected the information for the various

---

* HEW was later split into three cabinet level agencies: the Department of Health and Human Services (HHS), the Department of Education (EDUC), and the Social Security Administration (SSA).

entitlement programs and it was stored on separate computer systems. Before long, HEW began what is referred to as "matching programs;" they compared data collected for one entitlement program with the data supplied for another to discern any discrepancies that might indicate fraud. Soon, personal information was shared across multiple federal agencies, not just within HEW, and all sorts of "matching programs" were underway, especially for law enforcement and so-called "historical research." The fear expressed in the 1930s that Social Security numbers would become social surveillance numbers was becoming real. Fortunately, a few people had the foresight to see what a Pandora's box had been opened in relation to the privacy of personal data, and there was a push to create some protections at the federal level — hence the HEW report and the Congressional hearings.

Today, the bill is referred to as the Privacy Act of 1974 (As Amended). The preamble to the Act is worth noting; it describes the challenge of privacy for electronic records head-on[108]:

- The privacy of an individual is directly affected by the collection, maintenance, use, and dissemination of personal information by Federal agencies.
- The increasing use of computers and sophisticated information technology, while essential to the efficient operations of the Government, has greatly magnified the harm to individual privacy that can occur from any collection, maintenance, use, or dissemination of personal information.
- The opportunities for an individual to secure employment, insurance, and credit, and his right to due process and other legal protections are endangered by the misuse of certain information systems.
- The right to privacy is a personal and fundamental right protected by the Constitution of the United States.
- In order to protect the privacy of individuals identified in information systems maintained by Federal agencies, it is necessary and proper for the Congress to regulate the collection, maintenance, use, and dissemination of information by such agencies.

The similarity between these six principles and the five principles contained in the HEW Code of Fair Information Practices is evident. Most importantly, the right to privacy is acknowledged as a fundamental right under the Constitution of the United States. However, the first bullet in the HEW report totally fell by the wayside. Also, there is a hint that the government may exempt itself in some cases from these lofty ideals.

The Privacy Act acknowledges the potential harm that can result from misuse of private personal data. However, the Act is limited to protecting private personal information that is collected and disseminated by federal agencies, as can be seen from its stated purpose[108]:

- Permit an individual to determine what records pertaining to him are collected, maintained, used, or disseminated by such agencies.
- Permit an individual to prevent records pertaining to him obtained by such agencies for a particular purpose from being used or made available for another purpose without his consent.

- Permit an individual to gain access to information pertaining to him in federal agency records, to have a copy made of all or any portion thereof, and to correct or amend such records.
- Collect, maintain, use, or disseminate any record of identifiable personal information in a manner that assures that such action is for a necessary and lawful purpose, that the information is current and accurate for its intended use, and that adequate safeguards are provided to prevent misuse of such information.
- Permit exemptions from such requirements with respect to records provided in this Act only in those cases where there is an important public policy need for such exemptions as has been determined by specific statutory authority.
- Be subject to civil suit for any damages which occur as a result of willful or intentional action which violates any individual's rights under this Act.

It is important to understand how certain terms are used within the Privacy Act, especially because the Act is limited to government agencies.

> **Individual:** a citizen of the United States or an alien lawfully admitted for permanent residence.[108]

Foreign students, tourists, temporary workers, and other non-citizens who have not yet established a permanent legal residence in the United States are not protected by the Privacy Act.

> **Maintain:** maintain, collect, use, or disseminate.[108]

Maintain is used as a generic term to represent any type of transaction related to private personal data.

> **Record:** any item, collection, or grouping of information about an individual that is maintained by an agency, including but not limited to, his education, financial transactions, medical history, and criminal or employment history and that contains his name, or identifying number, symbol, or other identifying particular assigned to the individual, such as a finger or voice print or a photograph.[108]

A record, as defined by the Privacy Act, includes any type of information, in any format or media, that can be associated with an individual.

> **Routine use:** with respect to the disclosure of a record, the use of such record for a purpose which is compatible with the purpose for which it was collected.[108]

Routine use of private personal data implies a use that is consistent with the prestated purpose for which the information was collected, not an entirely new or unforeseen use of that information by the same or a different agency.

> **Source agency:** any agency which discloses records contained in a system of records to be used in a matching program, or any state or local government, or agency thereof, which discloses records to be used in a matching program.[108]

> **Recipient agency:** any agency, or contractor thereof, receiving records contained in a system or records from a source agency for use in a matching program.[108]

Notice that these two definitions move beyond federal agencies to include state and local governments, as well as their contractors. As a result, the same rules apply to contractors who build and operate information systems for federal, state, and local governments. It is not evident that all of these contractors are fully aware of their accountability. A source agency is any agency that releases data to a matching program run by another agency. Note that the definition does not require the source agency to be the original source of the information. An agency can be receive data in one matching program and release it as a source agency in the next matching program. This provision makes it rather difficult, if not impossible, to (1) control how many times and to how many agencies (federal, state, or local) private personal information is released, and (2) control release of private personal data in relation to the original prestated use.

The provisions of the Privacy Act have been tinkered with in the 30 years since the bill took effect. Section 6 of the Act, which was repealed and replaced by subsection (v), assigned some responsibilities to the Office of Management and Budget (OMB) that are discussed later. Section 7 of the Act stated that it was unlawful to withhold any legal right or benefit that an individual is entitled to under federal, state, or local law, if they refused to supply their social security number. This provision was not applicable to information systems in place prior to 1 January 1975. In that case, the system owner was required to tell the individual whether supplying a social security number was voluntary or mandatory, how it would be used, and the statutory authority under which this information was collected. While a part of the original Act, Section 7 was never codified and remains listed as a non-binding note. Section 9, the Rules of Construction, was also repealed. This section contained an explicit statement that the Act did not authorize the establishment of a national data base that (1) combines, links, merges, personal information in other federal agency systems; (2) directly links federal agency information systems; (3) matches records not authorized by law; and (e) discloses information except for federal, state, or local matching programs. In short, the prohibition against massive data mining, aggregation, and inference by federal agencies, and their state and local partners, was repealed. The Computer Matching and Privacy Act, Public Law 100-503, as codified at 5 U.S.C. § 552a, was issued in 1988. In essence, this was a restatement of the 1974 Privacy Act, with a few minor edits. An exemption was added for matches performed for the Internal Revenue Service or Social Security Administration.

The Freedom of Information Act (FOIA) is the only bill specifically mentioned in the Privacy Act. The FOIA was passed prior to the Privacy Act and signed by President Johnson. The Privacy Act contains a general statement that the Privacy Act is not in conflict with the FOIA, which makes sense because the FOIA and Privacy Act are contained in the same Chapter and Title of the U.S.C. Later we will see how legislation that was enacted after the Privacy Act relates to it.

Several scenarios are listed in the bill whereby an organization is exempt from the provisions of the Privacy Act[108]:

- Fraud investigations
- Central Intelligence Agency (CIA) information systems
- Law enforcement activities
- Presidential protective services
- Background checks for federal or military employment, access to classified information, promotion boards
- Use only as statistical records

The CIA exemption is a bit odd because the CIA is prohibited by law from conducting intelligence operations on U.S. citizens within U.S. borders. It is also odd that only the CIA is mentioned and not the Federal Bureau of Investigation (FBI); Drug Enforcement Agency (DEA); Alcohol, Tobacco and Firearms (ATF); or National Security Agency (NSA). The Department of Homeland Security (DHS) had not been created when the Privacy Act was originally issued, but it is surprising that it has not been added to the list by amendment. Perhaps that is because the phrase "law enforcement activities" is being interpreted rather broadly.

The Privacy Act also contains a clause entitled "Conditions of Disclosure." The clause states that no record from a government system shall be disclosed by any means of communication by or to any agency without a written request from the individual and their written consent. That was a noble start, but then the Act goes on to list 12 exceptions to this principle — almost one for every agency in the government! In essence, this clause is an extension to the exemptions cited above[108]:

- To staff (federal employees or contractors) who maintain the record system
- In response to a Freedom of Information Act request
- To the Bureau of the Census
- For statistical research
- Records that become part of the National Archives
- In response to written requests from law enforcement officials
- To protect the health and safety of the individual
- To the U.S. Congress
- To the Government Accountability Office (GAO)
- By Court Order
- To a consumer reporting agency
- For an agency's routine use

The "statistical research" exemption is a bit troubling. The use of private personal records for statistical research assumes that the records are rendered anonymous prior to disclosure, but no one is assigned responsibility for verifying that this is done. Also, what kind of statistical research are we talking about: average ages, average incomes, average number of children per family, average education levels, or what? Some of the results of this statistical research could be put to malicious purposes. In the 1930s and 1940s, the Nazi party did similar "statistical research" to identify Jews, Gypsies, Seventh Day Adventists, gays, people with disabilities, and other so-called "undesirables" prior to initiating massive genocide policies. Not to mention that the Census Bureau already collects this information every ten years through its persistent census takers who knock on your door every night until you fill out the forms. The "to protect the health and safety of the individual" exemption also lacks credibility. Corporations issue recalls for unsafe food, consumer, and pharmaceutical products — not the government. The legal basis or need for the federal government to exchange private personal data with consumer reporting agencies is also difficult to explain. The federal government sends these groups product safety information, such as cars with faulty brakes, toys that represent potential hazards to small children, and contaminated food, but there is no private personal information involved. In addition, the phrase "consumer reporting agency" is rather broad and could be interpreted to mean almost anything, including your local newspaper. In summary, it is difficult to think of a situation in which private personal data would be disclosed, for a legitimate or illegitimate reason, from one government agency to another, whether federal, state, or local, that does not fall into one of these 18 exemptions.

Agency Responsibilities

To help compensate for the multitude of exemptions, agencies are required to keep an accurate record of every time they disclose personal data to another party. This accounting includes the date the information was disclosed, the purpose of each disclosure, and the name and address of the recipient agency and contact person. Agencies are required to keep disclosure information for as long as the personal information is kept or five years after the disclosure, whichever is longer. Agencies must make disclosure records available to individuals upon request; the one exception is disclosures to law enforcement agencies. Agencies are required to keep this information for another reason — so that they can notify anyone to whom information has been disclosed of corrections or notation disputes initiated by the individual.

Other requirements are levied on agencies in regard to their record maintenance activities. Government agencies can only maintain personal data records that are needed to perform their primary mission. Agencies are encouraged to collect the information directly from the individual involved whenever possible. Prior to data collection, agencies must cite the statutory authority for collecting such information and explain whether providing this information is voluntary or mandatory. Individuals must be told why the information is being collected, the routine uses to which the information will be put, and the consequences of not providing all the information requested. Agencies are responsible for ensuring the accuracy, relevancy, currency, and completeness of all personal data records they maintain, and must verify this before any disclosure. Agencies are responsible for employing appropriate administrative, technical, and physical safeguards to ensure the security, confidentiality, and integrity of personal data records and prevent substantial harm, embarrassment, inconvenience, or unfairness to individuals that could result from unauthorized disclosures or the release of information, especially inaccurate information.[108] To make sure employees understand the seriousness of the Act, agencies are expected to issue a code of conduct, including penalties for noncompliance, for staff involved in the design, development, operation, and maintenance of record systems that contain personal data. The Privacy Act prohibits an agency from maintaining records about how an individual exercises his First Amendment rights, unless authorized by the individual or law enforcement officials. Likewise, individuals must be notified when the disclosure of their records is likely to become part of the public record.

In an attempt to keep the public informed, agencies are required to post two biennial notices in the *Federal Register*. The first notice documents the existence of agency record systems that contain personal data. The notice must contain the name and location of the system; the categories of individuals whose records are kept; the types of records that are kept; routine uses of the data; policies and procedures for storage, retrieval, access control, retention, and disposal of such information; procedures for finding out if records about an individual are maintained; procedures for obtaining copies and challenging the content of such records; categories of sources for the data; and the title and business address of the official responsible for the record system. The second notice concerns agency rules that govern how, when, and where they interact with individuals whose records they maintain. However, not too many people living on Main Street, USA, whether in a metropolis or small city, are regular subscribers to or readers of the *Federal Register*. So, it is not clear what these notices really accomplish. Should an agency decide to use personal data for a purpose other than that for which it was collected, it must take several steps. First, it must notify and obtain approval from the House Committee on Government Operations, the Senate Committee on Government Affairs, and the Office of Management and Budget (OMB) for any proposed significant change in a record system or a matching program. In addition, the agency must place a notice in the *Federal Register* 30 days beforehand.

Matching programs cannot be entered into haphazardly or at the whim of an individual government employee. Instead, there must be a prior written agreement between the two parties that states the purpose of the matching program, as well as the legal authority and cost-benefit justification for the matching program. The agreement explains how personal data records will be matched and used by each agency, the number of records involved, the data elements that will be examined, the start and end dates of the matching exercise, and the oversight role of the Data Integrity Board of each agency. An important part of the agreement is the procedures for verifying data accuracy, the retention and destruction or return of records, and ensuring appropriate administrative, physical, and technical security controls by both parties. A standard clause prohibits recipient agencies from re-disclosing the data records, except to another matching program. A copy of all agreements must be sent to the Senate Committee on Government Affairs and the House Committee on Government Operations and made available to the public upon request. Matching agreements do not take effect until 30 days after they are sent to Congress. The duration of matching agreements is limited to 18 months; the Data Integrity Board has the option of renewing an agreement for a maximum of one year. Federal agencies are not required to share personal information with a non-federal agency if there are any doubts about the recipient agency's compliance with the provisions of the Act. Under such circumstances, the source agency cannot enter into or renew a matching agreement unless the recipient agency certifies compliance with the Act and the certification is credible.

One interesting provision concerns mailing lists. Government agencies, whether federal, state, or local, are prohibited from selling mailing list type information that is extracted from personal data records that they maintain.

The following metrics can be used to measure whether or not an agency is fulfilling its responsibilities under the Privacy Act. These metrics can be used by agencies to monitor their own performance, individuals and public interest groups, and independent oversight authorities in the public and private sectors.

Number of times personal data records have been disclosed without the written consent of the individual(s) involved and not in accordance with a stated exemption: 1.9.1

    a. Number of personal data records involved per disclosure

Number of times the accuracy and completeness of disclosure records has been verified: 1.9.2

    a. Date of most recent verification
    b. Frequency of verification
    c. Number of problems found during most recent review, the type and severity of these problems
    d. Average time required to correct deficiencies

Number of instances in which disclosure records were not kept or were not kept long enough.   1.9.3

Number of times an agency failed: 1.9.4

    a. To tell the individual the purpose for which personal information was being collected
    b. To tell the individual the routine use of the personal information
    c. Cite the statutory authority for collecting the personal data

    d. Inform the individual whether supplying the information is voluntary or mandatory

    e. Inform the individual of the consequences of not supplying the requested information

Number of times an agency maintained more personal data records than needed for the stated purpose and the number of records involved.　　1.9.5

Distribution of times an agency did and did not verify the accuracy, completeness, currency, and relevance of personal data before disclosing it to a third party.　　1.9.6

Distribution of times an agency did and did not notify an individual that his records had been disclosed and were likely to become part of the public record.　　1.9.7

Number of times personal data records were subject to unauthorized access, copying, disclosure, or sharing due to inadequate:　　1.9.8

    a. Administrative security controls
    b. Physical security controls
    c. Technical security controls

Distribution of times an agency did or did not submit a complete *Federal Register* notice on time.　　1.9.9

Number of matching agreements:　　1.9.10

    a. Participated in either as a source or recipient agency and the number of personal data records involved in each
    b. Renewed by the Data Integrity Board
    c. Disapproved by Congress
    d. Disapproved by the Data Integrity Board
    e. Made available to the public upon request
    f. Disapproved by the OMB
    g. Where the Inspector General disagreed with the Data Integrity Board and notified OMB and Congress

Number of times an agency refused to participate in a matching program because of doubts about the recipient agency's compliance with the provisions of the Privacy Act.　　1.9.11

Individual Rights

Despite all the exemptions noted above, individuals do retain some rights under the Privacy Act. Individuals have the right to access, review, and copy personal data records that an agency maintains about them. With prior written notice, individuals have the right to have someone, such as legal counsel, accompany them when they review agency records. Individuals have the right to request that an agency correct any information that they consider to be inaccurate, incomplete, irrelevant, or out of date. Information is considered irrelevant if it is immaterial to (1) the prestated reason for which the information was collected, or (2) the prestated use of the information. Agencies must acknowledge receipt of a correction request within ten business days and make the correction or refuse to do so. If an agency refuses to make the correction, it is required to inform the individual of the reason for doing so, explain the procedures for appealing the refusal, and provide contact information for the official in charge. An agency must respond to a refusal appeal within 30 days. The head of an agency is responsible for reviewing appeals. If the agency head upholds a refusal to grant an individual access to his own records, it must provide a reason and explain the procedures for taking the matter to the courts. Should an agency disclose any information about an individual to another agency after the individual has filed a challenge, the agency is required to inform the recipient agency that a challenge has been filed and the source agency's reason for disagreeing.

A recipient agency, whether a federal agency or not, may not use data from a matching program to deny an individual any federal benefit or take any adverse action (firing, denying employment, denying a security clearance, denying a student loan, etc.) unless the recipient agency has independently verified the information. The Data Integrity Board of the recipient agency must also indicate that it has a high degree of confidence in the accuracy of the information. The recipient agency must notify the individual of the information leading to the adverse action and give him an opportunity to contest the information. In general, individuals have 30 days to respond. An agency may take a prohibited action without giving the individual time to respond if it believes that the public health and safety is at risk.

Individuals have the right to resort to the courts to seek civil or criminal penalties if they believe their rights under the Privacy Act have been abused by an agency. If an agency fails or refuses to comply with the provisions of the Act and the failure results in an adverse effect on an individual, that individual has the right to pursue civil action in a U.S. District Court. A legal guardian may act for the individual if he is under age or incapacitated due to a physical or mental disability. The suit can be brought to the District Court where the individual resides, has his business, the agency records are located, or to the District Court in Washington, D.C. The court can order an agency to correct an individual's record and force an agency to release records it is withholding from an individual. The suit must be filed within two years of the date the event occurred, or in the case of intentional or willful mishandling of personal data, within two years after that fact is discovered. A suit cannot be brought against an agency for events that occurred prior to the enactment of the Act in December 1974. If the court determines that the agency's actions were intentional or willful, the U.S. Government is liable for fines payable to the individual of actual damages, but not less than $1000, and court costs plus reasonable attorney's fees. In addition, government employees can be fined for their role in such proceedings. Government employees who willfully violate the limits on disclosing personal information can be found guilty of a misdemeanor and fined up to $5000. Government employees who keep personal data records for their own use, without meeting the requirements of the *Federal Register* notice, can be found guilty of a misdemeanor and fined up to $5000. Any person who obtains personal data records from a government agency under false pretenses can be found guilty of a misdemeanor and fined up to $3000. These fines were established in 1974 and have not been updated in the 31 years since the Act was passed. They seem ridiculously low today. Suppose an identity theft ring offers a government clerk typist $50,000 for the personal data on all employees in the agency. It is doubtful that a misdemeanor charge or a $5000 fine will serve as much of a deterrent.

The following metrics can be used to measure whether or not individuals are exercising their rights under the Privacy Act and whether agencies are honoring or interfering with these rights. These metrics can be used by agencies to monitor their own performance, individuals and public interest groups, and independent oversight authorities in the public and private sectors.

Number of times individuals requested access to their personal data records maintained by an agency: 1.9.12

   a. Number and percentage of times individual requests for access to personal data records was refused and the distribution among the reasons given

Number of times individuals requested corrections to their personal data records maintained by an agency: 1.9.13

   a. Number and percentage of correction requests that were refused and the distribution among the reasons given
   b. Number and percentage of times a refusal to release or correct personal data records resulted in an appeal to the agency head
   c. Number and percentage of times a refusal to release or correct personal data records resulted in a suit being filed in District Court
   d. Number and percentage of corrections for which agencies or persons to whom the information had been disclosed earlier, were notified of the correction
   e. Number and percentage of times agencies or persons to whom information had been disclosed earlier, were notified of information the individual disputed, like refused corrections

Number and percentage of suits brought to District Courts in which: 1.9.14

   a. The court ordered the agency to release personal data records it was withholding from an individual
   b. The court ordered the agency to make a correction to personal data records that it was refusing to make
   c. The individual was awarded damages and court costs
   d. Government employees were charged with a misdemeanor and fined
   e. Government contractors were charged with a misdemeanor and fined
   f. A person was charged with a misdemeanor for obtaining personal data records under false premises

Number of times an agency informed an individual of impending adverse action against them and gave them the opportunity to review and challenge the associated personal data records.   1.9.15

Organizational Roles and Responsibilities

The Privacy Act and subsequent legislation established several specific organizational roles and responsibilities in regard to implementing the provisions of the Act. This is an attempt to create some form of checks and balances among the three branches of government. To understand the dynamics involved, remember that the Director of the Office of Management and Budget is a political appointee, as are the judges in federal District Courts. Members of Congress are elected officials and most agency employees are career civil servants. We have already discussed the source and recipient agency responsibilities, as well as the role of the District Courts. Additional roles and responsibilities are assigned to:

- An agency's Data Integrity Board
- An agency's Privacy Officer
- The Office of Management and Budget
- The U.S. Congress
- The Office of the Federal Register

Each agency that conducts or participates in a matching program is required to have a Data Integrity Board. The Data Integrity Board is composed of senior agency officials, including the Inspector General, designated by the agency head. While the Inspector General is required to be a member of the Board, he is not allowed to chair the Board. Several responsibilities are assigned to the Data Integrity Board. The Board is responsible for reviewing, approving, and maintaining all written agreements for matching agreements to ensure complete compliance with the Privacy Act and other relevant laws and regulations. One of the reasons for reviewing matching agreements is to confirm the cost-benefit of participating in such a program. The Data Integrity Board cannot approve a matching agreement unless it contains a valid cost-benefit analysis. If the matching program is mandated by statute, an agency can participate the first year, but no longer, without a cost-benefit analysis. The Data Integrity Board also reviews and approves justifications for continued participation in a matching program; the Board has the authority to grant a one-year extension beyond the maximum 18-month duration of matching agreements. Record-keeping and disposal policies and procedures are reviewed regularly by the Data Integrity Board. A major responsibility of the Board is to serve as a clearinghouse for the accuracy, completeness, and reliability of personal data records maintained by the agency. Once a year, the Data Integrity Board must submit a report to the head of the agency and the Office of Management and Budget; this report must be made available to the public upon request. The report documents matching programs the agency participated in the previous year, either as a source or recipient agency, any matching agreements that were disapproved and the reason, changes in the membership of the Data Integrity Board throughout the year, waivers granted in response to the requirement for a cost-benefit analysis, any actual or alleged violations of the Act and the corrective action taken in response, and any other information the Board deems relevant. Also, the Act makes a vague reference to "matching activities that are not matching programs" and states that they can be aggregated in the report to protect ongoing law enforcement or counterintelligence investigations.

On February 11, 2005, the Office of Management and Budget, an agency that is part of the Executive Office of the President, issued a memo requiring each federal agency to appoint a Privacy Officer at the assistant secretary or senior executive service (SES) level. The provision for a Privacy Officer was included in the fiscal 2005 omnibus appropriation bill. This bill included the requirement for agencies to appoint a Privacy Officer to "create policies for privacy rules to ensure that information technology does not erode privacy protections related to the use, collection, and dissemination of information."[193a] Agencies were instructed to designate such an individual by March 11, 2005. The intent is for the Privacy Officer to be a senior-level official who has overall agency-wide responsibility for information privacy issues. It is assumed that this person will reside in the Office of the Chief Information Officer.[193] The memo gives the Privacy Officer the authority within an agency to consider privacy issues at a national and agency-wide level and the responsibility and accountability for implementation and compliance with the Privacy Act. In particular, the Privacy Officer is responsible and accountable for[108a]:

- Ensuring that appropriate safeguards are implemented to protect personal information from unauthorized use, access, disclosure, or sharing consistent with the Privacy Act and the Federal Information Security Management Act (FISMA)
- Ensuring that agency information systems, whether operated by government employees or contractors, are protected from unauthorized access, modification, disruption, and destruction
- Documenting compliance activities, conducting periodic audits, and promptly identifying and remedying any weaknesses uncovered
- Overseeing, coordinating, and facilitating compliance activities and compliance-related training
- Drafting and reviewing federal and agency privacy-related legislation, regulations, and policies
- Performing privacy impact assessments for new, upgraded, and legacy information systems

Furthermore, Privacy Officers are required to submit an annual report to Congress documenting the agency's privacy-related activities, complaints from individuals, employee training, etc. They are also required to sponsor an independent assessment of the effectiveness of their privacy policies, procedures, and practices every two years. Privacy Officers were given 12 months (until March 11, 2006) to get their agency's privacy protection initiatives in place. The relationship between the Data Integrity Board and the Privacy Officer is not explicitly defined in the memo. Presumably, the Data Integrity Board reports to the Privacy Officer.

The Office of Management and Budget has several responsibilities under the Privacy Act. Subsection (v) directs the Director of the Office of Management and Budget to develop guidelines and regulations to assist agencies in implementing the provisions of the Act and to perform an ongoing monitoring and oversight role in regard to implementation. The Privacy Officer memo is an example of this. The Director of the Office of Management and Budget can approve an exception to the requirement for a cost-benefit analysis in a matching agreement and, in effect, overrule a disapproval by the Data Integrity Board. The Office of Management and Budget is also a recipient of the annual reports submitted by the Data Integrity Boards. This information is used to prepare a biennial report to the Speaker of the House of the Representatives and the President *pro tempore* of the Senate describing the activities during the previous two years within the federal government related to the Privacy Act. In particular, four items must be addressed: (1) the extent of individuals exercising their rights to access and correct information, (2) changes in or additions to any federal system maintaining individuals' personal data, (3) the number of waivers granted for cost/benefit analyses, and (4) the effectiveness of federal agencies in implementing the provisions of the Act.

Congress made itself an active participant in the execution of the provisions of the Privacy Act. The House Committee on Government Operations and the Senate Committee on Government Affairs must be notified of and approve any proposed new use of personal data that has already been collected, any change to a federal record system that contains personal data, and any change to a matching agreement. Congress has 30 days to review and approve such items before they take effect. Matching agreements must also be reviewed and approved by these Congressional Committees. The House Committee on Government Operations and the Senate Committee on Government Affairs are the recipients of the biennial report produced by the Office of Management and Budget. Congress does not receive the annual reports produced by the Data Integrity Boards; presumably they could request a copy if they wanted one.

As mentioned previously, federal agencies communicate to individuals through the *Federal Register*. In addition, the Office of the Federal Register is responsible for compiling and publishing descriptions of all the federal record systems maintained on individuals by federal agencies, agency record-keeping policies and procedures, and the procedures for individuals to obtain information about their records. This information is captured from individual agency notices posted in the *Federal Register* and published every two years. Known as the Privacy Act compilation, this information has been available online as ASCII text since 1995 through GPO Access (www.gpoacess.gov).

The following metrics can be used to measure whether or not the appropriate organizational checks and balances specified in the Privacy Act are being exercised responsibly. These metrics can be used by agencies to monitor their own performance, individuals and public interest groups, and independent oversight authorities in the public and private sectors.

Distribution of agencies that do and do have a functioning Data Integrity Board. 1.9.16

Date of most recent meeting of the Data Integrity Board: 1.9.17
    a. Average frequency with which the Board meets
    b. Average annual turnover in Board membership

Number of matching agreements the Data Integrity Board: 1.9.18
   a. Reviewed
   b. Approved
   c. Disapproved
   d. Extended

Frequency with which Data Integrity Board reviews policies and procedures for maintaining, accessing, copying, disclosing, verifying, retaining, and disposing of personal data records.   1.9.19

Number and percentage of times the Data Integrity Board submitted their annual report to the OMB on time and the report was accepted by the OMB.   1.9.20

Distribution of agencies that do and do not have a functioning Privacy Officer.   1.9.21

Frequency with which the Privacy Officer reviews the adequacy of security controls to prevent unauthorized use, access, disclosure, retention, and destruction of personal data records.   1.9.22

Number of compliance audits conducted by the Privacy Officer.   1.9.23

Number of privacy impact assessments conducted by the Privacy Officer: 1.9.24

   a. For new or planned information systems
   b. For existing or upgraded information systems
   c. For legacy information systems
   d. Average number of problems found per audit and privacy impact assessment and the average time frame required to complete the remedial action

Number of independent assessments of the effectiveness of privacy policies, procedures, and practices requested by the Privacy Officer per fiscal year.   1.9.25

Number and percentage of times the Privacy Officer submitted his annual report to Congress on time and the report was accepted by Congress. 1.9.26

Number and percentage of times OMB submitted its biennial report to Congress on time and the report was accepted by Congress.   1.9.27

Number and percentage of times OMB granted a waiver for a matching program without a cost/benefit analysis.   1.9.28

Number and percentage of times the OMB Director overruled an agency's Data Integrity Board and approved a matching agreement.   1.9.29

Number and percentage of matching agreements Congress disapproved of.   1.9.30

Number of times either House of Congress expressed its displeasure at: 1.9.31

   a. An agency's compliance with the Privacy Act
   b. An agency's Data Integrity Board

      c. An agency's Privacy Officer

      d. OMB's oversight of federal agencies compliance with the Privacy Act

Number and percentage of times the Office of the Federal Register released the Privacy Act compilation on time.   1.9.32

Number and percentage of times the Privacy Act compilation prepared by the Office of the Federal Register was found to be incomplete or inaccurate.

1.9.33

Comparison of Privacy Regulations

Let us see how the five privacy regulations stack up against one another. Because Canada, the United Kingdom, and the United States are all Member States of the OECD and the European Commission is a participant in the OECD, it is appropriate to compare the regulations against the OECD Guidelines. As shown in Table 3.10, the Data Protection Directive, the U.K. Data Protection Act, and the Canadian PIPEDA are in complete conformity with the OECD Privacy Guidelines; they even incorporate some of the principles of the OECD Cryptography and Security Guidelines. The odd man out is the Privacy Act of the United States, which only addresses five of the eight principles in the OECD Privacy Guidelines and limits their application to just personal data records maintained by agencies of the federal government. The collection limitation and openness principles are neither adhered to, nor is any one person held accountable for noncompliance.

Unlike the OECD Guidelines, the Data Protection Directive, the U.K. Data Protection Act, or the Canadian PIPEDA, the U.S. Government has followed a practice of separate legislation for different privacy scenarios, versus a single, all-encompassing privacy bill. Here is a small sampling:

- The 1978 Right to Financial Privacy Act, Public Law 95-630, codified at 12 U.S.C. Chapter 35
- The 1980 Privacy Protection Act, Public Law 96-440, codified at 42 U.S.C. § 2000aa
- The 1986 Electronic Communication Privacy Act, Public Law 99-508, codified at 18 U.S.C. Chapter 121
- The 1988 Video Privacy Protection Act, Public Law 100-618, codified at 18 U.S.C. § 2710
- The 1991 Telemarketers Protection Act, Public Law 102-243, codified at 47 U.S.C. § 227

This practice highlights the need stated previously for a guide to writing object-oriented legislation. It is neither logical nor practical to write a separate privacy bill for every new electronic device or usage scenario that comes along. Technology and the use of such technology changes much faster than salient legislation can be enacted. At the rate the United States is headed, soon there will be separate privacy bills for PDAs, cell phones, automobile GPS, DVD players, and our Dick Tracy watches. One all-encompassing

Table 3.10   Consistency of Privacy Regulations with the OECD Guidelines

OECD Principles	Directive 95/46/EC	U.K. Data Protection Act	Canadian PIPEDA	U.S. Privacy Act
I. Privacy Guidelines				
Collection Limitation	x	x	x	
Data Quality	x	x	x	*
Purpose Specification	x	x	x	*
Use Limitation	x	x	x	*
Security Safeguards	x	x	x	*
Openness	x	x	x	
Individual Participation	x	x	x	*
Accountability	x	x	x	
II. Cryptography Guidelines				
Trust in Cryptographic Methods				
Choice of Cryptographic Methods				
Market Driven Development of Cryptographic Methods				
Standards for Cryptographic Methods				
Protection of Privacy and Personal Data			x	
Lawful Access				
Liability				
International Cooperation				
III. Security Guidelines				
Awareness				
Responsibility	x	x	x	
Response				
Ethics				
Democracy				
Risk Assessment	x	x		
Security Design and Implementation				
Security Management				
Reassessment				

* Only applies to personal data records maintained by federal agencies.

enforceable privacy bill, based on the OECD Privacy Guidelines, would be much better than 30 overlapping, conflicting, half-way measures.

The Privacy Act falls short in several important areas. As mentioned, the Act only applies to agencies of the federal government. The Privacy Act does not make provision for a single nationwide Supervisory Authority or Privacy Commissioner who is tasked with oversight, enforcement, and keeping the public informed. Instead, each federal agency has a Data Integrity Board and Privacy Officer. The OMB and Congress have minimal oversight of and insight into federal agencies' activities. Political appointees and elected officials come and go. In essence, the agencies are left to regulate themselves, which leads to lax enforcement. Self-regulation by federal agencies does not work, as the following two examples illustrate. It was recently discovered that the Social Security Administration, from September 2001 onward, had a policy in effect of broad ad hoc disclosures of personal information, in violation of the Privacy Act, to various law enforcement officials, supposedly under the guise of preventing terrorism.[239] These disclosures are rather odd because none of the 9/11 hijackers had social security numbers. Neither Congress[103] nor the OMB were informed; it is unclear whether the Data Integrity Board was consulted; in short, the checks and balances in the Privacy Act did not work. Likewise, it was recently reported that the Transportation Security Agency made unauthorized disclosures of 12 million passenger records to third parties, inside and outside the federal government.[236] While the stated purpose of the Privacy Act is noble, the subsequent provisions do not live up to these goals. Given the 18 exemptions, there are no real limits on the collection, use, or dissemination of information, particularly by recipient agencies that may or may not be part of the federal government. The civil and criminal penalties are ridiculously low. Because probably less than 1 percent of the population in the United States has heard of the *Federal Register*, this is not an effective means of communicating with the public. The Privacy Act leaves several important responsibilities unassigned. For example, no one is assigned the responsibility to:

- Verify that personal data is rendered anonymous before being disclosed for "statistical or historical research" purposes
- Verify that personal data records are in fact destroyed at the end of their prestated use (the government is notorious for never deleting any records)
- Determine which personal data records are or are not of "sufficient historical value" such that they should become a permanent part of the National Archives
- Monitor "matching activities" that are not part of an approved matching program
- Verify that disclosure records are indeed accurate, complete, and up-to-date
- Monitor the activities of recipient agencies
- Verify that use of the exemptions is not being abused

The implications and results of the shortfalls of the Privacy Act are obvious and serious. In the old days, an individual had to worry about having his checkbook or credit cards stolen and the accounts being misused. Today, at least once a week there is a story in the news about an identity theft ring stealing thousands of individuals' financial and other personal information. The company from whom the information is stolen wrings their hands and says it cannot imagine how that could have happened. The victims are left to fend for themselves at an average cost of $6000 and six months to clean up the mess. Congress holds hearings and talks about passing "safe harbor" legislation to absolve the companies from whom personal information is stolen from any liability.[231] The idea is that if the company had only done "x," it would not be responsible. This is an overly simplistic view of the situation, analogous to saying that if everyone wore seat belts there would not be any more fatal car accidents. It is not possible to write safe harbor legislation for the simple reason that all information systems, networks, connectivity arrangements, operational environments, operational procedures, etc. are quite different, not to mention constantly changing. Accordingly, Congress should specify what needs to be done, not how to do it. Instead of safe harbor legislation, the OECD Privacy and Security Guidelines should be implemented and enforced across all public- and private-sector organizations. Then organizations should be required to provide metrics to prove that they did in fact exercise due diligence and due care. If they are unable to do this, they should face stiff fines for allowing identify theft and other cyber crime to occur.

HOMELAND SECURITY

The following four policies represent attempts to enhance the security of key national assets and resources under the homeland security umbrella. Three of the four policies were issued by the federal government, while the fourth was issued by a non-government organization (NGO). The differences in approaches between the federal and NGO policies are striking.

3.11 Federal Information Security Management Act (FISMA) — United States

The E-Government Act, Public Law 107-347, was passed in December 2002. The intent was to make the acquisition, development, and operation of IT within the federal government efficient and cost-effective; to weed out duplicate, unnecessary, and overlapping systems; to ensure that site licenses are negotiated on a department-by-department basis, instead of at a branch or division level consisting of only 20 to 30 employees; etc. Needless to say, this is not the first such attempt, as is evident by several previous bills such as the Brooks Bill, none of which have been successful. How do you make a bungling 200-year-old bureaucracy embrace the ideals of efficiency and cost-effectiveness when (1) there are no profit and loss statements, no bottom line, no customers, no stockholders, and no Board of Directors to report to; (2) there are no competitors; (3) promotions and performance appraisals are based on the size of one's budget and the number of people one supervises; and

(4) there is no penalty for taking six years to do something that could and should have been done in six months, or six months to do something that could and should have been done in six weeks? Governments are good at performing some functions; efficiency and cost-effectiveness are not among the traits associated with any government, past, present, or most likely future.

Title III of the E-Government Act is known as the Federal Information Security Management Act, or FISMA. Likewise, this is not the first attempt to legislate adequate security protections for unclassified information systems and networks operated by and for the U.S. Government. The Computer Security Act and the Government Information Security Reform Act (GISRA) are a few of the predecessors. Again, the intent is reasonable; it is the implementation that is flawed. People in industry chafe under government regulations. If you think that situation is bad, try to imagine one government agency regulating the others — what a scary thought — and you begin to understand FISMA. FISMA is an example of wanting to do "something" so we can all feel good about the security of the federal government's information systems and networks. In this case, the "something" is to generate a lot of paperwork. This bill has kept a lot of technical writers and word processors employed. Has it made the information systems and networks of the civilian agencies in the federal government more secure? That is debatable, given the cookie-cutter approach pursued by most agencies. Paper does not make systems or networks secure; good security engineering practices throughout the life of a system or network, staff who have the appropriate education and experience, and the proper use of metrics do. Ironically, FISMA is considered an expansion of the Paperwork Reduction Act. Another interesting twist is that FISMA is limited to IT security. IT security cannot be achieved in a vacuum. There are many interdependencies among physical, personnel, IT, and operational security. This fact has led to some entertaining turf battles in federal agencies among the people responsible for FISMA and the people responsible for physical, personnel, and operational security. Needless to say, this has not contributed to efficiency or cost-effectiveness. If the scope of FISMA was that of a Chief Security Officer, not a Chief Information Security Officer, federal agencies would be in a better position to accomplish real reform.

FIMSA amends existing legislation, Chapter 35 of Title 44 USC and Section 11331 Title 40 USC. The stated purposes of FISMA are to[72]:

- Provide a comprehensive framework for ensuring the effectiveness of information security controls over information resources that support federal operations and assets
- Recognize the highly networked nature of the current federal computing environment and provide effective government-wide management and oversight of the related information security risks, including coordination of information security efforts throughout the civilian, national security, and law-enforcement communities
- Provide for development and maintenance of minimum controls required to protect federal information and information systems

- Provide mechanisms for improved oversight of federal agency information security programs
- Acknowledge that commercially developed information security products offer advanced, dynamic, robust, and effective information security solutions, reflecting market solutions for the protection of critical information infrastructures important to the national defense and economic security of the nation that are designed, built, and operated by the private sector
- Recognize that the selection of specific technical hardware and software information security solutions should be left to individual agencies from among commercially developed products

The inherent conflicts in FISMA are already apparent just from reading the list of stated purposes on the first page of the bill: (1) trying to manage information security government-wide, while at the same time letting individual agencies make their own decisions; (2) trying to promote specific controls, while promoting the use of commercial security solutions; and (3) coordinating information security efforts among the civilian, national security, and law enforcement agencies, which has always been a non sequitur. FISMA is currently funded through fiscal year 2007. If history is any indicator, it is likely that the law will be replaced rather than renewed.

FISMA assigns roles and responsibilities for information security to the Director of the Office of Management and Budget (OMB), civilian federal agencies, the Federal Information Security Incident Center, and the National Institute of Standards and Technology (NIST), each of which is discussed below.

Director of the OMB

The Director of the OMB has the primary role and responsibility for overseeing the implementation and effectiveness of information security in the civilian federal agencies. In effect, the Director of the OMB functions as the Chief Information Security Officer (CISO) of the federal government, as far as unclassified systems and networks are concerned. The Director is to oversee the development of information security policies, principles, standards, and guidelines. Ensuring that agencies comply with FISMA requirements and, when necessary, enforcing accountability are major initiatives. The OMB has considerable leverage in this regard. The GAO can audit any programs or agencies it wants to investigate, and all agencies must submit their budget requests, including funding for IT and security, to the OMB for approval. The OMB Director is also responsible for overseeing the operation of the Federal Information Security Incident Center. Each March, the Director of the OMB must submit an activity report to Congress, summarizing its findings from the previous year. In particular, (1) any significant information security deficiencies and the planned remedial action, and (2) the status of the development and acceptance of NIST standards must be reported. This report is compiled from the annual and quarterly reports agencies are required to submit to the OMB.

Federal Agencies

Federal agencies are responsible for developing, documenting, implementing, and verifying an agency-wide information security program. Generally, ultimate responsibility for this function lies within the Office of the Chief Information Officer (CIO), who appoints a Chief Information Security Officer for the agency. Federal agencies are to ensure compliance with information security policies, procedures, and standards. A major responsibility in this area is to ensure that information security management processes are integrated with the agency's strategic and operational planning processes. Physical, personnel, IT, and operational security controls are to be evaluated at least annually and the appropriate remedial action taken. Risk assessments are to be conducted regularly to ensure that risk mitigation activities are commensurate with the risk and magnitude of harm that could result from unauthorized access, use, disclosure, disruption, modification, or destruction of information or systems. For both new and legacy systems, the results of risk assessments are to be used to determine the extent, type, and robustness of security controls needed. In the case of legacy systems, this determination should be compared with the existing controls to identify any deficiencies. Federal agencies are responsible for putting policies and procedures in place to advance cost-effective risk mitigation and remedial action throughout the security engineering life cycle. Security awareness and training activities, which are tailored to the agency's mission and information systems, are to be held regularly to motivate employees to be responsible and accountable for their actions. Federal agencies are responsible for deploying a capability to detect, report, and respond to security incidents, with the goal of containing incidents before much damage is done. Oddly enough, FISMA is silent on the subject of intrusion prevention. Security incidents of any significance must be reported to the Federal Information Security Incident Center and law enforcement because government agencies, equipment, and information are involved. Contingency and disaster recovery plans and procedures, as well as continuity of operations plans and procedures, should be prepared and practiced regularly by federal agencies as part of their information security program. Federal agencies are also responsible for preparing several reports, including:

- An annual report to the agency head about the effectiveness of the information security program
- An annual performance plan documenting the schedule, budget, staff, resources, and training needed to execute the information security program
- A quarterly report describing progress in achieving the annual performance plan
- An annual report to the OMB Director; the House Government Reform and Science Committees; the Senate Governmental Affairs and Commerce, Science, and Transportation Committees; and the Comptroller General describing the adequacy and effectiveness of the agency's information security program in relation to its budget, IT management performance, financial management, internal accounting, and administrative controls; any deficiencies are to be noted

■ An annual inventory of major information systems and interfaces, submitted to the Comptroller General, that is to be used for planning, budgeting, monitoring, and evaluating security controls

In addition, the Inspector General of each agency is to submit an annual report to the Director of the OMB that documents (1) their results from independent testing of a representative sample of information system security controls; (2) their independent assessment of the agency's compliance with FISMA and information security policies, procedures, standards, and guidelines; and (3) their assessment of how well agency information is protected against known vulnerabilities. In 2005, the OMB began requiring agencies to include privacy issues as part of their FISMA reports.

The OMB provides direction to federal agencies about what information to include in their quarterly and annual FISMA reports and how to present it. The emphasis is on quantitative information. The intent is to standardize the information across agencies so that comparisons can be made among agencies and from one year to the next for a single agency. A series of report templates were given to agencies. Some tweaking of the templates takes place from year to year. Those discussed below were in effect during fiscal 2006.[72d]

The first set of metrics is for the annual report submitted by each agency. The questions focus on whether or not the agency is performing the activities required by FISMA. The questions do not evaluate whether an agency is being proactive in its approach to information security, nor do they address a fundamental issue — getting the security requirements right as the first step in the security engineering life cycle and designing security into systems and networks from the get-go.

Information Required for Agency Annual Report:

By risk category (high, moderate, low, not categorized) and bureau: 1.10.36
    a. Total number of systems
    b. Number of agency owned and operated systems
    c. Number of contractor owned and operated systems

By risk category (high, moderate, low, not categorized) and bureau: 1.10.37
    a. Number of systems certified and accredited
    b. Number of systems for which security controls have been tested and evaluated in the last year
    c. Number of systems for which contingency plans have been tested in the last year

NIST SP 800-53 (FIPS 200) security controls: 1.10.38
    a. Is a plan in place to implement the recommended security controls? (yes/no)
    b. Has implementation of the recommended security controls begun? (yes/no)

Incident detection: 1.10.39
    a. What tools and techniques does the agency use?
    b. What percentage of systems and networks are protected?

Number of security incidents reported internally, to US-CERT, and to law enforcement: 1.10.40

    a. Unauthorized access
    b. Denial of service
    c. Malicious code
    d. Improper usage
    e. Other

Security awareness and training: 1.10.41

    a. Total number of employees in current fiscal year
    b. Number of employees that received security awareness and training in current fiscal year
    c. Total number of employees with significant IT security responsibilities
    d. Number of employees with significant IT security responsibilities that received specialized security awareness and training in current fiscal year
    e. Total costs for providing IT security training in current fiscal year

Is there an agency-wide security configuration policy? (yes/no)   1.10.42

Using the following scale: (rarely 0–50 percent, sometimes 51–70 percent, frequently 71–80 percent, mostly 81–95 percent, always 96–100 percent, or N/A no such systems), indicate the extent of implementing product configuration guides across the agency: 1.10.43

    a. Windows XP Professional
    b. Windows NT
    c. Windows 2000 Professional
    d. Windows 2000 Server
    e. Windows 2003 Server
    f. Solaris
    g. HP-UX
    h. Linux
    i. Cisco Router IOS
    j. Oracle
    k. Other

Security incident policies and procedures: 1.10.44

    a. Documented policies and procedures are followed by identifying and reporting incidents internally (yes/no)
    b. Documented policies and procedures are followed by identifying and reporting incidents to law enforcement (yes/no)
    c. Documented policies and procedures are followed by identifying and reporting incidents to US-CERT (yes/no)

Has the agency documented security policies and procedures for using emerging technologies to counter new threats? (yes/no)   1.10.45

The second set of metrics is for the annual report required by the Inspector General of each agency. This report accompanies that prepared by the agency. Some of the questions seek to validate the information in the agency report; other questions ask the Inspector General to evaluate how well an agency is performing certain activities. The Inspector General metrics lack an overall assessment of the agency's security engineering life cycle and practices. They also do not evaluate personnel resources. Does the agency have the right number and right skill level of people assigned to perform information security engineering tasks? If people do not have the appropriate education and experience, they will not be able to specify, design, develop, test, operate, or maintain secure systems and networks or perform ST&E, C&A, and other FISMA functions correctly.

Information Required for Inspector General Annual Report:

By risk category (high, moderate, low, not categorized) and bureau: 1.10.46

    a. Total number of systems
    b. Number of agency owned and operated systems
    c. Number of contractor owned and operated systems

By risk category (high, moderate, low, not categorized) and bureau: 1.10.47

    a. Number of systems certified and accredited
    b. Number of systems for which security controls have been tested and evaluated in the last year
    c. Number of systems for which contingency plans have been tested in the last year

Agency oversight of contractor systems: 1.10.48

    a. Frequency of oversight and evaluation activities, using the following scale: (rarely 0–50 percent, sometimes 51–70 percent, frequently 71–80 percent, mostly 81–95 percent, always 96–100 percent, or N/A no such systems).
    b. Agency has developed an inventory of major information systems, including an identification of the interfaces between each such system and all other systems or networks, using the following scale: 0–50 percent complete, 51–70 percent complete, 71–80 percent complete, 81–95 percent complete, 96–100 percent complete
    c. Inspector General (IG) agrees with CIO on the number of agency owned systems (yes/no)
    d. IG agrees with CIO on the number of information systems used or operated by contractors (yes/no)
    e. Agency inventory is maintained and updated at least annually (yes/no)
    f. Agency has completed system e-authentication risk assessments (yes/no)

Plan of actions and milestones (corrective action plan): 1.10.49

    a. Is the plan of actions and milestones an agency-wide process, incorporating all known IT security weaknesses associated with information systems used or operated by the agency or by a contractor, using the following scale: (rarely 0–50 percent, sometimes 51–70 percent, frequently 71–80 percent, mostly 81–95 percent, always 96–100 percent)

b. When an IT security weakness is identified, program officials develop, implement, and manage a plan of action and milestones for their system(s), using the following scale: (rarely 0–50 percent, sometimes 51–70 percent, frequently 71–80 percent, mostly 81–95 percent, always 96–100 percent)

c. Program officials, including contractors, report to the CIO at least quarterly on their remediation progress, using the following scale: (rarely 0–50 percent, sometimes 51–70 percent, frequently 71–80 percent, mostly 81–95 percent, always 96–100 percent)

d. CIO centrally tracks, maintains, and reviews plans of action and milestones at least quarterly, using the following scale: (rarely 0–50 percent, sometimes 51–70 percent, frequently 71–80 percent, mostly 81–95 percent, always 96–100 percent)

e. IG findings are incorporated into the plan of actions and milestone process, using the following scale: (rarely 0–50 percent, sometimes 51–70 percent, frequently 71–80 percent, mostly 81–95 percent, always 96–100 percent)

f. Plan of action and milestone process prioritizes IT security weaknesses to help ensure significant IT security weaknesses are addressed in a timely manner and receive appropriate resources, using the following scale: (rarely 0–50 percent, sometimes 51–70 percent, frequently 71–80 percent, mostly 81–95 percent, always 96–100 percent)

IG assessment of the certification and accreditation process, using the following scale: excellent, good, satisfactory, poor, failing.   1.10.50

Is there an agency-wide security configuration policy? (yes/no) Using the following scale: (rarely 0–50 percent, sometimes 51–70 percent, frequently 71–80 percent, mostly 81–95 percent, always 96–100 percent, or N/A no such systems), indicate the extent of implementing product configuration guides across the agency: 1.10.51

    a. Windows XP Professional
    b. Windows NT
    c. Windows 2000 Professional
    d. Windows 2000 Server
    e. Windows 2003 Server
    f. Solaris
    g. HP-UX
    h. Linux
    i. Cisco Router IOS
    j. Oracle
    k. Other

Security incident policies and procedures: 1.10.52

    a. Documented policies and procedures are followed by identifying and reporting incidents internally (yes/no)

    b. Documented policies and procedures are followed by identifying and reporting incidents to law enforcement (yes/no)

    c. Documented policies and procedures are followed by identifying and reporting incidents to US-CERT (yes/no)

Has the agency ensured security awareness and training of all employees, including contractors and those with significant IT security responsibilities, using the following scale: (rarely 0–50 percent, sometimes 51–70 percent, frequently 71–80 percent, mostly 81–95 percent, always 96–100 percent)?

1.10.53

Does the agency explain policies regarding peer-to-peer file sharing in IT security awareness training, ethics training, or any other agency-wide training? (yes/no)

1.10.54

During 2005, the OMB directed each agency and department to appoint a Chief Privacy Officer. As part of the annual FISMA reports, the Chief Privacy Officer is to report on the status of complying with privacy laws and regulations in his agency.

Information Required for Agency Privacy Officer Annual Report:

Can your agency demonstrate through documentation that the privacy official participates in all agency information privacy compliance activities? (yes/no)

1.10.55

Can your agency demonstrate through documentation that the privacy official participates in evaluating the ramifications for privacy of legislative, regulatory, and other policy proposals, as well as testimony and comments under Circular A-19? (yes/no)

1.10.56

Can your agency demonstrate through documentation that the privacy official participates in assessing the impact of technology on the privacy of personal information? (yes/no)

1.10.57

Does your agency have a training program to ensure that all agency personnel and contractors with access to Federal data are generally familiar with information privacy laws, regulations, and policies and understand the ramifications of inappropriate access and disclosure? (yes/no)

1.10.58

Does your agency have a program for job-specific information privacy training, i.e., detailed training for individuals (including contractor employees) directly involved in the administration of personal information or information technology systems, or with significant information security responsibilities? (yes/no)

1.10.59

Section 3, Appendix 1 of OMB Circular A-130 requires agencies to conduct and be prepared to report to the Director of the OMB on the results of reviews of activities mandated by the Privacy Act. Indicate the number of reviews conducted by bureau. Which of the following reviews were conducted in the last fiscal year?

1.10.60

    a. Section M of contracts

    b. Records practices

    c. Routine uses
    d. Exemptions
    e. Matching programs
    f. Training
    g. Violations: (1) civil action, (2) remedial action
    h. Systems of records

Section 208 of the E-Government Act requires that agencies conduct privacy impact assessments under appropriate circumstances, post Web privacy policies on their Web sites, and ensure machine-readability of Web privacy policies. Does your agency have a written process or policy for (yes/no):   1.10.61

    a. Determining whether a privacy impact assessment is needed?
    b. Conducting a privacy impact assessment?
    c. Evaluating changes in business process or technology that the privacy impact assessment indicates may be required?
    d. Ensuring that system owners, privacy, and IT experts participate in conducting the privacy impact assessments?
    e. Making privacy impact assessments available to the public in the required circumstances?
    f. Making privacy impact assessments available in other than required circumstances?

Does your agency have a written process for determining continued compliance with stated Web privacy policies? (yes/no)   1.10.62

Do your public-facing agency Web sites have machine-readable privacy policies, i.e., are your Web privacy policies PGP enabled or automatically readable using some other tool? (yes/no) If not, provide date for compliance. 1.10.63

By bureau, identify the number of information systems containing federally owned information in an identifiable form: 1.10.64

    a. Total number of systems
    b. Agency systems
    c. Contractor systems

By bureau, identify the number of information systems for which a privacy impact assessment has been conducted during the past fiscal year: 1.10.65

    a. Total number of systems
    b. Agency systems
    c. Contractor systems

Number of systems from which federally owned information is retrieved by name or unique identifier: 1.10.66

    a. Total number of systems
    b. Agency systems
    c. Contractor systems

By bureau, number of systems for which one or more systems of records notices have been published in the *Federal Register:*   1.10.67

    a. Total number of systems
    b. Agency systems
    c. Contractor systems

OMB policy (Memorandum 03-22) prohibits agencies from using persistent tracking technology on Web sites except in compelling circumstances as determined by the head of the agency or designee reporting directly to the agency head.   1.10.68

    a. Does your agency use persistent tracking technology on any Web site? (yes/no)
    b. Does your agency annually review the use of persistent tracking? (yes/no)
    c. Can your agency demonstrate through documentation the continued justification for an approval to use the persistent technology? (yes/no)
    d. Can your agency provide the notice language used or cite the Web privacy policy informing visitors about the tracking? (yes/no)

Does your agency have current documentation demonstrating review of compliance with information privacy laws, regulations, and policies? (yes/no) If so, provide the date the documentation was created.   1.10.69

Can your agency provide documentation demonstrating corrective action planned, in progress, or completed to remedy identified privacy compliance deficiencies? (yes/no) If so, provide the date the documentation was created.
                                                                        1.10.70

Does your agency use technologies that allow for continuous auditing of compliance with stated privacy policies and practices? (yes/no)   1.10.71

Does your agency coordinate with the agency Office of Inspector General on privacy program oversight by providing to the Inspector General the following materials: 1.10.72

    a. Compilation of the agency's privacy and data protection policies and procedures? (yes/no)
    b. Summary of the agency's use of information in identifiable form? (yes/no)
    c. Verification of intent to comply with agency policies and procedures? (yes/no)

Does your agency submit an annual report to Congress and OMB detailing your privacy activities, including activities under the Privacy Act and any violations that have occurred? (yes/no) If so, when was this report submitted to OMB for clearance?   1.10.73

Agencies are also required to submit a quarterly report of metrics highlighting progress in performing corrective action. The focus is on resolving weaknesses that were identified during security certification and accreditation, internal audits, external audits, or from other sources. Greater insight would be gained if the weaknesses were reported by severity categories and the length of time the weaknesses remained open prior to resolution.

Information Required for Agency Quarterly Reports:

By bureau, total number of weaknesses identified at the start of the quarter.
1.10.74

By bureau, number of weaknesses for which corrective action was completed, including testing, by the end of the quarter.   1.10.75

By bureau, number of weaknesses for which corrective action is ongoing and is on track to be completed as originally scheduled.   1.10.76

By bureau, number of weaknesses for which corrective action has been delayed.   1.10.77

By bureau, number of new weaknesses discovered following the last quarterly update and distribution by method of discovery.   1.10.78

Federal Information Security Incident Center

The Federal Information Security Incident Center functions as a central clearinghouse for information about security events and coordinates federal agencies' response to them. The Federal Information Security Incident Center is tasked to provide technical assistance to operators of agency information systems regarding security incidents and keep them informed about current and potential information security threats and vulnerabilities. Today, most federal agencies have their own security incident response centers. Security incidents above a certain threshold of severity are reported to the Federal Information Security Incident Center. The center is responsible for compiling, analyzing, and sharing security incident information across the government to maximize preparedness and the implementation of best practices.

National Institute of Standards and Technology

The National Institute of Standards and Technology (NIST) is part of the Department of Commerce. Under FISMA, the Secretary of Commerce is responsible for prescribing IT standards developed by NIST that federal agencies must follow. These standards represent a minimum set of security requirements; agencies can employ more robust standards as the case warrants. The President retains the authority to disapprove or modify any prescribed NIST standard via a *Federal Register* notice. NIST is tasked with developing information security standards and guidelines for use by federal agencies that[72]:

- Categorize information and information systems by risk level
- Recommend types of information and information systems to be included in each category
- Identify minimum information security requirements for each category
- Provide guidelines for detecting and handling security incidents

NIST is specifically tasked to (1) evaluate private-sector information security policies and practices ... to assess their potential application by federal

Table 3.11   NIST FISMA Standards

Standard	Title	Page Count
FIPS 199	Standard for Security Categorization of Federal Information and Information Systems	9
FIPS 200	Security Controls for Federal Information Systems	258
SP 800-18	Guide for Developing Security Plans for Information Technology Systems	95
SP 800-53A	Guide for Assessing Security Controls in Federal Information Systems	158
SP 800-50	Building an IT Security Awareness and Training Program	70
SP 800-37	Guide for the Security Certification and Accreditation of Federal Information Systems	64
SP 800-30	Risk Management Guide for Information Technology Systems	48
SP 800-60	Guide for Mapping Types of Information and Information Systems to Security Categories	345
SP 800-26	Guide for Information Security Program Assessments and System Reporting Form, Rev. 1	106
Total		1153

agencies, and (2) use appropriate information security policies, procedures, and techniques to improve information security and avoid unnecessary and costly duplication of effort.[72] NIST was funded $20 million a year for fiscal years 2003 through 2007 to produce such standards and guidelines. NIST is also tasked with providing advice to the Secretary of Commerce and the Director of the OMB on issues related to the Information Security and Privacy Advisory Board.

Table 3.11 lists the standards NIST developed for agencies to use in implementing their FISMA requirements. The total page count of these standards (1153 pages) exceeds the total page count of all 13 security and privacy regulations and standards discussed in this chapter! This is where FISMA took a wrong turn. Here we have a set of standards that were developed and are used only by U.S. Government agencies, and not even all of them. Why was the $20 million a year not invested in developing international or at least national consensus standards? The International Electrotechnical Commission (IEC), in which the United States actively participates, has already developed 70 information security standards and more are in the works; surely one or more of these standards could have been used. Why has one set of information security standards for the U.S. federal government and another set of standards for industry and the rest of the world? When Dr. Perry was Secretary of Defense, one of his major initiatives was to use consensus standards whenever and wherever possible and move the Department of Defense (DoD) away from DoD only standards. He had more than enough evidence that the use of DoD-only standards was the prime cause for the $600 screwdrivers that made the evening news and other wasteful practices. DoD employees were strongly encouraged to participate in the IEEE, Society for Aerospace Engineers (SAE), IEC, and other standards bodies and the end result was mutually beneficial for DoD and the standards bodies.

FISMA appears to be determined to repeat the $600 screwdriver scenario. Security certification and accreditation (C&A) is only one piece of FISMA, yet agency costs for C&A are rather high. On average, an agency spends $40,000 to certify a system. The program office spends about two thirds of that cost preparing the system and documentation for certification; the agency CISO spends the other third to review and accredit the system. These figures do not include any other FISMA activities performed by the program office or the Office of the CIO or related activities performed by the agency's Inspector General. When you multiply these amounts by the number of information systems in the federal government, the costs add up quickly.

The other security standards discussed in this chapter are considerably shorter, more concise, and much more to the point. This is true for both those issued by the government to regulate industry and those issued by industry for its own use. The GLB, HIPAA, and Sarbanes-Oxley security rules, as codified in the *CFR*, are all 12 pages or less. Can you imagine the outcry if NIST attempted to publish a 1153-page final security rule in the *Federal Register*? Industry would not tolerate it. The Payment Card Industry Data Security Standard is only 12 pages long and it covers more topics than the NIST standards. Surely the financial and personal data processed by the Payment Card Industry is just as sensitive, if not more so, than the data processed by civilian agencies in the federal government. The NERC Cyber Security Standards (discussed in Section 3.13 of this chapter) also cover more territory than the NIST standards; they are only 56 pages long. For example, an assessment methodology and compliance levels are defined in the NERC Cyber Security standards. And, it did not cost the taxpayers $20 million a year for five years to produce the Payment Card Industry Data Security Standard, the NERC Cyber Security Standards, the GLB, HIPAA, or Sarbanes-Oxley final security rules. One of these five security standards or rules could have easily been adopted for use by FISMA. It appears that NIST missed the statement in FISMA that directed it to evaluate private-sector information security policies and practices to assess their potential application by federal agencies.[72]

Two other aspects of the NIST FISMA standards are troubling as well. First, if NIST believes that federal employees who are responsible for performing information security duties at civilian agencies need 1153 pages of guidance to carry out their jobs, there is a much more serious problem to be solved — one that legislation and standards cannot correct. Second, FIPS 200 is a replica of ISO/IEC 15408, known as the Common Criteria for IT Security Evaluation. The U.S. Government was one of the seven countries that led the development of ISO/IEC 15408. NIST is part of the National Information Assurance Partnership (NIAP) that is responsible for promulgating the Common Criteria standards in the United States. The goal was to develop a standardized methodology for specifying, designing, and evaluating IT products and systems that perform security functions which would be widely recognized and yield consistent, repeatable results.[155] That is, the goal was to develop a full life-cycle, consensus-based security engineering standard.[155] Instead of spending time and the taxpayers' money to develop a standard that duplicates the Common Criteria, these resources would have been better spent developing additions to the Common Criteria (Part 4, Part 5, etc.) that address issues the Common Criteria currently do not cover, such as physical and personnel security. There is nothing to be gained by taking Federal agencies back to the days of stovepipe government-only standards. Surely information security is too important a topic for backward thinking. In addition, an independent infrastructure is already in place to measure compliance with the Common Criteria standards, through the accredited worldwide Common Criteria Testing Labs.

Six months after FISMA was enacted, NIST published SP 800-55, which defined security metrics for federal agencies to use to demonstrate compliance with the Act. They measure security process issues, not the robustness or resilience of a system. FISMA reporting requirements have changed since then, but there is still some overlap.

3.12 Homeland Security Presidential Directives (HSPDs) — United States

How many of you non-government types even knew there was such a thing as Homeland Security Presidential Directives? Well, now you do and if you are in the security business, it is probably a good idea to stay informed about the latest developments in this area.

Homeland Security Presidential Directives (or HSPDs) were initiated in October 2001, in the wake of 9/11. Three days after the Patriot Act (which is discussed below in Section 3.14 of this book) was passed and before the Department of Homeland Security was created, the first HSPD was issued. HSPDs are similar to Executive Orders (EOs), Presidential Decision Directives (PDDs), and other mechanisms the executive branch of the U.S. Government uses to push the policies, procedures, and practices of the federal agencies in a certain direction. Congress, the legislative branch, passes laws and budgets that guide the strategic direction and priorities of the federal government, similar to a corporate board of directors. The President is responsible for managing the tactical day-to-day operations of the executive branch and the federal agencies that comprise it, similar to a corporate CEO. HSPDs are one tool that the President uses to accomplish this task. HSPDs and the like do not carry the weight or authority of a law or statute; rather, they represent policy, similar to a memo from your third-level boss. HSPDs and other directives often repeat provisions from a law or statute, with a fair amount of philosophy thrown in for good measure. Sometimes, directives are issued simply for public relations (PR) purposes, while other times the reasons are legitimate. Occasionally, the real reason for issuing a directive is not the same as that claimed. Why do non-government organizations and individuals need

Table 3.12 Summary of Homeland Security Presidential Directives

Number	Title	Date Issued
HSPD-1	Organization and Operation of the Homeland Security Council	10/29/2001
HSPD-2	Combating Terrorism through Immigration Policies	10/29/2001
HSPD-3	Homeland Security Advisory System	3/2002
HSPD-4	National Strategy to Combat Weapons of Mass Destruction	12/2002
HSPD-5	Management of Domestic Incidents	2/28/2003
HSPD-6	Integration and Use of Screening Information	9/16/2003
HSPD-7	Critical Infrastructure Identification, Prioritization, and Protection	12/17/2003
HSPD-8	National Preparedness	12/17/2003
HSPD-9	Defense of United States Agriculture and Food	1/30/2004
HSPD-10	Biodefense in the 21st Century	4/28/2004
HSPD-11	Comprehensive Terrorist-Related Screening Procedures	8/27/2004
HSPD-12	Policy for a Common Identification Standard for Federal Employees and Contractors	8/27/2004

to pay attention to HSPDs? Because the scope of the directives often goes well beyond government agencies and employees and includes government contractors, state and local agencies, and private-sector institutions, particularly when critical infrastructure is involved. At the time of writing, 12 HSPDs had been issued. They are listed in Table 3.12 and are discussed individually below.

As noted, HSPD-1 was "...the first in a series of HSPDs that shall record and communicate presidential decisions about the homeland security policies of the United States."[83] HSPD-1 established the Homeland Security Council, the principle members being the Secretaries of the Treasury, Defense, Transportation, and Health and Human Services; the Attorney General; Director of the CIA; Director of the FBI; the Director of the Federal Emergency Management Agency; and designated White House staff. The Council is chaired by the Secretary of the Department of Homeland Security. Other departments and agencies are invited to participate on an as-needed basis. The Council presides over 11 Policy Coordination Committees, each of which is chaired by a Department of Homeland Security employee, that integrate specific security policy initiatives across the federal government and with state and local agencies.

HSPD-2 reiterates many of the provisions found in the Patriot Act, and defines and elaborates the roles and responsibilities the Department of Homeland Security would inherit when the Homeland Security Act was passed in 2002. HSPD-2 launched five specific initiatives. The foreign terrorist tracking task force was established to (1) deny entry into the United States of anyone suspected of, associated with, or engaged in terrorist activities; and (2) locate, detain, prosecute, and deport any such persons already in the United States.[84] The foreign terrorist tracking task force was to encourage coordination among federal, state, local, and foreign governments in this effort. The second initiative involved enhancing enforcement of immigration and customs laws through joint investigation and intelligence analysis capabilities. Third, the status of international students began to be more closely observed for possible visa abuses and other actions detrimental to the United States. In addition to monitoring the expiration dates of student visas, the course of study, classes taken, full-time student status, and the source of funds for tuition, etc. are inspected. The fourth initiative was to promote compatible immigration laws, customs procedures, and visa practices between the United States, Canada, and Mexico. Finally, the fifth initiative was a temporary precursor to the automated entry/exit identity verification system mandated in the Patriot Act. The emphasis was on data mining of federal, commercial, and foreign databases to locate possible adverse information related to individuals requesting visas to enter the United States.

HSPD-3 launched the Homeland Security Advisory System or the color-coded threat warning system that you hear about on the news every now and then. This is perhaps the best known of the HSPDs. The intent was to devise a "comprehensive and effective means to disseminate information regarding the risk of terrorist acts to federal, state, and local authorities and the American public."[85] The color-coded system is used to represent a graduated set of threat conditions, based on the severity of the consequences and the likelihood of occurrence, and report warnings about them. The color-coded threat level chosen at any given time is a qualitative assessment of the threat credibility, whether or not the threat has been corroborated, the specificity and imminence of the threat, and the severity of the potential consequences. Depending on the specific circumstances, the threat level may apply to the entire country, a given region, or industrial sector. The goal is for protective measures to be in place beforehand for each threat level and scenario to reduce the vulnerability and increase the response capability. Compliance with HSPD-3 is mandatory for federal agencies and voluntary but suggested for state and local agencies and the private sector. Federal agencies are responsible for having plans and procedures in place for a rapid, appropriate, and tailored response to changes in the threat level, as that affects the agency's mission or critical assets. Federal agencies are expected to test and practice these preparedness procedures on a regular basis; just to make sure they do, each agency is required to submit an annual report to the Department of Homeland Security on their preparedness activities.

Table 3.13 is a practical example of HSPD-3 at one agency; it reflects preparedness at the IT security architecture level. The U.S. Federal Aviation Administration issued FAA Order 1370.89, which defines information operation (or INFOCON levels) that correspond to the national color-coded threat levels, for agency information systems and networks. As part of this initiative, the configuration and operation of different security appliances has been defined by INFOCON level. The configuration and operation of these devices adapts

Table 3.13   Sample Implementation of HSPD-3: Configuration and Operation of Security Appliances by INFOCON Level per FAA Order 1370.89

Product: IPS	Low Green	Guarded Blue	Elevated Yellow	High Orange	Severe Red
Attack intent severity levels 1–3	Tracking	Tracking	Tracking	Tracking	Tracking
Attack intent severity levels 4–5	TCP reset	TCP reset	TCP reset, consider blocking	TCP reset and blocking	TCP reset and blocking

Note: The configuration and operation of security appliances should adapt to the threat level.

to the threat level to ensure that critical assets are neither over- nor under-protected for a given scenario. As shown in the example, for low attack intent severity and threat levels, there is no change in the configuration of an intrusion prevention system (IPS). As the attack intent severity and threat level increases, different features and functions are enabled or disabled. Note that a separate worksheet is prepared for each security appliance and automated procedures are used to rapidly change the configurations enterprisewide.

There has been some concern in the media and elsewhere that the designation of national threat levels, as announced to the public, has not been as consistent or informative as it could have been. As a result, Congress has encouraged changes to "...provide more specific threat information to officials in the states, cities, and industries most affected."[229]

HSPD-4 concerns weapons of mass destruction. The intent is to foster cooperation with friends and allies of the United States to prevent the development and proliferation of weapons of mass destruction, through tighter export controls and monitoring of access to the resources and funding needed to build them.

HSPD-5 established the National Incident Management System (NIMS). The goal is to have a single, comprehensive national incident management system for use by federal, state, local, and private-sector organizations. Joint communication and cooperation is to enhance the ability of all to prevent, prepare for, respond to, and recover from terrorist attacks, major disasters (natural and man-made), and other emergencies.[87] Although HSPD-5 was signed in February 2003 and considerable funding has been spent on its implementation, this capability failed miserably during the initial response to hurricane Katrina.

The Terrorist Threat Integration Center was formed in response to HSPD-6. All federal, state, and local government agencies are required to report any relevant information they have to the Center, which is to become a repository for thorough, accurate, and current information about individuals known or suspected to be or have been engaged in terrorist activities.[88]

HSPD-7 zeroes in on critical infrastructure protection. This is probably the best example of cooperation between federal, state, local, and private-sector organizations, for the simple reason that governments are dependent on the services provided by critical infrastructures that are owned and operated by the private sector. HSPD-7 redefines the critical infrastructures, originally spelled out in PDD-63, as: IT, telecommunications, chemical, transportation (rail, mass transit, aviation, maritime, ground and surface, and pipeline), emergency services, and postal and shipping. This list includes critical infrastructures and key resources that are essential to providing the services that underpin the United States society and economy, or that of any other country as well. A combination of physical security, personnel security, IT security, and operational security controls are needed to identify, prioritize, and protect critical infrastructures and key resources. HSPD-7 calls for coordination across sectors to promote uniform methodologies, risk management activities, and metrics to assess the effectiveness of these protection mechanisms. A few paragraphs are particularly noteworthy:

- Paragraph 16 states that an organization should be maintained to serve as the focal point for the security of cyberspace. This organization is to lead the analysis, warning, information sharing, vulnerability reduction, mitigation, recovery efforts, investigation, and prosecution of cyber crime (actual or attempted).
- Paragraph 22 encourages more research in the academic community in relation to critical infrastructure protection, in particular critical information infrastructure protection. NIST is to head up this initiative. The Office of Science and Technology Policy is tasked with coordinating federal critical infrastructure protection research, while the Office of Management and Budget is to oversee government-wide policies, standards, and guidelines for computer security programs such as FISMA. The Federal CIO Council, which includes the CIO from each federal department and agency, is responsible for improving the design, acquisition, development, modernization, use, and operation of information systems and information security.
- Paragraph 25 promotes the sharing of information about physical and cyber security threats, vulnerabilities, indications and warnings, protective measures, and best practices.

National Preparedness is the focus of HSPD-8, in particular the polices and procedures that need to be in place to prevent and respond to threatened or actual domestic terrorist attacks, major disasters (natural and man-made), and other emergencies. HSPD-8, a companion to HSPD-5, promotes all-hazards preparedness throughout the public and private sectors. This directive also makes grants available to state and local first responders for preparedness training, planning, exercises, and equipment. HSPD-8 was signed in December 2003. Based on the initial response to hurricane Katrina, one can only conclude that to date implementation of this HSPD has itself been a disaster.

HSPD-9 gets a little more personal; it concerns protecting the food and water supply from terrorist acts. The Secretary of Agriculture and Secretary of Health and Human Services have the lead role, with help from the Environmental Protection Agency and Department of Interior, when needed. The goal is to develop robust comprehensive surveillance systems to monitor animal, plant, and wildlife diseases that could impact the quality, safety, and availability of the public food and water supplies. A nationwide biological threat awareness capability is envisioned through a series of interconnected labs and other facilities that support rapid identification, recovery, and removal of contaminated products, plants, or animals.

HSPD-10 addresses biological defenses that protect humans. This directive is mostly philosophy and a list of accomplishments by the date of issuance.

HSPD-11 builds upon HSPD-6 and strengthens provisions for terrorist screening. Comprehensive and coordinated procedures are specified for the screening of cargo, conveyances, and individuals known or suspected to be or have been engaged in, preparing for, or aiding terrorism and terrorist activities.[93] One of the technologies used is referred to as backscatter x-ray machines. The radiation dosage is low enough that it does not penetrate semisolid objects, but rather bounces off of them to create an image. The Transportation Security Agency recently announced the use of backscatter x-ray machines to search travelers at the following airports: Baltimore Washington International, Dallas Fort Worth, Jacksonville, Florida, Phoenix, Arizona, and San Francisco.[236] Atlanta, Boston, Chicago O'Hare, Gulfport, Mississippi, Kansas City International, Las Vegas, Los Angeles, Miami, Minneapolis St. Paul, New York's John F. Kennedy, and Tampa, Florida will be added later.[236] This technology is used to detect would-be drug smugglers as well as terrorists. While the technology is touted to be less invasive than a pat-down search, it amounts in effect to an electronic strip search. A full frontal and rear image is created of an individual's body contours and more detail is captured about the sags, bags, folds, and body parts than most people would consider decent, ethical, or acceptable.[236] Fortunately, a side view is not created. While most passengers consider this a temporary embarrassment or invasion of privacy, akin having to take off your shoes, there is nothing temporary about it. The images can be and are stored on a hard disk or floppy disk and can be viewed on any PC.[236] Objections to this technology increase when the application of it to your spouse, children, parents, or 92-year-old Aunt Sarah is discussed, in no small part due to the lack of policies and procedures to control the viewing, storing, retrieval, copying, retention, and distribution of the images.[236] It has been reported that this technology, while expensive — $100,000 to $200,000 per machine — is actually less effective than physical inspection and routine screening with a magnetometer, because it cannot detect weapons hidden in body folds or cavities.[236]

HSPD-12, the Common Identification Standard for Federal Employees and Contractors, was issued the same day as HSPD-11 and is equally as popular. Some consider it a precursor to a national ID card. Like most corporations, the federal government uses photo ID cards, some with and some without magnetic stripes, to identify employees and grant them access to government facilities. To date, each agency issues its own ID cards and procedures, consistent with the classification level of the facility and the assets being accessed. HSPD-12 is an attempt to move toward a single government-wide ID card. NIST was tasked to develop an identification standard for a secure and reliable identification that was[94]:

- Based on sound criteria for verifying an individual's identity
- Strongly resistant to identity fraud, tampering, counterfeiting, and terrorist exploitation
- Capable of rapid electronic verification
- Issued only by providers whose reliability has been established by an official accreditation process
- Based on a set of graduated criteria, to reflect the level of security and integrity needed

Federal agencies were to have a plan in place for implementing the new ID card four months after NIST issued the standard. Eight months after NIST issued the standard, federal agencies were to use the new ID card to control physical and logical access to federal facilities, assets, and information systems. The Office of Management and Budget was to identify, within six to seven months after issuance of the standard, other "federally controlled information systems and other federal applications that are important for security" that should be required to use the new ID card.[94] In reality, these deadlines proved to be highly optimistic. Ironically, national security systems, the most sensitive assets in the federal government, and employees of the intelligence agencies are exempt from the new standard.

On the surface this all sounds fine. But when you dig into the details of the standards, the red lights start flashing. FIPS PUB 201, Personal Identity Verification (PIV) of Federal Employees and Contractors, was signed by the Secretary of Commerce on 25 February 2005. FIPS 201 defines the technical and operational requirements of the PIV standard, both for the ID card and the information system that validates it.[166] FIPS 201 defines two implementation phases: PIV I addresses the control objectives and security requirements of HSPD-12, while PIV II addresses the technical interoperability requirements of HSPD-12. The standard facilitates both human or visual and automated identity verification. The standard is up-front in acknowledging that the main vulnerabilities lie in the area of operational security, not IT security; that is, the implementation of the new ID card, which is left for the most part to each agency[48]:

- Correctly verifying the identity of the individual to whom the PIV card is issued
- Protecting the information stored on the card and while it is transmitted to or from a reader from unauthorized access and disclosure
- Protecting the PIV database, system, and interfaces from unauthorized access and disclosure

The Texas state government is piloting a biometric identity authentication system to reduce Medicaid fraud; it already employs a similar system to combat welfare fraud. This system uses two techniques to avoid privacy problems[257]:

1. Instead of storing actual fingerprint images, these images are converted to a mathematical representation of an image that cannot be reproduced or reengineered to become the actual image.

2. The representation of the fingerprint image is only stored on the ID card, not in any database. The identity verification process involves comparing a person's fingerprints to the mathematical representation on the card — not validating an ID card against a database.

These techniques could be adopted easily to resolve some of the privacy problems with HSPD-12 and the proposed new PIV cards.

FIPS PUB 201 is supplemented by four other standards that provide more detailed specifications to promote interoperability across federal agencies:

1. SP 800-73, which defines the data elements stored on the PIV card and its interfaces
2. SP 800-76, which defines the requirements for collecting and formatting data stored on the PIV card
3. SP 800-78, which defines the cryptographic algorithms and key sizes that are acceptable for use with the PIV card and system
4. SP 800-79, which presents guidelines for certifying organizations that issue PIV cards

SP 800-73 specifies detailed interface requirements for retrieving and using the identity credentials stored on the PIV card. These specifications are quite detailed and posted on the NIST Web page in the open to facilitate vendor compliance. So what is to prevent would-be cyber criminals from taking advantage of this information? They have a complete specification, and there is not much left for them to figure out. The discussion of the security object buffer, container ID 0x9000, is particularly interesting. The statement is made that[48d]:

> *...is in accordance with Appendix C.2 of PKI for Machine Readable Travel Documents Offering ICC Read-Only Access Version 1.1 Tag '0xBA' is used to map the container ID in the PIV data model to the 16 data groups specified in the Machine Readable Travel Documents (MRTD). This enables the security object to be fully compliant for future activities with identity documents.*

Machine readable travel documents? Future activities with identity documents?

This is supposed to be just a standard for an identity card for government employees and contractors who need to access federal facilities and information systems in order to perform their job on a day-to-day basis.

SP 800-76, biometric data specification for personal identity verification, gets even more interesting. This standard specifies detailed data elements for collecting and formatting the biometric data stored on the PIV card and in the PIV database, including fingerprints and facial images. And we are not talking about a digital photo taken with your home camera. The standard requires collecting and storing all ten fingerprints, assuming they are available, although the PIV card and database only need or use two fingerprints. The reason for this is explained[48c]:

> Specifically, SP 800-76 involves the preparation of biometric data suitable for transmission to the FBI for background checks.

This is odd because all federal employees are subjected to a background check as part of the hiring process; the rigor of the background check is commensurate with the sensitivity of the position they will occupy and whether or not a security clearance is required. Also, as part of the hiring process, all federal employees are fingerprinted. The same is true for government contractors. In essence, the government already has this information and in some cases has had it for 20 or more years, depending on the individual's length of federal employment. No justification is provided of why (1) this information is being collected again, (2) individuals are being reinvestigated, or (3) why this information needs to be stored on an identity card or in a central database that is used to control access to federal facilities. Individuals who have security clearances are already reinvestigated every five to ten years, depending on their clearance level. Do people in non-sensitive positions really need to be reinvestigated also? No specific vulnerability or threat is identified that is driving this initiative. Nor are any rules defined about how the access, use, disclosure, dissemination, or retention of this biometric information will be controlled. This is particularly troubling because physical and personnel security professionals are not usually knowledgeable or adept at IT or operational security.

SP 800-78 specifies which encryption algorithms and key sizes are acceptable for use in encrypting information stored on the PIV card and in the PIV database. Unfortunately, it does not specify how to implement or manage cryptographic operations. This could have been valuable information because few civilian agencies have any expertise in this matter.

SP 800-79 is an attempt to ensure the integrity of the organizations that issue PIV cards. These organizations will also be responsible for collecting and storing the biometric data, as well as other personally identifiable information. What a gold mine of information this would be in the wrong hands. If a terrorist cell wanted to plant an individual in a certain federal agency, all it would have to do is insert that individual's biometric data into this database and issue them a PIV card. Hence the need for ultra-high controls over these organizations, their employees, and information systems. Each federal agency has the responsibility to certify the integrity of the organization issuing its PIV cards.[252] To be frank, some agencies are more qualified and prepared to do this than others.

These five standards are supplemented by a Federal Identity Management Handbook, which for the most part takes the requirements in the standards and says "do it." Appendix C contains a sample PIV request form, which includes among other things the individual's date and place of birth, social security number, home address, home phone, home e-mail address, work address, work phone, and work e-mail. What a treasure trove for an identity theft ring — there is nothing else they need to know! What ever happened to the tried and true security engineering principles of "need-to-know" and "least privilege?" Since when does a building guard need to know someone's birthday, home phone, home e-mail, or even their work e-mail? What does anyone's home e-mail address have to do with their access control rights and privileges for a given information system? And just in case you have not figured it out by now, the Handbook reminds us that "all individuals within an organization are capable of violating privacy rights."[48b] Unfortunately, nothing is done to remedy this situation.

At the request of Congress, the General Accountability Office (GAO) conducted an audit of federal agencies and their intended use of radio frequency identification (RFID) technology for physical access control to facilities, logical access control to information systems, and tracking assets, documents, and other materials. In that audit, 11 of the 24 agencies surveyed said they had no plans to implement RFID technology, including the Department of Commerce that issued the PIV standards,[74, 253] and 16 agencies responded to the questions relating to the legality of such use and one identified problems related to privacy and the tracking of sensitive documents and evidence.[74] Although the E-Government Act of 2002 and the OMB Privacy Officer Memo require privacy impact assessments, it is a well-known fact that passive RFID tags can be read from 10 to 20 feet, while active RFID tags can be read from 750 feet without the holder's knowledge. That is because all tags designed to respond to a given reader frequency will do so.[74] RFID tags come in different frequencies. Higher frequencies can be read at greater distances, while lower frequencies can penetrate walls better. As the GAO report notes, there are several security concerns associated with the use of RFID tags[74]:

- Controlling access to the data on RFID tags to only authorized readers and personnel
- Maintaining the integrity of the data on the RFID chip and in the database
- The ease of counterfeiting, cloning, replay, and eavesdropping attacks
- The frequency of collisions when multiple tags and readers are collocated
- The difficulty in authenticating readers
- The ease with which unauthorized components can read, access, or modify data

The GAO report is also quite clear about the privacy problems associated with RFID tags[74]:

> *Among the key privacy issues are notifying individuals of the existence or use of the technology; tracking an individual's movements; profiling an individual's habits, tastes, or predilections; and allowing secondary uses of the information.*

These concerns have led the state of California to ban the use of RFID tags by public agencies, such as those that issue driver's licenses, student ID cards, library cards, health insurance cards, etc.[248]

The U.S. State Department is pursuing a similar PIV objective via passports, hence the not-so-subtle reference earlier to "machine readable travel documents." This stipulation applies to U.S. passports issued in 2006 and beyond as well as the passports of countries that do not require visas to visit the United States by 26 October 2006. The RFID chip in the passports will hold a digital photo, the individual's name, date of birth, and place of birth at a minimum, and 64 KB of writeable memory for future use. The State Department is exploring ways to prevent unauthorized access to the passport information; to date, no decision has been made. One option is to encrypt data sent to or from readers; another is for the information to not be readable until the passport is opened. These issues are being discussed on an international basis because of the differences in the privacy laws of each country. As EPIC has reported[232]:

> *It has been well documented that cyber criminals are able to use readers to break the encryption systems in RFID tags. ... Once a biometric identifier has been compromised, there can be severe consequences for the individual whose identity has been affected. It is possible to replace a credit card or Social Security numbers, but how does one replace a fingerprint, voice print, or retina scan? It would be difficult to remedy identify fraud when a thief has identification with a security-cleared federal employee's name on it, but the thief's biometric identifier. Or, in a more innocuous scenario, the identities of employees with different security clearances and their biometric identifiers are mismatched in the files due to human or computer error.*

A 1930s radio broadcast of the *Shadow* program featured a case where the fingerprints left at the crime scene were that of a convicted criminal who had been executed three years prior. The Shadow finally figured out that the Deputy County Coroner was the culprit, using the opportunity, motivation, expertise, and resources equation. If a 1930s radio fiction writer can figure out how to steal fingerprints, surely cyber criminals can today. The integrity of stored and current biometric data samples is a concern — biometric data is not immune to misuse and attacks any more than other types of data, such as PINs and passwords.[254]

HSPD-12 lacks credibility — not the technical rigor behind the five standards, but the rationale for its issuance. Security solutions are supposed to be based on security requirements that are derived as a function of system risk, information sensitivity, and asset criticality. HSPD-12 skipped the vulnerability, threat, risk, and requirements analyses and went straight to a solution. What difference does it make if civilian agencies not engaged in national security systems have different ID cards? Do the Fish and Wildlife Service and the Census Bureau really need color-coordinated matching ID cards? Do employees of unclassified civilian agencies really need more scrutiny and surveillance than their counterparts in the intelligence community? If an individual from one agency needs to visit another agency, there are established procedures for sending a visit request, escorting the individual, and, if need be, transferring a security clearance. Also, there are neutral conference facilities where such meetings can take place. The number of federal employees or contractors who need to visit another agency on a regular basis is probably less than 1 percent of the total population; this 1 percent is already following the established procedures. This massive collection, storage, and dissemination to who knows where of biometric data for over 2 million people would not have caught Aldrige Ames, Robert Hansen, Timothy McVeigh, or deterred the nineteen 9/11 hijackers.

The principle of storing date of birth, place of birth, social security number, and biometric data on the PIV card is seriously flawed. All that should be stored on the card is the name, photograph, federal agency that employs the individual, and an expiration date. Biometric systems are supposed to function in two simple steps:

1. Enrollment: capturing and storing the unique biometric data of an individual in a secure database.
2. Authentication: verifying than an individual's current biometric characteristics match that stored in the database.

That is, an individual's hand, face, or eye is scanned in real-time as part of the authentication process. Storing biometric information on an identity card defeats the purpose of using a biometric system. All that is verified is that the data on the card matches the data in the database — the individual who has the card is not verified at all. Putting sensitive personal and biometric information on a card, knowing that it can be transferred to or from authorized and unauthorized readers without the holder's knowledge or consent, creates an incredible single point of failure, especially when one considers that the intent is to use the PIV cards for logical access to an agency's information systems also. The unsoundness of this approach is magnified tenfold when one considers that the database will be accessible by all federal agencies government-wide.

Furthermore, this approach ignores the fact that people lose things: purses and backpacks are stolen; items are left in hotels, airports, and taxis; things are dropped when running to catch the subway or bus or while out to lunch. A case in point — when agents switched to laptops in the mid-1990s, the FBI had such a problem with laptops containing sensitive data being left in taxis and airports that it had to resort to full disk encryption. Because complete specifications for the PIV cards and data are in the open, there is nothing to prevent criminals from retrieving and altering data on lost cards or making their own spoofed PIV cards.

HSPD-12 is an example of physical security engineers trying to use technology they do not understand (especially the broader ramifications for cyber security or privacy) to solve a physical, not IT, security problem. An analogy would be for IT security engineers to put concrete barricades around the Internet to protect it. In summary, HSPD-12 will create hundreds more security problems than it will solve. And in the meantime, individuals are left totally exposed, with no course of remedy or protection from loss, damages, or harm because there is no way to recover from biometric identity theft.

A standardized ID card for federal employees and contractors could be obtained by much simpler means, with no need for a mass invasion of biometric data privacy rights. During the 1950s, Senator Joseph McCarthy created mass hysteria by proposing that there was a communist behind every rock and that the federal government was infiltrated by communists. Hopefully we are not headed toward similar hysteria in regard to terrorists. I hate to think what would happen if someone akin to Senator Joseph McCarthy had access to the entire federal workforce's (civilian, military, and contractors) PIV data, or that of every citizen of the United States through their national identity card or passport, or that of every visitor to the United States through standard "machine readable travel documents."

The following metrics can be used by government agencies, oversight authorities in the public and private sectors, public interest groups, and individuals to monitor whether or not the HSPDs are (1) being implemented correctly, (2) achieving their stated goals, and (3) being misused.

HSPD-2

Per the Foreign Terrorist Tracking Task Force, by fiscal year: 1.11.1
  a. Number of individuals denied entry into the United States
  b. Number of individuals detained, prosecuted, and deported

Number of international student visa violations, by fiscal year: 1.11.2
  a. In the United States after the visa expired
  b. Taking prohibited courses
  c. Not maintaining full-time student status

HSPD-3

Number of federal agencies, per fiscal year, that: 1.11.3
  a. Had preparedness plans and procedures in place
  b. Tested and practiced their preparedness plans and procedures
  c. Submitted their annual report to Congress about their preparedness plans and procedures on time

HSPD-6

Number of times information was reported to the Terrorist Threat Integration Center, by fiscal year: 1.11.4
  a. By federal agencies
  b. By state agencies
  c. By local agencies

HSPD-7

Number of specific recommendations, by fiscal year, from the federal CIO Council about how to improve the design, acquisition, development, modernization, use, and operation of information systems and information security.

1.11.5

Number of physical and cyber security threats, vulnerabilities, indications and warnings, protective measures, and best practices disseminated government-wide.   1.11.6

HSPD-8

Number of grants made to state and local first responders for preparedness training, planning, exercises, and equipment, and the total funding by jurisdiction per fiscal year.   1.11.7

HSPD-9

Percentage of food sources nationwide that are subject to comprehensive safety monitoring and surveillance.   1.11.8

Percentage of water sources nationwide that are subject to comprehensive safety monitoring and surveillance.   1.11.9

HSPD-11

Number of terrorists, drug smugglers, or other criminals caught by the use of backscatter x-ray technology: 1.11.10

    a. Number and percentage prosecuted
    b. Number and percentage convicted
    c. Number and percentage of convictions as a percentage of the total population scanned

Number of individuals who objected to submitting to backscatter technology:

1.11.11

    a. Number of formal complaints filed

HSPD-12

Number and percentage of individuals who, by agency and fiscal year:

1.11.12

    a. Objected to having their biometric data collected and stored
    b. Had their PIV card or data stolen
    c. Had their PIV card or data misused or mishandled by an authorized employee
    d. Lost their PIV card

    e. Were incorrectly barred from accessing a federal facility or information system

    f. Had their PIV data used without their permission for other than the pre-stated purpose

    g. Filed suit over the loss, harm, and damages resulting from the loss, mishandling, or misuse of their PIV data

Number of employees disciplined or fined, by agency and fiscal year: 1.11.13

    a. For misusing or mishandling PIV data

    b. For accidental unauthorized disclosure of PIV data

    c. For intentional unauthorized disclosure of PIV data

    d. For unauthorized retention or dissemination of PIV data

Number of individuals who were able to gain access to federal facilities or information systems through the use of fraudulent PIV cards or fraudulent data in the PIV database, by agency and fiscal year.   1.11.14

3.13 North American Electrical Reliability Council (NERC) Cyber Security Standards

The North American Electrical Reliability Council (NERC), with encouragement from the Department of Energy and the Department of Homeland Security, developed and issued a series of eight cyber security standards, partly in response to the cascading failure of the power grid in the northeast on 14 August 2004.[170] The NERC standards development process, which is approved by the American National Standards Institute (ANSI), included public review, comment, and balloting prior to adoption by the NERC Board of Directors. NERC is a non-government organization composed of the reliability coordinators, balancing authorities, interchange authorities, transmission service providers, transmission owners, transmission operators, generator owners, generator operators, and load serving entities that own and operate the power grid in North America. The importance of NERC's role has increased in recent years with deregulation of the electric power industry and the opening up of markets to competition.

    The set of cyber security standards was developed and issued for a straightforward purpose[39]:

> *...to ensure that all entities responsible for the reliability of the bulk electric systems of North America identify and protect critical cyber assets that control or could impact the reliability of the bulk electric systems.*

Table 3.14 lists the eight NERC cyber security standards.

    The NERC cyber security standards took effect June 2006. At the same time, the NERC Reliability Functional Model will be put into effect. The NERC Compliance Enforcement Program, through ten regional reliability compliance programs, will begin assessing compliance against the new cyber security

Table 3.14   NERC Cyber Security Standards

Designation	Title	No. of High-Level Security Requirements	No. of Mid-Level Security Requirements	No. of Low-Level Security Requirements
CIP-002-1	Cyber Security — Critical Cyber Assets	4	4	9
CIP-003-1	Cyber Security — Security Management Controls	5	8	—
CIP-004-1	Cyber Security — Personnel & Training	4	—	—
CIP-005-1	Cyber Security — Electronic Security	6	3	—
CIP-006-1	Cyber Security — Physical Security	6	3	—
CIP-007-1	Cyber Security — Systems Security Management	11	20	—
CIP-008-1	Cyber Security — Incident Reporting and Response Planning	4	—	—
CIP-009-1	Cyber Security — Recovery Plan	5	—	—
Total		45	38	9

standards in 2007. A phased implementation process is planned. During 2007, the nine functional entities that make up the power grid will be sent self-certification forms. The entities will rank their current level of compliance with each requirement in the standards, then return the forms to the NERC Regional Reliability Council. Individual responses will be treated as confidential. The Regional Compliance Manager will summarize the results for the region and send them to the NERC Compliance Enforcement Program. Ultimate responsibility for compliance rests with each functional entity. The implementation plan distinguishes between auditable compliance (AC) and substantially compliant (SC). Auditable compliance implies that the functional entity "meets the full intent of the requirement and can prove it to an auditor," while substantially compliant infers that the functional entity has "begun the process to become compliant with a requirement, but is not yet AC."[39] The implementation plan sets an AC/SC timetable for each requirement in each cyber security standard for each type of functional entity. All entities are to be AC on all cyber security requirements by 2010. During 2008, an exemption for an SC status is granted for only two requirements[39]:

- CIP-004-1 R4: Personnel Risk Assessment — The Responsible Entity shall subject all personnel having access to Critical Cyber Assets, including contractors and service vendors, to a documented company personnel risk assessment process prior to being granted authorized access to Critical Assets.[33]
- CIP-007-1 R2: Test Procedures — Unattended Facilities — The Responsible Entity shall not store test documentation, security procedures, and acceptance procedures at an unattended facility but at another secured attended facility. The Responsible Entity shall conduct security test procedures for Critical Cyber Assets at the unattended facility on a controlled non-production environment located at another secure attended facility.[36]

The NERC standards cover the full scope of physical, personnel, IT, and operational security in an integrated, comprehensive, and efficient manner. The NERC cyber security standards are applicable to all nine types of functional entities, as listed previously. They are not applicable to nuclear facilities, which are regulated by the Canadian Nuclear Safety Commission and the U.S. Nuclear Regulatory Commission. The NERC cyber security standards are expressed in a uniform, no-nonsense style without the superfluous text or philosophy found in most government regulations. Any considerations that must be taken into account for regional differences or differences in entity types or attended versus unattended facilities are noted in the standards. Because the NERC cyber security standards cover a broad range of functional entities and organizations of varying size and geographical distribution, they should be considered a minimum set of security requirements.[265] Reality may necessitate that a given organization deploy more robust security practices.[265]

There are three key components to each standard:

1. Requirements, numbered R_x, which say what to do
2. Measures, numbered M_x, which explain how to perform the requirement and assemble the proof that it was indeed achieved
3. Compliance, which describes how to independently verify that each R_x and M_x was accomplished and completed correctly

There is a direct mapping between the requirements (R_x) and measures (M_x), as will be seen in the discussion of each standard below. Compliance activities are described in terms of a compliance monitoring process, compliance monitoring responsibilities, the compliance monitoring period and reset time frame, data retention requirements, additional compliance information, and levels of noncompliance. Each of the standards defines four levels of noncompliance. Level 1 indicates that a functional entity is almost compliant, but missing a few small items. Level 2 indicates that a functional entity is making progress, but has only completed about half of the requirements. Level 3 indicates that a functional entity has started the required activities, but still has a long way to go. Level 4, the lowest level of noncompliance, indicates that for all practical purposes no effort has been undertaken to comply with the standard. Note that compliance and noncompliance is assessed for each of the eight NERC cyber security standards. During the implementation phase, an SC rating would equate to a Level 1 or Level 2 noncompliance.

This approach is similar to that used in Part 3 of the Common Criteria standards, ISO/IEC 15408-3, Evaluation of IT Security — Security Assurance Requirements, which uses:

- Developer action elements, which are analogous to the NERC requirements
- Content and presentation of evidence elements, which are analogous to the NERC measures
- Evaluator action elements, which are analogous to the NERC compliance activities

In both cases, the end result is objective, verifiable criteria.

The NERC cyber security standards make some interesting and important distinctions through terminology[31–38]:

Critical Asset: those facilities, systems, and equipment which, if destroyed, damaged, degraded, or otherwise rendered unavailable, would affect the reliability or operability of the bulk electric system.

Cyber Asset: those programmable electronic devices and communication networks including hardware, software, and data associated with bulk electric system assets.

Critical Cyber Assets: those Cyber Assets essential to the reliable operation of Critical Assets.

The installed base of a functional entity is divided into Critical Assets, which keep the power grid up and running smoothly, and Cyber Assets, IT that helps make the Critical Assets work. A subset of the Cyber Assets is deemed Critical Cyber Assets if they are essential to the reliable operation of the Critical Assets. That is, a Cyber Asset cannot be "critical" in and of itself; rather, it must perform some function that is essential to the sustained operation of a Critical Asset. This is an important distinction; unfortunately it is often overlooked during ST&E and C&A.

Electronic Security Perimeter: the logical border surrounding the network or group of sub-networks (the "secure network") to which the Critical Cyber Assets are connected, and for which access is controlled.

Physical Security Perimeter: the physical border surrounding computer rooms, telecommunications rooms, operations centers, and other locations in which Critical Cyber Assets are housed and for which access is controlled.

The NERC cyber security standards acknowledge the reality of two separate security perimeters: one logical and one physical. The logical security perimeter is determined by the configuration and operation of IT and telecommunications equipment and is independent of the physical security perimeter. In contrast, the physical security perimeter is defined by the physical boundaries of equipment stored on-site. This observation is significant because radically different protection mechanisms are needed for each type of security perimeter.

> **Cyber Security Incident:** any malicious act or suspicious event that (1) compromises or was an attempt to compromise, the electronic or physical security perimeter of a Critical Cyber Asset, or (2) disrupts or was an attempt to disrupt the operation of a Critical Cyber Asset.

The NERC cyber security standards use the term "cyber security incident" as a global term encompassing attacks, anomalies, and security incidents. Given the critical nature of the power grid, NERC obviously felt that an extra layer of granularity in analyzing security events was not needed.

CIP-002-1 — Cyber Security — Critical Cyber Assets

The first standard in the series is CIP-002-1, which requires that assets critical to the operation of the interconnected bulk electric system be identified through a risk assessment. The standard puts this procedure in perspective[31]:

> *Business and operational demands for managing and maintaining a reliable bulk electric system increasingly require Cyber Assets supporting critical reliability control functions and processes to communicate with each other, across functions and organizations, to provide services and data. This results in increased risks to these Cyber Assets, where the loss or compromise of these assets would adversely impact the reliable operation of critical bulk electric system assets. This standard requires that Responsible Entities identify and protect Critical Cyber Assets that support the reliable operation of the bulk electric system.*

CIP-002-1 applies to all nine types of functional entities. Next we will look at the requirements and measures and the interaction between them.

R1 requires each functional entity to identify its Critical Assets through a risk assessment. Nine examples of assets to consider are given, related to monitoring and control, load and frequency control, emergency actions, contingency analysis, special protection systems, power plant controls, substation controls, and real-time information exchange. There are two corresponding measures. Per M1, a current list of Critical Assets must be maintained by each functional entity; M2 adds the requirement to document the risk assessment used to identify the Critical Assets, including the methodology and evaluation criteria.

R2 carries the analysis one step further and requires the identification of the Critical Cyber Assets associated with each Critical Asset identified under R1. This step is to include devices within the electronic security perimeter that are accessible by a routable protocol or dial-up modem. R3 expects that other cyber assets within the same electronic security perimeter will be protected to the same degree as the Critical Cyber Assets. M3 requires that a current list of Critical Cyber Assets, identified by R2, be maintained; this list is to include other cyber assets that are within the same electronic security perimeter. To make sure that this list is kept current, M4 requires that the documentation produced under M1, M2, and M3 be verified annually, at a minimum. Any changes to the list of assets or their configuration must be reflected in the list within 30 days of the change.

To add some accountability and veracity to this exercise, R4 requires senior management to approve the lists of Critical Assets and Critical Cyber Assets. A signed and dated record of each periodic approval must be maintained per M5 and M6.

The Regional Reliability Organization is responsible for inspecting and assessing compliance with CIP-002-1. Requirements and measures are required to be verified annually. The functional entity and compliance monitor are required to keep their records related to CIP-002-1 activities and audits for three years.

This standard has several noteworthy features. To start with, the Critical Asset list is determined first, and then the Critical Cyber Assets are identified. Critical Cyber Assets are not designated in a vacuum; they must have an essential link to a Critical Asset. Most organizations overlook this fact. All Cyber Assets within the same electronic security perimeter must have the same degree of protection. In effect, this means that all equipment within an electronic security perimeter is operating at system high; NERC is avoiding the complexity of operating in a multi-level secure environment. The lists of Critical Assets and Critical Cyber Assets must be justified through an explanation of the risk assessment method and evaluation criteria used. To reinforce this, senior management is required to signify its approval by signing and dating the lists.

CIP-003-1 — Cyber Security — Security Management Controls

The second standard in the series focuses on security management controls. These controls are not some abstract notion in response to a perceived generic security need. Rather, they are a direct result of the criticality of functions performed by Cyber Assets[32]:

> *Critical business and operational functions performed by Cyber Assets affecting the bulk electric system necessitate having security management controls. This standard defines the minimum security management controls that the Responsible Entity must have in place to protect Critical Cyber Assets.*

The five cyber security requirements specified in CIP-003-1 and the measures that enact them cover the waterfront of security management controls. R1 is sort of a super requirement in relation to the others; it requires that the functional entity create, implement, and maintain a cyber security policy that executes all of the requirements in CIP-003-1. The cyber security policy is not to just give lip service to the requirements. On the contrary, M1 expects that the level of detail in the policy will demonstrate the functional entity's commitment to protecting Critical Cyber Assets. The cyber security policy is to be kept up-to-date and regularly reviewed and reaffirmed, per M2.

R2 zeroes in on an area overlooked by many organizations — that of implementing a program to protect all critical information linked to Critical Cyber Assets. The scope is information that in the wrong hands could be used to compromise the reliability and availability of the power grid. A rather complete list of examples is provided: operations and maintenance procedures, Critical Asset inventories, network topologies, facility floor plans, equipment configuration and layout diagrams, contingency and disaster recovery plans, and security incident response plans. Functional entities are to categorize this set of information by sensitivity and develop procedures to limit access to it to only authorized personnel. Four measures map to this requirement. Per M5 and M6, the information security protection program is to be assessed at least annually. To do this, M7 requires that the procedures used to secure critical information be documented. Likewise, M8 requires that the sensitivity categorization of critical information be validated at least annually.

To make sure all this happens, R3 requires that a senior management official be designated as being responsible for implementing and ensuring compliance with all the provisions of the NERC cyber security standards. This individual must define the roles and responsibilities (1) of Critical Cyber Asset owners, custodians, and users; and (2) for accessing, using, and handling critical information. He is also responsible for authorizing any deviations or exemptions from the cyber security policy. Six measures are defined to ensure this requirement is achieved. M10 reinforces the accountability theme by requiring that the name, title, telephone number, business address, and appointment date of the designated senior management official be documented and readily available. The roles and responsibilities of Critical Cyber Asset owners, custodians, and users must be verified at least annually, per M12. The policy for accessing, using, and handling critical information must be documented, per M9. M3 requires all authorized deviations or exemptions to the cyber security policy to be documented. M4 requires that all deviations and exemptions to the cyber security policy must be reviewed, renewed, or revoked at least annually — deviations and exemptions are not to be issued once, and then stay in place indefinitely.

R4 reiterates the accountability provisions to an even greater extent, which makes sense. How can an organization enforce security management controls if there is no accountability? Specifically, the relationships and decision-making process at the executive level that demonstrate a commitment and ability to secure Critical Cyber Assets are to be defined and documented. Issues that are to be addressed include ST&E for new and replacement systems and software patches, configuration control and management, security impact analysis for hardware and software, regression ST&E, and rollback procedures if the new system or modification fails. M13 requires that the controls, tools, and methods that demonstrate that executive-level management has accepted its accountability and is engaged in protecting Critical Cyber Assets be documented and verified at least annually.

R5 expands upon a provision of R3 by requiring that the process for controlling access to critical information be documented in detail. In particular, the list of people who can authorize access to Critical Cyber Assets must be kept current, and all authorized accesses must be recorded. Individuals' access rights to critical information need to be verified regularly. Likewise, the procedures for modifying, suspending, and terminating access rights must be validated regularly. And, all changes to access rights, especially revocations, must be documented. Five measures emphasize the imperative nature of this requirement. Per M14 and M15, the name, title, telephone number, and appointment date of each authorized user and the systems, applications, and equipment they are authorized to access must be documented and kept current. M17 and M18 require that this list of access rights be reviewed and verified at least annually. M16 requires that the procedures for assigning, changing, and revoking access control rights be reviewed and verified or updated at least annually.

The Regional Reliability Organization is responsible for inspecting and assessing compliance with CIP-003-1. Requirements and measures are required to be verified annually. The functional entity and compliance monitor are required to keep their records for three years. The four levels of noncompliance represent various combinations of missing reviews and documentation or lack of assigned roles and responsibilities, of increasing severity or length of deficiency.

This standard has several features worth noting. A fair amount of emphasis is placed on protecting critical information that is linked to Critical Cyber Assets for the simple reason that this information could be misused for malicious purposes. However, most organizations ignore this practice out of ignorance, naiveté, or cost-cutting measures (i.e., they just do not want to be bothered). While a lot of standards talk about accountability, this standard eliminates the wiggle room. The accountability, commitment, and engagement of executives as well as the designated compliance officer are not just to be on paper, but demonstrated in reality. ST&E is given a prominent role in several different scenarios: new systems, replacement systems, patch management, and regression testing. Unfortunately, most organizations only perform ST&E on initial system deployment. CIP-003-1 also hits hard on another area of security management that is often given lip service "because it takes too much time" or "is too hard to keep up-to-date" — that of regularly reviewing, monitoring, and verifying individual access control rights and privileges.

CIP-004-1 — Cyber Security — Personnel & Training

Human nature being what it is, people are always the weakest link in any attempt to secure an operational environment. Insiders, outsiders, or insiders colluding with outsiders through accidental or intentional malicious action or inaction can and do exploit vulnerabilities in a security program. The actions of outsiders cannot be controlled completely, but the opportunity for them to cause damage can be minimized. The actions of insiders can be monitored and controlled somewhat, but again not completely. The risk from insiders can be minimized through four activities, as stated by CIP-004-1[33]:

> *Personnel having authorized access to Critical Cyber Assets, as defined by CIP-002-1, are given a higher level of trust, by definition, and are required to have a higher level of screening, training, security awareness, and record retention of such activity, than personnel not provided access.*

This standard applies to all nine types of functional entities, unless they do not have any Critical Cyber Assets.

R1 covers security awareness. Each functional entity is to develop, maintain, and document an ongoing security awareness program for employees to reinforce sound security practices. M1 gives several examples of activities that can be conducted to promote security awareness, such as e-mail or memo reminders, computer-based training, posters, Web pages, and all-hands meetings.

Security awareness programs should be supplemented with more in-depth security training. Because of FISMA (discussed in Section 3.11 of this book) and other policies, many organizations have security training programs today. However, the vast majority of these programs totally miss the mark because the training is very general and not focused — it is not something employees can take back to their desks and apply to their everyday job. In contrast, CIP-004-1 R2 requires that cyber security training be company specific and address information security policies and procedures, physical and electronic access control to critical assets, proper handling and release of sensitive information, contingency and disaster recovery procedures, security incident response procedures, and other directly relevant topics. M2 requires that this training be conducted for all employees annually, at a minimum.

R4 mandates that all staff having access to Critical Cyber Assets, including contractors and service vendors, undergo a personnel risk assessment prior to being given access to such assets. The background check is to be proportional to the criticality of the position an individual will occupy and include a check of his criminal record for the previous seven years. M4 ups the ante by requiring that a current list be maintained of all personnel with access rights to Critical Cyber Assets, along with the dates of their most recent security training activity and background check. The list is to detail who has access to what Critical Cyber Assets, detailing both their physical and electronic access rights. The list of access rights is to be updated within seven days of a normal change or within 24 hours of a revocation for cause. Background checks are to be updated every five years or for cause.

R3 requires that the functional entity prepare contemporaneous records that document the security awareness activities conducted, the security training conducted with attendee lists, and the status of personnel background screening. Likewise, M3 requires proof that the activities required by R1, R2, and R3 took place.

CIP-005-1 — Cyber Security — Electronic Security

As noted earlier, the NERC cyber security standards make a distinction between logical (or electronic) and physical security perimeters. Different security perimeters and different types of security perimeters may be at different security levels. Furthermore, different techniques are used to secure each type of security perimeter. The first step, however, is to define the security perimeter[34]:

> *Business and operational requirements for Critical Cyber Assets to communicate with other devices to provide data and services result in increased risks to these Critical Cyber Assets. In order to protect these assets, it is necessary to identify the electronic perimeter(s) within which these assets reside. When electronic perimeters are defined, different security levels may be assigned to these perimeters depending on the assets within these perimeter(s). In the case of Critical Cyber Assets, the security level assigned to these Electronic Security Perimeters is high.*

CIP-005-1 applies to all nine types of functional entities, unless they have no identified Critical Cyber Assets. CIP-005-1 takes a straightforward approach to securing electronic security perimeters, as will be shown in the discussion of the requirements and measures.

Not surprisingly, R1 requires that all electronic security perimeters be defined. This includes identifying not just the electronic security perimeter, but also the access points to that perimeter and the communications endpoints. M1 requires that this information be documented and kept current. When capturing this documentation, functional entities need to verify that the list of Critical Cyber Assets accurately reflects all interconnected Critical Cyber Assets within the electronic security perimeter. That is, this step is used to cross-check the results of CIP-002-1 R2.

R2 requires that all unused network ports and services within the electronic security perimeter be disabled. Only those network ports and services that are used for normal or emergency operations are allowed to remain active. All others, including those used for testing, are to be disabled. Following suit, M2 requires that current documentation be maintained on the status and configuration of all network ports and services available on all Critical Cyber Assets.

Dial-up modem lines always present a potential security problem. R3 requires that dial-up modem lines be secured, in part by deactivating them when they are not in use and authenticating their use prior to granting access to critical resources. The policies and procedures for securing dial-up modem lines must be documented per M3. And, at least once a year, all dial-up connections and their configurations must be audited for compliance with these policies and procedures.

Electronic access controls are defined in R4. Organizational, technical, and procedural controls for permitting or denying access within the electronic security perimeter, via the access points, must be defined and documented. Per CIP-005-1, the default is to deny access. As a minimum, R4 requires that either strong two-factor authentication, digital certificates, out-of-band authentication, or one-time passwords be used; for dial-up connections, automatic number verification or call back verification is required. Authentication is to be accompanied by a banner stating what is considered acceptable and unacceptable use of the resources accessed. M4 adds the requirement to document and periodically review the effectiveness of the controls for each access point and authentication method.

R5 mandates 24/7 monitoring of electronic access controls. This capability monitors and detects any attempted or actual unauthorized access to controlled resources. Organizational, technical, and procedural methods for implementing the continuous monitoring capability must be documented and kept current, per M5. Actual monitoring records must be kept as proof that the monitoring capability is functioning correctly and that this information is being reviewed and acted upon in a timely manner.

Together, R6 and M6 reinforce the mandate that all records and documentation required by CIP-005-1 are kept current. To do this, it is expected that these records and documentation will be reviewed and verified at least every 90 days. Updates are to be made within 30 days of any change.

The compliance activities require that all documentation, including security incident reports, are kept for three years. Normal access control logs, during an interval in which there were no security incidents, only need to be kept for 90 days. Audit records demonstrating compliance with this standard are to be kept for three years. The seriousness of these requirements and measures is evident in the definition of levels of noncompliance. A level 1 noncompliance is caused by missing less than 24 hours of monitoring data. If monitoring data is missing for one to seven days, a level 2 noncompliance results.

CIP-006-1 — Cyber Security — Physical Security

As a concurrent engineering activity to CIP-005-1, the physical security perimeter must be defined as well in order to protect Critical Cyber Assets. While physical security does not play as large a role as it did in the days of stand-alone systems, it is still an essential part of any security engineering program. As CIP-006-1 states[35]:

> *Business and operational requirements for the availability and reliability of Critical Cyber Assets dictate the need to physically secure these assets. In order to protect these assets, it is necessary to identify the Physical Security Perimeter(s) (nearest six-wall boundary) within which these Cyber Assets reside.*

This standard applies to all nine types of functional entities, unless they have no identified Critical Cyber Assets. The six requirements and measures in CIP-006-1 correspond to their counterparts in the electronic security standard.

R1 requires that the functional entities document and implement a physical security plan. The first task is to define each physical security perimeter and the access points to the perimeter, along with a strategy to protect them. This plan is to explain the processes, procedures, and tools that will be used to control physical access to facilities and key resources. M1 and M2 require that the physical security plan be reviewed and verified at least annually. Updates are to be made within 90 days of any change to the physical security perimeter, access points, or physical access controls. Furthermore, the functional entities must verify that all Critical Cyber Assets are within the physical security perimeter.

R2 expands the requirements for physical access controls. Access to the access points in the physical security perimeter are to be managed and controlled in response to a risk assessment. One or more physical access control methods are to be employed, as appropriate for the type of access point, per M3: card keys, special locks, security officers, security enclosures, keypads, or tokens. In addition, the physical controls, access request authorizations, and revocations must be documented. And, as expected, physical access rights are to be reviewed and validated regularly.

Physical access control points are to be monitored 24/7, per R3, just like logical access control points. One or more monitoring techniques are to be employed, per M4, such as closed-circuit television; alarm systems on doors, windows, and equipment cabinets; and motion sensors. Functional entities are to document the physical access controls they implement, along with proof that (1) they have been verified, and (2) the reports they generate are being reviewed and acted upon in a timely manner.

R4 requires that all physical access to controlled facilities and equipment rooms be logged, especially unattended facilities. This logging can be accomplished by manual logging (at attended facilities), computerized logging, or video recordings, per M5. The functional entity is responsible for documenting the method used to generate the physical access logs and retaining the logs for 90 days.

R5 requires that functional entities ensure that all physical security controls are in place and operating correctly through regular maintenance and testing activities. M6 reinforces this requirement by mandating that physical security controls should be tested at least annually. The testing results are to be documented and maintained for one year.

R6 reiterates that all documentation and records related to implementing and verifying the implementation of the physical security plan are to be prepared, kept current, and reviewed and verified regularly.

CIP-007-1 — Cyber Security — Systems Security Management

As of today, we are not at a point where a security infrastructure can be deployed and left to operate on its own. Maybe that will happen some time in the future. Actually, that might be preferable to the situation today, where people forget to change, configure, or update devices through forgetfulness, laziness, or a rush to leave for the weekend — a computer would never do that. In the meantime, security infrastructures must be astutely managed to adapt to ever-changing operational conditions. As CIP-007-1 states[36]:

A System Security Management Program is necessary to minimize or prevent the risk of failure or compromise from misuse or malicious cyber activity.

The standard applies to all nine functional entities unless they have no identified Critical Cyber Security Assets. When necessary, differences in the requirements for attended and unattended facilities are noted.

R1 hits home by laying down requirements for security test procedures for attended facilities. Functional entities are required to document *and* use (documentation is not allowed to just sit on the shelf) security test procedures to *augment* functional test procedures and acceptance test procedures. The key message here is that ST&E is a radically different beast than traditional functional, performance, integration, and acceptance testing. ST&E ensures that a network, system, and the data it transmits, receives, stores, and processes is protected against unauthorized access, viewing, use, disclosure, copying, dissemination, modification, destruction, insertion, misappropriation, corruption, and contamination. ST&E does not care if the system has a nice GUI or can print pretty reports. ST&E procedures are to be developed for all new systems and applications, and significant changes to existing systems and applications, such as patches, service packs, new releases, and upgrades to operating systems, database management systems, and other third-party software, hardware, and firmware. ST&E plans and procedures are also required as part of regression testing. Security test procedures are expected to demonstrate that the risks from identified vulnerabilities have been mitigated. ST&E is to be conducted in a controlled environment so that the results are legitimate and repeatable. Testing results, including details of the testing environment, are to be documented. Finally, the functional entity is required to ensure that all ST&E activities are completed successfully before deploying a new system or upgrade. R2 notes the difference for unattended facilities: ST&E procedures and records are not to be stored at unattended facilities for obvious reasons. All ST&E related procedures, records, results, and approvals must be retained for three years, per M1.

R3 zeroes in on the management of user accounts and passwords. The functional entity is responsible for implementing the necessary controls to ensure reliable and accurate identification, authentication, auditing, and administration of user accounts and passwords. To reduce the risk of unauthorized access to Critical Cyber Assets, several provisions are mandated. Strong passwords are to be used and changed periodically. Generic accounts and default passwords should be disabled. The use of group accounts should be minimized and approved on a case-by-case basis. Access control rights and privileges should be reviewed and verified at least semi-annually, in part to ensure that unused, expired, invalid, and unauthorized accounts are being disabled in a timely manner. M2 follows up on this by requiring that access control rights and privileges be reviewed within 24 hours following a termination for cause, and within seven days for a normal departure. The user account and password management policy must be documented and kept current. Likewise, the semi-annual audit records are to be retained for three years.

Security patch management is the subject of R4. The functional entities are to develop a robust program to track, evaluate, test, and install security patches and other upgrades to Critical Cyber Assets. The evaluation process needs to be thorough enough so that unnecessary and unproductive patches and upgrades can be weeded out before they are deployed. A configuration control board is expected to conduct monthly reviews of the patch management program to ensure that patches and upgrades are adequately evaluated prior to deployment or rejected for valid reasons. M3 captures this effort by keeping current documentation of all security patches tested and the test results, rejected and the reasons, installed and the date of installation. If for some reason a security patch is needed but cannot be installed, the functional entity is expected to employ and document the compensating measures taken.

R5 requires functional entities to ensure the integrity of custom developed and commercial off-the-shelf (COTS) software before installation or dissemination, as part their strategy to prevent the propagation of malware. This activity should be folded into the configuration control process. The version of software that is operational at each location should be documented, along with the installation date, per M4.

R6 focuses on the identification of vulnerabilities and managing the response to them. A vulnerability assessment should be conducted annually, at a minimum. This is to include diagnostic testing of the electronic security perimeter and access points, scanning for open ports and modems, checking for default passwords and user accounts, and an evaluation of security patch management and anti-virus software installations. Unattended facilities are required to undergo a vulnerability assessment prior to any upgrades. The results of the vulnerability assessments are to be documented, in particular the corrective action plan and progress to date in resolving these deficiencies. M5 captures the details of the vulnerability assessment by documenting the tools and procedures used to uncover vulnerabilities, in addition to proof that remediation activities are taking place.

R7 specifies time frames for the retention of the mandatory audit trails and system logs. Under normal conditions, audit trails and system logs are required to be kept for a rolling 90-day period. If a security incident occurs or is expected, audit trails and system logs are required to be kept for three years from the first date of suspicious activity. M6 requires that the location, content, and retention schedule of audit trails and system logs from Critical Cyber Assets should be indexed, readily available, and in a format that is usable for internal and external investigations.

Change control and configuration management are the subjects of R8. A detailed process, for both hardware and software, is to be developed that explains, among other topics, version control, change control, release control, acceptance criteria, regression testing, installation and dissemination of updates, audit trail generation, problem identification, and roll-back and recovery. Proof that the change control and configuration management tools and procedures are being followed is required by M7.

R9 reinforces CIP-005-1 R2, which discusses the electronic security perimeter. Again, functional entities are reminded that all unused ports and services should be disabled. Only those that are required for normal and emergency operations are to remain active; all others, including those used for testing, are to be deactivated before deployment. The current status and configuration of all ports and services of Critical Cyber Assets are to be documented, per M8.

Functional entities are expected to employ status monitoring tools that provide a real-time reporting capability for system performance, utilization, operating state and health, and security alarms, per R10. These metrics should be collected manually during each visit to an unattended site, if they cannot be gathered electronically. M9 requires that the functional entities document the tools and operational procedures they use to provide the real-time status monitoring; and for obvious reasons, this documentation should be kept current.

Finally, R11 addresses backup and recovery. Information that is critical to the operation or management of Critical Cyber Assets is to be backed up regularly and the backup media stored in a secure location. Making backups is a good idea, but it is an even better idea to verify them before an emergency. Consequently, M10 requires that the location, content, and retention schedule of backup media be indexed and readily available. This information should include recovery procedures, records documenting the results of annual restoration tests, and proof that the backup media are capable of being recovered.

CIP-008-1 — Cyber Security — Incident Reporting and Response Planning

Organizations cannot control the number or type of security attacks they experience. They can, however, control the opportunity attackers have to launch an attack and the expertise needed; that is, organizations have the ability to prevent an attack from becoming a security incident by reducing the (1) likelihood of an attack being successful, and (b) severity of the consequences. The answer, in part, lies in preparedness to deal with security incidents[37]:

> *Security measures designed to protect Critical Cyber Assets from intrusion, disruption, or other forms of compromise must be monitored on a continuous basis. This standard requires responsible entities to define the procedures that must be followed when Cyber Security Incidents are identified. This standard requires: (a) developing and maintaining documented procedures, (b) classification of incidents, (c) actions to be taken, and (d) reporting of incidents.*

CIP-008-1 applies to all nine types of functional entities unless they have no identified Critical Cyber Assets.

Functional entities are required to develop, implement, and maintain a security incident plan that describes "assessing, mitigating, containing, reporting, and responding" to security incidents, per R1.[37] As a concurrent activity under R2, a security incident classification scheme is developed. This scheme should characterize different types of security incidents, the appropriate action to be taken in response to them, and the organizational roles and responsibilities for incident handling, escalation, and communication. The functional entity is also responsible for reporting security incidents, above a certain severity level, to the electrical sector information sharing and analysis center, as part of the NERC indications, analysis, and warning standard operating procedures. Consistent with NERC's integrated approach to managing security, the security incident classification and reporting requirements apply to both physical and electronic security. The security incident classification scheme, handling procedures, and reporting procedures are to be thoroughly documented, reviewed and verified at least annually, and updated within 90 days of any changes, per M1. Security incident records are to be retained for three years, per M2.

CIP-009-1 — Cyber Security — Recovery Plans

Another important aspect of preparedness is contingency and disaster recovery planning. Being prepared for contingencies can minimize their impact in terms of both duration and severity. The purpose of CIP-009-1 is to ensure that the appropriate cyber security recovery planning is in place, while recognizing the differing roles of each functional entity in the operation of the grid, the criticality and vulnerability of the assets needed to manage grid reliability, and the risks to which they are exposed.[38] CIP-009-1 applies to all nine types of functional entities, unless they have no identified Critical Cyber Assets.

To start, R1 requires that functional entities create a contingency and disaster recovery plan for all Critical Cyber Assets and exercise it at least annually. M1 and M4 require that the contingency and disaster recovery plan be thoroughly documented and readily available. The attendee records and results of each annual drill are to be kept for three years. R1 is sort of a super requirement; the other four requirements in this standard are inputs to R1.

R2 is an incredibly insightful requirement, something most organizations do not even think of, let alone practice. R2 requires that a matrix be developed documenting different anomaly, contingency, and disaster situations. Then the duration and severity of each is varied to show (1) when it would trigger a recovery effort, and (2) how the recovery efforts are different for each unique situation, duration, and severity. This is a significant move away from the usual cookie-cutter contingency and disaster recovery plans. To illustrate, consider a network outage as the triggering event. Then vary the duration of the outage; use two minutes, two hours, two days, and two weeks as sample durations. It is pretty obvious that the recommended response in the contingency and disaster recovery plan would be different for each duration. Next, vary the severity or extent of the outage, from a single router, to a single network segment, single facility, single region, and the entire enterprise. Again, it is obvious that the recommended response in the contingency and disaster recovery plan would be different for each level of severity. The purpose of the contingency and disaster recovery planning matrix is to ensure that all possible scenarios are identified beforehand, along with the appropriate responses. This matrix is to be reviewed and verified at least annually and included in the contingency and disaster recovery plan, per M2.

R3 requires that the contingency and disaster recovery plan be updated within 90 days of any change. M3 reinforces the requirement to review and verify the plan at least annually.

R4 requires that the contingency and disaster recovery plan, including any changes or updates, be communicated to all parties who are responsible for implementing it within seven days of approval.

R5 requires that a training program be developed around the contingency and disaster recovery plan and conducted regularly for all parties who are responsible for implementing the plan.

In summary, the NERC cyber security standards are probably one of the most comprehensive sets of security standards in existence today. Unlike other standards that only address IT security, information security during system development, or C&A, these standards encompass the full spectrum of physical, personnel, IT, and operational security in a practical, logical, and well-thought-out manner. The NERC cyber security standards realize that not all security incidents are cyber in origin; there are also physical security incidents and a combination of both. The need for ST&E and security impact analyses to consider hardware, software, *and* the operational environment, and the concept that ST&E goes way beyond traditional functional, performance, integration, and acceptance testing are highlighted. Differences in logical and physical security perimeters and the unique techniques to protect each are acknowledged. The NERC cyber security standards promote the role of change control and configuration management as an integral part of an effective security management program, like having security awareness and training activities that are tailored for specific locations and job functions. The NERC cyber security standards can easily be adapted for use in other industrial sectors and most definitely should be.

The levels of compliance and noncompliance defined in the NERC cyber security standards indicate the degree of conformance with each individual standard as a whole. The following metrics provide an additional level of granularity by zeroing in on specific shortcomings. These metrics can be applied to a single functional entity, holding company, regional reliability compliance program, or the entire power grid.

CIP-002-1

Number of Critical Assets by functional entity type, and: 1.12.1
  a. Number of Critical Cyber Assets per Critical Asset
  b. Percentage change from last reporting period
  c. Number and percentage of Cyber Assets determined not to be critical

Number and percentage of functional entities who, by calendar year: 1.12.2
  a. Kept a current approved list of Critical Assets, reviewed and verified the list annually, and updated it within 30 days of any change

b. Kept a current approved list of Critical Cyber Assets, reviewed and verified the list annually, and updated it within 30 days of any change

c. Documented the risk assessment method and evaluation criteria used to identify Critical Assets and Critical Cyber Assets

CIP-003-1

Number and percentage of functional entities who, by calendar year: 1.12.3

a. Kept their cyber security policy up-to-date

b. Documented deviations and exemptions to the cyber security policy and reviewed and validated the deviations and exemptions annually

c. Implemented and enforced a program to protect sensitive information

d. Reviewed and validated the identification, categorization, and handling procedures for sensitive information at least annually

e. Designated a senior level official to be held accountable for compliance with NERC cyber security standards

f. Have a current definition of the roles and responsibilities of the owners, custodians, and users of Critical Cyber Assets

g. Have a current definition of the organizational roles and responsibilities related to authorizing, changing, and revoking access control rights and privileges, change control, and configuration management

CIP-004-1

Number and percentage of functional entities who, by calendar year: 1.12.4

a. Executed a security awareness program that is tailored for their specific site and mission

b. Executed a security training program that is tailored for their specific site and mission

c. Required all in-house, contractor, and vendor staff to undergo a risk-based background assessment prior to being granted access to Critical Assets and Critical Cyber Assets

d. Maintained current and complete records showing the status of security awareness, training, and background check activities

CIP-005-1

Number and percentage of functional entities who, by calendar quarter:
1.12.5

a. Identified and defined their electronic security perimeter(s) and access points

b. Identified and disabled all unused ports and services

c. Implemented policies and procedures to secure dial-up modems

d. Implemented electronic access control mechanisms and procedures

e. Implemented continuous monitoring of electronic access control mechanisms

f. Maintained current and complete documentation about the electronic security perimeter(s) and access points, and the electronic mechanisms, procedures, and monitoring used to control access to the electronic security perimeter

CIP-006-1

Number and percentage of functional entities who, by calendar quarter:

1.12.6

a. Identified and defined their physical security perimeter(s) and access points
b. Implemented physical access control mechanisms and procedures
c. Implemented continuous monitoring of physical access control mechanisms
d. Logged all physical access to Critical Assets and Critical Cyber Assets
e. Performed regular maintenance and testing of their physical security mechanisms
f. Maintained current and complete documentation about the physical security perimeter(s) and access points, and the mechanisms, procedures, and monitoring used to control access to the physical security perimeter

CIP-007-1

Number and percentage of functional entities who, by calendar year: 1.12.7

a. Employed rigorous ST&E procedures, in addition to traditional functional, integration, and acceptance testing
b. Employed a rigorous user account and password management program that included strong passwords, disabling generic accounts, and regular reviews and verification of access control rights and privileges
c. Employed a robust security patch management program to verify all patches before they are installed and reject unnecessary or unstable ones
d. Verified the integrity of all custom and COTS software before deploying it to prevent the proliferation of malware
e. Implemented a comprehensive vulnerability assessment and mitigation program
f. Retained audit trails and system logs, as required by CIP-007-1
g. Included change control and configuration management as an integral part of their security engineering program
h. Implemented a continuous security monitoring capability
i. Regularly backed up and tested recovery of information critical to the operation or management of Critical Cyber Assets

CIP-008-1

Number and percentage of functional entities who, by calendar year: 1.12.8

    a. Documented and implemented a security incident response program
       for both physical and cyber security incidents
    b. Defined a security incident classification scheme for both physical and
       cyber security incidents
    c. Defined and practiced security incident handling procedures
    d. Clarified and adhered to NERC security incident reporting requirements

CIP-009-1

Number and percentage of functional entities who, by calendar year: 1.12.9

    a. Developed and exercised a contingency and disaster recovery program
    b. Identified and defined specific responses to different scenarios, includ-
       ing their duration and severity
    c. Updated the contingency and disaster recovery plan within ninety days
       of any change
    d. Communicated the contingency and disaster recovery plan, including
       any updates and changes, to all parties responsible for its implemen-
       tation within seven days of approval

3.14 The Patriot Act — United States

This bill was supposedly passed to remedy the shortcomings by federal
agencies and the failure of local, state, and federal authorities to cooperate
that allowed the tragedy of 11 September 2001 to occur. Afterward there was
tremendous pressure to do something to show that the government was on
top of the situation and calm the public. But anyone who has lived in the
Washington, D.C. area as long as I have knows that 142-page bills are not
written, passed in Committee, passed in both Houses of Congress, reconciled,
and enacted in 45 days. A goodly portion of this bill was written long before
9/11, in fact before the 2001 summer recess. The bill was given a politically
correct title that would play well in the press and stampeded through the
process. Unlike the normal procedure, this bill was "introduced with great
haste, passed with little debate, and without a House, Senate, or conference
report," as noted by the Electronic Privacy Information Center (EPIC).[232] A
common joke around Washington, D.C. is, "Did anyone (members of Congress)
read this thing before they voted on it?" Now that some of the more unpopular
provisions are coming to light and being expanded or extended, the mass
mantra has become, "Well, … 142 pages … we did not have time to read it."
In addition, who would or could vote against a bill with a title like the Patriot
Act? Despite its name, this bill is a random and odd assortment of unrelated
provisions that sponsors were unable to get into other bills. To paraphrase
an old expression, this bill has everything in it including five kitchen sinks!
How do I know? I am one of the few people in town who have actually read
all 142 tedious pages. There is no other way to find your way through this
hodgepodge than to jump in with both feet … so here goes.

Background

The Patriot Act, Public Law 107-56, was approved by Congress on 24 October 2001 and signed into law by the President two days later. The complete title of this bill is "Uniting and Strengthening America by Providing Appropriate Tools Required to Intercept and Obstruct Terrorism Act (USA Patriot Act) of 2001. According to the preamble, the purpose is[104]:

> *To deter and punish terrorist acts in the United States and around the world, to enhance law enforcement investigatory tools, and for other purposes*

The last clause hints at some of the miscellaneous provisions. In effect, the purpose of the Patriot Act is to ensure the (1) physical security of public and private U.S. assets at home and abroad, and (2) integrity of financial systems within the United States. The first goal is readily understandable in light of the events of 9/11. The second goal links the social and economic instability associated with acts of terror; it will make more sense when Title III is discussed below. Congress felt this was an important issue — 36 percent of the total pages in the Patriot Act are devoted to preventing, intercepting, and prosecuting financial crimes.

The Patriot Act is organized into ten titles:

I — Enhancing Domestic Security against Terrorism
II — Enhanced Surveillance
III — International Money Laundering Abatement and Anti-Terrorist Financing
IV — Protecting the Border
V — Removing Obstacles to Investigating Terrorism
VI — Providing for Victims of Terrorism, Public Safety Officers, and Their Families
VII — Increased Information Sharing for Critical Infrastructure Protection
VIII — Strengthening Criminal Laws against Terrorism
IX — Improved Intelligence
X — Miscellaneous

A major portion of the Patriot Act amends other existing bills. As a result of that and the constant references to other bills, it is difficult to understand what is really being said unless you have all of the amended and referenced bills in front of you. Some of the amendments are minor edits, referred to as "technical and conforming amendments" or "clerical amendments," and others are more significant. To illustrate, the following amendment is an example of a minor edit[104]:

> Title II § 218, "… strike 'the purpose' and insert 'a significant purpose'."

That change is not exactly a big deal. In contrast, the following amendments are substantial[104]:

Title II § 214, "… strike 'for any investigation to gather foreign intelligence information or information concerning terrorism' and insert 'for any investigation to obtain foreign intelligence information not concerning a United States person or to protect against international terrorism or clandestine intelligence activities, provided that such investigation of a United Stated person is not conducted solely upon the basis of activities protected by the First Amendment to the Constitution'."

Title II § 204, "… striking 'wire and oral' and inserting 'wire, oral, and electronic'."

The first example expands the scope to include United States persons as potential sources of terrorist acts or clandestine intelligence activities. The second example, instead of just applying wiretaps to voice communications, adds e-mail and e-mail attachments sent and received, voice-over-IP (VoIP), Internet searches, downloads, chat rooms, and other such activities to the scope of surveillance. In total, more than 20 major bills were amended by the Patriot Act, as shown in Table 3.15.

Table 3.15   Major Bills Amended by the Patriot Act

Immigration and Nationality Act, 8 U.S.C. 1105, 1182, 1202
Bank Holding Company Act of 1956, 12 U.S.C. 1842(c)
Federal Deposit Insurance Act, 12 U.S.C. 1828, 1829
Bank Secrecy Act, 12 U.S.C. 1953(a), Public Law 91-508
Right to Financial Privacy Act of 1978, 12 U.S.C. 3412(a), 3414
Federal Reserve Act, 12 U.S.C. 248
Fair Credit Reporting Act, 15 U.S.C. 1681
Telemarketing, Consumer Fraud and Abuse Prevention Act, 15 U.S.C. 6101
Money Laundering Control Act of 1986, 18 U.S.C. 981
General Education Provisions Act, 20 U.S.C. 1232
Controlled Substances Act, 21 U.S.C. 413
Foreign Assistance Act of 1961, 22 U.S.C. 2291
DNA Analysis Backlog Elimination Act of 2000, 42 U.S.C. 14135
Victims of Crime Act of 1984, 42 U.S.C. 10602, 10603
Omnibus Crime Control and Safe Streets Act of 1968, 42 U.S.C. 3796
Crime Identification Technology Act of 1998, 42 U.S.C. 14601
Communications Act of 1934, 47 U.S.C. 551
National Security Act of 1947, 50 U.S.C. 403
Foreign Intelligence Surveillance Act of 1978, 50 U.S.C. 1825
International Emergency Powers Act, 50 U.S.C. 1702
Trade Sanctions Reform and Export Enhancement Act of 2000, Public Law 106-387

Another interesting point is that the Patriot Act creates and defines the term "computer trespasser"[104]:

> **Computer trespasser:** a person who accesses a protected computer without authorization and thus has no reasonable expectation of privacy in any communication transmitted to, through, or from the protected computer.

To connect the term "trespassing" with unauthorized access to computers was rather clever, as a large body of law already exists for trespassing. A "protected computer" is defined in a referenced bill as any computer "used in interstate or foreign commerce or communications." This can reasonably be inferred to include federal, state, and local government computer systems, public or private financial computer systems, computer systems critical to national security and defense, computers essential to the operation and monitoring of critical infrastructure systems, computer systems containing corporate research and development and other intellectual or proprietary property, and university computer systems, especially those for research labs, and the like. In theory (but not in practice), your home computer is included if you have Internet access.

To introduce some order, coherency, and understandability to the Patriot Act, the ten titles that compose it will be discussed in terms of (1) the roles and responsibilities of government agencies, (2) the roles and responsibilities of private sector organizations, and (3) individual rights. Yes, individuals do have rights under the Patriot Act; they are buried here and there but they do indeed exist. This discussion includes the provisions that are in effect today as well as proposed changes. Keep in mind that the Patriot Act was signed before the 9/11 Commission issued its report and recommendations and before the Department of Homeland Security was created.

Government Roles and Responsibilities

The Patriot Act represents a paradigm shift from the Cold War to the War on Terrorism. The sweep of the bill is not limited to suicide bombers; rather, it encompasses all forms of terrorism that could disrupt the physical security, economic security, and social stability of the United States. Unlike the Cold War, acts of terrorism are planned and executed by transnational groups operating across and within multiple geographic locations. State and local governments are equal partners with the federal government in the War on Terrorism — unlike the Cold War days. And hence the need to update so many existing laws to reflect the dramatic change in the threat profile and the emerging partnerships between federal, state, and local agencies.

Title I, Enhancing Domestic Security Against Terrorism, establishes a "Counterterrorism Fund" for use by the Department of Justice and other federal agencies to reimburse costs incurred as a result of a terrorist incident. Funding for the FBI Technical Support Center is also increased. The Secret Service is tasked with developing a national network of electronic crime task forces to prevent, detect, and investigate electronic crimes against financial institutions and critical infrastructures. The intent is to coalesce several independent initiatives at different levels of government into a unified and mutually supportive whole. Finally, the President is given the authority to confiscate the property of foreign persons, organizations, or countries that is within the United States, when the United States has been attacked or is engaged in armed hostilities with these individuals or groups.

Title II, Enhanced Surveillance Procedures, for the most part amends existing bills to remove constraints and limitations on electronic surveillance within the borders of the United States. Title II is the most controversial title in the Patriot Act because of concerns about the potential to violate the civil and privacy rights of American citizens. Here we see an inherent conflict between the approach to enhanced physical security for the public at large and individual privacy rights.

Per Section 203, information, that in the past was only available to a grand jury in a criminal proceeding, can now be shared with any federal law enforcement, intelligence, protective, immigration, national defense, or national security official. An attorney for the government is responsible for telling the court to whom the information was disclosed. The information is only to be used for the performance of official duties and re-disclosure is limited. The same arrangement applies to oral, wire, and electronic intercepts. Section 207 contains an unusual provision. Surveillance of non-United States persons is limited to 120 days or the period specified in the application; surveillance can be extended for a period not to exceed one year. No such time limitations are placed on surveillance of U.S. citizens anywhere in Title II or the remainder of the Patriot Act. That seems a bit backward. Section 209 adds the ability to seize stored voice mail messages with a warrant, as opposed to a subpoena. Why is that significant? Search warrants are much easier to obtain than subpoenas and are executed on-site by the government official. With a subpoena, the information requested is collected and delivered, by the individual or organization, to the location specified. Section 210 defines what type of information related to electronic communications is subject to a subpoena. As defined, this includes almost anything, including the name, address, local and long distance telephone call records (who you called, who called you, date, time, and duration of each call), date the telephone service was started and terminated, what service features were subscribed to, and the credit card or bank account number used to pay the bill. Per section 211, the same applies to cable or satellite television services — with one exception: records related to what programs you watch cannot be subject to a subpoena. Do not worry; the government does not know that you watch Donald Duck and Mickey Mouse reruns on Sunday afternoon; and even if they do know it, they will not admit it.

Section 212 has raised a few eyebrows. It has a nice title — Emergency Disclosure of Electronic Communications to Protect Life and Limb — but then goes on to talk about "voluntary disclosure of customer communications or records." The statement is made that "a provider of remote computing services or electronic communication services to the public shall not knowingly divulge a record or other information pertaining to a subscriber or customer of such service (not including the contents of communications covered by paragraph (1) or (2)) to any government entity."[104] However, less than a page later, the bill states that "if a provider reasonably believes that an emergency involving immediate danger of death or serious physical injury to any person requires disclosure of the information without delay,"[104] they may do so. This would imply, of course, that the service provider is already listening to your electronic communications in real-time. The section goes on to add a new section, "Required disclosure of customer communications or records," which undoes the earlier prohibition. Section 213 also slips in an odd provision. The issuance of warrants for the search and seize evidence can be delayed if notification of the execution of the warrant would interfere with the collection of evidence. That is a politically correct way of saying that investigators should obtain as much evidence as they can through extra-legal means, before resorting to a search warrant, which requires the individual or organization to be notified; when the stakes are high, sometimes rules are bent. The pen register and trap and trace authority in Section 214 is not very popular. It allows any form of electronic communication to be monitored, intercepted, and recorded if there is reason to believe that the information collected is related to international terrorism or clandestine intelligence activities. Again, any records related to the communications are subject to subpoena. As noted above, the scope of this clause was expanded to include U.S. citizens, and no time limits were set on how long personal communications can be monitored. Given that none of the 9/11 hijackers were U.S. citizens, nor were they working for a foreign intelligence service, it is unclear why the scope of this section was expanded.

Section 215 broadens the definition of what types of personal information are subject to subpoena. The legal term "any tangible things" is used. Theoretically, this could include records from airlines, hotels, car rental companies, rental properties, bookstores, video rentals, pharmacies, educational institutions, employers, frequent shopper programs, etc. An application to collect such information is made to a federal court and must certify that the information is needed for a terrorism or clandestine intelligence investigation. Twice a year, the Attorney General must "fully inform" the House Permanent Select Committee on Intelligence and the Senate Select Committee on Intelligence concerning all requests made under this section. In addition, the Attorney General must report, to the Judiciary Committees of the House and the Senate twice a year, the total number of applications made for the production of tangible things and the total number of orders granted, modified, or denied. The intent is to make sure that this provision is not over- or mis-used. Think about this provision for a minute. Assume you are a terrorist and you know this type of information is being collected. Would you not use your credit card or frequent buyer card to obtain the things you want the government to know about and pay cash and remain anonymous for everything else? While this provision is very invasive, it is not clear that it is very effective. Section 216 extends the pen register and trap and trace authority to ongoing criminal investigations. To prevent abuse, records must be kept about[104]:

- The officers who installed or accessed the device to obtain information
- The date and time the device was installed and uninstalled
- The date, time, and duration of each time the device was accessed to obtain information
- The initial and subsequent configurations of the device
- Any information collected by the device

This report must be submitted to the court that authorized the electronic surveillance within 30 days after the termination of the court order. Hypothetically, if the court order were renewed every year for 20 years, the report could be delayed for 20 years and one month. One would hope, however, that the court would require some evidence way before then that the electronic surveillance was legitimate and not harassment due to an individual's religious or political beliefs.

Section 217 introduces the eleventh commandment: "Thou shall not trespass on thy neighbor's protected computer." In such circumstances, it is legal to intercept the trespasser's communications to, through, and from the protected computer if[104]:

- The owner or operator of the protected computer authorizes the interception
- The interception is part of a legally authorized investigation
- There is reason to believe the contents of the interception are relevant to the investigation
- Such interception does not acquire communications from individuals other than the trespasser

Those limitations sound reasonable; however, there is no required reporting or oversight to enforce them. The fourth bullet raises particular concerns in regard to privacy rights and enforcement. The lack of enforcement and oversight leaves the door open for this provision to become an umbrella for monitoring any computer system for some undefined attack that might occur someday in the future. Consider the timeline of a computer attack. Unless extremely sophisticated intrusion prevention systems, honey pots, or decoy systems are deployed, it is unlikely that you will know about precursor events to an attack or an attempted attack in real-time. Therefore, this implies that the permission to intercept trespasser communications is granted *before* the protected computer is attacked, unless the intent is to trap a repeat offender. If the government agent knows that an individual is going to attack a particular protected computer beforehand, would it not be better to tell the system owner so he can prevent or preempt the attack? Why just sit back and let the attack happen?

Sections 219 and 220 eliminate single jurisdiction search warrants for electronic evidence. Previously, warrants were limited geographically to correspond to the physical jurisdiction of the court that issued them. Now warrants can be issued to collect electronic evidence nationwide. Section 221 adds some countries, organizations, and activities to the list of trade sanctions.

Section 222 allows companies that provide information and other tangible items to an investigator to be compensated for their time and expenses. To promote some sense of self-regulation, Section 223 describes disciplinary action to be taken against government agencies and employees that "willfully and intentionally" violate provisions of the Patriot Act; special concerns are expressed about improper disclosure of information obtained during an investigation.

Now to Section 224 — the sunset clause that has recently received much attention in the news. Knowing that some of the sections in Title II might not be popular with the public and had the potential to be abused, Congress built in a sunset provision. That is, certain clauses were given an expiration date of 31 December 2005, or four years, two months, and one week after enactment. Congress felt that in this amount of time they could tell if the expanded measures were really needed, effective, and being used appropriately. Sections 203(a), 203(c), 205, 208, 210, 211, 213, 216, 219, 221, and 222 are exempt from expiration. The other sections were to expire on 31 December 2005 unless Congress renewed or modified them. An exception is made for ongoing foreign intelligence investigations. If such an investigation began prior to 31 December 2005, the expanded powers under Title II of the Patriot Act can be used until the conclusion of the investigation. No maximum time limit is specified in this regard. Table 3.16 lists the sections that were set to expire and the number of times they have been used, as reported by the Department of Justice. The "number of times used" is a bit vague however. For example, it does not tell you how many telephone lines or computers were tapped or the duration of the monitoring and intercepts per each "use." An increased level of granularity in this reporting would be useful. The usage numbers would provide more insight into the need for such expanded powers if they were accompanied by conviction statistics. That is, if Section 206 was used 49 times, how many different cases were involved in the 49 uses, and how many convictions resulted from those 49 uses? Such ratios would help illuminate whether or not these expanded powers are being used effectively. Curiously, the Department of Justice provided no usage information for seven of these sixteen sections, or almost half of them. Why would a number — 48, 612, 327, or 1099 — be classified? I am sure most mathematicians are not aware of this! Numbers alone do not reveal anything about sources, methods, or ongoing investigations. Unless the number of uses in these cases equals 280 million, meaning that every citizen in the United States is subject to this type of surveillance, or the number equals 0, meaning that the FBI has no need for this extended power, it is difficult to understand why the number of uses is being withheld. Also, why the aggregate numbers? Surely this information could be provided by fiscal year. The metrics provided later in this section are examples of the type of information that would be much more useful to report, to see if (1) these new powers are really needed, and (2) they are being used for legitimate purposes.

There was much debate about whether or not to renew or perhaps modify these 16 sections of Title II of the Patriot Act. There is a consensus that greater openness or transparency about the application of the Act would help alleviate

Table 3.16   Title II Sections of the Patriot Act That Were Set to Expire 31 December 2005 and How Often They Have Been Used

Title II Section	Latest Department of Justice Reported Usage Statistics[232]
201 – Authority to intercept wire, oral, and electronic communications relating to terrorism	As of 3/10/05, used four times in two separate investigations
202 – Authority to intercept wire, oral, and electronic communications relating to computer fraud and abuse offenses	As of 3/10/05, used twice in a single investigation
203b – Sharing wiretap information	The Department Justice acknowledged making disclosures to the intelligence community, but declined to quantify them
203d – Sharing foreign intelligence information	As of 7/26/02, used 40 times
204 – Clarification of intelligence exceptions from limitations on interception and disclosure of wire, oral, and electronic communications	Usage information not made public
206 – Roving surveillance authority	As of 3/20/05, used 49 times
207 – Duration of surveillance of non-U.S. persons	Usage information not made public
209 – Seizure of voice mail	Usage information not made public
212 – Emergency disclosure of electronic communications records	As of 5/03, used in three cases
214 – Pen register, trap and trace authority	Usage information not made public
215 – Other tangible items	As of 3/30/05, used 35 times
217 – Computer trespasser intercepts	Usage information not made public
218 – Foreign intelligence information	Usage information not made public
220 – Nationwide search warrants for electronic evidence	Usage information not made public
223 – Civil liability for unauthorized disclosures	As of 5/13/03, no civil lawsuits had been filed
225 – Immunity for compliance with wiretaps	Usage information not made public

public concerns about violations of civil and privacy rights. Specific recommendations have been made to require (1) a public report on the uses, abuses, and results of having expanded surveillance powers; and (2) continued periodic reauthorization of why such extensive surveillance is really needed.[243] Most sources are against adding administrative subpoenas for nonregulatory investigations because (1) of the potential for civil rights abuses, (2) the FBI has not demonstrated the need for them, and (3) they are contrary to the 9/11 Commission Report recommendations.[230, 234, 235, 243, 245] An agency can give itself an administrative subpoena, thereby bypassing oversight by a court. Another proposed addition to the Patriot Act concerns "mail covers." That is the legal term for allowing the government to record the to and from addresses of all mail you send or receive and to read the contents of items of interest. At present, the Chief Postal Inspector has the final authority to approve or reject such requests. This authority was taken away from the Department of Justice and intelligence community in 1976 in response to the Church Committee Report, which documented extensive abuses related to mail covers.[235]

Another concern surrounds the retention and destruction of personal information records. As just discussed, Title II grants expansive powers in the area of electronic surveillance, including that of U.S. citizens. Later we will see that Title III expands monitoring of financial transactions and Title V removes all sorts of checks and balances in the investigation process. Yet nowhere in the Patriot Act is there any mention of how long information gathered through this increased surveillance and sharing between law enforcement, intelligence, immigration, and customs officials, with both foreign and domestic government agencies, can be kept or, conversely, must be destroyed. This omission is troubling, especially because government agencies rarely dispose of any records — even when required to do so — and there is no requirement to verify the accuracy of the information collected under the Patriot Act. Congress did not make the 31 December 2005 deadline. However, on 7 March 2006, these 16 provisions of Title II were renewed with minor cosmetic changes.

Finally, Section 225 ensures that individuals and organizations cannot be sued for supplying information or assistance to a government official under this Act. This section would have more merit if two items were added: (1) the individual or organization was required to verify that the request for information was indeed legitimate, lawful, and backed by a signed court order or warrant before cooperating; and (2) the individual or organization was required to verify and certify the accuracy of all information they disclosed beforehand. This would prevent: (1) rogue officers from bluffing their way to obtain information, and (2) individuals and organizations accidentally or intentionally disclosing false or misleading information.

Title III, International Money Laundering Abatement and Anti-Terrorist Financing Act of 2001, is by far the longest title in the Patriot Act. So why does money laundering receive such attention in a bill to fight terrorism? Congress is attempting to draw the connection between drug trafficking and terrorist groups — the so-called "narco-terrorists" and the use of profits from drug sales to finance terrorist organizations. At the same time, there is concern about the extent of money laundering worldwide and the potential impact on the stability and integrity of financial institutions in the United States. This is not an idle concern. The International Monetary Fund (IMF) estimates that money laundering accounts for $600 billion annually, or between 2 and 5 percent of the global gross domestic product (GDP).[104] Furthermore, the United States is a member of the Basel Committee on Banking Regulation and

Supervisory Practices as well as the Financial Action Task Force on Money Laundering, both of which have adopted international anti-money laundering principles and recommendations.

The Department of the Treasury is the lead agency for this title, and the Secretary of the Treasury is given broad discretion when implementing its provisions. Regulations may be applied to offshore financial institutions if they conduct business or participate in a transaction with an institution based in the United States. For example, the Secretary may require U.S. banks to keep records of all transactions to and from foreign banks, including the name and address of the sender and receiver, the account numbers, and the details of the transaction. Similar records of accounts held in U.S. banks by non-citizens may be required. The Secretary is required to notify the House Committee on Financial Services and the Senate Committee on Banking, Housing, and Urban Affairs in writing of any action taken in this regard.

Section 312 levies extra due diligence requirements on correspondent banks, payable through accounts, and private banking accounts to detect money laundering. Section 313 prohibits U.S. banks from having correspondent accounts with foreign shell banks or banks that do not have a physical presence in any country; they are often called banks without borders. Section 314 promotes cooperation among financial institutions, regulatory authorities, and law enforcement agencies to enhance the prevention and detection of money laundering to or through the United States. These organizations are encouraged to pay special attention to the transfer of funds, particularly repeated transfers of funds, to and from charitable, non-profit, and non-governmental organizations, that may indicate a narco-terrorism connection. To facilitate this initiative, the Secretary is required to submit a semi-annual report to the financial services industry and state and local law enforcement agencies detailing patterns of suspicious activity and other insights derived from current investigations. Section 317 gives federal district courts jurisdiction over foreign assets and accounts seized under this Act. Other property of equal value can be seized, per Section 319, if the laundered funds or funds from other criminal activities are not available. Section 321 adds credit unions to the list of financial institutions that must comply with Title III of the Patriot Act. The Secretary, Attorney General, and senior executives from the Federal Deposit Insurance Corporation, National Credit Union Administration, and the Securities and Exchange Commission are tasked to periodically evaluate the effectiveness of the provisions of Title III, per Section 324.

The Secretary is required to provide minimum standards for financial institutions to use to verify the identity of customers opening new accounts, per Section 326. No mention is made of applying these standards to existing account transactions or requests to close an account. The minimum standards are to include[104]:

- How to verify the identity of the individual
- How to maintain records of the information used to verify the person's identity, including name, address, and so forth

- The need to consult lists of known or suspected terrorists or terrorist-related organizations issued by the State Department, Justice Department, and Treasury

Section 328 tasks the Secretary of the Treasury, the Secretary of State, and the Attorney General to work together to "encourage" foreign governments and financial institutions to cooperate by supplying the identity of the originator of wire transfers sent to the United States. The intent is for this information to remain intact from the point of origination to the point of disbursement. The Secretary of the Treasury is further tasked to submit an annual report to the House Committee on Financial Services and the Senate Committee on Banking, Housing, and Urban Affairs detailing progress and impediments to achieving this goal. Likewise, Section 330 "encourages" inter national cooperation during the investigation of money laundering, financial crimes, and the financing of terrorist groups.

Criminal penalties are invoked in Section 329 for government employees or contractors who demand, seek, receive, accept, or agree to accept anything of value in return for aiding, committing, or colluding in any fraud or omitting to do any official act in violation of Title III.[104]

The criminal penalty is set at three times the monetary value of the item offered and/or 15 years in prison.

Section 351 protects financial institutions that voluntarily disclose information about a possible violation of law from any and all liability lawsuits, including failure to notify the individual about the disclosure. Without an accompanying requirement for the financial institution to verify and certify the accuracy of the information and its supposition, individuals are left in a very precarious position while the financial institution is blameless. This provision ignores the potential harm to an individual — the difficulty and expense of recovering from false or misleading information that was accidentally or intentionally attributed to him. This inequity and absence of accountability, which occurs in several sections of the Patriot Act, needs to be corrected.

Section 360 provides incentives for foreign countries to cooperate in preventing, detecting, or responding to international terrorism. Section 361 expands the scope of the duties of the Financial Crimes Enforcement Network (FinCEN) within the Department of the Treasury. FinCEN is tasked to coordinate with financial, intelligence, and anti-terrorist groups in other countries. One amusing statement talks about "… the submission of reports through the Internet *or other secure network*…." Heaven help us if FinCEN thinks the Internet is secure! Because FinCEN data is shared, the Department of the Treasury is tasked to develop standards and guidelines for complying with the Right to Financial Privacy Act of 1978. This is about the only mention of privacy rights in the Patriot Act. By Section 362, Congress realized its earlier *faux pas* and tasked the Secretary to expedite the development of a highly secure network for use by FinCEN. This network will be used by financial institutions to file various reports and by the Treasury to send financial institutions alerts and other information about suspicious activities. Just to make sure financial institutions understand that the federal government is serious, Section 363 stipulates civil and criminal penalties of two times the amount of a transaction, up to $1 million, for participating in money laundering. Armed law enforcement officials are authorized to protect the facilities, operations, and employees of a federal reserve bank under Section 364, including members of the Federal Reserve Board. Section 371 defines "bulk cash smuggling" and the penalties for doing so. To be considered smuggling, there must be an attempt to conceal the funds and not report them on U.S. Customs entry forms. Also, the amount must total $10,000 or more, in any combination of cash or checks. The penalty is up to five years in prison; other property can be confiscated as well. Sections 374 and 375 update laws relating to counterfeiting to bring them into the digital age. Finally, Section 377 clarifies that crimes committed abroad using credentials or instruments issued by United States financial institutions will be prosecuted by the United States.

Title IV, Protecting the Border, tightens many loopholes in immigration laws relating to tourists, foreign students, and other temporary visitors. The intent is to increase physical and personnel security at border entry points. For example, Section 401 tripled the staffing level of Immigration and Naturalization Service (INS) and U.S. Customs officials on the northern border and increased funding for related technology. State, local, and federal law enforcement officials are permitted to exchange records related to criminal offenses and fingerprints with the State Department to facilitate processing of visa applications, per the amendments in Section 403. Some limits are placed on the confidentiality, redistribution, and retention of this information, but no explanation is given on how this will be enforced.

The most interesting part of Title IV appears under the heading "Technology Standard to Confirm Identity," also part of Section 403. The Attorney General, Secretary of State, and NIST are specifically tasked to[104]:

> ... *develop and certify a technology standard that can be used to verify the identity of persons applying for a United States visa or such persons seeking to enter the United States pursuant to a visa for the purposes of conducting background checks, confirming identity, and ensuring that a person has not received a visa under a different name or such person seeking to enter the United States pursuant to a visa.*

This was the genesis of the U.S. Visit program, which has since been transferred to the Department of Homeland Security. Furthermore, Section 403 specifies that the solution must be integrated and interoperable[104]:

> ... *a cross-agency, cross-platform electronic system that is a cost-effective, efficient, fully integrated means to share law enforcement and intelligence information necessary to confirm the identity of such persons.*

The end result is to be accessible to U.S. consular offices around the world, border agents, law enforcement, and intelligence officers throughout the United States. The intent is to make sure the appropriate officials know who (1) is applying for visas and whether they should get them, and (2) is in the country at any given time, which entry point they came through, and how long they are authorized to stay. This system will also help identify people who have overstayed their welcome. The Attorney General, Secretary of State, and Secretary of the Treasury are required to submit a status report to Congress every two years on the development, implementation, efficacy, and privacy implications of the technology standard and information system deployed. Section 405 initiated a feasibility study to see if the FBI's existing integrated automated fingerprint identification system (IAFIS) could be integrated with the border entry system described in Section 403, to promote technology reuse by the government. Section 413 allows the Secretary of State to decide whether information in this database can be shared with foreign governments on a reciprocal basis. The exchange is limited to information about aliens and does not include U.S. citizens. In essence, the United States could give information it has about criminal activity attributed to a non-citizen to the alien's home or other country. This type of exchange is not limited by any U.S. privacy laws.

Sections 411 and 412 define and designate certain activities and groups as being terrorist related. These definitions are then used as the basis of denying admittance or expelling an individual from the United States, or detaining them. The Attorney General is required to submit a report to the House Committee on the Judiciary and the Senate Committee on the Judiciary every six months documenting the[104]:

- Number of aliens detained due to suspected terrorist-related activities
- Factual grounds for their detention
- Nationality of each detainee
- Length of their detention
- Number of aliens deported and released in the current reporting period

In addition, seven days before designating an organization as being terrorist related, the Secretary of State must notify the Speaker and Minority Leader of the House, the *President pro tempore,* Majority Leader and Minority Leader of the Senate, and members of the relevant committees of the House and Senate. This notification is to be done by written communication through classified channels and include the factual basis for such a designation. Seven days later, the designation of an organization as being terrorist related is published in the *Federal Register.*

Section 414 is also rather interesting. The Secretary of State and Attorney General are encouraged to fully implement the integrated entry and exit system described in Section 403 "with deliberate speed and expeditiously" for airports, seaports, and land border ports of entry. Three other requirements are levied[104]:

1. The use of biometric technology
2. The development of tamper-resistant machine-readable documents
3. The ability to interface with existing law enforcement databases

The first requirement caused a slight diplomatic storm when first introduced; *bona fide* tourists and VIPs from other countries took offense at being finger-printed like a common criminal. A few countries retaliated by doing the same to U.S. citizens traveling abroad. Diplomatic niceties aside, the focus now is to define and implement a standard machine-readable passport worldwide that contains the necessary personal identification information along with some biometric data, as noted in Section 417. The State Department lunged ahead in this direction in regard to replacing U.S. passports, only to retreat due to opposition in Europe and elsewhere because of potential privacy violations and the inherent insecurity of RFID technology.[74] Notice the similarities between the requirements of Sections 403 and 414 of Title IV of the Patriot Act, and HSPD-12 and FIPS 201 discussed earlier in Section 3.13 of this book. This has raised concerns in some quarters that the next step is a biometric-based national ID card that replaces the driver's licenses currently issued by each state.

Section 415 expands the increased monitoring and surveillance of aliens to include foreign students, probably the single group with the largest number of visa violations. Sections 421 through 428 close out Title IV by defining special privileges of immigrants and their families who are themselves victims of terrorism.

Title V, Removing Obstacles to Investigating Terrorism, lifts various restraints on investigations and provides incentives for cooperating with investigators. For example, the Attorney General and Secretary of State may offer rewards for assistance in combating terrorism. Section 503 promotes the ability to use DNA identification for terrorists, just as for other violent criminals. Information collected from electronic surveillance and physical searches can be shared with other federal law enforcement officers to further investigations or preempt a terrorist activity, per Section 504. Section 505 lowers the level of approval needed to obtain electronic communications records, financial records, and consumer reports as part of an investigation. Sections 507 and 508 add educational records to the list of items that can be easily obtained during an investigation.

Title VI defines various federal benefits available for victims of terrorism and their families, as well as public safety officers who are injured or killed as a result of a terrorist incident, and their families.

Title VII, Increased Information Sharing for Critical Infrastructure Protection, promotes the secure multi-jurisdictional exchange of information to facilitate the investigation and prosecution of terrorist activities at the federal, regional, state, and local levels.

Title VIII, Strengthening Criminal Laws Against Terrorism, does just that. Section 801 establishes a 20-year prison term for threatening, conspiring, or attempting a terrorist attack against any type of mass transit system under U.S. jurisdiction; if there are any fatalities, the sentence reverts to life. These are serious sentences, but probably not much of a deterrent for a suicide bomber. Section 802 defines domestic terrorism, in an attempt to distinguish it from international terrorism[104]:

> *... activities that involve acts dangerous to human life that are a violation of the criminal laws of the United States or any State and appear to be intended to: (a) intimidate or coerce a civilian population, (b) influence*

the policy of a government by intimidation or coercion, or (c) to affect the conduct of government by mass destruction, kidnapping, or assassination and occur primarily within the jurisdiction of the United States.

Section 803 explains the prohibitions against and the penalties for harboring, concealing, aiding, or abetting terrorists, along with procedures for confiscating their property. Section 808 provides a lengthy definition of what constitutes the federal crime of terrorism. The statute of limitations for terrorist-related crimes is extended or abolished by Section 809. Sections 810 and 811 modify the penalties for terrorist acts.

Then along comes Section 814 — Deterrence and Prevention of Cyber Terrorism. Unfortunately, despite the title, no prevention strategies are provided. Instead, loss and damage are defined, along with various fines and prison terms ranging from 1 to 20 years[104]:

Damage: any impairment to the integrity or availability of data, a program, a system, or information.

Loss: any reasonable cost to any victim, including the cost of responding to an offense, conducting a damage assessment, and restoring the data, program, system, or information to its condition prior to the offense, and any revenue lost, cost incurred, or other consequential damages incurred because of interruption of service.

These two terms will resurface in Chapter 5 during the discussion of security ROI. Just to add a little humor to the Patriot Act, the statement is made that a lawsuit cannot be filed under Section 814 "for the negligent design or manufacture of computer hardware, software, or firmware."[104] Why not? Buggy COTS hardware or software that is distributed nationwide comes close to the definition of domestic terrorism — intimidating or coercing a civilian population! Section 816 adds $50 million a year to enhance regional cyber security forensic capabilities at the federal, regional, state, and local levels through collaboration and information sharing.

Title IX, Improved Intelligence, anticipated the 9/11 Commission Report and encouraged further cooperation between the FBI and CIA, particularly in the areas of joint tracking of foreign assets and sponsorship of a national virtual translation center.

Several of the kitchen sinks can be found in Title X — Miscellaneous; we will skip them and focus on the highlights. Section 1001 requires the Inspector General of the Department of Justice to establish an office to receive and review complaints of civil rights abuses under the Patriot Act. A semi-annual report must be submitted to the Committee of the Judiciary of both Houses of Congress detailing implementation of this section and the alleged abuses. Section 1005 makes grants available to first responders to prevent terrorism. Section 1009 makes the FBI responsible for creating and disseminating the "No Fly List" to the airlines. Section 1011 takes the wind out of the fraudulent solicitation of donations for charities. Section 1012 defines the Department of

Transportation's role in limiting the issuance of licenses to transport HAZMAT across state lines. Sections 1013 through 1015 discuss bio-terrorism and domestic preparedness. Section 1016 establishes the National Infrastructure Simulation and Analysis Center within the Department of Defense.

The following metrics can be used to measure whether or not an agency is fulfilling its responsibilities under the Patriot Act. These metrics can be used by an agency to monitor its own performance, individuals and public interest groups, and independent oversight authorities in the public and private sectors.

Title I § 105	Total number and distribution of participants in the Electronic Crimes Task Force: (a) federal, (b) regional, (c) state, and (d) local	1.13.1
Title II § 203	Number of times grand jury information was shared with federal law enforcement, intelligence, protective, immigration, and national defense officials.	1.13.2
Title II § 209	Number of times voice mail messages were seized in accordance with a warrant:	1.13.3

a. Percentage of times this prevented a terrorist attack
b. Percentage of times this resulted in a conviction

Title II § 210	Number of times electronic communications records were subpoenaed, number of cases involved, and percentage that resulted in legal action.	1.13.4
Title II § 211	Number of times electronic communications records were subpoenaed, number of cases involved, and percentage that resulted in legal action.	1.13.5
Title II § 213	Number of times the issuance of a search warrant was delayed.	1.13.6
Title II § 214	Number of individuals and organizations that were subject to pen register and trap and trace:	1.13.7

a. Duration of each
b. Percentage of which prevented a terrorist attack
c. Percentage of which resulted in a conviction

Title II § 215	Number of times the Attorney General submitted the biannual report detailing the number of requests to produce "tangible things," the number granted, denied, and modified, to Congress on time and it was approved.	1.13.8
Title II § 216	Number of times investigators submitted eavesdropping records, detailing the officer(s) who installed or accessed the device to obtain information, the date and time the device was installed and uninstalled, the date, time, and duration of each time the device was accessed to obtain information, the initial and subsequent configuration(s) of the device, and any information collected by the device, to the appropriate court on time and it was approved.	1.13.9

Distribution of times the electronic information collected did and did not: 1.13.10

a. Relate to the investigation as claimed on the application
b. Result in a conviction
c. Relate to other individuals, not under surveillance

Title II § 217   Number and percentage of times computer trespasser intercepts: 1.13.11

a. Prevented a computer crime
b. Prevented a serious computer attack
c. Resulted in another type of conviction
d. Accidentally intercepted unrelated information

Title II § 220   Number of nationwide search warrants issued for electronic evidence: 1.13.12

a. Duration of each
b. Percentage of which prevented a terrorist attack
c. Percentage of which resulted in a conviction

Title II § 222   Number of organizations and individuals that requested reimbursement for cooperating under the Patriot Act, per fiscal year, and the total amount paid out. 1.13.13

Title II § 223   Number of government employees disciplined, per fiscal year, for violations of the Patriot Act: 1.13.14

a. Number of government contractors disciplined, per fiscal year, for violations of the Patriot Act
b. Number of lawsuits filed by individuals or organizations for abuses of the Patriot Act, by fiscal year

Title III § 312   Number of banks disciplined or fined for failure to comply with extra due diligence requirements of the Patriot Act, by fiscal year. 1.13.15

Title III § 313   Number of banks disciplined or fined for failure to terminate correspondent accounts with shell banks, by fiscal year. 1.13.16

Title III § 314   Number of times Secretary of the Treasury submitted the semiannual report about patterns of suspicious activity to the financial industry, state and local governments on time. 1.13.17

Title III § 317   Number of property seizures, by fiscal year, and total value of the property seized. 1.13.18

Title III § 324   Number of times Secretary of the Treasury, Attorney General, and senior executives from the FDIC, NCUA, and SEC met to discuss ways of improving the effectiveness of Title III, by fiscal year, and the number of recommendations made to Congress. 1.13.19

Title III § 326   Number of times minimum identity verification standards were violated by financial institutions, by fiscal year.   1.13.20

Title III § 328   Percentage of wire transfers to the United States that did and did not contain the identity of the originator.   1.13.21

Title III § 329   Number of government employees who received a criminal penalty for violations of Title III, by fiscal year: 1.13.22

    a. Number of government contractors who received a criminal penalty for violations of Title III, by fiscal year

Title III § 361   Number of times FinCEN, by fiscal year, underwent: 1.13.23

    a. Independent security audits
    b. Independent privacy audits
    c. The number of serious problems found
    d. The number of serious problems resolved

Title III § 371   Number of arrests and convictions for bulk cash smuggling.   1.13.24

Title III § 377   Number of financial crimes prosecuted abroad.   1.13.25

Title IV § 403   Number of times Attorney General, Secretary of State, and Secretary of the Treasury submitted status report to Congress on time and it was approved, detailing progress and privacy implications of the automated entry/exist identity verification system.   1.13.26

Title IV § 413   Number of times information from the automated entry/exit identity verification system was shared on a reciprocal basis with foreign countries and the distribution by country.   1.13.27

Title IV § 411   By fiscal year, the number of individuals and groups: 1.13.28

    a. Added to the terrorist watch list
    b. Deleted from the terrorist watch list

Title IV § 412   Number of times Attorney General submitted a status report to Congress on time and it was approved, detailing the number of aliens detained, the factual grounds for their detention, the nationality of each detainee, the length of their detention, and the number of aliens deported and released in the current reporting period.   1.13.29

Title IV § 414   By fiscal year, the number and percentage new entry/exit identity verification systems that have been installed at: 1.13.30

    a. Airports
    b. Seaports
    c. Land border ports

Title V   Number of rewards offered, and the total amount paid, for assistance in combating terrorism: 1.13.31

        a. By Attorney General § 501

        b. By Secretary of State § 502

Title VII 701   Number of times federal government participated in multi-jurisdictional sharing of terrorist-related information: 1.13.32

        a. With regional agencies

        b. With state agencies

        c. With local agencies

Title VIII § 801   Number of incidents of domestic terrorism by fiscal year, locality, and group. 1.13.33

Title VIII § 803   Number of criminal penalties imposed for concealing, harboring, aiding, or abetting a terrorist. 1.13.34

Title VIII § 808   Number of incidents of international terrorism by fiscal year, locality, and group. 1.13.35

Title X § 1001   Number of complaints received about abuses or misuses of the provisions of the Patriot Act, by fiscal year: 1.13.36

        a. From individuals

        b. From organizations

Title X § 1005   Number of grant awards made to first responders and total amount by fiscal year and organization. 1.13.37

Title X § 1009   Number of names on the "No Fly List" that were: 1.13.38

        a. Added

        b. Deleted, no longer a concern

        c. Deleted due to an error

        d. Source of a complaint from an individual

Private Sector Roles and Responsibilities

Private sector and non-profit organizations need to be aware of their roles and responsibilities under the Patriot Act for several reasons:

- To ensure complete compliance with the Act, no more and no less
- To ensure that information is not disclosed to unauthorized sources or in unauthorized situations
- To ensure that the volume and extent of information disclosed is neither too much, nor too little
- To ensure that all requests received for information or other forms of cooperation are legitimate under the Act and backed up with the appropriate signed and authorized documentation
- To protect the vital interests of the organization from potential lawsuits, fines, or other negative publicity resulting from some misstep related to the first four bullets

The federal government takes the Patriot Act seriously — so should your organization.

Title II, Enhanced Surveillance Procedures, primarily concerns communications services providers (landlines, cell phones, Internet access, cable and satellite television). Wiretapping by the federal government is not new, so the telephone companies are already equipped to handle these requests; the Internet access and television providers are the new kids on the block. The following is a review of the new regulations as a result of the Patriot Act.

Per Section 210, a company may be asked to supply the following communications records, *if* the request is accompanied by a subpoena[104]:

- Customer name
- Customer address
- Local and long distance telephone connection records, records or session times and durations
- Length of service, start date, types of services utilized
- Subscriber number or identity, including any temporary network address
- Means and source of payment, including credit card or bank account numbers

Section 211 clarifies that companies shall not disclose "records revealing cable subscriber selection of video programming from a cable operator." No explicit statement is made like this in reference to satellite television, but it is logical to conclude that the same prohibition is true.

Section 212 is where the discussion of "voluntary disclosure of customer records" can be found. First there is the prohibition[104]:

> (3) a provider of remote computing services or electronic communications services to the public shall not knowingly divulge a record or other information pertaining to a subscriber or customer of such service (not including the contents of communications covered by paragraph (1) or (2)) to any governmental entity.

Then the caveat[104]:

> (C) if the provider reasonably believes that an emergency involving immediate danger of death or serious physical injury to any person requires disclosure of the information without delay.

So the best approach is to use common sense and proceed with caution.

Section 215 describes the requirement of an organization to provide "tangible things" in response to a court order. This may include books, records, papers, documents, and other things such as lease information, book buying, video rental, hotel or rental car information, etc. An organization should verify the court order before supplying any information. Have a competent legal authority review the court order and if there are any questions or concerns, challenge it. Organizations are not at liberty to inform anyone that it disclosed or was requested to disclose such information.

Section 217 concerns computer trespassers. The federal government cannot intercept the communications of a computer trespasser to, through, or from your protected computer *unless* you authorize it. Even so, no communications other than that of the computer trespasser can be intercepted.

Title III, Section 319, concerns the forfeiture of funds in interbank accounts. Per this section, financial institutions have 120 hours to comply with a request for anti-money laundering information. The specific information requested must be supplied within that time frame and delivered to the location specified. No exemptions are made for weekends or holidays. Note also that the request must come from an "appropriate Federal banking agency" to be legitimate. A summons or subpoena may be issued by the Secretary of Treasury or the Attorney General for foreign bank records to any foreign bank that has a correspondent account in the United States. Similar written requests from authorized law enforcement officials must be responded to in seven calendar days; verbal requests are not legitimate or binding. In addition, a financial institution may be ordered to terminate a correspondent relationship with a foreign bank not later than ten business days after receiving a written request from the Attorney General or Secretary of the Treasury. Failure to comply can result in civil penalties of up to $10,000 per day until the relationship is terminated.

Section 326 requires financial institutions to verify the identity of customers who open new accounts, keep records of the information they used to verify their identity, and to consult terrorist watch lists from the Departments of State, Treasury, and Justice before opening an account. To address the identity verification requirement in Section 326, many banks require two forms of government issued IDs, such as a driver's license and a passport. Some banks carry it a step further and also require a utility statement (gas, electric, or telephone bill) at the address for which the account is being opened. I quit buying Certificates of Deposit because of this requirement; each CD is considered a separate account and I got tired of having to present the same information over and over again, especially when the bank representative knew me and could already read the information on his computer screen.

Section 328 requires organizations that send wire transfers to the United States to include the identity of the originator. Financial institutions in the United States that receive such wire transfers should "encourage" their overseas partners to comply.

Section 351 expects financial institutions to be proactive in preventing money laundering. This is to be demonstrated, at a minimum, by (1) having robust internal policies, procedures, and controls in place to detect and prevent money laundering; (2) designating a Patriot Act compliance officer; (3) ongoing employee training programs about the policies and procedures; and (4) a periodic independent audit to verify the effectiveness of the policies and procedures.

Sections 355 and 356 encourage, and in some cases require, the reporting of suspicious activities by individuals, financial institutions, securities brokers, investment companies, and related firms. While financial institutions have a legal duty to file suspicious activity reports, they also have an ethical duty to verify the accuracy of such information before submitting it to weed out any accidental or intentional errors. Financial institutions can be sued for intentional malicious reporting.

Section 358 requires consumer reporting bureaus to supply information in an individual's file, when presented with an authorized written request. Consumer reporting bureaus are not allowed to inform an individual that such information has been disclosed.

Section 363 stipulates that a financial institution that participates in a money laundering transaction may be subject to a civil or criminal penalty of not less than twice the amount of the transaction, up to $1 million.

Section 365 requires all business organizations to report any transaction for $10,000 or greater in which the customer pays by cash (coin, currency, or check). The report must include the name and address of the customer, the amount of each type of cash received, the date and nature of the transaction, and the name of the organization and individual filing the report and their contact information.

The following metrics can be used to measure whether or not an organization is fulfilling its responsibilities under the Patriot Act. These metrics can be used by an organization to monitor its own performance, individuals and public interest groups, and independent oversight authorities in the public and private sectors.

Title II § 210	Number of times an organization responded to a request for electronic communications records.	1.13.39
Title II § 211	Number of times customer video program selections were accidentally disclosed.	1.13.40
Title II § 212	Number of times customer electronic communications records were voluntarily disclosed.	1.13.41
Title II § 215	Number of times an organization responded to a request for "tangible things."	1.13.42
Title II § 217	Number and percentage of times an organization did and did not authorize computer trespasser intercepts.	1.13.43
Title III § 319	Distribution of times a financial organization did and did not meet the 120-hour rule to turn over information.	1.13.44
	Distribution of times a financial organization did and did not meet the 7-day rule to turn over information.	1.13.45
Title III § 326	Number of times a financial institution was unable to verify the identity of a customer and refused to open a new account.	1.13.46
Title III § 351	Number and percentage of organizations that, within the past fiscal year, did and did not:	1.13.47

    a. Have Patriot Act policies, procedures, and controls in place
    b. Designate a Patriot Act Compliance Officer
    c. Have ongoing training programs for employees about the
       Patriot Act
    d. Have an independent audit to assess compliance with the
       Patriot Act

Title III § 355, 356	Number of suspicious activity reports filed.	1.13.48

Title III § 358	Number of times consumer reporting bureaus responded to written requests for information.	1.13.49
Title III § 363	Number of financial institutions fined by participating in money laundering transactions, by fiscal year, and the total amount of the fines.	1.13.50
Title III § 365	Number of cash transactions reported by organizations that were $10,000 or more.	1.13.51

Individual Rights

Much concern has been expressed about the potential for misusing the provisions in the Patriot Act and the abuses of individual civil and privacy rights that could result due to its invasive nature. These concerns fueled the debates about the sunset provisions in Title II, which deals with electronic surveillance. From the beginning, Congress was aware of the prospect of something going wrong — an overzealous investigator, an unethical government employee, a data entry error — so they built in some protections for individuals, as described below. Some additional protections would be nice, but these at least provide a start. So if things do not seem quite right — mail that has always come on Thursdays starts arriving on Tuesday or Wednesday of the next week, radio or television stations that have always come in clear start having a lot of interference, your computer screen seems to flicker a lot more than it used to, people start asking you questions about comments you made in the privacy of your home when no one else was around — and you think you may have been confused with Osama bin Laden, take advantage of the protections provided in the Patriot Act. Remember that organizations and individuals that were ordered to cooperate cannot tell you what is going on; however, sometimes body language can tell you all you need to know. No one else is going to stick up for your rights for you. After all, if the names of two U.S. Senators can end up on the "No Fly List," just imagine what can happen to you.

Under Title II, Section 223, if an individual feels that he has been the subject of unwarranted electronic surveillance under the Patriot Act, he can file suit under the procedures of the Federal Tort Claims Act. The suit must pertain to "willful or intentional" violations of the Patriot Act, or the modifications it makes to the Foreign Intelligence Surveillance Act, by a government agency or employee, such as unwarranted collection or disclosure of personal electronic communications. The suit should be filed in a U.S. District Court within two years after the individual learns of the violation. The case will be heard by a judge without a jury. The court can award damages equal to the actual damage incurred, but not less than $10,000, plus reasonable litigation costs.

Under Title III, Section 316, an individual may contest the confiscation of property that was seized under the Patriot Act. The individual may file a claim according to the procedures specified in the Federal Rules for Civil Procedure (Supplemental Rules for Certain Admiralty and Maritime Claims). The individual should assert that (1) the property is not subject to confiscation under such provision of law, and (2) the innocent owner provisions of Section 983(d) of Title 18 U.S.C. apply to the case. The suit should be filed in U.S. District Court as soon as confiscation proceedings begin.

Under Title III, Section 355, an individual may file suit against a former employer (an insured financial institution) who supplied a derogatory employment reference, concerning potentially unlawful activities, with malicious intent.

Under Title III, Section 365, all business organizations are required to report any transaction amounting to $10,000 or more in which the customer paid by cash (coin, currency, or check). So, if you do not want your name to show up on a terrorist watch list or be subjected to extra electronic surveillance, do not pay cash for items that cost $10,000 or more. The limit for U.S. Postal Money Orders is less — just $3,000 will trigger the extra unwanted scrutiny. Remember that it is much easier to keep your name off the list than to remove it once it is there.

Both Title II, Section 214, and Title V, Section 505, make it clear that an individual's electronic communications (voice, video, fax, Internet, etc.), financial records, and consumer reports cannot be scrutinized solely on "the basis of activities protected by the first amendment to the Constitution of the United States." If individuals or organizations believe they are being harassed in this manner, they should seek legal counsel and a legal remedy in accordance with Title II, Section 223, and Title X, Section 1001, of the Patriot Act. Title X, Section 1001, requires the Department of Justice Inspector General to establish an office to receive, review, and act upon complaints of abuse from the public. There is no requirement to file a complaint under Title X before filing a suit under Title II; one or both avenues may be pursued at your discretion. Do not be shy about using these legal avenues to protect your rights — that is why Congress included them in the bill.

The following metrics can be used to measure whether or not individuals are exercising their rights under the Patriot Act and whether agencies are honoring or interfering with these rights.

Title II § 223   Number of individuals who filed suit over unwarranted electronic surveillance and percentage in which damages were awarded.   1.13.52

Title III § 316   Number of individuals who contested the seizure of property under the Patriot Act.   1.13.53

Title III § 355   Number of individuals who sued a former financial employer for a malicious negative employment reference.   1.13.54

Title X § 1001   Number of individuals who filed complaints with the Department of Justice Inspector General for being unfairly targeted or harassed by electronic surveillance under the Patriot Act.
                                                                          1.13.55

3.15 Summary

Chapter 3 navigated the galaxy of compliance metrics and the security and privacy regulations to which they apply. Security and privacy regulations have been issued at a dizzying pace around the world in the past few years in an attempt to bring laws and regulations in line with state-of-the-art technology and in recognition of the rapid advent of cyber crime. These regulations are intended to prevent mishandling, misuse, and misappropriation of sensitive information, whether financial, personal, healthcare, or related to critical infrastructure protection. Given the delta between the speed at which regulations are passed and the speed with which technology changes, this effort is almost a "mission impossible." A common problem in the regulatory environment is the dichotomy of complying with the "letter of the law" versus complying with the "spirit of the law." Some organizations and auditors take a minimalist approach to compliance, while others take a broader view by determining what needs to be done not only to comply with regulations, but also to ensure safety, security, and reliability. Some organizations and auditors just want to check off the boxes, while others focus on the big picture and how the safety, reliability, and security of their product or service will be perceived by the public at large. The latter view compliance as an opportunity to increase an organization's performance and efficiency.[205] Metrics provide the objective evidence needed to ensure big-picture regulatory compliance.

Most people have their own ideas about what privacy means, especially to themselves. Some even question the possibility of privacy in the age of the global information grid. A clear understanding of privacy and what it does and does not entail is necessary before delving into regulations. Privacy is a legal right, not an engineering discipline. That is why organizations have privacy officers, not privacy engineers. Security engineering is the discipline used to ensure that privacy rights are protected to the extent specified by law and company or organizational policy. Privacy is not an automatic outcome of security engineering. Like any other security feature or function, privacy requirements must be specified, designed, implemented, and verified to the integrity level needed. Privacy is not just another regulatory issue — identity theft is the most spectacular example of a violation of privacy rights.

Many authorities have taken the position that an individual's right to privacy must be sacrificed to ensure the physical safety of the public at large. "National security" has become a catch-all phrase; in many cases when government officials want to do something that conflicts with existing privacy laws and regulations, all they have to do is claim it is for "national security reasons. (Note the numerous exceptions in the five privacy regulations and the Patriot Act.) The logic in this supposition is flawed. First, society is composed of individuals; if individuals do not matter, then neither does society. Second, protecting an individual's nonpublic personal information has no impact, positive or negative, on the resilience of physical security controls. The U.S. Government knew Osama bin Laden's name, face, date of birth, place of birth, residence, financial status, etc. before 9/11. It even knew that his family was in the United States at that time. Knowing that personal information did nothing to prevent the tragedy. Personal information (names, social security numbers, birthdays, etc.) cannot be used to mitigate physical security vulnerabilities. The resilience of physical security measures depends on (1) eliminating a vulnerability in a physical security control or reducing the opportunity to exploit it, (2) making the expertise required to exploit a physical security vulnerability time or cost prohibitive — it is too difficult to exploit, and (3) preventing, controlling, and restricting access to the resources needed to exploit the physical security vulnerability (i.e., explosive, chemical, biological, and nuclear materials, as well as the cash needed to procure these items).

Identity cards and international airline travel are the areas where this flawed thinking has most gone awry. In December 2004, the OECD issued a study on the use of biometrics to enhance the security of international travel.[70] At the same time, the Transportation Security Agency (TSA) was beginning to deploy backscatter scanners at airports and the State Department was experimenting with RFID tags in passports. These agencies seem to have forgotten that all 9/11 hijackers had legitimate passports and did not carry any explosives or weapons — only box cutters. Put another way, these agencies seem determined to pursue high-tech solutions to low-tech terrorism. The OECD report documents the types of advance passenger information (API) and passenger name records (PNR) international flights are required to submit to government authorities before landing, and in some cases before take-off when people on the No Fly List pop up. This information includes[70]:

- Number and type of travel documents submitted (passport, driver's license, etc.)
- Nationality
- Full name
- Date of birth
- Place of birth
- Gender
- Point of entry
- Departure and arrival time
- Initial point of embarkation
- Mode of transport
- Total number of passengers

Other information can easily, and often is, gleaned from the carriers and travel agencies[70]:

- Date and method of payment
- Home address
- Telephone numbers, e-mail addresses
- Frequent flyer status
- Hotel and rental car information
- Seating and meal preference

Canada, for example, keeps this information for six years. Other countries' retention rules are not specified, nor are any rules specified about controlling access to this information, verifying its accuracy, limiting the use of this information after arrival, etc. No limitations (selling, disclosing, retaining) are placed on the airlines and others who collect and transmit this information. In the United States, this information is transmitted electronically before departure and prior to arrival, and may be shared among multiple government agencies. No mention is made of security requirements during transmission or sharing. Whatever happened to the tried and true security engineering principle of "need-to-know?" Privacy impact assessments have been waived for "national security" reasons. No distinctions are made between citizens, tourists, and "high risk individuals."

The GLB Act "modernized" the financial services industry by eliminating the barriers between banks, brokerage firms, and insurance companies that were erected in response to the Great Depression of the 1920s and 1930s.[141] Now these other types of financial institutions have to adhere to the same security and privacy regulations as banks.[183] The GLB Act consists of seven titles; most deal with financial issues. Title V specifies privacy requirements for personal financial information. The intent is for financial institutions to think about the security and privacy of customers' nonpublic personal information as a standard part of their broader business practices and regulatory compliance process, instead of just as an afterthought. The Federal Trade Commission, Federal Reserve Bank, Office of Thrift Supervision, Office of the Comptroller of the Currency, National Credit Union Administration, Securities and Exchange Commission, Commodities and Futures Traders Commission, and state insurance authorities are responsible for enforcing the GLB Act. Each of the above agencies codified the GLB Act through a separate Security Rule and Privacy Rule; the Act applies to the industries regulated by these agencies.

The GLB Act requires the financial services industry to exercise due diligence when protecting the security and privacy of individuals' nonpublic personal information — yet identity theft cases abound. Identity theft would imply that due diligence was not practiced. So why are these cases not being prosecuted? It stands to reason that if a few cases were prosecuted and stiff fines imposed, identity theft would cease. The thefts to date have used very low-tech methods. Robust enforcement and stiff fines, which are turned over to the victims, would bring a quick end to this situation. On the contrary, the exact opposite happened in a recently publicized case where 40 million MasterCard records were stolen. Instead of prosecuting the offending company, the FBI told MasterCard not to inform its customers.[247] After two weeks, MasterCard and Visa both stepped up to the plate anyway. All major credit card companies canceled their contracts with Card Systems Solutions Inc. because they violated the Payment Card Industry Data Security Standard. Without robust enforcement of the GLB Act, this situation will be repeated. As Dan Clements points out, merchants and individuals bear the cost of identity theft, not the credit card companies — they charge for reversing unauthorized charges![247] Senator Feinstein; Orson Swindle, Chairman of the Federal Trade

Commission; and others favor adding a liability clause to the GLB Act to "encourage" stronger compliance with the due diligence clause.

The Corporate and Auditing Accountability, Responsibility, and Transparency Act, known as the Sarbanes-Oxley Act, was enacted on 23 January 2002. This Act was in response to the stream of corporate meltdowns that resulted from extremely creative accounting practices at places such as Enron, World-Com, and Tyco, just to name a few. The Sarbanes-Oxley Act has been likened to the "most significant law affecting public companies and public accounting firms since the passage of the Securities and Exchange Commission Act of 1934,"[151] which was enacted in response to the stock market crash that precipitated the worldwide Great Depression of 1929–1934. The Securities and Exchange Commission was tasked with the responsibility of codifying the Act in the Code of Federal Regulations (CFR). The provisions of the Act apply to any public corporation or organization that is required to file annual reports to the U.S. Securities and Exchange Commission. In a survey of 217 companies with average annual revenues of $5 billion, the average one-time start-up cost of compliance was $4.26 million[171, 244] — or 0.0872 percent of the annual revenue. The annual cost to maintain compliance was considerably less. The Sarbanes-Oxley Act mandates adequate internal controls to ensure the accuracy and reliability of the IT systems and operational procedures used to generate financial reports; this means ensuring data, information, systems, and network integrity.

The Health Insurance Portability and Accountability Act, known as HIPAA, was passed by Congress in August 1996. There were concerns about an individual having the right to transfer medical insurance from one employer to another and continue medical insurance after ending employment with a given employer, while at the same time protecting the privacy of medical records as they were being transferred among physicians, hospitals, clinics, pharmacies, and insurance companies. HIPAA was codified by the Department of Health and Human Services (HHS) by amending 45 CFR Parts 160, 162, and 164. Two separate rules were issued: (1) the Security Standards Final Rule[81] and (2) the Standards for the Privacy of Individually Identifiable Health Information Final Rule.[82] The Security Rule mandates a combination of administrative, physical, and technical security safeguards. HIPAA provisions represent mostly common-sense best practices that the healthcare industry should be doing already.[206] HIPAA applies to the healthcare industry across the board[81]:

- Medical health plans
- Healthcare providers (physicians, clinics, hospitals, pharmacies)
- Healthcare clearinghouses (organizations that process and maintain medical records)

The Personal Health Information Act became part of the statutes of Canada on 28 June 1997. Each Provincial legislature subsequently passed the bill and it took effect at the end of 1997. Six specific purposes or objectives are stated for the Act[61]:

1. To provide individuals with a right to examine and receive a copy of personal health information about themselves maintained by a trustee, subject to the limited and specific exceptions set out in this Act
2. To provide individuals with a right to request corrections to personal health information about themselves maintained by a trustee
3. To control the manner in which trustees may collect personal health information
4. To protect individuals against the unauthorized use, disclosure, or destruction of personal health information by trustees
5. To control the collection, use, and disclosure of an individual's personal health identification number
6. To provide for an independent review of the decisions of trustees under this Act

The scope of the Personal Health Information Act encompasses almost anything related to biological or mental health, such as diagnostic, preventive, and therapeutic care, services, or procedures, including prescription drugs, devices, and equipment. Non-prescription items are not included. Personal health information includes any recorded information about an individual's health, healthcare history, genetic information, healthcare services provided, or payment method and history. Trustees are required to implement "reasonable" administrative, technical, and physical security safeguards to protect personal health information. In addition, the safeguards are to be in proportion to the sensitivity of the information being protected.

The OECD had the foresight to see the need for security and privacy regulations almost two decades before most organizations or individuals were aware of the dark side of the digital age. Three pioneering sets of guidelines, and supporting documentation, issued by the OECD laid the groundwork in this area:

1. OECD Guidelines on the Protection of Privacy and Trans-border Flows of Personal Data, 23 September 1980
2. OECD Guidelines for Cryptography Policy, 1997
3. OECD Guidelines for the Security of Information Systems and Networks: Towards a Culture of Security, 25 July 2002

The OECD Privacy Guidelines have been in effect for 25 years. In 1998, the OECD released a Ministerial Declaration reaffirming the importance of the Privacy Guidelines and encouraged Member States to make progress within two years on protecting personal information on global networks.[71c] The OECD Privacy Guidelines apply to any personal data that is in the public or private sectors for which manual or automated processing or the nature of the intended use presents a potential "danger to the privacy of individual liberties."[69] The Guidelines are presented in eight principles:

1. Collection Limitation Principle
2. Data Quality Principle

3. Purpose Specification Principle
4. Use Limitation Principle
5. Security Safeguards Principle
6. Openness Principle
7. Individual Participation Principle
8. Accountability Principle

The OECD Cryptography Guidelines were issued in 1997, some 17 years after the Privacy Guidelines. The Guidelines are applicable to both the public and private sectors, except in situations where national security is a concern. Like the Privacy Guidelines, the Cryptography Guidelines are organized around eight principles that form an interdependent set:

1. Trust in Cryptographic Methods
2. Choice of Cryptographic Methods
3. Market Driven Development of Cryptographic Methods
4. Standards for Cryptographic Methods
5. Protection of Privacy of Personal Data
6. Lawful Access
7. Liability
8. International Cooperation

The OECD Guidelines for the Security of Information Systems and Networks were issued on 25 July 2002. The Guidelines, subtitled "Toward a Culture of Security," replaced the 1992 OECD Guidelines for the Security of Information Systems. The purpose of the Security Guidelines is to promote proactive, preventive security measures, versus reactive ones. The Guidelines emphasize the importance of security engineering activities early in the system engineering life cycle. In particular, attention focuses on specifying security requirements and the design and development of secure systems and networks. This is an intentional shift from the old way of viewing information security as an afterthought during the operational phase. The Guidelines apply to all levels of government, industry, non-profit organizations, and individuals.[68] At the same time, the Guidelines acknowledge that different participants have different security roles and responsibilities. The OECD Security Guidelines are presented as a complementary set of nine principles that address the technical, policy, and operational aspects of information security:

1. Awareness
2. Responsibility
3. Response
4. Ethics
5. Democracy
6. Risk Assessment
7. Security Design and Implementation
8. Security Management
9. Reassessment

Directive 95/46/EC, known as the Data Protection Directive, was issued on 24 October 1995 by the European Parliament and Council. The purpose of the Directive is to protect an individual's personal data and the processing and free movement of this data necessary for economic integration and the flow of goods and services among Member States. Prior to the Directive, Member States had different levels of protection for the rights and freedoms of individuals, notably their right to privacy. As a result, the need for a consistent level of protection was identified, to protect individuals and promote economic integration. At the same time, a uniform provision for judicial remedies, damage compensation, and sanctions was created, should individual privacy rights be violated. The Directive applies to data that is in electronic form online, offline in electromagnetic or electro-optical archives, or in hard-copy form in filing cabinets. Textual, sound, and image data are included within the scope of the Directive if they contain any personally identifiable data. The protections of the Directive apply to individuals residing in any of the Member States. The provisions of the Directive apply to any organization residing within a Member State that collects and processes personal data, not just government agencies. The Directive does not apply to communication between individuals or personal records, such as address books. The Directive also does not apply in cases of criminal investigations, public safety or security, or national defense. The originator of the information is considered the owner of the data, not the organization collecting, processing, storing, or transmitting it, unlike the current situation in the United States.

The Data Protection Act is an example of a national law that was derived from the Data Protection Directive. The Data Protection Act was enacted by the U.K. Parliament on 24 July 1998 and took effect on 24 October 1998. The purpose of the Act is to "make new provision for the regulation of the processing of information relating to individuals, including the obtaining, holding, use or disclosure of such information."[64] Unlike the Directive, the Data Protection Act does not mention any economic reasons for enactment. The scope of the Data Protection Act is equivalent to that of the Directive. The Data Protection Act applies to any personally identifiable data that is in electronic form online, offline in electromagnetic archives, or in hardcopy form in filing cabinets, including textual, sound, and image data. The protections of the Act apply to individuals "ordinarily resident" in the United Kingdom.[64] The provisions of the Act apply to any organization residing within the United Kingdom that collects and processes personal data, not just government agencies. The Act requires that its provisions be extended to third parties with whom the organization that collected data has a contractual relationship regarding processing of that data. Like the Directive, the Act does not apply in cases of criminal investigations, public safety or security, or national defense. The Data Protection Act fills in certain details, like the role of courts in enforcement actions, required time frames to perform certain tasks, and when fees are applicable. These types of items were left out of the Directive because they are unique to each Member State's legal system. A fair amount of detail is provided about the rights of data subjects. The Data

Protection Act expands the scope of risk assessments to include the magnitude of harm the data subject could experience, should the technical or organizational security controls prove inadequate.

Bill C-6, the Personal Information Protection and Electronic Documents Act (PIPEDA), was issued by the Canadian Parliament on 13 April 2000. The Act is intended to protect individuals while at the same time promoting E-commerce. The PIPEDA assigns everything that can be done to or with personal information to three categories of activities: (1) collection, (2) use, and (3) disclosure. Provincial legislatures were given three years from the date of enactment (13 April 2000) to implement the Act within their provinces. Healthcare professionals and organizations were given less time — one year from the date of enactment. The PIPEDA also established the federal office of Privacy Commissioner, who is tasked with receiving, investigating, and resolving reports of noncompliance. The PIPEDA applies to any organization that collects, uses, or discloses personal information, whether for a commercial activity, government-related work, or for employment purposes within the legal boundaries of Canada. Personal information that is used by individuals or government agencies covered by the Privacy Act are excluded. Exemptions are also made for journalistic, artistic, or literary purposes; however, it seems that it would easy to misuse this exemption for malicious purposes. The PIPEDA rearranged the OECD privacy principles in order of priority and dependency. The PIPEDA also expanded the eight principles from the OECD Privacy Guidelines into ten principles and augmented them. The OECD Use Limitation principle was expanded to include disclosure and retention and renamed accordingly. Obtaining consent from individuals, before collecting, using, or disclosing their personal information, was broken out as a separate principle to emphasize the importance of this activity. Likewise, the right of individuals to challenge an organization's compliance with any provision of the PIPEDA was made into a new principle, separate from their right of access, to reinforce the fact that individuals are an active participant in this process.

The Privacy Act was originally issued in 1974 as Public Law 93-579 and codified in the United States Code at 5 U.S.C. 552a. Today, the bill is referred to as the Privacy Act of 1974 (As Amended). The preamble to the Act is worth noting; it describes the challenge of privacy for electronic records head-on[108]:

- The privacy of an individual is directly affected by the collection, maintenance, use, and dissemination of personal information by federal agencies.
- The increasing use of computers and sophisticated information technology, while essential to the efficient operations of the government, has greatly magnified the harm to individual privacy that can occur from any collection, maintenance, use, or dissemination of personal information.
- The opportunities for an individual to secure employment, insurance, and credit, and his right to due process and other legal protections are endangered by the misuse of certain information systems.
- The right to privacy is a personal and fundamental right protected by the Constitution of the United States.

- In order to protect the privacy of individuals identified in information systems maintained by federal agencies, it is necessary and proper for the Congress to regulate the collection, maintenance, use, and dissemination of information by such agencies.

The Privacy Act acknowledges the potential harm that can result from misuse of private personal data. However, the Act is limited to protecting private personal information that is collected and disseminated by federal agencies, as can be seen from its stated purpose[108]:

- Permit an individual to determine what records pertaining to him are collected, maintained, used, or disseminated by such agencies.
- Permit an individual to prevent records pertaining to him obtained by such agencies for a particular purpose from being used or made available for another purpose without his consent.
- Permit an individual to gain access to information pertaining to him in federal agency records, to have a copy made of all or any portion thereof, and to correct or amend such records.
- Collect, maintain, use, or disseminate any record of identifiable personal information in a manner that assures that such action is for a necessary and lawful purpose, that the information is current and accurate for its intended use, and that adequate safeguards are provided to prevent misuse of such information.
- Permit exemptions from such requirements with respect to records provided in this Act only in those cases where there is an important public policy need for such exemptions as has been determined by specific statutory authority.
- Be subject to civil suit for any damages that occur as a result of willful or intentional action which violates any individual's rights under this Act.

Title III of the E-Government Act is known as the Federal Information Security Management Act, or FISMA. This is not the first attempt to legislate adequate security protections for unclassified information systems and networks operated by and for the U.S. Government. FISMA is limited to IT security. IT security cannot be achieved in a vacuum. There are many interdependencies among physical, personnel, IT, and operational security. If the scope of FISMA was that of a Chief Security Officer, not a Chief Information Security Officer, federal agencies would be in a better position to accomplish real reform. The inherent conflicts in FISMA are already apparent just from reading the list of stated purposes on the first page of the bill: (1) trying to manage information security government-wide, while at the same time letting individual agencies make their own decisions; (2) trying to promote specific controls, while promoting the use of commercial security solutions; and (3) coordinating information security efforts among the civilian, national security, and law enforcement agencies, which has always been a *non sequitur*. FISMA is currently funded through fiscal year 2007. FISMA assigns roles and responsibilities for information security to the Director of the Office of Management and Budget (OMB), civilian federal agencies, the Federal Information Security Incident Center, and the National Institute of Standards and Technology (NIST). The Director of the OMB has the primary role and responsibility for overseeing the implementation and effectiveness of information security in the civilian federal agencies. Federal agencies are responsible for developing, documenting, implementing, and verifying an agency-wide information security program. Federal agencies are to ensure compliance with information security policies, procedures, and standards. A major responsibility in this area is to ensure that information security management processes are integrated with the agency's strategic and operational planning processes. The OMB provides direction to federal agencies about what information to include in their quarterly and annual FISMA reports and how to present it. The emphasis is on quantitative information. The intent is to standardize the information across agencies so that comparisons can be made among agencies and from one year to the next for a single agency. The annual report submitted by each agency focuses on whether or not the agency is performing the activities required by FISMA. The questions do not evaluate whether an agency is being proactive in its approach to information security, nor do they address a fundamental issue — getting the security requirements right as the first step in the security engineering life cycle and designing security into systems and networks from the get-go. The annual report required by the Inspector General of each agency accompanies that prepared by the agency. Some of the questions seek to validate the information in the agency report; other questions ask the Inspector General to evaluate how well an agency is performing certain activities. The Inspector General metrics lack an overall assessment of the agency's security engineering life cycle and practices. They also do not evaluate personnel resources. Does the agency have the right number and right skill level of people assigned to perform information security engineering tasks? If people do not have the appropriate education and experience, they will not be able to specify, design, develop, test, operate, or maintain secure systems and networks or perform ST&E, C&A, and other FISMA functions correctly. During 2005, the OMB directed each agency and department to appoint a Chief Privacy Officer. As part of the annual FISMA reports, the Chief Privacy Officer is to report on the status of complying with privacy laws and regulations in his agency. Agencies are also required to submit a quarterly report of metrics highlighting progress in performing corrective action. The focus is on resolving weaknesses that were identified during security certification and accreditation, internal audits, external audits, or from other sources. Greater insight would be gained if the weaknesses were reported by severity categories and the length of time the weaknesses remained open prior to resolution.

Homeland Security Presidential Directives (or HSPDs) were initiated in October 2001. HSPDs are similar to Executive Orders (EOs), Presidential Decision Directives (PDDs), and other mechanisms the Executive Branch of the U.S. Government uses to push the policies, procedures, and practices of the federal agencies in a certain direction. HSPDs are one tool that the U.S. President uses to accomplish this task. HSPDs and the like do not carry the weight or authority of a law or statute, rather they represent policy, similar to a memo from your third-level boss. HSPDs and other directives often repeat provisions from a law or statute, with a fair amount of philosophy thrown in for good measure. Why do non-government organizations and individuals need to pay attention to HSPDs? Because the scope of the directives often goes well beyond government agencies and employees, and includes government contractors, state and local agencies, and private-sector institutions, particularly when critical infrastructure is involved. At the time of writing, 12 HSPDs had been issued:

HSPD-1   Organization and Operation of the Homeland Security Council
HSPD-2   Combating Terrorism through Immigration Policies
HSPD-3   Homeland Security Advisory System
HSPD-4   National Strategy to Combat Weapons of Mass Destruction
HSPD-5   Management of Domestic Incidents
HSPD-6   Integration and Use of Screening Information
HSPD-7   Critical Infrastructure Identification, Prioritization, and Protection
HSPD-8   National Preparedness
HSPD-9   Defense of United States Agriculture and Food
HSPD-10   Biodefense in the 21st Century
HSPD-11   Comprehensive Terrorist-Related Screening Procedures
HSPD-12   Policy for a Common Identification Standard for Federal Employees and Contractors

The North American Electrical Reliability Council (NERC), with encouragement from the Department of Energy and the Department of Homeland Security, developed and issued a series of eight cyber security standards, partly in response to the cascading failure of the power grid in the Northeast on 14 August 2004.[170] The set of cyber security standards was developed and issued for a straightforward purpose[39]:

> *...to ensure that all entities responsible for the reliability of the bulk electric systems of North America identify and protect critical cyber assets that control or could impact the reliability of the bulk electric systems.*

The eight NERC cyber security standards are:

CIP-002-1   Cyber Security — Critical Cyber Assets
CIP-003-1   Cyber Security — Security Management Controls
CIP-004-1   Cyber Security — Personnel and Training
CIP-005-1   Cyber Security — Electronic Security
CIP-006-1   Cyber Security — Physical Security
CIP-007-1   Cyber Security — Systems Security Management
CIP-008-1   Cyber Security — Incident Reporting and Response Planning
CIP-009-1   Cyber Security — Recovery Plan

The NERC cyber security standards took effect in June 2006. At the same time, the NERC Reliability Functional Model will be put into effect. The NERC Compliance Enforcement Program, through ten regional reliability compliance programs, will begin assessing compliance against the new cyber security standards in 2007. The NERC standards cover the full scope of physical, personnel, IT, and operational security in an integrated, comprehensive, and efficient manner. The NERC cyber security standards are applicable to all nine types of functional entities. They are not applicable to nuclear facilities, which are regulated by the Canadian Nuclear Safety Commission and the U.S. Nuclear Regulatory Commission. The NERC cyber security standards are expressed in a uniform, no-nonsense style without the superfluous text or philosophy found in most government regulations. Any considerations that must be taken into account for regional differences, or differences in entity types or attended versus unattended facilities, are noted in the standards. Because the NERC cyber security standards cover a broad range of functional entities and organizations of varying size and geographical distribution, they should be considered a minimum set of security requirements.[265] Reality may necessitate that a given organization deploy more robust security practices.[265] There are three key components to each standard:

1. Requirements, numbered R_x, which say what to do
2. Measures, numbered M_x, which explain how to perform the requirement and assemble the proof that it was indeed achieved
3. Compliance, which describes how to independently verify that each R_x and M_x were accomplished and completed correctly

There is a direct mapping between the requirements (R_x) and measures (M_x). Compliance activities are described in terms of a compliance monitoring process, compliance monitoring responsibilities, the compliance monitoring period and reset time frame, data retention requirements, additional compliance information, and levels of noncompliance. Each of the standards defines four levels of noncompliance. Level 1 indicates that a functional entity is almost compliant, but missing a few small items. Level 2 indicates that a functional entity is making progress, but has only completed about half of the requirements. Level 3 indicates that a functional entity has started the required activities, but still has a long way to go. Level 4, the lowest level of noncompliance, indicates that for all practical purposes, no effort has been undertaken to comply with the standard. The NERC cyber security standards are probably one of the most comprehensive sets of security standards in existence today. Unlike other standards that only address IT security, information security during system development, or C&A, these standards encompass the full spectrum of physical, personnel, IT, and operational security in a practical, logical, and well-thought-out manner. The NERC cyber security standards realize that not all security incidents are cyber in origin — there are also physical security incidents and a combination of both. The need for ST&E and security impact analyses to consider hardware, software, *and* the operational environment, and the concept that ST&E goes way beyond traditional functional, performance, integration, and acceptance testing is highlighted. Differences in logical and physical security perimeters and the unique techniques to protect each are acknowledged. The NERC cyber security standards promote the role of change control and configuration management as an integral part of an effective security management program, like having security awareness and training activities that are tailored for specific locations and job functions. The NERC cyber security standards can easily be adapted for use in other industrial sectors and most definitely should be.

The Patriot Act, Public Law 107-56, was approved by Congress on 24 October 2001 and signed into law by the President two days later. The purpose of the Patriot Act is to ensure (1) the physical security of public and private U.S. assets at home and abroad, and (2) the integrity of financial systems within the United States. Thirty-six percent of the total pages in the Patriot Act are devoted to preventing, intercepting, and prosecuting financial crimes. The Patriot Act is organized in ten titles:

   I — Enhancing Domestic Security against Terrorism
   II — Enhanced Surveillance
   III — International Money Laundering Abatement and Anti-Terrorist Financing
   IV — Protecting the Border
   V — Removing Obstacles to Investigating Terrorism
   VI — Providing for Victims of Terrorism, Public Safety Officers, and Their Families
   VII — Increased Information Sharing for Critical Infrastructure Protection
   VIII — Strengthening Criminal Laws against Terrorism
   IX — Improved Intelligence
   X — Miscellaneous

More than 20 major bills are amended by the Patriot Act. The Patriot Act represents a paradigm shift from the Cold War to the War on Terrorism. The sweep of the bill is not limited to suicide bombers; rather, it encompasses all forms of terrorism that could disrupt the physical security, economic security, and social stability of the United States. State and local governments are equal partners with the federal government in the War on Terrorism. Title I, Enhancing Domestic Security against Terrorism, established a "Counterterrorism Fund," increased funding for the FBI Technical Support Center, and tasked the Secret Service with developing a national network of electronic crime task forces to prevent, detect, and investigate electronic crimes against financial institutions and critical infrastructures. Title II, Enhanced Surveillance Procedures, for the most part amends existing bills to remove constraints and limitations on electronic surveillance within the borders of the United States. Title II is the most controversial title in the Patriot Act because of concerns about the potential to violate the civil and privacy rights of American citizens. Here we see an inherent conflict between the approach to enhanced physical security for the public at large and individual privacy rights. Title III, International Money Laundering Abatement and Anti-Terrorist Financing Act of 2001, is by far the longest title in the Patriot Act. So why does money laundering receive such attention in a bill to fight terrorism? Congress is attempting to draw the connection between drug trafficking and terrorist groups — the so-called "narco-terrorists" and the use of profits from drug sales to finance terrorist organizations. At the same time, there is concern about the extent of money laundering worldwide and the potential impact on the stability and integrity of financial institutions in the United States. Title IV, Protecting the Border, tightens many loopholes in immigration laws relating tourists, foreign students, and other temporary visitors. Title V, Removing Obstacles to Investigating Terrorism, lifts various restraints on investigations and provides incentives for cooperating with investigators. Title IX, Improved Intelligence, anticipated the 9/11 Commission Report and encouraged further cooperation between the FBI and CIA, particularly in the areas of joint tracking of foreign assets and sponsorship of a national virtual translation center.

Private-sector and non-profit organizations need to be aware of their roles and responsibilities under the Patriot Act for several reasons:

- To ensure complete compliance with the Act, no more and no less
- To ensure that information is not disclosed to unauthorized sources or in unauthorized situations
- To ensure that the volume and extent of information disclosed is neither too much, nor too little
- To ensure that all requests received for information or other forms of cooperation are legitimate under the Act and backed up with the appropriate signed and authorized documentation
- To protect the vital interests of the organization from potential lawsuits, fines, or other negative publicity resulting from some misstep related to the first four bullets

Much concern has been expressed about the potential for misusing the provisions in the Patriot Act and the abuses of individual civil and privacy rights that could result due to its invasive nature. From the beginning, Congress was aware of the prospect of something going wrong — an overzealous investigator, an unethical government employee, a data entry error. So they built in some protections for individuals, such as the ability to file suit over unwarranted electronic surveillance, contest confiscation of property that was seized under the Patriot Act, file suit against a former employer (an insured financial institution) who supplied a derogatory employment reference concerning potentially unlawful activities with malicious intent, seek legal remedies for harassment for exercising First Amendment rights, and to file complaints with the Inspector General of the Department of Justice about abuses related to the Patriot Act.

Compliance metrics measure whether or not or how often some activity was performed. For the most part, compliance metrics are process metrics. They are important, but inadequate by themselves because they do not indicate how well or how thoroughly an activity was performed; nor do they measure the robustness or integrity of a security feature, function, or architecture. Many of the 13 security and privacy regulations discussed make the statement that the physical, personnel, IT, and operational security controls should be commensurate with the sensitivity of the information and the harm that could result from unauthorized access, use, disclosure, alteration, destruction, or retention. In addition, physical, personnel, IT, and operational security controls are to be tailored based on the complexity, nature, and scope of an organization's activities.

Compliance metrics alone cannot answer whether or not either of these two requirements have been met. That is why a comprehensive security and privacy metrics program includes metrics that measure the resilience of physical, personnel, IT, and operational security controls, which are presented next in Chapter 4.

3.16 Discussion Problems

1. How many of the security and privacy regulations were you aware of before you read this chapter? Now that you are familiar with them, how many apply to your organization?
2. Why are security and privacy regulations needed?
3. The importance of defining good metrics and using valid primitives has been discussed several times. In this hypothetical question, you are asked to apply your understanding of these principles. Suppose you are asked to measure how ethical a group of people is. Do you count how many times per day they prayed or did other good deeds, or do you measure how many times per day they sinned? Why?
4. Explain how the legal definition of breach of privacy relates to (a) IT security, and (b) operational security.
5. Describe a scenario is which personal information that (a) was collected in a legitimate manner, (b) was accurate at the time of collection, and (c) is only being used for the prestated purpose, would need to be updated? What is the correct way to do this per the OECD Guidelines, the U.K. Data Protection Act, the Canadian PIPEDA, and the U.S. Privacy Act? Note the similarities and differences in the regulations.
6. Why is a privacy impact analysis needed? When should it be performed?
7. Give examples of public and nonpublic information for different scenarios. Describe the similarities and differences among the regulations in their use of these terms.
8. What IT equipment is missing from the list provided in the scope for the Payment Card Industry Data Security Standard? What people organizations are missing? How serious are these oversights?
9. How do the internal controls required by the Sarbanes-Oxley Act relate to data integrity? How often are these internal controls assessed, and what is done with the assessment results?
10. Which of the security and privacy regulations has the most severe fines and penalties for violations? Why do you think this situation exists?
11. Describe the similarities and differences in measures used to control use versus control disclosure of nonpublic information. What factors determine how strong the controls must be?
12. What factors should an organization take into account when tailoring security requirements? Note any differences in the regulations.
13. Which regulations do and do not specify personnel security requirements? For the regulations that do not specify personnel security requirements, does that create a potential vulnerability?

14. Which regulations do and do not require that a person be designated to be accountable for implementing security and privacy requirements? What are the potential consequences of not designating such a person?

15. HIPAA security requirements are defined as being required or addressable. Select an addressable requirement and describe a situation in which (a) the requirement is not applicable and provide the rationale for not implementing it; (b) the requirement can be satisfied through an alternate strategy and provide the rationale for doing so; and (c) the requirement is applicable, but a more robust implementation is needed.

16. Compare the GLB and HIPAA privacy requirements with those contained in the OECD Privacy Guidelines.

17. Which regulations require consent from an individual before nonpublic information can be disclosed? What happens if it is not possible to obtain that consent?

18. The United States is a member of the OECD. What is needed to make the Privacy Act consistent with the OECD Privacy Guidelines?

19. How does the role of the Privacy Officer, as created by the OMB Memo of 11 February 2005, compare with the Supervisory Authority and Data Protection Commissioner?

20. What metrics can be used to determine if the roles and responsibilities of the Supervisory Authority, Data Privacy Commissioner, and Privacy Officer are being performed appropriately?

21. What are the benefits of using compliance metrics? What are the limitations of compliance metrics?

22. Compare the structure of the NERC Cyber Security Standards and the Payment Card Industry Data Security Standard.

23. What do non-government organizations need to know about the Homeland Security Presidential Directives?

24. How do physical security, personnel security, IT security, and operational security relate to the Patriot Act?

25. Is it necessary to have a trade-off between personal privacy of individuals and physical security of the public at large? Explain your reasoning.

Chapter 4

Measuring Resilience of Physical, Personnel, IT, and Operational Security Controls

---

The news finally arrived in August [1839], and came from Amyot, the Baron's assistant. No, the Czar [Nicholas I] had decided, no telegraph. It troubled him, Amyot explained, that electrical communication might easily be interrupted by acts of malevolence.

—**Kenneth Silverman**
Lightning Man: The Accursed Life of Samuel F.B. Morse
Knopf, 2003, p. 194

4.1 Introduction

In 1839, Samuel Morse went on an international marketing spree in an attempt to sell his latest invention, the electrical telegraph. Like any shrewd marketeer, he extolled the virtues of his design and pointed out the many weaknesses and limitations of his competitors. He made a point of visiting the leading European courts and scientific communities, seeking collaborators and funding, as a precursor to the lucrative government contracts of today. One such prospect was Czar Nicholas I. After a lengthy period of consideration, the czar turned him down. Why? Because the czar correctly surmised that electrical forms of communication were subject to disruption by "malevolent acts" and hence could be unreliable and insecure. While this fact is common knowledge today, it was a rather insightful observation in 1839 given that no form of electrical communication had been deployed anywhere in the world. The telephone had not yet been invented. Computers, the Internet, and wireless networks were more than 100 years in the future. The czar based his decision on deductive logic. In contrast, the other European powers declined Morse's offer due to a desire to keep their indigenous scientists and engineers employed, in a foreshadowing of future trade wars. In the end, this uppity Yankee conducted his proof-of-concept demonstration and pilot tests at home in the United States, with a little help from Congress. The rest is history.

These "acts of malevolence" that troubled the czar are still with us. Some attack methods are the same today as those envisioned by the czar: cable cuts, damaging or stealing equipment, and burning down buildings. Other attack methods evolved over the decades and are more tightly coupled to the technology of the target under attack, such as jamming, masquerading, man-in-the-middle attacks, and eavesdropping. In essence, physical and personnel security threats are pretty much the same as then, while IT and operational security threats have spawned whole new genres of attack methods. Measuring the resilience of security controls and their ability to prevent, preempt, delay, mitigate, and contain these attacks is what this chapter is all about.

The security solutions an organization deploys — whether physical, personnel, IT, or operational security — are or should be in response to specific threats. Countermeasures are or should be proportional to the likelihood of a specific threat or combination of threats being instantiated and the worst-case consequences should this occur. Nearly all the standards and regulations discussed in Chapter 3 state the requirement to deploy security controls that are commensurate with the risk. There are standardized methods by which to assess risk. However, unless the resilience of the security controls is measured, there is no factual basis on which to make the claim that the security controls are indeed commensurate with risk. Likewise, it is not possible to determine the return on investment (ROI) in physical, personnel, IT, and operational security controls unless their resilience has been measured against the risk — and hence the need for resilience metrics.

Resilience is defined as:

> **Resilience:** the capability of an IT infrastructure, including physical, personnel, IT, and operational security controls, to maintain essential services and protect critical assets while preempting and repelling attacks and minimizing the extent of corruption and compromise.

Resilience is not a Boolean or yes/no function: a system or network is or is not secure. Rather, security is a continuum. That is why metrics are needed to determine where the organization falls on this continuous scale. (See Figure 4.1.) Resilience does not imply that something is free from vulnerabilities. Rather, resilience emphasizes how well vulnerabilities are managed and attempts to exploit them are thwarted. By the same token, a person's character is not measured when everything is rosy and going his way. Instead, strength of character is measured by how well a person responds to the challenges,

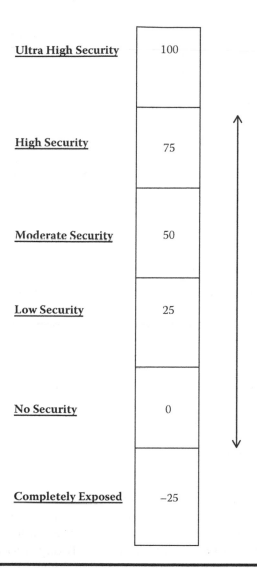

Figure 4.1 Security as a continuum.

hurdles, and upsets that life throws his way. The parallels in telecommunications engineering are error detection and correction protocols. The parallel in software engineering is error handling routines. Resilience can be measured for a single mechanism, a cluster of mechanisms, a system, network, or the enterprise security architecture. Resilience can be measured for physical, personnel, IT, and operational security controls, individually or in any combination. Resilience metrics highlight how strong or weak a given security control is. This information is compared against the operational risk to determine acceptability or the need for further work and resources. Often, it is useful to compare the resilience of different types of security controls. Perhaps it is cheaper and just as or more effective to mitigate a given vulnerability with an operational security control than an IT security control, or with a physical security control than an operational security control, etc. These comparisons can be quite enlightening and cost effective.

Resilience metrics provide the factual basis necessary to answer the two basic recurring questions every Chief Security Officer (CSO) and Information Security Manager (ISM) ask themselves:

1. How secure is the organization?
2. How secure do we need to be?

The intent is to ensure that an effective and complementary set of physical, personnel, IT, and operational security controls are implemented, so that there are no gaps or overlapping features and assets are not over- or under-protected. Hence, the GQM for Chapter 4 is:

GQM for Chapter 4

G: Ensure that all assets are neither over- nor under-protected.
Q: Are all logical and physical assets protected consistent with the assessed risk for their operational environment and use?
M: See resilience metrics defined in Chapter 4 for physical, personnel, IT, and operational security controls.

4.2 Physical Security

Physical security is perhaps the most well known of the four types of security controls. People can easily grasp the concept of physical security, especially when talking about the physical security of their persons and their property. Not long ago, some people were questioning the value of physical security in the advent of the global information grid. Today, those views are in the minority. Current events throughout the world have reminded us all of the importance of physical security. Physical security is a key component of contingency and disaster recovery planning and preparedness, as well as day-to-day operations. While basic physical security measures such as locks, guards, and fences are generally understood, the more subtle and sophisticated techniques are not. As a result, this section explains the goal, purpose, tools, and techniques for achieving and assessing the effectiveness of physical security controls.

Physical security has its own set of terms, like any other discipline. These terms are often misused by the non-specialist. So the best place to start to understand physical security is with the underlying concepts and terms.

> **Physical security:** protection of hardware, software, and data against physical threats, to reduce or prevent disruptions to operations and services and loss of assets.[156]

> **Physical safeguards:** physical measures, policies, and procedures to protect a covered entity's electronic information systems and related buildings and equipment from natural and environmental hazards, and unauthorized intrusion.[60, 80]

The underlying goal of physical security is to protect assets from physical threats, such as theft, tampering, disruption, destruction, and misappropriation. The physical threats from which assets need protection can be accidental or intentional, natural, man-made, or a combination of both. Physical threats can occur as the result of specific action or inaction. Physical security controls include tools, techniques, devices, and operational procedures to prevent unauthorized access, damage, and interference to an organization's premises and information.[28]

> **Loss:** any reasonable cost to any victim, including the cost of responding to an offense, conducting a damage assessment, and restoring the data, program, system, or information to its condition prior to the offense, and any revenue lost, cost incurred, or other consequential damages incurred because of interruption of service.[104]

> **Damage:** (*Black's Law Dictionary®*)loss, injury, or deterioration caused by the negligence, design, or accident of one person to another, in respect of the latter's person or property.

Physical security controls seek to protect against loss and damage. The notion of loss includes the total cost of the loss and the total cost of the impact of the loss, both short-term and long-term. The loss or damage can be experienced by an individual or a collection of people or a legal entity, such as an organization, company, city, government, etc. Damage can take many forms[16]:

- Causing a violation of law or regulations
- Impairing an organization's performance or mission
- Causing the loss of goodwill or having a negative effect on an organization's reputation
- Causing a breach of privacy (commercial or personal)
- Endangering personal safety
- Precipitating a loss of public order
- Triggering a financial loss, directly or indirectly, by affecting assets or revenue
- Endangering environmental safety

> **Asset:** something of importance or value and can include one or more of the following types of elements: (a) human — the human aspect of an asset includes both employees to be protected and the personnel who may present an insider threat, (b) physical — the physical aspect may include both tangible property and the intangible, e.g., information.[98]

> **Criticality:** the relative importance of an asset to performing or achiev-
> ing an organization's mission.

The purpose of physical security controls is to protect assets. People, of course, are any organization's chief asset. Few would dispute that the intrinsic value of human life is far above that of any other asset. Also, most organizations would find it impossible to accomplish their mission without their current skilled workforce.[116] A few temporary workers could be hired in the short-run, but it is not possible to re-staff an entire operation with new people. The corporate history is gone — the knowledge of the people, the organiza-tion, what work needs to be done, how and when to do it, who does what, and all the associated idiosyncrasies of the operation and its stakeholders. In addition, a combination of tangible and intangible assets need protection for a variety of different reasons. Some assets are more important than others, and hence require more robust protection; this aspect is referred to as *asset criticality*. Asset criticality can change over time and depends on one's per-spective and role. That is why it is crucial to (1) have all stakeholders involved in determining asset criticality, and (2) reassess asset criticality on a regular basis. There are three standard categories of asset criticality, as shown below. Note that these definitions correlate to an asset's criticality to achieving or performing the organization's mission.

1. **Critical:** systems, functions, services, and information that, if lost, would *prevent* the capability to perform the organization's mission and achieve the organization's business goals.
2. **Essential:** systems, functions, services, and information that, if lost, would *reduce* the capability to perform the organization's mission and achieve the organization's business goals.
3. **Routine:** systems, functions, services, or information that, if lost, would *not significantly degrade* the capability to perform the organization's mis-sion and achieve the organization's business goals.

> **Critical asset:** those facilities, systems, and equipment, which if destroyed, damaged, degraded, or otherwise rendered unavailable, would affect the reliability or operability of the … system.[31-38]

> **Key asset:** individual targets whose destruction could cause injury, death, or destruction of property, and/or profoundly damage national prestige and confidence.[98]

Here we see the link between physical security and critical infrastructure protection. The ramifications of losing a critical asset may go beyond the immediate organization and impact a larger group of organizations and people. That is why physical security is a key component of critical infrastructure protection, and physical security was given so much attention in the Patriot Act and several Homeland Security Presidential Directives (HSPDs), as dis-cussed in Chapter 3.

Physical security is one of four security domains; the other three are personnel security, IT security, and operational security. Is physical security the most important security domain? No. Is physical security the least important security domain? No. None of the four security domains is more important or less important than the others. All four security domains are equally essential to achieving, sustaining, and assessing enterprisewide security. This is true because there are many interdependencies between the four security domains. To illustrate, consider the definition of a computer security contingency:

> **Computer security contingency:** an event with the potential to disrupt computer operations, thereby disrupting critical mission and business functions, for example, a power outage, hardware failure, fire, or storm. If the event is very destructive, it is often called a disaster.[80]

Notice that the definition refers to "an event" — not an IT or cyber-security event, but rather any event that can disrupt operations. Why is this event noteworthy? Because of its potential to affect the ability of an organization to achieve its mission. Several examples of events are given: a power outage, a hardware failure, a fire, or a storm. The power outage, fire, and storm are types of physical security threats whose root cause could be natural, man-made, or a combination of the two. The hardware failure could be the result of inadequate reliability engineering in regard to availability (IT security), poor maintenance (operational security), or deliberate tampering (personnel and physical security). That is, the symptom is a failure of IT equipment. However, the source of the failure could be any of the four security domains. Consequently, it does not make sense to expend all your money and resources on IT security to the neglect of the other three security domains. Attackers will take the time to find and then attack the weakest link or the path of least resistance in your security posture. Mother Nature also has the uncanny knack of finding this weakest link — remember the Titanic? Likewise, it does not make sense to distribute the responsibility, authority, and accountability for physical, personnel, IT, and operational security to different warring fiefdoms within an organization that (1) do not even talk to (or in some cases acknowledge) each other, and (2) compete for funding. This approach is a certain recipe for (man-made) disasters. All hazards preparedness is not intended to precipitate all-out intra-organizational warfare. Rather, it is essential to have ongoing in-depth communication, coordination, and cooperation in order to design, deploy, operate, and maintain a comprehensive, complementary, and effective set of physical, personnel, IT, and operational security controls enterprisewide.

While physical security is closely intertwined with the other three security domains, its first cousin is physical safety. Physical safety and physical security are not synonymous, but they do seek to accomplish many of the same goals, as is evident from the definition of physical safety:

> **Physical safety:** freedom from those conditions that can cause death, injury, occupational illness, damage to or loss of equipment or property, or damage to the environment. [MIL-STD 882D]

Both physical safety and physical security seek to prevent, eliminate, and mitigate natural and man-made hazards, regardless of whether they are accidental or intentional in origin. Many of the same analysis, design, and verification tools are used by both safety and security engineers. In several industrial sectors, such as civilian aviation, power generation and distribution, and biomedical, the underlying interest in security engineering is due to the recognition that certain types of security incidents could have a significant safety impact.

To highlight the relationship between physical safety and physical security, think about an elevator in a high-rise office building. The physical safety engineering team would be responsible for verifying that:

- The equipment is properly sized to accommodate the anticipated weight and frequency of trips (i.e., the duty cycle).
- The equipment and controls are installed correctly.
- The equipment, including alarm systems, functions correctly under normal and abnormal situations, like emergency stops and starts.
- The passenger control panel, especially the alarm notification system, is easy to understand by all passengers, including the visually challenged.
- The elevator shaft adheres to building and fire safety codes.
- The elevator and shaft are properly vented.
- The elevator master controls, gears, and cables are tamper-proof.
- Routine preventive maintenance is performed correctly and on schedule with first-quality parts.
- Elevator design and operation comply with ANSI, UL, and other applicable safety standards.

These actions are undertaken to ensure that operation of the elevator is free from conditions that could cause death or injury to passengers and operators, damage to equipment and other property transported on the elevator, and damage to the environment as a result of a mechanical or electrical fire in the elevator shaft.

In contrast, the physical security engineering team would be responsible for verifying physical access controls to the elevator, elevator shaft, elevator equipment and control rooms, and the emergency control buttons in the elevator. These activities are undertaken to prevent (1) unauthorized access to restricted parts of the building, and (2) unauthorized access to, operation of, and tampering with the elevator, and its associated equipment and controls. The first physical access control point is the elevator itself. Is use of the elevator open to anyone, or restricted to people with the appropriate credentials or tokens? Can people go directly from the underground parking garage to the upper floors, or must a second elevator be taken from the lobby? Can all passengers exit on all floors, or is access to specific floors controlled by elevator keys? The second physical access control point is the elevator shaft. Who has access to the elevator shaft? By what methods can the elevator shaft be accessed? On television and in the movies, people are frequently climbing out of the elevator and into the elevator shaft for benign and malevolent reasons. How is this activity prevented? The third physical access control point is the elevator equipment and control rooms. Surely these spaces should be off-limits to all except known, trusted authorized personnel. Likewise with the emergency control buttons inside the elevator. Most elevators are equipped with buttons for emergency operation by police or firemen. Physical security controls are needed to prevent tampering with these and other elevator operation buttons and deliberate incorrect operation.

In the introduction, resilience was defined as:

> **Resilience:** the capability of an IT infrastructure, including physical, personnel, IT, and operational security controls, to maintain essential services and protect critical assets while preempting and repelling attacks and minimizing the extent of corruption and compromise.

What does this mean in terms of physical security? The IT infrastructure is able to withstand (prevent, preempt, mitigate, delay, and contain) physical security attacks. The IT infrastructure can keep rolling or bounce back and not miss a beat despite a physical security attack, regardless of the type, timing, time interval, and duration of the attack. Here are a few basic examples:

- In an earthquake-prone region of the world, IT equipment is bolted down, to prevent toppling, and housed in a vibration-proof or vibration-neutralizing chamber.
- In a geographical location prone to fierce windstorms, and hence power outages, facilities are equipped with backup generators.
- In areas where a lot of new construction is going on, facilities are equipped with sensors to immediately detect cable cuts and other loss of telecommunications circuits, and automatically switch to diverse telecommunications paths with no interruption of service.
- Organizations with highly sensitive operations house IT equipment in facilities that are fire, water, and explosion proof.
- Design extremely sensitive equipment to be tamper-proof. Generate audible and visible alarms if tampering is attempted; in addition, have devices that zero-out memory or self-destruct.

Resilience is not a Boolean function, such that a physical security is or is not resilient. Rather, resilience is a continuum and there are different levels of intensity or resilience — hence the need for resilience metrics. The resilience of physical security controls should correlate to the likelihood and severity of specific physical security threats. Natural physical threats such as hurricanes, earthquakes, etc. cannot be eliminated or prevented. As a result, it is necessary to plan and prepare for the worst-case likelihood and severity scenario. That is, the resilience of physical security controls should be proportional to the risk of a physical security threat being instantiated. If physical security threats are deployed that provide a higher degree of resilience than the assessed risk warrants, you have wasted limited security funds. On the other hand, if physical security controls are deployed that provide a lower degree of resilience than the assessed risk, you have under-spent and created a vulnerability and a weak link that most likely will be exploited. A third possibility is deploying robust physical security controls for which there is no measurable threat. This happens all too frequently. An extreme example would be earthquake-proofing a server room in an area that has never had a measurable earthquake. The equipment may look very impressive when the executives stop by for a tour, but the funds have been totally wasted when they probably could have been spent on something constructive. Balance and proportionality are the answer. Consider the lock on your home's front door. Depending on who you are, where you live, and the marketable valuables in your home, a different level of resilience for the lock is needed. For some people, a simple lock will do. Others may need a deadbolt as well. For a few among the rich and famous, an electromagnetic lock with remote controls may be appropriate. But not too many of us need the huge locking steel doors used for bank vaults. Remember that unless a thorough and specific risk assessment is performed, you do not know what level of resilience is needed. Likewise, unless resilience metrics are used, you do not know what level of resilience has been achieved.

Chapter 2 introduced the concept of opportunity, motive, expertise, and resources (OMER) in relation to security attacks. Like other security domains, physical security controls seek to minimize the opportunity to execute a successful attack, increase the expertise required to carry out a successful attack, and restrict the availability of the resources needed to initiate a successful attack or make them cost prohibitive. The key to neutralizing the opportunity, expertise, and resources part of the attack equation is to deploy physical security controls with the appropriate level of resilience. The resilience is just far enough over a certain threshold to make the attack too difficult, take too long, or cost too much. The thinking is that under these conditions, the attacker will choose another target. This assumes, rightly or wrongly, that the "other" target is not another physical security control in the same organization that lacks sufficient resilience. Of course the perception of resilience, if well managed, can be used as a *temporary* substitute until real resilient physical security controls are in place. There is little any organization can do about motive, except perhaps engage in psychological warfare (I mean public relations), and that is beyond the scope of this book.

Figure 4.2 illustrates the taxonomy of physical security parameters. Keep in mind that this is a taxonomy of physical security parameters, not physical security controls. In simplest terms, an organization protects its facilities to safeguard assets and thereby ensure the ability to perform its mission. Conversely, for an organization to reliably achieve its mission, it must safeguard its assets by protecting the facilities that house them. Think of this as a three-layered onion. The core is the organization's mission. The middle ring is composed of the organization's assets that are needed to perform the mission, some of which are more important or essential than others. The outer layer consists of the facilities that contain the organization's assets. Starting from the outside, let us walk through these three layers and examine the physical security parameters associated with each.

<u>Facility Protection</u>
- Location (geography, climate, and social and political environment)
- Surrounding facilities, infrastructure, and transit patterns
- Design, layout, and construction
- Physical security perimeters/Access control points
    - o Exterior: campus, sidewalk, landscaping, parking lot or garage, entrances and exits, loading docks, windows, roof, connections to public utilities, above ground walkways, underground tunnels
    - o Interior: lobby, hallways, stairwells, elevators, flooring and ceiling materials, offices, conference rooms, break rooms, restrooms, work areas, operational centers, equipment cabinets, etc.
- Physical security systems
    - o Exterior
    - o Interior
- Hazard protection
    - o Hazard detection, reporting, response
    - o Natural: wild fire, flood, earthquake, hurricane, tornado, dust or sand storm, extreme heat, cold, or humidity, pestilence
    - o Manmade: environmental, fire, explosion, water or liquid, electrical, chemical, biological, radiological, mechanical, structural
- Building services
    - o HVAC, electrical, mechanical, plumbing, water, gas, utilities, etc.
- Building support services
    - o Isolating pick-ups and deliveries (supplies, trash, food and beverages, mail, packages, etc.)

<u>Asset Protection</u>
- Protection of staff
- Asset inventory, criticality, and value (tangible and intangible)
- Communications and IT systems
    - o Equipment location and accessibility
    - o Tamper protection and alarms
    - o Power supplies
    - o Cable plant
    - o Storage media
    - o Remote and portable equipment, property passes
    - o Employee owned equipment and media, property passes
    - o Disposal and reuse of equipment, storage media, hardcopies
- Equipment operations and maintenance
    - o Configuration management
    - o Controlling service and maintenance
    - o Clean desk and screen

<u>Mission Protection</u>
- Security Master Planning and Preparedness
- Contingency and Disaster Recovery Planning and Preparedness
- Indemnity

Figure 4.2   Taxonomy of physical security parameters.

Facility Protection

A facility can be any type of structure of any size at any location: a high-rise office building, a floor or suite in an office building, an unmanned equipment facility, an underground bunker, a command center, a server room, a switching center, off-site archival storage, a backup operations center, or the dumpster behind your building. That is, a facility can stand on its own or be inside another facility. A facility can be manned or unmanned. Most organizations, whether or not they realize it, make use of a variety of different types of facilities.

A multiplicity of physical security parameters must be evaluated, individually and in combination, in order to plan, choose, and deploy effective physical security controls. Of course there are vast differences between designing and planning for a new facility and assessing or updating an existing facility. In the latter case, the choice of physical security controls, the options available, the integrity, and cost most likely will be quite constrained. The location of a facility is the first physical security parameter to consider. In what type of geography and climate is the facility located? A mountaintop, a river valley, a desert, or in a temperate zone? Are there extreme heat, cold, humidity, precipitation, wind, or other climatic issues that must be dealt with, such as hurricanes, mud slides, or tornadoes? What is the social and political environment of the location in which the facility is located? Is the facility in a major metropolitan area, a small town, or a rural area? Is the area economically stable? Is it a high crime area? Is there overt political unrest or instability? Are there reliable police, emergency medical, and fire department services in the area? Are they familiar with the facility and its layout?[222] If possible, the facility location should avoid public areas.[28] Similarly, a building housing sensitive assets and operations should be as unobtrusive as possible, so as to not draw attention to itself, and give little indication of what goes on inside.[28]

The surrounding facilities, infrastructure, and transit patterns are the next concerns. Do you know what organizations occupy the surrounding facilities or floors and suites of your building? Are these neighbors trustworthy or compatible with your organization and its mission? Are these organizations conducting legitimate businesses? Are any of these facilities processing hazardous materials?[222] Do they have a history of fires, chemical spills, thefts, or other property destruction? Are sufficient sprinkler systems, fire alarms, fire hydrants, hazmat teams, and other safety resources readily available? Are the utility providers in the area reliable, such as the electric grid, or are you pretty much on your own when there are problems? What about transit patterns around the facility? Is it easy to get to and from the facility? Are there alternate routes? Is public transportation (bus or subway) nearby? Is the facility near a major transportation hub or artery? How far back is the facility situated from the nearest roads? What is the distance from the building to parking facilities? Is air travel permitted over the building? Are there regularly scheduled commercial flights that traverse over the building? What about helicopters, private airplanes, and military aircraft? Are the roads well maintained? What about snow and ice removal? Is air or noise pollution a problem?[222]

A facility's design, layout, and construction can contribute to or detract from physical security. A facility's internal and external design can facilitate or complicate the implementation of physical security perimeters and physical security access control points. An open atrium-style design may be aesthetically pleasing, but at the same time make physical access control and the ability to conceal certain assets, operations, and visitors difficult. Similarly, stylish glass buildings, unless properly shielded, promote visual and electronic snooping. There are also trade-offs to consider between one-story and multi-story buildings. Restricted areas should be as far removed as possible from common areas and high-traffic hallways. Restricted areas and sensitive assets should be kept off the beaten path and evidence of their existence minimized. A building's design and construction materials are a major factor in determining its ability to withstand a physical threat. For example, are the various supporting structures designed to distribute temperature, pressure, and weight loads and to compensate for the loss of a given module? Are sections, floors, and stairwells equipped with fire doors to stop the spread of a fire or hazmat spill? Are building materials fire-retardant? Are the interior and exterior structures designed and built of materials that can absorb and contain explosions? Is the design of the ventilation system modular so that individual sections can be shut down and isolated to prevent the spread of airborne hazards? Does the building design permit a quick evacuation of all occupants, including the visually and physically challenged? Are there alternate evacuation paths and means, should one method become unavailable? How easy is it to get equipment and other non-human assets out of the facility in an emergency? Are the floors, walls, and ceilings real and robust, or are they a facade made of flimsy materials that can easily be bypassed? Are exterior windows of sufficient strength and in appropriate locations to prevent unauthorized breaking and entering? Are mechanical vents, ducts, and equipment on the sides and roof of the building robust enough to prevent unauthorized tampering, breaking, and entering?

Most organizations employ a variety of different types of nested physical security perimeters, each with different control objectives. In simplest terms, a physical security perimeter is a physical boundary or barrier that is used to protect specific assets and prevent or restrict access to them. In the latter case, designated controlled access points are located along the perimeter. All security perimeters must be clearly defined, especially in relation to one another, to ensure that there are no gaps.[28] The design, implementation, and operation of physical security perimeters should eliminate, as far as is technically feasible and economically practical, the ability for it to be defeated or bypassed.[28] The resilience of physical security perimeters should be proportional to asset criticality and reflect whether the security perimeter is a primary, secondary, or supporting perimeter. Nested physical security perimeters are often referred to as different lines of security. Each line of security can be thought of as a sieve, reducing the types of attacks that can pass through the perimeter and be successful.[45]

Exterior physical security perimeters can take many forms, such as fences, parking restrictions, concrete barriers, and creative landscaping. Connections to public utilities, above-ground walkways, and underground tunnels also should be controlled. The intent is to (1) limit access to the property on which the facility resides, as well as the facility itself; (2) control the traffic patterns on the property and in and around the facility; and (3) monitor and control all potential entry and exit points, both authorized and unauthorized, such as a broken window or the roof. Generally, a combination of guards (human and canine), CCTV, and other technology is employed to accomplish the latter. Equip all external doors, windows, and other potential entry points with internal locks and audible and visible alarms.

Loading docks and other receiving areas can pose special challenges. First, unless the delivery company and personnel are known, there also may be

personnel security issues to handle. Second, the contents of the delivery may
be in question. Is the delivery expected? Are the contents known and correct?
Have the packing materials been tampered with? Perhaps it is a good idea to
scan all deliveries or at least suspect deliveries for the presence of chemical,
biological, explosive, or other hazards. Third, the delivery vehicle itself might
be a concern. Is the vehicle under the ownership and operation of a known
trusted source? How close does the vehicle come to the facility? Is the vehicle
left unattended, such that it could be tampered with to become a delivery
mechanism for chemical, biological, or explosive materials? If so, there may
be a case for scanning vehicles prior to admitting them onto the property.
For these reasons it is often recommended that loading and receiving areas
be isolated from the main facility, even at times in separate facilities. All
incoming and outgoing materials should be registered and examined for
potential hazards.[28] Deliveries and pickups should be restricted to specific
holding areas that have separately controlled front and rear, external and
internal doors.[28] Delivery and pickup areas should be manned or monitored
electronically at all times. This approach is considerably more severe than that
practiced by most organizations, where packages are left at will at the guard's
desk or the secretary's desk and pizza lunches are delivered directly to the
break room. But do you *really* know these people and what is inside the
packages they are delivering?

Internal physical security perimeters can also take many forms: lobbies,
hallways, elevators, flooring and ceiling materials, offices, conference rooms,
break rooms, restrooms, work areas, operational centers, equipment cabinets,
etc. Lobbies can be used as holding areas for visitors awaiting escorts; they
can also be used to prevent people from wandering off to who knows where.
That is why it is always a good idea to have a separate restroom available in
the visitor lobby. Also, it is not a good idea to put a building directory,
organization phone book, a "you are here" map, or photographs of notable
employees in the lobby.[28] Hallways, if cleverly designed, can route traffic away
from sensitive areas and even hide their existence. Separate hallways can be
designed for sensitive and nonsensitive areas in the ideal setting. Concerns
about elevators were discussed previously. Separate offices, work areas, and
conference rooms can be set aside for handling and discussing sensitive
information and other critical assets. Of course, they should be clearly designated as such — perhaps not to the casual observer, but to those who need
to know. Extremely sensitive areas or critical rooms within a facility should
be windowless; have real floors and ceilings; and have their own heating,
ventilation, and cooling systems (HVAC), uninterrupted power supplies (UPS),
fire protection, etc.[222] Equipment cabinets and wiring closets present a special
challenge. Connectivity between equipment cabinets or wiring closets should
be limited or eliminated, if possible, to prevent tapping into or damaging
critical assets from noncritical cabinets. At the same time, physical access to
these resources should be tightly controlled to known trusted individuals who
have a need to access these resources. Equipment cabinets and wiring closets
are a wonderful opportunity to do a lot of damage that may or may not be
visible right away. Why make things easy for a would-be attacker, whether

insider or outsider? Employ mechanical, magnetic, or electronic locks to limit access to buildings, rooms, cabinets, and safes. Protect other equipment from unauthorized use as well, such as copiers, faxes, telephones, and printers. Place this equipment in secure areas to avoid unauthorized access and requests from outsiders to use this equipment.[28] Use separate office space and facilities for direct employees and third parties, such as consultants, vendors, and contractors.[28] Limit access to secure work areas on a need-to-know basis. There is no reason unauthorized personnel need to know that these facilities exist or what or who is in them. If any secure areas are temporarily vacant, they should be secured and inspected regularly.[28] And it goes without saying that equipment in vacant secure work areas should be removed or disabled, preferably the former. Likewise, photographic, video, audio, and other recording equipment should be prohibited from secure areas.[28] Asking people to leave their equipment out front is highly ineffective. Ever count how many people illegally record movies on their cell phones these days? No, people need to be scanned for the presence of this type of equipment before granting them access to sensitive areas. Otherwise, a lot of time and money has been wasted on physical and IT security controls.

Each physical security perimeter has one or more access control points associated with it. The purpose of the access control points is to[116, 266]:

- Permit or deny entry to, and exit from, or presence in a given space.
- Monitor access to key assets.
- Increase or decrease the rate or density of movement to, from, or within a given space.
- Protect people, materials, or information against unauthorized observation or removal.
- Prevent injury to people or damage to material.

Access control points, like security perimeters, correlate directly to asset criticality and the likelihood of a physical security threat being instantiated and the severity of the consequences, should this happen.[35] At the same time, access control points must be designed and implemented so that they do not conflict with building or fire safety codes.[116]

Access control points can be implemented through a variety of access control mechanisms and policies, each of which will yield a different level of resilience. In some instances, like tamper-proof equipment, physical access control mechanisms may be the last line of defense, after other technical and procedural controls have failed or been bypassed.[20] The most well-known access control mechanism is the badge or token an employee must present to gain admission to the workplace. These can take several different forms, such as badges or tokens with magnetic stripes, resonant circuits, optical memory cards, smart cards, proximity or contact readers, biometric features, or RFID tags (as discussed in Chapter 3). The badges or tokens can be inspected by humans or read by machines. Depending on the specific technology used, the badge or token may contain information about the person, his access level, the facilities and assets he has access to, and his normal work location. A prime concern of any badge or token is its inability to be duplicated or read by unauthorized means.

Other access control mechanisms include mechanical, magnetic, and electronic locks, turnstiles for people and vehicles, and mechanical ramps that prevent vehicle entry or exits without approval from an operator or badge reader. Often, the vehicle, trunk, and undercarriage are inspected prior to granting approval. Also, it is important to implement a method for rapidly identifying authorized vehicles. Something more sophisticated than the usual parking permits is needed because they are too easy to forge. Audio or visual monitoring systems, while they do not control access to a given space, may serve as a deterrent to unauthorized access.[222] If installed intelligently, such physical access control monitoring systems can also provide detection capability, especially if multiple viewing points and angles are used, and unlike human observation, facilitate recording, reviewing, and rerunning the evidence collected.[222]

Physical access control policies are used to supplement access control mechanisms and reinforce specific physical access control objectives. Physical access control policies define the who, what, how, why, and when of physical security controls.[222] A key requirement is to maintain audit trails of who accessed what resources and when they left the premises and returned the resources. Furthermore, physical access rights should be regularly reviewed, reaffirmed or revoked, and updated.[28, 35] Some examples of physical access control policies include[35, 116, 266]:

- Invoking the two-man rule, whereby sensitive assets and work areas can only be used when two people are present at all times
- Limiting the authorized hours of operation
- Logging and monitoring access to sensitive areas manually and with CCTV, intercoms, video, or digital recording media
- Retaining physical access logs for at least 90 days
- Excluding pedestrian traffic near or through the building and parking facility
- Only allowing admittance or exits through certain places after normal business hours
- Having individuals sign in and out after normal business hours
- Requiring employees to lock computers and workspaces at the end of their shift; independently verifying that these items are locked
- Inspecting purses, briefcases, backpacks, etc. prior to granting admittance
- Verifying property passes
- Requiring multiple forms of identification for visitors
- Having cleaning crews work during the day when the facility is occupied
- Shredding or incinerating all trash
- Using card readers to control use of copiers, faxes, computers, shredders, and telephones; keeping a current inventory of who has what cards
- Having separate elevators or stairwells to sensitive areas that are controlled by card readers
- Screening incoming packages and visitors for chemical, biological, explosive, and other hazardous materials, like weapons
- Documenting access requests, the authorization process, the revocation process, and the review/reaffirm/update cycle

- Requiring visitors to surrender temporary ID when leaving the facility
- Maintaining logs of who has certain access cards, keys, or the combination to cipher locks; the frequency with which the lists are updated and the locks changed
- Defining how often badges and other tokens must be updated and inventoried

Hazard protection is a major component of physical security. Hazard protection includes elements of preparedness, detection, reporting, and response to natural and man-made hazards, whether they are accidental or intentional. This concept is often referred to as "all-hazards preparedness." The key is to (1) acknowledge that certain adverse events may happen, and (2) be prepared to prevent, preempt, mitigate, delay, and contain or limit the consequences, so that critical assets are protected and the organization can continue to perform its mission. Keep in mind that human action or inaction beforehand and at the time of occurrence can make the outcome of a natural or man-made hazard better or worse.

Humans have no control over natural hazards such as wild fires, floods, earthquakes, hurricanes, tornadoes, typhoons, volcanic eruptions, dust or sand storms, extreme heat, cold, or humidity, and pestilence. Humans may engage in unwise environmental practices that precipitate or increase the frequency of such events. But as of today, there is no way to prevent or preempt such occurrences. All that can be done is to plan and prepare for the worst-case likelihood and severity scenario.

Man-made hazards, on the other hand, are more difficult to predict but easier to prevent and preempt. Man-made hazards include environmental hazards or damage, fires, explosions, water or liquid hazards, electrical hazards, chemical hazards, biological hazards, radiological hazards, and mechanical and structural hazards. Man-made hazards can be as simple as storing flammable and other hazardous materials incorrectly in a janitor's closet. Industrial disasters such as explosions, fires, chemical spills, and equipment malfunctions can occur without warning. Man-made hazards can be introduced accidentally or intentionally by insiders or outsiders. The prevalence of downsizing has increased the number of potential disgruntled employees. Civil disturbance, vandalism, conflicts of interest, and workplace violence can precipitate man-made hazards.[116] Accidental hazards lack a motive. In contrast, the objectives of intentional man-made hazards can include stealing or disrupting information, equipment, and material, monetary or political gain, and publicity.[45] A diverse set of tactics can be used to initiate man-made hazards, such as covert entry and deliberate acts of sabotage, the release of airborne or water-borne contaminants, and the delivery of explosives through vehicles, people, or packages.[45]

Proactive planning and preparedness for natural and man-made hazard scenarios is essential to avoid being caught in a reactive crisis management mode. Planning and preparedness should be based on a risk assessment and concentrate on loss avoidance and loss prevention. Potential loss event profiles should be developed for all conceivable natural and man-made hazard scenarios, which identify *a priori* the kinds of loss events that could be experienced, the relationships between specific conditions, circumstances, objects, activities, and (human and non-human) players that could trigger a loss event.[116] Keep in mind that the number of ways or opportunities to effect a loss increases the loss probability and the probability of repeatable loss events.[116] When planning for natural and man-made hazards, remember to ensure that secure off-site storage and backup operations are far enough away to avoid being damaged by the same hazard that affected the primary location.[28] Planning for natural and man-made disasters should take into account health and safety regulations and neighboring facilities.[28] For example, what is the facility's fire hazard rating? Are there smoke detectors, sprinkler systems, or gaseous fire control systems? Is the fire extinguishment capability fixed or portable?[116] Are the archives stored in a fire-proof vault? Are all security control, monitoring, and alarm systems interconnected, leading perhaps to a single point of failure? What about emergency backup lighting, utilities, and telecommunications?[222] Emergency lighting and exit signs are needed to evacuate interior workspaces. Do they have adequate battery power to effect a complete evacuation under less than ideal situations or a temporary shelter in place? Are generators required to supply long-term alternate sources of electricity to operate essential environmental equipment? Is this equipment being tested regularly? Does the equipment have adequate ventilation to avoid carbon monoxide poisoning? Do the water sources and telecommunications equipment have diverse and redundant connections and paths to avoid single points of failure?

It is necessary to conduct a through and methodical physical threat assessment to adequately plan and prepare for natural and man-made hazards. A cursory "somebody might do this" or "you know we are overdue for a major hurricane" just does not cut it. In the case of man-made hazards, the physical threat assessment needs to zero in on what groups and individuals are likely to initiate an attack; what their preferred tactics, attack methods, tools, and weapons are; and the physical security control (weakest link) they are likely to attack.[45] The exposure, duration, concentration, immediate effect, and delayed effect of a physical attack are key factors in determining the appropriate countermeasure.[45] This is often referred to as the design basis threat.

A multi-step process is used to perform a physical threat assessment for a specific facility. IT equipment and systems are subjected to type certification, whereby a system or network undergoes security certification and accreditation and then is deployed to multiple locations throughout the enterprise. Type certification is acceptable for IT systems that are simply being replicated. This approach is not acceptable for facilities because of the variation in location, use, surrounding neighborhood, design, layout, construction, and physical security perimeters. Facilities require individual physical threat assessments and security controls. This latter approach is referred to as site certification. The first step is to calibrate parameters related to the opportunity, expertise, and resources needed to execute a physical security attack. As shown in Table 4.1, there are seven parameters to calibrate for a man-made physical threat. These parameters are calibrated over a four-tier continuum. The first parameter is access to agent or the ease with which the source materials needed to carry

Table 4.1 Man-Made Physical Threat Criteria Weighted by Opportunity, Expertise, and Resources Needed[45]

Weight	Access to Attack Agent	Knowledge/ Expertise	Facility History of Threats	Asset Visibility, Symbolism	Asset Accessibility	Facility Population	Collateral Damage/ Distance to Facility
9–10	Readily available	Basic knowledge, open sources	Local incident, occurred recently, caused great damage, building function and tenants were primary target	Existence widely known	Open access, unrestricted parking	>5000	Within 1000 foot radius
6–8	Easy to produce	Bachelor's degree or technical school, open scientific or technical literature	Regional or state incident, occurred a few years ago, caused substantial damage, building function and tenants were one of the primary targets	Existence locally known, landmark	Open access, restricted parking	1001–5000	Within 1 mile radius
3–5	Difficult to produce or acquire	Advanced training, rare scientific or declassified literature	National incident, occurred some time in the past, caused important damage, building functions and tenants were one of the primary targets	Existence published, well known	Controlled access, protected entry	251–1000	Within 2 mile radius
1–2	Very difficult to produce or acquire	Advanced degree or training, classified information	International incident occurred many years ago, caused localized damage, building functions and tenants were not the primary targets	Existence not well known, no symbolic importance	Remote location, secure perimeter, armed guards, tightly controlled access	1–250	Within 10 mile radius

out the attack can be acquired.[45] Access to agent can range from materials that are readily available to those that are very difficult to acquire or produce. Those agents that are readily available are given a higher weighting than those that are not because they pose a greater potential threat. The knowledge and expertise required to create the attack mechanism and execute the attack is the second parameter to calibrate. There is quite a range here as well, from basic knowledge that is easy to acquire from open sources, to advanced specialized training at the graduate student level and access to classified information.[45] A third parameter to assess is the history of physical security attacks against the facility and its tenants. Perhaps the facility or tenants are an easy or popular target. This parameter can range anywhere from a recent local incident with extensive damage to an international incident that occurred several years ago with minor damage. Asset visibility and symbolism generally increase the likelihood of a facility becoming a target of a physical security attack. Here we see a link to motive — greater publicity is generated from successfully attacking a highly visible or symbolic target and the result is a greater impact psychologically on a greater number of people. This fact is illustrated in the range of weights for this parameter. Asset accessibility is another key parameter to evaluate in terms of the opportunity to execute a physical security attack. The easier it is to access a facility, especially in terms of how close unauthorized people and vehicles can get to a facility, the more likely the facility could become a target. Target richness is also increased by the number of people that might be in the facility at any given time. Again, the amount of publicity generated and the extent of the psychological impact increases proportionally to the number of people affected. Accessibility restrictions may prevent a would-be attacker from penetrating the target facility. In that case, a fallback option might be to attack a nearby facility, which is more accessible, with the intent of causing collateral damage to the real target facility. Hence the need to know the neighborhood and plan for such an eventuality.

A careful examination of these seven parameters provides detailed insight into the opportunity, expertise, and resources needed to formulate and execute a physical security attack on a given facility. Two of these parameters, asset visibility or symbolism and site population, also touch on the motive of an attack. Three of the seven parameters are constants and do not vary with the type of attack: asset visibility or symbolism, asset accessibility, and site population.[45] The other four parameters do vary, sometimes considerably, by the type of attack.

Table 4.2 demonstrates the equivalent process for natural physical threats. In this case, there are five parameters to calibrate. Again, the parameters are calibrated over a four-tier continuum. The first parameter is the facility's history of being subjected to natural disasters. For example, does this facility have a history of regularly being subjected to earthquakes or hurricanes? Here we see the importance of the location of a facility relative to geographical and climatic conditions and the ability to provide adequate physical security. In any given location, certain natural disasters may be common, infrequent, or unheard of; this is usually measured in years between occurrences. Asset

Table 4.2 Weighted Natural Physical Threat Criteria

Weight	Facility History of Natural Disasters	Asset Visibility, Symbolism	Asset Susceptibility to Natural Threats	Facility Population	Collateral Damage, Potential Radius of Disaster Impact
9–10	This type of natural disaster has occurred in the region within last 5 years	Existence widely known, loss would have major psychological impact	Asset design and construction do not take natural disasters into account	>5000	>10 mile radius
6–8	This type of natural disaster has occurred in the region within last 6–15 years	Existence locally known, landmark, loss would have regional psychological impact	Asset design and construction take natural disasters into account somewhat	1001–5000	5.1–10 mile radius
3–5	This type of natural disaster has occurred in the region within last 16–49 years	Existence published, well known, loss would have local psychological impact	Asset design and construction have a medium amount of preparation for natural disasters	251–1000	2.1–5 mile radius
1–2	This type of natural disaster has not occurred in the region within last 50 years	Existence not well known, no symbolic importance, limited psychological impact	Asset design and construction fully prepared for natural disasters	1–251	0.1–2 mile radius

visibility and symbolism are of concern, not because they have anything to do with the type of natural disaster, but rather because of the extent of the psychological impact should an asset be damaged or lost. How deeply and wide will the loss be felt — nationally, regionally, locally, or on a more limited scale? The third parameter is the asset's susceptibility to natural disasters. The design and construction of a facility, as well as its age, the building codes in effect at the time of construction, and the frequency of inspections play a major role in determining whether or not a facility will "weather the storm." One building may be right on top of a fault line and emerge from an earthquake unscathed, while another building five miles away totally tumbles to the ground. Similarly, it is important to consider the geographic area that could be affected by a specific type of natural disaster. Being at the center of a tornado, an earthquake, a hurricane, or flood zone is quite different because each type of hazard has a different potential damage radius. It is also essential to know the number of people at a given facility on a normal day and any peak situations. This total should include employees, visitors, customers, contractors, vendors, maintenance personnel, consultants, trainers, children in day care — anyone who might be in the facility. This number is important because it reflects the number of people that might need to be evacuated or rescued from the facility or need medical attention following a natural disaster.

The next step in assessing physical security threats is to correlate these parameters to specific threat scenarios. Table 4.3 illustrates this process for man-made physical threats. The seven parameters just discussed form the columns, with the addition of a "total score" column. The rows are types of specific physical security threats. Six categories of man-made physical threat scenarios are used in this example: (1) arson and explosives, (2) explosives carried by aircraft or ships, (3) chemical agents, (4) biological agents, (5) radiological agents, and (6) armed attacks. Using the criteria from Table 4.1, a weighting is given to each of the seven parameters for each specific threat scenario. The values assigned to each of the seven parameters are added together to derive a total score for each specific threat scenario. Then the total scores are compared to determine the most likely threat scenario for a given facility. When reviewing Table 4.3, it is important to remember three things. First, this table is just an example. True weights, scores, and threat scenarios should be developed for the particular facility being assessed. Second, once developed, the weights, scores, and threat scenarios need to be re-validated and updated at least quarterly, given the rapid changes in world events, the rapid advances in science and technology, and the almost-instantaneous dissemination of such information. Third, Table 4.3 only provides a sample worksheet for man-made hazards. An equivalent process should be followed and a worksheet developed for natural hazards.

Table 4.4 demonstrates this process for natural physical threats, using the Washington, D.C. area as an example. The Washington, D.C. area does have tornadoes and snowstorms, but not mud slides or avalanches. Many of the buildings have a symbolic and historic importance related to the federal government. Most of the facilities are more than 50 years old and few were designed with natural disasters in mind. Given that Washington, D.C. is a

Table 4.3 Sample Weighted Man-Made Physical Threat Criteria and Scenarios[45]

Scenario	Access to Agent	Knowledge/ Expertise	Facility History of Threats	Asset Visibility, Symbolism	Asset Accessibility	Site Population	Collateral Damage	Score
I. Arson and Improvised Explosive Device								
Deliberate arson, theft, or sabotage	9	9	5	8	3	10	3	47
1-lb. Mail bomb	9	9	3	8	3	10	1	43
5-lb. Pipe bomb	9	9	3	8	3	10	2	44
50-lb. Briefcase, suicide bomber	8	8	6	8	3	10	3	46
500-lb. Car bomb	6	8	7	8	3	10	3	45
5000-lb truck bomb	4	8	5	8	3	10	3	41
20,000-lb. Truck bomb	2	6	1	8	3	10	3	33
Natural gas	2	8	1	8	3	10	5	37
II. Bomb Delivered by Aircraft or Ship								
Small aircraft	9	6	3	8	3	10	3	42
Medium aircraft	5	4	7	8	3	10	3	40
Large aircraft	2	3	7	8	3	10	3	36
Ship	0	0	0	8	3	10	3	24

Table 4.3   Sample Weighted Man-Made Physical Threat Criteria and Scenarios[45] (continued)

Scenario	Access to Agent	Knowledge/ Expertise	Facility History of Threats	Asset Visibility, Symbolism	Asset Accessibility	Site Population	Collateral Damage	Score
III. Chemical Agent								
Chlorine	5	7	2	8	3	10	2	37
Phosgene	3	10	2	8	3	10	1	37
Hydrogen cyanide	3	8	2	8	3	10	1	35
Lewisite	3	6	2	8	3	10	1	33
Sarin	3	4	6	8	3	10	4	38
IV. Biological Agent								
Anthrax	4	5	9	8	3	10	2	41
Plague	4	5	3	8	3	10	2	35
Tularemia	4	5	2	8	3	10	2	34
Smallpox	2	5	2	8	3	10	2	32
Botulism	5	5	5	8	3	10	2	38
Ricin	8	8	9	8	3	10	2	48

V. Radiological or Other Energy Agent

Dirty bomb	5	7	1	8	3	10	5	39
Spent fuel storage	2	6	1	8	3	10	1	31
Nuclear plant	1	6	1	8	3	10	1	30
High-altitude electromagnetic pulse	2	3	3	8	3	10	2	31
High-power microwave electromagnetic pulse	2	3	3	8	3	10	2	31

VI. Armed Attack

Workplace violence	9	9	5	8	3	10	3	47
Hostage situation	9	9	5	8	3	10	3	47
RPG/LAW/mortar	4	5	2	8	3	10	2	34
Ballistic	10	10	5	8	3	10	2	48

Table 4.4 Sample Weighted Natural Physical Threat Criteria and Scenarios

Scenario	Facility History of Natural Disasters	Asset Visibility, Symbolism	Asset Susceptibility to Natural Threats	Facility Population	Collateral Damage, Radius of Potential Disaster	Score
Avalanche	1	9	9	7	2	28
Drought	6	9	9	7	7	38
Dust, sand storm	1	9	9	7	4	30
Earthquake	1	9	9	7	5	31
Extreme cold, ice or snow storm	8	9	8	7	7	39
Extreme heat	1	9	9	7	7	33
Extreme humidity	5	9	9	7	7	37
Flood	5	9	9	7	5	35
Hurricane	5	9	9	7	7	37
Mudslide	1	9	9	7	4	30
Pestilence	4	9	8	7	7	35
Tornado	9	9	8	7	4	37
Tsunami	1	9	9	7	9	35
Typhoon	1	9	9	7	7	33
Wild fire	1	9	6	7	7	30

major metropolitan area, the majority of office buildings have a high occupancy rate. Again note that asset visibility/symbolism and facility population are constants; they do not vary by the type of physical threat. This fact is reflected in the spread of the total scores. It is important to remember that natural disasters may affect the facility being protected directly or indirectly. For example, a natural disaster may:

- Affect the ability to ship products out of the facility
- Affect the ability for supplies to be delivered to the facility
- Affect the ability of people to travel to or leave the facility
- Interfere with the availability of public utilities, such as electricity, gas, water, and sewage
- Cause leakage of hazardous or toxic materials into the ground or waterways
- Interfere with telecommunications
- Increase the likelihood of the spread of disease

These factors must be taken into account when selecting physical security controls and when planning and preparing for contingencies and disasters.

So far we have (1) evaluated the opportunity, expertise, and resources needed to cause a natural or man-made physical security attack; and (2) correlated these parameters to specific threat scenarios to determine the most likely types of attacks. The next step is to identify the most likely targets within the facility, should it be subject to a physical security attack. There are two ways to look at this. One approach is to examine the functions within the building that might be the main target of the attack. Another approach is to examine the different infrastructure components within the facility that might be the main target of the attack. If a facility is small or the man-made attack planning cycle is cut short or unsophisticated, the attackers may not take the time to target a particular building function or infrastructure component. Instead, they may just attack the facility as a whole and see what happens. Natural disasters, of course, do not "target" specific facilities, functions, or building infrastructures either. However, certain facilities, functions, or infrastructure components may be more susceptible to a particular type of natural disaster. These functions or infrastructure components are then mapped to the specific threat scenarios just evaluated. A likelihood rating is assigned for a specific threat scenario being used to attack a specific building function or infrastructure component, based on the total scores from Tables 4.3 and 4.4 and knowledge of the building particulars. The standard likelihood categories discussed in Chapter 2 are used. This process is illustrated in Table 4.5. Again, these tables are just examples. Worksheets should be developed for the particular facility being evaluated. Table 4.5 only addresses man-made hazards. Equivalent worksheets should be developed to represent natural hazards, to accomplish all hazards preparedness.

Next, the consequences and impact, both locally and globally, of the natural or man-made hazard are determined. This is where the loss event profile comes into play. Table 4.6 illustrates the components of a loss event profile. A separate row is developed for each physical security threat. The first column

Table 4.5   Sample Worksheet: Likelihood of Man-Made Physical Threat Scenarios[45]

I. To Facility Functions

Facility Function	Improvised Explosive Device	Bomb Delivered by Aircraft or Ship	Chemical Agent	Biological Agent	Radiological or Other Energy Agent	Armed Attack
Administration						
Engineering						
Finance						
R&D						
Marketing/PR						
Legal						
Warehouse						
Data center						
Food service						
Security						
Housekeeping						
Day care						

II. To Facility Infrastructure Components

Facility Infrastructure Component	Improvised Explosive Device	Bomb Delivered by Aircraft or Ship	Chemical Agent	Biological Agent	Radiological or Other Energy Agent	Armed Attack
Site						
Architecture						
Structural systems						
Envelope systems						
Mechanical systems						
Plumbing and gas systems						
Electrical systems						
Fire alarm and protection systems						
IT/communications systems						
Stairwells, escalators, elevators						
Public address system						

Key:

Incredible: Unlikely to occur in the life of an item, with a probability of occurrence less than 10^{-7}.

Improbable: So unlikely it can be assumed occurrence may not be experienced, with a probability of occurrence less than 10^{-6}.

Remote: Unlikely, but possible to occur in the life of an item, with a probability of occurrence of less than 10^3 but greater than 10^{-6}.

Occasional: Likely to occur sometime in the life of an item, with a probability of occurrence of less than 10^{-2} but greater than 10^{-3}.

Probable: Will occur several times in the life of an item, with a probability of occurrence of less than 10^1 but greater than 10^{-2}.

Frequent: Likely to occur often in the life of an item, with a probability of occurrence greater than 10^1.

Table 4.6 Sample Loss Event Profile for Physical Security Threats — Part I. Damage Assessment

Physical Threat	Immediate Consequences	Local Impact and Duration	Global Impact and Duration
What might happen or has already happened	Impact on the facility and the assets it contains Range from most likely to worst-case scenario	Impact on products and services provided by this location Impact to local community	Impact on the organization as a whole and its ability to achieve its mission Impact on the community at large
Hurricane Katrina strikes New Orleans	Wind and flood damage to radar, control tower, and other equipment Equipment is repairable	Need to close New Orleans airport for five days	Need to reroute traffic to/from New Orleans airport for five days Aircraft and crews need to be reassigned Aircraft and crews in New Orleans must stay put

identifies the specific physical threat being examined, that is, what might happen or what has happened. This information can be extracted from Tables 4.3 and 4.4. Ideally, loss event profiles are developed as part of planning and preparedness. Loss event profiles can also be developed after the fact, as part of the post-event analysis and to derive lessons learned. The second column captures the immediate consequences or impact on the facility and the assets it contains. This can be expressed as a range from the most likely to the worst-case scenario, or as an absolute event. The third column describes the local impact of the consequences. How does this event impact the facility's ability to generate its normal products and services? What is the duration of the local impact — when will things be back to normal? Finally, the global impact of this event is assessed for the organization involved as well as stakeholders, business partners, and the community at large. Again, the duration of the global impact is projected.

There are two parts to a loss event profile. The first part is the damage assessment. Table 4.6 illustrates Part I or the damage assessment for a real event, Hurricane Katrina striking New Orleans, and the effect on the U.S. Federal Aviation Administration (FAA). The immediate consequences the FAA experienced included wind and flood damage to some critical and essential assets, such as radar and control towers. At the time, it was determined that the equipment was repairable. The local impact to the organization (the FAA) was the need to close the New Orleans airport for five days while repairs were made. It was difficult to get evacuees out or emergency supplies and personnel in with the airport closed, so time was of the essence. The global impact was the need to cancel and reroute flights to and from New Orleans during the interim. The airlines had to reassign aircraft and crews on short notice and notify passengers. The FAA air traffic controllers and the airlines worked together to reroute domestic and international flights. During the day, most flights carry passengers. At night, most flights are by overnight package delivery services.

The second part of the loss event profile is the cost assessment. This assessment will vary, depending on whether an organization is a government agency, non-profit organization, or public or privately held for-profit corporation. The size and geographical distribution of the organization will also effect the cost assessment, simply because it may be easier and faster for a large distributed organization to recover. Continuing with the FAA example, the local cost impact included items such as the cost for spare parts and new equipment; labor costs, including overtime for the crews that repaired the equipment; and the cost of paying employees who were scheduled to work, but could not while the facilities were shut down. Because the FAA is not a for-profit corporation, lost revenue was not a concern. In contrast, the global cost impact to the community at large was much more significant. This cost was spread across many organizations and included items such as lost revenue to the airlines, airport, ground transportation, hotels, restaurants, etc.; the cost of paying employees who could not work; the cost to airline passengers who had to seek alternate transportation; the cost to package delivery services that could not make deliveries or pickups on time; and the cost to companies that did not receive supplies on time. This fact highlights the interconnectedness of not just the global economy, but also the local economies. It also brings home why certain segments of the economy, such as transportation, are classified as critical infrastructures — if they are lost, damaged, or experience extended downtime, there is a ripple effect way beyond the immediate organization. This fact must be taken into account by the organization as well as local, regional, and national authorities when selecting physical security controls and planning and preparedness for disasters and contingencies.

The cost impact is also referred to as the total cost of the loss: (1) what assets will be damaged, and hence unusable for a period of time, but are repairable, and assets that will be totally destroyed and unrecoverable; (2) losses associated with the inability to achieve the organization's mission due to these losses; and (3) other related costs.[116] For example, what is the impact on the rest of the organization if this facility or function is lost? How readily can the function performed or the products produced at this facility be restored at this facility or replaced at another facility? The cost of loss normally includes such items as permanent replacement costs; the cost of temporary substitute workspace, equipment, and personnel; the cost impact on the rest of the organization; lost income; (re)training; and other related expenses.[116] The cost of loss can be expressed as[116]:

$$K = (C_p + C_t + C_r + C_l) - (I - a) \qquad\qquad 2.1.2.10$$

where:
K = Total cost of loss
C_p = Cost of permanent replacements
C_t = Cost of temporary replacements

C_r = Total cost of related costs
C_l = Lost income cost
I = Insurance or indemnity
a = Allocable insurance premium

Of course, to have any meaning, K must be calculated for a specified time frame. The loss is bounded by a specific time interval, which is referred to as the loss duration. Usually there is a combination of immediate loss, short-term loss, and long-term loss durations.

To put this all together, a variety of physical security parameters (Figure 4.2) determine the ability to protect a facility and the type of physical security controls needed. These parameters include the location of the facility, the surrounding neighborhood, the design, layout, and construction of the facility, physical security perimeters, access control points, and primary and support building services. To prepare for potential hazards, first analyze the conditions that could precipitate such a hazard. For man-made hazards, the opportunity, expertise, and resources needed to execute the hazard are evaluated (Table 4.1). For natural hazards, various aspects of a facility's susceptibility to a specific natural hazard are analyzed (Table 4.2). This information is correlated to particular threat scenarios to identify which hazard scenarios are most likely to be experienced. (Tables 4.3 and 4.4). In some cases, it may make sense to carry the analysis to a finer degree of granularity. If so, an assessment is performed to see if a particular building function or infrastructure component is a more likely target than another (Table 4.5). Now that the most likely physical threat scenarios have been identified, it is time to investigate the consequences should those threats be instantiated. A loss event profile is developed for each of the most likely physical threats. The loss event profile examines the immediate consequences, as well as the local and global impact and the duration of each (Table 4.6). The loss event profile is expressed in terms of a damage assessment and a cost assessment for both the facility, the immediate organization, and the community at large. This information is used to select, prioritize, and allocate resources for physical security controls.

The following metrics can be used to measure the resilience of different aspects of physical security controls related to facility protection. Many facility protection metrics are sorted by asset criticality. If multiple assets of differing criticalities are stored at a single facility, the highest criticality should be used.

Location and Surrounding Infrastructure

Percentage of facilities, by asset criticality, that are at risk of collateral damage from a neighboring facility because: 2.1.1.1

    a. The facility does not meet building and fire safety codes
    b. Hazardous materials are processed or stored there
    c. The facility has a history of being targeted by various groups for physical attacks
    d. Other

Percentage of facilities, by asset criticality and potential severity, that have implemented specific physical security controls in proportion to the risk of collateral damage from a neighboring facility because: 2.1.1.2

    a. The facility does not meet building and fire safety codes
    b. Hazardous materials are processed or stored there
    c. The facility has a history of being targeted by various groups for physical attacks
    d. Other

Percentage of facilities for which the surrounding occupants are known, trustworthy, and compatible with the organization's mission and goals.
                                                                      2.1.1.3

Percentage of facilities that have adequate: 2.1.1.4

    a. External lighting
    b. Lighting for parking facilities
    c. Emergency lighting and back-up power to support it

Percentage of business operations that are conducted in high crime areas or other areas of social unrest that might be a target of violent physical attacks, by asset criticality.   2.1.1.5

Percentage of business operations that are conducted in a politically sensitive area that might be a target of violent physical attacks from any group, by asset criticality[163]:   2.1.1.6

By facility and asset criticality, the proximity of public pedestrian and vehicle traffic: 2.1.1.7

    a. Red — less than one block
    b. Yellow — 1 to 2 blocks
    c. Blue — 2 to 3 blocks
    d. Green — over 3 blocks

By facility and asset criticality, the reliability and availability of emergency services:
                                                                      2.1.1.8

    a. Red — emergency services are remotely located and/or not reliable
    b. Yellow — emergency services usually respond within 30 minutes
    c. Blue — emergency services usually respond within 15 minutes
    d. Green — emergency services are readily available and completely reliable

Percentage of facilities that have multiple diverse ways of communicating with emergency services, by asset criticality.   2.1.1.9

Percentage of facilities, by asset criticality, that are equipped with anti-vehicle ramming protection that is proportional to the maximum achievable speed.
                                                                      2.1.1.10

By facility and asset criticality, the distance between parking facilities and the building: 2.1.1.11

   a. Red — parking is beneath the building
   b. Yellow — less than 1 block
   c. Blue — 1 to 2 blocks
   d. Green — over 2 blocks

Percentage of facilities, by asset criticality, for which external trash receptacles are: 2.1.1.12

   a. Secured
   b. Monitored
   c. Immune to explosives

Distribution of facilities by asset criticality that are unobtrusive and do not give an indication of their contents, activities, or operations.   2.1.1.13

Distribution of facility accessibility by the public at large, by asset criticality:
                                                                                    2.1.1.14

   a. None
   b. Very limited
   c. Limited
   d Controlled access
   e. Completely accessible (public building, mixed tenant facility, etc.)

Distribution of facilities, by asset criticality, for which facility protection measures have been designed to mitigate local climatic concerns: 2.1.1.15

   a. Extreme heat
   b. Extreme cold
   c. Extreme humidity
   d. Flood zone
   e. Earthquake zone
   f. Frequent hurricanes
   g. Frequent tornadoes
   h. Excessive rain or snowfall
   i. Drought

Design, Layout, and Construction

Percentage of facilities for which supporting structures are designed to distribute temperature, pressure, and weight loads and compensate for the loss of a given module, by asset criticality.   2.1.1.16

Within a facility, percentage of work areas, floors, and stairwells that are equipped with fire doors to stop the spread of a fire or HAZMAT spill.
                                                                                    2.1.1.17

Percentage of facilities that are constructed with fire retardant materials.
                                                                                    2.1.1.18

Percentage of facilities that have modular HVAC systems so that individual sections and intakes can be shut down and isolated to prevent the spread of airborne hazards.   2.1.1.19

Percentage of facilities that have multiple alternate evacuation paths. 2.1.1.20

Distribution by facility of how well the exterior of the facility is designed and constructed to prevent unauthorized entry: 2.1.1.21

   a. 0 — can easily be penetrated, such activity may be detected by an alarm
   b. 3 — can be penetrated with difficulty, such activity would be detected by one or more alarms within minutes
   c. 7 — exterior walls, roofs, windows, doors, and basements cannot be penetrated, except with extreme difficulty; such activity would be detected by multiple alarms instantaneously
   d. 10 — exterior walls, roofs, windows, doors, and basements cannot be penetrated

Distribution by facility, how well the interior of the facility is designed and constructed to prevent unauthorized entry and mitigate natural and man-made hazards to which the facility is likely to be subjected: 2.1.1.22

   a. 0 — few if any critical and essential assets are in spaces defined by real doors, floors, and ceilings that are capable of blocking natural or man-made hazards
   b. 2 — some but not all critical and essential assets are in spaces defined by real doors, floors, and ceilings, however they are not capable of blocking natural or man-made hazards
   c. 5 — all critical and essential assets are within spaces defined by real doors, floors, and ceilings, however they are not resistant to natural or man-made hazards
   d. 8 — all critical and essential assets are within spaces defined by real doors, floors, and ceilings that are capable of minimizing or delaying natural and man-made hazards
   e. 10 — all critical and essential assets are within spaces defined by real doors, floors, and ceilings that are capable of blocking natural and man-made hazards

Distribution by facility, percentage of fire doors that are alarmed and shut completely: 2.1.1.23

   a. 0 — none or few of the fire doors shut completely and are alarmed
   b. 3 — some of the fire doors shut completely, but they are not alarmed
   c. 7 — all of the fire doors shut completely, but they are not alarmed
   d. 7 — most of the fire doors shut completely and all are alarmed
   e. 10 — all fire doors shut completely and are alarmed or monitored 24/7 in real-time

By facility and asset criticality, percentage of external door locks that are:
                                    2.1.1.24

   a. Simple key locks
   b. Simple key locks with a single deadbolt
   c. Complex key locks with multiple deadbolts
   d. Electromagnetic locks
   e. Electromagnet locks with remote controls
   f. Alarmed and monitored 24/7

By facility and asset criticality, percentage of internal door locks that are:
                                                                    2.1.1.25

  a. Simple key locks
  b. Simple key locks with a single deadbolt
  c. Complex key locks with multiple deadbolts
  d. Electromagnetic locks
  e. Electromagnet locks with remote controls
  f. Alarmed and monitored 24/7

By facility and asset criticality, percentage of external doors and windows that are bullet proof and blast proof.   2.1.1.26

By facility and asset criticality, percentage of internal doors and windows that are bullet proof and blast proof.   2.1.1.27

By facility and asset criticality, type of vehicle identification system used for employee parking: 2.1.1.28

  a. Red — simple paper tags that are hung from the rear-view mirror or displayed
  b. Yellow — simple paper tags that are hung from the rear-view mirror or displayed; they are changed monthly
  c. Blue — a decal or token is used that cannot be duplicated, except with extreme difficulty
  d. Green — a decal or token is used that cannot be duplicated, except with extreme difficulty; they are changed monthly; an employee ID must be presented also when entering the parking facility

By facility and asset criticality, distance between visitor and employee parking:
                                                                    2.1.1.29

  a. Red — collocated
  b. Yellow — separate adjoining lots or lots are <25 feet apart
  c. Blue — separate lots 26–99 feet apart
  d. Green — separate lots 100+ feet apart

Physical Security Perimeter/Access Control Points

By facility and asset criticality, percentage of assets for which multiple nested physical security perimeters have been defined.   2.1.1.30

By facility and asset criticality, percentage of physical security perimeters for which access control points are defined and enforced through a combination of technical, organizational, and procedural controls.   2.1.1.31

By facility and asset criticality, percentage of physical security perimeters that implement processes, tools, and procedures to monitor physical access control points 24/7.   2.1.1.32

Distribution by facility, how well are the physical security perimeters defined and documented: 2.1.1.33

  a. 0 — not at all
  b. 3 — vaguely

    c. 7 — reasonably well, but there are some gaps or overlaps
    d. 10 — completely, there are no gaps or overlaps

Distribution by facility, how well is access to facilities and secure work areas controlled and restricted to authorized people with appropriate credentials?:
    2.1.1.34

    a. 0 — not at all
    b. 5 — access is somewhat controlled or restricted
    c. 10 — access is strictly controlled and enforced at all times

By facility and asset criticality, distribution of physical security perimeters for which physical access is logged manually or automatically: 2.1.1.35
    a. Percentage of facilities that validate this information against other sources

Percentage of critical and essential information assets that have been reviewed from the perspective of physical risks, such as controlling physical access and physical protection of the backup media.[105]   2.1.1.36

Percentage of critical IT assets in locations with controlled physical access.[105]
    2.1.1.37

Number and percentage of systems for which strict physical access controls are implemented and routinely enforced, by system criticality and information sensitivity.   2.1.1.38

By facility, percentage of network jacks for which physical access is restricted.
    2.1.1.39

By facility, percentage of wireless access points, gateways, and handheld devices for which physical access is restricted.   2.1.1.40

Percentage of facilities that have controlled access to: 2.1.1.41
    a. Parking facilities
    b. Elevators
    c. Stairwells
    d. Restrooms

By facility and asset criticality, percentage of equipment cabinets and wiring closets that are secured and to which access is strictly controlled.   2.1.1.42

By facility and asset criticality, percentage of copiers, printers, telephones, and fax machines that are secured and to which access is strictly controlled.
    2.1.1.43

Distribution by facility, percentage of access rights for employees and visitors to facilities and secure work areas that are regularly reviewed and updated, according to the following scales (40 point max):   2.1.1.44
    a1. 3 — 100 percent are reviewed and updated annually
    a2. 7 — 100 percent are reviewed and updated semi-annually
    a3. 10 — 100 percent are reviewed and updated quarterly
    b1. 3 — 100 percent of the most sensitive positions are reviewed and updated annually

b2. 7 — 100 percent of the most sensitive positions are reviewed and updated quarterly

b3. 10 — 100 percent of the most sensitive positions are reviewed and updated monthly

c1. 3 — 100 percent of the access control rights for employees facing disciplinary action are reviewed and updated within 1 week

c2. 7 — 100 percent of the access control rights for employees facing disciplinary action are reviewed and updated within 48 hours

c3. 10 — 100 percent of the access control rights for employees facing disciplinary action are reviewed and updated within 24 hours

d1. 3 — 100 percent of the access control rights for employees that are being transferred to a new assignment are reviewed and updated within one week

d2. 7 — 100 percent of the access control rights for employees that are being transferred to a new assignment are reviewed and updated within 48 hours

d3. 10 — 100 percent of the access control rights for employees that are being transferred to a new assignment are reviewed and updated within 24 hours

By facility, distribution of people in the facility that are required to wear a token that identifies them as an employee or visitor: 2.1.1.45

a. Percentage of employees that wear visible tokens all of the time that identify them as employees

b. Percentage of visitors that wear visible tokens all of the time that identify them as visitors

c. Percentage of employees who forget or lose their token who are required to wear a temporary ID that must be surrendered before leaving the building

d. Percentage of individuals seen in the facility without identification tokens who are immediately challenged all of the time

e. Percentage of logs of temporary employee IDs issued and returned that are reconciled daily

f. Percentage of logs of visitor IDs issued and returned that are reconciled daily

g. Percentage of ID tokens that must be presented and verified prior to granting access to the facility

h. Percentage of facilities that track the movement of employees and visitors automatically via the tokens to prevent unauthorized entry into restricted areas

By facility, percentage of secure work areas that are not accessible from main hallways or stairwells: 2.1.1.46

a. Percentage of secure work areas that are remotely located

b. Percentage of secure work areas that are not accessible or visible to the general population

c. Percentage of secure work areas that are labeled in an unobtrusive manner

    d. Percentage of secure work areas for which knowledge of the contents and activities performed is restricted on a need-to-know basis

    e. Percentage of unused secure work areas that are locked, sensitive equipment and information have been removed, and they are inspected weekly

    f. Percentage of secure work areas that can only be used during designated hours and when at least two people are present

Percentage of facilities for which procedures are in place to easily distinguish between employees and visitors.   2.1.1.47

Percentage of facilities that enforce the requirement for visitors to be authorized before entering sensitive work areas: 2.1.1.48

    a. Percentage of visitors that are given a time limited token that identifies them as a visitor, their need to be escorted, and the areas to which their access is limited

    b. Percentage of visitors that are required to return their token before leaving

    c. Percentage of facilities that verify daily that all visitor tokens were returned on time

Percentage of facilities that maintain an audit trail of visitor activity: 2.1.1.49

    a. Distribution by facility of the length of time this data is kept, using the following scale: Green — 3 months or more, Blue — 1 to 2 months, Yellow — less than 1 month, Red — 1 week or less

Physical Security Systems

Number and percentage of sensitive work areas that are monitored by cameras: 2.1.1.50

    a. Distribution by work area of the frequency with which this data is audited and correlated with other sources

    b. Distribution by work area of the length of time this data is kept, using the following scale: Green — 3 months or more, Blue — 1 to 2 months, Yellow — less than 1 month, Red — 1 week or less

By facility, percentage of physical security systems that are subject to regular maintenance and testing, by asset criticality: 2.1.1.51

    a. Percentage of facilities that retain test results for at least one year

Percentage of facilities, by asset criticality, for which external security monitoring systems have an unobstructed view of: 2.1.1.52

    a. All exterior walls and entrances

    b. The roof and all equipment located there

    c. Landscaping and courtyard

    d. Parking facilities

    e. Roadways and walkways leading to the facility

    f. Surrounding facilities and property

Percentage of facilities that prohibit photographic, video, audio, scanning, and other recording equipment in the facility, by asset criticality: 2.1.1.53

   a. Percentage of employees and visitors that are asked to deposit such equipment in a container at the building entrance
   b. Percentage of employees and visitors that are scanned for such equipment prior to being granted access to secure work areas
   c. Percentage of employees and visitors that are scanned for such equipment prior to being allowed to leave secure work areas
   d. Percentage of facilities that employ electronic countermeasures to disrupt the operation of unauthorized recording equipment and media

Hazard Protection

Percentage of critical and essential assets exposed to physical risks for which appropriate risk mitigation actions have been implemented in proportion to the likelihood and severity of the risk.[105]   2.1.1.54

Percentage of critical and essential assets that have been reviewed from the perspective of environmental risks such as temperature, humidity, dust, vibration, fire, flooding, etc., whether natural or man-made.[105]   2.1.1.55

Percentage of facilities that have completed a physical threat assessment per Tables 4.1 through 4.5.   2.1.1.56

Percentage of facilities that have developed loss event profiles as part of their hazard preparedness and planning, per Table 4.6.   2.1.1.57

Percentage of facilities that have current and comprehensive all hazards preparedness plans in place, by asset criticality.   2.1.1.58

Percentage of facility all hazards preparedness plans that address worst-case scenarios, by facility and criticality.   2.1.1.59

Percentage of facilities that have maximized the expertise and resources needed to execute a man-made hazard and minimized the opportunity to do so, per Tables 4.1 and 4.3.   2.1.1.60

Percentage of facilities that minimized their susceptibility to natural hazards, per Tables 4.2 and 4.4.   2.1.1.61

Percentage of facilities that correctly store and identify all hazardous materials.   2.1.1.62

Building Services

Percentage of facilities that have secured entry points for public utilities and environmental systems, by asset criticality: 2.1.1.63

   a. Water and sewage
   b. Electric
   c. Gas
   d. HVAC
   e. Water for fire protection systems

  f. Power for fire alarm, public address system, and other building alarm systems

Percentage of facilities that have multiple diverse sources and distribution systems for public utilities, by asset criticality: 2.1.1.64

  a. Water and sewage
  b. Electric
  c. Gas
  d. HVAC
  e. Water for fire protection systems
  f. Power for fire alarm, public address system, and other building alarm systems

How long will backup supplies or sources of public utilities last, by facility:
                         2.1.1.65

  a. Water and sewage
  b. Electric
  c. Gas
  d. HVAC
  e. Water for fire protection systems
  f. Power for fire alarm, public address system, and other building alarm systems

Percentage of facilities that protect utility systems within a building or on rooftops from unauthorized access and tampering, by asset criticality: 2.1.1.66

  a. Water and sewage
  b. Electric
  c. Gas
  d. HVAC
  e. Water for fire protection systems
  f. Power for fire alarm, public address system, and other building alarm systems

By facility and asset criticality, distance to nearest external fire hydrant:
                         2.1.1.67

  a. Red — over 100 feet
  b. Yellow — 50 to 100 feet
  c. Blue — 21 to 50 feet
  d. Green — 20 feet or less

Building Support Services

By facility, percentage of pick-up and delivery areas and mail rooms that are isolated and enforce strict access controls, using the following scales: 2.1.1.68

  a1. 10 — Pick-up and delivery areas are housed in a separate facility apart from the main facility
  a2. 5 — Pick-up and delivery areas are part of the main facility, however they are self-contained

    a3. 0 — Pick-up and delivery services are free to go directly to the work area requesting service

    b1. 10 — Pick-up and delivery areas are monitored 24/7 electronically and by humans

    b2. 5 — Pick-up and delivery areas are staffed during normal business hours and alarms are activated at other times

    b3. 0 — Pick-up and delivery areas are staffed on an "on call" basis

    c.   Percentage of pick-ups and deliveries that are inspected to ensure that: (a) no unauthorized material is leaving the facility, and (b) no hazardous material is entering the facility

    d.   Percentage of pick-ups and deliveries that are logged

    e.   Percentage of facilities that only use known and trusted pick-up and delivery services

Asset Protection

Numerous physical security parameters must be evaluated when planning for asset protection, for example, protecting employees, conducting an asset inventory to determine the criticality and value of tangible and intangible assets, securing communications and IT systems, and managing equipment operations and maintenance activities. Assets need protection from physical security threats originating not just from outsiders, but insiders as well. The retail industry is probably more aware of this fact than any other industrial sector. Annual retail losses due to theft, fraud, and procedural weaknesses are staggering. In 2002, the estimated losses were £884M in the United Kingdom, €29B in the European Union, and $31B in the United States.[198] This amounts to approximately 1.8 percent of the annual retail turnover. The startling part is that 46.6 percent of these losses are the result of deliberate employee theft (or insiders), while only 31.8 percent are from shoplifting (outsiders).[198] Another 12.8 percent are the result of accidental administrative errors by insiders, which makes the insider threat responsible for 59.4 percent of the total losses.[198] Granted, a small percentage of employees is involved, but they are doing a lot of damage.

People are any organization's greatest asset: employees, consultants, contractors, business partners, stakeholders, and customers. Organizations do not run very well or stay in business very long without people. But after reviewing most organizations' asset protection plans, you would never know that. In fact, most asset protection plans fail to make provision for or even mention the organization's most important asset — people. This is a tremendous oversight. Protecting people who are in a facility comes down to two things: (1) protection against natural and man-made hazards, and (2) providing a safe and healthy environment during normal and abnormal circumstances. The types of natural and man-made hazards that are most likely experienced can be determined through a physical threat assessment, as discussed above under facility protection. Use that information to plan and prepare for how a safe and healthy environment can be sustained during normal and abnormal conditions. Plan and practice how the facility can be quickly evacuated, including by people who are physically or visually challenged. Plan and practice where people should gather if the evacuation or rescue must be delayed for any period of time. Plan and have emergency medical, food, water, and other supplies such as flashlights on hand. Have key personnel trained in basic medical care. Ensure that all exits are clearly marked, well known, well lit, and unobstructed. Ensure that there are multiple exits in case one is damaged or unusable. Have smoke evacuation hoods readily available. If a facility is a likely target of a man-made airborne agent, have gas masks readily available also. All of these preparations are common sense, economical, and easy to implement, but it surprising how few organizations take the time to do them. Companies are more willing to expend funds for holiday parties, company picnics, and logo merchandise than for emergency preparedness for their greatest asset. That does not make any sense — business or otherwise. It may also create legal problems in the long run. Several of the nursing homes and hospitals in New Orleans that were caught unprepared for the disaster (no backup electricity, inadequate food, water, and medical supplies) are now facing negligence lawsuits in relation to unnecessary deaths.

A case in point: the airlines. Most all of us fly on a regular basis. Commercial aircraft, airlines, pilots, crews, and mechanics all have to adhere to various safety regulations. But one simple item has been overlooked: individual smoke evacuation hoods. New aircraft are equipped with individual movie screens, headphones, cell phones, blankets, pillows, magazines, all creature comforts, but not a simple safety device. This is unfortunate and illogical. Most fatalities related to fires and explosions are due to inhaling carbon monoxide and other toxic fumes, not the fire or explosion itself. The 15 minutes of clean air an individual smoke evacuation hood provides could make a big difference. That is why many hotels in Asia that are located in earthquake-prone regions equip guest rooms with smoke evacuation hoods. Let us look at the economics of this situation:

- Cost of one smoke evacuation hood: $70 retail, discounts available for bulk purchases.
- Usable life span of a smoke evacuation hood: five years.
- Assume an aircraft makes two flights per day, five days a week, or 520 flights a year.
- Assume the average flight occupancy rate is 66 percent.
- Then the retail cost of providing a smoke evacuation hood is 4¢ per flight — considerably less than a bag of peanuts and soda. With a bulk discount, the cost is probably closer to 2¢ per flight.

Asset protection is an essential component of managing assets. Asset protection is vital to the ability of an organization to carry out its mission; as a result, it should be considered a major responsibility of all levels of management.[14] Before assets can be protected, they must first be identified through an asset inventory; afterward, sensitivity, criticality, and value can be determined.[14] It goes without saying that to be of any use, asset inventories must be complete and current. That is not always an easy task, given the rapid change in technology and the non-stop restructuring and mergers of organizations, not to mention frequent changes in locations. Ever try to track down a computer from a two-year-old inventory for a facility and office that no longer exists? It is essential to verify that all assets are accounted for and that all assets are in fact needed.[28] The process of inventorying assets can be a good time to get rid of superfluous equipment and services. By the same token, it is also important to ensure that all assets have a designated and accountable owner.[28] If no one or no organization is willing to step forward and assume this responsibility for an asset, perhaps it is time to pull the plug. While conducting the inventory, it is a good idea to note dependencies within and among internal and external assets. This information is used to normalize sensitivity, criticality, and value ratings. For example, the value of a dependent asset: (1) can only be less than or equal to that of the independent asset on which it relies, and (2) is proportional to the degree of dependency and the value of the other assets.[16] Asset value can also be thought of in terms of the degree of debilitating impact that would be caused to the organization as a whole by the incapacity or destruction of that asset.[45] That is, there is a direct correlation between asset value and the severity of the consequences of the loss of that asset. To illustrate, what impact would be felt across different or nested physical security perimeters if that asset was lost? What assets are essential to a minimum operational capability?[45] What assets are essential to ensure the health and safety of the occupants?[45] What are the primary services or outputs generated at this facility, and how essential is this asset to their production? Are there any required inputs from external organizations? What happens if those external assets are lost or unavailable? Asset sensitivity, criticality, and value are the factors that determine the level of resilience needed in physical security controls. These factors also drive contingency and disaster recovery planning.

Table 4.7 illustrates how to determine asset value. First of all, note that the value of an asset does not equate to its unit cost or price. This fact is going to come as a shock to some readers, so let me repeat: the value of an asset does not equate to its unit cost or price. Buying and selling prices are only valid in the marketplace. As an analogy, consider your home. Inside your home you probably have some items that are expensive and many that are not. Perhaps you collect rare works of art, stamps, coins, or antique silver. You also have water, which sells for $1 per gallon bottled or less out of the tap. If there is a natural or man-made incident and you run out of water and there is none to buy in the city, you, your family, pets, and plants will die in a matter of days. So what asset of yours is more valuable: the $1 gallon jug of water or the $25,000 painting on your wall?

To determine the true value of an organization's assets, follow the process illustrated in Table 4.7. List all the assets identified in the asset inventory in the first column. Asset importance is then derived as a function of asset criticality and sensitivity. Criticality reflects how critical a given asset is to achieving an organization's mission. There are three standard categories of asset criticality: (1) critical, (2) essential, and (3) routine. Critical assets are those systems, functions, services, or information that, if lost, would prevent

Table 4.7 Asset Value Determination Worksheet

I. Asset Value Ranking

Asset ID	Asset Importance		Impact of Asset Loss			Asset Value Ranking*
	Criticality	Sensitivity	Loss Severity	Scope of Loss	Loss Duration	
Asset 1						
Asset 2						
Asset 3						
Asset x						

* Minimum 17, maximum 200.

II. Weighting Factors

Criticality	Sensitivity	Loss Severity	Scope of Loss	Loss Duration
60 — critical	20 — high	60 — catastrophic	40 — beyond single enterprise (critical infrastructure)	20 — >1 month
30 — essential	10 — moderate	30 — moderate	32 — enterprisewide	15 — 1 to 4 weeks
15 — routine	5 — low	15 — minor	24 — region-wide	10 — 1 to 6 days
	0 — none	7 — marginal	20 — campus-wide	8 — 1 to 23 hours
		0 — none	16 — facility-wide	4 — 1 to 59 minutes
			4 — single work area	0 — <1 minute
			2 — single device	

an organization from achieving its mission or business goals. The loss of essential assets would reduce the ability of an organization to achieve its mission, but not prevent it all together. In contrast, the loss of a routine asset might be a nuisance or require some temporary workarounds; however, it would not significantly degrade the ability of an organization to achieve its mission. Determine the appropriate criticality for each asset and enter the weighting factor from Part II of the table in column 2. Sensitivity assesses the relative degree of confidentiality and privacy protection a given asset needs. Most organizations have many sensitive assets, information or otherwise. Corporate R&D, marketing strategies, expansion plans, and prototypes of new products may all be considered sensitive. The location, contents, and activities conducted in certain facilities may also be sensitive. Sensitivity ratings are assigned to assets based on the potential adverse effect on organizational operations, reputation financial status, other assets, or individuals resulting from the compromise of that asset. Ascertain the appropriate sensitivity rating for each asset and enter the weighting factor from Part II of the table in column 3.

Next, the impact of the loss of each asset is examined in terms of the severity of the loss, the scope of the loss, and the duration of the loss. Severity represents the worst-case consequences. There are four standard categories of severity; they are defined in terms of property loss, financial loss, death, injury, illness, and environmental damage. Catastrophic consequences could result in loss, death, permanent total disability, property loss (including information assets) exceeding $1M, or irreversible severe environmental damage. Critical consequences could result in loss, permanent partial disability, injuries, or occupational illness that may result in hospitalization of at least three personnel, property loss (including information assets) exceeding $200K but less than $1M, or reversible environmental damage. Marginal consequences could result in loss, injury, or occupational illness resulting in a lost workday, property loss (including information assets) exceeding $10K but less than $200K, or mitigable environmental damage. Insignificant consequences could result in loss, injury or illness not resulting in a lost workday, property loss (including information assets) exceeding $2K but less than $10K, or minimal environmental damage. Determine the severity of the loss of each asset and enter the weighting factor from Part II of the table in column 4. The scope of the loss of an asset also affects the impact. There is quite a broad spectrum for the scope of a loss, from impacting a single device to a facility, region, or the entire enterprise. In some instances, the impact may even be felt way beyond the primary organization. The impact on business partners, stakeholders, customers, and the community at large must be factored in. The weighting factor for the scope of loss is entered in column 5. The third aspect of the impact of losing an asset is the duration of the loss, which can range from minutes to days, weeks, or more. Here there are many alternate scenarios for an organization to consider. Perhaps a catastrophic loss of a minute or less is easier to tolerate than a sustained minor loss that goes on for more than a month. The duration should reflect the total time required to remedy the loss and return operations to normal, locally and enterprisewide. Select the appropriate duration weighting factor and enter it in column 6. Now total the weighting factors across the row for each asset. The asset value ranking can range from a minimum of 17 to a maximum of 200. Asset value rankings will highlight which assets need the most resilient physical security controls and robust protection. This information should be a key input to planning and preparedness for contingencies and disasters. Very high asset value rankings may also indicate the need for spares, hot standbys, alternate suppliers, diverse paths, and other factors related to ensuring availability and eliminating single points of failure.

Organizations concentrate most of their protection strategies on IT and telecommunications assets. The need for these assets to function reliably is readily understood. IT and telecommunications assets include portable and fixed equipment, power supplies, the cable plant, and storage media (hard- and softcopy). The fundamental question to answer is, "what are you trying to protect these assets from: theft, sabotage, downtime, or natural or man-made hazards?" Then plan and implement asset protection strategies accordingly. Equipment location and accessibility have a direct effect on the ability to protect it and the type of protection needed. Equipment should be located so as to prevent unauthorized and unnecessary access or viewing and susceptibility to natural or man-made hazards.[28] This is common sense. You do not install your most critical assets on an earthquake fault line, in a region prone to mud slides, or below the water table, or place your most sensitive assets on public display if you want to stay in business for very long. Do not wait for the phone to ring to tell you something is wrong. Monitor the operational environment for critical and essential assets in real-time. Check for potential problems such as smoke, dust, humidity, water, vibration, chemicals, power fluctuations, or problems with the electrical supply.[28] And to avoid inducing these problems on yourself, it is a good idea to have policies in place that prohibit eating, drinking, or smoking near critical and essential equipment.[28] Given the prevalence of insider attacks, it is also a good idea to make critical equipment tamper-proof. This can be accomplished in a variety of ways. The equipment itself can be designed to be tamper-proof, such as tamper-proof enclosures, encapsulation, or shielding.[20] Equipment can also be installed in tamper-proof racks. The intent is to detect attempted tampering, collect evidence of such, and take predetermined action such as triggering an alarm, zeroing out memory, or automatically switching operation to another device or location.[20, 196] The design for tamper-proofing should also deter and resist unauthorized modification and substitution of equipment and components.[20] In very high risk environments, it may make sense to encapsulate critical hardware components in epoxy and include detection mechanisms in and under the epoxy boundary.[196] Epoxy can also be used to disguise chips to prevent reverse-engineering.[196] In short, the solution should reflect the type of tampering it is intended to prevent.

Power supplies are often overlooked when planning for asset protection. Very little IT or telecommunications equipment will operate very long or very well without power. Asset protection necessitates being prepared to provide alternative sources of power to ensure uninterrupted service should the primary source become unavailable. A determination must be made about how long the alternate source should be able to operate.[28] Equipment that does not have backup power supplies needs the ability to gracefully but rapidly power down, without compromising safety or security.[28] Alternate power sources need to be ensured for emergency lighting and equivalent functions. Equipment needs to be protected from dramatic power surges or drops as well. Due to the critical role power plays in the operation of IT and telecommunications equipment, it goes without saying that the policies, operational procedures, and equipment that provide alternate power sources should be tested regularly, so that when they are needed, they work as planned. To prevent deliberate misuse, minimum and maximum operating limits should be established for power supplies.[196]

Today, very few LANs (local area networks) or WANs (wide area networks) are completely wireless. Consequently, network cable plants need protection from natural and man-made hazards. Cable plants should be installed in secure, locked, and shielded conduit.[28] Separate conduit should be used for power and telecommunications cables to prevent interference.[28] A cable plant should have its own physical security perimeter to prevent unauthorized access and tampering. It is a good idea to sweep cable plants frequently to detect unauthorized devices.[28] Design cable plants so that they prevent or eliminate environmental hazards, such as water damage. Also, it is useful to implement a cable plant so that it is as unobtrusive as possible, so that it is not visible or at least not readily noticeable. That way, as little information as possible is revealed about the network and would-be curiosity seekers are deterred.

Storage media needs protection from natural and man-made hazards. This protection should be proportional to the criticality and sensitivity of the information stored on the media. Preventing unauthorized duplication or creation of storage media and controlling the movement of storage media, given its small size and portability, are two major asset protection challenges. A combination of physical and operational security controls, such as searching backpacks, briefcases, purses, etc. upon entry and exit, is needed to stay on top of the situation. Hard- and soft-copy storage media should be physically secured and access to it tightly controlled.[266] This includes the output from printers, copiers, fax machines, monitoring, and test equipment. Label hard- and soft-copy storage media to indicate its sensitivity.[266] Control the internal and external distribution of hard- and soft-copy storage media and require management approval prior to distribution.[266] If storage media is distributed externally, only use secured couriers.[266] To know what is really going on, it is a good idea to keep a current and complete inventory of storage media: who has what, how long they have had it, when it is due to be returned or destroyed, and the criticality and sensitivity category of the media. It is an even better idea to regularly verify the inventory and conduct surprise audits. Storage media should be stored in cabinets that are resistant to natural and man-made hazards. Backup storage media should be stored off-site, at a location far enough away that the backup location is not taken down by the same natural or man-made physical hazard as the primary location. To avoid being caught by surprise, verify the integrity of electromagnetic and electro-optical storage media regularly. It is always better to find out that an item is unreadable during a test than during an emergency.

Portable assets and assets at remote and unmanned sites are often overlooked in asset protection plans. Portable equipment complicates the usual notion of asset protection simply because the equipment is portable and the fact that much of it is employee owned. Concern centers around (1) loss or damage to the equipment itself, and (2) any sensitive information the equipment might contain or reveal about the operation or organization and the ensuing damage from such a loss or revelation. Portable equipment is subject to the hazards associated with portability: being dropped; being caught in the rain; being left in taxis, airports, or hotels; or outsiders eavesdropping on wireless connections. On the other end of the spectrum is the damage that can be done, accidentally or intentionally, from unauthorized equipment being brought into a facility. This can range from misappropriating sensitive information to altering the configuration and operation of IT systems, or introducing malware into an organization's IT infrastructure. Consequently, some common-sense principles are in order. Require property passes for all equipment entering or leaving a facility, regardless of whether it is owned by the organization or an employee.[28] Keep current and complete logs of property passes and their use.[28] Inspect all incoming and outgoing backpacks, briefcases, purses, boxes, and other places portable equipment might be stashed.[28] This is a particular challenge for USB drives. Enforce configuration control, virus signature updates and scanning, and malware detection policies, as well as rigorous identification and authentication controls, on all remote and portable equipment prior to allowing connectivity or access to the organization's IT infrastructure. Block or drop noncompliant equipment. Develop and enforce other telework policies as needed in accordance with the operational risk.[28]

Another topic that is often neglected is asset disposal and reuse. Organizations must carefully consider how and under what conditions assets can be reused or need to be disposed of to avoid potential compromises. Detailed procedures for asset reuse should specify what assets can or cannot be reused and who has the authority to approve and control asset reuse. Before assets are allowed to be reused, they must be sanitized. A variety of sanitization methods exist, each of which provides a different degree of resilience. Choose a sanitization method robust enough to be proportional to the risk of the operational environment. Sanitization refers to removing all traces of prior user activity and stored information. This includes sanitizing all fixed and portable drives, memory, user IDs, passwords, browser favorites, temporary and user files, access statistics, logs, etc. This information should not just be deleted but erased, purged, or degaussed so that it cannot be reconstructed, at least not in any reasonable period of time. Inspect all sanitized assets after the sanitization process to verify that is was effective and thorough, and a second time before allowing reuse.[28] Assets should also be sanitized before disposal. Sensitive assets should be sanitized, and then physically destroyed (shredded, turned into powder or pulp, or incinerated) as part of the disposal process.[28] It is always a good idea to destroy and dispose of information when it is no longer needed. For paper reports this is an easy task. CDs, DVDs, key tape, and other optical and electromagnetic media pose special challenges. That is why standards, such as the NSA/CSS Spec 04-01 for key tape destruction devices, have been developed to ensure that devices exist to properly destroy this type of media.

Do not forget about equipment operation and maintenance when planning for asset protection. This topic is usually thought of as part of IT or operational security, but there are physical security concerns as well. Always maintain equipment in accordance with its specification.[28] This may be a specification supplied by the vendor or one specifically developed by the organization. For this exercise to have any value, it is implied that (1) the specification is accurate, complete, and current; and (2) inspections are conducted regularly to ensure compliance with the specification. All known or suspected anomalies and any preventive or corrective maintenance should be documented: what work was performed, who performed it, when it was performed, and who and when the work was verified.[28] This information should be reviewed regularly, to look for potential trends and to compare it against the specification. Perhaps every time Dick Jones performs a maintenance action, further problems arise or a second trouble ticket must be filed to get the original problem fixed. This could be accidental, due to a lack of training or attention to detail, or intentional. That is why it is essential to limit maintenance personnel, insiders or outsiders, to known, authorized, and trusted staff.[28] It is also a good idea to make sure that maintenance personnel do not leave spare parts, test equipment, drawings, or other items laying around while they are working or after they leave. Make sure that maintenance personnel only work on the equipment or problem on which they are supposed to be working. Letting them roam free invites opportunities for benign or malicious tampering. Also make sure that maintenance personnel do not leave with any "additional" equipment, tools, or information. Be sure to sanitize all memory and storage media before sending equipment offsite for repair.

Operational staff and end users also have a role to play in physical security, specifically in preventing theft, compromise, or unauthorized disclosure of sensitive assets. One technique is known as the clean desk/clean screen policy.[28] This means that when employees leave their work areas, no sensitive information or media is left laying about; rather, everything is locked up and their desktops are clean. This policy should be applied to printers, fax machines, copiers, and interoffice mailboxes as well.[28] To facilitate the clean desk policy, hard and soft media should be labeled to reflect its sensitivity. [28] Generally, these labels are color coded as a vivid reminder. Check safes and lockable file cabinets at the end of each shift to ensure that they are locked.[28] It is best to have this done by an independent third party. Likewise, ensure that computer screens cannot be viewed or read by unauthorized personnel. Simple techniques such as standing at an angle from the screen, looking over someone's shoulder, or viewing activities through windows or glass walls are often used to snoop around. This can be defeated by careful placement of computer screens in work areas, such as screens that are sunken into a desktop, or by special screens that distort images read from an angle or a distance. Of course, if employees leave their computers on when they leave their work areas, all bets are off. To prevent this security lapse, employees should log off or lock their computers with a benign screen saver whenever they leave their work areas for more than ten minutes. If employees fail to do this, the computer system should do so automatically. That is, a clean screen policy should be enforced.

The following metrics can be used to measure the resilience of different aspects of physical security controls related to asset protection.

Protection of Staff

Distribution of facilities that can be evacuated in: 2.1.2.1

  a. Red — over 30 minutes
  b. Yellow — 21 to 30 minutes
  c. Blue — 11 to 20 minutes
  d. Green — 10 minutes or less

Percentage of facilities that continuously monitor air quality for: 2.1.2.2

  a. Chemical contaminants
  b. Biological contaminants
  c. Radiological contaminants
  d. Other harmful pollutants, like carbon monoxide

Distribution of the strength of the air filtration system, by facility: 2.1.2.3

  a. MERV — minimum efficiency reporting value
  b. HEPA — high efficiency particulate air

Percentage of facilities that have emergency medical, food, water, and other supplies on hand in preparation for natural and man-made disasters. 2.1.2.4

Percentage of facilities that have personnel on staff that are trained in basic emergency medicine. 2.1.2.5

By facility, the frequency with which emergency evacuations and shelter in place drills are practiced. 2.1.2.6

Percentage of facilities that are equipped to evacuate people with physical or visual disabilities. 2.1.2.7

By facility, percentage of the normal and peak population for which smoke evacuation hoods are available: 2.1.2.8

  a. Percentage that are child size, if day care is on premises

By facility, percentage of normal and peak population for which gas masks that neutralize chemical and biological airborne agents are available: 2.1.2.9

  a. Percentage that are child size, if day care is on premises

Asset Inventory, Criticality, and Value

Cost of loss $= (C_p + C_t + C_r + C_l) - (I - a)$[116]   2.1.2.10

where:
C_p = Cost of permanent replacements
C_t = Cost of temporary replacements
C_r = Total cost of related costs
C_l = Lost income cost
 I = Insurance or indemnity
 a = Allocable insurance premium

By organizational entity and asset criticality, frequency with which asset inventories are verified and updated.   2.1.2.11

By organizational entity and asset criticality: 2.1.2.12

    a. Percentage of assets that have been inventoried during the past quarter
    b. Percentage of assets that have a designated and accountable owner

By organizational entity, percentage of critical and essential assets for which internal and external asset dependencies have been identified.   2.1.2.13

By organizational entity, distribution of assets: 2.1.2.14

    a. Critical assets without dependencies
    b. Critical assets with dependencies
    c. Essential assets without dependencies
    d. Essential assets with dependencies
    e. Routine assets without dependencies
    f. Routine assets with dependencies

By organizational entity, distribution of asset value determinations, per Table 4.7.   2.1.2.15

    a. Low: 16–53
    b. Minor: 54–89
    c. Moderate: 90–126
    d. High: 127–163
    e. Very High: 164–200

By organizational entity, frequency with which asset value determinations are verified and updated, per Table 4.7.   2.1.2.16

By organizational entity, percentage of information assets that have been assigned a sensitivity category and labeled as such.   2.1.2.17

Percentage of critical and essential assets for which a loss event profile has been developed per Table 4.6:   2.1.2.18

    a. Frequency with which the loss event profile is updated and verified

Communications and IT Systems

Percentage of systems that have a data retention and disposal policy that is current and enforced, by information sensitivity.   2.1.2.19

Percentage of media backups that are stored in a secure off-site facility, by information sensitivity.   2.1.2.20

By facility, percentage of hard- and soft-copy media that are physically secured, by information sensitivity. 2.1.2.21

By facility, percentage of hard- and soft-copy media for which strict controls are enforced over internal and external distribution, by information sensitivity: 2.1.2.22

    a. Percentage of media that are labeled to reflect the sensitivity
    b. Percentage of media that are distributed via a secured courier or delivery mechanism that can be tracked

Percentage of facilities that enforce the requirement for management approval prior to removing media from a secured area. 2.1.2.23

Percentage of facilities that enforce strict control over the storage and accessibility of media, by information sensitivity: 2.1.2.24

    a. Percentage of facilities that maintain current and accurate media inventories
    b. Percentage of facilities that conduct regular audits to verify that the inventories are correct and the media is stored securely

Percentage of facilities that regularly destroy old information when it is no longer needed for business or legal reasons: 2.1.2.25

    a. Percentage of hard-copy materials that are shredded, incinerated, or pulped, by information sensitivity
    b. Percentage of electronic or optical storage media that are purged, degaussed, shredded, or otherwise destroyed so that data cannot be reconstructed, by information sensitivity

By organizational entity, percentage of critical and essential assets that are tamper-proof. 2.1.2.26

By organizational entity, percentage of critical and essential assets for which minimum and maximum operating limits have been established for power supplies. 2.1.2.27

Frequency with which cable plants are scanned for unauthorized devices, by organizational entity and asset criticality. 2.1.2.28

By information sensitivity, percentage of organizational entities that maintain current and complete inventories of all storage media: 2.1.2.29

    a. Percentage of organizational entities that verify their media inventories through regular audits

Frequency with which the integrity of backup storage media is verified, by organizational entity and information sensitivity. 2.1.2.30

Percentage of critical and essential communications and IT equipment for which environmental conditions are continuously monitored. 2.1.2.31

Percentage of critical and essential communications and IT equipment that is adequately protected from natural and man-made hazards, per Tables 4.1 through 4.5. 2.1.2.32

Percentage of critical and essential communications and IT equipment that is specifically located to minimize unauthorized access or observation.

2.1.2.33

Percentage of critical and essential communications and IT equipment that is protected from power fluctuations and the unavailability of the primary power source.   2.1.2.34

Percentage of communication lines that are protected from lightning strikes.

2.1.2.35

Number and percentage of cable plants that are in secure conduit, including at termination and inspection points.   2.1.2.36

Percentage of critical and essential communications and IT assets for which preventive maintenance is performed at regular intervals specified by the vendor or the organization: 2.1.2.37

    a. Percentage of maintenance records that are kept for at least one year

Percentage of operations for which primary and alternate telecommunications service providers have been brought under contract.   2.1.2.38

Percentage of operations for which no single point of failure exists for either the primary or the alternate telecommunications service.   2.1.2.39

Percentage of operations that monitor physical access to communications and IT equipment, by asset criticality.   2.1.2.40

Percentage of operations that protect power equipment from accidental or intentional malicious activity and tampering.   2.1.2.41

Percentage of operations that have the capability to execute an emergency shutdown of communications and IT equipment that allows the equipment to be shutdown quickly, but safely and securely (fail safe/fail secure).   2.1.2.42

Percentage of storage media that are labeled to indicate their sensitivity.

2.1.2.43

Percentage of organizational entities that strictly enforce physical access controls to storage media, by information sensitivity.   2.1.2.44

Percentage of organizational entities that strictly enforce controls over the duplication, alteration, and distribution of storage media, by information sensitivity.   2.1.2.45

Percentage of storage media that are sanitized using approved techniques and equipment prior to reuse or disposal, by information sensitivity.   2.1.2.46

Percentage of storage media for which the sanitization process is verified prior to reuse or disposal, by information sensitivity.   2.1.2.47

Frequency with which the sanitization equipment and technique is verified, by organizational entity.   2.1.2.48

Percentage of equipment that is sanitized using approved techniques and equipment prior to reuse, disposal, or repair by a third party.   2.1.2.49

Percentage of sanitized equipment for which the sanitization process is verified prior to reuse, disposal, or repair by third party personnel.   2.1.2.50

Percentage of facilities that enforce the requirement for property passes for all portable equipment and storage media entering and leaving a facility, regardless of whether it is owned by the employee or organization.   2.1.2.51

Percentage of facilities that keep current and complete logs of property passes and their use: 2.1.2.52

   a. Percentage of facilities that verify property pass logs on a monthly basis

Percentage of IT assets that enforce configuration controls, virus signature updates and scanning, and malware detection policies on all remote and portable equipment before allowing connectivity or access to the IT infrastructure.   2.1.2.53

Percentage of organizational units that enforce policies that define when assets can and cannot be reused and who has the authority to approve and control such reuse.   2.1.2.54

Percentage of entities covered by sanitization policies and procedures, by information sensitivity: 2.1.2.55

   a. Fixed disks and drives
   b. Portable disks and drives
   c. Memory
   d. User IDs
   e. Passwords
   f. Browser favorites
   g. Temporary files
   h. User files
   i. Access statistics
   j. Hardcopy output
   k. Other

Percentage of organizational units that enforce policies that define how and when to dispose of assets and who is responsible for verifying that assets are disposed of correctly, by asset criticality.   2.1.2.56

Equipment Operations and Maintenance

Percentage of operations that verify on a monthly basis that all communications and IT equipment is being maintained according to specification: 2.1.2.57

   a. Frequency with which specifications are verified to be current and complete

Percentage of operations that record and analyze, through to closure, all system anomalies, by system risk.   2.1.2.58

Percentage of operations that only use known trusted third-party maintenance personnel.   2.1.2.59

Percentage of operations that sanitize all equipment before sending it off-site
for repair.   2.1.2.60

Percentage of operations that enforce clean desk and clean screen policies.
                                                                           2.1.2.61

Mission Protection

Mission protection is the ultimate goal of facility and asset protection —
ensuring that an organization is able to achieve its mission and business
objectives under normal and abnormal conditions. Enterprisewide security
master planning and preparedness, and contingency and disaster recovery
planning and preparedness, are conducted to coordinate and confirm facility
and asset protection. This is no small task and it requires acute thoroughness,
attention to detail, and in-depth knowledge of the organization's operations
and idiosyncrasies by an interdisciplinary team. In addition, these plans require
constant updating, verification, and rehearsing by all involved. Conduct regularly announced and surprise inspections to ensure that the planning and
preparedness measures are being followed. If any problems are found during
the inspections, track them through to resolution. Financial continuity can be
eased by purchasing insurance to cover the loss from natural and man-made
hazards, theft, sabotage, and business interruption.[116]

The following metrics can be used to measure the resilience of different
aspects of physical security controls related to mission protection:

Percentage of facilities that maintain current and comprehensive Physical
Security Plans and verify, update, and test them quarterly, by asset criticality.
                                                                           2.1.3.1

Percentage of facilities that have current and complete contingency and disaster
recovery (CDR) plans that address unavailable services, degraded mode services, and systematic recovery of services, by asset criticality: 2.1.3.2

   a. Percentage of CDR plans that have been verified, updated, and tested
      in the past three months
   b. Percentage of CDR plans that address losses of varying types, severity,
      and duration
   c. Percentage of CDR plans that define staff responsibilities for activating
      the plan
   d. Percentage of CDR plans that define staff responsibilities for recovery
      activities
   e. Percentage of CDR plans that describe recovery activities in sufficient detail
   f. Percentage of CDR plans for which adequate additional resources (spare
      parts, alternate power supplies, alternate telecommunications paths,
      etc.) are already available

Percentage of off-site storage facilities and backup operational sites that are:
                                                                           2.1.3.3

   a. Green — 100 miles or more away from the primary location
   b. Blue — 50 to 99 miles away from the primary location

    c. Yellow — 25 to 49 miles away from the primary location
    d. Red — 24 miles or less away from the primary location

Distribution by facility and asset value, of the assets covered by insurance to protect against losses from: 2.1.3.4

    a. Natural hazards
    b. Man-made hazards
    c. Theft
    d. Arson
    e. Sabotage
    f. Business interruption

Percentage of Contingency and Disaster Recovery Plans that are based on a current physical threat assessment, per Tables 4.1 through 4.6.   2.1.3.5

Percentage of organizational units that conduct quarterly reviews to verify compliance with intellectual property rights and legislation: 2.1.3.6

    a. Copyrights
    b. Patents
    c. Trademarks
    d. Software licenses

Percentage of organizational units that conduct quarterly reviews to verify compliance with legal requirements for record retention: 2.1.3.7

    a. Information is retained for the proper period of time
    b. Information is in a format that is retrievable
    c. Information is stored in a media that is usable
    d. Access to the information is restricted
    e. Information is stored securely on-site and at a secure backup facility
    f. Information cannot be altered; such attempts are detected and preempted
    g. A current and complete record inventory is maintained and verified quarterly
    h. Retention mechanisms and procedures comply with privacy regulations

Percentage of operations, by asset criticality, that have alternate off-site storage and operational centers: 2.1.3.8

    a. Backup operational center is fully staffed and equipment is configured
    b. Can switch to the backup operational center automatically in a matter of minutes
    c. Backup operational center can handle normal and peak processing loads, capacity, and throughput
    d. Backup operational center can only handle a degraded mode processing load, capacity, and throughput

Dependency on multinational operations to accomplish mission and/or maintain current revenue stream, using the following scale: 4 — ultra high, 3 — high, 2 — moderate, 1 — minor, 0 — none.[105]   2.1.3.9

Percentage of business operations that are dependent upon third parties, by asset criticality.   2.1.3.10

Physical Security Metrics Reports

At times, a single metric will suffice. On other occasions, a collection of related metrics is required. The quantity and specific type of metrics needed depend on the Goal being measured and the Questions being investigated in order to measure progress toward achieving or sustaining that Goal. Table 4.8 provides a sample template for a physical security metrics report that analyzes the results from multiple metrics. The header information sets the context for the report, to help ensure that the results are not misinterpreted. First of all, the security domains, sub-elements, and focus of the report are identified. The domain can be one or more of the four security domains: (1) physical, (2) personnel, (3) IT, or (4) operational security. One or more sub-elements within the selected security domains can be examined. The sub-elements are those listed in the second column of Table 1.1. The focus clarifies the particular topic within the sub-element that is being investigated. Next, the measurement boundary and time interval used during the collection and analysis of the metrics are defined. Finally, the header indicates whether the metrics reported are estimates or actual values. This is an important distinction. Be careful not to mix both types of metrics in a single report, or the results could be very misleading. There are four main parts to the report: (1) the metric, (2) the target value, (3) the observed value, and (4) the interpretation of the observed value. The metric is identified by its reference number and a short definition. Then a target value is established for the metric. This is the ideal value for the metric, given your organization, mission, and operational environment. There may be a single value for this metric. More often, the value will be tailored according to system risk, information sensitivity, or asset criticality — in which case there would be three target values. The next column captures the value that was observed for this metric during the given measurement boundary, time interval, and other constraints specified by the measurement process. The final column interprets the meaning of the observed results in light of the specified target value. If necessary, explanatory notes can be added below the table. The last row in the table summarizes the overall observations.

Now let us walk through a completed physical security resilience metric report to see how it works. Assume the following:

Goal: Provide adequate protection for organizational assets

Question 1:   Do we have a complete picture of our organization's assets?

This is a fundamental goal of all organizations. However, most organizations fail to ask the first and perhaps most important question, in this regard. Put more bluntly, if an organization does not know in detail (1) what its assets are, (2) how important each asset is to achieving the organization's mission, and (3 who is responsible for each asset, it is impossible to provide adequate protection for these unknown, unvalued assets that no one is accountable for. And, in this situation, any funds spent for asset protection are most likely being thrown down the drain for a "feel-good" facade.

In contrast, Table 4.9 highlights what can be learned by investigating this fundamental question. As shown, Asset Protection is a sub-element of Physical

Table 4.8   Resilience Metric Report Template

Security Domain(s):   Sub-element(s):   Report Date:

Measurement Boundary: Time Interval: Reporting Entity:

Focus:

Prediction or Actual Value:

Metric			Target Value			Observed Value	Interpretation
ID	Definition		Low Risk/ Routine Asset	Moderate Risk/ Essential Asset	High Risk/ Critical Asset		
Summary			Total Possible			Actual Score	
						Overall Rating	

Notes

Table 4.9   Resilience Metric Report — Asset Protection

Report Date: 10 Nov 2005

Reporting Entity: Dept. 450

Security Domain(s): Physical Security   **Sub-element(s):** Asset Protection   **Focus:** Asset inventory and criticality

Measurement Boundary: Organizational entity   **Time Interval:** Aug 2005 – Oct 2005   **Prediction or Actual Value:** Actual value

	Metric	Target Value			Observed Value	Interpretation
ID	Definition	Routine Asset	Essential Asset	Critical Asset		
2.1.2.11	Frequency with which asset inventories are verified and updated	Semi-annually	Quarterly	Monthly	R - 0 E - quarterly C - quarterly	R - Red E - Green C - Yellow
2.1.2.12	Percentage (%) of assets inventoried this quarter	50%	100%	100%	R - 0 E - 100% C - 100%	R - Red E - Green C - Green
	Percentage (%) assets with a designated owner	100%	100%	100%	R - 0 E - 50% C - 75%	R - Red E - Yellow C - Yellow
2.1.2.13	Percentage (%) of assets for which dependencies have been identified	100%	100%	100%	R - 0 E - 50% C - 75%	R - Red E - Yellow C - Yellow

	Metric	Target Value				
ID	Definition	Routine Asset	Essential Asset	Critical Asset	Observed Value	Interpretation
2.1.2.14	Percentage (%) of critical assets without dependencies	N/A	N/A	N/A	25%	A high % of critical and essential assets have dependencies.
	Percentage (%) of critical assets with dependencies				75%	
	Percentage (%) of essential assets without dependencies				50%	See note 1.
	Percentage (%) of essential assets with dependencies				50%	
	Percentage (%) of routine assets without dependencies				?	
	Percentage (%) of routine assets with dependencies				?	
2.1.2.15	Distribution of asset value, per Table 4.7	N/A	N/A	N/A		Asset value distribution is normal.
	Low: 16–53				20%	
	Minor: 54–89				30%	
	Moderate: 90–126				30%	
	High: 127–163				15%	
	Very high: 164–200				5%	

Table 4.9   Resilience Metric Report — Asset Protection (continued)

Metric		Target Value			Observed Value	Interpretation
ID	Definition	Routine Asset	Essential Asset	Critical Asset		
2.1.2.16	Frequency with which asset value determinations are verified and updated	Semi-annually	Quarterly	Monthly	R - semi-annually E - quarterly C - quarterly	R - Green E - Green C - Yellow
2.1.2.17	Percentage (%) of information assets that have been assigned a sensitivity category and labeled as such	100%	100%	100%	R - 100% E - 100% C - 100%	R - Green E - Green C - Green
2.1.2.18	Percentage (%) of assets for which a loss event profile has been developed	100%	100%	100%	R - 0 E - 50% C - 75%	R - Red E - Yellow C - Yellow
	Update frequency	Semi-annually	Quarterly	Monthly	R - 0 E - semi-annually C - quarterly	R - Red E - Yellow C - Yellow
Summary Red = 0 points Yellow = 5 points Green = 10 points		**Total Possible** Routine - 80 points Essential - 80 points Critical - 80 points			**Cumulative Score** Routine - 25 points or 31% Essential - 60 points or 75% Critical - 50 or 62.5% **Overall Rating** Yellow	

Note 1: A high percentage of both critical and essential assets have dependencies. Recommend further analysis of the IT infrastructure architecture and workflow to: (a) look for opportunities to reduce the extent of dependencies, and (b) determine the distribution of dependency on internal and external assets.

Security. To answer Question 1, the focus is on how well and how thoroughly the organization understands its asset inventory and criticality. In this example, the measurement boundary is by organizational entity. Depending on the size of an organization, that could be a department, division, group, or wholly owned subsidiary. Using organizational entity as a measurement boundary leaves open the possibility of aggregating the metrics to obtain an enterprise-wide view later. First, the reports are captured by organizational entity to pinpoint where the problems are; then the information is aggregated to see the big picture. The reporting interval is the preceding three months and actual values are reported. In this report, eight metrics that relate to asset inventory and value are examined. No target values were established for two of the metrics: 2.1.2.14 and 2.1.2.15. These metrics represent information an organization needs to know, but it is difficult if not impossible to establish target values. Target values are established for the other six metrics by asset criticality. Looking at the observed values we see that the most effort has focused on essential and critical assets; hence information for routine assets is incomplete. The interpretation column translates the results into a color-coded scale: Red — serious problems, Green — everything is OK, Yellow — somewhere between Red and Green. This is an easy way of communicating the results to senior management. For the summary, a point value is assigned to each Red, Yellow, and Green rating by asset criticality. As shown, for routine assets, a score of 31 percent was achieved. For essential assets, a score of 75 percent was achieved; while for critical assets, a score of 62.5 percent was achieved. This indicates that there is still a fair amount of work to do; hence the overall rating is Yellow. In this example routine, essential and critical assets were assigned an equal weight. In some instances, it may be useful to weight the risk or asset criticality categories. To illustrate, if in this example essential assets were double-weighted and critical assets were triple-weighted, the summary and overall assessment would have been:

Routine — 25 points or 5 percent
Essential — 120 points or 25 percent
Critical — 150 points or 31 percent
Overall Rating — Red

4.3 Personnel Security

Mention the term "personnel security" and most people think immediately, and usually exclusively, of background investigations. Personnel security is associated with attempts to determine if the lowly peon who dared to apply for a job with an organization is a "good guy" or a "bad guy." Is he someone who can be trusted, or is he someone who is going to pilfer the cash drawer or the holiday party fund, rummage through the supply room and help himself to whatever he or his children or friends need, "borrow" office equipment and never return it, or sell trade secrets or other sensitive information on the black market? Many positions with government agencies and government contractors require special background investigations to determine if this low life is likely to hand out state secrets like Halloween candy or leave them lying around like food for the pigeons. To the uninitiated (and perhaps those with a slightly guilty conscience), this conjures up all sorts of nefarious images of super-snoops tapping your cell phone, reading your private e-mail, and interrogating your third-grade teacher about how many times you had to stay after school and why. If you have ever been a political appointee subject to confirmation hearings by Congress, this is all old hat. Fear not, in modern times, the polygraph exam has replaced the rack as the instrument of truth. Never mind the fact that many states have outlawed polygraph exams as part of the pre-employment process and as evidence in court, because they are about as accurate as a Ouija™ board.

There is a broad spectrum when it comes to background investigations. The high school student working as a cashier at a fast food restaurant needs a different type and intensity of background investigation than someone who is in charge of operating the U.S. Treasury's financial payment system. By the same token, background investigations are only one sequence in the array of personnel security measures. As mentioned previously in this chapter, people are any organization's greatest asset. When it comes to security, people can be an organization's greatest liability. People, not technology, are undoubtedly the weakest link in any security program.[14] Usually but not always, this is due not to malevolence, but rather to a lack of (1) proper security education, (2) awareness of the consequences of a given act, and (3) accountability.[14] Did you ever hear of IT equipment committing fraud or treason of its own free will? No. IT equipment does what it is told to do by the humans who design, develop, install, operate, and use it. And while IT equipment will always do what it is designed, instructed, or configured to do, rightly or wrongly, humans on the other hand are not infallible. That is why year after year the statistics show that insiders or insiders colluding with outsiders account for approximately 80 percent of all security incidents — and hence the need for a broad spectrum of ongoing personnel security measures.

So what is personnel security? Government regulations do not define personnel security. For the most part, regulations speak in nebulous terms of accountability and trustworthiness. Government and industry standards do not define personnel security. Rather, these standards jump into the details of how to conduct, adjudicate, and renew background investigations; for example, how to collect and transmit fingerprint files. So I will boldly go where no other security engineer has gone before and define personnel security:

> **Personnel security:** a variety of ongoing measures that are undertaken to reduce the likelihood and severity of accidental and intentional alteration, destruction, misappropriation, misuse, misconfiguration, unauthorized distribution, and unavailability of an organization's logical and physical assets, as the result of action or inaction by insiders and known outsiders, like business partners.

Personnel security measures are an attempt to minimize the risk of an organization incurring damage to or loss of its assets by people who routinely have approved access to them. Damage or loss can be accidental or intentional and the result of action or inaction. Someone can accidentally or intentionally crash a system. A file cabinet or desktop system can be accidentally or intentionally left open. A system administrator can "forget" to perform backups or update virus signatures. Damage can be very visible, such as deleted files or corrupted applications, or very subtle, such as slight changes to data or system configurations that do not generate any error messages and go undetected for a period of time. Physical security provides physical access controls. IT security implements logical access controls. Operational security governs how IT is developed, operated, used, and maintained. In contrast, personnel security attempts to determine whether people who have logical and physical access rights to develop, operate, use, and maintain an organization's assets are likely to abuse or misuse these privileges for personal motives or gain or act irresponsibly, such that damage or loss occurs. The people in question include permanent and temporary employees, contractors, consultants, vendors, service personnel, and a host of other business partners that have regular access to an organization's assets.

Personnel security is all about finding and acknowledging human weaknesses. Human beings are not perfect and never will be. People can be careless, inattentive, in a hurry, preoccupied, or in a bad mood; they can also be deliberately deceitful or destructive, or just lose control. It is essential to design and implement personnel security measures that acknowledge this fact. Why not go a step further? Design personnel security controls so that there is a buffer zone, between just a paper policy violation and a serious security impact, that will serve as a wake-up call to the individual who is about to do something really stupid. Consider the following analogy. Originally, if drivers left their car lights on when they parked, they came back to find the battery drained. That situation can be a real nuisance if it is 11 p.m. and you are 50 miles from home. So, automobile manufacturers added alarms that either beeped or told drivers that their headlights were on. Some people paid attention, but others were oblivious and used one false pretense after another: "I won't be gone long," "I don't have time," etc. If you have had to help jump-start a car late at night in the rain, you understand. Automobile manufacturers realized that human beings are not capable of making right decisions, even simple decisions, 100 percent of the time. So they added a timer to automatically shut off the headlights if a car remained parked for a period of time. The same kind of buffer zone should be applied to personnel security measures. This buffer zone is equivalent to the internal controls required by many of the security and privacy regulations discussed in Chapter 3. Internal controls are designed and intended to detect and preferably prevent security violations.

Personnel security is a delicate matter due to the long-term consequences to the individual and the organization, and the fact that this area is more of a soft science than physical, IT, or operational security — not to mention the possibility of lawsuits for wrongful action on part of the organization. Personnel security also raises a multitude of privacy issues that must be dealt with in an ethical, legal, fair, and consistent manner. It is reasonably easy to weed out the psychopaths and those with a long criminal history who would jump at the chance to do damage their first day on a new job. It is not so easy to identify who, among the vast majority of the populace that are honest, ethical, and law abiding, might sometime in the future do damage should the world situation or their personal situation, attitudes, or beliefs change. That is why an organization needs a variety of different ongoing personnel security measures.

Personnel security's first cousin is personnel safety. Personnel safety concerns accidental or intentional action or inaction that could have a safety impact, such as injury, illness, death, or environmental damage. Safety engineers spend a lot of time analyzing how a system, device, or asset is intended to be used, versus how it will be or might be used, human nature being what it is. Normal and abnormal operational profiles and scenarios are developed and analyzed with the assistance of human factors engineers and domain experts. The goal is to find and eliminate or minimize the opportunity for induced or invited errors — ways in which a system, device, or asset could accidentally or intentionally be misused. All sorts of design considerations are evaluated and optimized in terms of usability and safety: screen layout, sizes, shapes, colors, viewing angles, task sequences, amount of recall required, minimum and maximum response times, fatigue, number of steps or operations, understandability, etc. In conjunction, a variety of checks and balances are built in to preempt potential human error that could have a safety impact. For example, alarms are triggered and action is taken to prevent reaching unsafe conditions as a result of illegal inputs or illegal command sequences. A simplistic analogy is a software application or operating system asking you if you really, really want to delete, replace, or overwrite a file. This is why (1) many consumer products come with warnings about correct and incorrect use, and (2) product liabilities are limited to correct use and maintenance. In summary, personnel safety measures attempt to prevent humans from doing something ignorant that could have serious safety consequences, regardless of whether it is the result of inattention, stupidity, or a "bad hair day." Personnel security is very similar, the difference being that the intent is to prevent or preempt incidents that have a security impact.

Figure 4.3 illustrates the taxonomy of personnel security parameters. As shown, they fall into five categories:

1. Accountability
2. Background investigations
3. Competence
4. Separation of duties
5. Workforce analysis

The first three categories focus on one individual at a time, while the last two look across the workforce as a whole. Together, these five areas provide insight into an organization's personnel security status. Each area and the metrics that support it are discussed below.

Accountability
- Security policies, procedures, and standards are published and distributed
- Security policies, procedures, and standards define specific roles and responsibilities
- Security policies, procedures, and standards are tied to specific job descriptions and assets
- Regular educational forums are held to promote understanding
- Individuals acknowledge agreement in writing
- Adherence is part of performance appraisals
- Consequences of not following security policies, procedures, and standards are defined
- Requirements are extended to all third parties through legal means

Background Investigations
- Correspond to position sensitivity, criticality, and risk
- Reflect level of trust
- Completed prior to hiring, grounds for retaining
- Are unbiased, consistent, objective, accurate, fair, current

Competence
- Security education requirements
- Formal education, experience, certification, licensing required to perform tasks
- Position description
- Domain knowledge
- Contractual requirements

Separation of Duties
- Internal control
- Least privilege
- Need to know
- Job rotation

Workforce Analysis
- Definite insiders, pseudo insiders
- Tenure, experience
- Citizenship
- Eligibility to retire
- Geography
- Proficiency at more than one job function

Figure 4.3   Taxonomy of personnel security parameters.

Accountability

The essence of accountability is to hold people responsible for their conduct and obligations, whether personal or professional. Responsible behavior — the ability to choose by oneself between right and wrong — marks the difference between being a child and being an adult. Accountability implies that a certain level of trust has been conveyed upon an individual; should that trust be violated, the individual is liable for the consequences and penalties. Accountability begins by informing individuals of their duties and responsibilities. This is only common sense — it is not ethical, legal, or possible to hold someone accountable for something about which you have not told him or her. Informing people does not mean just a casual remark in passing, such as, "Be sure to turn off your computer before going home each night." Nor it is some generic fluff that is repeated and passed from organization to organization, such as, "Like wow! Security is really important dude; better pay attention to this." Rather, accountability means, first of all, that the organization is responsible for publishing and distributing all of its security policies, procedures, and standards. Publication and distribution can be electronic as long as the information is equally available to all involved. These security policies, procedures, and standards must, to be effective and enforceable, be detailed, define specific roles and responsibilities, and be tied to specific job functions and organizational assets.[14, 28, 52] They should explain what does and does not constitute sound security practices under all sorts of different scenarios, both normal and abnormal, such as correct logical and physical access control procedures, correct procedures for the use and release of sensitive information, and action to be taken and by whom during a known or suspected security incident.[33] Tailor security policies and procedures for each position and risk level.[14, 28, 52] Clearly assign and demarcate roles and responsibilities to ensure that (1) all security tasks are accomplished, independently when necessary, and (2) there are no overlaps or gaps.[15] Define all security duties unambiguously.[15] Once published, security policies and procedures should not be considered carved in stone. Instead, they need to be reviewed, updated, and reaffirmed at regular intervals.[52]

This is an area where most organizations fall short — they try to impose a single security policy across the entire organization, regardless of the organization's size, an individual's job function, or the position sensitivity or risk. That approach is a definite recipe for disaster. Do the receptionist in charge of visitor control, the head of network operations, and the head of accounts payable all have the same security roles, responsibilities, procedures, and standards to follow? Do all positions in an organization have the same sensitivity, criticality, and risk associated with them? The answer to both questions is a resounding no! That is exactly why (1) many of the security and privacy regulations discussed in Chapter 3 require security awareness and training to be focused and job specific, and (2) generic fluffy policies are not effective or enforceable.

Real commitment at all levels of an organization is needed to make accountability work.[15] As more and more organizations are coming to realize, security is a business responsibility that must be shared by all members and layers of the organization.[28, 105] This is definitely a situation where leading by example is the best practice. Conversely, security is not an area where a minimum wage employee should be terminated for a minor infraction, while a vice president gets away with one serious violation after another without any repercussions. Talk about sending the wrong message. Security accountability is not designed to be used as a "gotcha" to get rid of an individual or business partner who you had it in for anyway. Accountability must be practiced and enforced equitably at all layers up and down the chain. Failure to do so will lead to nasty and expensive lawsuits, not to mention severe damage to an organization's reputation. This is the exact scenario that precipitated issuance of several of the security and privacy regulations discussed in Chapter 3.

It is not practical to shove security policies and procedures into employees' mailboxes and declare "mission accomplished." Let us be reasonable. How many of you pay attention, particularly serious attention, to all the unsolicited and for the most part irrelevant paper that ends up in your mailbox? Beyond publication and distribution, accountability implies that all involved understand the security policies, procedures, and standards for which they are being held accountable. Hence, regular educational forums should be conducted to promote this understanding and reinforce its importance.[15, 28, 33, 266] People should feel free to ask questions and clarify issues then and at any time in the future.[28] They should be encouraged to recommend changes to policies that they think are not working or could work better.[28] Use this opportunity to direct people to additional documents, references, and resources they can consult for supplementary detailed information related to the security policies, procedures, and standards.[28] Explain the context and objectives behind security policies and procedures or, in other words, why the policies and procedures are needed.[15, 16]

At the same time, it is important to explain the consequences to the asset, organization, and individuals of not following security policies and procedures.[15] Do not make any assumptions. Often, people do not understand the seriousness of why something must be performed, or why it must be performed a certain way, or the severity of the potential damage if the situation is not explained to them. This is especially true when talking about safety and security. New employees and younger employees tend to need the most coaching in this regard.[28] Explain the consequences clearly and concisely, especially the sanctions that will be imposed according to the type, number, and severity of security violations committed. It goes without saying that sanctions must be applied fairly, consistently, and legally for all people.[28, 52] Sanctions may include disciplinary action, termination, revocation of a security clearance, financial fines, and other legal penalties.

Have each individual acknowledge in writing that he has received, understands, and agrees to the security policies, procedures, and standards that apply to his position and the assets that he owns, provides, and uses.[14, 52, 266] This is a good way to verify the effectiveness of the educational forums and the clarity and completeness of the policies, procedures, and standards. Require acknowledgment prior to granting access to facilities or assets.[52] The acknowledgment process is also a good time to explain and obtain signatures for information access agreements, such as non-disclosure agreements, use limitations, and conflicts of interest.[52] These documents serve as a formal written notice of asset sensitivity and criticality, and the legal protection requirements.[28] These documents should explain the consequences and penalties for any violations and how long the provisions are applicable after the individual severs his relationship with the organization.[28] As a friendly reminder, it is a good idea to review and resign these documents whenever an individual leaves or transfers to another part of the organization.[28]

Systematic internal controls are needed to enforce accountability. Examples include audit trails for IT systems and networks, records of logical and physical access rights and privileges, and records of actual logical and physical access, including remote access, by date, asset, and individual, records of participation in regular security policy educational forums, and conducting surprise audits to see how well security policies, procedures, and standards are being followed.[52, 266] Design internal controls to meet the legal requirement for non-repudiation and make this ability well known. Group, shared, and generic accounts, such as SYS ADMIN or TRAINING, defeat accountability and should

Definite Insiders
- Permanent employees, full-time and part-time

Pseudo Insiders
- Temporary employees
- Employees on extended leave of absence
- Retired employees
- New hires who have not reported to work
- Summer interns
- Employees stationed off-site
- Spouses and families of employees
- Contractors
- Consultants
- Vendors, suppliers
- IT maintenance personnel
- Business partners
- Customers

Pseudo-Outsiders
- Contract cleaning crew
- Delivery services (postal service, contract carriers)
- Public utility employees (water, gas, electric, telephone)
- Trash removal service
- Parking lot attendants
- Landlord

Definite Outsiders
- Individuals and organizations that have no business, financial, legal, educational, or social relationship with your organization

---

Figure 4.4   Who are insiders and outsiders?

be avoided at (almost) all costs. If there is a perception that accountability is not being enforced and is just another passing organizational psychology fad, adherence will be lax indeed. An easy technique to overcome a lax attitude is to include adherence to security policies, procedures, and standards as a key element in annual performance appraisals. Strict accountability requirements, explicit consequences and penalties for violations, and rigorous enforcement can have a very strong deterrence effect. Once people realize that an organization is serious about security and accountability, they will take these matters seriously as well.

To whom do accountability requirements apply? In security circles, it is common to speak of insiders and outsiders, as if everyone can easily be assigned to one bucket or the other. If this concept is considered more closely, it becomes apparent that this is not the case at all, regardless of the size of the organization. Of course there are a few who are definite insiders and a few who are definite outsiders. However, there are a lot of people who fall in the gray area between insiders and outsiders. Let us look at a few examples to see why (see Figure 4.4). The term "insiders" is generally used to refer to employees, but there are many categories of employees: permanent employees, temporary employees, employees who are on extended leaves of absence, former employees, retired employees, summer interns, new hires who have accepted a job offer but not yet reported to work, and employees who are stationed elsewhere, such as at a supplier's facility. Are all of these categories of employees really insiders? What about their spouses and other family members? Perhaps the only definite insiders are permanent employees, both full- and part-time. But then again, perhaps some of these people are in the process of interviewing with one of your competitors. Then we come to a group of pseudo-insiders who regularly interact with the organization, such as contractors, consultants, vendors, suppliers, IT maintenance personnel, customers, and other business partners. Should each of these groups be treated as insiders or outsiders? Why? A business partner today may be a competitor tomorrow.

Next there is a group of pseudo-outsiders who are not involved in the internal workings of an organization, but are essential to keeping an organization up and running. This group includes people who may be seen in your facility on a daily basis year after year, like the contract cleaning crew and delivery service personnel. People who are seen on a rare basis (usually during an emergency or when new services are started), such as employees of the public utilities, are also pseudo-outsiders. Some organizations lease facilities, in which case the landlord may have personnel on-site. They are responsible for the building services but not helping your organization accomplish its mission. Finally, we come to the group that can be considered definite outsiders: individuals and organizations who have no current or potential future business, financial, legal, educational, or social relationship with your organization. Consequently, rather than referring to just insiders and outsiders, it is more appropriate to refer to a spectrum of people who range from definite insiders to definite outsiders, and acknowledge that the mix changes over time.

Previously we stated that personnel security is concerned about potential, accidental, or intentional action or inaction by insiders and known outsiders. This means that security policies, procedures, and standards need to reflect this spectrum of insiders and outsiders, especially logical and physical access control rights and privileges. Define accountability requirements and liabilities for all categories of insiders and outsiders. Accountability requirements should be passed on to all third parties through their contracts to make the third parties legally liable and responsible for compliance.[52, 266] Require third parties contractually to (1) be subject to scheduled and surprise compliance audits, and (2) cooperate with responses to ongoing security incidents and after the fact incident investigations.[28, 52] Furthermore, it is a good idea to require third parties to produce evidence of insurance or other indemnities in this regard.[28] The same accountability provisions should be applied to outsourcing contracts, perhaps even more rigorously. A note of caution: the popular offshore outsourcing craze raises serious security concerns because of the questionable ability to enforce accountability provisions in the international legal arena. The prime organization's only recourse may be to cancel a contract or not pay for services rendered. However, that does not provide much of a deterrence capability, as recent scandals in India have shown, once the third party has your sensitive data or other critical assets.[250]

Accountability requirements often follow an individual long after he has left an organization or a contract has ended, especially if he was handling extremely sensitive or critical assets. That is why it is important to have a security exit interview during which all badges, keys, tokens, hard- and soft-copy files, etc. are turned in and accounted for to both parties' satisfaction.

This is a good time to remind the individual of his ongoing security responsibilities and verify that all logical and physical access rights have been revoked. Make sure the individual has a copy of all the paperwork from the security exit interview and is given a point of contact should any questions or concerns arise in the future.

The following metrics can be used to measure different aspects of the resilience of accountability personnel security controls. Note that the term "individuals" is used frequently, rather than employees, to indicate that the metric also applies to pseudo-insiders and pseudo-outsiders.

By organizational unit, percentage of individuals who have received current copies of all the security policies, procedures, and standards that are applicable to their job function and the assets they provide, own, operate, or use:

2.2.1.1

    a. Definite insiders
    b. Pseudo-insiders
    c. Pseudo-outsiders

By organizational unit, percentage of security policies, procedures, and standards that are: 2.1.1.2

    a. Current (reviewed, updated, and reaffirmed within the past 12 months)
    b. Detailed enough to implement on a daily basis
    c. Define specific roles and responsibilities
    d. Tied to specific job functions
    e. Tailored to position sensitivity, criticality, and risk
    f. Tied to specific assets
    g. Reflect normal and abnormal operational scenarios

Percentage of information security management roles for which responsibilities, accountability, and authority are assigned and required skills identified.[105]

2.2.1.3

Percentage of position descriptions that define the security roles, responsibilities, skills, and certifications for: (a) security managers and administrations, (b) IT personnel, and (c) general staff and system users.[105]   2.2.1.4

By organizational unit, frequency with which educational forums are held to explain security policies, procedures, and standards: 2.2.1.5

    a. Date of most recent class
    b. Percentage of affected individuals who have attended an educational forum within the past six months
    c. Number of recommended changes and enhancements to security policies and procedures that were received during educational forums held within the past six months

By organizational unit, percentage of security policies, procedures, and standards that define sanctions according to the type, number, and severity of violations.   2.2.1.6

Percentage of job performance reviews that include evaluation of information security responsibilities and information security policy compliance, appropriate for the sensitivity level of the position.[105]   2.2.1.7

By organizational unit, percentage of affected individuals who have acknowledged in writing that they have received, understand, and agree to the security policies, procedures, and standards that apply to them.   2.2.1.8

Percentage of accountability requirements in security policies, procedures, and standards that are enforced: 2.2.1.9

   a. Through technical controls
   b. Through management controls
   c. Through a combination of technical and management controls

Percentage of third parties for which accountability requirements have been conveyed through legal means: 2.2.1.10

   a. Pseudo-insiders
   b. Pseudo-outsiders
   c. Offshore business partners
   d. Outsourcing firms

Percentage of affected individuals for whom security exit interviews were conducted during the past 12 months: 2.2.1.11

   a. At contract expiration for third parties
   b. Prior to transfer to another part of the organization
   c. Prior to normal termination of employment
   d. Prior to termination for cause

Percentage of individuals whose logical and physical access privileges have been reviewed this quarter[105]:   2.2.1.12

   a. Definite insiders
   b. Pseudo-insiders
   c. Pseudo-outsiders
   d. Prior to transfer to another part of the organization
   e. Prior to normal termination of employment
   f. Prior to termination for cause

Background Investigations

Background investigations are a quasi-scientific attempt to determine if the level of trust that can be placed in individuals is equivalent to that required by the position for which they have applied. Different positions within an organization require different levels of trust. Different job functions and organizations require different types of trust. Level of trust refers to the degree of trust placed in an individual who occupies a certain position — the extent to which the organization trusts that individual to perform these duties accurately and efficiently, as instructed, to further the organization's goals. What

Ultra High
> Individual can be trusted under all situations to act responsibly, honestly, honorably, and ethically. Individual is not subject to coercion, manipulation, bribery, blackmail, lapses in judgment, or reneging on promises and commitments.

High
> Individual can be trusted under almost all situations to act responsibly, honestly, honorably, and ethically. Individual is not likely to be subject to coercion, manipulation, bribery, blackmail, lapses in judgment, or reneging on promises and commitments.

Medium
> Individual can be trusted most of the time to act responsibly, honestly, honorably, and ethically. Individual probably will not be subject to coercion, manipulation, bribery, blackmail, lapses in judgment, or reneging on promises and commitments.

Low
> Individual can be trusted somewhat to act responsibly, honestly, honorably, and ethically. For the most part the individual is not subject to coercion, manipulation, bribery, blackmail, lapses in judgment, or reneging on promises and commitments.

None
> Individual cannot be trusted to act responsibly, honestly, honorably, and ethically. Individual is likely to be subject to coercion, manipulation, bribery, blackmail, lapses in judgment, or reneging on promises and commitments in the near future.

Figure 4.5   Levels of trust.

the organization is trying to determine, through a background investigation, is whether or not the trust level of the position matches the trust level of the individual. As shown in Figure 4.5, there is a continuum of trust levels, from Ultra High all the way down to None. In essence, trust levels are a reflection of self-discipline, self-control, and personal and professional ethics, or the resilience of one's character. At the Ultra High level, an individual is relied upon under all situations to act responsibly, honestly, honorably, and ethically. The individual is not subject to coercion, manipulation, bribery, blackmail, lapses in judgment, or reneging on promises and commitments. A High level of trust means that the individual can be trusted under almost all situations to act responsibly, honestly, honorably, and ethically. The individual is not likely to be subject to coercion, manipulation, bribery, blackmail, lapses in judgment, or reneging on promises and commitments. At a Medium level of trust, the individual can be trusted most of the time to act responsibly, honestly, honorably, and ethically; he is not likely to be subject to coercion, manipulation, bribery, blackmail, lapses in judgment, or reneging on promises and commitments. At a Low level of trust, the individual can be trusted somewhat to act responsibly, honestly, honorably, and ethically; for the most part, he is not subject to coercion, manipulation, bribery, blackmail, lapses in judgment, or reneging on promises and commitments. As we see, each trust level flows into the next; there are not hard demarcations between one level and the next. The situation is similar to the debate about giving a student an A– versus a B+ or a B– versus a C+; cases that fall on the margins become rather subjective. The final trust level is not debatable: None. There are instances when an individual cannot be trusted at all to act responsibly, honestly, honorably, and ethically. This occurs when the individual is highly likely to be subject to coercion, manipulation, bribery, blackmail, lapses in judgment, or reneging on promises and commitments in the near future. A person may occupy a Low trust position today and a high trust position tomorrow. His position only reflects the trust level to which the background investigation was conducted. By the same token, a person may qualify for a High trust level, but not an Ultra High trust level. As we will see later, position trust levels correlate to the sensitivity and criticality of the assets an individual produces, owns, uses, and has access to within the organization.

Similarly, an individual makes many decisions about the level of trust he is willing to extend to another person or organization when managing his day-to-day affairs: a parking lot valet, landlord, insurance representative, veterinarian, physician, bank teller, loan officer, school bus driver, teacher, auto mechanic, repairman, swimming coach, baby sitter, neighborhood children, etc. It is common today for landlords to check an applicant's criminal record and whether or not that applicant is listed in a sex offender database, in addition to his financial history, before leasing an apartment or house. In some locales, it is possible to query public databases to determine if a physician or member of the clergy has a prior history of malfeasance. In each case, a determination is being made about the appropriate level of trust to extend, much like when an organization is evaluating a prospective employee; however, a much less formal "background investigation" is conducted.

The second dimension of trust is the type of trust that is being extended. That is, what is the individual being trusted to do or not do? The type of trust correlates to the specific job function; the assets produced, owned, used, and accessed; the scope of responsibility; and the ability to do harm. As shown in Figure 4.6, there are several different types of trust. A given position may require one or more types of trust.

Financial
> Financial industry (banks, brokerages, payment card, mortgages, insurance), retail, payroll, accounts payable, accounts receivable, financial audits, taxes

National Security
> Defense, intelligence, diplomatic, economic, strategic resources, advanced scientific research

Public Safety
> Law enforcement, fire department, emergency responders, public utility employees (water, gas, electric, telecommunications), transportation system employees, manufacturing (chemicals, food, medical products, consumer products), construction workers

Dependent Safety and Security
> Daycare, teachers, medical care workers, social workers, clergy, Boy Scouts, Girl Scouts

Public Trust
> Government services, legal counsel, landlords, charities, other positions that involve handling of sensitive personal information and personal property

Corporate
> Intellectual property, trade secrets, business plans, marketing strategies

Figure 4.6   Types of trust.

A position may require trust in financial matters. For example, an organization may need to have confidence that an individual will not commit fraudulent acts or otherwise steal financial resources. An organization needs to be confident that an individual will not abuse his position for direct financial gain, whether stealing from the cash drawer, fiddling with account books, misusing customers' sensitive financial data, or embezzlement. A financial institution can suffer irreparable damage to its reputation should an employee or business partner abuse his position. This type of damage can be more devastating than the actual financial loss, because the underpinning of the entire financial industry is trust. Recently, all major credit card companies canceled their contracts with Card Systems Solutions Inc. after approximately 40 million account records were stolen and the company was found not to be in compliance with personnel or operational security requirements.[247] As a result, the company quickly went out of business.

The type of trust most people are familiar with or have heard of concerns national security. Much of the information processed and generated by governments is quite sensitive; hence it is essential that this information be handled correctly in order not to compromise national security. Examples include information about defense plans, strategies, and logistics, intelligence information and operations, ongoing diplomatic initiatives, and information about strategic resources, economic information, and advanced scientific research. Governments must be confident that individuals will process, store, release, and use this information in accordance with established security policies and procedures. Governments do not function very well at home or abroad if this type of information is leaking all over the place.

A third type of trust involves public safety. Whenever you drive across a bridge, ride a train, or fly in an airplane, you expect the equipment to function safely and reliably and get you to your destination. Whenever you call 911, you expect competent police, firemen, or other emergency responders to arrive and resolve the situation quickly and effectively. Whenever you move into a dwelling, eat in a restaurant, or stay in a hotel, you expect the water, gas, and electric systems to operate safely and not flood, burn down, or blow up the facility or asphyxiate the inhabitants. The same is true of a variety of other positions that are directly related to public safety: construction workers, employees at companies that manufacture chemicals, food products, medical devices and drugs, and other consumer products. None of this happens automatically without a lot of people being involved and the appropriate checks and balances to ensure the public's safety. A tremendous amount of trust has been placed in these individuals that they will not accidentally or intentionally endanger public safety. The expectation in all these situations is that the product or service will function safely. In fact, this expectation is, for the most part, taken for granted, so much so that many people have no concept of what could go wrong.

A similar type of trust is placed in individuals who are responsible for providing leadership, direction, or taking care of others who are in a dependent status. People in these positions are trusted not to take advantage of, mislead, or harm those entrusted to their care. Examples include daycare employees, teachers, social workers, medical care workers, clergy, and groups such as the Boy Scouts. Several recent scandals at organizations like these underscore the importance of thorough and effective personnel security measures that are tied to the type and level of trust.

Public trust positions involve another type of trust. Generally, people think of government services, particularly government social services, when they hear the term "public trust position." Many government positions do involve public trust, but there also are many non-government positions that do involve the public's trust. Public trust implies that an individual will act responsibly when acting on behalf of, making decisions for, or giving advice to the public at large. That is, these individuals will act in the public's best interest. Government public trust positions involve setting economic policy, making decisions about protecting the environment, planning for major natural disasters and epidemics, and establishing strategic energy goals. Non-government public trust positions involve the handling of an individual's sensitive personal information or personal property, or the solicitation of funds. Examples include landlords, legal counsel, and charities. Let us look at the landlord–tenant trust relationship. As part of the application process, a landlord collects sensitive personal information. The landlord also has the keys to your apartment. A tenant trusts the landlord to (1) not misuse or mishandle his personal information, (2) not be careless with the keys or who he gives them out to, and (3) not to hire people with a criminal history as office or maintenance staff. What about contracts for specialty services such as termite prevention or cleaning the dryer vent? Some landlords just hand over the keys to the whole building and let the contractors roam freely. Responsible landlords have an employee escort the contractor from unit to unit, simply because it is good business — the landlord is liable for any personal property that is stolen or damaged. It is also good for customer relations. Do you really know who your apartment or condo office is handing out your keys to? During a four-year period at an apartment I lived at, the property manager disappeared after the IRS attempted to garnish her wages; the maintenance manager was jailed for attempting to murder his wife — she asked for a divorce and he said no with a gun; and a second maintenance employee was jailed for two scams. First, he would send appliances out for repair and then order the residents new appliances. The repaired appliances never came back to the property. He gave them to his friends and family or sold them. The second scam should have been obvious before he was caught by a surveillance camera. He was the type of maintenance employee who was just a little too friendly and seemed to remember too much about your possessions. As it turned out, he was learning people's schedules and the contents of their apartments so his friends could come in clean them out while they were gone. Charities and other non-profit foundations rely on the public's trust as well. The public must be convinced that the organization is legitimate and honest and is actually providing the service it claims and is not lining its own pockets or the organization is going to have difficulty raising funds. For a long time, government public trust positions have required strict personnel security measures. It is time for non-government public trust positions to follow suit.

The final area is positions involving corporate trust. Corporate trust is different from a position of financial trust because no financial resources are involved, only information. This information includes intellectual property, trade secrets, strategic marketing plans, long-term business plans, secret business partners, etc. — items that give an organization its leverage in the marketplace. This information is usually closely held by a small trusted inner circle. Should the information or similar misinformation leak out, a major business deal could be undone, shareholders might panic, employees might become unmotivated, or a competitor might gain a major advantage. As a result, an organization must have complete confidence in the people given access to this information. The organization must be convinced that individuals will not print out all the corporate secrets and take them with them to a new job across the street for a 20 percent pay raise.

Each of these six categories involves a specific type of trust, confidence that an individual (1) will follow established security policies and procedures to further the organization's goals, and (2) will not act in a manner that is damaging to the organization or the public for personal motives or gain. A specific individual may qualify for one, multiple, or all types of trust. For example, he may qualify for a public safety position, but not a financial one. Or he may qualify for a financial position, but cannot be trusted around children. Or he may qualify for all six trust types. Public and private sector organizations are responsible for determining this before they hire or contract with an individual. Failure to do so could qualify as negligence or reckless endangerment. This is where background investigations enter.

A background investigation is an attempt to use the past to predict the future. Investigators examine a person's previous behavior to see if there are any indications that the individual might not be a good candidate for a position requiring a certain trust level and type of trust. Reliability engineering speaks of "the fitness for use" of a system or component for a specified operational environment. Similarly, a background investigation tries to determine a human's "suitability" for a particular job function. Suitability is an assessment that an individual's character traits and past conduct indicate that he is eligible for employment in terms of his ability to carry out a job with effectiveness and efficiency and that he is unlikely to commit future actions that could have an adverse impact.[44] A background investigation attempts to gauge the resilience of a person's character, not just during the good times, but also during adversity because that is when one's real strength of character becomes apparent. Adverse conditions are also when an organization needs the most trust in an individual. An organization must be confident that should the world situation change, or the individual's situation or beliefs change, that individual can still be trusted. An organization may require a background investigation to be conducted on employees, consultants, contractors, vendor maintenance personnel, and other business partners prior to allowing them to work on a project. This type of screening is conducted to minimize the likelihood of insider attacks.[266]

A background investigation should not be an uncontrolled, unbounded, never-ending inquisition into one's past and personal life. That would be quite illegal. Rather, a background investigation is supposed to be directly proportional to the sensitivity and criticality of the position, and the type and level of trust being extended. The higher the level of trust, the more in-depth the background investigation will be. The more types of trust extended, the broader the scope of the background investigation. Trust levels and trust types that have not been verified through a background investigation should not be extended. The outcome of a background investigation is a major input into determining an individual's logical and physical access control rights.

The sponsor is responsible for determining the position sensitivity and risk level, prior to initiating a background investigation so that it can be focused accordingly. Position sensitivity and risk levels should be reviewed and reaffirmed at least annually to ensure that they are still accurate and needed. For national security positions, the process is straightforward — the position sensitivity and risk is tied directly to the classification level of the material that will be handled: confidential, secret, top secret, or above. For non-national security positions, a sequential decision-making process is followed. It is important for this decision-making process to be methodical, and not a cavalier "I think Joe's position needs a moderate level of trust," or an organization may find itself on the wrong side of a serious security incident.

Position sensitivity and risk is determined by examining several factors as they relate to the overall program the person will be working on and his individual role within that program, such as:

- Impact
- Scope
- Importance
- Influence
- Authority
- Independence

Refer to Figure 4.7. Every program contributes to an organization achieving its mission. If not, there is no reason for the program to exist. How well the program functions; whether the work is completed on time, correctly, and within budget; and other factors determine the organization's success. Some programs are more essential than others in achieving an organization's mission, and hence the distinction between line and staff or support functions. In terms of position sensitivity, this distinction is referred to as impact. A program can have anywhere from a major to a limited impact on the ability to achieve the organization's mission, depending on the direct operational impact on effectiveness and efficiency, the economic impact, and the number of people and organizations involved. Likewise, the scope of the program's operations is ranked. For example, is the program office responsible for a worldwide telecommunications network or a LAN in a single facility? The impact and the scope of the position are then correlated to determine the overall importance of the program to achieving the organization's mission. Note that Section I of Figure 4.7 is filled out the same for all positions within a given program. The other sections of the form are unique to the individual and job function.

Sample Position Risk/Sensitivity Level Designation	
Name	Organization Code or Cost Center
If not employee, name of Contracting Firm	Employment Status:
Position Title and Function	

If the position is a national security position (security clearance required) Sections I, II and III are optional.

RISK DESIGNATION

I. Program Sensitivity

Impact on ability to deliver product or service	Major	Substantial	Moderate	Limited
Scope of operations	World Wide	Nationwide	Multiple Organizations	Single Organization
Importance to organization's mission	Major	Substantial	Moderate	Limited

II. Individual's Position Sensitivity

a. Trust level	(high 5 - 0 low)	_____
b. Trust type(s)		_____
c. Influence	(high 5 - 0 low)	_____
d. Authority	(high 5 - 0 low)	_____
e. Independence	(high 5 - 0 low)	_____ TOTAL POINTS:_____

III. Risk/Sensitivity Level

Ultra High Risk - 4
High Risk - 3   Low Risk - 1
Moderate Risk - 2   None - 0   RISK LEVEL:_____

IV. Adjustment Factor(s)

Level of Security Clearance Required, if trust type = national security
□ TOP SECRET   □ SECRET   □ CONFIDENTIAL   □ NONE

V. Final Risk / Sensitivity Level

Final Risk/Sensitivity Level - _____
Comments:

Level of Investigation Required
□ CNACI   □ NACI   □ NACIC   □ MBI   □ LBI   □ BI   □ SSBI

Operating Office *(providing input)* and Org Code	Signature of Operating Office *(providing input)*	Date
Approving Security Official *(Type or Print name)*	Signature of Approving Security Official	Date

Figure 4.7   Sample position risk/sensitivity level designation.

Part II of Figure 4.7 examines the sensitivity of the specific job function. First the trust level and the type of trust are defined. Next the degree of influence this position has on the program as a whole is ranked. Likewise, the decision-making authority or control over the program's outcome is ranked. Finally, the degree of independence with which the individual operates is ranked. When ranking influence, authority, and independence, be sure to consider the potential degree of adverse impact, should the position be misused. A point value between 5 (highest) and 0 (lowest) is assigned to each of these factors, except trust type. In that case, the types of trust associated with the position are listed. A maximum total of 20 points is possible.

Table 4.10 Correlation of Program Importance and Job Function to Determine Position Sensitivity and Risk Level

Sensitivity/ Risk Level	Section I Ranking from Figure 4.7	Section II Ranking from Figure 4.7
Ultra High	Major	12–20
High	Major Substantial	8–11 16–20
Moderate	Major Substantial Moderate Limited	4–7 8–15 8–20 16–20
Low	Major Substantial Moderate Limited	0–3 0–7 0–7 1–15
None	Limited	0

Part III of Figure 4.7 correlates the information captured in Sections I and II to determine the position sensitivity and risk, which can range anywhere from Ultra High to None. The exact correlation will depend on the nature of an organization's mission and operations. However, Table 4.10 can be used as a guideline. Part IV of Figure 4.7 provides an opportunity to capture any additional information that may be useful in assigning an accurate position sensitivity and risk level. An example might be the fact that this program is in an emergency status and will provide a temporary solution until the real system is delivered. Another example might be that the job function is temporary or the individual is a new hire with no prior history in security matters.

Part V of Figure 4.7 is used to document the final determination of the position sensitivity and risk level and the type of background investigation needed. In Figure 4.7, the type of background investigation is encoded using the standard types of investigations[43]:

- **CNACI:** childcare national agency check consisting of a national agency check, written inquiries, state criminal history checks, and record searches covering specific areas of a person's background during the most recent five years.
- **NACI:** a national agency check with written inquiries and record searches covering specific areas of a person's background during the most recent five years.
- **NACIC:** a national agency check with written inquires from law enforcement agencies, record searches, and a credit check covering specific areas of a person's background during the most recent five years.
- **MBI:** a national agency check with inquiries, subject interview, a credit search, and telephone inquiries to follow up on written inquiries not returned.

- **LBI:** a national agency check, credit search, personal interviews of subject and sources, written inquiries of selected sources covering specific areas of a person's background during the most recent 3 years, and record searches for a total of 5 years coverage.
- **BI:** a national agency check, credit search, personal interviews of subject and sources, written inquiries, and record searches covering areas of a person's background during the most recent five years, and additional record searches during the most recent seven years.
- **SSBI:** a national agency check, birth records search, credit search, personal interviews of subject and sources, written inquiries, and record searches covering specific areas of a person's background during the most recent ten years.

Many of these investigations include a national agency check. During a national agency check, files maintained by the Federal Bureau of Investigation (FBI) Records Management Division, the FBI Identification Division, the Office of Personnel Management (OPM) Index of Security/Suitability Investigations, and the Department of Defense (DoD) Index of Clearances and Investigations are searched for information relating to the subject of the investigation. Most of these investigations include record searches covering specific areas of a person's background; that is shorthand for saying the investigation is tailored to the type of trust involved. These types of investigations are common to the United States. Similar investigations are conducted in other countries. Given that we live in the digital age and the speed and ease with which data mining expeditions can be conducted, for the most part background investigations are performed electronically today.

A variety of information obtained from the applicant and his sources is examined during a background investigation. One source or reference may lead to another source or reference; all relevant sources and leads are explored if they are within the scope of the investigation and time permits. An obvious place to start is with an identity check: is the person who he claims to be?[28, 33] If not, there is no point in continuing the investigation. Information on the application is verified, such as residences, previous employment, education, and references.[28, 44] The applicant's criminal history and financial status are also examined. Fingerprints are usually collected. Generally, a pre-employment drug test is given. Other medical records, particularly mental health records, may also be consulted. If the investigation is for a national security position, foreign travel may also be examined. Friends, neighbors, co-workers, and former employers, clergy, and instructors may be interviewed. Affiliations, such as social and professional organizations, and hobbies may be evaluated, although in theory it is not ethical or legal to consider religious affiliation (or lack thereof) when processing a background investigation. Depending on the trust level, the background investigation may extend to roommates, family, and relatives. The intent is to see if there are any skeletons in the closet that could cause the applicant to be subject to coercion, manipulation, or blackmail because of family or social ties. This can be a sticky issue when some family members live overseas or are not citizens, or there has been a divorce. Voter registration, selective service registration, and military service records are usually inspected too, especially when applying for a national security position.

Investigators collect and sift through all this information not just because they are professional busy bodies, but because they are trying to determine what makes a person tick. Are they honest? Are they reliable? Did they supply accurate and complete information? Have they lived up to their previous obligations and commitments? The intent is not to determine if the applicant is Mr. Personality or the winner of popularity contests in college. Rather, the intent is to determine the applicant's strength of character, moral certitude, and trustworthiness. Investigators are looking for any red flags that might indicate the potential for trouble in the future should the person be accepted for a position of trust. Perhaps the person is obsessed with money or material status. Maybe the person craves attention and company and, as a result, can easily be manipulated. A history of alcohol or drug abuse is a cause for concern, as is an inability to manage one's finances. A pattern of animal cruelty or other physical violence is a definite red flag, as is continual reckless or irresponsible behavior. What are the person's real or changing loyalties — to the organization or what? Perhaps the person is jealous because he did not get the same promotion, bonus, or new office as a co-worker. Maybe he is threatened by an impending organizational change, new boss, or new employee. Or he is experiencing a family or financial crisis. The background investigation tries to predict whether or not this person is likely to become a disgruntled, disruptive employee prone to security violations.

Information collected during a background investigation comes from a variety of sources and is assembled by a team of investigators, especially if prior employment and residences were in different locales. Investigators have a professional responsibility to report accurate, objective, reliable, timely, and relevant information.[116] They are required to be consistent and thorough when verifying information and to discard obvious fabrications from people who hold a grudge against the applicant. It is also essential for investigators to restrain their personal biases, prejudices, and preconceived ideas when reporting information, whether for or against an applicant. Sometimes that is easier said than done. The lead investigator assembles the information into a composite report and may add a summary and a recommendation. Adjudication is the final step in the background investigation process. Adjudication is usually performed by a panel separate from the investigators, but it can be performed by an individual. The adjudicators review the final background investigation report and make a decision about whether or not the person should be approved for the specified trust level and trust types. The organization is responsible for ensuring that the adjudicators have the proper training and credentials, especially in the relevant state and federal laws.

The background investigation process must include procedures for (1) granting temporary or interim access while an investigation is ongoing, and (2) an applicant to appeal a negative decision. Temporary access should only be granted in special situations, such as when the person is already an employee and has one trust level and is being upgraded to another, or an emergency situation exists. Individuals must be given the opportunity to appeal a negative decision because of the financial, career, and personal ramifications. Furthermore, an applicant must be given the opportunity to explain, deny, or refute any information gathered in a background investigation *before* it is used as the basis for an adverse action or negative decision; secret tribunals are not allowed.[44] The applicant must be supplied with the adverse information that caused the negative decision, but not necessarily the source. And the applicant should be given adequate time to challenge and disprove such information. The right to an appeal is required by law as part of due process. Strict controls must be placed on the access and dissemination of unfavorable information. The background investigation process must specify how the information collected will be stored, how long the records will be retained, and who will and will not have access to them. Background investigations contain a lot of sensitive personal information; hence, this information must be protected in accordance with the Privacy Act and other state and federal laws or the applicable laws in countries other than the United States. As a general rule, background investigations are updated and reaffirmed on a regular basis, generally every five years. Investigations may also be updated for cause should some new information or behavior raise concerns.

While the background investigation process attempts to be fair and impartial, there are many opportunities for flaws to seep in because the process is essentially subjective in nature. This is particularly troubling given the growing intolerance and polarization of society, where some groups accuse anyone who disagrees with them of being immoral or unpatriotic. The fundamental flaw in the background investigation process is that information about people is collected by people from people. We are not talking about information that can be scientifically measured with an instrument or mathematically proven. The issues being investigated are not subject to hard and fast definitions; rather, they are soft areas such as trustworthiness, reliability, and loyalty, which are subject to interpretation. A major weakness in the background investigation process is that it is far too easy for an investigator's personal biases and prejudices to cause information to be slanted or distorted, either for or against the applicant. These same biases can taint the information an investigator receives. This situation is referred to as the "like me/not like me" syndrome.

Investigators, like most people, have conscious and subconscious biases and prejudices for and against certain ethnic, religious, economic, occupational, educational, professional, gender, and age groups. Many people acquire their prejudices at home or from the community they grow up in. These prejudices may be so ingrained that a person is unaware of them; they assume everyone thinks like they do, so it is difficult to even acknowledge these biases and prejudices. Other biases and prejudices may be acquired later as a result of some real or imagined slight or through peer pressure. These latter prejudices and biases may be acknowledged but are difficult to overcome without concerted effort.

Once jealousy and the inexplicable need of a few to (in their minds) put other people below themselves in the social pecking order are removed, the underlying cause of prejudices is fear — fear of someone who is different. People tend to gravitate toward, are more comfortable with, and accept people who are "like" themselves. This phenomenon manifests itself every day. Given a choice on the subway, in a meeting, or at a luncheon, people tend to sit by people who appear to be "like" them, even if they are total strangers. This subconscious bias has led to some class action lawsuits for discrimination in hiring and promotion practices. One such case involved the U.S. Secret Service. White Christian males from a blue collar background were routinely hired and promoted faster than people from other backgrounds with identical or better credentials. The explanation was that the hiring managers "could relate to" people who had the same background as they did. Maybe, but as the courts pointed out, this practice is illegal. A conscious effort and independent oversight are necessary to overcome such biases.

Unfortunately, these conscious and subconscious biases creep into the background investigation process and again the "like me/not like me" syndrome is manifest, to the detriment of the individual and the organization. Perhaps the applicant prays on the "wrong" day or not at all. Perhaps the applicant has too many vowels or consonants in his last name. Perhaps he observes strange holidays, customs, or traditions that the investigator does not understand and misinterprets. Maybe he looks, talks, eats, or dresses differently. Maybe his family just arrived in the country or lived here before the country was a country. An investigator with conscious or unconscious biases may use any of these items as a false pretext for claiming that the applicant is different, not "one of us," an outsider and therefore not deserving of trust. In turn, an investigator will hold someone who is "like" himself to less stringent standards. There have been several high-profile cases in the news where such biases have severely damaged national security. Robert Hansen at the FBI and Aldridge Ames at the Central Intelligence Agency (CIA) are two recent examples. Both were good old boys, the consummate insiders, "one of us"; they could not possibly be doing anything wrong. So although there were glaring red flags to the contrary, they both were allowed to continue working against the agencies they were (supposedly) employed by for over 20 years.

There are also many opportunities for abuse during the conduct of a background investigation. The form an applicant signs gives the investigator the legal right to collect information from the designated sources (credit bureaus, employers, landlords, medical records, education records, etc.) for one year from the date of signature. A copy of the form is supposed to be presented when requesting information. Unfortunately, investigators have been known to use these forms more than a decade later with altered dates. Some investigators, instead of trying to get "just the facts," are on a power trip or a personal vendetta. Perhaps they automatically do not like the applicant because he has multiple graduate degrees while the investigator barely made it through junior college. Or the applicant served as an officer in the military while the investigator served in the enlisted ranks. Perhaps the applicant grew up in a comfortable middle-class home while the investigator grew up poor. A frequent problem is that the applicant's salary is much higher than the investigator's. Investigators have been known to be abusive, manipulative, and accusatory during interviews and misrepresent who they are and why they are asking questions in order to try and get the answer they want rather than the truth. Much like polling, they make an accusation, and then frame the question to get the answer they want.

During the 25 years I have been in the world of security clearances, I have witnessed a lot of inappropriate behavior. Let us face it: people who are not familiar with the background investigation process are startled when out of the blue they get a knock at the door, a telephone call, or a form to fill out from the government. They immediately assume something bad has happened. Some unscrupulous investigators prey on this state of anxiety and uncertainty, hoping to get the person to accidentally confirm some false accusation. The ethical thing for investigators to do would be to explain that John Doe, who the person knows, has applied for a position that requires a security clearance, and that they need to ask a few questions to confirm his suitability for a position of trust. This should all be handled like a normal employment reference check. The smart thing for an applicant to do is to let everyone know ahead of time that an investigator will be coming. I had one employee come to me in tears first thing Monday morning. An investigator had showed up at her house unannounced over the weekend. She already had a security clearance; her sister was going through the process. The investigator made one false accusation after another about her sister — "You know she ...." — and threatened my employee that if she did not agree; her clearance was in jeopardy. One time when my own clearance was being processed, an investigator showed up at the house of an 83-year-old friend of the family. Instead of saying who he was or why he was there, he lied and said he was a friend of mine from work, just stopping by to say hello. Now, 83-year-old ladies like to talk, especially when they live alone. So they chatted for a couple hours about my dance recitals, swimming lessons, bike rides, birds, and Girl Scout work, but he did not get any of the negative information he had hoped to obtain under false pretenses. Fool that he was, he should have known that she would call me as soon as he walked out the door. She did and I was scolded for not telling her he was coming. She could have made some cookies or had the photo albums handy....

When working on classified projects, a person is frequently asked to comment about co-workers, subordinates, and superiors during a background investigation. In this instance, investigators are required to show an ID and explain who they are and why they are there — they cannot simply walk into secure facilities. Over the years, I have participated in several such interviews; it is an interesting situation to be able to comment on your boss! These interviews tend to be more professional but there have still been some outliers. Investigators accused one boss of being an alcoholic, a co-worker of being gay, a subordinate of being beaten by her husband, etc. This tactic is nothing more than a fishing trip, an unethical attempt to trick the interviewee into saying something or plant a falsehood in their mind. Many of the same scenarios are repeated in the world of polygraph exams, which if you are not aware, only measure your heart rate, blood pressure, and pulse. One examiner leaned over the table and asked me if I thought he was cute. Another tried to convince me that my brother's birth date was mine and vice versa, as if I would not know the difference. A third examiner could not keep his pronouns (you, we, they, he, she) straight during the questions. I have seen people I would not trust to feed my goldfish pass the highest level security clearance, while people I would trust with my life, minuscule fortune, family, and pets be denied a low-level clearance. The background investigation process is far from being an exact science. In summary, background investigations are like parking tickets. Investigators must meet their quota of people they flunk or they are not doing their jobs. If you suspect abuses in the processing of your background investigation, appeal it loudly, clearly, and persistently, just like you would a bogus parking or speeding ticket.

And what about privacy during the conduct of a background investigation? Sensitive personal information is required under the Privacy Act and others to be protected. But who is independently monitoring the investigators to see that this happens? If investigators go blabbing their mouths all over town, they have violated this requirement. If investigators go all over town making false accusations — we all know how fast malicious gossip spreads — they are liable for defamation of character and slander lawsuits. It is more than apparent that an independent body is necessary to oversee that background investigations are, in fact, conducted fairly, impartially, consistently, ethically, honestly, and in accordance with privacy legislation. When they are not, the negligent investigators should be sanctioned. Given the many weaknesses and opportunities for abuse and bias, an organization should not rely on background investigations alone, but rather employ a complementary set of personnel security measures.

The following metrics can be used to measure the resilience of the background investigation process and whether or not it is being conducted efficiently, fairly impartially, consistently, ethically, honestly, and in accordance with privacy legislation.

Percentage of definite insiders, pseudo-insiders, and pseudo-outsiders who have undergone current background investigations, by position trust level and trust type.[105]   2.2.2.1

By organizational unit, distribution of positions by trust level and trust type:
                                                                          2.2.2.2

    a. Percentage that have been reviewed and reaffirmed within the last six months

By organizational unit, percentage of background investigations that: 2.2.2.3
    a. Have been approved
    b. Are in process, waiting for approval
    c. Are in process, waiting for renewal
    d. Were renewed within the mandatory time frame
    e. Expire in the next six months
    f. Have not been initiated yet

By organizational unit, average time to process a background investigation, by trust level and trust type.   2.2.2.4

Distribution of security incidents by severity and the trust level and trust type of the individuals involved, for: 2.2.2.5

a. The current month
b. The past 12 months

By organizational unit, during the last 12 months the number of: 2.2.2.6

a. Interim or temporary trust levels and trust types granted and the average length of time they were in effect
b. Background investigations that were updated for cause
c. Reported abuses during the conduct of a background investigation
d. Appeals filed against negative decisions from a background investigation
e. Appeals upheld to overturn a negative decision from a background investigation

Percentage of organizational units that implement documented procedures, and sanctions if the procedures are not followed, for: 2.2.2.7

a. Collecting records relating to a background investigation in accordance with privacy legislation
b. Storing records relating to a background investigation in accordance with privacy legislation
c. Retaining records relating to a background investigation in accordance with privacy legislation
d. Disposing of records relating to a background investigation in accordance with privacy legislation
e. Controlling access to records relating to a background investigation in accordance with privacy legislation
f. Reporting abuses during a background investigation
g. Appealing a negative decision from a background investigation

Number of times sanctions have had to be imposed on investigators or others during the past 12 months for: 2.2.2.8

a. Inappropriate behavior during the conduct of a background investigation
b. Mishandling information related to a background investigation

By organizational unit, distribution of positions by trust level and trust type held by: 2.2.2.9

a. Definite insiders
b. Pseudo-insiders
c. Pseudo-outsiders
d. Offshore personnel

Competence

Competence is a fundamental component of personnel security, like accountability. Competency is an essential precursor to accountability and making internal controls function. The significant role competence plays in personnel security is often not understood or ignored, to the detriment of an organization. Incompetent people, whether definite insiders, pseudo-insiders, or definite outsiders, represent a major security vulnerability waiting to be exploited. Simply put, incompetent people, at any level of an organization, do not know (1) what needs to be done, (2) why something needs to be done, (3) how to do something, (4) when to do something, or (5) how to verify that something was done correctly. Some incompetent people are oblivious to their state. They may be very sincere in trying to accomplish their duties, but are clueless. Some incompetent people are aware of their state and try to deflect it by taking a cavalier attitude toward their duties or tap dancing through their career. Then there are those who are painfully aware of their incompetence. A few try to get the training and experience they need to be productive. The rest become defensive, disruptive employees who spend their time trying to shift the blame for their shortcomings onto others through all sorts of she-nanigans. This latter group represents a particular security nightmare. Incompetent managers tend to hire incompetent employees, so they do not look bad by comparison; then again, maybe they are so incompetent that they do not know any better! Managers of a more devious nature hire incompetent employees to cover up their own questionable behavior. Anyone who has worked for a living has seen these situations repeated over and over.

Competence implies that an individual has the requisite abilities, qualities, and capacity to function in or respond to a given situation in the prescribed manner. A competent individual has sufficient training, knowledge, experience, and skills to perform his assigned duties accurately, effectively, efficiently, securely, and in a timely manner. Competence encompasses carrying out one's job function, including security roles and responsibilities. The ISO 9000 quality management compendium requires, as part of the certification process, that employees be competent to perform their assigned duties.[13, 158] This is not a simple, "Yes, John knows what he is doing"; rather, the standard specifies that (1) competency requirements be specified for each position; (2) individuals be required to furnish proof of the required formal education, knowledge, experience, licensing, and certifications; and (3) the employer keep records of both the competency requirements and the proof.[13, 158] Several other international standards follow suit, such as the ISO/IEC 61508 safety engineering series. ISO/IEC 61508-1 is quite explicit that individuals must be competent to carry out their responsibilities, whether technical, financial, acquisition, or management.[1] Competency requirements for each position have to be not only stated, but justified.[1] IEC 61508-1 identifies several factors that need to be considered when assigning competency requirements for a position and assessing an individual's competency relative to those requirements[1]:

- Domain knowledge related to the specific application
- Technical knowledge related to the specific engineering or administrative discipline
- Knowledge of the safety engineering concerns related to the specific technology and application
- An understanding of the consequences of a safety-related failure
- Knowledge of the different safety integrity levels, how they are achieved and assessed

- The novelty of the design, technology, or operational procedures
- Knowledge of legal and regulatory requirements
- Relevance of previous experience and qualifications to the specific duties and technology

It is expected that the specification and assessment of competency will be more rigorous as the competence and safety integrity levels increase. This approach is only common sense — incompetent people working in the area of safety engineering can cause fatalities, injuries, and environmental damage. The same process and rigor needs to be applied to defining security competency requirements, given the damage that can be done. Likewise, security competency requirements need to be applied to all personnel, not just security engineers.

Competency requirements extend to individuals and organizations. An individual may be competent to perform assigned tasks, but the organization he is assigned to may not be competent. An organization is competent if it is able to perform its mission accurately, effectively, efficiently, securely, and in a timely manner. Organizational competency involves having sufficient appropriate resources ready and available when needed.[158] If an organization has not identified rigorous competency requirements for all positions, especially security roles and responsibilities, or staffed all positions with competent personnel, there are going to be problems. An organization may be competent to perform one function, but not another. Be wary of business partners who try to reinvent themselves to meet your every need. Reinventing an organization is not impossible, but it does take time, commitment, and serious (re)training and, most likely, restructuring.

It takes time to establish legitimate competency requirements for all positions, but it is time well spent. What can be more important than ensuring that an organization has a workforce with the appropriate depth, breadth, and mix of skills to reliably accomplish its mission? Private sector organizations have no choice but to do this if they want to stay in business. Public sector organizations' budgets spiral out of control when this is not done. Business partners may specify competency requirements in terms of formal education, number of years of experience, licensing, and certification requirements. They are looking for proof that an organization can perform the work, and hence minimize the risk of defective products, the need for rework, and cost and schedule overruns. Different job functions within the same discipline may have different levels of competence. For example, it is common in the IT industry to distinguish between entry-level engineers, senior engineers, principle engineers, and staff engineers. The education requirements may be the same (a Master's degree in electrical engineering or computer science), but the years' experience, specialized experience, level of expertise, and scope of responsibility are different. The same is true with security competency requirements. As a result, when defining professional and security competency requirements, it is important to clarify the specific skills and qualifications needed, as well as the assumed limitations — the individual is expected to know how to do x, but not necessarily y. An organization can avoid potential security vulnerabilities that arise from false competency assumptions by taking the time to define competency limitations.

Many organizations have come to rely — or perhaps over-rely — on certifications as a measure of competence. Certifications have become a cottage industry, particularly in the IT industry. Some certifications have merit, while others do little more than provide a steady revenue stream for the organization that sponsors them. Before placing too much trust in a certification, find out exactly what the exam does and does not cover. Is it a high-level, broad brush type exam, or does it go into the details? Does the exam require the individual to apply the knowledge or simply recall information? What are the requirements for taking the exam? Are there minimum formal education and specialized experience requirements? If not, beware. What is the average pass rate of the exam? How many people in this field have this certification? If either of these last two numbers is high, what is the value of the certification? Almost every adult has a driver's license. Looking at the rate of traffic violations, accidents, and fatalities, it would seem that having a driver's license (a form of certification) does not necessarily mean a person knows how to drive. Ditto the plethora of IT certifications. What an organization really needs to know is whether or not the individual has previously performed the specific job function. Has he specified, designed, implemented, or tested a security architecture? Has he installed, configured, initialized, and operated encryption equipment? How many security audits has he conducted? What type of operational security procedures has he written? What type of security test and evaluation has he performed, and in what type of environment? It takes more time to discern and verify this information than a certification, but it is well worth the effort. Think about it for a minute. It is quite a different skill set to take a one-week course and pass an exam than to have been in the trenches doing the work for 20 years. Would you go to a surgeon who had only taken a one-week course and passed a written exam?

Many organizations avoid dealing with competency requirements and instead go into a state of denial. They mistakenly think employees are interchangeable. A 20-year veteran can be replaced with a new graduate and paid half as much, or an operations and maintenance engineer can be swapped for a design engineer, or vice versa. This shortsighted approach never works out and is the root cause of most schedule and cost overruns. When programs get behind schedule and over budget, corners are cut; and security funds are usually the first to be cut. Here we see a ripple effect between a lack of competency and security. It all goes back to understanding what work needs to be done, how to do it, etc.; this is not something bean counters who are only focused on maximizing profit are qualified to do. Organizations avoid acknowledging competency requirements by giving all personnel in a group the same performance ratings, awards, and bonuses. That is a sure-fire way to encourage the top talent (the competent employees) to leave. On the contrary, performance ratings and promotions should be tied to specified and demonstrated competency requirements. As Schulmeyer points out, it is counterproductive to ignore differences in employee competency. For example, a poor performer may insert more defects than productive lines of code in a software program.[210] Often it is more effective for an organization to remove a poor performer than to add a new good performer.[210] Poor performers affect the morale of good performers, because it is the good performers who have to work twice as hard to compensate for the poor performers and clean up the mess the poor performers leave behind.

A lack of competency, whether related to one's job function or security roles and responsibilities, can have a major impact on the security posture of an organization. Accountability is difficult if not impossible to achieve without competency. It is unlikely that an individual could pass the suitability test of a background investigation (ability to provide effective and efficient service) without meeting competency requirements. A lack of competency in being able to perform security roles and responsibilities indicates that the security awareness and training function (part of operational security) is not properly focused. Here are just a few examples of what can happen when competency requirements are not defined or met. Keep in mind that almost all identity theft cases and other cyber crime are the result of negligence and a lack of competence.

- **Specification.** Personnel lacking the appropriate level of competency will not be able to specify a set of complete, consistent, accurate, unambiguous, and verifiable security requirements. They may not understand what security requirements are needed or why. Or worse, they may not even know what a security requirement is. Wrong or missing security requirements spawn vulnerabilities that are waiting to be exploited. Wrong or missing security requirements are also very expensive to fix after the fact.

- **Design.** Personnel lacking the appropriate level of competency will not be able to design resilient security perimeters or IT systems or networks. They may not even understand the concept of different levels of resilience, the need for multiple diverse countermeasures, or how to verify design integrity. The vast majority of COTS products today are full of vulnerabilities — not because they have to be, but because the designers lacked competency in how to design a secure product. The emphasis was on functionality, not security.

- **Development/implementation.** Personnel lacking the appropriate level of competency will not be able to develop effective operational security procedures, physical security access controls, or secure telecommunications networks. They may not even understand the specialized tools and techniques needed to develop these items. Concepts such as designing a system or network to detect, prevent, and preempt security incidents will be foreign to them. They will implement a system that has no security requirements the same as one that has ultra-high security requirements. As the saying goes, ignorance is bliss — until the security incidents are broadcast all over newspaper front pages.

- **Security test and evaluation (ST&E), Security Audits, Certification and Accreditation (C&A).** Personnel lacking the appropriate level of competency will not be able to perform effective, comprehensive, or in-depth ST&E or security audits. They may be very sincere about going through the motions but do not know what questions to ask, do not understand what they are looking for, what step or sequences of action must be performed, what the results should be or really mean, or why these functions should be performed by independent parties. They will not be in a position to determine if the security requirements, design, or implementation is correct or meets the specified resilience level. They may be very dutiful about generating a lot of pretty reports, but they may not even be able to find a vulnerability if it were staring them in the face! Because deployment decisions are made based on these reports, would it not be better to have competent people perform these tasks?

- **Operations and maintenance.** Personnel lacking the appropriate level of competency may understand how to install, configure, and operate IT equipment, but that does not mean they know how to do so securely. They may not understand why one command sequence or configuration is more (or less) secure than another. The equipment is up and running — and that is all that is needed, right? Wrong! Operations and maintenance personnel need an in-depth understanding of why security procedures must be followed to the letter, because of the extent of their access rights and privileges. If they do not have this understanding, they may cut corners to save time, bypass internal controls, do favors for friends or superiors, and in general create a security nightmare. Operations and maintenance personnel who lack the appropriate level of competency will not know how to troubleshoot, respond to, or prevent security incidents. They may not even notice that a security incident is ongoing until it is too late. They will not be able to assess the security impact of proposed upgrades. Lack of competence in the operations and maintenance staff can leave an organization totally exposed. Few critics consider naked security architectures a work of art.

- **Project management.** Personnel lacking the appropriate level of competency will not understand the importance of security tasks, roles, and responsibilities. They will not understand what should be done or why it should be done. As a result, they will not assign the appropriate resources or allocate the necessary time frames to perform security tasks. Project managers tend to be cost and schedule driven, and security requirements are left behind in the dust at the starting gate. Many spectacular security failures can be traced back to this ignorant mind-set. Ignorance may be bliss but it does not absolve an organization of liability and negligence lawsuits.

- **Contracts, procurement.** Personnel lacking the appropriate level of competency will emphasize buying the cheapest products and services that can be delivered the fastest. They have no concept of the magnitude of harm that can result from substandard parts or materials, unqualified suppliers, or incompetent outsourcing firms. When negotiating prices and contracts, they will drop security requirements on the floor, like popcorn at the movies, without a second thought. Conversely, when negotiating work for their organization, they will sign up to impossible deadlines just to get the contract, and security will be the first corner cut. Acquisition personnel rarely understand or are familiar with the legal ramifications of due care and due diligence or regulatory requirements related to security engineering. Acquisition personnel at all levels of an organization need to understand that security requirements are not negotiable. Failure to do so leaves the organization liable for negligence.

The following metrics can be used to measure the resilience of personnel security controls related to competence.

By organizational unit, number and percentage of positions for which detailed competency requirements have been defined for the job function and security roles and responsibilities   2.2.3.1

   a. Definite insiders
   b. Pseudo-insiders
   c. Pseudo-outsiders
   d. Offshore personnel
   e. By position sensitivity/risk

By organizational unit, number and percentage of individuals who meet or exceed the competency requirements for their job function and security roles and responsibilities: 2.2.3.2

   a. Definite insiders
   b. Pseudo-insiders
   c. Pseudo-outsiders
   d. Offshore personnel
   e. By position sensitivity/risk

By organizational unit, number and percentage of positions for which stated competency requirements for the job function and security roles and responsibilities have been reviewed and verified within the past 12 months or within 3 months following a reorganization: 2.2.3.3

   a. Definite insiders
   b. Pseudo-insiders
   c. Pseudo-outsiders
   d. Offshore personnel
   e. By position sensitivity/risk

Distribution of organizational units that have taken action to remedy competency weaknesses: 2.2.3.4

   a. No action has been taken
   b. Need for retraining has been identified
   c. Specific classes for specific individuals have been initiated
   d. Remedial training has been completed
   e. New hires have been brought on board to provide missing skills

By organizational unit, number and percentage of positions for which performance appraisals and promotions are tied to specific competency requirements for the job function and security roles and responsibilities.   2.2.3.5

Number and percentage of security incidents during the past 12 months that involved individuals that did not meet the competency requirements for their position or competency requirements were not defined for their position, by incident severity.   2.2.3.6

By organizational unit, number and percentage of positions for which different levels of competency within the same discipline are defined.   2.2.3.7

By organizational unit, number and percentage of positions for which competency limitations are defined in addition to competency requirements.

2.2.3.8

Separation of Duties

Separation of duties is the fourth major component of a comprehensive personnel security program. Mention separation of duties at any security conference and the audience will politely nod in agreement, "Yes, we need that." But why, if separation of duties is so important, is it not mentioned in 99.9 percent of the security publications to date? Not even ISO/IEC 17799, the current international standard for security management, discusses the topic. The problem is twofold. First, most security engineers only understand the concept of separation of duties at a very high or abstract level. They lack the in-depth understanding necessary for implementation. Or worse, they lack the authority to implement separation of duties. Second, separation of duties, like accountability and competence, is one of those "people issues" that most organizations go out of their way to avoid like the plague. This sidestepping routine is based on ignorance, and sometimes just plain laziness, and can have severe consequences for an organization. Here again we will see the fallacy of placing all of an organization's attention and funding on IT security (or technology). After all, who designs, implements, operates, and uses technology? People. And people can be any organization's greatest security liability.

Separation of duties refers to the practice of dividing and distributing the responsibility for different steps in a process, procedure, or system function among several individuals or user roles to prevent a single individual from subverting that process, procedure, or system function. Separation of duties is an attempt to make sure that employees do not "have their cake and eat it too" at the organization's expense. For example, very few employees have the authority to submit, approve, and disburse funds to pay their own expense vouchers. Separation of duties is an extension of the "need-to-know" concept. Need-to-know is a method whereby information assets are isolated based on an individual's need to have access to that asset, or in some cases even know of its existence, but no more in order to perform his job. For example, a personnel officer needs access to sensitive personnel records and a marketing manager needs to access sensitive marketing information, but not vice versa. The fact that if the company wins the DEF contract, the organization will need to add 200 staff quickly is a data point that could be shared between these two functions. A sure giveaway that something is not quite right is when an individual starts asking a lot of questions about information that is not related to his job function. The term "need-to-know" is generally applied to people, while "least privilege" is generally applied to IT access rights.[158]

Separation of duties is neither a new idea nor is it limited to the high-tech industry. The intent is to help spot and prevent accidental and intentional internal misuse of an organization's assets.[222] The basic premise is that it is less likely for two (or more) individuals to decide to cooperate in a preplanned malevolent act or series of actions, than for one person to do so by himself.

Detection of malicious activity is also easier when two or more people are involved. The likelihood is thought to decrease geometrically in proportion to the number of positions the duties are distributed among. Statistics from the past 20 years tend to prove this hypothesis correct. The vast majority of cases of cyber crime and compromises of national security have been committed by individuals acting on their own — the exception being the Walker brothers. The financial industry originated the idea of separation of duties in the 1970s as an internal control to prevent fraud.[222] Since then the idea has spread to several other industries and is applied to many different types of critical operations. The nuclear industry has been a major proponent of separation of duties for years; in this instance, it is referred to as the two man rule. A variation of separation of duties is known as independence. Almost all international safety engineering standards and many quality engineering standards require independence during validation and verification activities. Independent teams validate the requirements, design, implementation, and testing results in order to reduce the likelihood of common cause failures. Separate teams may be used to generate the requirements, design, implementation, and conduct testing as well. That is, individuals cannot be involved in validating products they helped create. Independence and objectivity are the goal because it is nearly impossible for someone to review his own work and find all the accidental errors. The intentional errors, of course, will not be "discovered" either. The need for independence increases in proportion to the integrity level of the product. The higher the degree of asset sensitivity and criticality, the greater the need for separation of duties. The lower the individual's trust level, the greater the need for separation of duties. Consequently, separation of duties is needed across the board and not just for IT processes. This is especially important in organizations that are moving to all-electronic processes.

Separation of duties can be applied hierarchically, laterally, and geographically within an organization or operation. Hierarchical separation distributes responsibilities among different layers within the same organization, such as an employee, his first-level supervisor, and his second-level supervisor. Lateral separation distributes responsibilities across different functions within an organization, such as engineering and finance, or separation between design engineers, production engineers, test engineers, and operations and maintenance engineers. Geographical separation distributes responsibilities among parts of an organization that are in different locations, either across town, across the country, or outside the country. These three types of separation of duties can be used individually or in combination with each other. The intent of each is to ensure that an individual cannot subvert or bypass an internal control for personal motives or gain. Separation of duties also helps prevent insiders from colluding with outsiders, because a single individual lacks authority to complete a transaction.

Job rotation is often discussed in the context of separation of duties. Job rotation can be used to supplement separation of duties. However, if not structured correctly, job rotation can defeat separation of duties. On occasion, individuals become very possessive of the job functions they perform. Over time, they begin to blur the distinction between the job function and their identity until the two are inseparable. This is not a healthy situation for the individual or the organization. Their ego, sense of importance or authority, or conversely feelings of being slighted, undervalued, or under-recognized, can become so intense that they lose all objectivity and balance when performing their duties. They "become" the process or system. Favors are bestowed on those who acknowledge their omnipotence. Work requests from those who do not are delayed, confounded, or deliberately sabotaged. And woe to the organization if they do not get the pay raise, bonus, or promotion they were expecting. Job rotation can be an effective tool in preventing this type of megalomania from setting in and an organization becoming too dependent on one individual. Job rotation can also contribute to continuity of operations. It is always a good idea to train people so that they are capable of performing two or three different job functions — they have a primary job function but are proficient at performing other tasks also. At some companies it is standard practice to put new graduates into a two-year rotation program. New hires spend six months in each of four very different assignments. The intent is to expose them to different parts of the company while giving them a more informed basis on which to decide in which area they would like to specialize. This practice helps to ensure that the organization is up and running during holidays, vacations, extended medical leaves, and other contingencies. In addition, job rotation can help minimize and pinpoint internal misuse of an organization's assets.[222] Design job rotation assignments so that the individual does not rotate among the separate tasks into which a function has purposely been divided. That is, do not rotate an individual from account creation, to account monitoring, to account deletion and revocation. The individual will know how all the separate tasks of a function are performed, how tasks and privileges are structured, how task records are kept, how well oversight is or is not enforced, when certain tasks are scheduled, the weaknesses in the process, what equipment is used and where it is located, and all the players involved. Armed with all this information, it becomes much easier to subvert a process. If technical means do not work, a phone call can always be made to a friend in the "old" department for a "favor."

Separation of duties must be (1) implemented for all the appropriate processes, procedures, and system functions; and (2) implemented to the proper degree, in order to contribute to an organization's security posture. Look for opportunities to implement separation of duties based on asset sensitivity and criticality, position sensitivity and risk, and by position trust level and trust type. Determine where and how to implement separation of duties so that it adds the most value to an organization. Often there are some natural breaks in a task sequence in which it is ideal to insert some checks and balances. Analyze each situation to identify which type of separation will be the most effective: lateral, hierarchical, geographic, or a combination. Different solutions may be more appropriate in different situations. Next, the degree of separation needed for each situation must be evaluated. Some situations may require a high degree of separation, while in others, a low degree of separation is acceptable. Be sure to verify on a regular basis that the separation of duties controls are being implemented correctly and function as expected. Surprise audits can be very insightful.

Some tasks within functions are natural candidates for separation of duties, as the following examples illustrate:

- **User account management:** requesting a new account, approving a new account, initiating a new account, changing account privileges, deleting or revoking an account, monitoring account usage.
- **Data management:** approving data prior to entry, entering data, validating data, editing data, deleting data, backing up data, archiving data.
- **System management:** network management, security management, operating system management, application software management, directory management, backups, help desk, performance monitoring.
- **Configuration management:** recommending a change, approving a change, testing a proposed change for its functional and performance impact, testing a proposed change for its security impact, implementing a change, verifying that the change or update was performed correctly, updating system documentation to reflect the change.
- **Incident management:** reporting an incident, responding to an incident, post-event analysis, approving recommendation to prevent incident recurrence.
- **Audit trail management:** implementing audit trail function, reading an audit trail, analyzing audit trail information, archiving audit trails, overwriting audit trails.

Let us look at how separation of duties could be implemented and how to assess the degree of separation. Account management will be used as the test case, following the chronology of events related to a general user account.

A new employee reports for duty. His supervisor submits a request to create a new account for him and identifies what systems, servers, software applications, and directories to which he needs access. Networking privileges are also identified. These privileges may be tied to a specific fixed desktop location, anywhere the individual logs in from within the corporate intranet, or include both local and remote access privileges. In most organizations, once the first-level supervisor signs off, the account is created. This is an example of one degree of hierarchical separation. This process could be strengthened to two degrees of hierarchical separation and one degree of lateral separation by (1) requiring the employee's second-level supervisor to also approve the new account request, and (2) requiring the manager of the IT staff to approve the request before acting upon it. This would allow the IT staff to independently verify the trust level, trust types, and the need to access certain resources. This practice would also help motivate line managers to quit taking the easy way out, by requesting that everyone be given access to all resources, and instead take the time to determine exactly what an individual needs and does not need to access.

The new account request is given to the IT staff to implement. The account is created and the individual is given a phone call and sent a welcome e-mail. And that is usually the end of it. This is an example of a process that has no checks and balances. A more resilient process would add the following steps. First, after an account is created, a second member of the IT staff independently verifies that the account was initialized correctly, with all the specified access rights and privileges, but no more. Second, before the new employee is allowed to access corporate assets, he must participate in an orientation course, demonstrate a level of proficiency, and be briefed on standard security policies and procedures. This approach adds one degree of separation hierarchically and laterally, and complements the organization's accountability and competence goals. Most new employees spend an inordinate amount of time in-processing. Why not use part of that time to do something constructive?

After an employee is on the job for a while, he may take on new responsibilities or transfer to another project. As a result, the assets he needs access to change. Often, this is taken care of by a simple phone call — "Can you add Jane to the list for ...?" — because the employee is now an insider. This is another example of a process without any checks and balances, one that could easily be misused. A more resilient process would require that changes to access rights and privileges be handled the same way as a new account request, with the hierarchical and lateral separation built in. Clearly identify the new assets the individual needs access to, the old assets the individual needs continued access to, and the old assets the individual no longer needs access to. To prevent access creep, all definite insiders', pseudo-insiders', and pseudo-outsiders' access rights and privileges should be independently verified, hierarchically and laterally, at least every six months. Do not just confirm their access rights on paper; also verify that they are implemented correctly in the IT system. Maintain records of the changes, approvals, and account verification activities.

Eventually the time comes to delete or revoke an account. Accounts are routinely deleted under normal circumstances when an employee leaves or transfers to another part of the organization. Accounts are revoked in an emergency as part of an adverse action or following a security violation. It is essential to split the responsibility to create and delete or revoke accounts, in order to prevent mischief and cover-ups. Separate the responsibility for deleting or revoking accounts from the authority to authorize the deletion or revocation; this separation should be lateral and hierarchical. Make first-line supervisors responsible for initiating the request to delete accounts. They should be held responsible for ensuring that accounts are deleted by the close of business on the day an individual leaves an organization. Put procedures in place to verify that accounts were in fact deleted on time. Establish a separate process for emergency account revocation. Ensure that the necessary approvals are obtained, but in an expeditious manner, so that revocation can be accomplished within ten minutes. It is best to design this process so that the personnel security office is involved. Designate alternates in case the key players are not available in the limited time frame. Document all action taken due to potential legal ramifications. Test normal account deletion and emergency account revocation processes on a regular basis to ensure that they work as planned and within the specified time frames.

Most organizations monitor account usage, some more rigorously than others. Account usage should be monitored by the security staff, not the IT staff that creates or deletes accounts, to ensure hierarchical and lateral separation. Internal misuse is detected by monitoring account usage. Repeated attempts to access resources an individual does not have access to, repeated attempts to bypass security features, a high volume of activity during off-hours or from strange locations, and perpetual unused accounts are all potential indications of malicious activity. The ability to monitor this activity must be separated from general account management functions to provide lateral separation from the IT staff and the individual's program office. To add hierarchical separation, the ability to monitor account usage should be separated from the authority to take preemptive action if malicious activity is expected. Account monitoring functions require a high degree of independence and a high level of trust to be effective Put another way, what better way is there to cover up malicious activity than to tamper with the account usage monitoring function?

So you think this is all too much bother and you do not have time? Well, let us look at what can go wrong when separation of duties is not implemented or is implemented ineffectively. As a test case, we examine the IT asset inventory management function.

The engineering capital planning program office initiates an annual inventory of IT assets. Fixed IT assets, mobile IT assets, spare parts, equipment out for repair, unused equipment, and current application, system, and networking software licenses are included within the scope of the inventory. Expendables such as printer paper, printer toner, disks, etc. are not included. The results of this inventory will be used for several purposes, such as determining the current IT asset value for the organization's annual financial report, determining the remaining useful life span of the IT assets, identifying the need to order new equipment and spares, identifying the need to update and consolidate software licenses, and highlighting the need to allocate sufficient funds to pay for the new equipment and software licenses. And as mentioned previously, inventories are a good time to identify asset owners. To obtain an accurate and complete inventory, hierarchical and lateral separation of duties should be employed. Assign the IT staff the responsibility for conducting a physical inventory of IT assets, whereby they go office to office and inventory the equipment and software installed and verify bar codes and serial numbers. Have a second-level supervisor on the IT staff approve the final report before it is sent to the program office. At the same time, task the network management staff to conduct an electronic inventory of all IP addresses; the equipment installed; the types and versions of software installed; and whether authorized, bootleg, or "home" software. Depending on the organization it may be appropriate to remove or quarantine any unauthorized equipment or software. Have a second-level supervisor on the network management staff approve the final report before sending it to the program office. Task the security management staff to independently compare the reports from the IT staff and the network management staff, looking for inconsistencies and conflicting information. At the same time, have the security management staff compare the inventories with documented access rights and privileges to see if there are any assets that are not accounted for or phantom assets. If need be, the security management staff should be allowed to conduct their own independent physical and electronic inventories to verify or disprove information. Have a second-level supervisor on the security management staff approve the final report before sending it to the program office. Establish the program office as the final decision maker for the veracity of IT asset inventory information provided by the other three offices. This approach provides three degrees of lateral separation and two degrees of hierarchical separation.

Today many organizations have trouble with computers, particularly notebooks, walking out the front door never to be seen or heard from again. This situation is not due to lax physical security controls, like the requirement for property passes, but rather the lack of effective separation of duties. Often, all aspects of responsibility for IT assets are (wrongly) placed in one organization, usually the IT staff. Worse still, one person within that organization usually has sole responsibility for a group of users and their IT equipment. Without the independence and separation of duties described in the above example, the door is wide open for abuse. There is nothing to prevent:

- Equipment or software from being ordered that is not needed or is never delivered to the organization
- Bogus inventories that distort the real type, quantity, configuration, and location of equipment
- An incomplete or inaccurate inventory in which phantom equipment appears or disappears
- Equipment being sent out for repair and never returning

In one location, the same individual ordered, installed, inventoried, and sent IT equipment out for repair. He had quite a scam going until someone in finance calculated that, based on the purchase orders, there should be three computers per employee in that division. The division was split between two buildings that were five miles a part. He was always moving equipment from one building to the next to "make sure everyone had the latest equipment." What he was really doing was moving the inventory bar codes from the real system to a lesser configuration and selling the new equipment on the side. The people he dealt with on a daily basis and his co-workers did not have a clue — that is why there needs to be more to accountability than being friendly and "helpful." The purchase orders and the fact that he worked so much on the weekends finally gave him away. Individuals on the IT staff have been known to declare that a system is "out of warranty" as an excuse for ordering new equipment and selling the old. Sometimes they get a kickback from the company they keep ordering the new equipment from. And it is unlikely that the old systems were sanitized before they were sold, thus compounding the organization's loss. It is also not uncommon to use an organization's software licenses to load friends' and neighbors' computers. In this instance, the organization is liable for violations of the software licenses.

Other problems can arise if an IT inventory is only conducted electronically. Sometimes organizations decide it is too much trouble or they do not have time to do a physical inventory so they just do an electronic inventory. Several things can go wrong in this case. Word gets around that an electronic inventory is being conducted so unauthorized equipment is temporarily disconnected or relocated. Employees have been known to disconnect equipment from the corporate intranet and reconnect through the Internet using their office phone and a modem. The electronic inventory may not be conducted properly, accidentally or on purpose, so that entire subnets or classes of equipment or software are missed. If there are not enough checks and balances in the electronic inventory process itself, data may be accidentally or intentionally corrupted or dropped, hiding the real situation. All organizations rely on the IT infrastructure to accomplish their mission. As the example above has shown, without the appropriate separation of duties, hierarchically and laterally, related to the IT inventory, an organization could be operating on a house of cards. The IT infrastructure could be compromised, limited IT funds wasted, and equipment and software stolen, with the organization being liable for the consequences. Not to mention, how do you design or implement a security architecture when you do not have any control over or insight into your real IT asset inventory? Similar unnecessary risks result when separation of duties is not implemented in other business processes.

The following metrics can be used to measure the resilience of personnel security controls related to separation of duties.

By organization unit, percentage of processes, procedures, and system functions that implement separation of duties: 2.2.4.1

    a. By asset sensitivity and criticality
    b. By position sensitivity and risk
    c. By position trust level and trust type
    d. Overall

By organizational unit, percentage of processes, procedures, and system functions that implement separation of duties: 2.2.4.2

    a. By lateral separation
    b. By hierarchical separation
    c. By geographical separation
    d. By a combination of types of separation

Distribution by organization unit of the degree of separation of duties implemented: 2.2.4.3

    a. By asset sensitivity and criticality
    b. By position sensitivity and risk
    c. By position trust level and trust type
    d. Overall

Distribution by organization unit of the degree of separation of duties implemented: 2.2.4.4

    a. By lateral separation
    b. By hierarchical separation
    c. By geographical separation
    d. By a combination of types of separation

Percentage of organizational units that have verified, within the past 12 months, that separation of duties is implemented for all applicable processes, procedures, and system functions (and not where it is not needed or of no value).
            2.2.4.5

Percentage of organizational units that have verified, within the past 12 months, that the implementation of separation of duties is working correctly, to the level of resilience specified, for all processes, procedures, and system functions:
            2.2.4.6

    a. Percentage of implementations that did not pass
    b. Percentage of failures for which remedial action has been taken
    c. Time frame for reassessment

During the past 12 months, the percentage of incidents that were traceable to ineffective or a lack of separation of duties, by incident severity.   2.2.4.7

Percentage of job rotation programs that are consistent with and complement the organization's separation of duties strategy: 2.2.4.8

    a. By asset sensitivity and criticality
    b. By position sensitivity and risk
    c. By position trust level and trust type
    d. Overall

Percentage of job rotation programs that have been reviewed during the last 12 months to ensure that they are consistent with and complement the organization's separation of duties strategy.   2.2.4.9

Workforce Analysis

The fifth major component of a comprehensive personnel security program involves analyzing the organization's workforce. This is another example of a people issue that many organizations do not understand or ignore, mistakenly thinking that is the politically correct thing to do. On the contrary, it is prudent for an organization to periodically analyze the composition of its workforce. The intent is to see if there are any indications of potential vulnerabilities inherent in the mix at a given point in time. The focus is on vulnerabilities that could impact or prevent an organization from reliably achieving its mission under normal and abnormal conditions. Workforce analysis is not an attempt to probe into an individual's personal affairs and use that information as an excuse for running him off. Rather, the scope of the analysis concerns the workforce as a whole and not individuals. Large organizations may want to perform the analysis facility by facility, then consolidate the results by locations, regions, and ultimately enterprisewide. Workforce analysis investigates the seven factors listed below. There may be additional factors that are unique to one organization and should be analyzed as well. These factors are examined in light of business continuity planning and potential security risks should the right mix of people not be available when needed.[158] In essence, workforce analysis attempts to find any single points of failure in an organization's workforce while there is still time to mitigate them:

- Definite insiders, pseudo-insiders
- Tenure, experience, and turnover
- Citizenship
- Offshore
- Eligibility to retire
- Geography
- Proficiency at more than one job function

Previously, during the discussion of background investigations, we looked at the array of different types of insiders and outsiders (refer to Figure 4.4). As part of workforce analysis, it is a good idea to periodically review the distribution along this spectrum. Contractors and consultants who work for an organization today may decide to team with their competitors tomorrow. Contractors and consultants may assign key staff to other projects. Key contractor staff members may be promoted, transferred, or simply leave the company. The departure of key staff may create a competency vacuum that takes a long time to fill, especially if several key people leave at the same time. Specific job skills, historical knowledge, and organizational familiarity can rarely be recreated overnight — neither can an in-depth understanding of security policies, procedures, and standards. The need for lengthy background investigations at the appropriate trust level and trust types may further delay filling key vacancies. Government contracts often include a clause about the transfer or reassignment of key personnel. For the most part, these clauses are not enforceable. If a top performer has earned a promotion or wants to transfer, a company cannot withhold this; if the company tries, the employee will simply leave and go to a new firm. Another potential vulnerability concerns suppliers and vendors. It is always wise to have secondary sources for all critical and essential supplies and services. Dependency on a single supplier or vendor can create cost and schedule vulnerabilities. Prices may not be competitive. Availability may be compromised. A supplier or vendor may go out of business, or be bought or merged with a competitor. During its heyday, Digital Equipment Corporation (DEC) maintained an internal second sourcing capability for all critical chip technology. This capability prevented delays in introducing new DEC products whenever a semiconductor manufacturer experienced production or fabrication problems, which occurred from time to time. Yes there was a cost associated with the second sourcing capability, but it was far less than the potential lost market share. Consequently, take the time to analyze the current workforce on a quarterly or semi-annual basis. Look for areas of over-dependence on pseudo-insiders. Verify that contingency plans and alternate modes of operation are already in place, should a pseudo-insider disappear overnight. The time to scramble is now, so that you do not find yourself up the proverbial creek without a paddle.

Tenure is another parameter that is evaluated as part of workforce analysis — in particular, the distribution of the workforce by the number of years they have been with the organization and their total number of years of experience. The intent is to determine how experienced and familiar the workforce is with company and security policies, procedures, and standards. Large organizations may want to perform this calculation by facilities, organizational units, regions, and enterprisewide to obtain a composite picture. Ideally, the distribution should be fairly even among the 0–5 years, 5–10 years, 15–20 years, and 20+ years categories. The distribution for critical and essential functions should be calculated separately to pinpoint specific vulnerabilities. Often, organizations find that most of their workforce falls into either the 0–5 years or 20+ years categories. This is not a good situation. People in the 0–5 years category tend to job-hop quite a bit, for two reasons: (1) they are still trying to figure out what they want to specialize in, and (2) to bump up their salary. This is a very transient group. At the other extreme is the 20+ years group. Some people in this category are very talented, hard-charging professionals. Others have let their skills become outdated and are just coasting to retirement. The strong center, the people with 5–20 years of experience, is missing. These people tend to be current in their field and are in the best position to teach operational procedures, explain the corporate culture, and mentor less-experienced workers. The larger the age and experience gap between mentor and mentoree, the less effective the relationship will be. Often, companies grow too fast and suddenly find that close to 50 percent of their workforce has less than five years' tenure. A common problem for small companies, this situation creates a very unstable workforce. Newcomers have yet to internalize the purpose, mission, vision, or culture of their new organization. As a result, they are unable to pass this on to the people they supervise or set a steady course for them. Instead, they try to recreate the work environment of their previous organization, that with which they are familiar. When approximately 50 percent of the staff do this, soon the organization is pulling in so many different directions, rather than everyone pushing together toward a common purpose, mission, and vision, that it eventually collapses. This explains in part why so many start-up firms die out between their fifth and tenth years. At the same time, security policies, procedures, and practices become a disjointed mess, riddled with vulnerabilities, and each small group doing (or not doing) things their own way. The leadership vacuum is filled by indecision, inaction, overlapping, conflicting, and incomplete policies — a cyber criminal's heaven. As a result, be sure to include tenure and experience as part of an ongoing workforce analysis initiative.

As a corollary to tenure and experience, another useful parameter to analyze is retention or staff turnover rates. In the high-tech industry, it is common for management, particularly senior management, to purposely ignore this number. They go into a state of denial, rationalizing the exodus by saying it "goes with the territory." Some people are perpetual job-hoppers, but most are not. When retention rates are low and turnover rates are high, it is a blunt indicator that something is wrong in the work environment; and contrary to popular myth, salary is not the only or most important issue. Perhaps a particular manager is abrasive or incompetent. The work is dull or not challenging for the level of people assigned to perform it. Project schedules are impossible and there is non-stop unpaid overtime nights and weekends, month after month. Maybe the cause of the ridiculous hours is that workers do not have the tools or training they need to perform their assignment. It is management's responsibility to determine and alleviate the root cause of the exodus. As the saying goes, the top talent are always the ones to leave — because they can. The dead wood never leaves — because they cannot. If the cause of high staff turnover is not corrected, an organization will soon find itself populated by an under-skilled, under-motivated staff — a situation that is ripe for an epidemic of security violations.

Citizenship also needs to be evaluated as part of workforce analysis. Are the majority of the workforce citizens of the country in which the organization operates? It is preferable for 90+ percent of the workforce overall and 100 percent of the workers who perform critical or essential job functions to be citizens. Specific trust levels and trust types may require citizenship. Citizenship by itself is not an automatic indicator of loyalty and responsibility. Likewise, lack of citizenship by itself is not an automatic indicator of a lack of trust-worthiness. The lack of citizenship, however, can create problems for an organization in the areas of stability and accountability. If someone is not a citizen, he may not stay in the area long, because he does not have any ties. On the other hand, a person who was employed by an organization as a non-citizen may leave for a new, better-paying position once he receives citizen-ship. I have witnessed several instances where a U.S. firm sponsored someone who had a "green card." For the company it was a bargain — non-citizens could usually be paid half as much as what U.S. citizens were paid. But once these individuals received their citizenship papers, they were out the door for a new job that paid more. The end result was constant turnover. The lack of citizenship may also cause morale problems should the international political or economic situation change. Accountability is complicated by a lack of citizenship. Should a non-citizen commit a security violation (accidentally or intentionally), instead of facing the sanctions, he may simply leave the country — because it is nearly impossible to enforce such sanctions across borders. As a result, it is a good idea to include citizenship as part of workforce analysis.

Another aspect of workforce analysis involves taking a close look at the distribution of local and offshore workers (definite insiders and pseudo-insiders). Many Western companies have become fascinated with the much cheaper labor markets in Asia, particularly in manufacturing and call center processing. Often, the daily wages in these areas are less than the minimum hourly wage back home. And the cost of benefits is also much lower. At the same time, many large corporations are inherently international in character. They have an engineering, sales, and maintenance presence in many countries around the world. Having an organization's operations spread across several geographic locations may offer economic advantages in the short term, such as lower labor costs and a buffer from a temporary economic downturn in one area. However, there may be significant long-term disadvantages. If history teaches us anything, it is that the international political situation changes constantly, often quickly and dramatically. Overnight trade embargoes are imposed and "foreign" firms are nationalized — not to mention the equally as quick currency fluctuations. During World War II, U.S. firms operating in territories controlled by Germany were transferred to German ownership and vice versa. IBM was perhaps one of the most well-known firms to go through this experience. During the 1970s, many Western oil companies woke up to find that their holdings in Venezuela and the Middle East had been nationalized — they could still buy crude oil but they no longer owned anything and there was nothing that could be done about it legally. How are spare parts for an airplane, computer, or electric power plant obtained when the local manufacturing capability and know-how has been lost, the international situation has become unstable, or a trade embargo has been imposed? Some experts project that the long-term consequences of globalization will be economic downturn and instability. The manufacturing of almost everything, from shoes to consumer electronics and automobiles, is being outsourced offshore. Fruits, vegetables, and flowers are being imported from around the world. All of these economic shifts are occurring at the same time the world's supply of oil is being depleted, while demand is skyrocketing. Soon, some experts hypothesize, it will be cost prohibitive to transport products around the world. Between January and December 2005, gas heating bills in the United States increased by an average of 37 percent, and that was just in one year. That fresh Hawaiian pineapple that costs $4 today may soon cost $20. As a result, organizations need to take a serious look at their distribution of local and offshore workers and how this is likely to impact the ability to reliably and securely provide and obtain the goods and services needed to achieve their mission, both in the short term and the long term. The time to do the analysis and make adjustments is before a crisis erupts.

Another part of workforce analysis concerns age distribution. At some point in time, everyone retires. Some people retire at 55, others at 65, and a few hang on until 75 or later. The "official" social security retirement age in the United States is currently 67.5. A host of very different and very personal reasons influence when an individual decides to retire. Some people announce when they are going to retire two or three years ahead of time; others change the date two or three times before they actually retire because they are nervous about making such a big change in their lives. To ensure smooth transitions, an organization should periodically monitor the percentage of its workforce that is eligible to retire. The idea is to plan ahead and make sure there are sufficient senior people on board who are thoroughly trained in the job function, company policies and procedures, and security practices, and can move up and assume new responsibilities as retirements occur. Adequate long-range planning is essential for these transitions to occur smoothly. This process needs to be handled professionally and delicately, so that it is not perceived as age discrimination or harassment to force people to retire before they are ready. Many organizations are surprised to discover, when they first analyze the age distribution of their workforce, that 30+ percent of the people are eligible to retire in two years or less. As the wave of retirements begins, they are caught unprepared. In desperation, vacancies are filled by junior people or temporary employees who do not have the appropriate knowledge, skills, or experience. Safety, reliability, and security fly out the door, with serious consequences to the organization's finances and reputation. This is definitely a case where an ounce of prevention (or preparation) is better than a pound of cure.

The geographical distribution of an organization's workforce is another parameter to analyze. The intent is to determine the percentage of the workforce that would be able to make it to work at their primary location, or a backup site, should a natural or man-made disaster strike. Are most workers located in the same city or metropolitan area? Are they spread around various parts of the city and hence use different routes to get to work, or concentrated in one area? Are workers distributed among different cities throughout the country? What is the average commute to the primary and backup locations? What are the primary modes of transportation, and how might they be effected by natural or man-made disasters? Most disasters commence with very little warning; that is why it is crucial to do the analysis, planning, and preparation beforehand. For example, in December 2005, a three-day transit strike in New York City almost shut down the city as 7.5 million people scrambled to find alternate transportation. What would happen to your organization if bus and subway service suddenly came to a halt? What would happen if a major bridge, tunnel, or other commuting artery was suddenly unavailable? Would workers still be able to get to and from work? Very few organizations can operate effectively, securely, or for any length of time if only 10 percent of their employees can make it to work. Now is the time to put alternate transportation plans in place, such as company vans, satellite work centers, and telecommuting.

The next question to ask is what percentage of the workforce is trained and proficient at performing more than one job function? This number can be critical in certain circumstances. Previously, during the discussion of competency, the need for cross-training was identified to provide coverage during holidays, vacations, and other extended absences. Cross-training is also an essential ingredient for continuity of operations under abnormal conditions. Should a natural or man-made disaster strike and only 40 percent of the workforce can make it to work, that is not going to be very helpful if no one knows how to perform certain key job functions. The 40 percent who arrived may end up spending their time looking at one another and wondering why they risked their necks coming to work. And the organization is no better off than if it had remained closed. The need for cross-training is also crucial during epidemics, when a large number of people are on an extended medical absence. The first step toward preparation is to classify all job functions at a facility as either critical, essential, or routine. Ideally, there should always be multiple people who are trained, proficient, and available to perform critical and essential job functions. Identify alternate and backup staff and ensure that their training is up-to-date. Make sure all the appropriate people in the management chain know who the primary, alternate, and backup people are for each critical and essential job function and how to contact them. And it is always a good idea to be certain that the individuals are aware that they have been designated as key staff; this is not something to be handled by a passive e-mail or memo. Establish primary and alternate modes of communications and transportation for these individuals. Conduct quarterly practice drills. Have workers perform their alternate assignments and verify alternate modes of communication and transportation. Note any retraining or changes that are needed to the plan.

The following metrics can be used to measure the resilience of personnel security controls related to workforce analysis.

Frequency with which workforce analysis is performed for each category and date of most recent analysis: 2.2.5.1

    a. Definite insiders and pseudo-insiders
    b. Tenure and experience
    c. Citizenship
    d. Offshore
    e. Eligibility to retire
    f. Geography
    g. Proficiency at more than one job function

Distribution of workforce by the categories below, by facility, organizational unit, region, and enterprisewide: 2.2.5.2

    a. Permanent employees
    b. Temporary employees
    c. Interns
    d. Contractors
    e. Consultants
    f. Vendors and suppliers

Distribution of workforce that is performing critical job functions by the categories below, by facility, organizational unit, region, and enterprisewide: 2.2.5.3

    a. Permanent employees
    b. Temporary employees
    c. Interns
    d. Contractors
    e. Consultants
    f. Vendors and suppliers

Distribution of workforce that is performing essential job functions by the categories below, by facility, organizational unit, region, and enterprisewide: 2.2.5.4

    a. Permanent employees
    b. Temporary employees
    c. Interns
    d. Contractors
    e. Consultants
    f. Vendors and suppliers

Distribution of workforce tenure by position criticality (critical, essential, routine):
2.2.5.5

    a. <1 year
    b. 1–5 years
    c. 5–10 years
    d. 10–15 years
    e. 15–20 years
    f. 20+ years

Distribution of workforce experience by position criticality (critical, essential, routine):
2.2.5.6

    a. <1 year
    b. 1–5 years
    c. 5–10 years
    d. 10–15 years
    e. 15–20 years
    f. 20+ years

Percentage of workforce that are not citizens, by position criticality (critical, essential, routine).
2.2.5.7

Distribution of workforce that is offshore by position criticality (critical, essential, routine):
2.2.5.8

    a. Africa
    b. Asia
    c. Europe
    d. North America
    e. South America
    f. South Pacific

Distribution of workforce that is eligible to retire by position criticality (critical, essential, routine):
2.2.5.9

    a. <1 year
    b. 1–2 years
    c. 2–3 years
    d. 3–5 years

Geographical distribution of the workforce, by facility and criticality and sensitivity of the products and services provided:
2.2.5.10

    a. Within 2 miles of the facility
    b. Within 2–5 miles of the facility
    c. Within 5–10 miles of the facility
    d. Within 10–15 miles of the facility
    e. +15 miles of the facility
    f. Percentage whose only option is to drive
    g. Percentage who can use bus service
    h. Percentage who can use subway service

Percentage of organizational units that have established alternate work sites, by the criticality and sensitivity of the products and services provided:

2.2.5.11

a. Backup locations
b. Satellite work centers
c. Telecommuting option

Percentage of the workforce that are trained and proficient at performing more than one job function.   2.2.5.12

Percentage of critical job functions for which alternate and backup workers have been designated and trained.   2.2.5.13

Percentage of essential job functions for which alternate and backup workers have been designated and trained.   2.2.5.14

Frequency with which practice drills are conducted to verify that alternate and backup workers can perform their assigned duties and alternate communication and transportation modes work as planned: 2.2.5.15

a. Date of most recent drill
b. Percentage of job functions that were performed correctly during most recent drill

Staff turnover rate by position sensitivity (ultra high, high, moderate, low, none) for the last 6, 12, and 18 months.   2.2.5.16

Personnel Security Metrics Reports

An effective personnel security program requires a combination of controls in the areas of accountability, background investigations, competence, separation of duties, and workforce analysis. Given the dynamic nature of personnel security, these controls must be monitored on an ongoing basis. At times it may be appropriate to probe into the details of one of these areas. On other occasions it may be preferable to take a composite view across the entire personnel security program. The quantity and specific types of metrics used in these situations will depend on the Goal being measured and the Questions being investigated in order to measure progress toward achieving or sustaining that Goal. The metrics report template presented earlier in Table 4.8 is also used for personnel security reports. Let us walk through two sample personnel security metrics reports to see the type of information they convey. The first report examines a single component — background investigations. The second report evaluates the personnel security program as a whole.

When monitoring background investigations, most organizations focus on how many have been submitted, are in progress, or have been completed. However, there is another whole dimension of information to be illuminated as well. For example, consider the following Goal and Question:

Goal: Ensure that background investigations are unbiased, impartial, fair, consistent, accurate, objective, and timely.

Question: What is the effectiveness of the background investigation process?

Table 4.11   Resilience Metric Report: Background Investigations

Report Date: 3 January 2006

Reporting Entity: Seattle Regional Office

Security Domain(s): Personnel Security

Sub-element(s): Background Investigations

Focus: Effectiveness of background investigation process

Measurement Boundary: Regional offices   **Prediction or Actual Value:** Actual value

Time Interval: 4th quarter

Metric		Target Value	Observed Value	Interpretation
ID	Definition			
2.2.2.1	Percentage (%) of staff that have current background investigations	100%	75%	Yellow
2.2.2.2	Percentage (%) trust levels and trust types that have been reviewed and reaffirmed within the last six months	100%	50%	Red
2.2.2.5	Number of security incidents by severity and the trust level and trust type of the individuals involved	0	Ultra High — 0 High — 0 Moderate — 1 Low — 1 None — 0	Red
2.2.2.6	Problems or delays with the background investigation process:			
	a. Number of interim approvals granted	a. 0	a. 5	a. Red
	b. Number updated for cause	b. —	b. 1	b. Yellow
	c. Number of reported abuses during background investigation	c. 0	c. 2	c. Yellow
	d. Number of appeals filed	d. 0	d. 3	d. Yellow
	e. Number of appeals upheld	e. —	e. 1	e. Red

Table 4.11   Resilience Metric Report: Background Investigations (continued)

Metric		Target Value	Observed Value	Interpretation
ID	Definition			
2.2.2.8	Number of times sanctions were imposed on investigators for:			
	a. Inappropriate behavior during a background investigation	a. —	a. 1	a. Red
	b. Mishandling information from a background investigation	b. —	b. 1	b. Red
Summary Red = 0 points Yellow = 5 points Green = 10 points		**Total Possible** 100 points	**Actual Score** 10 or 10% **Overall Rating** Red	

Note: It would appear that some inexperienced or overzealous investigators were involved. Corrective action should be taken to (1) remedy investigator shortcomings, and (2) determine why the adjudication process did not filter out erroneous information.

Five metrics can be used to answer that question, as shown in Table 4.11. First, we want to know the percentage of background investigations that are current. Most investigations expire and are to be renewed at five- or ten-year intervals. In this example, a single target value is given: 100 percent of all background investigations are to be current. In some circumstances it may be preferable to establish different target values for different trust levels, such as ultra high 100 percent, high 100 percent, moderate 90 percent, and low 80 percent. The observed value is 75 percent; this is not out of the ordinary as many organizations fail to stay on top of background investigations. The second metric involves verifying that the designated trust levels and trust types for each position have been reviewed and reaffirmed within the past six months. This is something all organizations should do, but again very few actually get around to doing. The target value is 100 percent, while the observed value is only 50 percent; there is definitely room for improvement. The third metric is one measure of whether or not the background investigation process is working. Security incidents for the quarter are itemized by the trust level and trust types of the individuals involved. All types of security incidents (physical, personnel, IT, and operational) are examined. All individuals possessing a trust level and trust type are included: definite insiders, pseudo-insiders, and pseudo-outsiders. If the background investigation process is working, this metric should be zero; hence the target value. The observed value indicates otherwise. Another factor to examine when measuring the effectiveness of the background investigation process is the number of problems or delays encountered. When investigations take too long, interim approvals are often granted. Once in awhile, or in an emergency situation, it may be acceptable to grant interim approvals (with the appropriate checks and balances). If interim approvals become part of the standard process, there is a problem that needs to be corrected; hence the target value is zero. In this example, the observed value is 5, indicating the need for corrective action. Another indicator of problems is the number of background investigations updated for cause. If the background investigation process was perfect and human behavior totally predictable, this number would always be zero. Because neither case is true, occasions arise when it is necessary to update an individual's background investigation for cause. If this number is always zero, updates may not be being performed when needed. On the other hand, if this number is always a non-zero value, the background investigation process itself may be defective. As a result, this number needs to be monitored closely, but no target value can be set. Other indicators of problems in the background investigation process are the numbers of abuses reported, appeals filed, and appeals upheld. In an ideal world, the number of abuses reported and appeals filed would be zero. If these numbers are always zero, that may indicate instead that people are either unaware of their rights, subject to intimidation, or fear retaliation — none of which is healthy for an organization. Investigators, as well as the investigation process, are imperfect. Consequently, checks and balances — such as the right to report abuses, file appeals, and have an independent and objective review of an appeal — are needed. The fifth metric evaluates whether or not misconduct is being dealt with seriously. Specifically, are sanctions being imposed on investigators for inappropriate behavior and mishandling of information? These numbers must be monitored closely; however, no target value can be set. Rather, sanctions should be imposed when necessary. Each of these five metrics has been evaluated separately. Finally, a summary rating is given based on the total score, which in this case is 20 percent (or red).

Periodically, a status check should be taken of the overall personnel security program, to see how well it is functioning. Often an organization will see a lot of activity going on and mistake that for an effective program. To illustrate, consider the following Goal and Question:

Goal: Ensure, on a regular basis, that the personnel security program is comprehensive and effective.

Question: How effective are ongoing personnel security controls that are not related to background investigations?

To answer that question, a composite report could be generated that includes the metrics shown in Table 4.12. Individual metrics are identified for each of the four categories: (1) accountability, (2) competence, (3) separation of duties, and (4) workforce analysis. The metrics focus on assessing how well the day-to-day personnel security controls are working. A value is reported for each individual metric. Each metric is compared to the target value and a rating is assigned. Ratings and scores are then calculated for each of the four categories and the personnel security program overall.

Table 4.12 Resilience Metric Report: Personnel Security Program

Report Date: 3 January 2006

Reporting Entity: Headquarters

Security Domain(s): Personnel Security

Sub-element(s): Accountability, Competence, Separation of Duties, Workforce Analysis

Focus: Status of overall personnel security program

Measurement Boundary: Enterprisewide   **Prediction or Actual Value:** Actual value

Time Interval: 4th quarter

Metric		Target Value	Observed Value	Interpretation
ID	Definition			
1. Accountability				
2.2.1.4	Percentage (%) of position descriptions that define security roles, responsibilities, and certifications:			
	a. Security managers	a. 100%	a. 100%	a. Green
	b. IT personnel	b. 100%	b. 80%	b. Yellow
	c. General staff and system users	c. 100%	c. 50%	c. Red
2.2.1.6	Percentage (%) of security policies, procedures, and standards that define sanctions according to the type, number, and severity of violations	100%	60%	Yellow
2.2.1.7	Percentage (%) of job performance reviews that include security roles and responsibilities	100%	30%	Red
2.2.1.9	Percentage (%) of accountability requirements that are enforced	100%	50%	Red
Subtotal	Total Possible: 60 points	Score: 20 or 33% Rating: red		

Table 4.12   Resilience Metric Report: Personnel Security Program (continued)

Metric		Target Value	Observed Value	Interpretation
ID	Definition			
2. Competence				
2.2.3.1	Percentage (%) of positions for which detailed competency requirements have been defined for the job function and security roles and responsibilities	100%	50%	Red
2.2.3.2	Percentage (%) of individuals that meet or exceed competency requirements by position sensitivity/risk:			
	a. Ultra High	a. 100%	a. 100%	a. Green
	b. High	b. 100%	b. 95%	b. Green
	c. Moderate	c. 100%	c. 80%	c. Yellow
	d. Low	d. 100%	d. 50%	d. Red
	e. None	e. 100%	e. 50%	e. Red
2.2.3.6	Number and percentage (%) of security incidents in the past 12 months that involved individuals that did not meet competency requirements	0	0	Green
Subtotal	Total Possible: 70 points	Score: 35 or 50% Rating: red		
3. Separation of Duties				
2.2.4.1	Percentage (%) of critical and essential processes, procedures, and system functions that implement separation of duties	100%	90%	Green
2.2.4.6	Percentage (%) of organizational units that have verified, within the last 12 months, that the implementation of separation of duties is working correctly	100%	75%	Yellow

Table 4.12　Resilience Metric Report: Personnel Security Program (continued)

Metric		Target Value	Observed Value	Interpretation
ID	Definition			
2.2.4.7	Percentage (%) of security incidents in the last 12 months that were traceable to ineffective or a lack of separation of duties	0	0	Green
2.2.4.8	Percentage (%) of job rotation programs that are consistent with and complement the separation of duties strategy	100%	75%	Yellow
Subtotal	Total Possible: 40 points	Score: 30 or 75%　Rating: yellow		
4. Workforce Analysis				
2.2.5.3	Distribution of workforce that is performing critical job functions:			
	a. Permanent employees	a. 100%	a. 85%	Red
	b. Temporary employees	b. 0	b. 0	
	c. Interns	c. 0	c. 0	
	d. Contractors	d. 0	d. 8%	
	e. Consultants	e. 0	e. 4%	
	f. Vendors, suppliers	f. 0	f. 3%	
2.2.5.4	Distribution of workforce that is performing essential job functions			
	a. Permanent employees	a. 95%	a. 90%	Yellow
	b. Temporary employees	b. 0	b. 0	
	c. Interns	c. 0	c. 0	
	d. Contractors	d. 2%	d. 5%	
	e. Consultants	e. 2%	e. 2%	
	f. Vendors, suppliers	f. 1%	f. 3%	

Table 4.12   Resilience Metric Report: Personnel Security Program (continued)

	Metric	Target Value	Observed Value	Interpretation
2.2.5.5	Distribution of workforce by tenure:			Red
	a. <1 year	a. 15%	a. 15%	
	b. 1–5 years	b. 17%	b. 10%	
	c. 5–10 years	c. 18%	c. 10%	
	d. 10–15 years	d. 18%	d. 10%	
	e. 15–20 years	e. 17%	e. 25%	
	f. 20+ years	f. 15%	f. 30%	
2.2.5.9	Distribution of workforce that is eligible to retire:			Red
	a. <1 year	a. 1%	a. 5%	
	b. 1–2 years	b. 1%	b. 10%	
	c. 3 years	c. 3%	c. 2%	
	d. 3–5 years	d. 5%	d. 3%	
2.2.5.11	Percentage (%) of organizational units that have established alternate work sites:			Yellow
	a. Backup location	a. 100%	a. 100%	
	b. Satellite work center	b. 100%	b. 50%	
	c. Telecommuting option	c. 60%	c. 40%	
2.2.5.13	Percentage (%) of critical job functions for which alternate and backup workers have been designated and trained	100%	80%	Yellow
2.2.5.16	Staff turnover rate for last 6, 12, and 18 months by position sensitivity:			Yellow
	a. Ultra High	a. 0%	a. 1%	
	b. High	b. 1%	b. 2%	
	c. Moderate	c. 1%	c. 3%	
	d. Low	d. 1%	d. 2%	
	e. None	e. 2%	e. 5%	
Subtotal	Total Possible: 60 points	Score: 20 or 33% Rating: red		

Table 4.12   Resilience Metric Report: Personnel Security Program (continued)

Summary	Total Possible	Actual Score
Red = 0 points Yellow = 5 points Green = 10 points	230 points	105 or 46% **Overall Rating** Red

Note: The most progress has been made in the area of separation of duties. However, more work is needed in all areas to meet our goals.

The composite report provides three levels of abstraction to highlight areas that are going well and those in need of improvement. In this example, the accountability metrics reflect that the organization has started to implement accountability but still has a long way to go. Not all position descriptions include accountability requirements. Not all security policies, procedures, and standards define sanctions for security violations. Only 30 percent of job performance reviews include security roles and responsibilities. And the real give-away is the fact that only half of the accountability requirements are enforced; this is a red flag that not everyone in the organization is on board with the accountability initiative. Hence, the overall rating is red. A similar situation exists in relation to competence. Some progress has been made in defining competency requirements for each position, but not enough. An attempt has been made to ensure that people occupying positions at the highest trust levels meet competency requirements; however, this practice should be extended to all trust levels. Finally, the correlation between a lack of competence and security incidents is assessed. Overall, half of the competence goals have been met. As a result, the rating is red. In this example, most of the progress and accomplishments have been in the area of separation of duties, the only category not to have any red ratings. For the most part, separation of duties has been implemented and verified; even job rotation programs adhere to the strategy. Because of this, the overall rating for separation of duties is yellow. Workforce analysis is a weak area, achieving only one third of the goals. In this case, the target values represent the goals an organization should work toward, while the observed values expose the organization's weaknesses. Again, the category rating is red, as is the composite summary rating. How would your organization stack up against the same metrics?

4.4 IT Security

The third security engineering domain is IT security. The general public hears more about this domain than the other three, if by doing nothing else than listening to the evening news or reading the newspapers. Some of the information disseminated in this fashion is actually true. Unfortunately, most of it is not and should be filed under hype (intentional?), misinformation (accidental?), or another rerun of *Ignorance is Bliss* (but not really).

The high-tech industry has been wandering in the wilderness for years when it comes to IT security metrics. Some false prophets have declared that return on investment (ROI) metrics represent the true manifestation of IT security metrics. Other equally misguided oracles have latched onto statistics emanating from IDS logs as the divine truth. A third group seeks an epiphany from monolithic high-level process metrics, while the remainder await divine revelation from the latest and greatest whiz-bang gizmo their anointed sales-man guided them (like sheep) to buy. Jelen describes this situation quite aptly[169]:

> *You have to know what "it" is before you can measure it!*

The problem is that many people, in all types of organizations and at all levels within an organization, have a vague, distorted, incomplete, fragmented, or microscopic understanding of IT security. Compounding the problem is the fact that most of these people are unaware of their knowledge gap, due to the barrage of misinformation from the general media and overzealous sales-men. Hence, the difficulty the industry has had in developing useful IT security metrics.

To overcome this situation, a clear, complete, and concise definition of IT security is needed:

> **IT Security:** inherent technical features and functions that collectively contribute to an IT infrastructure achieving, and sustaining, confidentiality, integrity, availability, accountability, authenticity, and reliability.

Notice that this definition does not mention anything about firewalls, IDS, or encryption. Rather, the definition refers to "… features and functions that collectively…." IT security is not about individual products. There is no one single product (or even two products) that will magically deliver IT security. The crux is for an IT infrastructure as a whole to be secure, not individual products. Consequently, the emphasis is on a combination of different complementary security features and functions that, working together, will achieve and sustain a specified level of confidentiality, integrity, availability, accountability, authenticity, and reliability under normal and abnormal conditions. The real measure of IT security is under abnormal conditions. That is why the selection, implementation, and configuration of security features should correspond to worst-case scenarios, not some idyllic notion of normal operations that never occurs. Worst-case scenarios determine the specific level of confidentiality, integrity, availability, accountability, authenticity, and reliability that is needed.

Notice also that the definition does not include the phrases "network security," "computer security," "database security," etc. On the contrary, IT security encompasses the totality of an IT infrastructure. If any aspect of the security of the IT infrastructure is neglected or shortchanged (i.e., operating

IT Security Control System (provide security functionality during normal operations)
- Logical access control
- Data authentication, non-repudiation
- Encryption, cryptographic support
- Flow control (operational and data)
- Identification and authentication
- Maintainability, supportability
- Privacy
- Residual information protection
- Security management

IT Security Protection System (protect assets from abnormal operations)
- Audit trail, alarm generation
- Availability (redundancy, diversity, fault tolerance, block recovery, dynamic reconfiguration, rollback, self-healing)
- Error, exception and incident handling
- Fail safe, fail secure, graceful degradation, degraded mode operations
- Integrity (hardware, software, network, active data, stored data, system)
- Domain separation (partitioning, information hiding, security kernels, encapsulation)
- Resource management (resource allocation, service priority, capacity management)

Figure 4.8   Taxonomy of IT security parameters.

system, e-mail, application, LAN, WAN, etc.), it will not be possible to achieve or sustain any level of IT security. The weakest link will be quickly compromised and used as an entry point for attacking the remaining infrastructure, and the domino principle will take over. Hence, the emphasis is on a combination of different complementary security features and functions working together. A complete set of security features and functions is needed that mitigates all types of risk at all layers of the protocol stack. Duplication and gaps in security features and functions need to be eliminated. The exact set of security features and functions needed is unique to each organization, based on that organization's particular IT infrastructure, the criticality of its mission and operations, the sensitivity of its assets, its risk exposure, and regulatory requirements, if applicable. The selection, implementation, and configuration of security features and functions should not be a case of chasing after the Joneses. Make no mistake; this is one area where it is essential to set your own style and do some serious custom tailoring.

IT security is limited to "inherent technical features and functions" — technology. Human interaction with technology and the processes followed to develop and assess technology are part of operational security, not IT security. This is a common area of confusion. Operational security, the fourth security engineering domain, is discussed in Section 4.5, which follows this section.

Conceptually, IT security is composed of two systems: (1) an IT security control system and (2) an IT security protection system. As shown in Figure 4.8, the IT security control system provides ongoing security functions during normal operations. These functions arbitrate access to and interaction with system assets on a regular basis. The corollary to this is the IT security protection system that protects system assets from and during abnormal operations. The IT security protection system is responsible for stepping in and taking proactive, preventive, and, if need be, reactive measures whenever anomalous operating conditions are suspected or confirmed. As technology moves closer and closer toward self-healing and autonomic responses, the relative importance of the IT security protection system increases.

Both the IT security control system and the IT security protection system are comprised of several components. Each of these topics is discussed individually below. To bring everyone to a common level of understanding and explain what "it" is, a brief synopsis of each topic is given. (Complete standards and books have been published on several of these topics. For a more in-depth treatment, readers are referred to the bibliography contained in Annex B.) The role each component plays in IT security and its relationship to resilience are examined. Then metrics are defined to ascertain where on the resilience scale a particular implementation and configuration of an IT security feature or function falls. Keep in mind that a low resilience rating is not necessarily bad, while a high resilience rating is not necessarily good. The objective is to achieve and sustain a resilience rating that is proportional to operational risk, so that assets are neither over- nor under-protected. Finally, examples of composite IT security resilience metrics reports are presented. IT security resilience metrics can be used in several ways; for example, to evaluate COTS products prior to purchase, to identify vulnerabilities in legacy systems, and to determine whether a new system is sufficiently robust and ready to deploy.

IT Security Control System

There are nine components of an IT security control system, each of which contributes to providing security functionality during normal operations:

- Logical access control
- Data authentication, non-repudiation
- Encryption, cryptographic support
- Flow control (operational and data)
- Identification and authentication
- Maintainability, supportability
- Privacy
- Residual information protection
- Security management, credential management, rules management

Logical Access Control

Logical access control complements physical access control by mediating access to IT and information assets. Logical access control prevents unauthorized and unwarranted access to networks, systems, applications, data, and other IT assets. Logical access control consists of two main parts: (1) access control rights that define which people and processes can access which system resources, and (2) access control privileges that define what these people and processes can do with and to the resources accessed.[270] Examples of access control privileges include read, write, edit, delete, execute, copy, print, move, forward, distribute, etc. Access controls should be operative at all layers of the protocol stack. For example, at the network layer, access control restrains access to networks and the establishment of network sessions. At the application layer, access control restricts access to, and the execution of, systems, applications, data, and other shared resources. Access may be permanently denied, permanently granted, or granted conditionally based on some variable parameters.

Access control mechanisms are activated immediately after identification and authentication. In simplest terms, an **initiator** (person or process) requests to perform an **operation** on a target **resource**. Access control mechanisms mediate these requests based on predefined access control rules. The initiator/resource combination reflects access control rights, while the initiator/operation combination reflects access control privileges. As noted by Rozenblit,[271] ISO/IEC 10164-9(1995-12) and ISO/IEC 10181-3(1996-09) access control rules can be defined three ways:

1. Through the use of access control lists that specify the approved initiators for each group of target resources
2. Through the use of access capability lists that specify the target resources accessible to a group of initiators
3. Through the use of security labels, such that each initiator and target resource is assigned to one or more security labels (confidential, secret, top secret, etc.), which in turn defines access control rights and privileges

A scope of control is associated with each unique combination of initiators, operations, and target resources — hence the need to define multiple access control rules. In a low risk operational environment, it may be acceptable to specify access control rules for the most critical subset of all possible operations on the target resources. In moderate and high risk operational environments, it is usually necessary to specify access control rules for all possible operations on the target resources.

Table 4.13 illustrates the three methods for specifying access control rules, using the same set of initiators, operations, and resources. Often, it is easier to think in terms of an access control list. It is useful to develop an access control list first, and then rotate the matrix to develop the corresponding access capability list. This serves as a cross-check to ensure that no unintended inferred access control privileges or information flow have been specified. As shown in Table 4.13, in order to execute application A, send and receive foreign e-mail, perform Internet searches, or import foreign files, access to the organization's LAN/WAN is inferred. Because Henani has explicit access rights to everything, that is alright. Through the access capability list, it is uncovered that Malachi and Omri would also have these access rights inferred. Because Malachi and Omri only have limited explicit access rights, design features must be employed to restrict them from LAN/WAN resources to which

Table 4.13   Comparison of Methods for Specifying Logical Access Control Rules

Initiators	Desktop PC, Printer	Application Server	E-mail Server, LAN/WAN	Web Server, Internet
I. Access Control List				
Malachi	Execute desktop office automation	None	Send/receive local e-mail	None
Omri	Execute desktop office automation	Execute application A (limited)	Send/receive local e-mail	None
Henani	Execute desktop office automation application	Execute application A (full)	Send/receive local e-mail Remote access	Send/receive foreign e-mail Perform Internet searches Import foreign files
II. Access Capability List				
Execute desktop office automation	Malachi Omri Henani			
Send/receive local e-mail			Malachi Omri Henani	

Table 4.13 Comparison of Methods for Specifying Logical Access Control Rules

	Resources			
Initiators	*Desktop PC, Printer*	*Application Server*	*E-mail Server, LAN/WAN*	*Web Server, Internet*
Send/receive foreign e-mail			*	Henani
Remote access			Henani	
Perform Internet searches			*	Henani
Import foreign files			*	Henani
Execute application A (limited)		Omri	*	
Execute application A (full)		Henani	*	
III. Security Label				
Confidential	Execute desktop office automation	None	Send/receive local e-mail	None
Secret	Execute desktop office automation	Execute application A (limited)	Send/receive local e-mail	None
Top Secret	Execute desktop office automation	Execute application A (full)	Send/receive local e-mail Remote access	Send/receive foreign e-mail Perform Internet searches Import foreign files

* Inferred right or privilege.

they do not have explicit access rights. The third option, security labels, is a variation of access control lists. Initiators are groups of people with a certain security clearance who have rights and privileges to access certain resources having the same or lower classification. This approach can be used to verify an access control list and an access capability list.

As far back as the *Orange Book,* a distinction was made between the use of access control lists and access capability lists, which is referred to as discretionary access controls, and the use of security labels for initiators and target resources, which is referred to as mandatory access controls. Discretionary access controls view target resources as lateral entities — an initiator has a need-to-know or use resource A, but not resource B. In contrast, mandatory access controls view target resources in a hierarchical manner corresponding to their security labels. An initiator is permitted to access and create target resources that have the same or lower security labels as their access rights. To illustrate, a user holding a secret clearance can access and create information assets that have a secret label or below; they cannot access or create information assets that have a security label above secret. Mandatory access controls require that all target resources have a current and accurate security label associated with them. This can be a difficult task, depending on the level of granularity to which the labeling is conducted. Likewise, the processing of security labels can add a significant amount of overhead. For this reason, mandatory access controls are generally only applied in high risk operational environments.

Access control rights and privileges are determined based on a variety of parameters, such as the user's need-to-know, trust level, trust type, asset sensitivity and criticality, and regulations.[28, 52] Adequate time must be taken to define access control rights and privileges to the appropriate level of detail. Unfortunately, too many organizations only specify access control rights for the corporate LAN and e-mail system and stop there; this is a major vulnerability related to insider threat. A default of "access denied" should be invoked if the system encounters an unknown or undefined state when mediating access rights and privileges. Access control rules should be regularly reviewed, updated, and revalidated or revoked if no longer needed.

Files defining access control rules must themselves be protected from unauthorized access and modification; otherwise, the access control function will become a farce. Organizations should prohibit redundant accounts, limit concurrent sessions, and implement session locking and session termination to support internal misuse detection. A capability must be implemented to provide immediate emergency revocation of access control rights and privileges. It is essential to define who has the right to update or modify access control rules, in both normal and abnormal situations. Failure to designate primary and alternate staff who have the authority to handle this function can cause an organization to be locked out while attackers take control of system resources. In addition to specifying who has the authority to change access rights and privileges, it is necessary to determine who has the authority to (1) approve that such changes be made and (2) determine a user's access rights and privileges.[28]

Specifying access control rights for information assets can be complicated. Depending on the sensitivity and criticality, access control rights can be specified at the field, record, file, or directory level. If access control rights are not specified carefully, a vulnerability is created for aggregation, inference, misuse, and compromise. Keep in mind that it is usually easier and less error-prone to (re)design data structures to accommodate a security architecture than to develop complex access control software.

Mobile and personally owned devices pose special access control concerns. In short, these devices should be assumed to be untrusted until proven otherwise. Access to corporate IT and information assets should be prohibited until it can be proven that these devices comply with security policies relating to configuration management, patch management, virus signature updates and scans, malware scans, disabling unused hardware and software components, etc.[52] This proof should be reestablished each time a device attempts to connect to the corporate IT infrastructure; after all, who knows what this device has been connected to in the interim. Devices that fail the compliance test should be blocked or quarantined.

Some novel ways of expressing access control rights include:

- Time-based access control:
  - A user or process may be allowed to access certain system resources only at certain times during the day.
  - A user or process may only be allowed to access system resources for a specified time interval after their identity has been authenticated.
  - Time-sensitive information may only be accessed "not before" or "not after" specified dates and times.
  - E-mail, public keys, and other security tokens may have built-in (hidden) self-destruct dates and macros.[272]
- Origin-based access control
- Owner-controlled access control
- Role-based access control

The particular method chosen to specify access control rights and privileges will depend on the nature of the IT infrastructure, the operational environment, asset sensitivity and criticality, and the usage profile. Whichever method is chosen, it must be consistent with accountability requirements of the personnel security program.

Due to the variety of resources needing protection, access control mechanisms are implemented throughout the IT infrastructure. For example, server and network configuration files, user name and password, file access privileges, default permissions, server log, server root access, etc. all need to be protected as well as data files.[272, 273] In some situations, the capabilities of commercial products may be employed, such as using an operating system to define shared directories. In other situations, custom scripts are written to operate stand-alone or as an enhancement to a commercial capability.

The following metrics can be used to measure the resilience of different aspects of logical access controls. To obtain a complete picture, these metrics measure:

- How thoroughly and how well logical access controls are implemented
- Whether appropriate logical access controls have been implemented for a given operational environment
- How well the logical access controls work
- The extent and types of logical access control failures experienced

Percentage (%) of inactive user accounts that have been disabled in accordance with policy this reporting period, by sensitivity of the assets accessed.[105]

2.3.1.1

Percentage (%) of user accounts assigned to personnel who have left the organization or no longer have need for access that have been closed this reporting period, by sensitivity level of the assets accessed.[105]   2.3.1.2

Percentage (%) of workstations with session time-out/automatic log-out controls set in accordance with policy, by information sensitivity.[105]   2.3.1.3

Percentage (%) of user accounts that have been reviewed within the past quarter for justification of current access rights and privileges in accordance with policy, by information sensitivity.[105]   2.3.1.4

Percentage (%) of systems and applications that assign user access rights and privileges according to role-based access control, by asset criticality.[105] 2.3.1.5

Percentage (%) of mobile and personally owned devices that are required to verify compliance with approved security and configuration policies prior to being granted access to IT and information assets, by asset criticality.[105]

2.3.1.6

Number of times administrative access was made or attempted outside of a valid maintenance window, by asset type and criticality.[117]   2.3.1.7

Number of times unauthorized users gained super-user privileges to network, server, or desktop operating systems, by asset type and criticality.[117]   2.3.1.8

Number of times changes in access rights and privileges could not be correlated with valid user account administration activity, by asset type and criticality[117]:

2.3.1.9

   a. Per end-user accounts
   b. Per administrative accounts

Number of times IT and information assets were successfully accessed without completing a valid identification and authentication function, by asset type and criticality.[117]   2.3.1.10

Percentage (%) of organizational units that have defined and enforce access rights and privileges for all layers of the protocol stack for their IT infrastructure.

2.3.1.11

By organizational unit, percentage (%) of IT and information assets for which access rights and privileges have been defined, by asset criticality.   2.3.1.12

Percentage (%) of organizational units that use access capability lists to verify that there is no unintended inferred access rights contained in access control lists and security labels.   2.3.1.13

Percentage (%) of systems and networks that default to "access denied" if an unknown or undefined state is encountered when arbitrating access rights and privileges, by asset criticality.   2.3.1.14

Percentage (%) of systems and networks that implement robust access controls to prevent unauthorized changes to the rules specifying access rights and privileges, by asset criticality.   2.3.1.15

Percentage (%) of organizational units that have designated who has the authority to: 2.3.1.16

   a. Change access rights and privileges during normal and abnormal situations
   b. Approve the change of access rights and privileges
   c. Determine a user's access rights and privileges

Percentage (%) of systems and networks for which access rights and privileges have been defined to a sufficient level of granularity to prevent accidental or intentional aggregation, inference, misuse, and compromise, by asset criticality.
2.3.1.17

Percentage (%) of low risk operational environments that implement access rights and privileges for the most critical subset of all possible operations on target resources.   2.3.1.18

Percentage (%) of moderate and high risk operational environments that implement access rights and privileges for all possible operations on target resources: 2.3.1.19

   a. Percentage (%) of high risk operational environments that implement mandatory access controls

Percentage (%) of systems and networks for which access rights and privileges have been tested during this reporting period and were found to work as specified under normal and abnormal conditions, by asset criticality: 2.3.1.20

   a. Distribution of problems found by problem type and severity, this reporting period and the previous three reporting periods

Percentage (%) of organizational units where access rights and privileges support accountability requirements of the personnel security program.
2.3.1.21

Data Authentication, Non-Repudiation

Data authentication is an attempt to validate the true source of a message or file. Data authentication is a feature that allows the recipient of a message or file to have confidence that the source of the information is known. This feature is particularly important when critical decisions must be made or critical actions taken based on receipt of a message or file. A common example is software patches and upgrades. It is a good idea to know that software patches and upgrades are from a known trusted source before implementing them.

Digital signatures are the most common method used for data authentication. Other proprietary methods often come bundled with e-mail applications, operating systems, and configuration management tools. Digital signatures provide reasonable evidence of the true sender of an electronic message or file, which is often referred to as non-repudiation of origin.[20] Digital signatures are created using public key encryption, such as RSA. A signature generation algorithm and a signature verification algorithm are involved. The initial Digital Signature Standard (DSS) was issued in May 1994. A digital signature consists of a fixed-length string of bits that is derived from the original message using public key encryption. This string of bits is attached to the original message before it is sent. Usually, a digital signature is generated on the cleartext message. The message is encrypted. Then the signature is attached and the message is transmitted.[271] The recipient decrypts the string to verify that the signature reflects the original message. In this way, the recipient knows (1) the message has not been altered and (2) the real origin of the message. Non-repudiation of receipt requires the recipient to sign the message and return it to the sender. This provides round-trip message delivery confirmation.

Non-repudiation helps prevent future claims that an individual did not send or receive a message or file.[52] Non-repudiation generates proof of the "who, when, and where" that can be used later to reconstruct a sequence of events.[17] Such evidence should be kept for seven years for legal reasons. A variety of reports can be generated related to non-repudiation[20]:

- The user who requested that such evidence be generated
- The date and time non-repudiation functions were invoked
- The source and destination of the information
- A copy of the evidence generated
- The user or process that generated the evidence

There are several implementation issues to consider when deploying digital signatures. First, not all messages or files require data authentication. Each organization must decide on a case-by-case basis where to employ data authentication and where it is not needed. Critical and essential IT assets and high and moderate sensitivity information assets are good candidates, as is critical operational information that is exchanged among business partners. Second, a decision should be made as to whether the invocation of data authentication features is mandatory — the feature is always on — or whether data authentication can be invoked manually, as needed. Third, keep in mind that digital signatures help establish the identity of a sender of a message or document. However, they do not necessarily prove that the sender created the contents of the message or document.[270] Fourth, digital signatures consume additional system resources and require that a reliable key management process be followed.

The following metrics can be used to measure the resilience of different aspects of an organization's implementation of data authentication. To obtain a complete picture, these metrics measure:

- How thoroughly and how well authentication has been implemented
- Whether data authentication has been implemented consistent with asset criticality and information sensitivity
- The extent and types of data authentication failures experienced

Percentage (%) of organization units that employ data authentication mechanisms to verify the exchange of information, by information sensitivity category: 2.3.2.1

a. Internally within in facility
b. Internally within a distributed corporate IT infrastructure
c. Externally with business partners
d. Externally with outsiders

Percentage (%) of organizational units that verify the origin of software patches and upgrades before acting upon them, by system risk and IT asset category. 2.3.2.2

Length of time non-repudiation evidence and related reports are kept, by organizational unit and asset criticality. 2.3.2.3

Distribution of organizations that employ mandatory or manual data authentication for: 2.3.2.4

a. Critical IT assets
b. Essential IT assets
c. High sensitivity information
d. Moderate sensitivity information

By asset criticality and information sensitivity, percentage of organizational units that have tested their data authentication mechanisms this reporting period and found that they worked as specified under normal and abnormal conditions: 2.3.2.5

a. Distribution by type and severity of errors found, this reporting period and the previous three reporting periods

Number and percentage of security incidents, by incident severity, related to: 2.3.2.6

a. Failure of a data authentication mechanism
b. Faulty implementation or configuration of a data authentication mechanism
c. Lack of data authentication
d. A combination of two or more of the above

The frequency with which the implementation of data authentication is reviewed, reaffirmed, or updated: 2.3.2.7

a. During normal operations
b. Following a major system upgrade or change
c. Following a change to the system operational profile and usage
d. Following a major security incident

Encryption, Cryptographic Support

Most organizations, and people for that matter, are familiar with the concept of encryption, if only at a high level. Discussions tend to center around what algorithm to use and which key length is best. As discussed below, there are many other equally important issues to consider when analyzing, planning, implementing, and operating encryption mechanisms.

Encryption provides confidentiality for data while it is stored or transmitted. This is accomplished by manipulating a string of data (cleartext) according to a specific algorithm to produce ciphertext, which is unintelligible to all but the intended recipients. Encryption does not provide a permanent solution to confidentiality, because all encryption algorithms can be broken, given enough time and computing resources.

A series of decisions must be made prior to implementing encryption, as shown in Figure 4.9. The first question to answer is: What data needs to be encrypted? This information is derived from an analysis of an organization's information security goals. Items such as e-mail; mission-critical, sensitive, and proprietary data; data covered by privacy regulations; authentication data; access control rules; encryption keys; and video teleconference sessions may

1. What data needs to be encrypted?
   a. E-mail
   b. Text, graphic, video files
   c. Database files
   d. Application data
   e. Telephone conversations and voice mail
   f. Fax transmissions
   g. Video teleconferences
   h. Authentication data files
   i. Private keys
   j. Access control rights and privileges

2. Where is the data:
   a. Created?
   b. Stored?
   c. Transmitted?

3. What strength of encryption is needed?
   a. Low
   b. Medium
   c. High
   d. Very high

4. At what layers in the ISO/OSI or TCP/IP reference models should encryption take place?
   a. Data link
   b. Network
   c. Transport
   d. Application

5. Should hardware or software encryption be used?

6. Should block or stream ciphers be used?

7. What cipher mode of operation should be used?
   a. ECB
   b. CBC
   c. OFB
   d. CFB
   e. Counter

8. Should symmetric or asymmetric keys be used?

9. What key management procedures should be used for?
   a. Key generation
   b. Key distribution
   c. Key verification
   d. Controlling key use
   e. Responding to key compromise
   f. Key change
   g. Key storage
   h. Key recovery, backup
   i. Destroying old keys

10. What encryption algorithm should be used?

Figure 4.9   Key decisions to make when implementing encryption.

be selected. At the same time, data that does not need to be encrypted is identified. For example, certain fields in a database record may need to be encrypted (i.e., a social security number or credit card account number), but not the entire record or file. Because of the time, cost, and resources utilized, it is important not to over-identify data needing encryption. Conversely, it is equally important not to under-identify data needing encryption and in so doing create opportunities for aggregation, inference, misuse, and compromise.

The second question to answer is: Where is the data created, stored, and transmitted? The intent is to uncover all instances of this data so that the most efficient and effective encryption strategy can be employed. Printouts, local and organizational hardcopy archives, and electronic backups, storage media, and archives should be accounted for as well. There is no point in encrypting active electronic data if printouts and archives are unprotected and can be accessed at will.

Third, the strength of encryption needed is determined. Encryption strength is determined by the sophistication of the encryption algorithms, the key length, and other factors that influence how easy or difficult it is to break.[271, 276, 291] As Schneier[276] and Ritter[290] point out, longer key lengths by themselves do not necessarily guarantee more security. Different information sensitivity and asset criticality categories need different levels of encryption strength. Privacy and regulatory requirements must also be taken into account when determining the encryption strength needed.

Fourth, a decision needs to be made about where to implement encryption, specifically in what layers of the ISO/OSI and TCP/IP reference models. Encryption can be implemented at the data link, network, transport, and application layers. Data link layer encryption encrypts all traffic on a single high-capacity, point-to-point link and is often referred to as bulk encryption. It is easy to implement because of well-defined hardware interfaces.[276] Data link layer encryption is transparent to higher level applications and provides protection against traffic analysis.[276, 291] However, data is exposed temporarily at network nodes because it must be decrypted to obtain routing information.[276, 291] To alleviate this vulnerability, data is often double encrypted prior to transmission.

Network and transport layer encryption utilize a key ID that explains the encryption algorithm, block size, integrity check, and validity period. ATM encryption standards are in the process of being finalized.[292] Transport layer encryption is implemented using the Transport Layer Security (TLS) protocol, which makes use of TCP virtual circuits. This permits different circuits between the same pair of hosts to be protected with different keys.[291] TLS encrypts the TCP header and segment, but not the IP header. Network layer encryption is implemented using either IPSec or the Network Layer Security (NLS) protocol, which make use of encapsulation. IPSec and NLS encrypt entire packets, including the original IP header, and generate a new IP header. IPSec, NLS, and TLS are transparent to higher level applications. IPSec and NLS protect subnets from traffic analysis,[291] while TLS does not. Key management is more complex at the network and transport layers, than for data link layer encryption.

Application layer encryption can be implemented in a variety of ways. For example, an application can encrypt data stored on a server or in a database. Financial data in spreadsheets can be encrypted on local workstations or shared directories on servers. Corporate personnel files can be encrypted. Perhaps the best-known instance of application layer encryption is e-mail. Several e-mail encryption protocols are available, including PEM, PGP, and S/MIME. In addition to encryption, some of these protocols support digital signatures and digital certificates. A common vulnerability of all application layer security is that the data can be attacked through the operating system before it is encrypted. Another concern is when encryption takes place relative to network transmission or the browser function, in the case of Web applications. That is, is the data exposed and accessible prior to being encrypted? To alleviate this vulnerability, it is beneficial to employ encryption at multiple layers of the ISO/OSI and TCP/IP reference models. To supplement application layer encryption, data should be encrypted while it is stored on a local workstation, on an application server, in backup files, archives, and other portable media. As discussed previously, the cleartext stores of this information must be controlled as well or the encryption will be to no avail.

The fifth decision is whether hardware or software encryption should be employed, inasmuch as encryption algorithms can be implemented in either. Hardware encryption is the primary choice for critical applications and is used almost exclusively by the defense and intelligence communities.[276] This occurs for several reasons:

- Hardware encryption provides algorithm and to some extent key security because the units are designed to (1) be tamper-proof, (2) erase keys if tampering is attempted, (3) eliminate emanations through device shielding.[276]
- Hardware encryption is considerably faster than software encryption and it offloads intensive calculations from the CPU, thus improving overall system performance.
- Hardware encryption is implemented in modules, boards, and boxes that are easy to install.

In contrast, software encryption, while easy to use and upgrade, presents several vulnerabilities not found in hardware encryption. For example, a software encryption task runs the risk of being preempted by a higher priority task or interrupt and being written to disk. This leaves both the key and the data exposed.[276] Software encryption algorithms are vulnerable to unauthorized and potentially undetected alterations. Key management is also more complex with software encryption.

The sixth decision is whether block or stream ciphers should be used. Block ciphers operate on a fixed number of bits or bytes; if necessary, the last block is padded. Both the ciphertext and cleartext have the same block size. Block ciphers can be implemented in hardware or software. Stream ciphers operate on asynchronous bit streams, transforming a single bit or byte of data at a time. Stream ciphers are implemented in hardware at the data link layer.

The next decision concerns the mode of operation for the block or stream cipher. Some modes are only applicable to block ciphers, while others work for both block and stream ciphers. The differences between the modes are, for the most part, subtle. A notable difference is the extent to which errors are propagated. The five most common operational modes are:

1. Electronic code book (ECB)
2. Cipher block chaining (CBC)
3. Output feedback (OFB)
4. Cipher feedback (CFB)
5. Counter

ECB mode produces the same results from the same block of data each time it is encrypted. This feature is convenient and simplifies verification, but facilitates crypto analysis.[276] In CBC mode, each block of cleartext is exclusive OR'd with the previous block of ciphertext before encryption. Initialization vectors are supplied for the first block of data. Block ciphers or stream ciphers can operate in OFB mode. In this mode, n-bits of the previous ciphertext are exclusive OR'd with the cleartext, starting at the right-most bit. This mode has the advantage that errors are not propagated. In CFB mode, the left-most n-bits of the last ciphertext block are exclusive OR'd with the first or next n-bits of the cleartext. Unfortunately, this mode propagates errors. In counter mode, sequence numbers (rather than previous ciphertext) are used as input to the encryption algorithm. The counter is increased by a constant value after each block is encrypted. Block ciphers or stream ciphers can operate in counter mode. Errors are not propagated.

The choice of what type of encryption key to use comes next. Symmetric or asymmetric keys can be used. When symmetric or secret keys are used, the same key is used for encryption and decryption. The use of symmetric keys is the traditional approach to encryption and was used in the past primarily for defense and intelligence applications. Bulk data link layer encryption makes almost exclusive use of symmetric encryption keys. Most sources recommend changing symmetric keys at least once a day.[271, 276, 291] In fact, in very critical applications, separate keys can be used for each session.[291] Symmetric keys are more appropriate in the following situations:

- The sender and receiver are known to each other and are in the same organization or cooperating organizations.
- The sender and receiver remain constant for a fixed period of time.
- The sending and receiving nodes remain constant for a fixed period of time.
- A long-term relationship between the sender and receiver is anticipated, with a regular need to exchange sensitive information.
- The sender and receiver have the ability to cooperate on key management and other encryption issues.

In contrast, with asymmetric keys, a pair of public and private keys is used. The public key (used for encryption) is shared, while the private key (used for decryption) is not shared. The two keys are mathematically related but it is not feasible (in any meaningful time frame) to uncover the private key from the public key. In practice, when A wants to send B a sensitive message, A encrypts the message with B's public key. Then, B decrypts the message with his private key. It is recommended that asymmetric systems employ time stamps to prevent replay.[271] The first asymmetric key cryptosystems were announced in the late 1970s. Since then, several other systems have been developed. Asymmetric key cryptosystems are considerably slower and use much longer key lengths than symmetric key systems. As Schneier[276] points out, symmetric and asymmetric key systems are designed for different operational profiles:

> *Symmetric cryptography is best for encrypting data. It is orders of magnitude faster and is not susceptible to chosen cipher text attacks. Public key cryptography can do things symmetric cryptography can't; it is best for key management and a myriad of other protocols [digital signatures, key exchange and authentication, digital cash, etc.].*

Key management issues are the next logical decision. Given that most encryption algorithms are publicly available, it is the keys that must be protected. The extent to which a key should be protected is proportional to the sensitivity of the information being encrypted. Several issues must be decided when developing key management plans and procedures; these include[16, 20, 28, 32, 52, 156, 266]:

- What algorithm to use to generate keys
- The frequency, process, and schedule for changing keys
- How to distribute keys securely
- Normal dates for activating and deactivating keys
- How to control access to keys
- How to store keys securely, both local and backup copies
- How to verify the authenticity of keys
- The process for recovering "lost" keys
- The process for controlling and revoking keys
- The process for destroying all instances of old keys
- The process for responding to the compromise of symmetric and asymmetric keys
- The process for logging and auditing all key management activities

These policies and procedures need to be established by an organization, with the involvement of all stakeholders, prior to implementing encryption. All staff should be thoroughly trained on how to use the procedures. Periodic audits should be conducted to verify that the procedures are being followed and to look for opportunities to improve them.

The final decision to be made is what encryption algorithm to use. Of course, several of the decisions made above will narrow this choice. Today there are a variety of proprietary commercial products to choose from, as well as commercial products that implement standardized encryption algorithms. AES, the Advanced Encryption Standard, is the newest publicly available encryption standard. FIPS 140-2 certification, by the Cryptographic Module Validation Program (CMVP), is the most recognized sign of encryption product integrity. There are several implementation details to consider when selecting an encryption algorithm. The processing efficiency of the algorithm, in terms of the time and resources used, is a major factor for both the sender and the receiver of encrypted data. Efficiency is improved if the encryption block size is consistent with the data bus size. Files should be compressed before they are encrypted, while error detection/correction codes should be added after encryption.[276] In situations where confidentiality is extremely important, it may be beneficial to implement multiple or cascade encryption to further inhibit opportunities for crypto analysis. In multiple encryption, the same encryption algorithm is repeated several times on the same block of data using multiple keys; triple DES is a well-known example of this. In cascade encryption, multiple different algorithms are performed on the same block of data. Finally, while encrypting e-mail increases privacy for the sender and receiver, it potentially decreases system and data integrity for the receiver because, as Garber[293] notes, many commercial anti-virus products have difficulty scanning encrypted e-mail effectively.

The following metrics can be used to measure the resilience of different aspects of an organization's implementation of encryption. To obtain a complete picture, these metrics measure:

- How thoroughly and how well encryption has been implemented
- Whether encryption has been implemented consistent with asset criticality and information sensitivity
- Whether both active and inactive data have been taken into account
- Whether key management procedures and other items related to cryptographic operations have been documented and disseminated
- The extent and types of encryption failures experienced

Percentage (%) of communication channels controlled by the organization that have been secured via encryption, by information sensitivity.[105] 2.3.3.1

Percentage (%) of critical and essential information assets stored on network accessible devices that are encrypted with widely tested and published cryptographic algorithms, by information sensitivity category.[105] 2.3.3.2

Percentage (%) of mobile computing devices that use encryption for critical and essential assets while they are stored and transmitted.[105] 2.3.3.3

Percentage (%) of passwords, PINs, and other authentication data that are encrypted.[105] 2.3.3.4

Percentage (%) of information assets for which encryption is implemented, by organizational unit, asset criticality, and information sensitivity: 2.3.3.5
   a. Data related to an organization's operations and mission
   b. Proprietary data
   c. Financial data
   d. Data covered by privacy regulations
   e. Authentication data

    f. Access control rules
    g. Corporate communications

Percentage (%) of active information assets for which encryption is implemented, by organizational unit, asset criticality, and information sensitivity:

    2.3.3.6

    a. On servers
    b. On desktops
    c. On mobile devices
    d. During transmission across a LAN
    e. During transmission across a WAN
    f. In hardcopy format
    g. On portable storage media (disk, tape, USB drive, etc.)

Percentage (%) of inactive information assets for which encryption is implemented, by organizational unit, asset criticality, and information sensitivity:

    2.3.3.7

    a. On servers
    b. On desktops
    c. On mobile devices
    d. In hardcopy format
    e. On portable storage media (disk, tape, USB drive, etc.)

The strength of encryption used, by organizational unit, asset criticality, and information sensitivity: 2.3.3.8
    a. Ultra high
    b. High
    c. Moderate
    d. Low

By asset criticality and information sensitivity, percentage (%) of organizational units that implement encryption at: 2.3.3.9
    a. The data link layer
    b. The network layer
    c. The transport layer
    d. The application layer
    e. At two of the above layers
    f. At three or more of the above layers

By asset criticality and information sensitivity, percentage (%) of organizational units that implement encryption through: 2.3.3.10
    a. Hardware encryption
    b. Software encryption
    c. A combination of both

By asset criticality and information sensitivity, percentage (%) of organizational units that implement encryption through: 2.3.3.11

　　a. Symmetric keys
　　b. Asymmetric keys
　　c. A combination of both

Percentage (%) of organizational units that have documented and implemented encryption key management procedures that address:　　　　　2.3.3.12
　　a. What algorithm to use to generate keys
　　b. The frequency, process, and schedule for changing keys
　　c. How to distribute keys securely
　　d. Normal dates for activating and deactivating keys
　　e. How to control access to keys
　　f. How to store keys securely, both local and backup copies
　　g. How to verify the authenticity of keys
　　h. The process for recovering "lost" keys
　　i. The process for controlling and revoking keys
　　j. The process for destroying all instances of old keys
　　k. The process for responding to the compromise of symmetric and asymmetric keys
　　l. The process for logging and auditing all key management activities

Percentage (%) of organizational units that conduct regular training about key management procedures.　　　　　2.3.3.13
　　a. Date of most recent training

Percentage (%) of organizations that implement multiple or cascade encryption for critical and essential assets.　　　　　2.3.3.14

By asset criticality and information sensitivity, percentage of organizational units that have tested their encryption mechanisms and implementation this reporting period and found that it worked as specified under normal and abnormal conditions:　　　　　2.3.3.15
　　a. Distribution by type and severity of errors found, this reporting period and the previous three reporting periods

Number and percentage of security incidents, by incident severity, related to:　　　　　2.3.3.16
　　a. Failure of an encryption mechanism
　　b. Faulty implementation or configuration of encryption
　　c. Failure to follow cryptographic or key management procedures
　　d. Lack of encryption
　　e. A combination of two or more of the above

The frequency with which encryption keys are changed, by organizational unit, asset criticality, and information sensitivity:　　　　　2.3.3.17
　　a. Symmetric keys
　　b. Asymmetric keys
　　c. After a key is lost, stolen, or compromised

Flow Control

Flow control is an extension of access control privileges; however, in this instance, the focus is more on controlling interactions between software entities than between humans and software. There are two different aspects to flow control:

1. Operational flow control
2. Data flow control

Operational flow control represents the flow of control both (1) internal to an individual system or network and (2) among multiple interacting systems and networks, whether they are local or geographically dispersed. It is particularly important to perform an analysis of operational control flow when integrating untrusted commercial software. Are the various components comprising the multiple interacting systems and networks, that are internal and external to an organization, cooperating as peer to peer entities, or is there a control structure in place to limit what each entity can do to and with another entity? Some everyday examples illustrate these concerns:

■ Can an unknown, untrusted Web application write cookies and other information to a user's hard drive?
■ Can an unknown, untrusted Web application read, copy, or edit information on a user's hard drive?
■ Can users bypass the LAN log-on script and use their desktop PC in stand-alone mode?
■ Suppose a user receives a message on a classified e-mail system that contains an active URL link. What prevents the user from activating that link within the e-mail system?
■ Is it possible to access database records or other files directly from the operating system, without going through the database or application system user interface/log-on screen?

The design, implementation, and configuration of system and application software, whether commercial products, custom developed, or a combination of both, creates the opportunity for normal or permitted operational control flows and potential abnormal or illicit operational control flows. To prevent the latter, it is necessary to (1) analyze all possible operational control flows within and among IT assets, (2) explicitly state which flows are permitted and which are denied, and (3) install and configure IT assets, through a combination of utilities, scripts, and middleware, to enforce the permitted operational control flows and prevent the prohibited operational control flows. Illicit operational control flows are a major vulnerability. They can be uncovered through static analysis and dynamic testing. It is an understatement to say that the analysis of all possible operational control flows must be thorough. If not, an organization's IT infrastructure is likely to have so many illicit control flows that it will be leaking like a sieve. Illicit control flows must be deliberately blocked. Do not assume that no one will ever try to exploit them. Problems from insiders tend to arise when a system is working too slow or they are up against impossible deadlines — insiders get creative and try to find some workarounds. As far as outsiders are concerned, their main goal is to find and exploit illicit operational control flows. Is it not more cost-effective (and less embarrassing) for an organization to take the time to find illicit operational control flows first?

In the days of stand-alone stovepipe application systems that were mostly custom software with a proprietary commercial operating system and a few utilities thrown in, an analysis of operational control flow was rather straightforward. That process is described below. In today's world of near-total interconnectedness and (over)reliance on commercial software, an analysis of operational control flow is more complex but the process is the same. Ideally, operational control flow analysis should be ongoing throughout the life of a system. Specify permitted and prohibited operational control flows during the requirements analysis phase. Tie the specification of permitted and prohibited operational control flows to detailed assumptions about processor speeds, system and network configurations, throughput, capacity, memory sizes, cache size, etc.[20] Confirm that the system architecture and design incorporate the permitted and prohibited operational control flows. Test the as-built system to verify that (1) all permitted operational control flows are enabled, and (2) all prohibited operational control flows are disabled, under normal and abnormal conditions. Repeat this testing regularly during the operations and maintenance phase, especially after changes, corrections, and upgrades. Pay particular attention to operational control flows across interfaces of products from different vendors and entities owned and operated by outsiders, such as outsourcing firms.

Operational flow control analysis is conducted to uncover weak and incorrect control logic that could compromise system integrity. Historically, operational flow control was referred to as reference mediation or the reference monitor concept.[20] Operational flow control analysis examines the logical structure of interactions within and among system components. A diagram is used to represent the control flow through the system components. Several automated tools are available to generate such a diagram. Unconditional jumps, unused and unreachable code, incomplete and uncontrolled operations, and a lack of exception handling, all of which could be used as an opening for an attack, are uncovered. The diagram is also reviewed for opportunities to optimize program structure and thereby enhance maintainability. The emphasis is on verifying correct control flow to, from, and within internal and external system components. Operational flow control analysis is useful for uncovering implementation errors before a system is tested or fielded. Inconsistencies between designs and implementations are highlighted. However, operational flow control does not verify timing, capacity, or throughput requirements.

The corollary to operational flow control is data (or information) flow control. An analysis of data flow control is used to uncover incorrect and unauthorized data exchanges, transformations, and operations that could compromise data confidentiality or integrity. Data flow control analysis examines the access and change sequence of critical data elements. Using the diagram developed for control flow analysis, each distinct operation performed on a data element and each distinct transformation of that element are evaluated. Actual data flow is compared to required data flow to detect erroneous conditions and potential leakage, which could lead to a system compromise or failure. Examples of items to check during data flow analysis include[7, 285]:

- Variables that are read before they are assigned a value
- Variables that are written more than once before they are read
- Variables that are written but never read
- Variables that are accidentally or intentionally overwritten
- Variables that are accidentally or incorrectly read (framing and addressing errors, etc.) or modified
- Leakage or co-mingling of data of one classification level with another classification level
- Memory leaks, buffer overflows, and other transitions that could corrupt data

Include all internal and external system components within the scope of data flow control analysis. Specify permitted and prohibited data control flows. For moderate to high risk systems, it may be appropriate to specify permitted and prohibited data control flows for all possible operations on all data types. For low risk systems, it may be appropriate to specify permitted and prohibited data control flows for the most critical subset of operations and data types. Data control flows can be specified based on security labels or other security attributes and should identify valid sources, destinations, and operations or state transitions. Historically, data control flow analysis focused on preventing the transfer of information from one security classification into a lower category. Today, data control flow analysis is concerned about preventing invalid hierarchical or lateral flows. The intent is to isolate or separate different data streams to prevent unauthorized disclosure, compromise, and loss of integrity. Data flow control analysis is useful for uncovering incorrect and unauthorized data transformation and operations before a system is tested or fielded. Inconsistencies between designs and implementations are highlighted. However, data flow control analysis does not verify timing, capacity, or throughput requirements.

The following metrics can be used to measure the resilience of different aspects of an organization's implementation of flow control. To obtain a complete picture, these metrics measure:

- How thoroughly and how well flow control has been implemented
- Whether flow control has been implemented consistent with asset criticality and information sensitivity
- The extent and types of flow control failures experienced

By system risk and asset criticality, percentage of IT assets for which permitted and prohibited operational control flows have been specified. 2.3.4.1

By system risk and asset criticality, percentage of systems and networks that have been implemented and configured to: 2.3.4.2

  a. Enable permitted operational control flows
  b. Prevent prohibited operational control flows
  c. Generate alarms when an attempt is made, or successful, to bypass operational control flow mechanisms

By system risk and asset criticality, percentage of systems and networks that have been tested this reporting period and the results indicated that all permitted and prohibited operational control flows worked as specified under normal and abnormal conditions: 2.3.4.3

  a. Distribution by type and severity of errors found, this reporting period and the previous three reporting periods

By asset criticality and information sensitivity, percentage of IT assets for which permitted and prohibited data control flows have been specified. 2.3.4.4

By asset criticality and information sensitivity, percentage of systems and networks that have been implemented and configured to: 2.3.4.5

  a. Enable permitted data control flows
  b. Prevent prohibited data controls flows
  c. Generate alarms when an attempt is made, or successful, to bypass data control flow mechanisms

By asset criticality and information sensitivity, percentage of systems and networks that have been tested this reporting period and the results indicated that all permitted and prohibited data control flows worked as specified under normal and abnormal conditions: 2.3.4.6

  a. Distribution by type and severity of errors found, this reporting period and the previous three reporting periods

Number, type, and severity of failures this reporting period, by asset criticality and information sensitivity of: 2.3.4.7

  a. Operational control flow mechanisms
  b. Data control flow mechanisms

Number and percentage of security incidents, by incident severity, related to: 2.3.4.8

  a. Failure of an operational control flow mechanism
  b. Failure of a data control flow mechanism
  c. Faulty specification, implementation, or configuration of an operational control flow
  d. Faulty specification, implementation, or configuration of a data control flow
  e. The ability to bypass an operational control flow
  f. The ability to bypass a data control flow
  g. Lack of an operational control flow

    h. Lack of a data control flow
    i. A combination of two or more of the above

The frequency with which: 2.3.4.9

    a. Specifications for operational control flows are reviewed, reaffirmed, or updated
    b. Specification for data control flows are reviewed, reaffirmed, or updated
    c. Operational control flow mechanisms are tested to ensure correct operation
    d. Data control flow mechanisms are tested to ensure correct operation

Identification and Authentication

Identification and authentication is a function that permits the claimed identity of a user, process, or system to be proven to and confirmed by a second party. The identification and authentication function is needed to ensure that the correct associations are made between users and their true identities, roles, trust levels, and trust types.[20] Absent this function, it is difficult if not impossible to separate authorized users from unauthorized users and attackers. Unfortunately, many organizations deploy a superficial identification and authentication function at best. Accurate identification and authentication of all users, processes, and systems is an essential first layer of defense, upon which access control, audit trail, and internal misuse detection functions depend.

If a user, process, or system does not (1) identify itself correctly, or (2) present a valid identity, it must be blocked from accessing system resources. Failed identification and authentication attempts are considered and logged as unauthorized activity. An unauthorized user should not be allowed to keep trying to guess a correct user name or password repetitively. Suppose the attacker already knows half the information. Should he be allowed to keep trying until he gets the rest of it correct? No. The identification and authentication function should log each unsuccessful attempt as potential malicious activity. After two or three unsuccessful attempts, the user should be blocked from any further activity by locking the user account or point of entry, such as the workstation and network node from which the attempt was made.[20] There are two alternatives at this point. Further log-on attempts can be locked for a specified period of time, such as a half hour, 12 hours, 24 hours, etc. Or, further log-on attempts can be blocked until an official request is made through appropriate channels to reset a user name/password pair. The latter approach is more robust because (1) it requires the user's identity to be confirmed as an authorized user, and (2) it blocks any further activity by unauthorized users, such as going on to the next name on the list. Why should unauthorized users be allowed to try again later?

Once authorized users pass the identification and authentication process, they should be presented with two pieces of information[28]:

1. The date and time of their most recent successful log-on
2. The details about all unsuccessful log-on attempts since their last successful log-on

This way, users can help system administrators identify any potential misuse, by pointing to activity they did not initiate.[28] Likewise, maximum session durations should be enforced, after which the user must be re-authenticated or the session terminated.[20, 28] This practice also helps prevent misuse of IT and information assets.

Identification and authentication credentials should be unique for all end users and operations and maintenance staff.[28] Group accounts should be avoided or limited to low risk systems processing low sensitivity information assets. Structure identification and authentication credentials so that they do not give any indication of a user's role and system privileges.[28] Do not limit identification and authentication to human users. Processes, sessions, devices, and systems can be identified through the use of MAC, IEEE 802.1x, and TCP/IP addresses, RADIUS/TLS, TACACS with tokens, VPNs with certificates, etc. It is also necessary to define what, if any, activities each specific user, process, or system is allowed to perform before being authenticated.[20] In moderate and high risk operational environments, it may be appropriate to implement single-use authentication or require multi-factor authentication. Robust authentication of remote access is essential. Employ a combination of authentication methods, such as hardware tokens and a challenge-response protocol, verifying the user's network address, or performing dial-back authentication.[28] Review, reaffirm, update, or revoke identification credentials at 30- to 90-day intervals. This practice (1) ensures that only current authorized users have valid identification and authentication credentials, and (2) limits the time interval during which stolen or compromised credentials can be misused.

Some common mistakes made during the identification and authentication process are [20, 28, 158]:

- Displaying system or application banners before the log-on process is complete
- Not encrypting passwords during transmission or storage
- Providing help messages during the log-on process
- Indicating where the errors are in the identification information provided during the log-on process

Remember at this point that you do not want to provide any information that might help would-be attackers walk through the front door, such as telling them what application system they have encountered, what operating system is running, that the password must be eight digits long and contain capital letters and numbers, etc. To paraphrase a native American proverb, do not put feathers in the arrow your enemy is trying to shoot at you.

Employ a combination of diverse but complementary identification and authentication functions at different places in the IT infrastructure and at different layers of the ISO/OSI and TCP/IP reference models. None of the mechanisms should assume anything about whether or not identification and authentication functions encountered beforehand worked correctly. If malicious activity is suspected or detected at any point, the user or process should be blocked and quarantined. Because it is unlikely that an attacker will be able to bypass all identification and authentication functions, this practice eliminates the vulnerability where the attacker is in if only one identification and authentication function is bypassed.

Authentication takes place at several levels within an IT infrastructure: logging on to a desktop PC, LAN, e-mail, WAN, specific application system, etc. In each instance, a user is required to identify himself and prove it through some supporting evidence. A user name and supposedly secret password are provided in most cases. There is movement toward the use of more sophisticated parameters because of the vulnerabilities associated with using just user names and passwords. For example, browsers store previous pages, including user names and passwords.[272] Fegghi, Fegghi, and Williams point out that when choosing authentication parameters, consideration should be given to what information is supplied, what information is derived, and what information can be faked.[274] As a result, common sense dictates that a combination of factors should be used to authenticate a user or process, such as[272, 274, 275]:

- Individual user name/passwords
- User role or category
- Trust level and trust type
- Security token or PIN
- Time of day
- Terminal ID or location
- Network node, traffic source
- Transaction type
- Biometric information

There are several authentication methods: unilateral, mutual, digital certificates, Kerberos, data origin, peer entity, smart cards, and biometrics. These methods are used for different purposes and at different layers in the protocol stack. Each method has its own strengths and weaknesses. Consequently, it is important to select appropriate and compatible methods to deploy throughout the IT infrastructure.

Authentication can be unilateral or mutual. When a user logs on to a system, the user is authenticated to the system but the system is not authenticated to the user. In many situations, particularly E-commerce, it is highly desirable to have mutual authentication in which all parties (users, processes, and systems) are authenticated to each other before any transactions take place. This practice eliminates the vulnerability of thinking you are interacting with one system or Web application, when actually you have been switched to another site and are not aware of it. A challenge-response protocol is commonly used to perform mutual authentication. This protocol makes use of public key encryption and requires a minimum of three message exchanges.[271] The association request can be aborted at any time if a discrepancy is detected. The basic exchange is as follows[271]:

X sends an association establishment request, plus a unique string to Y.
Y encrypts the string and sends it back to X along with a new unique string.

X decrypts the string, verifies that it is the string sent, then encrypts the second string and sends it to Y.
Y decrypts the message and verifies that it is the string sent.

Digital certificates are used to authenticate the distribution of public keys, software, and other material. Trusted certificate authorities (CAs) issue digital certificates. Certificates can be revoked before they expire; hence, it is prudent to check current certificate revocation lists (CRLs) maintained by trusted CAs. Digital certificates should be bound to a specific request to prevent replay.[271] It is important to remember that digital certificates guarantee the source; they do not guarantee the integrity of the message or file contents.[272] The format of digital certificates has been standardized since June 1996 through CCITT X.509 version 3[271, 274]:

X.509 version identifier
Certificate serial number assigned by CA
Algorithm used to generate the certificate signature (k)
CA name
Certificate validity period (start and end dates)
Subject name (unique individual or entity)
Subject public key information (public key, parameters, algorithm)
Optional issuer unique identifiers
Optional subject unique identifiers
Optional extensions
CA digital signature of preceding fields

Kerberos provides trusted third-party authentication for TCP/IP networks.[276] Kerberos supports unilateral and mutual authentication, primarily user to host, and provides a reasonable degree of confidentiality. Kerberos utilizes tickets as its basic security token. Kerberos is generally available as shareware, although some commercially supported products are beginning to emerge.[277]

Data origin authentication ensures that received messages are indeed from the claimed sender and not an intruder who hijacked the session.[271, 274] Data origin authentication is initiated after an association setup is established and may be applied to all or selective messages.[271]

Peer entity authentication provides mutual application to application authentication. As Rozenblit reports[271]:

Peer entity authentication provides a (usually successful) second line of defense against intruders who have successfully bypassed connection access control.

Smart cards are a physical security token that a user presents during the authentication process. Smart cards represent an evolution of ATM or credit cards with magnetic strips, in that they contain a limited amount of processing power. Smart cards are currently used to access mobile phone networks, store electronic funds, and perform debit and credit card transactions. In the near future, they may replace employee badges for authentication purposes: entry into secure office spaces, desktop log-on, etc. such as that specified for HSPD-12, as discussed in Chapter 3.

Chadwick cites the advantages and disadvantages of smart cards[279]:

- Advantages:
    - Increased security: private key is unlikely to be copied unless the smart card is stolen and the third party knows the password and PIN
    - Potential mobility of users: however, mobility is dependent on the availability of compatible smart card readers
    - Sequential access to one desktop PC or other machine by multiple users
- Disadvantages:
    - Cost: which may improve over time
    - Slower performance: 5 to 100 percent slower during message signing and encryption
    - Interoperability problems with new technology

Biometric systems are one of the newest modes of authentication. In simplest terms, a biometric system is a pattern recognition system that establishes the authenticity of a specific physiological or behavioral characteristic possessed by a user.[278] A biometric system has two major components: (1) a high-resolution scanner that acquires and digitizes information, and (2) computer hardware and software that perform pattern recognition. The two major functions of a biometric system are enrollment and identification. Enrollment involves registering biometric information with a known identity and consists of three steps[281]:

1. Capturing a raw biometric data sample from a scanner
2. Processing the raw biometric data to extract the unique details
3. Storing a composite of raw and unique data with an identifier

Identification involves comparing a current biometric sample to known stored samples to verify a claimed identity or to identify a person.[281, 282] Identification repeats the capture and processing steps. Then, pattern recognition algorithms are invoked to perform the comparison. Current and planned future applications of biometric identification include access to secure facilities, access to desktop PCs, verification for receipt of welfare payments, verification for home banking privileges, and verification for bank ATM access. Biometric identification can be combined with smart card technology.

Nine types of biometric systems are currently in use or under development. Each measures a different physical characteristic[282, 283]: fingerprints, iris, retina, face, hand, ear, body odor, voice, and signature.

Fingerprint scanning is the oldest technology. Automated fingerprint identification standards began appearing in 1988. Fingerprint scanning offers 40 degrees of freedom. Lerner[283] reports that the false positive rate, which can be improved if two fingers are scanned, is approximately 1 percent. Fingerprint scanning may replace passwords in the near future for access to desktop computers.

The algorithm for iris scanning was developed in 1980 by John Daugman of the Cambridge University Computer Science Department. It is only recently, given improvements in computer processing power and cost, that iris scanning technology has become commercially viable. IrisScan, Inc., of New Jersey, currently holds the patent for this technology. In simplest terms, iris scanning involves wavelet analysis on a 512-byte pattern, similar to Fourier analysis. As reported by Lerner,[283] iris scanners support 266 degrees of freedom and can perform 100,000 scans per second.

Biometric authentication can also be performed through voice verification. In this case, the enrollment process consists of extracting unique feature vectors from a passphrase that is recorded and stored in a voice-print database. Biometric authentication through voice verification is geared toward reducing fraud in three environments: (1) E-commerce over the Internet, (2) T-commerce over fixed-line telephones, and (3) M-commerce over mobile and wireless devices. An advantage of voice verification is that it requires "little or no additional infrastructure investment due to the wide availability and low cost of computer microphones and telephones, whether fixed-line or cellular."[284]

A drop in the cost of biometric systems has expanded their usage. The use of biometric identification systems raises performance and privacy issues. While biometric systems are considered more accurate than non-biometric systems,[282] they still raise concerns about false positives and false negatives given the variability in biometric characteristics.[278] For example, changes in makeup, hair style or color, tinted contact lenses, plastic surgery, a suntan, and presence or absence of facial hair would all change facial characteristics, as would an illness or the normal aging process. Also, what is to prevent a person from placing a photograph or hologram in front of the scanner, or in the case of a voice recognition system, playing a tape recording? The accuracy of biometric systems is, not surprisingly, tied to cost. Some experts think that multi-mode biometric identification may be more accurate than single mode;[282] however, this has not yet been proven. The integrity of stored data samples and current data samples is another concern. Biometric data is not immune to misuse and attacks any more than other types of data.[283] Enrollment fraud is a major concern for the system owners and the individual whose identity has been hijacked.[255] How does a person recover from biometric identity theft? Personal biometric characteristics cannot be changed like a credit card account number. Likewise, the privacy and confidentiality of biometric data is a major concern. Until standardization efforts take hold, system integration and interoperability issues will remain. In summary, biometric identification systems are expected to reduce fraud, forgery, and theft[283]; but like other authentication methods, they are not a panacea.

The following metrics can be used to measure the resilience of different aspects of an organization's identification and authentication function. To obtain a complete picture, these metrics measure:

- How thoroughly and how well the identification and authentication function has been implemented throughout the IT infrastructure
- Whether the identification and authentication function has been implemented consistent with system risk and asset criticality

- Whether identification and authentication credentials are being properly managed
- The extent and types of identification and authentication failures experienced

Number and percentage of active user IDs assigned to only one person, by criticality of assets accessed.[105]   2.3.5.1

Percentage of systems and applications that perform password policy verification, by system risk.[105]   2.3.5.2

Number of system accesses by unauthorized users through channels protected by strong identification and authentication, by type of failure.[169]   2.3.5.3

Number of active user passwords that are set to expire in accordance with policy, by system risk.[105]   2.3.5.4

Percentage of systems with critical and essential information assets that use stronger authentication than IDs and passwords.[105]   2.3.5.5

Percentage of systems where vendor-supplied or default accounts and passwords have been disabled or reset, including maintenance back doors, by system risk.[105]   2.3.5.6

Percentage of systems and networks that lock user accounts or the point of entry after two or three failed log-on attempts, by system risk and asset criticality.[105]   2.3.5.7

Percentage of IDs created, deleted, or modified this reporting period, by system risk.[143]   2.3.5.8

Percentage of user IDs that also require use of a token or smart card, by information sensitivity.[143]   2.3.5.9

Number of failed log-on attempts this reporting period, by system risk and asset criticality.[169]   2.3.5.10

Number of unauthorized changes made to authentication credentials this reporting period[117]:   2.3.5.11

   a. Percentage that were used to successfully access IT and information assets

By system risk and asset criticality, percentage of systems and networks that, following a failed log-on attempt: 2.3.5.12

   a. Lock the account and/or point of entry for a specified period of time
   b. Lock the account or point of entry until an official request is approved to reset it

By system risk and asset criticality, percentage of systems and networks that, following a successful log-on attempt: 2.3.5.13

   a. Display the date and time of the user's most recent successful log-on, for confirmation
   b. Display details about all unsuccessful log-on attempts since the user's last successful log-on, for confirmation

By system risk and asset criticality, percentage of systems and networks that: 2.3.5.14

    a. Limit maximum session durations

    b. Require sessions to be re-authenticated or terminated after a specified time interval

By system risk and asset criticality, percentage of systems and networks that require processes, sessions, devices, and systems to be authenticated. 2.3.5.15

By system risk and asset criticality, percentage of systems and networks that require: 2.3.5.16

    a. Unique identification and authentication credentials for all users

    b. Identification and authentication credentials to be structured so that they do not reveal anything about a user's role or system privileges

    c. Single use authentication

    d. Multi-factor authentication

    e. Robust authentication for remote access

By system risk and asset criticality, percentage of systems and networks that employ complementary identification and authentication mechanisms at: 2.3.5.17

    a. Different points in the IT infrastructure

    b. Different layers of the ISO/OSI and TCP/IP reference models

By system risk and asset criticality, percentage of organizational units that have tested their identification and authentication mechanisms this reporting period and found that they worked as specified under normal and abnormal conditions: 2.3.5.18

    a. Distribution by type and severity of errors found, this reporting period and the previous three reporting periods

Number and percentage of security incidents, by incident severity, related to: 2.3.5.19

    a. Failure of an identification and authentication mechanism

    b. Faulty implementation or configuration of an identification and authentication mechanism

    c. The ability to bypass one or more identification and authentication mechanisms

    d. Failure to follow identification and authentication procedures

    e. Lack of an identification and authentication mechanism at some point in the IT infrastructure

    f. A combination of two or more of the above

The frequency with which identification and authentication credentials are reviewed, reaffirmed, and updated or revoked, by organizational unit, asset criticality, and information sensitivity. 2.3.5.20

Maintainability, Supportability

Industrial sectors, such as aerospace engineering, where safety and reliability are paramount, have a mature understanding of supportability and maintainability and have developed robust programs, procedures, and standards to ensure it. A case in point is the following standards that were issued by the Society for Aerospace Engineering (SAE) in the late 1990s and are used worldwide:

- SAE AIR 5121 Software Supportability Overview
- SAE JA 1006 Software Support Concept
- SAE JA 1004 Software Supportability Program Standard
- SAE JA 1005 Software Supportability Program Implementation Guide

In contrast, the security engineering community has yet to absorb or apply this wealth of experience and best practices. Supportability and maintainability are ignored and not considered a security engineering issue. Or, at most maintainability is (incorrectly) thought of in terms of updating virus signatures, firewall rule sets, and routing tables.

Supportability is a set of attributes associated with the design of a product or system, the development tools and methods used, and the support environment infrastructure that enable support activities to be conducted.[40–42] Support activities are performed to ensure that an operational product or system fulfills its original requirements and any subsequent modification of those requirements.[40–42] By default, supportability determines the operational readiness of a product or system, and the cost and resources needed to sustain this state.

Maintainability is one aspect of supportability. The others include topics such as availability and configuration management, which are discussed later in this chapter. Maintainability refers to the ease with which a product or system can be modified to correct faults, improve performance or other attributes, or adapt to a new operational environment, and the effort required to do so.[40–42] Maintainability includes activities such as change impact analysis and regression testing and is a function of the ease of the ability to modify, enhance, and adapt a product or system throughout its operational life, with a low probability of introducing new errors. While availability is concerned with mean time between failures (MTBF) and mean time to failure (MTTF) measures, maintainability focuses on the mean time to repair (MTTR).

Supportability and maintainability issues should be evaluated and addressed throughout the life of a product or system, beginning long before it is deployed and becomes operational. Often, organizations become engulfed in the acquisition or development of a product or system and fail to recognize that, on average, most products or systems spend 80 percent of their life span in the operations and maintenance phase (not acquisition or development). That is why issues such as supportability and maintainability are crucial, especially when making IT capital investment decisions. Cost and schedule constraints can easily dominate acquisition and development efforts and drive legitimate technical concerns under the rug. That is very shortsighted and ultimately can be very expensive, regardless of whether you are talking about COTS or custom-developed products and systems. Failure to give supportability and maintainability concerns appropriate attention up-front can result in[40–42]:

- Low product or system supportability and maintainability in the field
- Inadequate life-cycle funding for supportability and maintainability
- No meaningful analysis and optimization of possible support alternatives
- Lack of good data from laboratory evaluations, proof of concept demonstrations, or operational field testing

A variety of technical attributes have a direct impact on the supportability and maintainability equation, including[40–42]:

- Design and implementation complexity
- Uniqueness or novelty of technical approach
- Platform dependencies: hardware, operating system, system utilities, etc.
- Operation profile and duty cycle
- Ease of installation and configuration
- Operational or environmental constraints: timing, size, interfaces, etc.
- Support tools and techniques
- A multi-vendor operational environment
- Mandatory recovery times and response time to failures
- Obsolescence and technology refresh
- Whether a product or system design and implementation adheres to national and international consensus standards
- Operational impact of scheduled (routine) and unscheduled (emergency) maintenance and support activities

An organization has control over some of these issues; other issues they have no control over. However, all these issues must be taken into account when planning for supportability and maintainability.

In addition, a variety of logistical issues must be calculated as part of the sum. A support profile needs to be developed that defines the support level, support agents, and support scenarios for the product or system, regardless of whether it is COTS or custom developed. The support level determines where each type of support activity will be performed: on-site, at a local or regional maintenance depot, at the vendor's facility, etc. The support agent determines who will perform each type of support activity: end users, customer's help desk staff, the supplier or vendor, or a third-party maintenance firm. The support agent also determines what type of training and skill level the person performing each support activity needs, how many people are needed, and how quickly they must be available under normal and abnormal conditions. For example, people of different skill levels are generally needed at different support levels, and they have different response times. Support scenarios define the standardized processes and procedures to be followed when performing each type of support activity. They also identify the resources and time required to complete each activity, along with any constraints.

So what does all this have to do with the resilience of IT security controls? A lot. The vast majority of the vendors of security appliances are small start-up companies. This is not surprising; small start-up companies tend to be more creative. The problem is that many of these companies are less than five years old; they and their products are here today and gone tomorrow. A select few are bought out by a larger, older company, usually to eliminate the competition, not to fold in the product line. Most of these small start-up companies offer a single product. Because these products are new, with little or no installed customer base, the MTBF, MTTF, and MTTR are unknown; there is not enough data available to construct a valid supportability plan. These companies have a questionable financial footing, immature engineering practices and procedures, limited or no product technical documentation, and usually high staff turnover. In short, they lack corporate stability and hence the ability to support a product. One product we evaluated had a total of one field support engineer assigned to support the entire federal government! On the other extreme, many of these companies like to think their products qualify as "shrink-wrapped," but they are far from it. One such product was advertised to be up and running in an hour — it took us three weeks to install and configure the device with full-time on-site support from the vendor. Often, small companies do not want to deal with support activities at all and farm it out to a third party who is as equally clueless and unmotivated. The fad now is a 24-hour maintenance guarantee, where replacement parts or products will be shipped overnight. That sounds great, but security incidents take seconds. In 24 hours, your whole IT infrastructure could be compromised.

Those are the supportability problems associated with a single security appliance. Given that most mid- to large-size organizations have between half a dozen to a dozen or more security appliances, all from different vendors, installed throughout their IT infrastructure, the supportability problems increase geometrically. Interoperability issues are always tenuous at best under such circumstances. Just when a steady state has been reached, it is time for an upgrade here, a patch there, and a new interface between this module and that. The steady state is no more and instead you have a herd of warring white elephants on your hands. You try to call the vendor for support, only to find out that the company has gone out of business or that your call is so important to them that they will get back to you sometime in the next three months. In the meantime, you have to shut down some of the appliances because of the performance impact, and security goes out the window. In summary, you can have the world's strongest identification and authentication function, access control function, encryption function, etc., but if these products are not supportable and maintainable, your security architecture will come tumbling down faster than the walls of Jericho and you will be as helpless as Humpty Dumpty.

Judicious use of the following metrics will let an organization evaluate the resilience of:

- The supportability and maintainability of an individual product or system
- The supportability and maintainability of an integrated set of products or systems
- Its overall supportability and maintainability program

By system risk and asset criticality, percentage of system development acquisition initiatives that: 2.3.6.1
  a. Include and evaluate supportability and maintainability requirements
  b. Analyze supportability and maintainability options
  c. Identify and reserve adequate funding for supportability and maintainability throughout the life of a system or product
  d. Develop and coordinate a comprehensive supportability plan that specifies support levels, support agents, and support scenarios, before a product or system is fielded
  e. Monitor the execution of the supportability plan at a senior level of management

Extent to which a product or system has been designed and developed with supportability attributes, using the following scale (high — 5, medium — 3, low — 1, none — 0), maximum total points 50:   2.3.6.2
  a. Modularity
  b. Testability
  c. Easy to install, configure, and operate
  d. Easy to update and modify, such as changing interfaces
  e. Design and implementation adheres to national or international consensus standards
  f. Lack of dependence on specific hardware or software platforms or external interfaces
  g. Adaptability to different operational profiles and duty cycles
  h. Percentage of support activities that can be performed without disrupting operations
  i. Expected useful life span with respect to technology refresh and obsolescence
  j. Product maturity

Extent to which logistical infrastructure is in place to ensure the support levels, support agents, and support scenarios defined in the supportability plan, using the following scale (high — 5, medium — 3, low — 1, none — 0), maximum total points = 45:   2.3.6.3
  a. Extent to which support agents have the necessary training and experience to perform their assigned support activities
  b. Extent to which the appropriate number of support agents with the appropriate training and experience are available when needed
  c. Completeness to which support scenarios have been defined
  d. Degree to which the accuracy and completeness of support scenarios have been validated

   e. Availability of non-human resources needed to perform support activities
   f. Degree to which the pre-coordination necessary to execute support scenarios has been carried out
   g. Currency, completeness, and availability of technical reference manuals and other documentation needed to execute the support scenarios
   h. Availability of operational data from the field, such as MTBF, MTTF, and MTTR
   i. Ability to meet mandatory response and recovery times

Vendor stability, using the following scale (high — 5, medium — 3, low — 1, none — 0), maximum total points = 45: 2.3.6.4
   a. Number of years company has been in business: +10 years — 5, 5 to 10 years — 3, 3 to 5 years — 1, less than 3 years — 0
   b. Number of products offered by company: +4 product — 5, 2 to 4 products — 3, 1 product — 1
   c. Installed customer base: +20 sites — 5, 11 to 20 sites — 3, 2 to 10 sites — 1, none — 0
   d. Availability of references
   e. Financial stability
   f. Turnover rate for engineering staff
   g. Maturity of corporate system engineering processes
   h. Number of trained field support engineers
   i. Long-term plans to support and continue offering the product
   j. Percentage of features and functions the product actually performs, compared to the advertising literature

Number of times supportability and maintainability issues across the IT infrastructure are assessed prior to selecting or deploying a new security appliance, by system risk and asset criticality: 2.3.6.5
   a. Interoperability issues are evaluated, for current and planned future configurations
   b. The security impact of patches, upgrades, and interface changes across the IT infrastructure are evaluated prior to implementation
   c. The planned evolution of the IT infrastructure takes into account the impact of supportability and maintainability of adding or removing various devices

Number of times one or more security appliances or other devices have had to be shut down or discarded due to supportability and maintainability problems, by system risk and asset criticality: 2.3.6.6
   a. Average duration of the time the appliance or device was shut down
   b. Total cost of appliances or devices involved

Number and percentage of security incidents, by incident severity, that were precipitated by inadequate or ineffectual supportability and maintainability. 2.3.6.7

Total downtime across the IT infrastructure this reporting period due to supportability and maintainability shortcomings, by asset criticality. 2.3.6.8

Frequency with which the supportability and maintainability program is reviewed for compliance and opportunities to improve it: 2.3.6.9

 a. Overall supportability and maintainability program
 b. Supportability and maintainability program for individual products or systems

By system risk and asset criticality, percentage of support activities that:
                                                                                2.3.6.10

 a. Can be performed by in-house staff, all resources needed are on hand
 b. Can only be performed by the vendor
 c. Can only be performed by third-party maintenance

Increase in maintainability of security appliances, functions, and systems due to implementing design features like partitioning, using an ordinal scale of 0 (none) to 10 (very high).   2.3.6.11

Privacy

Privacy is a legal right, not an engineering discipline. That is why organizations have privacy officers, not privacy engineers. Security engineering is the discipline used to ensure that privacy rights are protected to the extent specified by law and organizational policy. Privacy is not an automatic outcome of security engineering. Like any other security feature or function, privacy requirements must be specified, designed, implemented, and verified to the integrity level needed.

There are several legal aspects to privacy rights. People living in the United States and other countries have a basic legal right to privacy. That means that their personal life and how they live it remains a private, not public, matter. The right to privacy is protected by privacy laws. Although the exact provisions of privacy laws in each country differ, the common ground is restricting access to private residences and property, personnel information, and personal communications. The intent is to prevent harassment and unwarranted publicity. The laws provide legal remedies should privacy rights be violated. A person's privacy is considered invaded when his persona is exploited or private matters are made public without his consent. Usually this is done with the intent of causing personal, professional, or financial harm. Whenever a breach of privacy or invasion of privacy occurs, the victim has the right to pursue a legal remedy based on the contents of the applicable privacy laws and regulations. Both the individuals and the organizations responsible for the privacy violation can be prosecuted.

A variety of laws and regulations have been enacted to protect privacy rights in the digital age, as discussed in Chapter 3. Privacy rights extend to personal data, which is understood to mean *any* information relating to an identified or identifiable individual.[69] Personal data includes financial, medical, scholastic, employment, demographic, and other information, such as purchasing habits, calling records, e-mail, and phone conversations, whether it is in the public or private sectors. The mere fact that this information is available in electronic form presents a potential danger to the privacy of individual liberties.[69] This is true due to the potential for malicious misuse of the information, which could have a serious negative economic or social impact on the individuals involved — and hence the genesis of the enactment and enforcement of robust privacy legislation worldwide.

Legislation passed to date coalesces around eight privacy principles[61, 62, 64, 69, 71, 75, 80, 108, 267]:

1. **Collection Limitation.** The minimum amount of data necessary to support the stated use is to be collected and no more. The individuals whose data is being collected have to be told what data will be collected and how it will be collected. Furthermore, individuals *must* give their consent beforehand to such data being collected.
2. **Data Quality.** Organizations that collect and use personal data are responsible for ensuring the accuracy, completeness, and currency of such data at all times.
3. **Purpose Specification.** Individuals must be told beforehand why their personal data is being collected, what the data will be used for, who the data will be disseminated to, and how long the data will be kept. If an organization wants to put the data to a new use in the future, they must contact the individuals and obtain their consent again.
4. **Use Limitation.** Personal data that has been collected from individuals can only be used for the purposes stated at the time of collection. Personal data must be securely destroyed or rendered anonymous after such use.
5. **Security safeguards.** Organizations that collect, process, store, transmit, or disclose personal information are responsible for implementing a combination of physical, personnel, IT, and operational security controls to protect that information. In particular, organizations are responsible for protecting personal data from unauthorized access, alteration, use, release, and destruction.
6. **Openness.** Organizations are responsible for informing individuals about what personal data they hold and the procedures the organization follows to protect it. In addition, individuals must be told that they have a right to view data held about them and how to contact the organization to do so.
7. **Individual participation.** Individuals have a right to obtain copies of their personal data held by an organization. Furthermore, individuals have the right to challenge the accuracy of that data and insist that errors be corrected.
8. **Accountability.** Organizations that hold or process personal data are liable for adhering to these eight privacy principles and are subject to prosecution and fines when they are not followed.

Consequently, the resilience of IT security controls relating to privacy is a function of how well and how thoroughly these eight privacy principles have been incorporated into the IT infrastructure, as the following metrics demonstrate.

Number and percentage of personal data elements collected that are beyond the scope needed for the stated purpose of collection: 2.3.7.1

    a. Distribution by type of data
    b. Disposition of extraneous personal data

Number and percentage of personal data elements that were collected without:
                                                                         2.3.7.2
    a. The individual's prior knowledge and consent
    b. Telling the individual what the data would be used for
    c. Telling the individual who the information will be disseminated to
    d. Telling the individual how long the data would be kept

Frequency with which the accuracy, completeness, and currency of personal data held by an organization is verified: 2.3.7.3
    a. Date of most recent verification activity
    b. Percentage of data found to be accurate, complete, and current during most recent verification activity

Number of times personal data was put to a new use without first obtaining the individual's approval.   2.3.7.4

Distribution of times personal data was and was not disposed of in a secure manner after the end of the stated usage time interval.   2.3.7.5

Frequency with which individuals are informed about: 2.3.7.6
    a. Personal data an organization holds about them
    b. The procedures the organization follows to protect personal data
    c. Their right to view their personal data
    d. How to contact an organization that holds their personal data

Speed with which an organization is able to respond to an individual's request to: 2.3.7.7
    a. Receive copies of their personal data
    b. Correct inaccurate data

Degree to which the IT infrastructure enforces accountability for privacy requirements: 2.3.7.8
    a. Ultra High/Completely
    b. High
    c. Medium
    d. Low
    e. None

By system risk, percentage of systems and networks that have been tested to verify their privacy controls this reporting period and found that they worked correctly under normal and abnormal conditions: 2.3.7.9
    a. Protecting personal data from unauthorized access
    b. Protecting personal data from unauthorized alteration
    c. Protecting personal data from unauthorized use
    d. Protecting personal data from unauthorized release
    e. Protecting personal data from unauthorized destruction

Number and percentage of security incidents, by incident severity, related to:
2.3.7.10

    a. Failure of a privacy mechanism
    b. Faulty implementation or configuration of a privacy mechanism
    c. The ability to bypass one or more privacy mechanisms
    d. Failure to follow privacy procedures
    e. Lack of a privacy mechanism at some point in the IT infrastructure
    f. A combination of two or more of the above

Frequency with which privacy mechanisms and procedures are reviewed, reaffirmed, and updated, by organizational unit and information sensitivity.
2.3.7.11

Customer sensitivity to information security and privacy (3 — high, 2 — moderate, 1 — low).[163]
2.3.7.12

Residual Information Protection

Like flow control, residual information protection is an extension of access control. While residual information protection is not known by the acronym RIP (commonly translated as rest in peace), it could be because the concept is not much different. The purpose of residual information protection is to ensure that information that has been deleted is no longer accessible by the same or other processes.[20] That is, data that has been logically deleted or released cannot be recovered — it can "rest in peace."

There are several inexpensive commercial utilities that specialize in recovering files that were accidentally deleted or data from hard drives that crashed. That is not the scenario we are talking about here — nor are backups, archives, or portable storage media involved. In contrast, residual information protection applies to dynamic data that is constantly being read and written within an active system. Residual information protection applies to memory, cache, buffers, registers, stacks, and heaps throughout a system or network, as well as active database fields, records, files, etc. These are resources that are serially reused by different subjects within a system,[20] usually within milliseconds or less. The concern centers around reusable resources where the destruction of the data object does not equate to the destruction of the resource or its information content.[20] For example, operating system registers are continually swapped by different processes. The problem is that this dynamic information, while logically deleted, may still be present and capable of being subsumed, accidentally or intentionally, into a newly created data object — and hence the need for residual information protection.

Residual information protection is not a user-invoked function, but rather a function that is triggered automatically. Residual information protection mechanisms can be set to trigger at the time a data object is released (de-allocation) or prior to allocating resources for a new data object. There are advantages and disadvantages to both approaches. Invoking residual information protection upon de-allocation ensures the immediate destruction of old data; however, it may complicate rollback.[20] Invoking residual information protection upon allocating resources ensures that the resources are clean before they are reused. However, if there is a significant time interval between the time a resource is de-allocated and allocated, there is a chance of the old data being compromised. As a result, in some high-risk scenarios, it may make sense to execute residual information protection mechanisms upon both de-allocation and allocation of dynamic reusable resources.

Due to cost and performance constraints, a decision must be made about where and when to implement residual information protection. Should residual information protection mechanisms be implemented for all dynamic data objects or just a subset? This will have to be decided by each organization on a case-by-case basis, after evaluating factors such as system risk, asset criticality, information sensitivity, and privacy concerns. If a system is operating in a multilevel secure mode, then, by default, complete residual information protection is needed to prevent opportunities for data of different sensitivity levels from becoming comingled, contaminated, or compromised. In low-risk environments, it may be acceptable to apply residual information protection to the most critical subset of data objects. Keep in mind that it is easier and cheaper to implement residual information protection when it is designed into a system from the beginning, than to retrofit an operational system.

The following metrics can be used to measure the resilience of different aspects of an organization's implementation of residual information protection. To obtain a complete picture, these metrics measure:

- How thoroughly and how well residual information protection has been implemented
- Whether residual information protection has been implemented consistent with asset criticality and information sensitivity
- The extent and types of residual information protection failures experienced

By information sensitivity and system risk, percentage of information assets for which residual information protection mechanisms are invoked upon:
2.3.8.1
a. Allocation of dynamic reusable resources
b. De-allocation of dynamic reusable resources
c. Both allocation and de-allocation of dynamic reusable resources

Percentage (%) of systems for which residual information protection has been implemented consistent with rollback requirements, by system risk.   2.3.8.2

By asset criticality and information sensitivity, percentage of organizational units that have tested their residual information protection mechanisms this reporting period and found that they worked as specified under normal and abnormal conditions.   2.3.8.3
a. Distribution by type and severity of errors found, this reporting period and the previous three reporting periods

Number and percentage of security incidents, by incident severity, related to:
2.3.8.4

    a. Failure of a residual information protection mechanism

    b. Faulty implementation or configuration of a residual information protection mechanism

    c. Lack of residual information protection

    d. A combination of two or more of the above

The frequency with which the implementation of residual information protection is reviewed, reaffirmed, or updated: 2.3.8.5

    a. During normal operations

    b. Following a major system upgrade or change

    c. Following a change to the system operational profile and usage

    d. Following a major security incident

Security Management

Once logical access control, data authentication, encryption, flow control, identification and authentication, privacy, and residual information protection mechanisms have undergone initial installation and configuration, they need to be managed. This is accomplished through the security management function (or security information management [SIM], or security management infrastructure [SMI] as it is sometimes called). Security management encompasses all devices and tasks that implement the security architecture and enforce security policies. The purpose of the security management function is to ensure that security appliances, individually and collectively, throughout the IT infrastructure, operate in a known secure manner at all times. A whole host of activities fall under the scope of security management, such as[266]:

- Configuring routers and firewalls in accordance with standards reflecting asset criticality and information sensitivity
- Ensuring that vendor-supplied default passwords and accounts and remote maintenance ports are disabled before devices are deployed
- Disabling unnecessary and unused device functions and features
- Restricting the release of internal network addresses
- Configuring devices to enable or disable external connectivity and public access, wired and wireless, consistent with security and operational needs
- Encrypting all administrative access

Security management activities fall into four major categories, all of which are intertwined. Security management activities are concerned with managing[20]:

1. Security attributes
2. Security data
3. Security functions
4. Security management roles

Security attributes are information associated with subjects, users, and objects that is used to enforce security policies.[20] Security attributes control the behavior of security functions. Logical access control rights and privileges are examples of security attributes. These security attributes are associated with initiators and determine what resources they can access and what operations they can perform on or with those resources. Identification and authentication credentials, digital certificates, firewall rule sets, and other parameters that control or mediate security functions are all security attributes. That is, a security function consults a security attribute or set of security attributes to determine (1) whether a function is allowed to be performed, and (2) how to perform the function.

Security attributes are rarely static for any period of time and, as a result, need to be managed. Access control rights and privileges change over time as system resources are added, removed, or modified. Identification and authentication credentials change over time as employees join or leave an organization, or are promoted or transferred. Digital certificates and other security tokens are issued to a given person (or process) for a specific purpose and a specific time interval. The security management function is responsible for ensuring that all security attributes are accurate, valid, and current at all times. Accurate, valid, and current security attributes are essential to ensuring that the IT infrastructure continues to operate in a secure state. Absent that state, the IT infrastructure will be quickly compromised due to incorrect behavior of security functions or the ease with which security functions can be bypassed.

Security attributes are initialized and can be queried, viewed, edited, and deleted through the security management function. The security management function also determines whether and under what conditions security attributes can be overridden. Due to the transient nature of security attributes, each attribute is linked to an expiration date. The time interval that a security attribute is valid is specified through the security management function. Expiration dates can be specified for individual security attributes: John's digital certificate expires before Jane's. Or, expiration dates can be specified by attribute type: all user name/password pairs expire the first of every month or all user name/password pairs expire every 30 days. The approach taken should be consistent with system risk, asset criticality, and information sensitivity. Conversely, the approach to managing security attributes should not be selected just because it is the easiest for the security management staff to implement. The action to be taken upon expiration of a security attribute needs to be specified as well. Is the subject to which the security attribute applies notified that the attribute is about to or has expired? Is an automatic notice sent to the security management staff that an attribute is about to or has expired? Who is contacted to confirm whether or not the expired attribute should be renewed, canceled, or modified? What is the time frame for each of these activities to be conducted? What happens in the interval during which an attribute has expired but has not yet been renewed? Suppose there is an unplanned delay or an emergency and a valid authorized user needs access.

The expiration of security attributes is a normal everyday occurrence, part of the built-in checks and balances of operating a secure IT infrastructure. In contrast, the revocation of security attributes is an emergency procedure. A security attribute has been lost through negligence or misappropriated through malicious activity and a lack of robust security controls, or a valid authorized user has suddenly gone over to the dark side and their security attributes need to be vaporized immediately. The security management function controls the rules that define how and under what conditions security attributes are revoked. Once the need to revoke security attributed has been identified, the revocation must be completed as quickly and completely as possible, to ensure that all instances of the security attributes are revoked before any (further) damage can be done. Contracts that include security service level agreements generally stipulate that revocation be completed within a matter of minutes after being directed to do so. Revocation rules must specify the action to be taken immediately after a security attribute is revoked. What happens to the accounts, files, directories, and storage media linked to the owner of that security attribute? Are these assets deleted, transferred to a secure holding area pending further review, or left as is? Who is notified that the security attribute has been revoked: the employee's manager, co-workers, IT help desk staff, business partners, or the director of personnel? What protective system activities are taken during the time interval between when a request is made to revoke a security attribute and the revocation is complete? What evidence is to be kept about why, how, and when the security attribute was revoked and attempts to use the security attribute after it was revoked? How long is this evidence kept? Revocation can be a messy business when personnel, legal, business, and financial issues are factored in. Consequently, it is important to evaluate and review all aspects of a revocation process very carefully, preferably before it is needed.

The execution and operation of security functions generates security data. To ensure that the IT infrastructure continues to operate in a known secure state, under normal and abnormal conditions, this data must be managed, just like security attributes. Critical decisions are made and actions taken, by humans and automatically by IT assets, based on security data. As a result, it is essential that security data be accurate, complete, and current. What better way is there to attack a system than to alter the security data so that no evidence of the attack is generated or kept? Or, what better way is there to disrupt operations than to alter the security data so that is shows an emergency situation when none exists? Various systems, services, and connections will be dropped or blocked. Devices will be reconfigured and diagnostics run, all playing into the hands of the attacker. Security data is generated and stored at a variety of places throughout the IT infrastructure. In some cases, there are interdependencies between one type of security data and another — all the more reason to ensure that security data is adequately protected. System logs, audit trail data, identification and authentication failures, successful and unsuccessful attempts to access resources and perform certain operations, remote access logs, and date and time stamps are all examples of security data.

The security management function is responsible for verifying and maintaining valid security data. The security management function monitors the value of security data to ensure that it stays within prespecified legal ranges. The action to be taken when security data reaches or goes beyond legal minimum or maximum values must be specified by the security management function, to ensure that a system stays in a known secure state at all times and does not encounter any unknown or undefined states. Is the event logged, an alarm generated, the requested activity or operation blocked, or further processing suspended until the system can take remedial action?

Security functions implement the security architecture and enforce security policies. Security functions consult security attributes before performing certain activities. Security data is generated in the process of executing security functions. Some security functions operate in continuous mode — they are always invoked. Other security functions operate in demand mode — they are invoked only when needed. Different security functions are implemented throughout the IT infrastructure. Multiple instances of the same security function may also be implemented through the IT infrastructure.

It is the responsibility of the security management function to manage all security functions and ensure their correct and reliable operation. As security appliances are added to and removed from the IT infrastructure or need to be upgraded or modified, this task can quickly become quite complex. Decisions must be made about whether security functions are going to be managed locally, through a centralized security management function, or through a series of security management tiers. Procedures must be defined and enforced to ensure consistent and compatible management of security functions throughout the enterprise. What is the standard configuration of each type of security appliance? What features and functions are enabled or disabled? What values are configuration parameters set to? How and when are patches and upgrades installed? How long does security data remain online and active? When is security data archived and overwritten? When do security attributes have to be consulted: before, during, or after an operation? If the operational environment consists of a nationwide WAN with thousands of nodes, are all security appliances that perform the same function configured the same? Or, does the configuration of security appliances vary by system risk, asset criticality, and information sensitivity? In short, managing security functions requires that a lot of serious decisions be made and monitored that have significant long-term consequences enterprisewide.

The management of a single security appliance, or a handful of the same security appliance, is not usually difficult. The challenges begin when more than a handful of security appliances or multiple devices from different vendors are deployed. Most of the security appliances on the market today do not scale up very well. One device we tested had no means of combining the management and reporting functions from multiple devices. If 50 of these devices were deployed throughout the enterprise, 50 different management and reporting screens had to be reviewed. Another common problem is that many products have no means to export data to or import data from a centralized security management console. You have to wonder what the product designers were thinking. If the security management staff have to switch to separate consoles or even screens for every security appliance and type of security appliance managed, it is highly unlikely that they will be able to perform their duties accurately, effectively, or in a timely manner. (However, it is highly likely that an organization will have a high turnover in security management staff under such conditions.) In addition to usability problems, there will be severe timing issues related to the propagation and replication of security attributes across distributed and interconnected systems.[20]

The lack of an ability to merge and synthesize data from multiple security appliances from multiple vendors is a third problem area. There are a couple of products that do a half-way job of this, but only if the data can be sent to them in a specific format. To manage the security functionality across an enterprise, a consolidated picture of security data from all vendors' products is needed. At present there is not a tool that does that well. Some organizations have rigged their own custom solutions. Other organizations have spent a considerable amount of funds and resources in pursuit of an event correlation capability — the ability to merge and make sense of event logs from a variety of different types and brands of security appliances and IT equipment. Almost none of these efforts have been successful. In addition, they become obsolete as soon as a new product is released, because the event correlation capability must be updated. Trying to build an event correlator is attempting to solve the wrong problem. Instead, what is needed is an industry-wide standard for capturing and reporting events. A standardized data and file format is needed that defines common mandatory fields and their legal values. In addition, there needs to be some optional industry-specific fields, such as needed for SCADA, process control, etc. This way, event information could easily be exchanged, merged, and analyzed from different types and brands of security appliances. It is time for the IT security industry to move away from proprietary standards and toward international consensus standards. Once that happens, security attributes, data, and functions can really be managed.

The fourth security management function is to define and implement the various distinct (human) security management roles, and their interaction and separation.[20] Security management roles determine the who, what, where, and when of managing security attributes, security data, and security functions. Who can create, view, edit, or revoke a security attribute? Who decides what security data is captured and how long it is kept? Who has the authority to enable, disable, configure, or execute security functions? What different security management roles are needed for network-based, operating system-based, and application layer security functions? What different security management roles are needed for shared resources (e.g., LANs, servers, and printers) versus single-user devices (e.g., desktop computers)? What is the security management role in relation to mobile and personally owned IT equipment?

Managing security roles involves controlling the assignment of specific roles to different users, along with the capability and authority associated with each role.[20] An explicit definition of the security management capabilities that are permitted and denied is needed for each role, to prevent overlapping and conflicting roles. The relationship between different security management roles must be defined. Are the security management roles defined laterally, hierarchically, or a combination of both? How are the security management roles defined in relation to the organizational structure and geographical distribution of the IT infrastructure? For example, are there headquarters, regional, and local security management roles?

Because security management roles involve humans, there is a link to personnel security. The accountability, background investigation, and competence requirements an individual must meet before they can be assigned to or assume a security management role need to be defined.[20] Furthermore, to prevent an individual from abusing his role, it is essential to implement separation of duties when creating security management roles and assigning individuals to them. Another key decision is to determine who has the authority to define or modify security management roles, and assign or modify the list of individuals assigned to each role. Security management roles and their membership tend to change over time, so some checks and balances are needed here as well. Finally, a key tool for monitoring security management roles is to audit every successful and unsuccessful use of a security management role[20] and tie this information back to a specific individual, not just the role.

The following metrics can be used to measure different aspects of the resilience of an organization's security management function. To obtain the big picture, several items are measured:

- How thoroughly and how well security management is implemented
- Whether security management is implemented consistent with system risk and asset criticality
- How well the security management features work
- The extent and type of security management failures experienced

Percentage of security attributes that were verified this reporting period and found to be accurate, valid, and current.   2.3.9.1

Percentage of security attributes that are linked to a specific expiration date.   2.3.9.2

Percentage of security attributes for which the action to be taken upon expiration is defined.   2.3.9.3

Percentage of security attributes for which revocation rules have been defined and verified, by attribute type.   2.3.9.4

Average time required to revoke security attributes, by attribute type: 2.3.9.5
   a. Number of security attributes revoked this reporting period

Percentage of security attribute revocation rules that specify the action to be taken upon revocation of an attribute: 2.3.9.6
   a. Percentage of security attribute revocation rules that specify what protective measures are to be taken between the time revocation is requested and completed

Percentage of security attribute revocation rules that specify what evidence is to be kept about why, how, and when a security attribute was revoked and attempts to use the attribute after it was revoked: 2.3.9.7

    a. Length of time this evidence is kept

Extent to which security data is protected against accidental or intentional unauthorized access, modification and deletion, using the following scale (completely protected — 5, high degree of protection — 4, moderate amount of protection — 3, limited protection — 1, and no protection — 0), by type of security data.   2.3.9.8

Percentage of security data that has been validated as being accurate, complete, and current by type of security data.   2.3.9.9

Percentage of security data for which valid legal ranges of values have been specified and are monitored, by type of security data.   2.3.9.10

Percentage of security data for which the action to be taken when an element reaches or goes beyond legal minimum or maximum values is defined, by type of security data.   2.3.9.11

Percentage of organizational units for which policies and procedures are defined, implemented, and enforced for standardizing the management of security functions, by asset criticality.   2.3.9.12

Percentage of organizational units that tailor policies and procedures for managing security functions by system risk, asset criticality, and information sensitivity.   2.3.9.13

Percentage of security functions that are scalable to the size and distribution of the IT infrastructure, by asset criticality.   2.3.9.14

Percentage of security functions that can export data to and import data from a centralized security management function.   2.3.9.15

Degree of completeness to which security management roles are defined, using the following scale (complete — 5, high — 4, moderate — 3, limited — 1, none — 0):   2.3.9.16

    a. Number of overlapping or conflicting security management roles

Degree to which the definition of and membership in a security management role complies with separation of duties principles using the following scale (complete — 5, high — 4, moderate — 3, limited — 1, none — 0): 2.3.9.17

    a. Number of individuals assigned to more than one security management role

Degree to which the definition of and membership in a security management role is linked to accountability, background investigations, and competence requirements, using the following scale (complete — 5, high — 4, moderate — 3, limited — 1, none — 0).   2.3.9.18

Extent to which successful and unsuccessful attempts to use security management roles are audited and linked to a specific individual, using the following scale (complete — 5, high — 4, moderate — 3, limited — 1, none — 0):
                                                                2.3.9.19

Degree to which the security management function is protected, using the following scale (complete — 5, high — 4, moderate — 3, limited — 1, none — 0). 2.3.9.20

Degree of security management functions that have been tested this reporting period and found to be working as specified under normal and abnormal conditions: 2.3.9.21

    a. Distribution by type and severity of errors found, this reporting period and the previous three reporting periods

Number and percentage of security incidents, by incident severity, related to: 2.3.9.22

    a. An incorrect, incomplete, missing, or compromised security attribute
    b. Incorrect, incomplete, missing, or compromised security data
    c. Failure of a security function
    d. Faulty implementation or configuration of a security function
    e. Failure to implement a security function
    f. Incorrect or undefined security management roles
    g. Failure to invoke a security function or security management role
    h. A combination of two or more of the above

Frequency with which the following items are reviewed, reaffirmed, updated, or withdrawn: 2.3.9.23

    a. Security attributes
    b. Collection and retention of security data
    c. Configuration and operation of security functions
    d. Definition of and membership in security management roles

IT Security Protection System

There are seven components of an IT security protection system, each of which contributes to protecting IT and information assets from and during abnormal operations:

- Audit trail, alarm generation
- Availability (redundancy, diversity, fault tolerance, block recovery, dynamic reconfiguration, rollback, self-healing)
- Error, exception, and incident handling
- Fail safe, fail secure, graceful degradation, degraded mode operations
- Integrity (hardware, software, network, active data, stored data, system)
- Domain separation (partitioning, information hiding, security kernels, encapsulation)
- Resource management (resource allocation, service priority, capacity management)

Audit Trail, Alarm Generation

An audit function records information that is needed to establish accountability for system events and for the actions of system entities that cause them. Audit information is captured in what is referred to as an audit trail. An audit trail is a set of records that collectively provides documentary evidence of system resources accessed by a user or process to aid in tracing from original transactions forward and backward to their component source transactions.[156] An audit trail provides a chronological record of system activities that is sufficient to enable the reconstruction, review, and examination of the sequence of operational environments and activities surrounding or leading to an operation, procedure, or an event in a transaction from its inception to final results, including all mode and state changes. For example, an audit trail could include a chronological record of when each user logs in, how long he is engaged in various activities (e.g., start and stop times), what he was doing (e.g., e-mail, Internet access, local word processing, etc.), and whether or not any actual or attempted security violations occurred.

A robust, comprehensive, and integrated audit capability is a prerequisite for (almost) all IT security control system functions and IT security protection system functions. It is difficult, if not impossible, to manage IT resources, monitor the integrity and availability of IT assets, or know when to invoke error, exception, and incident handling routines or a controlled failure mode without the information supplied by an audit function. An audit capability functions as the sensory system for an IT infrastructure. It senses changes in throughput, capacity, and system loading, and normal and abnormal activity patterns enterprisewide. Information about the status, performance, and health of the IT security control system functions and IT security protection system functions is gathered, along with data points about internal, external, and environmental stress factors. An audit trail performs several security functions, such as:

- Capturing information about which people and processes accessed what system resources and when
- Generating real-time and historical logs of system states, transitions, and resource usage
- Developing normal system and user profiles
- Supplying information with which to reconstruct events during post-event analysis

Audit information is captured locally, regionally, and enterprisewide. As measurement boundaries expand and contract, audit information from different sources throughout the IT infrastructure is merged, analyzed, and dispatched (as needed) to the appropriate IT security control or protection system functions to initiate proactive preventive or reactive remedial action.

An organization needs the ability to quickly analyze audit information if it is to be in a position to take proactive preventive action in real-time to keep the IT infrastructure in a known secure state. The ability to analyze audit information quickly is needed to support post-event analysis. After all, the purpose of post-event analysis is to derive "lessons learned" so that action can be taken quickly to prevent the recurrence of the same or similar incidents. Audit information is captured from a variety of sources at layers 2 to 7 of the

ISO/OSI Reference Model, such as operating system logs, application system transaction logs, desktop and server usage statistics, network filters, network event and traffic reports, and Internet access point usage. Audit information is generated by IT security control and protection system functions, for example, successful and unsuccessful mediation of security attributes for logical access control or identification and authentication mechanisms. An audit function must be able to sift through this information rapidly to identify potential, imminent, or actual security violations.[20] Individual events as well as sequences of events are analyzed. The analysis of historical audit data, particularly information collated from different sources, can help identify persistent, previously undetected, low-level attacks and improvements needed in operational procedures.[271]

Several approaches have been developed to expedite and automate the analysis of audit data: (1) the creation of profiles for "normal" system and user behavior, (2) the definition of signature events that represent known attack sequences, (3) anomaly or pattern detection, (4) the use of attack heuristics, and (5) behavior-based models. Each approach has strengths and weaknesses and provides a different perspective from which to conduct the analysis. As a result, when practical, it is preferable to analyze audit information using more than one approach. Today there are many tools available that provide graphical displays of audit information, which facilitate its rapid analysis.

An organization needs to manage its audit function to ensure that the information of interest is captured, instead of a lot of information that is not of interest. To start, the type of events to be captured needs to be defined.[20] Some events are of interest; others are not. It is neither logical nor practical to capture audit information for all events. Thresholds must be defined for events that are of interest.[20] For example, how may times is an access control or identification and authentication operation rejected before an alarm is triggered? If this happens once, probably not. But, if this happens twenty times in five minutes, most likely a significant event threshold has been exceeded. Rules need to be established for what audit information is captured and when it is captured.[20] That is, are all audit functions continuously invoked? Or, are various audit functions turned on and off based on some operational scenario or other triggering event? Parameters that are used for defining "normal" profiles of system and user behavior, signature events, attack sequences, etc. should be kept current. If not, the audit function may miss some significant events or lock on to benign events by mistake.

To recognize significant events, an audit function must capture information about[20, 271]:

- The type of event that took place
- When it happened, including complete system date and time stamps
- What resources were involved and their logical and physical addresses
- The initiators of the event (users or processes)
- The configuration or parameters that triggered the event
- The severity of the event (indeterminate, catastrophic, critical, major, minor, warning)

Events must be traceable to preceding and succeeding events in the same execution thread. Events need to be attributable directly to the user who initiated the event, or indirectly to the user who initiated the process that triggered the event.[20] This linkage enforces personnel security accountability requirements. An alarm is generated and dispatched to designated primary and secondary recipients whenever a potential or imminent security compromise is expected, or an actual security compromise is confirmed. The recipients include a combination of human users, such as security management staff, and security appliances that are configured to take automatic protective action. Depending on the nature, extent, and severity of the alarm, the response can vary from a simple warning, to terminating a process, disabling a service, dropping or blocking a network connection, closing a user account, or quarantining a subset of IT resources.

Real-time audit data is needed to facilitate preventive and corrective action. Audit data is used in the short term to support post-event analysis. Audit data is used in the long term to demonstrate regulatory compliance, enforce accountability requirements, and substantiate legal actions. For all these reasons, it is essential that audit data be captured and stored securely. Audit data is often the second target of an orchestrated attack, the intent being to cover up all traces of the attack method and source. Due to the significance of the decisions made and action taken, it is of paramount importance to ensure the integrity of audit data while it is active and after it is stored. Audit data should be protected from unauthorized access to prevent (1) masking current events that should never trigger an alarm, and (2) analysis of historical information to facilitate a masquerade attack.[156] Access to audit data should be restricted to authorized users. A thorough analysis should be conducted to ensure that these access controls cannot be bypassed. Audit data should be exempt from modification at all times. If erroneous data is captured, it should be left intact and an annotation made elsewhere. In many industrial sectors, legal requirements define how long audit data must be kept. Senior management should establish corporate policies, consistent with legal requirements, that define how long audit data is kept online and offline in backups and archives, how quickly offline audit data can be retrieved, and the physical and IT security controls that will prevent unauthorized access, alteration, or destruction.

There are several implementation considerations to evaluate when deploying an audit capability. An audit function consumes system resources, such as processor time to identify and capture auditable events, online and offline storage to record parameters associated with events of interest, and network bandwidth to transmit the audit data captured, reported, and stored. Thus, care should be exercised when determining what events to record and how frequently they should be recorded. Otherwise, IT assets may become overwhelmed with resource requests from the audit function, so much so that all other processes are blocked or delayed. A determination must be made about the interval at which audit data should be archived and overwritten. Another decision is whether or not a separate audit trail should be used to capture events from IT security control and protection system functions, to facilitate rapid identification of significant events and enhance data integrity.

A final consideration concerns privacy issues. Depending on what information is captured, what it is used for, how it is captured, who has access to the information, and who the information is released to, there may be an inherent conflict between the implementation of an audit capability and privacy legislation. Some common examples include auditing employees' Internet usage or monitoring or recording their telephone conversations. These concerns are raised because of the potential for the information to be taken out of context and misused. A case in point is the privacy concerns linked to the use of RFID tags in employee badges, driver's licenses, passports, Easy Passes for tollways, and smart cards for subways. In such scenarios, it would be easy to compile information about where a person is, what he is doing, and, with cell phones and VoIP, what he is saying 24 hours a day.

The following metrics can be used to measure the resilience of an organization's implementation of an audit capability. In particular, these metrics measure:

- How well and how thoroughly an audit capability has been implemented throughout the IT infrastructure
- Whether the implementation of the audit capability is consistent with asset criticality and system risk
- How well the security audit function is managed
- The extent and nature of audit function failures experienced, and how this has contributed to the overall pattern of security incidents

By asset criticality, percentage of IT assets that have or are covered by a robust audit capability: 2.3.10.1

   a. Percentage of IT assets that are covered by more than one type of audit mechanism

By asset criticality, percentage of IT assets for which audit data is captured and reported: 2.3.10.2

   a. Locally
   b. Regionally
   c. Enterprisewide

By asset criticality, percentage of IT assets for which audit data can easily be sent to a centralized security audit management function: 2.3.10.3

   a. Locally
   b. Regionally
   c. Enterprisewide

By asset criticality, percentage of IT assets for which audit data can easily be merged with data from other audit mechanisms: 2.3.10.4

   a. Locally
   b. Regionally
   c. Enterprisewide

By asset criticality, distribution of audit mechanisms by type of IT asset:
2.3.10.5

 a. Operating systems
 b. System utilities
 c. Software applications
 d. Shared IT resources
 e. Single-user IT resources
 f. Mobile devices
 g. LAN
 h. WAN
 i. LAN/WAN interfaces
 j. Internet access points
 k. Other external interfaces

By asset criticality, percentage of IT assets for which the audit capability
supports: 2.3.10.6

 a. Initiating proactive preventive action in real-time
 b. Initiating reactive corrective action in real-time
 c. Enforcement of personnel security accountability requirements
 d. Post-event analysis to derive "lessons learned"
 e. Claims made by the organization during legal action about misuse,
    misappropriation, or destruction of IT assets
 f. Demonstration of regulatory compliance
 g. Linking sequences of events and not just identifying isolated events

Speed and effectiveness of enterprisewide audit capability: 2.3.10.7

 a. Time it takes to report a significant event that occurred in one location
    to the local, regional, and enterprisewide security audit management
    function
 b. Time it takes to report a significant event that occurred in multiple
    locations within a region to the local, regional, and enterprisewide
    security audit management function
 c. Time it takes to report a significant event that occurred in multiple
    locations throughout the IT infrastructure to the local, regional, and
    enterprisewide security audit management function
 d. Time it takes to associate audit data from different sources as belonging
    to the same significant event thread
 e. How quickly thresholds and other parameters for monitoring significant
    events can be changed

By asset criticality, percentage of IT assets for which the audit capability
distinguishes: 2.3.10.8

 a. Potential security violations
 b. Imminent security violations
 c. Actual security violations

Frequency with which the following items are routinely reviewed and reaffirmed or updated: 2.3.10.9

    a. The types of events to be audited
    b. The definition of thresholds for significant events
    c. Conditions for enabling and disabling each type of audit function
    d. Normal system and user activity profiles
    e. Definitions of signature events that represent known attack sequences
    f. Anomaly and pattern detection schemes
    g. Attack heuristics
    h. Behavior-based models

Integrity of online and offline audit data: 2.3.10.10
    a. Percentage of audit data sources that have been tested this reporting period to ensure that access controls cannot be bypassed
    b. Percentage of audit data sources that have been tested this reporting period to ensure that the audit data is accurate and complete
    c. Percentage of audit data sources that have been tested this reporting period to ensure that audit data cannot be accidentally or intentionally corrupted
    d. Percentage of audit data sources that have been tested this reporting period to ensure that physical security controls used to protect audit data work as specified
    e. Distribution by type and severity of errors found, this reporting period and the previous three reporting periods

By information sensitivity, percentage of audit functions that have been designed to operate in compliance with privacy regulations and policies.
             2.3.10.11

Number and percentage of security incidents, by incident severity, this reporting period and the previous three reporting periods, related to: 2.3.10.12
    a. Incorrect, incomplete, missing, or compromised audit data
    b. Failure of an audit function
    c. Faulty implementation of an audit function
    d. The ability to bypass an audit function
    e. Lack of an audit capability
    f. A combination of two or more of the above

Percentage of systems for which event and activity logs are monitored and reviewed in accordance with policy, by system risk and asset criticality.[105]
             2.3.10.13

Percentage of systems for which audit log size and retention duration have been specified and implemented in accordance with legal and policy requirements, by system risk and asset criticality.[105]   2.3.10.14

Availability

The term "availability" is known to most security engineers through the confidentiality, integrity, and availability model — the need for IT resources to be available when needed. But what does availability really mean in reference to securing the IT infrastructure enterprisewide? And why is the absence of availability of such concern? Availability is a security goal that generates the requirement for protection against (1) intentional or accidental attempts to perform unauthorized deletion of data or otherwise cause a denial of service or data, and (2) unauthorized use of system resources.[50] Availability is the property that data, information systems, and communication networks are accessible and usable upon demand by an authorized person.[80] Availability reflects the ability of an item (under combined aspects of its reliability, maintainability, and supportability) to perform its required function at a stated instant in time or over a stated period of time.[197] Availability is an objective measurement indicating the rate at which systems, data, and other resources are operational and accessible when needed, despite accidental and intentional subsystem outages and environmental disruptions.[156] Availability implies that IT assets are not just available for use, but that they are functioning correctly and are able to meet performance requirements for throughput, capacity, response time, processing load, number of concurrent users, etc. Availability implies a normal mode of operations; that is, all systems are go. The terms "reliability" and "availability" are often confused, and hence it is important to clarify the distinctions. Reliability refers to the ability of a system or component to correctly perform its function under certain conditions in a specified operational environment for a stated period of time. Availability is a measurement indicating the rate at which systems, data, and other resources are operational and accessible when needed, despite accidental and intentional outages and other disruptions. Availability is an outcome of reliability and a reflection of integrity.

A lack of availability means some portion of the IT infrastructure is not operating in a normal mode of operations — it has entered a failure mode. The system or service is down and is either not available at all or available in some diminished capacity. The severity of the consequences of a lack of availability can range from a nuisance (slow e-mail) for a routine system to catastrophic for a critical system or service (loss of a telecommunications network for an air traffic control system). The nature of the consequences of a lack of availability varies by industrial sector and can include an extreme financial loss or a major safety impact.

Availability is defined as[153]:

$$A_i = \text{MTBF}/(\text{MTBF} + \text{MTTR})$$

where
MTBF = Mean time between failures
MTTR = Mean time to repair

A point of clarification should be made here. Some system components can be repaired and others cannot. Non-repairable items are replaced. MTBF is used for repairable items, while mean time to failure (MTTF) is used for non-repairable items. MTBF is the ratio of the mean value of the length of time between consecutive failures, computed as the ratio of the cumulative observed time to the number of failures under stated conditions, for a stated period of time in the life of an item.[197] MTBF is expressed as[197]:

$$MTBF = \text{Total time/Number of failures}$$

MTTF is the ratio of cumulative time to the total number of failures during the period, under stated conditions for a stated period in the life of an item.[197] MTTR, on the other hand, is the total maintenance time divided by the total number of corrective maintenance actions during a given period of time.[197]

There are three variations of the availability calculation: (1) inherent availability, (2) operational availability, and (3) achieved availability The three availability calculations measure availability differently because the measurements are taken at discrete points during the life of a system using diverse primitives. With the minor modifications shown below in the list of metrics, the operational and achieved availability calculations can be used to measure the operational resilience of a single security appliance, an information system security architecture for a single system or network, a facility or campus, or the entire IT infrastructure. The definition of the measurement boundaries determines the scope of the availability measurement.

Inherent availability is the estimated availability while a system or subsystem is still in the development phase.[197] The same calculation cited above is used, but it is a prediction rather than an actual measurement. Inherent availability is also referred to as potential availability.

Operational availability is the observed availability following initial system deployment.[197] Operational availability is also referred to as actual availability. Operational availability is expressed as[197]:

$$A_0 = MTBMA/(MTBMA + MDT)$$

where
MTBMA = Mean time between maintenance actions (preventive and corrective)
MDT   = Mean down time

Achieved availability is the observed availability once a system has reached a steady state operationally.[197] Achieved availability is also referred to as final availability. Achieved availability is expressed as[197]:

$$A_a = MTBMA/(MTBMA + MMT)$$

where
MTBMA = Mean time between maintenance actions (prevention and corrective)
MMT   = Mean maintenance action time
       ((Number of corrective maintenance actions per 1000 hours ×
         MTTR for corrective maintenance) +
       (Number of preventive maintenance actions per 1000 hours ×
         MTTR for preventive maintenance))/
       (Number of corrective maintenance actions +
         Number of preventive maintenance actions)

Availability requirements should be determined long before a product or system is deployed. Allocate availability requirements across the IT infrastructure based on the criticality of each IT asset. Specify availability requirements in service contracts, as for telecommunications. Tell the vendors the availability requirements they need to meet. These requirements may vary by time of day, time of month, etc. This lets the vendors know what is expected of them, and they can plan and cost their services accordingly. When contractual availability requirements are not met, financial penalties should be imposed. Availability requirements should also be specified for COTS products. Require vendors to submit MTBF, MTTF, and MTTR values as part of their proposals. Then use the metrics at the end of this section to monitor whether or not availability goals are being met and what corrective action needs to be taken.

A variety of techniques can be used to enhance availability, such as:

- Redundancy
- Diversity
- Fault tolerance
- Block recovery
- Dynamic reconfiguration/self healing
- Rollback

Redundancy is a technique employed to increase hardware reliability and system availability.[197, 285] IEEE Std. 610.12-1990 defines redundancy as:

> The presence of auxiliary components in a system to perform the same functions as other elements for the purpose of preventing or recovering from failure.

In this context, identical components are used to perform identical functions. Redundancy, and the increased hardware reliability and system availability it provides, are important for several reasons. The historical computer security model focused on confidentiality, integrity, and availability; without reliability, none of these can be achieved. To be effective, security features must function reliably. To do so, they are dependent on the reliable operation of hardware components, communications equipment, etc. If a hardware or communications component is not reliable, security features can be bypassed and defeated. For example, if firewall hardware is subject to intermittent faults, unauthorized users and processes may slip through. Unreliable hardware and communications equipment can yield incorrect results. Transient memory or CPU faults can lead to data corruption and compromise. Unreliable hardware and communications equipment may cause a critical function, service, or mission not to be performed on time, or at all; this could have severe security and safety consequences. Reliability is essential in achieving security goals and should not be overlooked. As Arbaugh et al.[302] succinctly state:

> *All secure systems assume the integrity of the underlying [hardware and] firmware. They usually cannot tell when that assumption is incorrect. This is a serious security problem.*

That is, these assumptions need to be backed up by engineering facts.

Hardware redundancy is implemented three ways: (1) active, (2) standby, and (3) monitored. Active redundancy utilizes multiple identical components operating simultaneously to prevent, detect, or recover from failures. The redundant components operate in parallel. If a fault is detected in the primary unit, control is switched to the redundant or "hot standby" unit. The transition can be automatic or manual. Standby redundancy also utilizes multiple identical components. However, the redundant or "cold standby" units are not switched on until a fault is detected in the primary unit. Monitored redundancy, often referred to as m-out-of-n redundancy, is a variation of active redundancy. This method monitors the outputs of the parallel components. If discrepancies are found, voting logic is activated (hence the name m-out-of-n) to determine which output is correct and what action should be taken (e.g., switching to a new primary component).[285] Monitored redundancy is frequently used in PLCs as triple modular redundancy (TMR).

There are several issues to consider when implementing redundancy. Active redundancy permits a faster transition — the redundant unit is already powered-up and initialized; however, this unit consumes additional power, space, and weight and has been subjected to the same environmental stresses as the primary unit.[303] Standby redundancy provides a slower transition because of the need to power-up and initialize the system.[285] However, the remaining life of this unit is longer than a hot standby because it has not been stressed.

Trade-off studies conducted early in the architecture and design phase evaluate which option is best for a given application. These studies should ensure that single points of failure are eliminated and that there are no common cause failure modes between redundant units. Redundancy can be implemented anywhere from low-level electronic components to major subsystems or systems. As O'Connor[197] notes:

> *Decisions on when and how to design in redundancy depend upon the criticality of the system or function and must always be balanced against the need to minimize complexity and [development and operational] costs.*

Redundancy is not implemented in software. Because software failures are systematic, all copies of a given version and release of software contain the same faults.[158, 285, 286] Instead, diverse software is implemented. The use of redundancy should be addressed in maintainability and supportability programs, operational procedures, and contingency and disaster recovery plans.

Diversity is a technique employed to enhance integrity by detecting and preventing systematic failures. While diversity does not prevent specification errors, it is useful for uncovering specification ambiguities.[285] Diversity can be implemented in hardware and software.

Software diversity, also referred to as n-version programming, deploys more than one algorithm or component to solve the same problem. The same input is supplied to the n versions, and then the outputs are compared. If they agree, the appropriate action is taken. Depending on the criticality of the application, 100 percent agreement or majority agreement can be implemented.[158] If the results do not agree, error detection and recovery algorithms take control. Diverse software can execute in parallel on different processors or sequentially on the same processor. The first approach increases hardware size, cost, and weight, while the second approach increases processing time.[285] Diversity can be implemented at several stages in the software life cycle:

- Development of diverse designs by independent teams
- Development of diverse source code in two or more different languages
- Generation of diverse object code by two or more different compilers
- Implementation of diverse object code using two or more different linking and loading utilities
- Implementation of two or more different COTS products that perform the same function

Hardware diversity employs multiple different components or modules to perform the same function. This contrasts with hardware redundancy in which multiple units of the same hardware are deployed. To the extent possible, components and modules are chosen that have different rates and types of failures. Diversity can also be implemented in telecommunications networks by having alternate diverse paths for the traffic to follow, should the primary path become unavailable.

The goal of diversity is to decrease the probability of common cause and systematic failures, while increasing the probability of detecting errors. Diversity may complicate supportability issues and synchronization between diverse components operating in parallel. Accordingly, diversity is only implemented for critical and essential functions.

Fault tolerance increases availability by providing continued correct execution in the presence of a limited number of hardware or software faults.[304] As Jajodia[287] notes:

> *Fault tolerance is a natural approach for dealing with information attacks because it is designed to address system loss, compromise, and damage during operation.*

Fault tolerance is a category of techniques that focuses on containing and mitigating the consequences of faults, rather than preventing them. In Chapter 2 we discussed the relationship between errors, faults, and failures. Fault tolerance attempts to prevent a fault from progressing to a failure, which could compromise a system or render it inoperable. Faults provide an opening for possible attacks, especially if the fault condition can be intentionally induced.

There are three types of fault tolerance: (1) hardware, (2) software, and (3) system. As Levi and Agrawala[180] point out, hardware faults are generated by design errors (overload, improper states, etc.) and environmental stresses, which cause physical degradation of materials, while software faults are caused by design errors and runtime errors. However, they note that[180]:

> *One cannot always distinguish hardware from software failures.*
> *...hardware failures can produce identical faulty behavior to that gen-*
> *erated by software. Memory failures are equivalent to software failures*
> *if they occur during instruction fetch-cycles of the processors, generating*
> *an erroneous execution of an instruction. A processor whose program*
> *counter is inappropriately altered produces an out of order execution*
> *of instructions as does a software design error.*

As a result, a combination of hardware, software, and system fault tolerance is needed.

Hardware fault tolerance is usually implemented through redundancy, diversity, power-on tests, built-in test equipment (BITE), and other monitoring functions. The concept is that if a primary component fails, the secondary component will take over and continue normal operations.

Software fault tolerance is usually implemented through block recovery, diversity, error detection and correction, and other techniques. The basic premise of software fault tolerance is that it is nearly impossible to develop software that is 100 percent defect-free; therefore, techniques should be employed to detect and recover from errors while minimizing their consequences. Software fault tolerance should be implemented in software applications, middleware, and operating systems.

System fault tolerance combines hardware and software fault tolerance, with software monitoring the health of both the hardware and the software. System fault tolerance is employed for critical and essential functions. Fault tolerance is an effective method to increase system reliability and availability. It may increase the physical size and weight of a system, which can conflict with specified constraints.

Block recovery is a technique that provides correct functional operation in the presence of one or more errors.[7] Block recovery is implemented to increase the availability and integrity of modules that perform critical functions. For each critical module, primary and secondary modules (employing diversity) are developed. After the primary module executes, but before it performs any critical transactions, an acceptance test is run. This test checks for possible error conditions, exceptions, and variables that are out of range.[285] If no error is detected, normal execution continues. If an error is detected, control is switched to the corresponding secondary module and another acceptance test is run. If no error is detected, normal execution resumes. However, if an error is detected, the system is reset either to a previous (backward block recovery) or future (forward block recovery) known safe/secure state.

In the world of IT, things do not always go as planned. An upgrade here causes an interoperability problem there. A new high-speed interface increases latency, rather than decreasing it. The mandatory transition to an enterprise data dictionary causes a few data elements to be left out. The migration to a new standardized desktop operating environment causes a whole department to be locked out for a week. As a result, recovery is the flip side of availability.

The purpose of recovery mechanisms is to minimize service discontinuities and maximize the availability of IT assets. Recovery mechanisms can be applied to an individual product or component or an entire system, network, or IT infrastructure. Needless to say, the larger the scope of the recovery effort, the more complex and challenging it is. Today there are several approaches to recovery: manual, semi-automatic, and automatic. Very sophisticated approaches to recovery are employed in the telecommunications industry, such as self-healing networks and dynamic reconfiguration. The goal of all these approaches is to return to a known stable secure state as quickly as possible. In fact, the more-proactive techniques may execute a "recovery" beforehand in order to preempt a potential failure.

Successful recovery operations, large or small, require extensive prior planning and analysis. There are different recovery scenarios. A system crashes on a "normal" day and there are no other extenuating circumstances. A system crashes due to an abnormal situation, such as an unplanned power outage. Or, some natural or man-made disaster causes a system to crash. In all three scenarios, a recovery effort is necessary to restore the system to a known stable and secure state. However, how the recovery is executed, what is recovered, and how quickly it is recovered will vary in each of these scenarios. That is why recovery should not be thought of only in terms of recovery efforts following a major disaster. "Normal" recovery efforts may be considerably easier but they are just as important.

Several factors must be considered and several parameters have to be analyzed when planning recovery efforts:

- The specific type of service discontinuities for which recovery efforts need to be planned
- The specific type of recovery effort to by applied to each type of service discontinuity
- Whether the recovery effort should be manual, semi-manual, or automatic
- Who has the authority and responsibility for initiating recovery efforts

First of all, the scope of recovery efforts needs to be bounded. Not all failures are of a sufficient severity that they require immediate recovery. In many instances, routine corrective maintenance will suffice. Second, the method of recovery should be spelled out in detailed operational procedures; the method will vary by type of failure. Third, a decision should be made about the feasibility and acceptability of automatic recovery. In some cases, automatic recovery may be the preferred approach. In other cases, the cost may be prohibitive or automatic recovery may introduce too much risk. Fourth, there needs to be some accountability for recovery efforts. Finally, to ensure the success of recovery efforts, they must be continually practiced and refined. Furthermore, recovery efforts must be coordinated at all levels and locations throughout an organization. Recovery efforts rarely succeed, and may in fact exacerbate the problem, if facility A uses one recovery method, location B uses a second recovery method, and region C uses a third recovery method.

Rollback is a special instance of recovery. Rollback is applied to software systems, in particular to database management systems. It is not possible to roll back telecommunications or hardware transactions. Rollback undoes the last operation or series or operations to return user data to a known secure state. Incorrect, incomplete, or failed transactions may create the need for a rollback.[20] Rollback is similar to backward block recovery. Limits are set on rollback operations in terms of how many previous transactions can be undone. These limits can be based on elapsed time or the number of transactions.[20] The types of transactions to which rollback can be applied must be specified. Usually, this is a small subset of the total possible transaction set. Who has the authority to execute a rollback must be specified, as well as the conditions under which a rollback can be executed. Be sure to exercise extreme caution when specifying the rules for rollback — what better way is there to cover up an unauthorized transaction than to execute rollback and cover up the fact that it occurred? In the wrong hands, rollback can be a very convenient feature for malicious insider attacks.

The following metrics can be used to measure different aspects of availability in relation to achieving and sustaining the operational resilience of an IT infrastructure.

Operational security availability: 2.3.11.1

$$A_0 = MTBMA/(MTBMA + MDT)^{197}$$

where

MTBMA = Mean time between security maintenance actions (preventive and corrective)
MDT   = Mean down time due to security failures

Achieved security availability: 2.3.11.2

$$A_a = MTBMA/(MTBMA + MMT)^{197}$$

where

MTBMA = Mean time between security maintenance actions (preventive and corrective)
MMT   = Mean security maintenance action time
            ((Number of corrective security maintenance actions per 1000 hours ×
              MTTR for corrective security maintenance) +
            (Number of preventive security maintenance actions per 1000 hours ×
              MTTR for preventive security maintenance))/
            (Number of corrective security maintenance actions +
              Number of preventive security maintenance actions)

Percentage (%) of operational time that critical services were unavailable (as seen by users and customers).[105]   2.3.11.3

Percentage (%) of IT assets for which availability: 2.3.11.4
   a. Requirements have been specified
   b. Is routinely monitored, measured, and reported

By asset criticality, percentage (%) of contracts that state availability requirements and impose penalties when they are not met: 2.3.11.5

    a. Services contracts
    b. Supplier contracts

Percentage (%) of critical and essential IT assets for which redundancy is
implemented: 2.3.11.6

    a. Active redundancy
    b. Standby redundancy
    c. Monitored redundancy

Percentage (%) of critical and essential IT assets and services for which diversity
is implemented: 2.3.11.7

    a. Hardware
    b. Software
    c. Telecommunications equipment
    d. Telecommunications paths

Percentage (%) of critical and essential IT assets and services for which fault
tolerance is implemented: 2.3.11.8

    a. Hardware
    b. Software
    c. Application systems
    d. Telecommunications networks

Percentage (%) of critical and essential IT assets for which block recovery is
implemented.   2.3.11.9

By asset criticality, percentage (%) of IT assets for which recovery procedures
have been defined and implemented.   2.3.11.10

Number of successful and unsuccessful attempts to execute recovery this
reporting period, by type of service discontinuity: 2.3.11.11

    a. Average time to execute a recovery
    b. Distribution by recovery method: manual, semi-automatic, automatic

Percentage (%) of systems with critical information assets or functions that
have been backed up in accordance with policy, by asset criticality.[105]

                                                        2.3.11.12

Percentage (%) of systems with critical and essential information assets or
functions where restoration from a stored backup has been successfully demonstrated this reporting period, by asset criticality.[105]   2.3.11.13

Percentage (%) of backup media stored off-site in secure storage, by information sensitivity and asset criticality.[105]   2.3.11.14

Number of successful and unsuccessful attempts to execute a rollback this
reporting period, by type of operation rolled back.[20]   2.3.11.15

Frequency with which rollback and recovery operations are practiced, by IT asset sensitivity: 2.3.11.16

    a. Date of most recent practice drill
    b. Distribution by type of error found

By asset criticality, percentage (%) of increase or decrease in availability this reporting period compared to the previous three reporting periods. 2.3.11.17

By asset criticality, number and percentage (%) of availability techniques implemented that have been tested this reporting period and were found to work as specified: 2.3.11.18

    a. Redundancy
    b. Diversity
    c. Fault tolerance
    d. Block recovery
    e. Recovery
    f. Rollback

Error, Exception, and Incident Handling

From the beginning of the computer age in 1943 to the present, computer hardware, operating systems, utilities, software applications, and data communications networks have never functioned 100 percent correctly 100 percent of the time. Neither will that lofty goal be achieved at any time in the foreseeable future. One of the earliest documented cases of a computer defect, and certainly the most famous, occurred in 1945 and involved the Mark II computer. As often happens, a program did not execute as expected. Dr. Grace Hopper discovered that the source of the problem was Relay #70 in Panel F.[308] The "problem" was a moth, which caused the relay to malfunction.[308] Although the problem was in the operational environment, the terms "software bug" and "debugging" were born and took root.[308]

As discussed in Chapter 2, humans introduce errors into products, processes, and operational systems through errors of omission (something that was not done) and errors of commission (something that was done wrong). The manifestation of an error is referred to as a fault — a defect that results in an incorrect step, process, data value, mode, or state.[125] A failure results whenever a fault condition is exercised. Humans make mistakes, even under the best of conditions. As a result, errors are introduced into IT equipment, systems, and networks, and always will be. Errors can be introduced accidentally or intentionally at any point during the life of a system, network, or component. Errors can be introduced while specifying the requirements for an IT system or network. In fact, several studies conclude that approximately 80 percent of the defects found in software systems after they are deployed can be traced back to wrong or missing requirements.[158, 285, 286, 298] Errors can be introduced when translating requirements into a design and when converting a design into an operational system. Errors can be introduced when interfacing a system to external systems and networks. Like the moth found in the Mark II, errors can be introduced in the operational environment. Most electronic equipment is very sensitive to power fluctuations, temperature and humidity extremes, dust, vibration, EMI/RFI, and changes in the operational profile and duty cycle. Furthermore, errors can be introduced by end users, system administrators, and maintenance staff. These concerns are equally applicable to COTS and custom-developed software. COTS just means someone else developed the software and they have the same opportunities to introduce errors. After all, most of the so-called never-ending "vulnerabilities" in COTS software products are nothing more than errors that are the result of sloppy software engineering.

The telecommunications industry has made extensive use of error, exception, and incident handling logic for several decades. Error detection and correction algorithms are used to increase data integrity during the transmission of data within and among networks. Error detection and correction algorithms examine data to determine if any data was accidentally corrupted or lost, and to discover if any unauthorized changes were intentionally made to the data.[294] These errors are compensated for by self-correcting codes at the receiving end or requests for retransmission. Common error detection and correction algorithms include longitudinal and vertical parity checks, Hamming codes, convolutional codes, recurrent codes, checksums, cyclical redundancy checks (CRCs), digital signatures, and hash functions.[294] The same principles can be applied to ensure secure operation of an IT infrastructure.

Given that errors, and the faults and potential failures they spawn, are a constant, it behooves responsible security engineers to take action rather than sitting back and helplessly waiting for the next vulnerability announcement and patch release. The reason security engineers are paid the big bucks is because they know how to prevent, control, contain, and minimize the effects of faults, so that a system or network remains in a known secure state at all times. Let us face it, anyone can write buggy software — there is plenty evidence worldwide to prove that fact. However, it takes special talents to neutralize the impact of defective hardware or software. These talents need to be applied to the entire threat control chronology[159]:

- *Anticipate and Prevent.* Anticipate the different ways in which a system, network, or component could fail and take proactive action to prevent or mitigate the failure
- *Detect.* Implement a robust capability to detect erroneous inputs, outputs, modes, and states before they cause a failure
- *Characterize.* Characterize and classify different types of fault conditions so that the appropriate corrective action can be determined
- *Respond and Contain Consequences.* Based on the event characterization, take the specified action to isolate, contain, and neutralize the consequences of the fault condition on the overall operation of the IT infrastructure
- *Recover.* Return to normal operations. If that is not possible, transition to a controlled failure mode (fail safe, fail secure, or fail operational). Conduct post-event analysis to derive lessons learned to prevent recurrence of the same or similar events.

Many organizations spend the vast majority, if not all, of their resources on responding to and recovering from incidents. That approach hardly meets the requirements of due diligence, as required by the regulations discussed in Chapter 3 — neither does it meet the test of common sense, as the biggest bang for the buck is found at the beginning of the threat control chronology: anticipate and prevent. All five activities of the threat control chronology are necessary; however, the most cost-effective solutions occur in the earlier activities. As the saying goes, "an ounce of prevention is worth a pound of cure."

Fault conditions can be present anywhere in the IT infrastructure and at any layer of the ISO/OSI Reference Model. Faults can exist in hardware or software, at the interfaces between different systems, components, and networks. Erroneous inputs and outputs can trigger fault conditions, as can transactions that occur too fast, too slow, out of sequence, or at an excessive volume. The key to error, exception, and incident handling is to identify (1) what could go wrong and (2) what type of corrective action should be taken in each instance. Equipping the IT infrastructure to respond correctly to anomalous conditions and events is a key component of resilience. Robustness and survivability do not happen by chance. Rather, robustness and survivability are the result of thorough planning, analysis, and design: (1) all possible error conditions are accounted for, (2) error handling paths are well defined, and (3) a graceful exit out of an error condition can be executed.[197] To do so, a system's behavior and properties must be characterized, along with normal, abnormal, and illegal modes and states.[112] Taking the time to define "must work functions" (MWFs) and "must not work functions" (MNWFs) can be a very enlightening and useful exercise upon which to build error, exception, and incident handling logic. Standard practice is to identify all possible known error conditions that could occur anywhere throughout the IT infrastructure; for example, an input parameter is too low or too high, an address is out of range, a request to transition to an illegal state, a framing error, a packet collision, an unauthorized operating system call, memory conflicts between COTS packages, etc.[17, 28, 112] The list includes automatic process-to-process errors, as well as user and operator errors. Then for each unique erroneous condition, the specific action to be taken is defined; such as rejecting the input, assuming a default value or state, requesting packet retransmission, executing a rollback, terminating or restarting a process or session, etc.

There are three parts to the logic of error, exception, and incident handling:

1. *Normal operations:* status parameter is within legal range; continue normal operations.
2, *Known error, exception and incident:* illegal status parameter is identified as a known error, exception, or incident. For each specific situation, execute predefined error, exception, or incident handling procedure.
3. *Unknown, undefined, irrevocable error, exception and incident:* status parameter does not match any known legal or illegal values. Assume a predefined default secure state, then transition to a controlled failure mode if needed.

System status is continuously monitored at selected critical checkpoints. If the status parameters meet certain conditions, normal operations are allowed to continue. On the other hand, if the status parameters do not meet certain conditions, an erroneous condition is present. The status parameters are then compared to the list of known errors, exceptions, and incidents. When a match is found, predefined error handling procedures are invoked. If no match is found, an unknown or undefined error condition has been encountered. Rather than doing nothing and letting the system fall into an unstable and insecure state, have the system assume a predefined secure state; then, if necessary, transition to a controlled failure mode. The third part of error, exception, and incident handling logic is critical. No matter how hard an organization tries, it is not possible to identify 100 percent of the potential erroneous conditions. This is especially true when concurrent, overlapping, or sequential faults are experienced.[112] The otherwise clause allows the behavior of these unknown and undefined faults to be controlled, leaving the IT infrastructure in a known stable and secure state. Furthermore, some error conditions are irrevocable. In this case, the only option to maintain the system in a known secure state is to transition to a controlled failure mode. It is best to acknowledge and plan for this eventuality up front.

Error, exception, and incident handling logic can be implemented within hardware, between hardware and software components, within custom developed software, between custom and COTS software, between systems and networks, and within networks. It is not practical or logical to monitor everything; instead, critical checkpoints are identified. This is where the audit function comes into play. Because of the prevalence of errors in COTS products and conflicts between COTS products, especially if they are from different vendors, it is wise to employ error, exception, and incident handling scripts between COTS products to monitor and mediate their interactions. This will definitely enhance the integrity of the operational control flows and the data control flows. By distributing error, exception, and incident handling logic throughout the IT infrastructure, errors are contained and mitigated locally, while opportunities for fault propagation are minimized. This technique is referred to as creating hardware error confinement areas (HECAs) and software error confinement areas (SECAs).[203]

The duration, distribution, and severity of an error, exception, or incident will impact the nature of the corrective action.[37] The preplanned response to a potential, imminent, or actual erroneous condition can be automatic (the system takes care of itself), semi-automatic (a combination of automatic and manual processes are involved), or manual (human action is required to correct the situation). Error, exception, and incident handling procedures, automatic and manual, should be tested regularly to verify their accuracy and speed.[52]

A decision must be made about whether or not to inform stakeholders when error, exception, and incident handling routines are invoked. If the erroneous condition was deliberately triggered by an insider attack, that would not be wise. On the other hand, if stakeholders are about to transmit very sensitive data, it might be a good idea to let them know to wait a few minutes. This is something that should be analyzed and decided on a case-by-case basis.

The following metrics can be used to measure the resilience of an organization's implementation of error, exception, and incident handling. In particular, these metrics measure:

- How well and how thoroughly error, exception, and incident handling has been implemented throughout the IT infrastructure
- Whether the implementation of error, exception, and incident handling is consistent with asset criticality and system risk
- The extent and nature of error, exception, and incident handling failures experienced, and how this has contributed to the overall pattern of security incidents

By asset criticality, percentage of IT assets that have a robust error, exception, and incident handling capability.   2.3.12.1

By asset criticality, percentage of IT assets for which robust error, exception, and incident handling is implemented: 2.3.12.2
    a. Within operating systems and utilities
    b. Within custom software applications
    c. Within COTS software applications
    d. Within hardware components
    e. Between hardware and software components
    f. Between operating systems and software applications
    g. Between different COTS software applications
    h. Between COTS and custom software applications
    i. Within networks
    j. At interfaces to external systems and networks
    k. Such that it is able to detect erroneous conditions in the operational environment

By asset criticality, percentage of IT assets that have a robust error, exception, and incident handling capability that: 2.3.12.3
    a. Defines normal system behavior, modes, states, and parameters
    b. Defines abnormal and illegal behavior, modes, states, and parameters and the specific corrective action to be taken for each
    c. Traps unknown and undefined erroneous conditions and specifies the appropriate corrective action to be taken

By asset criticality and asset type: 2.3.12.4
    a. Time it takes to initiate proactive preventive action once an error, exception, or incident has been identified
    b. Time it takes to initiate reactive remedial action once an error, exception, or incident has been identified

By asset criticality, percentage of IT assets for which error, exception, and incident handling capabilities cover the entire threat control chronology.
                                       2.3.12.5

By asset criticality, percentage of critical checkpoints throughout the IT infrastructure for which error, exception, and incident handling has been implemented.   2.3.12.6

By asset criticality, percentage of IT assets for which error, exception, and incident handling is implemented locally through the use of HECAs and SECAs.
                                                                              2.3.12.7

By asset criticality, percentage of error, exception, and incident handling mechanisms that have been tested this reporting period and were found to work as specified under normal and abnormal conditions: 2.3.12.8
   a. Distribution by type and severity of errors found

Number and percentage of security incidents, by incident severity, this reporting period and the previous three reporting periods, related to: 2.3.12.9
   a. Failure of an error, exception, or incident handling mechanism
   b. Faulty implementation of error, exception, or incident handling
   c. The ability to bypass error, exception, or incident handling mechanisms
   d. Lack of an error, exception, or incident handling mechanism
   e. A combination of two or more of the above

By severity, percentage of errors, exceptions, and incidents for which post-event analysis was conducted.   2.3.12.10

Number, operational impact, and business impact, including damage and loss, of all security incidents this reporting period, by type of incident.[105, 143]
                                                                              2.3.12.11

Number of vulnerability mapping/scanning exercises conducted this reporting period, by system risk.[143]   2.3.12.12

Percentage of errors, exceptions, and incidents that were managed in accordance with established policies, procedures, and processes.[105]   2.3.12.13

Percentage of externally exposed systems with an IDS/IPS capability, by system risk.[169]   2.3.12.14

Percentage and number of successful external network penetrations this reporting period, by information sensitivity.[169]   2.3.12.15

Fail Safe/Fail Secure, Fail Operational/Fail Soft/Graceful Degradation/Degraded Mode Operations

The conglomerate of logical and physical devices that is referred to as an IT infrastructure is not always well-behaved. Not all of the "children" have learned how to "play well together" inside the family or out in the neighborhood. Some of the "adults" get cranky at times also. As a result, it is sometimes necessary to implement a timeout and shut down everything. The entire IT infrastructure or some logical or geographical subset of it may need to be shut down. The need to perform a shutdown may be known and scheduled in advance, so that all stakeholders and operational staff have time to prepare.

Or, the need to perform a shutdown may arise suddenly without warning. In either situation, it is essential to perform the shutdown in a methodical manner to ensure that all IT and information assets remain in a known secure state throughout the procedure, and again afterward when systems and services are restored. This does not happen by chance; rather, a lot of planning, coordination, and analysis are involved.

There are two primary approaches to shutting down an IT infrastructure, each of which is used for different purposes and in different scenarios: (1) the systems or networks can be completely shut down, or (2) the systems or networks can be partially shut down, with a minimum of services remaining operational. The former is referred to as fail safe/fail secure, while the latter is known by several names: fail operational, fail soft, graceful degradation, and degraded mode operations. On occasion, a variation of these two states is executed, whereby a fail operational state is assumed for a temporary period until some critical activity is completed, and then a transition is made to a fail safe/fail secure state. In either case, the intent is to enter a controlled failure mode. Controlled failure modes are implemented through a combination of system design and integration practices and operational procedures.

Fail safe emphasizes the elimination or mitigation of potential safety hazards associated with a shutdown, while fail secure emphasizes the elimination or mitigation of potential security compromises associated with a shutdown. Fail safe/fail secure is defined as:

> **Fail safe/fail secure:** (1) a design wherein the component or system, should it fail, will fail to a safe/secure condition[307]; (2) the system can be brought to a safe/secure condition or state by shutting it down; for example, the shutdown of a nuclear reactor by a monitoring and protection system.[298]

Fail safe/fail secure are techniques that ensure that a system remains in a known safe and secure state following an irrecoverable failure. To fail safe or fail secure means that a component automatically places itself in a known safe or secure mode or state in the event of a failure. In many instances, known safe or secure default values are assumed. Then the system is brought to a known safe/secure mode/state by shutting down.

To fail operational means that a system or component continues to provide limited critical functionality in the event of a failure. In some instances, a system cannot simply shut down; it must continue to provide some level of service if it is not to be hazardous, such as an aircraft flight control system.[298] Fail operational, fail soft, graceful degradation, and degraded mode operations all refer to the same concept. These terms are defined as follows:

> **Fail operational:** (1) maintaining the availability of the more critical system functions, despite failures, by dropping the less critical functions[7]; (2) selective termination of non-essential processes, when a hardware or software failure is determined to be imminent.[100] Also referred to as fail soft, graceful degradation, and degraded mode operations.

The purpose of degraded mode operations — or graceful degradation as it is sometimes called — is to ensure that critical system functionality is maintained in the presence of one or more failures. Critical and essential functions can rarely just cease operation in response to an anomalous event, suspected attack, or compromise. Instead, some minimum level of service must be maintained. Degraded mode operations allow priorities to be established for maintaining critical and essential functions, while dropping routine ones, should insufficient resources be available to support them all. The total system (hardware, software, and communications equipment) is considered when planning for degraded mode operations; often, a (partial) system reconfiguration is necessary.[285]

The prioritized set of critical and essential functions should be specified during the requirements analysis and design phases, if not sooner. Criteria for transitioning to degraded mode operations is specified. The maximum time interval during which a system is allowed to remain in degraded mode operations is also defined, along with the action to be taken when this time limit is reached. Degraded mode operations should include provisions for the following items, at a minimum:

- Notifying operational staff and users that the system has transitioned to degraded mode operations
- Error, exception, and incident handling
- Logging and generation of warning messages and alarms
- Reduction of processing load (execute core functionality only)
- Masking nonessential interrupts
- Signals to external resources to slow down inputs
- Trace of system states to facilitate post-event analysis
- Specification of the conditions required to return to normal operations

Degraded mode operations provides an intermediate state between full operation and system shutdown; hence the name graceful degradation. This allows the minimum priority system functionality to be maintained until corrective action can be taken. Degraded mode operations is a preventive strategy in which decisions are made beforehand about how to respond to a potential crisis situation. Without this prior planning and preparation, the ensuing system degradation and compromise will be most ungraceful indeed.

Fail safe/fail secure and fail operational ensure that a system responds predictably to failures by making proactive design decisions. The first step is to identify all possible failure modes. This is done by developing transaction paths and using analysis techniques such as fault tree analysis (FTA), failure mode effects analysis (FMEA), and HAZOP studies, as discussed in Chapter 2. Next, the appropriate response to each failure is specified so that the system will remain in a known safe/secure state. The correct response to one failure may be to fail safe/secure, while the correct response to another failure in the same system may be to fail operational. The operational mode/state will influence the choice of a controlled failure mode.

Fail safe/fail secure and fail operational designs should be implemented for all critical and essential functions at the hardware, software, system, and network levels. This is essential for maintaining system integrity. Fault tolerance prevents a limited number of faults from progressing to failures. Those that cannot or are not expected to be handled sufficiently by fault tolerance must be dealt with by fail safe/fail secure and fail operational designs and operational procedures. Combining fault tolerance with fail safe/fail secure and fail operational designs is one way to enhance the resilience of IT security controls. Planning for controlled failure modes should be a major ingredient of operational procedures and contingency plans.

The following metrics can be used to measure the resilience of an organization's implementation of a fail safe/fail secure and fail operational capability. In particular, these metrics measure:

- How well and how thoroughly fail safe/fail secure and fail operational modes have been implemented throughout the IT infrastructure
- Whether the implementation of fail safe/fail secure and fail operational modes is consistent with asset criticality and system risk
- The extent and nature of fail safe/fail secure and fail operational failures experienced

By asset criticality and system risk, percentage of assets, systems, and networks for which failure modes have been thoroughly identified.   2.3.13.1

By asset criticality, system risk, and failure mode severity, percentage of identified failure modes that are not mitigated by fault tolerance, for which fail safe/fail secure and/or fail operational controls and procedures have been implemented.   2.3.13.2

By asset criticality and system risk, percentage of systems and networks for which controls and procedures are in place to execute controlled failure modes on short notice: 2.3.13.3
   a. Fail safe/fail secure
   b. Fail operational
   c. Both

By asset criticality and system risk, percentage of controlled failure mode implementations that address all sources of failures: 2.3.13.4
   a. Hardware failures
   b. Software failures
   c. Network failures

By asset criticality and system risk, percentage of controlled failure mode implementations that define or perform: 2.3.13.5
   a. The criteria for transitioning to a fail safe/fail secure or fail operational mode
   b. The maximum allowable time interval to remain in a fail operational mode

c. The action to be taken when the maximum allowable time interval to remain in a fail operational mode has been reached
d. How to notify operational staff and users that a system has transitioned to a controlled failure mode
e. Error, exception, and incident handling
f. Logging and generation of warning messages and alarms
g. Reduction of processing load
h. Masking of nonessential interrupts
i. Signaling to external resources to slow down inputs
j. Traces of system states to facilitate post-event analysis
k. The conditions required to return to normal operations

By asset criticality and system risk, percentage of systems and networks for which service priorities have been specified for all critical and essential functions, services, and tasks, while operating in a fail operational mode. 2.3.13.6

By asset criticality and system risk, average amount of time it takes to transition to a controlled failure mode: 2.3.13.7

a. Fail safe/fail secure
b. Fail operational

By asset criticality and system risk, percentage of systems and networks for which the definition of service priorities during controlled failure modes has been verified to be compatible with capacity management scenarios and the resources expected to be available.   2.3.13.8

Number and percentage of security incidents and other system failures or downtime, by incident severity, that were related to: 2.3.13.9

a. A failure of a fail safe/fail secure or fail operational control or procedure
b. Incorrect implementation of a fail safe/fail secure or fail operational control or procedure
c. Lack of provisions for a controlled failure mode
d. Failure to identify a failure mode
e. Failure to follow specified procedures for a controlled failure mode
f. A combination of two or more of the above

Percentage of controlled failure mode controls and procedures that have been tested this reporting period and were found to work as specified under normal and abnormal conditions: 2.3.13.10

a. Distribution by type and severity of errors found, this reporting period and the previous three reporting periods

Frequency with which the following controlled failure mode components are reviewed, reaffirmed, and updated, by organizational unit and asset criticality:
                                                                   2.3.13.11

a. Identification of potential failures
b. Conditions for transitioning to a specific controlled failure mode
c. Specification of service priorities during each type of controlled failure mode

  d. Maximum allowable time interval for remaining in a fail operational mode
  e. Action to be taken after the maximum allowable time interval for remaining in a fail operational mode has been reached
  f. Controlled failure mode procedures
  g. Selection of assets that are and are not covered by a controlled failure mode capability
  h. The acceptability of the time interval that it takes to transition to a controlled failure mode

Integrity

Integrity is a prerequisite for the correct operation of any IT security control and the foundation of the security of any IT infrastructure. Webster's Dictionary defines integrity as "an unimpaired condition, soundness, completeness." This definition is not far off the mark when considering the integrity of IT security. There are several different aspects to the integrity of IT security:

- The integrity of the hardware on which the IT infrastructure operates
- The integrity of all the software operating within the IT infrastructure, including operating systems, firmware, utilities, middleware, and applications, whether custom developed or COTS
- The integrity of the telecommunications networks, services, and equipment
- The integrity of fixed and portable online and offline storage media
- The integrity of system and user data
- The integrity of the logical and physical interfaces and interactions among all of the above items

The integrity of the people who develop, use, administer, operate, and maintain the IT infrastructure is addressed by personnel security controls (see Section 4.3 of this chapter). The integrity of the procedures employed to develop, use, administer, operate, and maintain the IT infrastructure is covered by operational security controls (see Section 4.5 of this chapter).
Security integrity is defined as:

> **Security integrity:** (1) a security goal that generates the requirement for protection against either intentional or accidental attempts to violate data integrity (the property that data has when it has not been altered in an unauthorized manner) or system integrity (the quality that a system has when it performs its intended function in an unimpaired manner; free from unauthorized manipulation)[50]; (2) quality of an information system reflecting the logical correctness and reliability of the operating system; the logical correctness and completeness of the hardware and software implementing the protection mechanisms, and the consistency of the data structures and occurrence of the stored data.[100]

System integrity encompasses the integrity of all the hardware, software, telecommunications, storage media, and interfaces within the IT infrastructure.

System integrity is a precondition for data integrity. Systems and system components must function correctly to generate and maintain system and user data that is accurate and complete. By the same token, data integrity is a precondition for system integrity. Systems do not operate very well, or in some cases for very long, if system or user data has become corrupt. Data integrity is defined as:

> **Data integrity:** (1) the state that exists when data is the same as the source information and has not been exposed to accidental or malicious addition, deletion, alteration, or destruction[158]; (2) the property that data or information has not been modified or altered in an unauthorized manner.[71, 80, 81]

The counterpart to security integrity is safety integrity. Safety integrity is defined as:

> **Safety integrity:** the probability of a safety-related system satisfactorily performing the required safety functions under all stated conditions within a stated period of time. Safety integrity relates to the performance of the safety-related systems in carrying out the specified safety functions.[5]

Both data integrity and system integrity are essential for ensuring that an IT infrastructure operates in a known secure state at all times. Humans and machines make critical decisions and take critical actions based on data — that is why data integrity is so important. A loss of system integrity can cause security to be compromised quickly, as IT security controls fail or are bypassed. Loss of system integrity will quickly lead to a loss of data integrity. System and user data is likely to be exposed, contaminated, corrupted, and subject to unauthorized addition, deletion, alteration, access, and release. The most difficult situations to catch are those in which a system appears to be operating normally but the data it is operating on, or generating, is bogus, although it is within the range of legal values. Depending on the operational environment, the loss of data integrity can have catastrophic consequences. In the financial sector, if a transaction was accidentally or intentionally changed from $10,000 to $10,000,000 or vice versa, the consequences would be dire. In the medical sector, if a prescription was accidentally or intentionally changed from 10 cc to 100 cc or vice versa or the patient's name was altered, the consequences would be dire. In several industrial sectors, a loss of data integrity can have safety consequences, such as a railway signaling system, a power plant control system, or an air traffic control system. A loss of system or data integrity can also have privacy implications. Concerns about data integrity are not limited to any one industrial sector or application. Information fuels each country's national economy, security, and stability. Decision makers at all levels in the public and private sectors must have confidence in the integrity of the information upon which they make decisions. In the absence of data integrity, intelligent, correct, and timely decisions cannot be made at any level in an organization, and eventually the organization is unable to perform its mission.

System and data integrity can be disrupted accidentally or intentionally. As a result, integrity is closely linked to reliability. Both hardware reliability and software reliability play an important role in maintaining security integrity. Resource management, domain separation, and design features discussed earlier under availability (like redundancy, diversity, and fault tolerance) are major contributors to security integrity. Another common feature is built-in self-tests that check the health and stability of hardware, software, and communications functions. Built-in self-tests can be used to check the correct operation of interfaces, memory chips, disk drives, and executables. Built-in self-tests can be scheduled to run at start-up, periodically at specified time intervals, and on-demand.[20] Should a built-in self-test uncover a problem, prespecified action is taken. For example, an alarm is generated, further processing is suspended until the condition is cleared, error correction routines are initiated, processing is switched to backup equipment, or the device enters a controlled failure mode.

Data integrity concerns extend to active system and user data that is being used, processed, or transmitted, as well as inactive data that is stored in online or offline backups and archives. Active data is subject to a whole host of attacks, which can lead to unauthorized access, alteration, deletion, addition, use, release, and replay. The sensitivity of information assets and the need for protection to ensure its integrity may increase or decrease over time.[192] The integrity of system data that is shared or replicated throughout the IT infrastructure raises particular concerns about consistency and currentness.[20] Data that is received from external sources also creates integrity concerns.[20]

A variety of techniques can be used to verify the integrity of data when it is initially created or received and to monitor the integrity of data while it is active, prior to acting upon it[20, 28, 52, 192, 214, 266]:

- Verifying that data falls within the legal range of values specified for that data element, including upper and lower limits
- Verifying that the data does not include any invalid characters
- Verifying that all required data fields are complete and that nothing is missing
- Performing plausibility checks
- Verifying consistency between input sources and the active data
- Verifying that data is not corrupted during processing or transmission
- Verifying that data is processed in the correct sequence
- Regularly confirming the validity of key fields, files, and parameters of system data

Stored data is subject to many of the same attacks, such as unauthorized addition, deletion, alteration, access, use, and release. Furthermore, stored data depends on the integrity of the backup and archival processes.[192] That is another point where accidental or intentional errors can be introduced. Sensitivity labels should be used to clearly indicate access and distribution restrictions on storage media.[20, 28, 52] Strict physical security controls should be imposed to prevent unauthorized access and tampering with stored data.

Physical security controls should also pay attention to environmental controls. Storage media can become unstable under temperature, humidity, dust, and EMI/RFI extremes. Policies that spell out (1) how long data is to be retained and (2) how storage media is to be sanitized or destroyed need to be defined and enforced.[28, 52, 266] Stored data should be encrypted to make it unreadable to all but authorized users.[266] The integrity of stored data should be monitored regularly through the use of checksums, hash functions, or digital signatures.[20, 28, 52, 266]

It is essential to specify the action to be taken when a data integrity error is detected, both for system data and user data. There is no point in just knowing that a data integrity error has occurred. The reason for knowing that a data integrity error occurred is so that proper action can be taken to prevent a larger problem. As a result, the response to each specific type of data integrity error must be spelled out, preferably so that action can be taken automatically, with an option for manual override. There may be some data integrity errors that fall into the "don't care" category; that is alright. The action to be taken can be specified as "generate a warning and continue processing." For other more severe data integrity errors, state the specific action to be taken and whether an attempt should be made to recover from the data integrity error.

The following metrics can be used to measure different aspects of system and data integrity. To see the big picture, several items are measured:

- How well and how thoroughly system and data integrity measures are implemented throughout the IT infrastructure
- How effectively system and data integrity measures are implemented
- The nature and extent of system and data integrity failures
- The impact of integrity failures on the organization and IT infrastructure

Percentage of IT integrity security controls that protect against: 2.3.14.1

    a. Accidental malicious activity
    b. Intentional malicious activity

Percentage of assets within the IT infrastructure for which integrity is continuously monitored, by asset criticality: 2.3.14.2

    a. Hardware
    b. Telecommunications equipment and services
    c. Operating systems software and utilities
    d. Applications system software
    e. User data (online and offline)
    f. System data (online and offline)
    g. External interfaces

Percentage of assets within the IT infrastructure for which the action to be taken (automatically and/or manually) upon the detection of an integrity error is defined, by asset criticality: 2.3.14.3

a. Hardware
b. Telecommunications equipment and services
c. Operating systems software and utilities
d. Applications system software
e. User data (online and offline)
f. System data (online and offline)
g. External interfaces

By asset type, distribution of assets for which integrity measures have been implemented consistent with their criticality and sensitivity.   2.3.14.4

By information sensitivity, percentage of assets for which system and user data integrity measures check for common attacks, such as: 2.3.14.5

a. Unauthorized alteration
b. Unauthorized deletion
c. Unauthorized addition or insertion
d. Unauthorized access
e. Unauthorized use
f. Unauthorized release
g. Replay

By information sensitivity, percentage of stored data assets for which:
     2.3.14.6

a. The integrity of backup and archival procedures has been verified this reporting period
b. Environmental controls have been verified this reporting period
c. Access and distribution physical security controls have been verified this reporting period

Number and percentage of integrity errors experienced by source of integrity error, this reporting period[20]:   2.3.14.7

a. Hardware
b. Telecommunications equipment and services
c. Operating systems software and utilities
d. Applications system software
e. User data (online and offline)
f. System data (online and offline)
g. External interfaces
h. Other (specify)

Distribution of system integrity errors this reporting period, by error type and severity.   2.3.14.8

Distribution of data integrity errors this reporting period, by error type and severity.[20]   2.3.14.9

Number and duration of failed attempts to monitor: 2.3.14.10

a. System integrity
b. Data integrity

By type of recovery method, distribution of successful and unsuccessful attempts to recover from[20]:   2.3.14.11
   a. A system integrity error
   b. A data integrity error

Impact of integrity errors: report minimum, maximum, and average values for system integrity errors, data integrity errors, and total integrity errors[214]:
                                                                    2.3.14.12

   a. Number of stakeholders affected
   b. Number of IT assets affected, by asset criticality
   c. Duration (time between detection of an integrity error and completion of remediation and restoral activities)

Number and percentage of security appliances, functions, control systems, and protection systems that implement boundary value analysis, by system risk and asset criticality categories: 2.3.14.13
   a. Percentage (%) of boundary value analysis routines that check for parameter values that are below or at the minimum threshold before acting upon them
   b. Percentage (%) of boundary value analysis routines that check for parameter values that are above or at the maximum threshold, before acting upon them
   c. Percentage (%) of boundary value analysis routines that check for zero or null data fields, before acting upon them
   d. Percentage (%) of boundary value analysis routines that check for correct data types, before acting upon them
   e. Percentage (%) of different types of error conditions identified by boundary value analysis routines for which there is a corresponding error/exception handling routine

Percentage of security appliances, functions, control systems, and protection systems that implement plausibility and range checks on: 2.3.14.14
   a. Inputs before acting on them
   b. Outputs before acting on them

Percentage of must work functions (MWFs) for which state transitions are monitored.

Percentage of must not work functions (MNWFs) for which state transitions are monitored.   2.3.14.15

Percentage of security parameters for which type, state, and range is validated at procedure entry, before any action is taken.   2.3.14.16

Percentage decrease in security incidents due to the implementation of boundary value analysis, by incident severity.   2.3.14.17

Comparison of the robustness of the security and privacy controls to information asset sensitivity categories, using a nominal scale of high, moderate, and low.   2.3.14.18

Percentage of host servers that are protected from becoming relay hosts[105]:

2.3.14.19

Percentage of mobile users who access enterprise facilities using secure communications methods.[105]

2.3.14.20

Percentage of IT assets with automatic protection in accordance with policy[105]:

2.3.14.21

    a. Workstations
    b. Servers
    c. Mobile devices
    d. Personally owned devices

Domain Separation

Domain separation is a class of techniques that protects data and operations from tampering and interference from untrusted subjects.[20] Trusted domains are logically and physically separated from untrusted domains. The underlying assumption is that an untrusted user, process, or product might accidentally or intentionally corrupt or compromise system or user data. In this instance, "untrusted" can mean several things. Either the untrusted subject is of a different or lower criticality or sensitivity category, or the security and integrity of the untrusted subject is unknown and has not been evaluated — hence the need to isolate or separate the trusted domain from the untrusted subject.

Historically, the primary application of domain separation was to isolate user data and processes of different sensitivity categories. For example, keeping top secret data and applications separate from secret data and applications. This is the classic multi-level secure processing model. Today, domain separation is used in several different scenarios, such as separating user functions and system management functions, network management functions and security management functions, etc.[52] Domain separation is also used to isolate IT assets by criticality categories. Operational flow control restrictions and data flow control restrictions are other examples of domain separation.

In all cases, the goal is to enhance integrity. External untrusted subjects are prevented from observing or modifying user or system data or operations within the domain.[20] Flows between domains are minimized and strictly controlled.[20, 52] Parameters are validated before they are transferred to or from a domain.[20] Commingling of resources from different sensitivity or criticality categories is prohibited. Unneeded and unused functions and resources are disabled and excluded. The end result is that (1) security domains are self-protecting to a degree, and (2) complexity is minimized, which facilitates testability and, by default, integrity. For many of the same reasons, domain separation is widely used in the safety engineering community.

One fundamental question routinely emerges in regard to domain separation: How separate is separate? In any operational environment there are finite technical limits to both logical and physical separation. In any organization there are finite cost constraints to implementing domain separation. To illustrate, most multinational corporations have some very sensitive data that they want to keep from all but a few trusted and authorized users. Perhaps the data spells out competitive pricing strategies, research trade secrets, or proprietary financial information. The need to keep this data in a separate domain, away from untrusted subjects inside and outside the corporation, is real. However, it is not practical to install a proprietary company-owned and -operated network from New York City to Los Angeles, Tokyo, Frankfurt, and London. At some point in the ATM or frame relay core, or on the satellite links, this data will be traveling with "foreign" data. Yes, VPNs (virtual private networks) can be implemented at the edges at Layer 3 of the ISO/OSI Reference Model, but it is wise to remember what the V in VPN stands for. Consequently, for each such scenario, an organization must decide the acceptable threshold for how separate each domain must be.

Domain separation is implemented in a variety of different ways and in a variety of different places within an IT infrastructure. Perhaps a separate domain is needed for interactions with each business partner.[28] Some of the more common techniques to implement domain separation are listed below. The different methods for implementing domain separation represent variations of a central theme, rather than distinctly different techniques. And as usual in the IT world, each technique is known by more than one name. To be effective, all domain separation techniques require thorough up-front analysis to determine how to restrict untrusted subjects and what to restrict them to.

- Partitioning
- Security kernels
- Information hiding
- Encapsulation
- Separation

Partitioning refers to isolating design components, functionality, and execution. Data, functions, operational control flows, and data control flows are separated and isolated based on information sensitivity or IT asset criticality. The intent is to prevent one partition from interfering with, corrupting, or compromising another, either accidentally or intentionally. In essence, partitioning is a miniature implementation of boundary protection within an IT infrastructure; individual partitions act as buffers to prevent accidental or intentional fault propagation from one partition to another. Partitioning can be implemented logically or physically and in hardware or software. Some everyday examples are partitioning hard drives, memory regions, server directories, and telecommunications paths, segments, nodes, and channels. Partitioning can be applied to the integration and operation of COTS products, as well as the design of custom-developed software. Effective partitioning creates the "you can't get there from here" scenario. Several national and international standards either mandate or highly recommend the use of partitioning for critical and essential functions and data. A fringe benefit of partitioning is that the higher risk components are identified and isolated; hence resources can properly focus on protecting the most critical items. Partitioning is also referred to as isolation, separation, separability, and confinement.

Information hiding is defined as:

> **Information hiding:** (1) a software development technique in which each module's interfaces reveal as little as possible about the module's inner workings and other modules are prevented from using information about the module that is not in the module's interface specification (IEEE Std. 610.12-1990); (2) a software development technique that consists of isolating a system function, or set of data and operations on those data, within a module and providing precise specifications for the module.[7]

Information hiding is a technique that enhances data and system integrity by:

- Preventing accidental access to and corruption of critical software and data
- Minimizing the introduction of errors during maintenance and enhancements
- Reducing the likelihood of common cause failures (CCFs)
- Minimizing fault propagation

Information hiding is a design technique employed during the development of custom software. Object-oriented designs are quite amenable to information hiding. Information hiding can be applied to system and user data and program logic. Information hiding increases reliability and maintainability by minimizing coupling between modules, while maximizing their cohesion. Data structures and logic are localized and as self-contained as possible. This allows the internal data structures and logic of a module to be changed at a later date without the ripple effect on the behavior of other modules or necessitating that they also be changed. Several national and international standards highly recommend the use of information hiding for critical and essential functions and data.

The idea of a *security kernel*, or *safety kernel* as it is known in the safety engineering community, has been around a long time. In simplest terms, a security kernel is a utility that executes between an operating system and an application, and between different applications, and functions as border police or customs agents. A security kernel mediates all access and operations among applications and operating systems, and enforces all security policies. To do so, the security kernel itself must be (1) exempt from unauthorized modification and (2) verifiable. The underlying premise is to separate and isolate all security control and protection functions into one self-contained security kernel. It is felt that it is easier to monitor, control, protect, and verify a self-contained security kernel than a couple dozen security features and functions that are scattered throughout a system and designed and developed by different vendors. Security kernels restrict untrusted programs from accessing system resources and executing system processes. The intent is to prevent an untrusted program from exhibiting unknown and unauthorized behavior, such as[299]:

- Accidentally or intentionally corrupt data. Untrusted components can overwrite vital information stored in common memory and used by trusted components.

- Accidentally or intentionally trigger the execution of critical sequences.
- Prevent or delay the execution of critical functions by restricting or preventing access to a shared resource. In particular, untrusted components can use too much CPU time, fail to terminate, or crash, and as a result prevent trusted components from executing.
- Open a covert channel through which sensitive data is misappropriated.

While the concept of a security kernel is old, it is very applicable to today's IT environment. Most organizations today are struggling with the challenge of how to certify the security of COTS products that were not designed or developed with security in mind, and for which the source code is proprietary and little or no life-cycle documentation exists. This is an example of asking the wrong question or trying to solve the wrong problem. Instead, organizations should (1) assume all COTS products are untrusted and always will be, and (2) insert a known trusted security kernel at various places in the system architecture to monitor and control interactions among COTS products and operating systems. It is orders of magnitude cheaper and easier to design, develop, certify, and deploy a security kernel than to retrofit security into a myriad of ever-changing COTS products. After all, this is the exact scenario for which the security kernel concept was developed.

Encapsulation is a variation of partitioning. Instead of separating security domains throughout the IT architecture, data is partitioned or encapsulated while it is transmitted. In essence, data is put in an opaque envelope while it is transmitted securely to its destination. Wrappers are a isolation technique that encapsulates datagrams to control invocation and add access control and monitoring functions.[272] They were originally developed for use with secure protocols, such as the encapsulated payload in IPSec or NLS. In the case of IPSec and NLS, the wrapper is used to protect what is encapsulated from the outside world.

There are several common points in an IT infrastructure where domain *separation* can be applied easily and to great benefit. COTS software, mobile code,[273, 288] reused software, shareware, and the active content of Web pages are all good candidates for isolation, which can be implemented by:

- Restricting a process to reading data it has written[272]
- Limiting the privileges of executables to the minimum needed to perform its function. For example, child processes do not inherit the privileges of parent processes[273, 289]

Gollmann[272] gives examples of language-based isolation:

- Applets do not get to access the user's file system.
- Applets cannot obtain information about the user's name, e-mail address, system configuration, etc.
- Applets can make outward connections only back to the server from which they came.

- Applets can only pop-up windows that are marked "untrusted."
- Applets cannot reconfigure the system, for example by creating a new class loader or a new security manager.

Mobile code is also a good candidate for isolation. Sander and Tschudin[288] cite several concerns about mobile code that isolation can help to mitigate:

- Protecting host computers from accidental or intentional errant mobile code
- Protecting mobile agent's code and data from accidental or intentional tampering, corruption, and privacy violations
- Secure routing of mobile code
- Protecting mobile code from I/O analysis

The following metrics can be used to measure different aspects of an organization's implementation of domain separation. To see the big picture, several items are measured:

- How well and how thoroughly domain separation is implemented throughout the IT infrastructure
- Whether domain separation is implemented consistent with IT asset criticality and information asset sensitivity
- Whether domain separation activities are properly managed
- The nature and extent of domain separation failures

Percentage (%) of IT assets for which domain separation is implemented, by asset criticality. 2.3.15.1

Percentage (%) of information assets for which domain separation is implemented, by information sensitivity. 2.3.15.2

By asset criticality, number and percentage of systems and networks for which: 2.3.15.3

a. User functions are separated from system management functions
b. Security management functions are separated from network and system management functions
c. Data and memory regions are partitioned

Number and percentage (%) of systems and networks that implement domain separation through: 2.3.15.4

a. Logical partitioning
b. Physical partitioning
c. Information hiding
d. Security kernels
e. Encapsulation

Number and percentage (%) of application systems that monitor and control the execution of COTS products through a security kernel, by system risk. 2.3.15.5

Number and percentage (%) of networks that protect data during transmission through encapsulation, by risk category. 2.3.15.6

Number and percentage (%) of security management information parameters that are shared with or accessible by non-security related functions. 2.3.15.7

Number and percentage (%) of security management functions that interface directly with non-security related functions. 2.3.15.8

Number and percentage (%) of security control system functions that are not partitioned from non-security related functions. 2.3.15.9

Number and percentage of security protection system functions that are not partitioned from non-security related functions. 2.3.15.10

Number and percentage (%) of IT assets for which the implementation of domain separation has been tested this reporting period and found to be working as specified under normal and abnormal conditions: 2.3.15.11

   a. Distribution by type and severity of errors found, this reporting period and the previous three reporting periods

Number and percentage (%) of security incidents, by incident severity, related to: 2.3.15.12

   a. Failure of a domain separation mechanism
   b. Faulty implementation of domain separation
   c. Lack of adequate domain separation
   d. The ability to bypass a domain separation mechanism
   e. A combination of two or more of the above

Frequency with which the following items are reviewed, reaffirmed, and updated: 2.3.15.13

   a. The need for domain separation
   b. Domain separation implementation specifics
   c. The effectiveness of domain separation mechanisms
   d. Opportunities to enhance and optimize the implementation of domain separation enterprisewide

Resource Management

Resource management is a key ingredient for protecting the IT infrastructure from abnormal conditions. We are not talking about managing just security appliances, but rather all IT resources. How can an organization expect its IT resources to be up and running and available when needed if they are not properly managed? It should be clear from the earlier discussion that availability does not just "happen." By the same token, neither does the absence of availability. Denial-of-service-like attacks do not succeed because of some super stealth attack method: they succeed because of poor resource manage-ment or a complete lack of resource management. The system owner creates this vulnerability; an attacker simply exploits it. Reliability engineers and safety engineers understand this point all too well. It is time for security engineers to learn this lesson also.

A simple analogy can be used to explain how resource management works and why it is important. Think of your local radio station for a moment. Occasionally these stations have contests where caller number x wins some sort of prize. Once the announcement is made, the station is flooded with calls. Eventually, the broadcaster comes on the air to announce that they have a winner, listeners are requested not to make anymore calls, and regular programming resumes. If a radio station did not do proper resource management before holding such a contest, they would invite (or inflict?) a denial-of-service attack upon their telephone system, knocking out service to all extensions connected to that private branch exchange (PBX), including the newsroom, advertising, and circulation. Instead, what happens is that the contest is planned ahead of time for a certain point during the show. A decision is made about which sequential caller will be the winner. This number determines how many calls need to be accepted. If caller number 9 is the winner, a total of nine calls must be accepted. The other calls are blocked and get a busy signal. Nine calls is the maximum capacity needed and it is only needed for a short period of time. Afterward, the radio station's telephone system can be reconfigured back to its normal state. Large telephone companies operate the same way. They have different resource configurations to accommodate peak, normal, and low capacity demands at various times by commercial and residential customers in different time zones. Now you know why you get a busy signal if you wait too late to call home on Mother's Day.

The purpose of resource management is to ensure that all IT resources are available when needed, with little or no interference or delay, and allocated to tasks in accordance with established priorities. Resource management includes the ability to preempt tasks or operations to ensure that the IT infrastructure remains in a known secure and stable state at all times. Resource management addresses all modes of operation: normal operations, degraded mode operations, parallel operations, graceful degradation, fail operational, and fail safe/fail secure. If resource management is performed correctly, denial-of-service-like attacks will not be successful. There are three major aspects to resource management[20]:

1. Resource allocation
2. Capacity management
3. Service priority

An IT infrastructure is built, usually incrementally over a period of time, from a combination of unique IT assets. IT infrastructures are rarely static. On the contrary, IT infrastructures are in a perpetual state of semi-planned evolution following the ebb and flow of the IT capital budget and advances in technology. IT infrastructures also tend to mutate following a series of mergers and leveraged buyouts, in which disparate IT infrastructures are suddenly stitched together. As a result, at any point in time, an organization's

IT infrastructure contains an odd assortment of antique, legacy, old, not so old, and new equipment. Usually, there is also a mixture of equipment that is (1) owned and operated by the organization, (2) leased but operated by the organization, and (3) owned and operated by a third party from whom the organization buys services, such as telecommunications. This mixture of equipment includes a myriad of different types, makes, and models of devices, platforms, and components that perform different functions within the IT infrastructure. In essence, there is no steady state. Phrased another way, the only steady state in the IT infrastructure is change — hence the need for robust resource management.

The constant state of flux within an IT infrastructure necessitates a comprehensive and methodical approach to resource allocation. An organization cannot simply install and initialize all this equipment, walk away, and everything will be fine. Far from it; instead, a free-for-all will ensue as competing and conflicting users, processes, and tasks quickly consume all available resources. A combination of saturation and deadlock will follow as operational flows and data flows are frozen in a holding pattern. Not to mention that systems that are unstable due to resource management problems make convenient targets to attack. Here we see a link between availability and resource management.

This rush-hour scenario can be avoided with a little common sense, planning, and analysis. Strategies should be devised that control the allocation and de-allocation of resources.[20] All use of resources by all initiators needs to be planned, monitored, and controlled to ensure that (1) adequate resources are allocated to the most important or time critical tasks, and (2) resources cannot be monopolized by any one task or a combination of low-priority tasks.[20] That is, resources are allocated but limits are placed on their use in terms of timing, capacity, and throughput.

A three-step process is followed for resource allocation. Given the dynamic nature of the IT infrastructure, this process is constantly repeated. The first step is to identify all the hardware, software (operating systems, utilities, middleware, applications, firmware, etc.), and telecommunications resources within the IT infrastructure. It is hard for an organization to allocate resources effectively if the organization does not know what resources it has. Here we see a link to physical security — the need to develop and maintain a current and complete IT asset inventory. The same inventory can be used for both purposes — all the more reason for the physical and IT security folks to talk. An organization needs to know:

- How much processing power it has locally and enterprisewide
- How much bandwidth is available on the various networks
- How much memory, primary online storage, and secondary offline storage is available
- How many wired and wireless internal and external access points there are
- How many output devices there are and their capacity
- What major application systems there are, what they are used for, and what information assets they consume and generate

- Which resources are shareable and which are not[20]
- Where all this equipment is located and how it is logically and physically interconnected or purposely separated

This information should be collected and reported at different levels of abstraction, consistent with the discussion in Chapter 2 about hierarchical views of metrics. For example, a high-level report may refer to a server farm that has 20 high-end servers that perform function y. A detailed report of the same information for the local administrator would include specifics about the memory, processors, hard drives, and interfaces on each server.

The second step is to identify what resources are needed by each organization, function, and "system," internally and externally. Resource needs should be specified by what is needed for a normal duty cycle, a maximum load scenario, and a minimum load scenario.[20] The minimum load scenario should reflect low processing demand, as well as the minimum resources needed to keep operating under a degraded mode operations scenario. In addition, resource requirements should be identified for today and on a sliding three- to five-year future window.[28]

At this point, an organization knows what IT resources it has on the one hand, and what requirements it has for those resources on the other hand. The third step is to identify the criticality and time sensitivity of the various resource needed, as they relate to achieving the organization's mission. Then resources are allocated accordingly. The criticality or time sensitivity of resource needs is referred to as a service priority. Service priorities determine the allocation of IT resources. Service priorities should be established for all classes and types of services, initiators, and operations.[20, 52] Whenever resource needs change — new resource requests are made, old resource requests are changed or withdrawn — service priorities must be reevaluated and adjusted.[20] Perhaps the new resource requests have a higher priority. Perhaps some old resource requests no longer have a high service priority; a medium service priority will suffice now. Operation under emergency conditions can dramatically change all service priorities. Consequently, the ease with which service priorities can be specified and changed is a key consideration. An audit trail of all resource allocation activities should be kept and continually monitored to ensure compliance with service priorities. This audit trail should include all resource allocation requests, whether they were accepted or rejected.[20] A careful analysis of this information will provide useful insights, such as attempts to bypass resource allocation or capacity management controls, and how well the service priority schema is working.

Service priorities cannot be established in a vacuum — they must be linked to capacity management. Every IT infrastructure has a finite resource capacity. There is only so much bandwidth, throughput, storage, processing power, and speed. This finite capacity will change as the IT infrastructure evolves, but the capacity is fixed at any given point in time. Capacity management balances the inherent conflicts between resource needs, service priorities, and the finite resources available. In almost all organizations, IT resource needs (real or perceived) exceed the resources available, due to technology constraints and limited

IT capital budgets. If resources are allocated simply based on service priority, 200 percent of available resources will soon be allocated, some services, processes, and tasks will be permanently locked out, and the IT infrastructure will come to a screeching halt. Capacity management puts the brakes on before saturation or deadlock scenarios are reached. If a server can only handle 50 concurrent sessions before it becomes unstable, capacity management controls will block any further session requests. If there is only 100 GB of online storage, capacity management controls will distribute the available storage in accordance with service priorities for peak, normal, and low load scenarios. The same capacity management principles apply to allocating telecommunications resources to ensure that saturation and deadlock do not occur. When there is a conflict and there are not enough resources available, perhaps each request is allocated 70 percent of the resources requested or some low-priority requests are temporarily dropped.

Capacity management decisions need to be informed and capacity management controls need to be flexible. Capacity management decisions should be made not by a first-level system administrator, but rather by a senior-level interdisciplinary team of stakeholders, senior-level managers, telecommunications engineers, security engineers, system engineers, and software engineers. Capacity management decisions should be made in terms of what is best for the enterprise so that the organization achieves its mission. Procedures need to be in place so that these decisions can be made, changed, and communicated rapidly under emergency conditions.

The following metrics can be used to measure different aspects of an organization's implementation of resource management. To see the big picture, several items are measured:

- How well and how thoroughly resource management is implemented throughout the IT infrastructure
- Whether resource management procedures and controls are implemented consistent with achieving the organization's mission
- Whether resource management activities are properly managed
- The nature and extent of resource management failures

By organizational unit and asset criticality, percentage of IT resources that are included in and covered by: 2.3.16.1
   a. Resource allocation procedures and controls
   b. Service priority procedures and controls
   c. Capacity management procedures and controls

By organizational unit and asset criticality, percentage of resource management procedures and controls that address: 2.3.16.2
   a. Normal operations
   b. Degraded mode operations
   c. Parallel mode operations
   d. Graceful degradation
   e. Fail operational
   f. Fail safe/fail secure

By organizational unit and asset criticality, percentage of resource management
procedures and controls that have the capability to: 2.3.16.3
   a. Preempt tasks or operations quickly
   b. Change and communicate the resource allocation schema quickly
   c. Change and communicate service priorities quickly
   d. Change and communicate capacity management strategies quickly

By organizational unit and asset criticality, percentage of IT resource needs
that have been identified for: 2.3.16.4
   a. Normal duty cycle
   b. A peak loading scenario
   c. A low load scenario
   d. The minimum resources needed for degraded mode operations

By organizational unit and asset criticality, percentage of resource allocations,
service priorities, and capacity management strategies that are consistent with
an enterprisewide view toward achieving the organization's mission. 2.3.16.5

By organizational unit and asset criticality: 2.3.16.6
   a. Percentage of resource requirements that identify current and future
      needs
   b. Percentage of capacity management strategies that take into account
      current and future needs

By organizational unit and asset criticality, percentage of resource allocation
activities that are continually captured in an audit trail and monitored.
                                                                         2.3.16.7

By organizational unit and asset criticality, percentage of capacity management
decisions that are made with the involvement of: 2.3.16.8
   a. Stakeholders
   b. Senior management
   c. Senior telecommunications engineers
   d. Senior security engineers
   e. Senior system engineers
   f. Senior software engineers

Number and percentage of security incidents and other system failures or
downtime, by incident severity, that were related to: 2.3.16.9
   a. A resource allocation error or failure
   b. A service priority error or failure
   c. A capacity management error or failure
   d. The ability to bypass a resource allocation control
   e. The ability to bypass a service priority control
   f. The ability to bypass a capacity management control
   g. Lack of a resource allocation control
   h. Lack of a service priority control
   i. Lack of a capacity management control

      j. Conflicts between resource requirements and available resources
      k. A combination of two or more of the above

Percentage of resource management functions that have been tested this reporting period and were found to work as specified under normal and abnormal conditions, and distribution by type and severity of errors found, this reporting period and the previous three reporting periods: 2.3.16.10

      a. Resource allocation
      b. Service priority
      c. Capacity management

Frequency with which the following resource management components are reviewed, reaffirmed, and updated, by organizational unit and asset criticality:
     2.3.16.11

      a. IT asset inventory (in coordination with physical security staff)
      b. Resource allocation procedures and controls
      c. Service priority procedures and controls
      d. Capacity management procedures and controls

Number of times this reporting period and average duration of each event that resource requirements exceeded available resources and contingency capacity management procedures had to be invoked.   2.3.16.12

IT Security Metrics Reports

We have just explored a total of 229 metrics that measure the resilience of IT security controls. The metrics are organized by the nine components of an IT security control system and the seven components of an IT security protection system. An organization will use different metrics at different points in time to measure the resilience of its IT security controls. While the resilience of IT security controls is measured continuously, the particular metrics evaluated at any given time will depend on the GQM: what goal the organization is trying to accomplish, and the questions being asked to measure progress toward achieving or sustaining that goal. An organization may be exploring a single issue in depth, like the resilience of their logical access controls. Measurements may be made locally, regionally, or enterprisewide, depending on the definition of the measurement boundaries for that GQM. An organization may be investigating a cross-cutting issue that involves the interactions between various components of the IT security control and protection systems. The resilience of the IT security control system or IT security protection system as a whole may need to be measured. Or, an organization may be required to measure the resilience of a particular IT security control to demonstrate compliance with security and privacy regulations, like those discussed in Chapter 3.

    The metrics report template presented earlier in Table 4.8 is also used for IT security metrics reports. Let us walk through a sample IT security metrics report to see the type of information that can be conveyed. This report examines the resilience of an organization's logical access controls and takes into account the dependencies between logical access controls and the identification and authentication function. The metrics are selected and evaluated in response to the following GQM:

Goal: Ensure access to IT assets is restricted to authorized users.

Question: How well does the IT infrastructure prevent unauthorized logical access to IT assets, by both insiders and outsiders?

Table 4.14 is a sample IT security metrics report that evaluates the effectiveness in preventing unauthorized access to IT assets. Metrics are selected that present an in-depth analysis of the resilience of an organization's logical access controls. This report measures how well and how thoroughly logical access controls have been implemented throughout the IT infrastructure, how well the logical access control mechanisms work, and, conversely, how often

Table 4.14 Resilience Metric Report: Logical Access Control

Report Date: 3 March 2006

Reporting Entity: Southwest Region

Security Domain(s): IT Security

Sub-element(s): Logical Access Control

Focus: Effectiveness in preventing unauthorized access

Measurement Boundary: Regional offices   **Prediction or Actual Value:** Actual value

Time Interval: previous 6 months

Metric		Target Value	Observed Value	Interpretation
ID	Definition			
2.3.1.1	Percentage (%) of inactive user accounts that have been disabled in accordance with policy this reporting period	100%	60%	Red
2.3.1.2	Percentage (%) of user accounts assigned to personnel who have left the organization or no longer have need for access that have been closed this reporting period	100%	75%	Yellow

Table 4.14   Resilience Metric Report: Logical Access Control (continued)

Metric		Target Value	Observed Value	Interpretation
ID	Definition			
2.3.1.3	Percentage (%) of workstations with session time-out/automatic log-out controls set in accordance with policy	100%	80%	Yellow
2.3.1.4	Percentage (%) user accounts that have been reviewed within the past quarter for justification of current access rights and privileges	100%	50%	Red
2.3.1.10	Number of times IT and information assets were successfully accessed without completing a valid identification and authentication function:			
	a. Critical assets	a. 0	a. 0	a. Green
	b. Essential assets	b. 0	b. 1	b. Red
	c. Routine assets	c. 0	c. 2	c. Red
2.3.1.11	Percentage (%) of organizational units that have defined and enforce access rights and privileges for all layers of the protocol stack for their IT infrastructure	100%	85%	Green
2.3.1.12	Percentage (%) of IT and information assets for which access rights and privileges have been defined:			
	a. Critical assets	a. 100%	a. 100%	a. Green
	b. Essential assets	b. 100%	b. 85%	b. Green
	c. Routine assets	c. 100%	c. 50%	c. Red
2.3.1.14	Percentage (%) of systems and networks that default to "access denied" if an unknown or undefined state is encountered when arbitrating access rights and privileges	100%	65%	Red

Table 4.14 Resilience Metric Report: Logical Access Control (continued)

Metric		Target Value	Observed Value	Interpretation
ID	Definition			
2.3.1.15	Percentage (%) of systems and networks that implement robust access controls to prevent unauthorized changes to the rules specifying access rights and privileges	100%	80%	Yellow
2.3.1.17	Percentage (%) of systems and networks for which access rights and privileges have been defined to a sufficient level of granularity to prevent accidental or intentional aggregation, inference, misuse, and compromise:			
	a. Critical assets	a. 100%	a. 100%	a. Green
	b. Essential assets	b. 100%	b. 85%	b. Green
	c. Routine assets	c. 80%	c. 50%	c. Red
2.3.1.19	Percentage (%) of operational environments that implement access rights and privileges for all possible operations and target resources:			
	a. High risk	a. 100%	a. 100%	a. Green
	b. Moderate risk	b. 100%	b. 85%	b. Green
2.3.1.20	Percentage (%) of systems and networks for which access rights and privileges have been tested during this quarter and were found to work as specified under normal and abnormal conditions:			
	a. Critical assets	a. 100%	a. 80%	a. Yellow
	b. Essential assets	b. 80%	b. 60%	b. Yellow
	c. Routine assets	c. 60%	c. 25%	c. Red

Table 4.14 Resilience Metric Report: Logical Access Control (continued)

ID	Definition	Target Value	Observed Value	Interpretation
	Metric			
2.3.5.6	Percentage (%) of systems where vendor-supplied or default accounts and passwords have been disabled or reset, including maintenance back doors, by system risk:			
	a. High risk	a. 100%	a. 100%	a. Green
	b. Moderate risk	b. 100%	b. 90%	b. Green
	c. Low risk	c. 80%	c. 50%	c. Red
2.3.5.12	Percentage (%) of systems and networks that, following a failed log-on attempt:			
	a. Lock the account and/or point of entry for a specified period of time	a. 100%	a. 100%	a. Green
	b. Lock the account and/or point of entry until an official request is approved to reset it	b. 80%	b. 65%	b. Yellow
2.3.5.14	Percentage (%) of systems and networks that:			
	a. Limit maximum session durations	a. 100%	a. 100%	a. Green
	b. Require sessions to be re-authenticated or terminated after a specified time interval	b. 100%	b. 65%	b. Red
2.3.5.15	Percentage (%) of systems and networks that require processes, sessions, devices, and systems to be authenticated:			
	a. Critical assets	a. 100%	a. 90%	a. Green
	b. Essential assets	b. 80%	b. 80%	b. Green
	c. Routine assets	c. 60%	c. 25%	c. Red

Table 4.14   Resilience Metric Report: Logical Access Control (continued)

Metric		Target Value	Observed Value	Interpretation
ID	Definition			
2.3.5.16	Percentage (%) of systems and networks that require:			
	a. Unique identification and authentication credentials for all users	a. 100%	a. 80%	a. Yellow
	b. Multi-factor authentication	b. 100%	b. 80%	b. Yellow
	c. Robust authentication for remote access	c. 100%	c. 75%	c. Yellow
2.3.5.18	Percentage (%) of organizational units that have tested their identification and authentication mechanisms this reporting period and found that they worked as specified under normal and abnormal conditions	100%	75%	Yellow
Summary Red = 0 points Yellow = 5 points Green = 10 points		**Total Possible** 350 points	**Actual Score** 190 or 54% **Overall Rating** Red	

they fail. Target values are established for each metric. The actual observed value is compared against the target value and interpreted. Overall, the report demonstrates that some progress has been made in this area, but not enough. Most of the effort has focused on critical IT assets, which is a good start. However, goals for essential and routine assets have not been met. This leaves open the possibility of a lower criticality asset being used as a vehicle to attack a critical IT asset. Particularly troubling is the observation that only 65 percent of systems and networks default to "access denied" if an unknown or undefined state is encountered when arbitrating access rights and privileges. Also, there appears to be an unnecessary delay when closing out inactive accounts and reviewing and rejustifying access rights and privileges. This report demonstrates the value of objective quantifiable metrics. A simple verbal review would pick up the items that have been performed and function correctly. The metrics capture that information *and* highlight the items that have been neglected or do not function correctly — such as the ability to bypass an identification and authentication function on essential and routine IT assets. A verbal report would leave the impression that the resilience of logical access controls is high. In contrast, the metrics report tells the complete story: only 54 percent of the resilience goals have been met and the overall rating is red.

4.5 Operational Security

The fourth security engineering domain is operational security. Operational security is perhaps the least well understood of the four security engineering domains. As a result, operational security is often ignored, neglected, or at best given lip service. A poor operational security program can undo an excellent IT security program. Hence, the lack of understanding surrounding operational security is extremely problematic. Mention the term "operational security" and the few people who have heard of it think you are talking about the security of a military campaign or intelligence operation. This is not the first technical term to have a dual identity.

Operational security is an essential part of security engineering because it represents the interaction between people and technology. Physical security focuses on protecting physical entities (facilities, assets, people) from natural and man-made hazards. Personnel security takes a deeper look at the people who might be given access to these facilities and assets, in particular in regard to their accountability and competence. IT security zeroes in on the inherent security features and functions of technology. In contrast, operational security represents the nexus of people and technology. Achieving an effective operational security program can be quite a challenge, because people are any organization's greatest security liability; but it is well worth the effort.

So what is operational security and how does it relate to resilience? Operational security is defined as:

> **Operational Security:** implementation of standard operational security procedures that define the nature and frequency of the interaction between users, systems, and system resources, the purpose of which is to: (1) achieve and sustain a known secure system state at all times, and (2) prevent accidental or intentional theft, release, destruction, alteration, misuse, or sabotage of system resources.[156]

Operational security defines how, when, under what circumstances, and why people in different roles interact with IT assets. These interactions are documented in formal procedures that are reviewed, reaffirmed, and updated on a regular basis, or following a major technology upgrade or change. Here we see a link between operational security and the accountability principle of personnel security. Employees and pseudo-insiders are held accountable for adhering to standardized operational security procedures. Operational security activities are undertaken to (1) achieve and sustain a known, secure system state at all times; and (2) prevent accidental or intentional theft, release,

<u>Security Engineering Life-Cycle Activities (COTS and custom)</u>
- Concept formulation
- Requirements analysis and specification
- Security architecture and design
- Development and implementation
- Security test and evaluation (ST&E), certification and accreditation (C&A), independent validation and verification (IV&V)
- Delivery, installation, and deployment
- Operations and maintenance
- Decommissioning (transition, sanitization, reuse, destruction)

<u>Ongoing Security Risk Management Activities (COTS and Custom)</u>
- Vulnerability assessment
- Security policy management
- Security audits and reviews
- Security impact analysis, privacy impact analysis, configuration management, patch management
- Security awareness and training, guidance documents
- Stakeholder, strategic partner, supplier relationships

Figure 4.10   Taxonomy of operational security parameters.

destruction, alteration, misuse, or sabotage of system resources. Contrary to a common misconception, operational security does not begin during the operations and maintenance phase, but rather long before then.

The resilience of operational security is measured according to the thoroughness, completeness, and robustness of an operational security activity. An organization may have all the required operational security procedures in place to pass an audit, but are they any good? Do the procedures have any depth, or do they merely skim the surface and mouth empty platitudes? Does anyone know about the procedures? Are they routinely followed and enforced? Are the procedures effective at preventing, preempting, and repelling cyber security attacks, while minimizing the extent of corruption and compromise? What kind of story do the results from performing operational security activities tell?

At a conceptual level, operational security comprises two different categories of activities: (1) security engineering life-cycle activities and (2) ongoing security risk management activities. As shown in Figure 4.10, security engineering life-cycle activities begin during concept formulation and carry on through system decommissioning. These security engineering life-cycle activities are applicable regardless of which system engineering life-cycle model is followed. Likewise, these activities are applicable regardless of whether the system is constructed entirely of COTS products, entirely of custom-developed components, or a combination of both. As will be seen, the exact nature of how these tasks are executed varies, depending on the COTS/custom equation, but they are still performed. In addition, there are ongoing security risk management activities that are performed repeatedly throughout the life of a system. The features and functions of IT security control and protection systems are specified and built during the security engineering life-cycle activities. The resilience of the features and functions of IT security control and protection systems are assessed and ensured by the ongoing security risk management activities.

There are a variety of system engineering life-cycle models. Each model has the same eight security engineering life-cycle activities discussed below; however, the sequence in which the activities are performed varies. The models are known by several names, such as structured analysis and design, Jackson structured design, functional decomposition, Yourdon-DeMarco, spiral, waterfall, object-oriented analysis and design, etc. About every five years or so, a new name and not necessarily a new model pop up. These models fall into three main categories: (1) "once through," (2) incremental, and (3) evolutionary. There are pros and cons associated with each of the three categories of life-cycle models. An organization needs to be aware of the pros and cons because they have security repercussions.

There is a linear progression through life-cycle activities in the "once through" category. Each life-cycle activity is performed only once and in succession; hence the name "once through." This category is preferred by procurement officials because it is easy to understand. End users like this category of life-cycle models because it *promises* to deliver all planned capabilities in one delivery and phase out old technology all at once. The key word is "promises" and there are significant risks associated with these promises. There is a risk that the requirements will be captured incorrectly or incompletely, and that fact will not be discovered until deployment to the field. There is a risk that the product or system is, in reality, larger or more complex than estimated and, as a result, cannot be completely specified, designed, developed, and delivered within the funding or staffing constraints. Large projects often take years to execute. With a linear progression through the life-cycle activities, there is a risk that the rapid evolution of IT may make parts of a product or system obsolete before it is deployed.

The incremental category of life-cycle models pre-plans a series of product or system improvements. This is the well-known version 1, version 2, … version x scenario. The requirements for all deliveries are defined up-front and more or less frozen. Then the product is delivered incrementally in the priority order that certain capabilities are needed, and as funding and staffing are available. This model makes some assumptions that may increase project risk. First, this model assumes that all requirements for all versions will be captured and prioritized correctly the first time around. That is a big assumption. Plus, what happens when priorities or requirements change? Second, this model assumes that funding and staffing projections for the out years will pan out. Very few organizations have static budget planning cycles. Sometimes budgets are higher than expected; more often, they are lower than expected. Budgets can change dramatically from one year to the next; that can cause a project to be constantly redefining the composition of the various increments, sometimes to the point where the last increment never happens. Third, the incremental category of life-cycle models can get caught in the trap of technology obsolescence. The requirements and design that were valid when the first increment was delivered become obsolete and invalid two years later when it is time to deliver the next increment. Often, the cost of rework and throw-away is more than the original development cost and the project spirals downhill from there.

The evolutionary category of life-cycle models recognizes and attempts to compensate for the shortcomings of the other models. In essence, a product or system evolves as the requirements are better understood and refined. An initial concept is defined for the product or system. The requirements for the first delivery are quite specific, while requirements for future deliveries are more of a vision, to be refined later. A project cycles repeatedly through the middle six life-cycle activities repeatedly until it is time to retire the product or system. Planned increments may be combined or skipped and new increments may be added as the project's needs and technology change. Also, earlier life-cycle activities may be repeated or revisited to resolve errors uncovered during later life-cycle activities. The evolutionary category of life-cycle models does not deliver "all" the capability at once and may give the appearance of a product or system never being finished. But, when in the past 30 years has a COTS or custom-developed product or system delivered all the capability that was promised at the outset, regardless of what type of life-cycle model it was developed under? The high-tech industry has never been good at managing expectations; in fact, many firms go out of their way to do the exact opposite. While the evolutionary category of life-cycle models is not perfect and confounds most procurement officials, it at least acknowledges some realities the other types of models do not. First, change is just as inevitable in the world of IT as it is in the rest of life — changes in requirements, changes in priorities, changes in funding, changes in staffing, changes in technology, changes in connectivity and interoperability. Evolutionary models allow the project to adapt to change easily, by iterating through life-cycle activities as needed. Second, errors of omission and errors of commission happen, human nature being what it is. Sometimes, errors are discovered in the life-cycle activity in which they were committed; usually, errors are not discovered until a later life-cycle activity. Only evolutionary models accommodate this fact by allowing earlier life-cycle activities to be repeated and revisited.

In summary, the "once through" and incremental categories of life-cycle models pose greater inherent security risks because of their lack of flexibility in regard to changes in requirements, technology, and the operational environment. For systems that incorporate a combination of COTS and custom-developed products, this lack of flexibility can dramatically increase the prevalence of vulnerabilities and exacerbate their severity. For example, a COTS product was selected based on a parameter that is no longer valid, a COTS product does not perform all the functions it was advertised to do, a COTS product does not perform a function the way it was advertised to do, interfaces or timing parameters have changed, a COTS product is not available according to the advertised schedule, etc. This mismatch between planned technical capabilities and reality is a beacon for attackers inside and outside an organization. And who is in a better position to exploit these vulnerabilities than the insiders who are well aware of them and the outsiders who helped create them?

Both the security engineering life-cycle activities and the ongoing security risk management activities consist of several components. Each of these topics is discussed individually below. To bring everyone to a common level of understanding, a brief synopsis of each topic is given. (Complete standards and books have been published on several of these topics. For a more in-depth treatment, readers are referred to the bibliography contained in Annex B.) The role each component plays in operational security and its relationship to resilience are examined. Then metrics are defined to ascertain where on the resilience scale a particular implementation of an operational security activity or the results from performing that activity falls. Keep in mind that a low resilience rating is not necessarily bad, while a high resilience rating is not necessarily good. The objective is to achieve and sustain a resilience rating that is proportional to operational risk, so that assets are neither over- nor under-protected. Finally, examples of composite operational security resilience metrics reports are presented. Operational security metrics can be used in several ways; for example, to evaluate the thoroughness and completeness of information security requirements, to evaluate the coverage and results from security test and evaluation (ST&E), to determine whether security impact analysis is being performed and the results taken into account before implementing a change or upgrade, and to determine the extent to which security requirements have been passed on to business partners.

Security Engineering Life-Cycle Activities

There are eight security engineering life-cycle activities; each represents a different step in specifying, building, and deploying a secure system:

1. Concept formulation
2. Security requirements analysis and specification
3. Security architecture and design
4. Development and implementation
5. Security test and evaluation (ST&E), certification and accreditation (C&A), independent validation and verification (IV&V)
6. Delivery, installation, and deployment
7. Operations and maintenance
8. Decommissioning (transition, sanitization, reuse, destruction)

Concept Formulation

There is a starting point for every system, product, or component. The original idea may come from an individual, a committee, a request from an end user for a new feature, or the need to stay competitive in the marketplace. Eventually the idea evolves into a concept describing the functions the system or product will perform and how it will be used. The first step toward defining and planning for a new technical capability is the most critical one. The further along a project is in the life cycle, it becomes more difficult, more time consuming, and more expensive to correct errors of omission and errors of commission from previous steps. An engineering life cycle is similar to introducing a child to the world of learning, regardless of whether the topic is math, science, art, history, or languages. A freshman in college cannot learn calculus if he was never taught basic math skills in grade school. In the world of IT, as in the world of learning, the fundamental concepts are paramount.

During concept formulation, the basic idea for a new technical capability is created and analyzed from many perspectives. An idea is expanded and augmented as understanding increases. As more avenues of thought are explored and more facts emerge, what was once thought to be a golden idea may turn out not to be so brilliant and end up being discarded. Or, perhaps the idea was almost right and a slight course correction will make it not only viable, but extremely useful. Concept formulation is the time to be open-minded and creative, and play the "what if" game. Innovation and thoroughness are the key to successful concept formulation. Unless a concept is being developed for a new proprietary product line, it is best to have an interdisciplinary team of stakeholders participate during concept formulation. That way, ideas can be viewed from as many different angles and needs as possible. Concept formulation should not be rushed, despite pressure from the top. At each step in the life cycle, technical choices and options become more and more limited. A project team does not want to find itself in the position of saying, "Wish we had thought of that sooner."

During concept formulation, a variety of considerations are probed until decisions can be made. A clear, concise statement of why the new system or product is needed and what functions it will and will not perform is developed first. This statement is compared to the IT asset inventory to determine what systems and components the new technology will enhance or replace. The proposed operational profile, which describes how the new technology will be used and by whom, is flushed out next, including internal and external interfaces and connectivity. The proposed duty cycle is defined, which spells out usage and loading parameters, such as normal and peak transaction volume, how quickly transactions must be processed, and the duration of normal and peak transaction loads. Constraints on the proposed operational environment are identified also. For example, is the new technology being deployed in an office environment, in the middle of a desert or jungle battlefield, across the Arctic circle, or on a satellite? What are the expected ambient temperature ranges, humidity, power sources, dust filtration, and vibration? Are there size and weight constraints? What about protection from EMI/RFI or deliberate jamming? During concept formulation, issues surrounding where the new technology is envisioned to be used are explored to the same depth as issues related to how it is going to be used.

Often, decisions that should be made during concept formulation are deferred due to an inability to reach a consensus or in a rush to get to the next step. This practice is extremely unwise. Concept formulation is the time to pin down all details related to what functions the new technology will and will not perform, how it will be used and by whom, how it will be integrated into the existing IT infrastructure, etc. Deferring these decisions may be politically correct, but it is not cost-effective. The longer these decisions are delayed, the more expensive it will be to incorporate them and the options and choices for incorporating them will have become very limited. Not to mention that on occasion the answer to a deferred question is that something cannot be done. In this case, all of the time, resources, and funds spent earlier were wasted. It is preferable to find out this fact during concept formulation, rather than later in the life cycle.

One item that must be dealt with early is whether the new technology is considered permanent or just a temporary stop-gap measure. The expected longevity of the new technology will have a major impact on other decisions. If an item is only expected to be used for 12 to 18 months, the time, resources, and funds an organization is willing to expend will be considerably less than for an item that is expected to be deployed for five or more years. That is why several feasibility studies, cost-benefit analyses, and other trade-off studies are conducted during concept formulation.

Concept formulation is a good time to review, reaffirm, and update the organization's IT asset inventory. In particular, the IT asset sensitivity, criticality, and risk assessments should be brought up-to-date. The introduction of new technology that enhances or replaces existing IT assets will most likely cause these ratings to be adjusted. Furthermore, this is the time to make an initial decision about the sensitivity, criticality, and risk of the new technology, so that it can be specified, designed, developed, and tested accordingly. A preliminary risk assessment is conducted based on the operational and functional concept, interfaces, and connectivity. Dependencies on internal and external assets are also identified and taken into account.

A security concept is developed for the new technology at this time. The goal is to clarify how the new technology will fit into the overall security architecture and IT infrastructure. Because very few organizations operate only one system or one network, this is an important exercise. Introduction of new technology can upset a delicate balance between diverse components, exacerbate known vulnerabilities that were previously controlled, and create new vulnerabilities or performance problems. The security concept encompasses three main items: (1) a discussion of the security features and functions to be performed by the new technology, (2) an explanation of how the security features and functions will be assured and what integrity level they need to be assured to, and (3) identification of the operational procedures that are needed to ensure that the security posture to which the new technology is certified will be maintained once the technology is deployed in the operational environment. The security concept must be consistent with the sensitivity, criticality, and risk ratings for the new technology. The security concept must reflect internal and external interfaces, connectivity, and dependencies. In addition, the security concept needs to include compliance with applicable security and privacy regulations, industry standards, and corporate policies. Other technical concerns should also be dealt with at this time, such as safety and reliability.

A variety of planning, coordination, and logistical issues are addressed during concept formulation. Real cost and schedule constraints should be pinned down. There is no point in developing a concept for new technology that will cost ten times what an organization can or is willing to pay. Likewise, there is no point in developing a concept for new technology that is so complex that it will take so long to develop that the deployment window is shut. A little reality needs to be brought into the creativity surrounding concept formulation.

Concept formulation is the time to delineate when the new technology is needed and the optimum deployment time frame. At this step, the need should be expressed as a "not before/not after" date to capture the earliest and latest dates the technology can be incorporated into the IT infrastructure without having a negative impact. If the new technology is incorporated too early, the internal and external entities to which it interfaces may not be ready for the transition. If the new technology is incorporated too late, the window of opportunity for the new technology to add value to the organization may have passed and the ROI or operational impact on the IT infrastructure may be negative. On occasion, the concept for new technology may become obsolete before it is completely developed or deployed. In this instance, it is best to discard the current project and move on to the next concept. Usually this is difficult because of the egos involved, but from an ROI perspective it is the best course of action. The federal government is infamous for taking twice as long as planned to develop and deploy systems and for keeping them operational long after they have ceased to be cost-effective, due to a cumbersome acquisition process. When planning the introduction of new technology, organizations need to remember that IT infrastructures are not static — rather, they are in a constant state of flux, with each system, network, component, and interface evolving and being upgraded or replaced on its own timeline. These changes may go faster or slower than originally expected. As a result, the timing of the introduction of new technology is a delicate matter and requires constant attention.

Concept formulation is the time to select an appropriate life-cycle model and development tools and techniques. Various go/no-go checkpoints are chosen throughout the project, along with pass/fail criteria. Strategies for conducting security test and evaluation (ST&E), certification and accreditation (C&A), and independent validation and verification (IV&V) activities should be identified. A first cut is made at which components will be COTS, which components will be custom developed, and how they will be integrated. A list of potential suppliers is formed, along with criteria for evaluating and selecting suppliers. Contingencies are put into place, should a supplier fail to deliver at any point during the project. Roles and responsibilities are clearly defined for insiders, pseudo-insiders, and pseudo-outsiders. The final concept is vetted by all stakeholders and supplies and adjustments are made as needed. At this point, the project is ready to proceed to formal requirements analysis and specification.

The following metrics can be used to measure the resilience of an organization's approach to concept formulation. In particular, these metrics assess the thoroughness and successful outcome from executing concept formulation activities.

Percentage of stakeholder organizations actively involved during concept formulation.   2.4.1.1

Average duration of concept formulation, by IT asset criticality and project
cost.   2.4.1.2

By IT asset criticality, number and percentage of the following items that were:
(1) produced during concept formulation, and (2) agreed to by all stakeholders:
                                                                            2.4.1.3

   a. A clear concise statement of need
   b. A description of the functions that will and will not be performed
   c. An updated IT asset inventory
   d. Preliminary risk assessment, including criticality and sensitivity ratings
   e. Proposed operational profile and duty cycle
   f. List of potential users
   g. Internal and external interfaces, connectivity, and dependencies
   h. Constraints for the operational environment

By IT asset criticality, number and percentage of projects for which the security
concept developed during concept formulation: 2.4.1.4
   a. Defined the security features and functions to be performed
   b. Defined how the security features and functions would be assured and
      the integrity level they need to be assured to
   c. Defined operational procedures needed to ensure that the security
      posture to which the new technology is certified will be maintained
      once it is deployed in the operational environment
   d. Addresses internal and external interfaces, connectivity, and dependencies
   e. Addressed compliance with security and privacy regulations, standards,
      and policies
   f. Defines strategies for conducting ST&E, C&A, and IV&V activities

By IT asset criticality, during concept formulation percentage of projects for
which: 2.4.1.5
   a. Cost and schedule constraints are identified
   b. Go/no-go checkpoints are identified throughout the project
   c. An initial list of suppliers is developed
   d. A first cut is made about what components will be COTS and which
      will be custom developed

By IT asset criticality: 2.4.1.6
   a. Percentage of projects that were discontinued during concept formula-
      tion and distribution by reason
   b. Percentage of projects that failed or were discontinued later in the life
      cycle due to an error of commission or error of omission during concept
      formulation
   c. Percentage of projects that failed or were discontinued later in the life
      cycle due to deferring a decision that should have been made during
      concept formulation

Security Requirements Analysis and Specification

During concept formulation, the functional concept, security concept, intended use, operational profile, duty cycle, and operational environment are defined. Once these items have solidified, the next step is requirements analysis and specification. Requirements are specified in an implementation-independent style. Requirements specify "what" needs to be done, not "how" it is to be done. The "how" comes later during the architecture and design step. A distinction is made between requirements (the "what") and the architecture and design (the "how") so that the utmost creativity can be employed to derive an efficient and cost-effective solution. Several types of requirements are specified for a new product, system, or network[158]:

- *Functional requirements:* the type of functionality to be provided.
- *Performance requirements:* the capacity, throughput, bandwidth, processor loading, number of concurrent sessions, transaction volume and speed, etc. to be supported.
- *Reliability requirements:* requirements to ensure that a certain level of accurate, consistent, and repeatable performance is maintained under specified operational conditions.
- *Security requirements:* security features and functions to be implemented by the IT security control and protection systems and the integrity level to which these feature and functions need to be verified.
- *Safety requirements:* requirements to ensure that a product or system performs predictably under normal and abnormal conditions and the likelihood of an unplanned event occurring is minimized and its consequences controlled and contained, thereby preventing accidental injury or death, environmental or property damage, whether accidental or intentional.

This discussion focuses on security requirements. Physical and personnel security requirements must also be specified. However, the emphasis here is on IT security requirements.

Security requirements specify what security features and functions must be implemented and the integrity level to which they should be verified. The security features and functions are drawn from the 16 components of the IT security control and protection systems. For example, what types of logical access controls are needed? How extensive do the error, exception, and incident handling procedures need to be? What degree of domain separation is needed? What levels of availability and integrity are needed? What types of supportability and maintainability are needed to ensure that availability requirements are met?

Security requirements are specified in a hierarchical manner, with each subsequent level adding additional details. The intent is to decompose the requirements to the lowest level of detail possible to ensure that the requirements are not misinterpreted, but without stating how the solution for the requirements should be designed. Consider the following example:

Goal: Prevent unauthorized logical access to IT assets.

1. The system shall authenticate all users prior to granting them access to any IT assets.
   1.1 The system shall perform authentication using strong two-factor authentication.
      1.1.1 A biometric parameter shall be used to authenticate local users.
      1.1.2 A security token shall be used to authenticate remote users.

High-level requirements are derived from the security goals and objectives stated in the security concept. These same goals are used to identify appropriate metrics in response to a GQM. In this example, one requirement that could be derived from the goal is to require that all users be authenticated prior to accessing IT assets. This is a high-level requirement. High-level requirements are qualified by mid-level requirements. In this case, the mid-level requirement adds the stipulation that strong two-factor authentication must be performed. Low-level requirements add or clarify certain details. In this example, a distinction is made between local and remote users. One authentication parameter for local users must be a biometric, while remote users must present a security token.

The integrity level to which security features and functions need to be verified is specified after the requirements decomposition is complete. The integrity level determines the depth and rigor of the security engineering lifecycle activities and the ongoing risk management activities. The integrity level is determined as a function of (1) the criticality of the IT assets, (2) the sensitivity of the information processed by the IT assets, (3) the preliminary risk assessment, and (4) the perceived motive, expertise, and resource of attackers, which is referred to as the attack potential. These four parameters are analyzed and an appropriate integrity level selected. In general, an integrity level is chosen for the entire product or system. The integrity level for an individual component may be higher than that specified for the entire product or system, but not lower.

Taking the time to specify good security requirements is not just an intellectual exercise or a paper chase. On the contrary, the best vulnerability prevention strategy an organization can pursue is to specify good security requirements. Several studies have concluded that approximately 80 percent of the defects found after a system is deployed are traceable to wrong or missing requirements.[158, 285, 286] It goes without saying that it is easier and cheaper to correct a wrong or missing requirement during the requirements analysis and specification step than after a product or system has been built and fielded — not to mention the cost of downtime and lost revenue because of the defect. Like concept formulation, the requirements analysis and specification step should not be rushed.

A good security requirement possesses several characteristics; a security requirement that does not meet these criteria needs more work[21, 158]:

- Clear
- Complete

- Concise
- Correct
- Consistent
- Verifiable

Security requirements must be specified in clear, unambiguous language — language that is not subject to multiple interpretations. The security requirements specified for a product or system must be complete and form a coherent set that is sufficient to achieve the security goals and objectives stated in the security concept. For the security requirements to be complete, all dependencies between requirements must be resolved.[21] All known or presumed threats to the technology or operational environment must be addressed.[21] In addition, dependencies on internal and external entities must be taken into account. There cannot be any missing requirements or gaps between the security concept and the specified security requirements. Good security requirements are correct and internally consistent. Security requirements must be consistent with each other and organizational security policies[21] and regulatory requirements. Security requirements must be consistent with the intended use and operational environment. Security requirements must correctly reflect the logical and physical boundaries of the technology and the security concept. Furthermore, security requirements must be verifiable. There is no point in specifying requirements for security features and functions that cannot be verified. A requirement that cannot be verified cannot be met or proven to work. Formal methods are often used to verify the correctness of security requirements in environments that have a very high criticality, sensitivity, or risk.

Security requirements should be specified for COTS as well as custom-developed products and systems. Unless security requirements are specified, there is no way for an organization to know (in fact) what products it needs to purchase. Unless security requirements are specified, there is no way for an organization to know if a product meets its needs, or which product best meets its needs. Some organizations take a haphazard approach to security requirements for COTS products. They decide to buy a little of this and a little of that based on misleading advertising and overzealous salesmen who lead them around like the pied piper. Security mechanisms are bought and installed without any requirements or testing. The first product does not work quite right or as promised, so a second and third product are purchased. Soon there are racks of very impressive-looking equipment and a request is made to double the IT security budget. However, if these purchases are not tied to *bona fide* security requirements, they will do little to nothing to secure the IT infrastructure. The security budget will be wasted and the security ROI will be zero or negative. It is time to grow up and put the engineering into security, and that means analyzing and specifying a complete set of security requirements.

The metrics listed below measure the resilience of an organization's approach to generating security requirements. The discussion that follows explains the thrust and necessity of some of the metrics, to reinforce the importance of this step.

Total number of security requirements by level: 2.4.2.1
  a. High-level requirements
  b. Mid-level requirements
  c. Low-level requirements

Requirements traceability: 2.4.2.2
  a. Percentage of security requirements that are traceable to the goals and
      objectives stated in the security concept
  b. Percentage of the goals and objectives stated in the security concept
      that are traceable to the security requirements

Percentage of security requirements for which internal and external dependencies have been identified and taken into account: 2.4.2.3
  a. Percentage of security requirements that are dependent on assumptions
      stated for internal entities for which the organization has control
  b. Percentage of security requirements that are dependent on assumptions
      stated for external entities, for which the organization has limited or
      no control

Number and distribution of security requirements across IT security control
system functions and IT security protection system functions.   2.4.2.4

Number and percentage of stakeholder groups that: 2.4.2.5
  a. Participated during security requirements analysis and specification
  b. Approved the final security requirements

Percentage of security requirements that are consistent with: 2.4.2.6
  a. Federal security and privacy regulations
  b. Corporate security and privacy regulations
  c. Industry standards

Percentage of security requirements that: 2.4.2.7
  a. Have been independently validated
  b. Are testable by static and/or dynamic analysis
  c. Are not testable by static or dynamic analysis
  d. Have been proven to be correct through the use of formal methods

Extent to which security requirements are consistent with criticality, sensitivity,
and risk ratings: 2.4.2.8
  a. Green — completely consistent, no changes needed
  b. Blue — the majority but not all requirements are consistent, changes
      are needed
  c. Yellow — a minority of the requirements are consistent, major changes
      are needed
  d. Red — not consistent at all

Distribution of security requirements errors found, by the severity of the error and the type of error[8, 9]: 2.4.2.9

    a. Ambiguous requirement
    b. Incomplete requirement
    c. Wrong requirement
    d. Inconsistent requirement
    e. Requirement not verifiable
    f. Missing requirement

Distribution of security requirements errors, by the severity of the error and the type of requirement: 2.4.2.10

    a. By IT security control system function
    b. By IT security protection system function
    c. Wrong integrity level specified (too high/too low)

Distribution of security requirements errors, by the severity of the error and the step in which the error was uncovered: 2.4.2.11

    a. Security requirements analysis and specification
    b. Security architecture and design
    c. Development and implementation
    d. Security test and evaluation (ST&E), certification and accreditation (C&A), independent verification and validation (IV&V)
    e. Delivery, installation, and deployment
    f. Operations and maintenance
    g. Decommissioning

Impact of security requirements errors: 2.4.2.12

    a. Operational impact (downtime, number of IT assets involved, number of users involved, etc.)
    b. Cost impact

The first metric is straightforward and provides a foundation for the metrics that follow; it is simply a count of the number of security requirements by level (i.e., number of high-, mid-, and low-level requirements). But do not stop here; there is a lot of useful information to be gleaned from the metrics that follow. Next, the effectiveness of the security requirements decomposition process is verified. A mapping is performed to verify that all lower-level requirements are traceable back to high-level requirements, and vice versa. The objective is to ensure that (1) no additional (untraceable) lower-level requirements have crept in, and (2) all high-level requirements have been adequately decomposed. The resolution of internal and external dependencies is measured next. As a simplistic illustration, access control requirements depend on identification and authentication requirements to function correctly. If no identification and authentication requirements are specified, the access control requirements will not function correctly. Unfortunately, this step is often overlooked, resulting in requirements gaps that are actualized as vulnerabilities and exposed as security incidents. Following this, there is a metric relating to the distribution of security requirements. The allocation of security requirements among the features and functions of IT security control and protection systems is measured, such as access control, authentication, and encryption. The intent is to make sure that the distribution of requirements is not lopsided. For example, if there are 95 access control requirements and only one identification and authentication requirement, either this is a very unusual system or something is wrong. The number of requirements should increase or decrease in proportion to the system risk, information sensitivity, and asset criticality. The distribution of requirements across high-level security functions and the level of decomposition should be relatively even. Often what happens is that the requirements in one area, such as identification and authentication, are elucidated in detail because people are familiar with the topic, while other areas they are not familiar with, such as encryption, are specified in one or two terse requirements. This metric will highlight this situation and the need for improvement in capturing security requirements.

On to another sticky wicket — stakeholder involvement in specifying security requirements. If the numbers are not high on both of these metrics, the requirements will not pass the completeness or cohesiveness test and the project is heading for trouble. Speaking of sticky wickets, the next metric measures compliance. If an organization is a government agency or a regulated industry, security and privacy requirements must adhere to federal regulations or the organization runs the risk of fines and other penalties, not to mention the loss of customer confidence. If security and privacy requirements do not comply with corporate standards, what is the point of having the standards? Do the standards need improving, or is more effort needed to enforce compliance? Some organizations are in a sector in which compliance with industry standards is a must to remain competitive or do business with trusted partners. It is better to find out during the requirements analysis and specification, rather than later, whether or not security and privacy requirements are compliant. Another way to measure compliance, completeness, and cohesion is to have an independent third party validate security requirements. This step can save a lot of time and expense in the long run. Determining whether or not security and privacy requirements are verifiable, either through static analysis or dynamic analysis, is a further measure of correctness. A security requirement that is not testable cannot be verified and increases system risk exposure.

Static analysis refers to analytical techniques that are used to assess the security of a system without executing it.[156] Static analysis can be used to analyze operational control flow, data control flow, data usage, and properties such timing, capacity loading, state transitions, and correctness and consistency when moving from requirements, to a design, and ultimately the as-built system. Static analysis techniques can be performed during all life-cycle phases. Examples of static analysis techniques include: critical path analysis, fault tree analysis (FTA), failure mode effects criticality analysis (FMECA), HAZOP studies, Petri nets, cause consequence analysis, change impact analysis, and sneak circuit analysis.[158] Dynamic analysis refers to exercising the system being assessed through actual execution.[156] This is the realm of traditional testing activities such as functional testing, logical testing (i.e., failure assertion, structural testing, and statistical-based testing), stress testing, and ST&E. Unlike static analysis, major system components must have been built before dynamic analysis can be performed. (For more information about static analysis techniques, see Reference 156.)

These metrics may sound like "everything you wanted to know about your security and privacy requirements, but were afraid to ask." Believe me, the consequences of not asking these questions during the requirements analysis phase are worse. The value of metrics in highlighting problem areas early in the life cycle, when it is much easier and cheaper to fix problems, is more than evident. It should also be apparent by now that there is a lot more to security engineering than bolting on some firewalls and IDSs to systems and networks that are already operational. Security and privacy do not "just happen" — they must be engineered like any other system function or property.

Security Architecture and Design

IEEE Std. 610.12 defines an architecture as "the organizational structure of a system or component," and a design as "the result of defining the architecture, components, interfaces and other characteristics of a system or component." A security architecture and design describes how the various features and functions specified in the security requirements will be implemented. The "what" specified in the security requirements is translated into the "how" in a security architecture and design. The security architecture represents the high-level or logical design, while the low-level or physical design captures precise implementation details. Several different levels of security architectures and designs are developed. A security architecture and design is developed for an individual component or product, an individual system or network, a collection of systems and networks within a facility or region, and enterprise-wide. The different levels of security architectures and designs assign security roles and responsibilities to different components, define interfaces and per-formance criteria, and address interoperability issues. The intent is to ensure that individual components, collections of components, and the enterprise as a whole operate in a known secure state at all times. A security architecture and design for a component or system details what goes on "inside the box," as well as how "the box" fits into and complements the overall security architecture. As a result, it is essential for all the different levels of security architectures and designs to be consistent and complementary, not just when initially issued but throughout the life of a component or system.

The same quality characteristics that apply to security requirements are applicable to a security architecture and design. A good security architecture and design is clear, complete, concise, correct, consistent, and verifiable. A good security architecture and design must be stated in a clear manner through a combination of text, diagrams, models, and other formal and informal representations. A clear design is easily understood by developers. A design that is not clear is subject to misinterpretation, multiple interpretations, and guesswork on the part of developers, all of which will lead to vulnerabilities and other problems in the final product. A good security architecture and design is a complete reflection of all stated security requirements. All of the security requirements have been incorporated into the architecture and design, yet no additional or unspecified functionality has crept in. A good security architecture and design is documented completely, but concisely. A developer should not have to wade through page after page of rambling, repetitive, unstructured design material. Understandability decreases and the likelihood of errors being introduced increases if an architecture and a design are not specified in a concise manner. A security architecture and design must implement specified security requirements correctly. If the requirements state that only two log-on attempts are allowed, the design must follow suit. If the requirements state that an account is to be locked after failing two log-on attempts, the design must lock the account and not allow the user to retry after a timeout period. A security architecture and design must be consistent. A security architecture and design must be consistent with specified security requirements. Internally, different parts of the security architecture and design must be consistent. Externally, a security architecture and design must be consistent with the other levels of security architectures and designs that are above, below, and parallel to it. It is pointless to develop a security architecture and design in a vacuum. If a security architecture and design are not (1) derived from *bona fide* security requirements, (2) internally consistent, or (3) consistent with the external security operational environment, do not waste time putting them into the recycle box — deposit them directly in the compost pile. Fiction, fantasy, and mystery are not attributes of good security architectures and designs. It is equally unwise to outsource the development of an organization's security architecture and design to vendors. Under such an arrangement, the security architecture and design will be developed in response to one and only one requirement: to maximize the sale of the vendor's products. Finally, a good security architecture and design can be verified as being a complete, correct, and consistent implementation of stated security requirements. Security architectures and designs that cannot be verified, cannot be built (correctly) and will flunk security test and evaluation (ST&E). Often, designs are difficult to verify because they lack a cohesive organization and structure, or they are overly complex. Usually more time and thought or support from higher-level staff are needed to remove this opaqueness.

An iterative process is followed to create and refine a high-level security architecture and the corresponding low-level security design. Ideally, representatives from all stakeholder groups should participate in this process, to ensure that critical domain knowledge is captured. The organization, structure, interactions, and internal workings of the specified security features and functions are defined and optimized. A series of feasibility studies, cost-benefit studies, and other trade-off studies are performed as inputs to the design process. The intent is to produce the most efficient and cost-effective security architecture and design possible, one that meets all stated security requirements for the IT security control and protection systems, while minimizing complexity and dependencies. Most technical requirements can be implemented in a variety of different ways. Some design solutions are cost-effective, while others are not. Some design solutions make efficient use of IT resources, while others do not. Some design solutions meet all performance requirements with a comfortable margin to spare, while other design solutions are minimally compliant with performance requirements and have no reserve capacity for future growth. As a result, it is important to take the time to develop and analyze alternative design solutions so that the optimum solution can be pursued.

The security architecture and design process may uncover errors in security requirements. In particular, conflicting requirements, overlapping requirements, and gaps in security requirements are highlighted. When this happens, that part of the design process should be put on hold until the requirements problems are corrected.

A security architecture and design must be specified and planned to be resilient — resilience does not happen by itself. As Kay[114] states, the best approach to securing cyberspace is to "proactively architecture secure, flexible IT infrastructures that are based on [*bona fide* security requirements], rather than responding reactively." That is why close attention must be paid to the selection, specification, and implementation of IT security control and protection system functions. Despite an organization's best efforts, on occasion an IT security control system function will fail. That is when the IT security protection system functions step in to prevent, preempt, and control the security incident and contain the consequences. Hence, the resilience of the architecture and design of IT security control and protection system functions must correspond to the criticality, sensitivity, and perceived risk of the system or component. As Clarke notes, "Organizations have to architect their systems to be fault tolerant and that means compartmentalizing the system so it doesn't all go down … and they have to design it in a way that it is easy to bring back up."[114]

Security architectures and designs can be documented in a variety of informal and formal nomenclatures and formats. The important thing is to focus on the content and quality characteristics of the security architecture and design, and not get hung up on the format (unless there are overriding corporate, legal, or regulatory reasons for doing so). A consistent nomenclature should be used throughout an organization, so that it is possible to understand and compare different levels of security architectures and designs. A security architecture and design records all design details and decisions, so that nothing is left to chance or guesswork during development. The high-level security architecture should specify the underlying hardware, software, firmware, communications services, etc. The low-level design should be as detailed as a blueprint for a house or office building. Complete specifications should be provided for the design and operation of all internal and external interfaces. How, when, and why these interfaces are used must be explained, along with the anticipated volume and frequency of data exchanges. Also, priorities for exchanging data across interfaces should be established. Operational control flows and data control flows should be completely specified. Required timing, sequences, conditions, precursor events, and control logic, including error, exception, and incident handling, should be explained in detail. Interoperability issues must be resolved, especially in relation to timing and data formats. The relationship to and interaction with higher-level, lower-level, and parallel security architectures and designs must be described. All assumptions and dependencies on internal and external entities (such as power, HVAC, and public networks) must be clearly stated. To facilitate accurate and efficient construction, a security architecture and design needs to detail and quantify the types of resources needed, such as hardware, operating systems and utilities, memory, disk storage, processor speed, throughput, and capacity, telecommunications bandwidth, maximum number of concurrent sessions, archival material, output capabilities, etc. The resources specified must be consistent with availability and integrity requirements. For example, if redundancy or diversity is specified, additional resources may be required, as well as higher performance resources. A complete operational profile and duty cycle are defined as part of the security architecture and design. Data elements that are created, manipulated, and stored are documented. In particular, the format, use, initial value, legal values, and memory locations of data elements are defined in a data dictionary. This is true for both end-user data elements and system control parameters. Rules for validating data inputs and outputs are also defined.

The accuracy and integrity of a security architecture are verified through a combination of static analysis techniques and security assurance activities. In high-criticality, high-sensitivity, or high-risk environments, formal proofs of correctness may be generated. It is best to use a three-tiered process to verify security architectures and designs. The design team verifies the security architecture and design first. The security architecture and design are evaluated against the six quality characteristics. Traceability to and from stated security requirements, both functional and performance, is assessed to ensure that (1) the architecture and design incorporate all requirements, and (2) no additional unspecified functionality is present. The design team verifies that overlapping security requirements, conflicting security requirements, and gaps in security requirements were resolved correctly. Finally, an assessment is made as to whether or not the security architecture and design has been sufficiently optimized, the organization and structure of the security architecture and design is logical, and complexity has been minimized. Next, representatives from all stakeholder groups verify the security architecture and design. The stakeholder representatives follow the same process as the design team, but focus on ensuring that domain knowledge has been captured correctly. Often, designs are presented in different views to ensure completeness and facilitate understanding by different audiences. For example, stakeholder representatives might evaluate a different view than the design team. Depending on the criticality, sensitivity, and risk, an independent team might also be called in to verify the security architecture and design. Each of the three review teams documents its findings and recommendations to correct design deficiencies separately. Once all deficiencies have been corrected or otherwise resolved (sometimes items noted as deficiencies are out of scope or not deficiencies), the project is ready to move to the development and implementation step.

The security architecture and design step is somewhat shorter if COTS components are employed as part of the design solution. The high-level security architecture of logical design is developed as usual. The low-level or physical design concentrates on the security functions assigned to each COTS component. Attention focuses on interfaces and interactions among COTS components and between COTS and custom-developed products. Operational control flows, data control flows, data formats, and timing issues are of particular concern. In addition, a thorough laboratory evaluation is conducted to (1) ensure that all unused functionality can be disabled, such that it cannot be accidentally or intentionally invoked, and (2) confirm the presence or absence of undocumented features and functions and how they will be controlled. Finally, the security architecture and design must define and implement hardware error confinement areas (HECAs) and software error confinement areas (SECAs) to contain latent defects found in a COTS product and prevent their propagation to other COTS or custom-developed products. The same process is followed to verify the security architecture and design.

The metrics listed below measure the resilience of an organization's approach to generating a security architecture and design. The discussion that follows explains the thrust and necessity of some of the metrics, to reinforce the importance of this step.

Percentage (%) of security requirements: 2.4.3.1

    a. Included in the security architecture and design, by level (high-level, mid-level, low-level)
    b. Not included in the security architecture and design, by level (high-level, mid-level, low-level)
    c. Distribution of security requirements not included by IT security control and protection system function

Number of security architecture and design features for which there is no corresponding security requirement. 2.4.3.2

Number of gaps that have been identified in the security requirements as part of the security architecture and design step: 2.4.3.3

    a. Distribution of gaps by severity
    b. Distribution of gaps by IT security control and protection system function

Number of security requirements errors that have been identified as part of the security architecture and design step: 2.4.3.4

    a. Distribution of errors by severity
    b. Distribution of errors by IT security control and protection system function
    c. Distribution of errors by type of requirements error (ambiguous, incomplete, incorrect, inconsistent, not verifiable)

Extent to which the security architecture and design meet the following criteria, using the following scale: 0 — none to 10 — highest, maximum 50 points: 2.4.3.5

    a. Logical organization and structure
    b. Efficient use of resources
    c. Complexity has been minimized
    d. Cost effective
    e. Function and performance have been optimized

Percentage of security architecture and design that has been: 2.4.3.6

    a. Verified by the design team
    b. Agreed to by all stakeholders
    c. Verified by an independent team

Security architecture and design verification: 2.4.3.7

    a. Number and type of static analysis techniques that were used to verify the security architecture and design
    b. Number and type of security assurance activities that were successfully completed to verify the integrity of the security architecture and design

Degree to which the security architecture and design complies with: 2.4.3.8

    a. Federal security and privacy regulations
    b. Corporate security and privacy policies
    c. Industry security and privacy standards

Percentage of organizational units that use the same nomenclature to document security architectures and designs.   2.4.3.9

Extent to which the organization's IT infrastructure is accurately captured in different levels of security architectures and designs that are complete and consistent hierarchically and laterally, using the following scale: 0 — not at all, to 10 — completely.   2.4.3.10

Extent to which the following items are completely and accurately specified in the security architecture and design, using the following scale: 0 — not at all, to 10 — completely, maximum 120 points: 2.4.3.11

    a. Internal interfaces
    b. External interfaces
    c. Interoperability issues
    d. Operational control flows
    e. Data control flows
    f. Assumptions
    g. Dependencies on internal and external entities
    h. Resources needed
    i. Operational profile and duty cycle
    j. Data elements, end-user data and control parameters
    k. Timing, critical event sequences
    l. Performance issues

Extent to which the following items are completely and accurately specified for COTS components in the security architecture and design, using the following scale: 0 — not at all, to 10 — completely, maximum 100 points: 2.4.3.12

a. Interaction between COTS components
b. Interaction between COTS and custom-developed products
c. Interfaces between COTS components
d. Interfaces between COTS and custom-developed products
e. Operational control flows to/from COTS products
f. Data control flows to/from COTS products
g. Ability and need to disable unused functionality
h. Need to confirm and contain presence of undocumented features and functions
i. Definition of hardware error confinement areas (HECAs)
j. Definition of software error confinement areas (SECAs)

Extent to which the security architecture and design is consistent with criticality, sensitivity, and risk ratings: 2.4.3.13

a. Green — completely consistent, no changes needed
b. Blue — the majority but not all of the security architecture and design is consistent, changes are needed
c. Yellow — a minority of the requirements are consistent, major changes are needed
d. Red — not consistent at all

Impact of security architecture and design errors: 2.4.3.14

a. Operational impact (downtime, number of IT assets involved, number of users involved, etc.)
b. Cost impact

Note: each review team (design team, stakeholder representatives, and independent review team) should complete score sheets for metrics 2.4.3.5, 2.4.3.10, 2.4.3.11, 2.4.3.12, and 2.4.3.13. Differences between the three score sheets should be resolved before proceeding to the development and implementation step.

Ensuring that a security architecture and design is accurate, complete, and consistent with the security requirements is the overriding goal of the security architecture and design step. The first question to ask, to see whether or not this goal will be achieved, concerns the responsiveness of the design to the security requirements. There are several different ways responsiveness can be measured. The percentage of the security requirements that are, or conversely are not, included in the design provides some initial insight. The distribution of missing security requirements across IT security control and protection system functions, such as access control, authentication, encryption, etc., indicates weak points in the security architecture and design. Perhaps the designers did not understand the requirements or the requirements were not detailed enough. Another perspective to examine is the number of design features for which there is no corresponding security requirement. Here, the designers got a bit carried away and strayed from their manifesto. These items should be deleted. Additional unspecified or unintended functionality is frequently a source of latent security defects.

Most likely, some gaps in the security requirements will be uncovered during the security architecture and design step. Requirements gaps occur through an error of omission. A security requirement may be missing, a dependency was not resolved, or a requirement was not decomposed to a sufficient level of detail. Knowledge of the distribution of gaps by severity category and across IT security control and protection system functions will help improve the requirements engineering process and cross-check for further gaps. The security architecture and design step is the time to find and remedy the situation, not after a system or component has been built.

Erroneous requirements are a corollary to requirements gaps. Erroneous requirements — wrong, inconsistent, conflicting, ambiguous, and incomplete requirements — occur as a result of errors of commission. An indication of the magnitude of the problem can be gleaned from the number of requirements errors and their distribution by severity category and across IT security control and protection system functions.

Two measures of the "goodness" of a design are (1) modularity, which should be high, and (2) complexity, which should be low. A logical organization and structure facilitates understandability, which in turn simplifies preventive, adaptive, and corrective maintenance. Modularity is a good feature to have, especially when the time comes to do an emergency patch. Complexity is the opposite of modularity and is a measure of the old "spaghetti code" syndrome. Complexity complicates verification and maintainability in a non-linear fashion and often indicates uncertainty or difficulty understanding the design on the part of the developer. Unnecessary complexity is often the source of vulnerabilities. Measuring modularity and complexity during the security architecture and design step can help to avoid expensive rework later.

Three percentages — the percentage of the design that has been verified by the design team, agreed to by stakeholders, and independently verified — measure the soundness of the security architecture and design. Independent verification is bound to catch some design errors that in-house staff missed, no matter how thorough they were; often, these errors are related to a lack of domain knowledge. Stakeholder agreement is a strong endorsement of the correctness of operational control flows and data control flows. The extent to which design integrity has been verified can be measured by two process metrics: (1) the number and type of static analysis techniques used to assess design robustness, and (2) the number and type of security assurance activities that were completed successfully. Security assurance activities include items such as configuration management, security test and evaluation (ST&E), and the preparation of life-cycle documentation. The more complementary static analysis techniques used and the more security assurance activities performed, the better (up to a point), because the different techniques and activities will catch different types of design errors.[158]

Finally, compliance with federal security and privacy regulations, corporate security and privacy policies, and industry security and privacy standards is measured. Compliance can be measured using an interval scale, because there are a specific number of provisions in a regulation, policy, or standard against which compliance can be assessed.

In their totality, these metrics can provide valuable and timely insight into the accuracy and completeness of a security architecture and design, and its consistency with the security requirements.

Development and Implementation

The development and implementation step turns the security architecture and design into the target product or system. Discipline is imposed on the development and implementation step to ensure that what comes out of this step is what is expected, and not a surprise. Some organizations like to start the security engineering life-cycle activities with the development and implementation step, as if they can shake a magic wand and, *voila*, the perfect IT security product or system will appear. However, if security requirements have not been specified and a security architecture and design has not been defined, how is this magic product or system going to solve undefined and unknown security problems? How will anyone know when or if these undefined and unknown security problems have been solved? How will anyone even know where to plug in this magic product or system — since the security architecture is nonexistent? As a professor of mine once said, it is a good idea to know whether you are building a bicycle or a tank before beginning the development and implementation step.

During the 1970s, there were debates about whether software development was an art (the result of unbridled creativity) or a science (the result of a disciplined methodology). The past 30 years have provided more than ample evidence that you cannot just turn the software developers loose. Their unbridled creativity is the root cause of decades of massive cost overruns, significant schedule delays, projects that fail to deliver 20 percent of the functionality promised, and a host of latent defects and security vulnerabilities. Creativity is great, but in this instance it needs to be channeled toward finding an efficient solution to the problem set expressed in the security requirements, architecture, and design. Adherence to a disciplined development methodology becomes more and more important as the number of developers and development teams increases.

The development and implementation step is when the IT security control and protection system functions transition from a paper design or prototype model into an "as-built" product or system. Features such as partitioning, information hiding, diversity, and security kernels take shape while functions such as resource management and security management are built. Features and functions are not constructed all at once. Rather, sub-components are developed and their functionality verified. Groups of sub-components are integrated and verification activities are repeated, while paying special attention to timing, interfaces, and other interoperability issues. The process is repeated as different groups or levels of sub-components are integrated and verified, until the entire product or system is constructed. On large projects, multiple teams, often located in different cities or countries, are involved in development; hence a disciplined methodology is needed to prevent total chaos during development and implementation.

Most development activities today are conducted with the assistance of computer-aided software engineering (CASE) tools. Depending on the specific tool, the entire design may be entered into the tool and the majority of the code automatically generated. In this scenario, security concerns are raised about the accuracy and integrity of the CASE tools and whether or not they are certified to any standards. Some old-timers still insist on doing development by hand; sometimes this is necessary when developing embedded real-time systems. From a security point of view, this practice does not raise any additional concerns.

Development activities frequently involve integrating COTS products from multiple vendors or a combination of COTS and custom-developed components. A disciplined methodology is needed to ensure that interface, timing, and interoperability issues are thoroughly evaluated at each integration stage to prevent vulnerabilities from creeping in. The vast majority of COTS products come with "fringe benefits" known as undocumented features and functions, not to mention latent defects. As a result, the development and implementation step must take the time to identify these fringe benefits and how they are going to be controlled and contained.

Rigor is imposed on the development and implementation step to ensure traceability to the security requirements, architecture, and design. All of the features, functions, and constraints specified in the security architecture and design must be present and accounted for in the as-built product or system. No additional unspecified functionality is allowed, nor is less functionality acceptable. Developers may think they are doing the customer a favor by adding some bells and whistles. In reality, they are creating vulnerabilities because they do not understand the big picture — the overall security architecture and how all the pieces fit together.

The same five quality characteristics apply to the development and implementation of a product or system. A quality output of the development and implementation step is clear, complete, concise, consistent, and verifiable. In addition, a sixth quality characteristic is added during this step: modifiable.[3] The first five quality characteristics are prerequisites for the sixth quality characteristic. The development and implementation of a product or system should be easy to understand. There should be a clear path from the approved security architecture and design to the as-built product or system. The purpose, function, structure, logic, interfaces, etc. of each component and sub-component should be obvious; otherwise, supportability and maintainability are in jeopardy. An as-built product or system must be a complete instantiation of the security architecture and design. Nothing can be left out or added during the development and implementation step. An as-built product or system must be complete or finished before moving on to the next step. Too often, COTS and custom-developed products are rushed through the development and implementation step. A product that is only ~80 percent complete is knowingly pushed out the door to meet an arbitrary schedule, with assurances from above that everything will be fixed later, but it never is. Incomplete defective products are fielded and disaster sets in. Development is development. Testing is testing. Operations and maintenance are operations and maintenance. Each of these steps serves different purposes. Deferring development activities until the operations and maintenance step puts the entire IT infrastructure at risk because of gaping security holes. Different skill sets and staff are associated with each step of the engineering life-cycle activities. It is quite likely that the operations and maintenance staff will not be able to complete the development activity as prescribed, and new vulnerabilities will be introduced in the process. It is also quite likely that development activities conducted under the operations and maintenance umbrella will not be subject to the same degree of rigor when it comes to security test and evaluation (ST&E), certification and accreditation (C&A), and independent verification and validation (IV&V). Hence, the real security integrity of the product or system will be unknown. Deferring problems never solves them; it merely delays the problems and magnifies the pain.

The development and implementation of a product or system should be concise. That means that the implementation itself is efficient and makes efficient use of system resources. Inefficient implementations contain a fair amount of unused, unreachable, and dead code. The software is not well structured and contains a lot of unnecessary repetitive logic. Some CASE tools perform optimization, and others do not. Inefficient implementations are vulnerability prone because their long and winding illogical structure is often difficult to verify and creates wonderful pockets in which to insert malware. Poor implementations tend to be resource hogs, using two, three, or more times as much memory, processor time, storage, bandwidth, and other finite resources than really needed. Other key processes are delayed or locked out in the interim.

The development and implementation of a product or system must be internally consistent in terms of how data elements are named, defined, and used, and how interfaces are specified, invoked, and controlled. Operational control flows, data control flows, and timing parameters must be consistent. Errors in the above items are exposed during component integration. The development and implementation of a product or system must also be consistent with the specification for the operational environment, the operational profile, and the duty cycle. These issues go beyond simple functional testing and need to be evaluated by a combination of static and dynamic analysis techniques. If the implementation of a product or system is not consistent with the specified operational environment or duty cycle, there is no point in deploying it — it will exhibit a hard failure right from the beginning and facilitate a major security compromise in the process. Many serious security incidents can be traced back to a mismatch between a COTS product and the operational environment or operational profile that caused the product or system to become saturated or unstable.

The development and implementation of a product or system must be capable of being verified against the security architecture and design. This is true regardless of whether the product or system is COTS or custom developed. If a product or system cannot be verified as being a complete and accurate instantiation of the security architecture and design, it should be rejected and sent back to the drawing board. Implementations that are 80 percent complete or 70 percent accurate are 100 percent insecure and represent a disaster waiting to happen.

A new quality characteristic is added during the development implementation step: modifiable.[3] For a product or system to be modifiable, it must first be clear, complete, concise, consistent, and verifiable. It is only logical that a requirement be added at this point for a product or system to be modifiable. There is not a single product or system in the world, from 1943 to the present, that from initial delivery and deployment remained untouched until the day it was decommissioned. On the contrary, change proposals, trouble reports, and preventive, adaptive, and corrective maintenance begin immediately. Consequently, it is essential for a product or system to be easily modified without disrupting the security posture to which it was certified. In fact, some international standards require or highly recommend that requirements that are likely to change in the future, due to planned enhancements or changes in the operational environment, be earmarked prior to the development and implementation step. Then partitioning, information hiding, and other techniques can be employed to minimize the disruption and ripple effect during modifications. Modifiability spans the bridge between the supportability and maintainability IT security control and the security impact analysis, configuration management, and patch management operational security control. Modifiability also determines the extent of regression testing needed after a change is made. Taking the time up front during the development and implementation step to ensure that a product or system is modifiable saves considerable time, resources, cost, and headaches later in the life cycle.

The development environment, tools, techniques, procedures, and standards are all defined as part of the discipline imposed on the development and implementation step. The tools, techniques, procedures, and standards selected must be appropriate for the type of product or system being developed, as well as the criticality, sensitivity, and risk. In general, the higher the criticality, sensitivity, and risk, the more formal the development methodology; in addition, there is a greater need for development tools and platforms to be certified. Another consideration is whether or not the same tools can be used during the operations and maintenance step. For example, there is a good chance of introducing or overlooking errors if different configuration management tools are used during the development and implementation and operations and maintenance steps. The process of setting up and using the development environment yields valuable information that can be used to fine-tune resource requirements prior to deployment. Since the development environment, particularly that used for integration, mimics the operational environment, this is a good time to see if the stated resource requirements are adequate for current and planned future use. Perhaps more memory or a more robust CPU is needed. Physical security and personnel security requirements must also be defined for the development environment. The last thing a project wants is for an unauthorized person to walk in and copy or modify prototypes and modules under development.

An important aspect of the development and implementation step is tracking the identification and resolution of errors. For each error, the following information should be captured:

- Type of error: requirements, security architecture and design, development and implementation, functional, performance, interface, timing, data element, addressing, etc.
- Conditions under which the error was exposed
- Root cause of the error
- Severity of the error
- Step in which the error was introduced
- How the error was resolved
- Impact of the error on other components

Errors must be investigated fully to ensure that they are understood and accurately resolved. The information listed above should be documented completely, regularly monitored, and independently verified. Analysis of this information provides valuable insights into the accuracy, integrity, and thoroughness of the development and implementation step, as well as earlier life-cycle activities. On large projects, especially those with distributed development teams, it is essential to define and implement standardized procedures for reporting and tracking errors.

Documentation created during the development and implementation step should be generated with an eye toward reusing it during ST&E and the operations and maintenance step. The development team should document all the design and implementation decisions it made and the rationale behind those decisions. Items such as the alternatives considered and the types of analysis performed should be captured. This information will save the operations and maintenance staff a lot of time and potential mistakes because they will not have to repeat the analysis or trade-off studies or guess at the rationale behind certain implementation specifics. Observations about changes or additions to resource requirements or testing strategies should be passed on as well. In addition, components and sub-components should be categorized as being security critical, security related, or not security related so that verification activities can be focused accordingly. Likewise, privacy-critical and privacy-related components and sub-components should be categorized. Again, this information is needed for verification purposes; it will also facilitate change impact analysis during operations and maintenance. Finally, the error history records should be made available to the operations and maintenance staff.

Why is so much time spent discussing development and implementation activities in this age of COTS-mania? For three very profound reasons. First, application layer security is the last best hope for securing the IT infrastructure, after all other protective layers, such as network security, operating system security, and physical security, have failed. Second, COTS just means that someone else developed the software. COTS does not mean that the software is of divine origin and without "sin" — far from it. Hopefully, this book is being read by some COTS software vendors and they will apply these lessons. That would certainly make life easier for the rest of us. Third, to highlight what can go wrong in a COTS product and to explain how to detect and be prepared for such an eventuality.

The metrics listed below measure the resilience of an organization's approach to development and implementation. The discussion that follows explains the thrust and necessity of some of the metrics, to reinforce the importance of this step.

Percentage of security design elements: 2.4.4.1
  a. Included in the as-built product or system
  b. Not included in the as-built product or system
  c. Distribution of design elements not included in the as-built product or system by IT security control and protection system functions

Number and percentage of as-built components for which there is no corresponding element in the security architecture and design.   2.4.4.2

Number of gaps that have been identified in the security architecture and design as part of the development and implementation step: 2.4.4.3
  a. Distribution of the gaps by severity
  b. Distribution of the gaps by IT security control and protection system function

Number of errors that have been identified in the security architecture and design as part of the development and implementation step: 2.4.4.4
  a. Distribution of errors by severity
  b. Distribution of errors by IT security control and protection system function
  c. Distribution of errors by type of error (ambiguous, incomplete, incorrect, inconsistent, not verifiable, not modifiable)

Extent to which the implementation of the as-built product or system meets the following criteria (0 — not at all, 10 — completely, maximum 60 points):   2.4.4.5
  a. Logical organization and structure
  b. Efficient use of resources
  c. Complexity has been minimized
  d. Cost-effective solution
  e. Performance has been optimized
  f. Supportable and maintainable

Percentage of the as-built product or system that has been: 2.4.4.6
  a. Verified by the development team
  b. Agreed to by all stakeholder representatives
  c. Verified by an independent team

Verification of development and implementation: 2.4.4.7

    a. Number and type of static analysis techniques that were used to verify the as-built product or system

    b. Number and type of security assurance activities that were successfully completed to verify the integrity of the as-built product or system

Degree to which the as-built product or system complies with the following items (0 — not at all, 10 — completely): 2.4.4.8

    a. Federal security and privacy regulations

    b. Corporate security and privacy policies

    c. Industry security and privacy standards

Degree to which the as-built product or system conforms to stated constraints for the operational profile, duty cycle, and operational environment. 2.4.4.9

Extent to which a disciplined methodology is imposed during the development and implementation step (0 — not at all, 10 — completely): 2.4.4.10

    a. Extent to which the methodology is consistent with the stated criticality, sensitivity, and risk

Extent to which standardized tools, techniques, procedures, and standards are specified for the development environment and are enforced (0 — not at all, 10 — completely): 2.4.4.11

    a. Extent to which the tools, techniques, procedures, and standards are consistent with the stated criticality, sensitivity, and risk

    b. Extent to which the tools, techniques, procedures, and standards are consistent with the operational environment

    c. Percentage of CASE tools that have been certified

    d. Percentage of tools that can continue to be used during ST&E and operations and maintenance

Extent to which the as-built product or system corresponds to the following quality characteristics (0 — not at all, 10 — completely): 2.4.4.12

    a. Clear

    b. Complete

    c. Concise/efficient

    d. Consistent

    e. Verifiable

    f. Modifiable

Percentage of projects that produce the following outputs as part of the development and implementation step: 2.4.4.13

    a. Updated resource requirements specifications

    b. Report of errors detected, resolved, and still open

    c. Implementation decisions and supporting rationale

    d. Analysis of alternatives

    e. Categorization of components as being security critical, security related, or not security related

  f. Categorization of components as being privacy critical, privacy related, or not privacy related

Percentage (%) of custom-developed and COTS sub-components that are verified: 2.4.4.14

  a. Prior to implementation
  b. As part of each integration step

Percentage (%) of component integration activities that evaluate: 2.4.4.15

  a. Security functionality
  b. Interfaces
  c. Interoperability
  d. Timing
  e. The ability to control and contain undocumented features and functions
  f. The ability to control and contain latent defects

Impact of development and implementation errors: 2.4.4.16

  a. Operational impact (downtime, number of IT assets involved, number of users involved, etc.)
  b. Cost impact

These metrics are a combination of (1) process metrics, which evaluate the thoroughness and appropriateness of the development and implementation step, and (2) product metrics, which evaluate the completeness and robustness of the as-built product or system, relative to the specified security requirements, architecture, and design. Earlier we measured the correspondence between the security architecture and design and the security requirements; now we shift to examine the correspondence between the as-built product or system and the security architecture and design. The intent is to ensure that the security architecture and design are completely incorporated in the as-built product or system and that they are incorporated correctly.

The percentage of approved design elements that are (or are not) included in the as-built product or system is measured first. The as-built product or system needs to incorporate all approved design elements. Some optimization of the allocation or implementation of security requirements is to be expected; however, all design elements must be accounted for in the final product or system. Weaknesses will be highlighted by examining the distribution of design elements not included in the as-built product or system across IT security control and protection system functions. In parallel, the number of as-built components for which there is no corresponding design element must be identified, to pinpoint problem areas, and then deleted. Unintended and unspecified functionality is a prime source of vulnerabilities in an operational system.

Designs are not always perfect, especially the first time around, so a gap analysis is performed next. In particular, gaps in the security architecture and design that were discovered as part of the development and implementation step are counted and characterized by severity and security functional area.

This information is used to go back and revalidate the security requirements, architecture, and design from which the as-built product or system was developed. Perhaps the gaps are legitimate. Perhaps the developers did not understand the design. Or, perhaps the developers found themselves in a schedule crunch and skipped a few items, which happens more often than not. The root cause of the gaps cannot be known unless this information is investigated; nor can appropriate corrective action be taken. Security metrics provide the insight needed to start the ball rolling. As a counterpart to the gap analysis, errors in the as-built product or system are analyzed next. Errors include wrong, inconsistent, conflicting, ambiguous, and incomplete implementation of the approved security architecture and design. Metrics capture information about both the number of errors and the distribution of errors by severity category and security functional area. The modularity and complexity of the as-built system are also assessed. Because similar metrics were generated during the requirements and security architecture and design steps, some trends should start to become visible.

The next metrics attempt to answer the question: why should anyone outside the development team have any confidence in the security of the as-built product or system? What percentage of the as-built product or system was (1) independently verified, and (2) agreed to by all stakeholder representatives? The higher the percentage, the better. The number and type of static analysis techniques used to verify the as-built product or system are also good indicators of robustness, assuming the results were acted upon. Likewise, the number and type of security assurance activities successfully completed during the development and implementation step are good indicators of the integrity of the as-built product or system.

Finally, to keep the project (and organization) out of trouble, it is a good idea to measure how well the as-built product or system complies with federal security and privacy regulations, corporate security and privacy policies, and industry standards. A further predictor of success is the degree to which the as-built product or system conforms to stated constraints for the operational profile, duty cycle, and operational environment.

Security Test and Evaluation (ST&E), Certification and Accreditation (C&A), Independent Validation and Verification (IV&V)

Security test and evaluation (ST&E), certification and accreditation (C&A), and independent validation and verification (IV&V) are not stand-alone life-cycle activities per se. Rather, these activities are ongoing throughout the security engineering life cycle. ST&E, C&A, and IV&V represent specialized validation and verification activities whose goals it is to ensure that a product or system conforms to security functional and integrity requirements. That way, when deployment time arrives, an organization can have confidence, which is backed up by evidence, in the security worthiness of the product or system.

ST&E, C&A, and IV&V are performed to ensure that a product or system operates according to its specification under normal and abnormal conditions.

The resilience of IT security controls is evaluated. A comparison is made between the actual resilience of a product or system and the level of resilience needed and specified. A variety of different techniques are used to accomplish this objective. Functional and structural testing are conducted. Tests are performed to determine the presence of unintended unspecified functionality and undocumented features, all of which could compromise security. Positive and negative tests are executed to verify (1) the correct operation of must work functions (MWFs) and must not work functions (MNWFs), (2) that illegal modes and sates cannot be reached accidentally or intentionally, and (3) that security policies have been implemented correctly and cannot be bypassed or violated.

Three attributes are generally used to measure the thoroughness and rigor of ST&E, C&A, and IV&V activities[21]:

1. Coverage
2. Depth
3. Independence

Functional testing evaluates the correct behavior of security features and functions. Formal test plans and procedures spell out the goals of the testing, test configurations, prescribed preconditions and sequences of events, and expected results. The tests are conducted in a controlled environment and evidence is collected to prove or disprove correct functional performance. Testing results are analyzed to assess the likelihood of undiscovered flaws and other undesired behavior.[21]

Test coverage evaluates the completeness of testing activities to determine whether or not they are sufficient to demonstrate that the product or system operates as specified.[21] For example, if twenty security functions are specified and only ten were tested, the test coverage could hardly be considered adequate. If only functional testing was conducted, and not structural testing, the test coverage would be inadequate. If only positive testing was conducted and not negative testing, the testing is incomplete. If a product or system was only tested in isolation and not in the operational environment, the test coverage is superficial. Inadequate test coverage leads to incomplete and misleading test results. The importance of adequate test coverage increases in proportion to asset criticality, information sensitivity, and risk.

Test depth evaluates the rigor of testing activities. That is, did the testing just skim the surface, or did it really exercise the features and functions under a variety of normal and abnormal conditions? Some testers approach testing as if IT components, particularly COTS products, are delicate fragile antiques that must be handled with care to avoid shattering them into a million pieces. But that is exactly what is needed — testing activities *are* undertaken to establish the exact breaking points of a product or system. This practice is common in hardware engineering and is referred to as destructive testing — an item is stressed until it crumbles or melts in order to find the real breaking point. Functionality, timing, interfaces, connectivity, and interoperability issues should all be evaluated in depth, under normal and abnormal conditions. What happens when events or commands occur out of sequence? What happens when events that are supposed to occur in sequence occur simultaneously? What is the maximum number of sessions that can be handled simultaneously? What is the maximum number of security credentials that can be arbitrated at one time? What is the maximum throughput, bandwidth, or processor load? What is the maximum number of data elements that can be indexed? All products and systems have finite processing capabilities. It is essential to learn where these breaking points are to facilitate effective resource management and prevent a product or system from becoming saturated or unstable once deployed — conditions which facilitate security compromises. These breaking points are frequently at much lower thresholds than advertising literature would lead one to believe. When minimum activity thresholds are breached, instability often results as well. Consequently, stress testing should force both minimum and maximum thresholds to determine the breaking points. Lack of adequate testing depth also leads to incomplete and misleading results.

To ensure objectivity and thoroughness, it is a good idea to have ST&E, C&A, and IV&V activities conducted by teams that are independent of the developers and system integrators. In-house staff may take a first cut at ST&E, but these activities need to be repeated by independent teams before any decisions are made. Developers and system integrators are too close to a project, under too much cost and schedule pressure, and have too much at stake to admit something is wrong and be completely objective at all times. Independent teams can compensate for deficiencies in test coverage and test depth; they are also free to repeat tests conducted by in-house staff, to see if they get the same results, and conduct new tests. The question that must be answered on a case-by-case basis is: what degree of independence is needed? Does the independent team need to come from another part of the same project, another part of the same organization or company, or an entirely separate organization or company? As a rule of thumb, the higher the asset criticality, information sensitivity, and risk, the higher the degree of independence needed during ST&E and C&A. Many of the regulations discussed in Chapter 3 require independent security testing or independent verification of the results. Because testing results are used to decide whether or not a product or system is ready to deploy and organizations are liable for negligent security violations, this is not an area in which to put on blinders.

As discussed previously, ST&E, C&A, and IV&V are not stand-alone activities in the security engineering life cycle. Instead, ST&E, C&A, and IV&V activities occur during each step of the security engineering life cycle, from requirements analysis and specification through decommissioning. ST&E, C&A, and IV&V activities verify that the requirements specified for security features and functions are clear, complete, concise, consistent, and verifiable, and that the integrity level is appropriate for the criticality, sensitivity, and risk. ST&E, C&A, and IV&V activities verify that a security architecture and design is understandable, complete, internally consistent, and consistent with the operational environment, operational profile, duty cycle, and external interface and connectivity requirements. ST&E, C&A, and IV&V activities also verify that a security architecture and design is traceable to the security requirements (no additional or missing features), verifiable, and appropriate for the criticality, sensitivity, and risk. ST&E, C&A, and IV&V activities verify that an as-built product or system is supportable, maintainable, complete, correct, consistent, and modifiable. These activities also verify that an as-built product or system makes efficient use of system resources and is traceable to the security architecture and design, again with no additional or missing features. The output from these activities is the basis upon which a decision is made about whether a product or system is ready to deploy — do the security features and functions operate as specified, and do they exhibit the necessary degree of resilience? ST&E, C&A, and IV&V activities continue during operations and maintenance to ensure that the security posture, to which the original product or system was certified, is maintained during preventive, adaptive, and corrective maintenance. During decommissioning ST&E, C&A, and IV&V activities, ensure that no security compromises occur as one product or system is shut down and the functions, services, and data are transferred to a new product or system. These activities also ensure that old equipment and storage media are sanitized and disposed of properly.

Because ST&E, C&A, and IV&V activities are ongoing throughout the life of a product or system, it is essential to budget sufficient funds to pay for these activities. Unfortunately, too many organizations are stuck in the 1960s mentality where "testing" is done after a product or system is built, and they budget accordingly. Why wait until after a product or system is built to find out that the security requirements, architecture, or design are wrong? The cost of fixing errors increases geometrically from one life-cycle activity to the next.

Different ST&E, C&A, and IV&V techniques are used at different points in the security engineering life cycle and for different purposes. A combination of static and dynamic analysis techniques is used to perform ST&E. Static analysis techniques can be used throughout the life of a product or system. Dynamic analysis techniques can only be used after a product or system is built. Static analysis techniques include Bayesian belief networks, cause consequence analysis, change impact analysis, common cause failure analysis, event tree analysis, fault tree analysis (FTA), failure mode effects criticality analysis (FMECA), hazard and operability studies, Petri nets, reliability block diagrams, response time memory constraint analysis, sneak circuit analysis, and usability analysis. (For a complete discussion of static analysis techniques, see Reference 156.)

The output from static analysis techniques can be used to guide dynamic analysis. Dynamic analysis exercises the as-built product or system; this is the realm of traditional testing activities. Dynamic analysis can be used as part of the selection process for COTS products. In general, dynamic analysis progresses through three tiers, assuming each previous tier was successful. To start, a laboratory evaluation is conducted to verify that the component performs all functions as stated. In the case of COTS products, this would involve comparing performance to the functionality stated in advertising literature, users manuals, and such. Assuming the anomalies noted during the laboratory evaluation are neither numerous nor serious, the dynamic analysis proceeds to a proof of concept demonstration. If not, the component is sent back for rework. If a COTS product is being evaluated and the anomalies are serious, the product may simply be rejected and another one evaluated. A proof of concept demonstration inserts the component under evaluation into a small-scale mock-up of the target operational environment. Functionality is verified in addition to performance issues such as timing and interfaces. Stress testing is conducted to determine the maximum load and processing. Usually, some rework is needed before continuing on to operational field testing. The third tier of dynamic analysis is the real proof of whether or not a product or system meets the security functional and integrity requirements, security architecture and design, and security worthiness test. This testing is conducted in a live operational setting. Tests are usually run for 30 to 90 days. Often, a configuration is set up whereby the new component or system executes in parallel to the existing equipment. That way, the performance of the old and new equipment under identical conditions can be compared. Anomalies are noted and resolved, and then a final deployment decision is made. The test coverage, test depth, and degree of independence during the three tiers of dynamic analysis are proportional to the asset criticality, information sensitivity, and risk.

As shown in Table 4.15, there are a variety of different ST&E techniques that can be used to verify the security functionality and integrity of an as-built product or system. These techniques include a combination of static and dynamic analysis techniques. Some of the techniques can be used prior to deploying a product or system and after deployment as part of the ongoing security assessments during operations and maintenance or in support of recertification and regression testing. Other techniques can only be used after deployment and only applied to an entire system or network — not individual components. Each of these techniques serves a different purpose. It is important to use a complementary set of ST&E techniques to obtain a comprehensive assessment. Deployment decisions should not be based on a single ST&E activity, unless you have already lined up a new job. (See reference 156 for a complete discussion of ST&E verification techniques.)

Certification and accreditation (C&A) encompasses ST&E but is broader. In addition to IT security controls, C&A examines operational security controls and physical security controls related to the IT infrastructure. C&A is a regulatory requirement. Federal regulations require that IT systems operated by or on behalf of the federal government undergo C&A every three years or following a major upgrade. NIST 800-37 is the current C&A standard for unclassified systems in the United States. C&A is required as part of FISMA, one of the regulations discussed in Chapter 3. Outside the United States, other standards and regulations are used to accomplish the same objectives. Individual components are not certified — only complete systems or networks.

Certification is a comprehensive assessment of the technical and nontechnical security features and other safeguards of a system associated with its

Table 4.15   ST&E Techniques That Can Be Used to Verify As-Built Products or Systems

Technique	Use Pre- and Post-Deployment for Components or Complete Systems and Networks	Only Use Post-Deployment for Complete Systems and Networks
I. Dynamic Analysis		
Boundary value analysis	x	
Equivalence class partitioning	x	
Interface testing	x	
Performance testing	x	
Statistical testing	x	
Stress testing	x	
Usability testing	x	
Network mapping		x
Vulnerability scanning		x
Brute force or penetration testing	x	
Security credential cracking	x	
File integrity checking		x
Virus and malware detection		x
War dialing		x
II. Static Analysis		
Control flow analysis (operational and data)	x	
Formal proofs of correctness	x	
Anomaly detection and pattern matching	x	
Testability analysis	x	
Common cause failure analysis	x	
Event tree analysis	x	
Fault tree analysis	x	
Failure mode criticality effects analysis	x	
Hazard and operability studies	x	
Petri nets	x	
Reliability block diagrams	x	
Response time memory constraint analysis	x	
Sneak circuit analysis	x	
Usability analysis	x	

use and operational environment to establish the extent to which a particular system meets a set of specified security requirements. The next step, accreditation, is a formal declaration by the Designated Approval Authority (DAA) that a system or network is approved to operate in a particular security mode using a prescribed set of safeguards, based on the residual risks identified during certification. The acceptability of the residual risk depends on the evidence of the resilience of IT and operational security controls and confidence in the plan of actions and milestones (POAM) to resolve deficiencies noted during ST&E and certification. Active involvement is required by the DAA to ensure that the deficiencies are actually resolved as planned; if not, any interim approvals to operate should be reevaluated. Serious thought must be given to planning, organizing, and conducting C&A activities. Otherwise, there is a high potential of C&A becoming a very expensive paper chase. Here we see a link between operational security resilience and ROI metrics, which is discussed in Chapter 5.

One last thought. Dynamic analysis and static analysis, particularly ST&E, C&A, and IV&V, are specialized skills. If these tasks are not assigned to staff members who have these specialized skills, understanding, and experience, an organization is wasting its time and money. People who lack this specialized competency will not know what to do, how to do it, when to do it, or what the results mean. They might generate a lot of pretty notebooks full of meaningless paper, but this facade will have no impact on the security of an organization's IT infrastructure. The end result will be just another "feel-good" gesture. Here we see a major link between operational security controls and the competence parameter of personnel security.

The metrics listed below measure the resilience of an organization's approach to ST&E, C&A, and IV&V. The discussion that follows explains the thrust and necessity of some of the metrics, to reinforce the importance of this step.

Percentage (%) of the following items that have been verified to perform according to specification in the operational environment: 2.4.5.1
  a. Security requirements
  b. Security architecture and design elements
  c. As-built security and privacy controls

Percentage (%) of the following items that have been verified to perform correctly during stress testing and under abnormal conditions: 2.4.5.2
  a. Security requirements
  b. Security architecture and design elements
  c. As-built security and privacy controls

Number and distribution of problems encountered during ST&E, C&A, and IV&V activities by: 2.4.5.3
  a. Life-cycle step and severity
  b. IT security control and protection system function
  c. Type of problem

Distribution of problem reports, open and closed, generated during ST&E by life-cycle step and: 2.4.5.4

    a. Severity
    b. IT security control and protection system function
    c. Verification activity that discovered them

Number and type of static and dynamic analysis techniques from Table 4.15 performed by life-cycle step.   2.4.5.5

Percentage (%) of ST&E, C&A, and IV&V activities and results that were:
                                                                       2.4.5.6

    a. Verified by the team who performed them
    b. Approved and agreed to by all stakeholder representatives
    c. Verified by an independent team
    d. Performed by an independent team

For each IT security control and protection system function, the extent to which security functional requirements were verified through (0 — not at all, 10 — completely):   2.4.5.7

    a. Functional testing under normal, abnormal, and stress conditions
    b. Structural testing under normal, abnormal, and stress conditions
    c. Positive testing under normal, abnormal, and stress conditions
    d. Negative testing under normal, abnormal, and stress conditions
    e. Adequate test coverage
    f. Adequate test depth
    g. Adequate degree of independence in the test teams

For each IT security control and protection system function, the extent to which security integrity requirements were verified through (0 — not at all, 10 — completely):   2.4.5.8

    a. Functional testing under normal, abnormal, and stress conditions
    b. Structural testing under normal, abnormal, and stress conditions
    c. Positive testing under normal, abnormal, and stress conditions
    d. Negative testing under normal, abnormal, and stress conditions
    e. Adequate test coverage
    f. Adequate test depth
    g. Adequate degree of independence in the test teams
    h. Testing for unintended unspecified functionality
    i. Testing for undocumented features and functions
    j. Testing the ability to reach illegal modes and states
    k. Testing correct operation of must work functions (MWFs) and must not work functions (MNWFs)
    l. Testing the ability to bypass or violate the IT security control and protection system functions

Extent to which ST&E and C&A activities were tailored in accordance with (0 — not at all, 10 — completely):   2.4.5.9

    a. Asset criticality
    b. Information sensitivity

     c. Risk

     d. Operational environment

     e. Operational profile

     f. Duty cycle

Percentage (%) of facility management staff, operations and maintenance staff, and end users that have been notified of the deployment schedule. 2.4.5.10

Percentage (%) of IT security control and protection system functions that have been independently verified to perform as specified during normal operations, stress testing, and abnormal conditions.   2.4.5.11

Extent to which ST&E, C&A, and IV&V activities (0 — not at all, 10 — completely):   2.4.5.12

     a. Are conducted in a controlled environment

     b. Are conducted throughout the life cycle

     c. Are conducted using the three-tiered approach to dynamic analysis

     d. Are adequately budgeted for throughout the life cycle

     e. Are performed by competent staff

Percentage (%) of projects for which there is consistent follow-up until all deficiencies from C&A are resolved.   2.4.5.13

The first metrics measure the correctness of the security requirements, architecture and design, and as-built product or system in the operational environment. Requirements are often conceived in an abstract manner and verified in a development or laboratory environment. Verification in the operational environment — correct operation under normal and abnormal conditions — is what really counts. The number and distribution of problems encountered during ST&E, C&A, and IV&V activities are evidence of the thoroughness of these activities. The distribution of the problems by severity category, life-cycle activity, and major security function can be enlightening. Ideally, the number and severity of problems will decrease from one life-cycle phase to the next. A parallel metric is the distribution of problem reports closed by life-cycle phase, severity, major security function, and the verification activity that exposed the problem. It is common to measure the time that problem reports remain open during the operations and maintenance phase. This practice should be expanded to include all life-cycle phases and the additional distribution factors mentioned above. The length of time that problem reports stay open, particularly serious ones, is one index of the maturity of the security engineering process.

The thoroughness and appropriateness of ST&E, C&A, IV&V activities can be measured, in part, by the number and type of static analysis and dynamic analysis activities performed. For example, if only dynamic analysis was performed (traditional testing), then the validation and verification was superficial. Independent confirmation of the results of verification activities, by third parties and stakeholders, is another measure of thoroughness. Verification activities should not be performed by in-house staff alone; that is akin to grading your own final exam. In-house staff are too close to the project and under too much pressure to meet schedules and budgets to be completely objective at all times. Testing must be realistic for the results to be an effective measure of the robustness and integrity of the as-built product or system. As a result, metrics have been identified to assess the test duration, use of live data, and tailoring of test scenarios commensurate with system risk, asset criticality, and information sensitivity. Test results will be inconsequential without appropriate test durations and tailoring of test scenarios; the results will not meet the correctness or validity tests for good metrics.

More than technology parameters need to be assessed to determine whether or not a product or system is ready to deploy. It is never a good idea to deploy a product or system and then say voila! Instead, notify all facility management staff, operations and maintenance staff, end users, and stake-holders well in advance of the deployment schedule and keep them up-to-date about any slips along the way. This is only common sense and a professional courtesy; after all, they also have arrangements to make. Not only do they need to be notified, but they must also receive position-relevant training and documentation about the security features and functions of the new system. Highlight the consequences of not following appropriate operational security procedures.

The designated approval authority (DAA) for security certification and accreditation should delve deeply into the ST&E, C&A, and IV&V metrics. Even if time is not available to look at any other metrics, these metrics will tell the DAA what he needs to know before signing on the dotted line.

Delivery, Installation, and Deployment

Contrary to popular belief, a product or system does not go directly from (successful completion of) ST&E, C&A, and IV&V into operations and maintenance. There is middle ground between these two steps: delivery, installation, and deployment. While project planners and schedulers may try to skip this step, it is inadvisable for the engineering staff to do so, due to the security ramifications. The delivery, installation, and deployment step does not necessarily have to be a lengthy, time-consuming step; by the same token, it should not be rushed.

The delivery, installation, and deployment step applies to COTS and custom-developed products and systems. ST&E, C&A, and IV&V have been completed successfully and all action items have been resolved. Now it is time to deliver the product or system to the designated operational environment and get it ready to turn over to the operations and maintenance staff. Delivery may be to a single location, multiple facilities, multiple regions, or the entire enterprise. Issues relating to type certification and site certification will have already been resolved. Type certification refers to certifying a single instance of a product or system. If 50 identical copies of an application are to be deployed throughout an enterprise, only one copy needs to undergo ST&E, C&A, and IV&V because they are all identical. On the other hand, if there are unique configuration and installation parameters or different operational constraints at each location, site certification may be necessary to account for the configuration variations. Depending on the nature of the product or system, delivery can be accomplished in a variety of ways. Equipment can be delivered manually to each location. Software can be delivered manually to each location or distributed electronically. Likewise, installation and configuration can be performed manually, electronically, or through a combination of the two. Interface, connectivity, cables for I/O and power, and a slew of other logistical issues must be dealt with also. Finally, an acceptance test is performed to ensure that the product or system was installed correctly and functions as expected.

The delivery, installation, and deployment step raises several security concerns. First, how well is the product or system controlled during delivery? Do procedures exist to control logical and physical access to a product or system during distribution?[21] Are these procedures documented and enforced?[21] What safeguards are in place to prevent modifications, tampering, or substitutions during delivery?[21] How can an organization know with certainty that the product or system delivered is identical to the one that passed ST&E, C&A, and IV&V? How can an organization know with certainty that the product or system delivered is exactly what was ordered? Perhaps it is an earlier version or later version and a few "enhancements" have been made. As part of the delivery, installation, and deployment step, an organization needs the capability to detect, and preferably prevent, modifications, tampering, and substitutions from being introduced. Furthermore, plans that spell out the correct action to take upon detection of a discrepancy need to be in place beforehand. Should installation be halted? Should installation continue, except for the step in which the discrepancy was detected? Is connectivity to external assets allowed in this situation? Who is notified of the discrepancy? How is the severity of the discrepancy determined? What information, if any, is given to end users about the discrepancy? How and when is the discrepancy reported to the supplier? Answers to these questions and others must be thought through carefully and decisions made long before a crisis exists. Because of the potential for a serious security compromise, these are not decisions for the field engineer conducting installation to make on the spot or in a vacuum.

The second security concern centers around installation, generation, and start-up.[21] In general, a whole series of parameters must be initialized and connections made whenever hardware or software is installed. This is true even with so-called "shrink-wrapped" COTS products, despite what the advertising literature says. Often, there are streamlined or default configuration options; they may save time but rarely contribute anything positive to security. On the contrary, these default parameters and configurations are often the source of vulnerabilities. On occasion, field engineers performing the installation are under pressure to get the job done. They hurry and in the process skip a few steps or make a few errors, which are not discovered until it is too late. A file is missing, so one from a test disk is inserted instead. The vendor sent the wrong initialization script, so one is made up on-the-fly. Time is running out, so "yes" is automatically typed in response to all the installation and configuration questions without reading them. As a result, it is essential that an organization put rigorous checks and balances in place over installation, generation, and start-up to ensure that each step is conducted in a secure manner. This is a good place to insist upon independence as part of the checks and balances. One such important step involves requiring that an exact log be made of the installation procedures followed and the configuration parameters initialized during setup. This log should be independently verified two ways: (1) that the as-built product or system was indeed installed and configured this way, and (2) that the steps indicated on the log are in fact the correct way to install and configure the product or system. This last step involves verifying that the installation and configuration complies with security policies for the IT infrastructure, including external connectivity. The installation and configuration log should be retained until decommissioning, in case there is a need to reinstall or reconfigure the product or system as part of normal operations and maintenance or contingency and disaster recovery procedures.

The third security concern during delivery, installation, and deployment involves people — specifically, who is responsible for what. An organization needs to define a clear division of responsibilities for all the activities during delivery, installation, and deployment. The "who" includes definite insiders, pseudo-insiders, and pseudo-outsiders. Vendors, development staff, security engineering staff, operations and maintenance staff, end users, and business partners all have a role to play. To avoid confusion, overlapping, and counterproductive efforts, not to mention frustration, it is best to clearly define:

- Who is and is not responsible for doing what during delivery, installation, and deployment
- When each activity must be performed
- Who is and is not responsible for verifying that an activity is complete and performed correctly
- Dependencies between activities
- Go/no-go milestones

In addition, it is essential to define who is and is not informed of progress and problems during delivery, installation, and deployment and the level of detail each person is permitted to receive. This advance planning will help ensure that delivery, installation, and deployment proceed in an orderly and secure manner.

The metrics listed below measure the resilience of an organization's approach to delivery, installation, and deployment.

By asset criticality and risk, percentage (%) of projects for which a separate delivery, installation, and deployment step is defined and monitored: 2.4.6.1
 a. Percentage (%) for COTS products and systems
 b. Percentage (%) for custom-developed products and systems

Extent to which procedures are documented and enforced to (0 — not at all, 10 — completely, maximum of 40 points):   2.4.6.2

    a. Control logical and physical access to a product or system during delivery

    b. Prevent modifications, tampering, and substitutions during delivery

    c. Detect modifications, tampering, and substitutions during delivery

    d. Ensure a preplanned methodical response when modifications, tampering, or substitutions are detected

Extent to which installation and configuration of products and systems are independently verified (0 — not at all, 10 — completely, maximum 50 points): 2.4.6.3

    a. Default configurations and parameters are replaced

    b. Installation and configuration logs are independently verified to ensure that they match the deployed product or system

    c. Installation and configuration logs are independently verified for compliance with security policies

    d. Installation and configuration logs are retained through decommissioning

Extent to which a clear division of roles and responsibilities during delivery, installation, and deployment are defined (0 — not at all, 10 — completely, maximum 70 points): 2.4.6.4

    a. Who is responsible for performing each activity

    b. When each activity is to be performed

    c. Who is responsible for verifying that each activity is complete and has been performed correctly

    d. Dependencies between activities

    e. Go/no-go milestones

    f. Who is informed of progress and problems and the level of detail provided

Operations and Maintenance

In the flurry of activity surrounding the planning, development, and acquisition of a new product, system, or network, organizations frequently forget that approximately 80 percent of the life cycle is spent in the operations and maintenance step. This fact underscores the importance of getting the security requirements, architecture, design, development, and implementation correct. Why? Because whatever comes out of those steps is what the organization will be stuck with for about 80 percent of the life cycle. Deferred problems will not magically go away during the operations and maintenance step; instead, they will be much more expensive and painful to solve.

    The operations and maintenance step is where the "rubber meets the road," so to speak. The real resilience of physical security controls, personnel security controls, IT security controls, and operational security controls become glaringly apparent. The act of transitioning a product or system to the operational environment has a knack for exposing latent vulnerabilities, usually at the most inopportune time, such as when the new capability is being demonstrated to senior management or in the middle of a class to introduce the new capability to reluctant end users. It is a good idea to remember this the next time there is pressure to rush ST&E, C&A, and IV&V. Because this situation is predictable, it is wise to consider a partial deployment for the first 30 to 90 days, rather than a full deployment all at once. That way, latent vulnerabilities can be dealt with on a small scale and the entire IT infrastructure is not put at unnecessary risk.

The purpose of the operations and maintenance step is to ensure that a product or system operates correctly and securely once deployed.[28] Specifically, the goal is to ensure that the security posture to which a product, system, or network was originally certified is maintained during the operations and maintenance step,[21] despite preventive, adaptive, and corrective maintenance actions. This implies that a current and complete set of operational procedures exists that defines in detail what needs to be done, when it needs to be done, who has the authority to authorize maintenance actions to be performed, who is responsible for performing the activity, and who is responsible for verifying that the activity was performed correctly and on time. Operational procedures should be documented and communicated to all responsible parties. To ensure that everyone is reading from the same script, operational procedures must be under strict configuration management. The operations and maintenance step provides a wonderful opportunity for insider attacks. To prevent deliberate or negligent misuse of resources and privileges, it is essential to design operational procedures according to the separation of duties and accountability principles.[28] Furthermore, operational procedures must be consistent with and contribute to supportability and maintainability goals.

A decision must be made about which maintenance activities will and will not be performed on-site and the security ramifications of such a course of action.[52] Several issues should be considered, such as the need for sanitizing equipment before it leaves the facility, how sanitization will be verified and by whom, how physical access to equipment taken off-site will be controlled, the need for off-site vendor and in-house personnel to undergo background investigations, potential damage that could result should the equipment be compromised, lost, or stolen while off-site, etc. Likewise, decisions should be made about whether components will be maintained according to vendor specifications alone, organizational specifications and policies, or a combination of the two. Again, the security ramifications of such decisions must be thoroughly evaluated.[52] Vendor specifications for maintaining equipment usually focus on functionality and performance; they are rarely optimized for security, nor are they optimized for each organization's unique operational environment, IT infrastructure, or security architecture. The downfall of COTS products is that they are designed for the (nonexistent) generic masses. Consequently, it is almost always necessary for vendor maintenance specifications to be supplemented with parameters that are specific to the organization.

A whole host of issues need to be delineated and defined in standardized operations and maintenance procedures. An important factor that should not be overlooked is defining the competence requirements for personnel assigned to perform operations and maintenance actions. Operations and maintenance is definitely not an area in which to go with the least expensive staffing arrangement. The following are examples of topics that should be addressed in operations and maintenance procedures, but this should not be considered an exhaustive list[21, 28, 52]:

- Procedures for handling, processing, storing, archiving, retaining, and destroying information, by information sensitivity level
- Procedures for scheduling operations and maintenance activities, given dependencies and interactions with other products, systems, and networks
- Procedures for reporting, tracking, and resolving errors, exceptions, and incidents
- Procedures for controlling the use, configuration, and management of IT assets
- Routine and emergency procedures for conducting patch management, configuration management, security impact analysis, and security audits
- Procedures for creating and retaining logs of maintenance activities
- Procedures for ensuring that compilers, editors, libraries, and system utilities are not directly accessible by end users
- Routine and emergency procedures for restarting IT assets
- Procedures for verifying the integrity of security features and functions after maintenance actions have been performed
- Routine and emergency procedures for monitoring the performance of IT security controls
- Procedures for identifying the appropriate support point of contact (POC) for each IT asset and disseminating that information to end users
- Procedures governing the conditions under which remote maintenance can and cannot be performed
- Routine and emergency procedures governing the conduct and verification of sanitization and secure disposal of IT assets and information
- Procedures governing the use of diagnostic and other maintenance tools that could capture vulnerabilities and other sensitive information

The metrics listed below measure the resilience of an organization's approach to operations and maintenance.

Percentage (%) of patches, upgrades, and enhancements for which security regression testing is performed before they are deployed.[105]   2.4.7.1

Percentage (%) of reusable media that are sanitized before reuse, by information sensitivity.   2.4.7.2

Ratio of attempted attacks to successful security incidents, by severity: 2.4.7.3
   a. Distribution of security incidents by severity
   b. Distribution of security incidents by IT security control and protection system function
   c. Distribution of security incidents by severity and length of time since the IT asset was deployed
   d. Distribution of security incidents by root cause

Percentage (%) of security incidents that: 2.4.7.4

    a. Caused hard failures
    b. Caused soft failures
    c. Percentage (%) of incipient failures that were preempted

Percentage (%) of new products, systems, and networks that are: 2.4.7.5

    a. Deployed throughout the enterprise all at once
    b. Deployed incrementally after a successful partial deployment

Extent to which operations and maintenance procedures (0 — not at all, 10 — completely, maximum 70 points): 2.4.7.6

    a. Are current
    b. Are complete
    c. Define precise roles and responsibilities
    d. Have been verified within the past 6 (six) months to be correct
    e. Are under configuration management control
    f. Implement the separation of duties and accountability principles
    g. Are consistent with supportability and maintainability goals

Percentage (%) of IT assets that are maintained off-site for which a security assessment has been performed. 2.4.7.7

Percentage (%) of IT assets for which a security assessment was conducted to determine whether maintenance should be performed according to vendor specifications, organizational policies, or a combination of the two. 2.4.7.8

Percentage (%) of operations and maintenance positions for which competence requirements have been defined. 2.4.7.9

Extent to which the following topics are adequately addressed in operations and maintenance procedures, for routine and emergency situations (0 — not at all, 10 — completely, maximum 140 points): 2.4.7.10

    a. Handling, processing, storing, archiving, retaining, and destroying information, by information sensitivity level
    b. Scheduling operations and maintenance activities
    c. Reporting, tracking, and resolving errors, exceptions, and incidents
    d. Controlling the use, configuration, and management of IT assets
    e. Conducting patch management, configuration management, security impact analysis, and security audits
    f. Creating and retaining logs of maintenance activities
    g. Ensuring that compilers, editors, libraries, and system utilities are not directly accessible by end users
    h. Restarting IT assets
    i. Verifying the integrity of security features and functions after maintenance actions have been performed
    j. Monitoring the performance of IT security controls
    k. Identifying the appropriate support point of contact (POC) for each IT asset and disseminating that information to end users

l. Conditions under which remote maintenance can and cannot be performed
m. Conduct and verification of sanitization and secure disposal of IT assets and information
n. Use of diagnostic and other maintenance tools which could capture vulnerabilities and other sensitive information

Number and percentage of security incidents, by incident severity, related to:
                                                                    2.4.7.11

a. Faulty operations and maintenance procedures
b. Failure to follow standardized operations and maintenance procedures
c. Lack of a standardized operations and maintenance procedure

Impact of security incidents due to erroneous operations and maintenance procedures: 2.4.7.12

a. Operational impact (downtime, number of IT assets affected, number of users affected, etc.)
b. Cost impact

Operations and maintenance metrics are the most commonly used and familiar category of security metrics. The goal is to ensure that no marginal, critical, or catastrophic security incidents occur during the operations and maintenance step. Several metrics are derived from one question that is used to measure achievement of this goal: is the security posture to which the product, system, or network was originally certified being maintained now that it is operational? In general, certifications are for a given operational environment, operational profile, and duty cycle. A particular configuration of a system and its components are certified. Once a system enters the operational state, change begins almost immediately. Something is different in the installation facility, the duty cycle changes, or the configuration must be modified to accommodate a new constraint. Any of these changes can disrupt the premise upon which the original certification was based. The astute use of metrics can help ensure that the as-certified security posture is being maintained, despite inevitable changes.

Determining the percentage of patches, upgrades, and other enhancements for which security regression testing was performed prior to deployment is a good place to begin. Except under very unusual situations, this number should be 100. To put it another way, if security regression testing is not performed, the operational system is no longer the one that was certified and the organization is "flying blind."

Reusable media raise concerns about unintended release of potentially sensitive information. Hence, it is important to verify, through the use of metrics, that these media are being sanitized before they are reused.

The relationship between attempted attacks and successful security incidents can tell a lot about the operational robustness and integrity of the deployed system, if the data is collected and analyzed with care. A system owner has no control over the number of attacks experienced. However, a system owner can prevent attacks from becoming successful security incidents. The judicious use of security metrics can make this job easier. Several security metrics can provide valuable information about the strength of the current security posture and areas needing improvement. The ratio of attacks to security incidents is a good place to begin. Also look at the distribution of security incidents by severity category, IT security control and protection system function, and over time. If the majority of security incidents are in the high severity categories, then there are some major security vulnerabilities that must be mitigated. If the majority of the security incidents are in one major security functional area, this area is in serious need of rework. Likewise, the number of security incidents should decrease over time as you batten down the hatches.

Unfortunately, today, most organizations spend the majority of their time analyzing attacks (and not incidents) and producing all sorts of reports and graphs about them. This is a waste of time, especially considering the volume of attack data. A system owner does not and never will have any control over the type or source of attacks. A system owner can *only* prevent attacks from being successful and becoming *bona fide* security incidents. So the effectiveness of prevention strategies should be measured instead, using the metrics above. Unlike attack data, this information is useful because it can be acted upon to improve the overall security posture.

To improve the security engineering process, be sure to take time to investigate security incidents of marginal or higher severity to determine the real root cause of each incident. Look at the overall distribution of root causes to expose trends that brought about these vulnerabilities. The effectiveness of preemption strategies can be measured (in part) by examining the distribution of incidents that caused hard failures, soft failures, or incipient failures that were successfully preempted.

Decommissioning

All good products, systems, and networks must eventually come to an end. Either the technology is so old it cannot be upgraded any longer, or it becomes cost prohibitive to do so. Amid all the fallacies associated with the Y2K scare, one legitimate but alarming fact came to light. Many organizations (most notably the federal government) "discovered" that they had antique operational systems for which no one outside retirement communities knew the source language in which the applications were written. That situation makes it a bit difficult to perform preventive, adaptive, or corrective maintenance. Despite this awakening, some organizations still insist on letting these senior systems run until they drop their last bit on the floor, or as happens more often, forget where they put it. Ever hear of Algol, Jovial, or MUMPS? Many of these senior systems are written in languages for which it is difficult to find any information, except in computer history books. And no, you really do not want to know what mission-critical systems are operating in this state of advanced dementia.

Other, more enlightened organizations (most notably the private sector) saw the light and began transitioning their IT infrastructure to technology that is more appropriate for the 21st century.

Products, systems, and networks cannot just be shut down, regardless of the state of decrepitness. The functionality or service provided must be replaced, augmented, or enhanced — it cannot simply just disappear. The stickier question concerns what should be done with the data generated by this old-timer. Usually, a lot of data has been produced over the years. Some of the data is in paper archives. Some of the data is stored offline in tape libraries. Other data is stored in online archives. The most recent data is probably still on an active server somewhere. Data formats and definitions tend to change over the years as data requirements become more specific: the length of a field is expanded, the definition of a field is changed to handle alphabetic and numeric fields, two extra decimal places are added for precision, or a new data element is added to a record definition. Old data may or may not be able to be read under the new definitions and new formats. This situation raises several questions. How much of the old data should be kept and for how long? What format and media should the data be kept in? How much of the old data will be transitioned to the new system? How will that be accomplished and verified? What part of this data should be destroyed in a secure manner? How will that be accomplished and verified? As is evident, there is a lot more to decommissioning than flipping the off switch.

Several security concerns are raised during decommissioning:

- Preventing equipment and data from being compromised
- Identifying and mitigating weaknesses during cutover
- Ensuring that IT assets and information assets are properly sanitized prior to disposal or reuse
- Providing continuity of services to end users so that business operations are not disrupted
- Providing continuity of data availability and integrity so that business operations are not disrupted
- Conducting appropriate planning and coordination with all stakeholders
- Notifying all end users and business partners of the decommissioning schedule
- Having a fallback plan in place in case problems are encountered while decommissioning the old product, system, or network and transitioning to the new one

If not carefully planned and monitored, risk exposure can increase dramatically when decommissioning one system and transitioning to another. That is where metrics come into play. The goal is to ensure that no marginal, critical, or catastrophic security incidents occur during decommissioning. One question from which metrics can be derived to measure achievement of that goal is: has the security impact of decommissioning and transition to a new system been adequately evaluated? Perhaps the timing or sequencing of decommissioning activities is critical. Perhaps certain segments, servers, or facilities have to be done first for some obscure reason. Maybe a break in service or data availability, however slight, creates an unacceptable risk. The order in which IT security control and protection system functions are shut down on the old system and activated on the new system can also create temporary vulnerabilities. All of these issues should be thought through carefully, because what can go wrong will go wrong during decommissioning. An organization needs to anticipate these scenarios and be prepared to prevent and detect when things are not going as planned.

Decommissioning is a tricky business; there are a million and one details that have to come together just at the right time for everything to work. Add in security and privacy concerns and it can be seen why nothing should be left to chance. The number of times the exact cutover sequence has been practiced can provide some level of confidence in a successful transition. Supplement this with the number of times the exact cutover sequence has been tested, and passed without any loss of system functionality or security integrity, and the result is a higher level of confidence in success. To go for the gold, determine the percentage of decommissioning plans and procedures that have been independently verified.

Systems that are about to be decommissioned contain reusable and non-reusable resources. These resources must be disposed of correctly to avoid unintended release of potentially sensitive information. Sanitize and destroy nonreusable resources. Sanitize reusable resources. In both cases, the sanitization process should be independently verified. The percentage of resources that were sanitized correctly should be measured by information sensitivity level. Establish chain-of-custody rules to ensure correct handling of these resources during and after sanitization. Any potential gaps will be identified by measuring the percentage of resources for which chain-of-custody rules have or have not been established.

In today's globally interconnected world, very few systems and networks can be shut down at 5 p.m. on Friday and the new system or network turned on Monday morning. Rather, most systems and networks need to be up and running 24/7. The challenge of how to continue to provide essential services during decommissioning and transition is real and should be taken seriously. Consult contingency and disaster recovery plans to identify and prioritize essential services. Determine which groups of users will receive what services and when to minimize disruption to business operations. Depending on the nature of the business, the consequences of a service disruption, no matter how short, can range from minor to catastrophic.

There is always the fear of losing or corrupting data during decommissioning and transition. Consequently, the frequency of backups, both online and offline, should be carefully measured to identify potential gaps. In addition, it is wise to monitor how many previous backups are kept until it is certain that the transition was successful. The lack of data integrity and availability during decommissioning and transition may itself create security incidents. Therefore, it is necessary to devise alternative means of getting data to end users securely, so that the data is available when needed during decommissioning and transition. The data must be controlled to prevent corruption, accidental duplication, and unauthorized release. If parallel operations were part of ST&E, decisions should be made about how to monitor and control the duplicate data streams until decommissioning and transition is complete. Archives are kept even after systems are decommissioned. Often, federal regulations, corporate security and privacy policies, and industry standards contain many stipulations relating to archives. Prior to decommissioning, measure archive retention, conversion, and destruction plans and procedures for compliance to these regulations, policies, and standards. Errors in these procedures cannot be corrected after the fact and may result in fines or other financial or legal penalties.

Systems do not operate in a vacuum. There are always a number of internal and external entities upon which a system depends, such as electricity. It is important to measure how many of these entities have been coordinated with, prior to starting the decommissioning sequence, or an organization may be in for some big and embarrassing surprises. A good place to start is with the people involved; for example, what percentage of facility management staff, operations and maintenance staff, end users, and business partners have been notified that the system is being decommissioned and the schedule for doing so? (On occasion, there may be security reasons for not telling everyone all the details.) In addition, the percentage of people who have been informed about special operational procedures to be followed during decommissioning and transition needs to be monitored, to avoid accidental security incidents.

Finally, it is essential to have a fallback plan in place in case something goes really wrong during decommissioning and transition. An organization does not want to find itself in the position of having completely shut down the old system and something goes wrong, thereby preventing transition to the new system. Getting stuck in this no man's land halfway between the old system and the new system certainly qualifies as a career-ending move. Unfortunately, it happens far more often than publicized. A few mergers ago, a local bank found itself in that situation. The newly acquired bank's IT assets were to be merged into the parent company during Memorial Day weekend. By 9:30 a.m. on Tuesday, duplicate account numbers and other problems were discovered. The branch offices in all states remained open but they could not process any transactions. No deposits could be made. No withdrawals could be made; even the ATMs were turned off. Checks could not be cashed. Accounts could not be opened or closed. This situation continued for four days. Needless to say, there were a lot of angry customers and it was all over the news. The moral of the story: do not start decommissioning unless you have a fallback plan for each step along the way.

The metrics listed below measure the resilience of an organization's approach to decommissioning.

> Percentage (%) of facility management staff, operations and maintenance staff, end users, and business partners who have been notified that the system is being decommissioned and the schedule for doing so.   2.4.8.1

> Frequency of online and off-site backups during the decommissioning and transition period.   2.4.8.2

Number and percentage of internal and external entities for which decommissioning planning and coordination has taken place.   2.4.8.3

Percentage (%) of non-reusable system resources that have been sanitized and destroyed, by information sensitivity, and the sanitization and destruction process verified[105]:   2.4.8.4

    a. Percentage (%) of reusable system resources that have been sanitized, by information sensitivity, and the sanitization process verified[105]

    b. Percentage (%) of decommissioned system resources for which chain of custody rules have been established and are monitored and enforced

Number of times the exact cutover sequence has been practiced: 2.4.8.5

    a. Number of times the exact cutover sequence has been tested, and passed without any loss of system functionality or security integrity

    b. Percentage (%) of decommissioning plans and procedures that have been independently verified

Percentage (%) of archives for which retention plans and procedures have been verified to comply with federal regulations and corporate security and privacy policies: 2.4.8.6

    a. Percentage (%) of archives for which conversion plans and procedures have been verified to comply with federal regulations and corporate security and privacy policies

    b. Percentage (%) of archives for which destruction plans and procedures have been verified to comply with federal regulations and corporate security and privacy policies

    c. Percentage (%) of unofficial system archives that have been disposed of correctly

Distribution of projects being decommissioned and transitioned: 2.4.8.7

    a. Due to normal preplanned system evolution

    b. Because the technology is so old it can no longer be supported

    c. Because the technology is so old it can no longer be supported in a cost-effective manner

Extent to which the decommissioning plan (0 — not at all, 10 — completely, maximum 30 points):   2.4.8.8

    a. Identifies and accounts for critical sequences and timing constraints

    b. Identifies and accounts for the order in which IT security control and protection system functions have to be shut down and re-initialized to prevent security compromises

    c. Puts procedures in place to prevent and detect problems during decommissioning

Extent to which the decommissioning plan (0 — not at all, 10 — completely, maximum 40 points):   2.4.8.9

    a. Identifies and prioritizes critical services that need to be provided throughout decommissioning and transition

    b. Determines which groups of users will receive what services and when
    c. Minimizes disruptions to business operations
    d. Has identified the severity of the impact of different types of service disruptions
    e. Has been independently verified

Completeness and realism of the fallback plan, should something go wrong during decommissioning and transition (0 — not at all, 10 — completely).

2.4.8.10

Extent to which the decommissioning plan has procedures in place to prevent a loss of data integrity and availability, or a privacy violation, during decommissioning and transition.

2.4.8.11

Ongoing Security Risk Management Activities

There are six ongoing security risk management activities; each focuses on a different aspect of achieving and sustaining a known secure system state:

1. Vulnerability assessment
2. Security policy management
3. Security audits and reviews
4. Security impact analysis, privacy impact analysis, configuration management, patch management
5. Security awareness and training, guidance documents
6. Stakeholder, strategic partner, supplier relationships

Vulnerability Assessment

Vulnerability is probably the most misused of all security engineering terms. Vulnerability is frequently and incorrectly used interchangeably with threat and risk, as if vulnerability assessments, threat assessments, and risk assessments were synonymous. While these three terms and activities are closely related, each has a distinct meaning. There are three widely recognized definitions of the term vulnerability, which are variations on a theme:

> **Vulnerability:** (1) weakness in an information system, system security procedures, internal controls, or implementation, that could be exploited or triggered by a threat source[51, 100]; (2) flaw or weakness in the design or implementation of an information system (including the security procedures and security controls associated with that system) that could be intentionally or unintentionally exploited to adversely affect an organization's operations or assets through a loss of confidentiality, integrity, or availability[60]; (3) a flaw or weakness in system security procedures, design, implementation, or internal controls that could be exercised (accidentally triggered or intentionally exploited) and result in a security breach or violation of the system's security policy.[50]

Note that all the definitions point out that vulnerabilities can exist in all four security engineering domains: physical security, personnel security, IT security, and operational security. Vulnerabilities can be triggered accidentally or intentionally. Successful exploitation of a vulnerability has a negative impact on an organization and its assets, the severity of which can range from minor to catastrophic. The weakness or flaw that the vulnerability represents is the result of an error of omission or an error of commission in a security engineering life-cycle activity.

Vulnerability assessments are one of seven different types of risk management activities. Vulnerability assessments are ongoing throughout the life of a product, system, or network, from initial concept formulation through decommissioning, regardless of whether it is COTS or custom developed. A vulnerability assessment is the formal process of identifying and documenting vulnerabilities, their cause, and options to eliminate or mitigate them. It is important to remember that the introduction of security safeguards may eliminate one vulnerability and at the same time introduce another vulnerability.[14] That is why vulnerability assessments are repeated before and after the introduction of safeguards, and the acceptability of residual risk should be reevaluated continuously.[14]

Vulnerability assessments investigate the IT security control and protection system functions, comparing actual resilience against the level of resilience specified and needed. The intent is to identify any weaknesses in the development or operation of IT security control and protection system functions. In particular, a vulnerability assessment looks for opportunities to defeat or bypass security features and functions, introduce instability and unknown and undefined states, and contribute to accidental or intentional misuse and misconfiguration.[21] Searches are also made for potential illicit operational control flows and data control flows. Poor human factors engineering as well as conflicting, misleading, and incomplete guidance documents can create vulnerabilities and hence must be examined as well.[21]

The outputs of vulnerability assessments are used as inputs to security engineering life-cycle activities. For example, a vulnerability assessment performed on the security requirements may indicate (1) the requirements need more work, or (2) the requirements are alright but some information needs to be passed to the security architecture and design step. The outputs from vulnerability assessments are key inputs to ST&E, C&A, and IV&V activities. This information is used to focus ST&E, C&A, and IV&V on identified weaknesses. Depending on the level of asset criticality and information sensitivity, it may be advisable to have vulnerability assessments performed by an independent third party, in addition to those performed by in-house staff. Undoubtedly, each group will uncover certain vulnerabilities that the other group missed. Also, there may be differences in the severity and likelihood ratings assigned by each group. It is always better to get these issues out on the table, discussed, and resolved, than to find out the hard way through an actual security compromise. Another issue should not be neglected either: controlling access to and distribution of the vulnerability assessment results, both interim and final. Because this information represents a "how-to guide" for would-be attackers, it is best to keep it under wraps.

There are several different steps in a vulnerability assessment. First the vulnerabilities are identified, through a combination of static and dynamic analysis techniques. Next the vulnerabilities are documented and assigned a severity rating and a rating indicating the likelihood and ease of exploitation. The root cause of the vulnerability is also documented, including the security engineering life-cycle step during which the vulnerability was introduced and how or why it was introduced. Vulnerability documentation should be complete and specific so that an independent party can understand and, if necessary, reinvestigate the vulnerability. Complete information is also necessary to identify options to eliminate or mitigate the vulnerability. Incomplete information might lead to an inappropriate mitigation strategy being recommended. Once vulnerabilities are identified, they are monitored continuously to ensure that they are resolved (versus being documented and then forgotten) and that the mitigation strategies are effective and do not introduce any new vulnerabilities. Monitoring information is updated each time a new vulnerability assessment is performed by an in-house or independent team. Vulnerability assessments are not a one-time event whereby a box is checked off and you are finished. (Actually, your career as a security engineer might be finished if you take that approach.)

Vulnerabilities can be characterized in a variety of different ways. One method that is particularly useful relates to the ease of exploitation. In this approach, all vulnerabilities fall into one of three categories[269]:

1. **Directly exposed:** vulnerabilities that can be exploited directly from internal or external threat sources.
2. **Indirectly exposed:** vulnerabilities that can be exploited only after a directly exposed vulnerability has been exploited.
3. **Inaccessible:** vulnerabilities that cannot be exploited due to existing security controls.

Here we see potential linkages between vulnerabilities. To illustrate, assume that a directly exposed vulnerability is assigned a minor severity rating and as a result no effort is spent on mitigation. Then, later it is discovered that this minor vulnerability unleashes the potential to exploit a major indirectly exposed vulnerability. If the protection mechanisms were weak because that vulnerability was rated as being only indirectly exposed, a security compromise could result. Furthermore, vulnerabilities are rarely 100 percent inaccessible. Usually, this inaccessibility rating is the result of it being too time consuming, too expensive, or too difficult to exploit the vulnerability. An inaccessible rating should be independently verified, reviewed, reaffirmed, and updated regularly, given the rapid changes in technology and attack methods. An organization does not want to find itself in the position of having its IT infrastructure compromised due to a false sense of security about supposedly inaccessible vulnerabilities. A vulnerability's ease of exploitation, using the three categories above, can be correlated with asset criticality and information sensitivity to determine mitigation priorities. However, it is essential to ensure that vulnerabilities have been properly categorized and that all linkages between directly exposed and indirectly exposed vulnerabilities have been uncovered. Otherwise, all bets are off.

A variety of common-sense practices can help prevent vulnerabilities throughout the security engineering life cycle. Some of these practices are well known, while others are not. The most familiar include activities conducted during the operations and maintenance step, such as keeping anti-virus software current; monitoring alerts; performing security impact analysis (SIA) and ST&E on all patches and configuration changes before deploying them; disabling all factory-set default parameters, maintenance back doors, and accounts; prohibiting anonymous file transfers; and rejecting inputs from untrusted sources.[36, 51, 149, 266] In addition, internal misuse detection capabilities should be continuously monitored to evaluate insider threat and the effectiveness of internal controls. Insider threat attacks are often successful due to a breakdown of a combination of physical security controls, personnel security controls, IT security controls, and operational security controls. When evaluating the insider threat potential, be sure to look for common threads across all four security engineering domains. Thoroughly evaluate all internal and external interfaces and control structures to see if they can be misused, defeated, or bypassed. A comprehensive and preferably independent analysis should be conducted to identify all potential access points to the electronic security perimeter. Regular scanning should be performed to locate open ports, renegade modems, and other vulnerabilities.[36] Careful consideration should be given to whether or not remote access is allowed — and if so, under what specific conditions. Likewise, the difference between logical access controls for remote access and local access needs to be defined carefully. Is remote access to stored data allowed?[266] What functions can and cannot be accessed remotely?[266] From what locations can remote access take place? These and other questions related to remote access deserve some serious thought.

A variety of vulnerability prevention practices can be used earlier during the design and development steps. This is when an organization can realize the greatest ROI for vulnerability prevention. These practices help prevent vulnerabilities from being introduced in the first place; they also help make unavoidable vulnerabilities inaccessible. These are common-sense practices. They do take a little extra time, but it is time well spent. This list, when combined with the appropriate IT security control and protection system functions and supplemented by appropriate static and dynamic analysis techniques, will provide a robust vulnerability prevention approach during design and development.[14, 36, 51, 149, 196, 266]

- *Ensuring that all possible modes and states that could be reached under normal and abnormal conditions are adequately accounted for in the control logic.* This means that a product or system will not reach an unknown or undefined state and not know how to respond; rather, should an illegal state be reached, the proper course of action is predefined. Hence, the product or system will remain in a known secure state.

- *Monitoring and controlling what is in memory at all times.* Read, write, execute, and direct memory access to specific memory regions should be restricted to specific types of functions and data emanating from specified sources. Otherwise, there are likely to be memory conflicts, memory leaks, and buffer overflows, as well as illicit operational control flows and data control flows. Other potential problems include data being used as instructions and script injections.

- *Validating all critical and essential inputs and outputs before acting upon them.* The nanosecond it takes to perform a range check or a plausibility check could prevent a catastrophic compromise. It is all too easy for data to be corrupted accidentally or intentionally — a packet collision, sloppy programming, a framing error, a power fluctuation, a data entry error, numeric overflows, an addressing error, etc. Inputs and outputs should not be assumed to be correct unless they have been validated.

- *Employing a robust suite of error, exception, and incident handling procedures that include rollback, block recovery, fail safe, fail secure, and fail operational capabilities.* Expect the unexpected, especially when integrating heterogeneous COTS and custom-developed products, systems, and networks. Be prepared to automatically preempt, prevent, and respond to anomalous events to ensure that the IT infrastructure remains in a known secure state at all times. Design in hardware error control areas (HECAs) and software error control areas (SECAs) to contain and minimize the consequences of anomalous events. Analyze operational control flows to see if deadlock or race conditions can be deliberately induced. Determine how logical access controls, session management, and authentication mechanisms can be broken. Do not just assume that everything will work correctly all the time.

- *Shielding components and cables to prevent accidental or deliberate interference or eavesdropping.* Electromagnetic interference (EMI), radio frequency interference (RFI), and electrostatic discharge (ESD) are frequently the root cause of unstable and unpredictable behavior. As our world becomes more and more interconnected, with both wired and wireless transmissions, interference is becoming more of a problem. The only way to eliminate this problem is through appropriate shielding of cables and components, which has the fringe benefit of preventing unauthorized eavesdropping. Shielding prevents interference from coming into an IT infrastructure; it also prevents an organization's information from emanating out of an IT infrastructure.

- *Using separate development, integration, and test environments.* The use of separate environments and even separate teams for development, integration, and ST&E minimizes the likelihood of vulnerabilities being introduced and remaining undetected because they are linked to a single environment. These are the types of vulnerabilities that do not become apparent until a product or system is moved to the operational environment. Something associated with the development environment masks the vulnerability until then. The use of independent teams is also useful for finding these obscure vulnerabilities. Once the product or system is transitioned to the operational environment, be sure to remove or disable all diagnostic functions, test points, debugger modes, etc. to prevent misuse.

Of course, vulnerability assessments should start at the beginning during concept formulation and requirements analysis and specification. At this time, the technical concept, operational concept, and requirements should be analyzed against the five quality characteristics (clear, complete, concise, consistent, testable) to uncover vulnerabilities. Static analysis techniques can be very helpful in this process.

The following metrics can be used to measure whether or not an organization has a robust approach to vulnerability assessments and is producing meaningful results.

Interval between the life-cycle step a security fault was introduced into a product or system and the life-cycle step in which the security fault was detected, by fault severity[8, 9]: 2.4.9.1

    a. Interval between the life-cycle step a security fault was introduced into a product or system and the life-cycle step in which the security fault was removed, by fault severity

    b. Interval between the life-cycle step a security fault was detected and the life-cycle step in which the security fault was removed, by fault severity

Percentage (%) of systems with critical IT assets, information assets, or functions that have been assessed for vulnerabilities, in accordance with policy[105]: 2.4.9.2

    a. Percentage (%) of vulnerability assessment findings that have been addressed since the last reporting period, by severity of the findings

Total number of faults prevented, by severity, as a result of conducting a vulnerability assessment: 2.4.9.3

    a. Number and percentage of stakeholder groups that were represented
    b. Number of errors in the human computer interface that were identified
    c. Number of errors in proposed operational procedures identified
    d. Number of illegal system states, prohibited parameter values, and operational constraints identified
    e. Number of must work functions (MWFs) and must not work functions (MNWFs) identified

Probability of physical, personnel, IT, and operational security controls failing individually and/or in combination, such that an internal control fails or insider threats are instantiated: 2.4.9.4

    a. Percentage (%) of physical, personnel, IT, and operational security controls that have been tailored by information sensitivity and asset criticality and independently verified

Severity of the impact to national security/stability or critical infrastructures in case of an outage or interruption to the systems, networks, and services the organization provides (4 — ultra high, 3 — high, 2 — moderate, 1 — low, 0 — none).[163] 2.4.9.5

Potential brand impact of a serious security incident (4 — ultra high, 3 — high, 2 — moderate, 1 — low, 0 — none).[163]   2.4.9.6

Percentage (%) of key IT and information assets for which a comprehensive strategy has been implemented to mitigate vulnerabilities and maintain the risk within acceptable thresholds[105]:   2.4.9.7

    a. Percentage (%) of identified risks that have a defined risk mitigation plan against which status is reported in accordance with policy
    b. Percentage (%) of information security risks related to system architecture identified in the most recent risk assessment that have been adequately mitigated
    c. Number of residual risks analysis reports that were reviewed and accepted this reporting period

Percentage (%) of key business objectives for which an information security vulnerability assessment has been conducted.[163]   2.4.9.8

Percentage (%) of key organizational functions for which a comprehensive strategy has been implemented to mitigate information security vulnerabilities and to maintain the risk within acceptable thresholds.[105]   2.4.9.9

Percentage (%) of key external security requirements for which the organization has been deemed by objective audit or other means to be in compliance.[105]
                                    2.4.9.10

Percentage (%) of IT assets within the system boundaries for which criticality assessments have been performed: 2.4.9.11

    a. Distribution of IT assets across criticality categories
    b. Percentage (%) of IT asset criticality assessments that have been independently verified
    c. Percentage (%) of IT asset criticality assessments that have been agreed to by all affected stakeholders
    d. Currency of IT asset criticality assessment

Percentage (%) of IT assets that are dependent on external entities that the organization has no control over, by criticality.   2.4.9.12

Percentage (%) of information assets within the system boundaries for which sensitivity assessments have been performed: 2.4.9.13

    a. Distribution of information assets across sensitivity categories
    b. Percentage (%) of information asset sensitivity assessments that have been independently verified
    c. Percentage (%) of information asset sensitivity assessments that have been agreed to by all affected stakeholders
    d. Percentage (%) of information asset sensitivity assessments that are consistent with federal security and privacy regulations
    e. Currency of information asset sensitivity assessments

Frequency with which vulnerability, threat, and risk assessments are updated:
                                    2.4.9.14

Complete Guide to Security and Privacy Metrics

    a. Frequency with which information sensitivity assessments are updated
    b. Frequency with which asset criticality assessments are updated

Percentage (%) of projects for which vulnerability assessments: 2.4.9.15
    a. Cover all four security engineering domains
    b. Are ongoing throughout the life cycle, from concept formulation through decommissioning
    c. Verify that safeguards do not introduce any new vulnerabilities
    d. Evaluate potential human factors engineering vulnerabilities
    e. Evaluate the potential for vulnerabilities to be introduced as a result of conflicting, misleading, or incomplete user and system documentation
    f. Are verified by independent third parties
    g. Are performed by independent third parties
    h. Are consistent with asset criticality and information sensitivity

Extent to which vulnerability assessments (0 — not at all, 10 — completely, maximum 70 points):   2.4.9.16
    a. Document each vulnerability formally
    b. Identify the root cause of the vulnerability
    c. Evaluate options for eliminating or mitigating the vulnerability
    d. Characterize vulnerabilities by severity and ease of exploitation
    e. Are regularly monitored from identification through resolution
    f. Control access to and distribution of interim and final results
    g. Evaluate vulnerability prevention strategies

By severity and type, the number of vulnerabilities that were not identified correctly over the last 12 months.   2.4.9.17

By quarter, the business impact of the failure to sufficiently identify vulnerabilities: 2.4.9.18
    a. Operational impact (downtime, number of assets affected, number of users affected, etc.)
    b. Cost impact

Security Policy Management

Security policy management is an essential part of an overall security engineering program. Security policies spell out the what, why, when, how, and who of security controls.[16] Security policies are not the panacea some people would like to believe — that security policies by themselves can solve all of an organization's security problems. On the other hand, security policies do not have to be a mindless repetitive paper chase either. The truth lies somewhere between these two extremes. Properly managed, security policies can establish a viable foundation upon which to build an effective security program.

Security policies should be written, communicated, and enforced for all four security engineering domains. Organize security policies according to the taxonomy presented for each security engineering domain. For example, organize physical security policies by facility protection, asset protection, mission protection, and the sub-elements for each of these topics as shown in Figure 4.2. Organize personnel security policies by accountability, background investigations, competence, separation of duties, and workforce analysis, as shown in Figure 4.3. Organize IT security policies around the IT security control system functions and IT security protection system functions, consistent with Figure 4.8. Likewise, operational security policies should correspond to the security engineering life-cycle activities and ongoing risk management activities, as depicted in Figure 4.10. Just as a comprehensive security engineering program needs to cover all four security engineering domains, so do an organization's security policies. Too many organizations tend to focus all their security policies on technical issues, such as passwords, firewalls, encryption, etc. These policies are necessary, but incomplete by themselves. Absence of a policy in a particular area creates a potential vulnerability. How can compliance be measured, execution standardized, or operations monitored if there is no policy to compare against? Without policies, each organizational unit will "do its own thing" or nothing at all, creating vulnerabilities across the enterprise.

I am often amused by salesmen at trade shows who market security policy software: COTS software that is guaranteed to write all of an organization's security policies in no time at all! That is a pretty amazing claim indeed. An inanimate piece of software written by a company I have never heard of and who knows nothing about my organization is going to automatically generate all the security policies my organization needs. What a scam! To write any type of security policy, it is necessary to first understand the organization and its mission. Then it is necessary to understand the organization's assets and the criticality, sensitivity, and risk associated with each.[16] Furthermore, technical security policies are tailored for each unique type of platform, product, system, and network. Sometimes there are regional, time-of-day, time-of-month, time-of-year, and other distinctions as well. Security policies are very specific to the organization and operational environment to which they apply. That is why "security policy in a box" solutions do not work well.

While security policies must be detailed and specific, they do not need to be lengthy. A security policy that is concise and to the point is easier to understand and more likely to be followed. The same five quality characteristics that are applied to security requirements, architectures, and designs should be applied to security policies: clear, complete, concise, consistent, and testable. In this instance, testable means that compliance with the policy can be measured. Some technical security policies can be modeled or simulated to verify that they are correct; for example, the specification of access control rights and privileges.[21] This practice provides an extra degree of confidence in the accuracy and completeness of a policy; however, it is usually time consuming and expensive. So policy modeling, particularly automated modeling, should be reserved for policies associated with high-risk activities.

The use of a standardized format for security policies facilitates understanding because employees and business partners know where to look to find the information they need. Each security policy should contain seven major sections:

1. **Scope:** the technical and organizational domains to which the policy applies, such as all database servers, all facilities in Southeast region, all temporary employees, etc.
2. **Purpose:** what the policy defines and why it exists, for example "define the criteria for approving remote access as part of a telework policy."
3. **Roles and Responsibilities:** who is responsible for implementing and adhering to the policy; who is responsible for verifying compliance with the policy; who is responsible for generating and retaining records and other evidence of compliance with the policy; how the records and evidence are to be captured and stored and how long they must be kept.
4. **Compliance:** how and when compliance with the policy will be measured; Consequences of noncompliance.
5. **Effective Dates:** when the policy goes into effect. The cycle under which the policy will be reviewed, reaffirmed, and updated or withdrawn.
6. **References:** pointers to related policies and other relevant information; Point of contact for the policy.
7. **Details:** specifics of the policy to be followed.

The development of security policies need not be a contentious issue. The first six sections of a policy are straightforward. The final section, details, is where consensus-based organizations often get enmeshed in prolonged turf battles and terminology tiffs. There is no need for that to happen, particularly for technical policies. Why not just point to an existing national or international standard, like those published by the International Organization for Standardization (ISO), the International Electrotechnical Commission (IEC), or the National Institute for Standards and Technology (NIST)? They already fought all the battles to reach consensus and get the standards through the balloting process. Why not benefit from their expertise and experience? To illustrate, instead of spending three years trying to write a C&A policy line by line, why not just state the following? A sentence or two can be added to do whatever tailoring is necessary, but there is no point — and certainly no ROI — in trying to rewrite an entire standard.

    7 Details

       7.1 All C&A activities shall be conducted in accordance with NIST SP 800-37 and FIPS PUB 199.

       7.2 All high-risk systems and networks shall undergo C&A annually and following a major upgrade or security incident of a severity level of moderate or higher.

       7.3 All moderate-risk systems and networks shall undergo C&A biannually and following a major upgrade or security incident of a severity level of moderate or higher.

       7.4 All low-risk systems and networks shall undergo C&A every three years and following a major upgrade or security incident of a severity level of critical or higher.

       7.5 The status of resolving weaknesses discovered during C&A shall be reported to the Chief Information Officer (CIO) and Chief Security Officer (CSO) monthly.

7.6 The status of systems and networks operating under an interim approval to operate or other type of waiver shall be reported to the CIO and CSO monthly.

Security policies should be communicated and accessible to all responsible parties. Just like the accountability principle, it is not possible or logical to hold people responsible for information they have not received or do not understand. Paper copies of all security policies should be distributed to all responsible parties. Electronic copies should also be available online. Supplement the paper copies with classes, as part of the Security Awareness and Training program, to ensure that everyone understands the content and has time to ask questions or make suggestions on how the policies could be improved. Periodic refresher courses are also a good idea. Keep security policies under strict configuration management controls to ensure that everyone is operating from the same approved version. Depending on the content, access to certain security policies may be restricted; other security policies may be freely exchanged with business partners.

Security policies should become part of standard business practices and the corporate culture. The best way for that to happen is for the senior executives to publicly endorse the security policies and reiterate their importance to achieving the organization's mission and business objectives. Enforcing security policies becomes much easier with this type of public endorsement. The few stragglers who need a little more incentive to get on board can always be reminded of the consequences of noncompliance.

Security policies are designed to protect the enterprise, not individual systems or networks. As a result, the security policy management function should be centralized under the auspices of the CSO. This will ensure that the suite of security policies is consistent and complete, and that implementation and enforcement is uniform. Organizations take different approaches to the actual development and approval of security policies. Depending on the corporate culture, security policies may be developed through a top-down, bottom-up, or consensus-based approach. The particular approach is not important, as long as all stakeholders are in the loop and have an opportunity to express their views and concerns before a policy is issued in final form. It may be a good idea to have an independent third party review the more critical policies to see if anything is missing, will not work, or could be accomplished more efficiently.

The following metrics can be used to measure the resilience of an organization's security policies and approach to developing those policies:

Extent to which physical security policies adequately cover the following topics (0 — not at all, 10 — completely, 150 maximum points) and the number of current approved policies in each area: 2.4.10.1

Facility Protection:

a. Location
b. Surrounding facilities, infrastructure, and transit patterns
c. Design, layout, and construction

    d. Physical security perimeters/access control points
    e. Physical security systems
    f. Hazard protection
    g. Building services
    h. Building support services

Asset Protection:

    i. Protection of staff
    j. Asset inventory, criticality, and value
    k. Communications and IT systems
    l. Equipment operations and maintenance

Mission Protection:

    m. Security master plan and preparedness
    n. Contingency and disaster recovery plan and preparedness
    o. Indemnity

Extent to which personnel security policies adequately cover the following
topics (0 — not at all, 10 — completely, 280 maximum points) and the number
of current approved policies in each area: 2.4.10.2

    Accountability:
    a. Security policies, procedures, and standards are published and distributed
    b. Security policies, procedures, and standards define specific roles and
       responsibilities
    c. Security policies, procedures, and standards are tied to specific job
       descriptions and assets
    d. Regular educational forums are held to promote understanding
    e. Individuals acknowledge agreement in writing
    f. Adherence is part of performance appraisals
    g. Consequences of not following security policies, procedures, and stan-
       dards are defined
    h. Requirements are extended to all third parties through legal means

Background Investigations:

    i. Correspond to position sensitivity, criticality, and risk
    j. Reflect level and type of trust
    k. Completed prior to hiring, grounds for retaining
    l. Are unbiased, consistent, objective, accurate, fair, current

Competence:

    m. Security education requirements
    n. Formal education, experience, certification, licensing required to per-
       form tasks
    o. Position description
    p. Domain knowledge
    q. Contractual requirements

Separation of Duties:

r. Internal control
s. Least privilege
t. Need to know
u. Job rotation

Workforce Analysis:

v. Definite insiders, pseudo-insiders
w. Tenure, experience
x. Citizenship
y. Offshore
z. Eligibility to retire
aa. Geography
bb. Proficiency at more than one job function

Extent to which IT security policies adequately cover the following topics (0 — not at all, 10 — completely, 160 maximum points) and the number of current approved policies in each area: 2.4.10.3

IT Security Control System:

a. Logical access control
b. Data authentication, non-repudiation
c. Encryption, cryptographic support
d. Flow control (operational and data)
e. Identification and authentication
f. Maintainability, supportability
g. Privacy
h. Residual information protection
i. Security management

IT Security Protection System:

j. Audit trail, alarm generation
k. Availability (redundancy, diversity, fault tolerance, block recovery, dynamic reconfiguration, rollback, self-healing)
l. Error, exception, and incident handling
m. Fail safe, fail secure, graceful degradation, degraded mode operations
n. Integrity (hardware, software, network, active data, stored data, system)
o. Domain separation (partitioning, information hiding, security kernels, encapsulation)
p. Resource management (resource allocation, service priority, capacity management)

Extent to which operational security policies adequately cover the following topics (0 — not at all, 10 — completely, 150 maximum points) and the number of current approved policies in each area: 2.4.10.4

Security Engineering Life-Cycle Activities (COTS and Custom):

a. Concept formulation
b. Security requirements analysis and specification

   c. Security architecture and design
   d. Development and implementation
   e. Security test and evaluation (ST&E), certification and accreditation (C&A), independent validation and verification (IV&V)
   f. Delivery, installation, and deployment
   g. Operations and maintenance
   h. Decommissioning (transition, sanitization, reuse, destruction)

Ongoing Security Risk Management Activities (COTS and Custom):

   i. Vulnerability assessment
   j. Security policy management
   k. Security audits and reviews
   l. Security impact analysis, configuration management, patch management
   m. Privacy impact assessment
   n. Security awareness and training, guidance documents
   o. Stakeholder, strategic partner, supplier relationships

Frequency with which security policies are reviewed, reaffirmed, and updated or withdrawn: 2.4.10.5

   a. Physical security policies
   b. Personnel security policies
   c. IT security policies
   d. Operational security policies

Frequency with which internal and external audits are conducted to verify compliance with security policies: 2.4.10.6

   a. Physical security policies
   b. Personnel security policies
   c. IT security policies
   d. Operational security policies

Percentage (%) of current security policies, standards, and procedures for which compliance has been verified this reporting period[143]:   2.4.10.7

   a. Percentage (%) of security policy compliance audits with no violations noted[105]

Percentage (%) of security policies that contain the following required information, by security engineering domain (physical, personnel, IT, and operational):   2.4.10.8

   a. Scope
   b. Purpose
   c. Roles and responsibilities
   d. Compliance
   e. Effective dates
   f. References
   g. Details

Frequency with which refresher courses are held for the people responsible for implementing security policies: 2.4.10.9
    a. Physical security policies
    b. Personnel security policies
    c. IT security policies
    d. Operational security policies

Extent to which security policies are tailored to reflect asset criticality, information sensitivity, risk, and the operational environment (0 — not at all, 10 — completely, 40 maximum points): 2.4.10.10
    a. Physical security policies
    b. Personnel security policies
    c. IT security policies
    d. Operational security policies

Percentage (%) of security policies that are: 2.4.10.11
    a. Under configuration management control
    b. Available online
    c. Part of standard business practices
    d. Publicly endorsed by senior executives
    e. Consistent across all four security engineering domains

Percentage (%) of information security program principles for which approved policies and controls have been implemented by management[105, 143]: 2.4.10.12
    a. Percentage (%) of information security program elements for which approved policies and controls are currently operational
    b. Percentage (%) of business unit heads and senior managers who have implemented operational procedures to ensure compliance with approved information security policies and controls

Percentage (%) of security management policies, standards, and procedures that have been reviewed and re-validated or updated this reporting period.[163] 2.4.10.13

Number of new security policies, standards, and procedures issued this reporting period.[143] 2.4.10.14

Number of policy exceptions requested and granted this reporting period, by asset criticality.[143, 169] 2.4.10.15

Number of security policy violations this reporting period, by severity and type.[169] 2.4.10.16

Business impact of security policy violations this reporting period and the last 12 months: 2.4.10.17
    a. Operational impact (downtime, number of assets affected, number of end users affected, etc.)
    b. Cost impact

Number of security incidents, by incident type and severity, this reporting period as a result of: 2.4.10.18

  a. An incorrect security policy
  b. Failure to follow an approved security policy
  c. Failure to inform all affected parties of their duties related to a security policy
  d. Lack of a security policy

Security Audits and Reviews

Security audits and reviews are an inevitable part of doing business if an organization is a government agency, a company that contracts with a government agency, or part of a regulated industry. In the United States, federal agencies are audited by other federal agencies, such as the Office of Management and Budget (OMB) and the General Accountability Office (GAO), as well as their own internal Office of the Inspector General (OIG). Organizations that are under contract to federal agencies must abide by the same rules and, as a result, are subject to audit by the same agencies. Companies that are in a regulated industry are audited to see if they are in compliance with the applicable security and privacy regulations discussed in Chapter 3. The global economy has made this situation even more common. The government agency responsible for monitoring, oversight, and enforcement of a regulation conducts the audit. In addition, internal security audits and reviews are (hopefully) conducted by the organization itself. In each instance, it is possible for an organization to pass an audit, fail an audit, or end up in the gray area between passing and failing. Passing an audit is good news — not to mention a relief. In contrast, failing an audit can have severe legal, financial, and business consequences.

Security audits and reviews encompass a broad spectrum. In essence, a security audit can be conducted at any time for any reason. The scope of a security audit can be very narrow or unbounded. The duration of a security audit can range from a few days, to a few weeks, to a few months, or longer. The size of the team conducting the audit varies also. It all depends on why the audit is being conducted, who is conducting the audit, and what questions need to be answered during the audit. The scope of a routine internal audit may be limited to a single topic, such as whether contingency and disaster recovery plans and training are up-to-date. The scope of an external regulatory audit can be very broad, especially if there were compliance problems in the past. In the latter case, auditors may look at anything and everything to get a sense of what is really going on.

Security audits and reviews take place throughout the security engineering life cycle. All four security engineering domains are subject to security audits and reviews. Security audits and reviews can be scheduled in advance or conducted on a surprise basis. The intent is to monitor compliance with approved security policies and controls.[14] The effectiveness and efficiency with which security policies and controls are implemented is analyzed.[16] The degree of conformance to security standards and procedures is measured.[16] For example, a new system under development may be audited to determine how many of the security requirements have been incorporated and how efficiently they have been incorporated into the system. An audit can be conducted to see if asset inventories and criticality ratings are current; determine whether security impact analysis, configuration management, and patch management procedures are being followed; or evaluate adherence to information handling procedures, such as labeling, media storage, controlling distribution inside and outside the organization, and keeping logs of who received what information and when. Internal controls, such as separation of duties, accountability, and background investigations are frequent targets of security audits and reviews.

Security audits can be conducted by internal or external staff; either way, the auditors are independent of the people and projects being audited. Common practice is to have internal auditors evaluate the same items that the external auditors are expected to evaluate, so that any deficiencies can be corrected ahead of time. To really be prepared for an external regulatory audit, why not hire an independent third party to conduct an audit beforehand? Their results are bound to be more objective than an internal audit. Having these results and acting upon them puts an organization in a better position to pass the official audit. Internal auditors can examine items that external auditors do not, and vice versa. Again, it all gets back to what the auditors are trying to find out. There may be legal issues involved during a security audit after a major security breach, such as preservation of evidence. Regardless of the type or purpose of a security audit, it is essential to ensure that auditors have access to accurate, current, and complete information. Supplying auditors old, incomplete, misleading, or bogus data only increases the pain. Does Enron ring a bell? If an organization knows it is weak in certain areas, it is better to admit that up-front to the auditors and explain to them what is being done to remedy the situation. The more an organization tries to dance around an issue, the hotter the coals will get under their feet.

A variety of different techniques can be used to conduct an audit. In summary, an audit is[100]:

> **Audit:** an independent review and examination of records and activities to assess the adequacy of security controls, to ensure compliance with established policies and operational procedures, and to recommend necessary changes in controls, policies, or procedures.

An audit can consist of interviews of key staff and inspections or sampling of visitor logs, system logs, maintenance records, system documentation, and ST&E results. An auditor can follow a prescribed checklist or proceed in ad hoc fashion, pursuing a line of inquiry that appears to be enlightening. Auditors can choose to monitor normal operations or emergency preparedness exercises. They have the option of repeating ST&E activities or conducting new tests on their own. Auditors should be considered "free range" creatures.

An audit can be conducted manually, by manually reviewing hardcopy reports or online files. Or, an audit can be conducted through the use of automated tools, such as those used to analyze system and IDS logs. It is the organization's responsibility to ensure that the date and time stamps for different reports and IT assets are synchronized.[52] Often, auditors do a little data mining of their own by merging and correlating records from diverse sources,[52] all the more reason for an organization to ensure that its records are accurate and complete.

Some sources consider security reviews passive in nature; security reviews tend to only report the results of the review. In contrast, security audits tend to be more interactive and yield results, action items, and recommendations on how to resolve the action items. (*Note:* some of the security and privacy regulations discussed in Chapter 3 prohibit auditors from making recommendations. Instead, auditors are only allowed to report their findings and the action items or weaknesses that need to be fixed.)

A key consideration for both the auditor and the audited is protecting the integrity of (1) the audit process and (2) the audit records. Because both parties' reputations are at stake, it behooves them to ensure that the audit is conducted in an open, honest, and thorough manner. That is, many of the same security principles that are being audited should be applied to the audit process to ensure data integrity and prevent unauthorized access, modification, and tampering.[52] Audit records should contain a sufficient level of detail to substantiate the findings and recommendations and adequate pointers to the source information that led to the findings.[52] That way, if the audit itself is audited, it will be easy to verify the findings. In addition, there are usually legal and corporate requirements for retaining audit records and source information for a period of time after an audit is complete.[52]

The following metrics can be used to measure the resilience of an organization's approach to preparing for, conducting, and responding to security audits and reviews.

Percentage (%) of security requirements from applicable laws and regulations that are included in the internal/external audit program and schedule[105]:

2.4.11.1

    a. Percentage (%) of security audits conducted in compliance with the approved internal/external audit program and schedule[105]

Percentage (%) of required internal and external audits completed and reviewed by senior management[105]:   2.4.11.2

    a. Percentage (%) of management actions in response to audit findings/recommendations that were implemented as agreed as to timeliness and completeness in the current reporting period[105]

    b. Percentage (%) of audit findings that have been resolved, by severity of finding and elapsed time interval[105]

Number and distribution of security audits conducted this reporting period and the last 12 months, by security engineering domain: physical security, personnel security, IT security, and operational security.   2.4.11.3

Percentage (%) of security and privacy systems, policies, procedures, and controls that were audited for effectiveness and compliance this reporting period, by asset criticality and risk[163, 169]:   2.4.11.4

    a. Percentage (%) of security and privacy systems, policies, procedures, and controls that were independently audited for effectiveness and compliance this reporting period, by asset criticality and risk[163, 169]

Number of weaknesses found by security engineering domain, security control, and severity, as a result of conducting all security audits: 2.4.11.5

    a. Number of weaknesses found by security engineering domain, security control, and severity, as a result of conducting internal security audits

    b. Number of weaknesses found by security engineering domain, security control, and severity, as a result of conducting independent third-party security audits

    c. Number of weaknesses found by security engineering domain, security control, and severity, as a result of conducting external security audits

Number of weaknesses, by security control and severity, that were prevented from reaching the as-built system and the operational procedures, as a result of conducting security audits: 2.4.11.6

    a. Number of weaknesses, by security control and severity, that were and were not detected and corrected in the same life-cycle step, as a result of conducting security audits

Frequency with which internal security audits are performed to verify ongoing compliance with federal regulations and corporate security and privacy policies: 2.4.11.7

    a. Average and worst-case interval for resolving deficiencies noted during security audits

Distribution of problems found during security audits conducted during this reporting period and the last 12 months, by type of problem and severity: 2.4.11.8

    a. Missing security control
    b. Ineffective security control
    c. Security control not enforced
    d. Inefficient implementation of a security control
    e. Wrong security control employed
    f. Staff not adequately trained on operational procedures associated with the security control
    g. Security control not deployed consistently throughout the enterprise
    h. The only information available during the security audit was old, incomplete, or misleading
    i. Incorrect record keeping associated with the security control
    j. Other (explain)

Percentage (%) of weaknesses from previous audits that were corrected prior to a follow-up audit, by severity: 2.4.11.9

    a. Percentage (%) of weaknesses that were not corrected and no concrete action had been taken to resolve them

    b. Percentage (%) of weaknesses that were not corrected and concrete action had been started to resolve them

During the last 12 months, the number of times a security audit was failed or terminated because the integrity of the audit process and/or records were compromised: 2.4.11.10

    a. Cost impact

    b. Operational impact

Security Impact Analysis, Privacy Impact Assessment, Configuration Management, Patch Management

Security impact analysis, privacy impact analysis, configuration management, and patch management are closely related risk management activities that are ongoing throughout the security engineering life cycle. The purpose of these activities is to ensure the security and privacy of IT and information assets despite the inevitable changes that occur along the way, from concept formulation through decommissioning. The security and privacy impacts of all proposed changes are evaluated, prior to approving the change, to prevent accidental or intentional errors from being introduced that could have serious security or privacy consequences. Security impact analysis, privacy impact analysis, and configuration management impose discipline and control during the refinement and modification of assets throughout their useful life spans.[21] Casual changes, changes that are not completely thought through, and changes that are not coordinated with all stakeholders can cause errors to be introduced, errors that will be manifested later as vulnerabilities and failures. Security impact analysis, privacy impact analysis, configuration management, and patch management are particularly important during operations and maintenance. The challenge is to ensure that a product, system, or network is maintained in a known secure state and changes do not disrupt the security posture to which the system was originally certified.[14] This is not an idle challenge — inadequate change control related to IT assets is a common cause of system and security failures.[28]

A further challenge, and one that is often overlooked, is to ensure that all changes are accurately reflected in all applicable system documentation, such as contingency and disaster recovery plans, operations and maintenance procedures, security roles and responsibilities, asset inventories, and security awareness and training materials.[14] If changes are made but not documented, it may not be possible to restore a product or system using old documentation. Testing results may appear to be valid when they are not. Addressing schemes may be out of date. In short, there are an unlimited number of ways to confound an IT infrastructure when using out-of-date documentation. Given the high turnover of IT staff, it is unwise to assume that the right people will know what changes were made, when they were made, and more importantly, why they were made. Verbal configuration management systems are not very reliable.

Security impact analysis, privacy impact analysis, and configuration management are applicable to all four security engineering domains, not just IT. The security and privacy impact of all proposed changes to physical security controls should be evaluated prior to implementation. The security and privacy impact of all proposed changes to personnel security controls should be evaluated before they take place. Likewise, the security and privacy impact of all proposed changes to IT and operational security controls should be evaluated before they are deployed. The scope of items to include as part of security and privacy impact analyses is quite broad. Here are just a few examples[14, 21, 28, 52]:

- Changes in the operational environment
- Changes to the operational profile or duty cycle
- Changes in user requirements
- Changes in internal or external interfaces
- New operational procedures, including contingency and disaster recovery preparedness
- New features or functionality
- Software updates, patches, and revisions to operating systems, utilities, middleware, and applications
- Hardware upgrades and revisions
- Changes to configuration settings
- Changes to the telecommunications infrastructure, connectivity, or carriers
- Replacing a COTS product with a similar product from a different vendor
- Replacing manual processes with automatic ones or vice versa
- Outsourcing agreements
- Changes in maintenance contractors
- Relocation to a new facility
- Replacing a custom-developed product with a COTS product, and vice versa
- Replacing discrete hardware logic with embedded software
- Replacing application layer software with firmware
- Changing or replacing online or offline storage media and mechanisms

Personnel roles and responsibilities for security impact analysis, privacy impact analysis, configuration management, and patch management must be clearly defined — specifically, who is responsible for performing what activities, who is responsible for verifying that the activities were performed correctly and on time, and who has the authority to authorize that activities be performed or changes made.[21, 52] A decision must be made about who has the authority to decide when an item is ready to be put under configuration control.[21] A clear-cut definition of these roles and responsibilities is necessary to avoid activities being duplicated or not performed at all. They can be assigned to an individual by name or an organizational unit. Spell out the relationship and reporting structure of the different organizational units involved. Make sure all stakeholders are aware of their assigned tasks and the point of contact for other tasks.

Similarly, security impact analysis, privacy impact analysis, configuration management, and patch management activities need to be scheduled. The schedule should depict the sequence of events, the duration of events, the interval between events, which events occur on a regular basis, and which events occur on an as-needed basis and what triggers them. Some events occur on a regular basis, such as a routine meeting of the configuration control board, and can be scheduled for a certain date, such as the tenth of each month. Other activities occur on an as-needed basis, such as privacy impact analysis. As-needed activities can be scheduled by stating that they must start so many days after the receipt of something, in this case a change request, and finish within a certain time frame, given certain parameters, such as complexity or severity. Dependencies between the start and completion of different activities should be shown on the schedule as well. Taking the time to develop a schedule will help ensure that an adequate amount of time is allocated so that each activity can be performed in a comprehensive manner. Of course, distinctions must be made between routine and emergency situations.

The schedule should be supplemented with a list of resources that are required to perform security impact analysis, privacy impact analysis, configuration management, and patch management. First and foremost, the number and type of personnel needed for each activity should be identified. What specific type of knowledge, skills, and experience do these people need? In short, the competence requirements for each of these positions must be defined. Are senior people needed? Can junior people be paired with senior people? How many years of each type of experience do they need? Are there any formal education or certification requirements? When and for how long is each specific skill set needed? It is illogical to ask someone to perform a privacy impact analysis of a Web-based employee benefits system if the person has no knowledge of privacy regulations or attack methods common to Web-based systems. They may try very hard and produce a pretty report, but the content will be questionable.

In addition, specific requirements for automated tools and other equipment, as well as standardized techniques and procedures, should be identified for each activity. It is wise to ensure that standardized methodologies are used to perform security impact analysis and privacy impact analysis and verify the correct implementation of configuration changes. That way, the enterprise will not be put at risk because security impact analyses in Milwaukee are performed differently than those in San Pedro. These methodologies must be documented and communicated to the appropriate people. Identify what specific automated tools and equipment are needed. Give make and model numbers if appropriate. State when and for how long the equipment is needed. Identifying resource needs up-front helps to ensure that (1) the resources will be available when needed, (2) adequate funds are set aside for these resources, and (3) security impact analysis, privacy impact analysis, configuration management, and patch management activities can be accomplished in an effective, efficient, and timely manner.

Security impact analysis, privacy impact analysis, configuration management, and patch management must be conducted as formal processes to be effective. Ad hoc attempts or lip service routines will accomplish nothing and might actually make the situation worse. There are five key process areas involved in security impact analysis, privacy impact analysis, configuration management, and patch management: (1) configuration identification, (2) configuration control, (3) ongoing status accounting, (4) periodic configuration audits and reviews, and (5) secure storage, retrieval, tracking, replication, distribution, retention, and backup of items under configuration management. The goal of each key process area is to ensure that all assets remain in a known secure state at all times.

Configuration identification involves two tasks. First, the items that do and do not belong under configuration management are delineated for each project and organizational unit.[21] Document assumptions upon which the delineation was made; should the assumptions change later, the list of items that are and are not under configuration management may change. Obvious items to place under configuration management include hardware components, COTS and custom-developed software components (operating systems, utilities, middleware, applications), network equipment, system documentation, operational procedures, security policies, facility drawings, ST&E procedures, equipment configuration parameters, contingency and disaster recovery plans and procedures, system and user guidance documents, and security training and awareness materials. For other items, a decision will have to be made on a case-by-case basis as to whether or not they belong under configuration management. Meeting minutes, briefing slides, individuals' engineering notebooks, and test equipment are some of the items that fall into this gray area.

Next, unique configuration items are identified and assigned an ID name, number, and version. Logical, physical, or functional boundaries can be used to identify a configuration item. Configuration items can be COTS, custom developed, or a combination of the two. The boundary of a configuration item can be as large or as small as practical. However, for consistency's sake, it is best to use the same level of granularity and nomenclature that was used in the IT asset inventory. A configuration item list identifies each unique item, while the IT asset inventory identifies all instances of each configuration item. Like the IT asset inventory, it is essential to keep the configuration item list current and complete. Over time, a configuration item list may change as the IT infrastructure, physical security controls, and personnel security controls evolve. Two separate configuration items can be combined into one configuration item. A single configuration item can be split into two configuration items. Or, a configuration item can be deleted because it is no longer needed or has been replaced by a new configuration item. All of these changes are legitimate as long as the configuration documentation is kept current and there is complete traceability back to previous configuration baselines.[52] Consequently, the configuration item list itself should be under configuration management.

The second process area is configuration control. Note that the configuration is controlled, not frozen. Within configuration control, change requests are evaluated, approved or disapproved, implemented, and verified. This is where security impact analysis, privacy impact analysis, and patch management come into play. Each proposed change request, no matter how small in scope it initially appears, must be evaluated in terms of the security and privacy impact of the proposed change. Proposed changes can come about as a result of preventive, adaptive, or corrective maintenance. Patches are another form of change request; hence they must be evaluated as well.[28] The same is true for routine upgrades of COTS products.[28] A variety of information is evaluated during security impact analysis and privacy impact analysis. Some of the information is produced by the organization that submitted the change request. Some of the information is generated by the team evaluating the change request. In moderate and high-risk environments, an independent third party may be asked to independently generate or verify some information.

Security impact analysis and privacy impact packages contain several key sections, such as those shown below. In addition, each change proposal should include an explanation of how a rollback is to be effected should the change be unsuccessful and it becomes necessary to return to a previous known secure state.[28]

- **Justification:** why the change is needed.
- **Description:** what will be changed and how it will be changed.
- **Scope:** the internal and external assets, end users, and business partners that will be impacted by the change.
- **Analysis:** security, privacy, and operational impact of the proposed change.
- **Priority:** urgency with which the change request must be dealt.
- **Evaluation:** whether the proposed change is approved or disapproved and why.
- **Implementation:** the version and release of the effected configuration items in which the change was implemented, applicable documentation that was updated to reflect the change, effective date.
- **Verification:** how and by whom the change was verified.
- Approval signatures.

One of the more difficult items during security impact analysis and privacy impact analysis is to accurately gauge the ripple effect of a proposed change.[21] Historically, operations and maintenance staff grossly underestimate the scope of the impact of a proposed change. This leads to the familiar situation where in the process of fixing one problem, two new problems are created. In security terms this means that "fixing" one vulnerability creates two new vulnerabilities. Or, as often happens, indirectly exposed vulnerabilities become directly exposed vulnerabilities and existing mitigation strategies are no longer effective. Frequently, new vulnerabilities are created at interfaces and integration points.[114] This is why ST&E and C&A reports should be consulted as part of security impact analysis and privacy impact analysis; particular attention should be paid to stated assumptions and anomaly reports.

Evaluators may agree that a change should be made, but disagree with the approach. Instead, the evaluators may recommend that other options be investigated.

<u>Security Impact Analysis</u>
- Does the change introduce a new vulnerability?
- Does the change exacerbate an existing vulnerability?
- Does the change convert any indirectly exposed vulnerabilities into directly exposed vulnerabilities?
- What evidence exists to substantiate the answers to the previous three questions?
- What is the impact on existing IT security controls? Are they still as effective? Are new or different IT security controls needed as a result of the change?
- What is the impact on existing operational security controls? Are they still as effective? Are new or different operational security controls needed as a result of the change?
- What is the impact on existing physical security controls? Are they still as effective? Are new or different physical security controls needed as a result of the change?
- What is the impact on existing personnel security controls? Are they still as effective? Are new or different personnel security controls needed as a result of the change?
- What assumptions made during ST&E and C&A are and are not still valid?
- What ST&E, C&A, and IV&V activities need to be repeated to verify the impact of the proposed change? What additional verification activities are necessary?
- What is the impact of the change on end users and business partners?
- What part of the IT infrastructure is the most and least impacted by the change?
- What is the fall back plan if implementation of the change is not successful?
- What is the operational impact while the change is being deployed?
- What other organizations have successfully implemented this change?
- What is the level of confidence in the estimate of the scope of the impact?

<u>Privacy Impact Analysis</u>
- Is personal information being collected about a person without their prior knowledge and consent?
- Is personal information about an individual being used for purposes other than that specified at the time the information was collected?
- Is more personal information being collected than is needed for the stated purpose?
- How is the accuracy of personal information verified? How often is the accuracy of personal information verified?
- Is personal information about an individual being disseminated to new sources that were not identified to the individual when the information was collected?
- Is personal information being kept longer than the individual was told at the time of collection?
- Is personal information destroyed in a secure manner or rendered anonymous after the specified use and retention period? How is this verified?
- Are there adequate physical, personnel, IT, and operational security controls to prevent unauthorized access, alteration, use, release, and destruction of personal information stored online, offline, and in hardcopy format?
- Has the organization informed individuals about the personal information it holds about them, their right to view the information, their right to obtain copies of the information, and their right to challenge inaccurate information and insist that it be corrected?

Figure 4.11   Items to consider during security impact analysis and privacy impact analysis.

Security impact analysis and privacy impact analysis should be conducted in parallel because a change may trigger a vulnerability that has both a security and a privacy impact. As part of the evaluation process, some ST&E activities may necessitate repeating. Also, a determination should be made about whether or not the proposed changes are so extensive that recertification is necessary.[21] Figure 4.11 summarizes some of the key issues to evaluate during security impact analysis and privacy impact analysis. These items are examples and should not be considered an exhaustive list. The exact list of items to be evaluated should be determined on a case-by-case basis.

The third key process area is ongoing configuration status monitoring. The configuration of IT and other assets should be continually monitored for

several reasons. Monitoring is the only way to ensure that approved configuration baselines — the baselines to which the assets were certified — are
being maintained. Not maintaining approved configuration baselines puts the
IT infrastructure and other assets at risk. An uncertified configuration can
expose new vulnerabilities or exacerbate existing vulnerabilities. Because the
configuration has not been evaluated, its security posture is unknown. To
mitigate this risk, some configuration status monitoring tools have the capability
to either force a change back to the approved configuration or block a device
from accessing corporate assets until it is restored to a compliant configuration.
Subtle unauthorized configuration changes can also indicate an imminent
attack or a sustained low-level attack. As a result, configuration status monitoring can also be used as part of an intrusion prevention strategy,[117] particularly
for insider attacks. Ongoing configuration status monitoring is usually accomplished through a combination of automated tools.[21, 52] However, surprise site
visits can be equally enlightening. This process area is responsible for keeping
a complete audit trail of all changes requested[28] and all changes implemented.[21]
This will help ensure that all changes that were made were indeed authorized.[21]

The fourth key process area is periodic configuration audits and reviews.
Periodic configuration audits and reviews supplement the ongoing configuration status monitoring. Configuration audits and reviews are performed by a
team that is independent from the team that performs the ongoing configuration status monitoring. This activity is a subset of the broader category of
security audits and reviews discussed previously. These particular audits and
reviews concentrate on determining compliance with approved configuration
parameters and standardized configuration management procedures. Configuration audits can be scheduled, or conducted on a stealth basis. Audit findings
are ranked by severity, so the most urgent items receive attention first. For
example, suppose an audit discovers that 60 percent of an organization's
servers are not in compliance with the approved baseline configuration. It is
unlikely that they can all suddenly be shut down. However, armed with that
information, some interim measures can be taken to minimize the risk exposure
until the configuration is brought into compliance.

The fifth key process area concerns the secure storage, retrieval, tracking,
replication, distribution, backup, and retention of approved configuration
items. That can be a daunting task when talking about an entire IT infrastructure. Online libraries are established for software configuration items, documentation, policies, and procedures under configuration control. However, it
is difficult to place IT hardware and telecommunications equipment into an
online library. Depending on asset criticality and availability requirements,
redundancy with hot standby, redundancy with cold standby, or spares that
are ready to go may be employed. In either case, the intent is to have a
master copy or adequate spares of each configuration item so that (1) there
is an approved reference standard to which compliance comparisons can be
made, and (2) there are sufficient resources from which to recreate or restore
a configuration item, should it become damaged. As a result, items under
configuration management are strictly controlled to prevent tampering, theft,
destruction, and environmental degradation. Critical assets can be stored in

multiple configuration libraries or storage areas that are geographically dispersed, similar to critical data archives. It is wise to keep at least two previously approved configuration baselines for each configuration item, in case an emergency situation arises and there is a need to revert back to a previously known secure state.

The following metrics can be used to measure the resilience of an organization's approach to security impact analysis, privacy impact analysis, configuration management, and patch management.

Percentage (%) of organizational units that perform security impact analysis, privacy impact analysis, and configuration management throughout the security engineering life cycle.   2.4.12.1

Percentage (%) of organizational units that perform security impact analysis, privacy impact analysis, and configuration management for all four security engineering domains.   2.4.12.2

Percentage (%) of change requests that undergo a thorough security impact analysis, privacy impact analysis, and operational impact analysis by an independent source prior to approval and implementation.   2.4.12.3

Extent to which documentation, plans, procedures, and policies are kept current to reflect approved configuration changes (0 — not at all, 10 — completely).   2.4.12.4

Extent to which personnel roles and responsibilities for security impact analysis, privacy impact analysis, and configuration management are clearly defined (0 — not at all, 10 — completely).   2.4.12.5

Extent to which security impact analysis, privacy impact analysis, configuration management, and patch management activities are adequately scheduled, including dependencies between tasks (0 — not at all, 10 — completely).
                                                                                                                 2.4.12.6

Extent to which the resources needed to conduct security impact analysis, privacy impact analysis, configuration management, and patch management are identified beforehand and available when needed (0 — not at all, 10 — completely).   2.4.12.7

Extent to which the items that need to be under configuration management control have been completely identified (0 — not at all, 10 — completely, 40 maximum points):   2.4.12.8
  a. Extent to which unique configuration items have been identified
  b. Degree of consistency between the configuration item list and the asset inventory
  c. Currency of configuration item list
  d. Degree of traceability between current configuration item list and previously approved baselines

Extent of confidence in the thoroughness and accuracy of the security and privacy impact analysis (0 — none, 10 — complete, 80 maximum points):
                                                                                                                 2.4.12.9

   a. Justification
   b. Description
   c. Scope
   d. Analysis
   e. Priority
   f. Evaluation
   g. Implementation
   h. Verification

Number of configuration changes made this reporting period that were[117]:

                                                                                                                     2.4.12.10

   a. Performed outside normal maintenance windows
   b. Not correlated with expected maintenance activities
   c. Made post installation to change file permissions
   d. Made to Web server security configuration parameters, such as root directory and ability to index

Percentage (%) of system architecture changes (additions, modifications, or deletions) that were reviewed for security and privacy impacts, approved by appropriate authorities, and documented via change request forms.[105, 163]

                                                                                         2.4.12.11

Percentage (%) of patches and other upgrades to COTS components for which security and privacy impact analysis was performed before they were deployed, by asset criticality.   2.4.12.12

Percentage (%) of custom and COTS software changes that were reviewed for security and privacy impacts in advance of installation, by asset criticality.[105]

                                                                                         2.4.12.13

Percentage (%) of critical information assets residing on systems that are currently in compliance with the approved system architecture, by risk and criticality.[105]   2.4.12.14

Percentage (%) of systems where permission to install non-standard software is limited or prohibited, by asset criticality.[105]   2.4.12.15

Percentage (%) of system and network components for which approved configuration settings have been implemented, as required by policy[105]:

                                                                                        2.4.12.16

   a. Percentage (%) of system and network components for which security-related configuration settings are documented and under configuration control, by risk and criticality[163]
   b. Percentage (%) of system and network components that do not deviate from approved standards, by risk and criticality[105]

Percentage (%) of system and network components that are continuously monitored for configuration policy compliance with out-of-compliance alarms or reports, by risk and criticality[105]:   2.4.12.17

    a. Percentage (%) of configuration status monitoring tools that have the capability to either force configuration compliance or block access until configuration compliance is restored

    b. Percentage (%) of systems whose configuration is compared with a previously established trusted baselines in accordance with policy, by criticality and risk[105]

Percentage (%) of systems where the authority to make configuration changes is limited in accordance with policy, by criticality and risk.[105]   2.4.12.18

Percentage (%) of systems with the latest approved patches installed, by system criticality and the severity of the vulnerability the patch claims to mitigate.[105]

    2.4.12.19

Mean time from vendor patch availability to patch approval to patch installation, by type of technology and asset criticality.[105]   2.4.12.20

Percentage (%) of workstation firewalls, host firewalls, sub-network firewalls, and perimeter firewalls that are configured in accordance with policy.[105]

    2.4.12.21

Percentage (%) of security incidents that exploited existing vulnerabilities with known solutions, patches, or workarounds[105]:   2.4.12.22

    a. Percentage (%) of systems affected by security incidents that exploited existing vulnerabilities with known solutions, patches, or workarounds[105]

Percentage (%) of desktops, laptops, and servers that have current anti-virus software installed, by system risk, as of the close of this reporting period.[143]

    2.4.12.23

Security Awareness and Training, Guidance Documents

The title of this activity, security awareness and training, has always amused me somewhat. Does one have to be "aware" before one understands that one needs security training, similar to the fact that an alcoholic or drug addict must acknowledge his addiction before he can be cured? In this case, an individual would have to acknowledge his emptiness relative to security engineering and hence his desperate need for training. Or, is it only through training that one can see the light and truly become aware? But if one is not "aware" and neither are one's first- or second-level managers, how are they going to have the insight to know they even need security training and what exactly this training should consist of? It is entirely possible for one to be ignorant of what one is ignorant of. Having visited many organizations in the Washington, D.C. area, it would appear that several of them are waiting for a divine epiphany in this regard. The politically incorrect truth is that this ongoing risk management activity is trying to ensure, after the fact, that an organization's personnel have the necessary competency to perform their assigned security roles and responsibilities. In the past decade, a lot of people in all four security engineering domains have inherited overnight significant security roles and responsibilities. Organizations are relying on this on-the-job training as a way of playing catch-up. Is this goal being achieved? We will let the auditors and the news media decide.

Many of the security and privacy regulations discussed in Chapter 3 require that (1) personnel be held accountable for their actions relative to security engineering, and (2) personnel be competent to perform their assigned duties, especially their security roles and responsibilities. Auditors expect to see *bona fide* evidence of this competence.[52] This is the void organizations are trying to fill with a security awareness and training program. Unfortunately, in too many organizations security awareness and training has become a random collection of generic feel-good fluff to make the training statistics look good. This is a waste of time and money because there is no "one-size-fits-all" approach to security awareness and training that is applicable to an entire organization, let alone multiple disparate organizations. Instead, what is really needed is focused training that is tailored for specific job functions, security roles, and position sensitivities. Security awareness and training accomplishments should be tied to specific job descriptions and performance appraisals, in an effort to close the loop between accountability and competence.

Security awareness and training emphasizes the correct implementation, use, and enforcement of security safeguards.[16] The intent is to tell personnel exactly what they need to know to perform their security roles and responsibilities on a day-to-day basis. This should include items such as:

- When ID badges must be worn and presented
- When and why people who are not wearing a badge should be challenged
- Why background investigations are performed and how frequently they are updated
- Procedures for challenging the results of a background investigation
- Information storage and handling procedures by information sensitivity level
- Media sanitization and reuse procedures
- Which hardcopy materials can be recycled and which must be shredded
- Remote access procedures
- Wireless access procedures
- Procedures for requesting, approving, and revoking security credentials
- What information may and may not be discussed over the phone, with co-workers, or people outside the organization
- What information can and cannot be sent by fax
- What information can and cannot be sent by e-mail
- Permitted and prohibited uses of corporate IT assets
- Permitted and prohibited uses of employee-owned IT assets

Often, people working in one security engineering domain are extremely knowledgeable about their domain but not the other domains. For example, personnel security specialists are generally meticulous about keeping paper files locked and not leaving papers laying around on their desks. At the same time, they generally do not think twice about faxing the same sensitive information over an open (unsecure) line, or worse, e-mailing it. I do not know how many e-mails I have received where the text goes to great length to point out that the attachment is FOUO and cannot be distributed further. Since when did e-mail over the public network become a secure means of distribution? This is an example of where an appropriate security awareness and training program can be extremely beneficial. In summary, the security training an individual receives should cover in detail every physical, personnel, IT, and operational security policy that applies to him and his current position.

The purpose of a security awareness and training program, as envisioned by the regulations in Chapter 3, is to explain the organization's security objectives, strategies, and policies and how they relate to achieving (or not achieving) the organization's mission.[14, 16, 21, 52] This information correlates to specific job functions and security roles and responsibilities. At the same time, the consequences — to the organization and the individual — of not performing assigned security roles and responsibilities are made clear.[14] The goal is for security roles and responsibilities to become second nature and part of standard business practices across the organization.[16] This means that security awareness and training activities should be applied to everyone in the organization, not just the IT security staff.[16] The exact content and depth of security awareness and training activities depend on the specific job function, trust level, and trust type. It is always a good idea to require an employee or business partner to demonstrate competence in performing his assigned security roles and responsibilities before giving him access to corporate assets.[52] Security awareness and training activities should be applied to all four security engineering domains and throughout the security engineering life cycle, from concept formulation through decommissioning. In particular, the impact of security incidents on the organization and the individual should be described, along with procedures for reporting security incidents of any kind.[16]

Security awareness and training activities should be conducted frequently, according to an ongoing schedule. Keep the material fresh and current with changing business needs; that way, the students will be engaged and in a receptive mode. Repeating the same old information over and over again is a guaranteed recipe for low participation and retention.

The success of a security awareness and training program is not counted by how many names are on the attendance list. Rather, the success of a security awareness and training program is measured by the knowledge gained, the knowledge retained, the extent to which the program is kept current, and the resulting improvement in security behavior.[16]

Guidance documents are a companion to security awareness and training. Guidance documents are common in the realm of IT security and operational security. Usually, two different types of documents are prepared: (1) those for end users and (2) those for system operations and maintenance staff. Incomplete, incorrect, misleading, and out-of-date documentation can create a vulnerability.[21] As a result, it is essential that accurate, current, and complete documentation be available to those who need and are authorized to received it. Guidance documents should place special emphasis on explaining the secure use and operation of IT assets. Assumptions about the intended operational environment and use of each IT asset should be made quite clear up-front.[21, 52] In particular, documentation needs to explain the security functions performed, internal and external interfaces, and legal and illegal values for security parameters.[21, 52] Guidance should be provided on how to interpret diagnostics, warnings, and error messages.[21, 52] A distinction should be made between what does and does not constitute a security relevant event and how to respond appropriately to each.[21] And it goes without saying that complete instructions are needed that describe how to (re)start, install, configure, optimize, monitor, shut down, and recover the IT asset in a secure manner.[21, 52] That is, guidance documents are expected to provide all the information systems operations and maintenance staff and end users need to be able to perform their security roles and responsibilities in an effective and efficient manner. Careful consideration must be given to what information does and does not belong in the end-user documentation versus the system operations and maintenance documentation, and vice versa. This is of particular concern when there are security features or parameters that are directly accessible by end users. Finally, decisions should be made about (1) how to control access to electronic and hardcopy guidance documents, and (2) to whom these documents are and are not released.

The following metrics can be used to measure the resilience of an organization's security awareness and training program, including guidance documents.

Extent to which the security awareness and training program closes the loop between accountability and competence requirements, relative to security roles and responsibilities (0 — not at all, 10 — completely).   2.4.13.1

Extent to which the security awareness and training program tailors each segment to the specific (0 — not at all, 10 — completely, 30 maximum points):
                                                                    2.4.13.2

    a. Job function
    b. Security roles and responsibilities
    c. Position sensitivity

Extent to which the security awareness and training program produces concrete evidence that an individual is competent to perform his assigned security roles and responsibilities (0 — not al all, 10 — completely).   2.4.13.3

Extent to which the security awareness and training program (0 — not at all, 10 — completely, 70 maximum points):   2.4.13.4

    a. Explains the organization's security objectives, strategies, and policies
    b. Explains how security relates to achieving the organization's mission
    c. Explains the consequences of not performing assigned security roles and responsibilities
    d. Embeds security into standard business practices
    e. Is applied to all organizational units and levels
    f. Is applied to all four security engineering domains
    g. Is applied to the entire security engineering life cycle

The frequency with which security awareness and training activities are conducted: 2.4.13.5

   a. The frequency with which the effectiveness of security awareness and training activities are verified

Percentage (%) of new employees hired this reporting period who satisfactorily completed security awareness training appropriate for the sensitivity level of their position, before being granted access to critical resources[105, 143]: 2.4.13.6

Percentage (%) employees who have satisfactorily completed periodic security awareness refresher training this reporting period, appropriate for the sensitivity level of their position[105 143]. 2.4.13.7

Percentage (%) of individuals with access to security controls who are trained and authorized security administrators, appropriate for the sensitivity level of their position[105]: 2.4.13.8

   a. Percentage (%) of individuals who are able to assign access control rights and privileges who are trained and authorized security administrators[105]

Number of training hours by security engineering domain and policy this reporting period and the number of people to which the training applied that attended. 2.4.13.9

Extent to which guidance documents are accurate, current, and complete when describing the secure installation, configuration, operation, and use of IT assets, relative to security roles and responsibilities: 2.4.13.10

   a. End-user documentation
   b. System operation and maintenance documentation

By IT asset criticality, percentage (%) of guidance documents for which access and distribution is controlled on a need-to-know basis. 2.4.13.11

Stakeholder, Strategic Partner, Supplier Relationships

What do stakeholders, strategic partners, and suppliers have to do with the resilience of an organization's operational security? A lot. Today, just as IT systems and networks do not stop at the exterior walls of a facility, neither does an organization. Due to globalization and increased specialization, companies throughout the world have become totally enmeshed, such that it is often difficult to tell where one company starts and another company stops. The economic repercussions of one company's fortunes are equally as unbounded. It is almost to the point where if a kangaroo sneezes in Australia, the price of apples in Washington state goes up and the availability of industrial-grade diamonds in Antwerp drops.

IT infrastructures become intertwined, out of necessity, as companies become enmeshed. These entanglements are common within the private sector, within the public sector, and between the public and private sectors. How could it be otherwise in this time of online shopping, electronic funds transfer, and credit cards? Not to mention the vast medical and insurance industries.... In the not so distant past, IT standards used to refer to supplier–acquirer and supplier–acquirer–certifier relationships. In this age of unbounded systems, networks, and organizations, these distinctions are not always so clear-cut. More often than not, who plays which of these roles at any point in time is a rather fluid situation.

As a result, stakeholders inside and outside the organization, strategic partners, and suppliers have the potential to have a major impact (positive or negative) on the resilience of an organization's operational security. For example, in the late 1990s, the federal government woke up to the fact that it was not as "in charge" of national security as it thought. The federal government found out that approximately 80 percent of the critical infrastructures essential for the nation's social stability and economic well-being were under the control the private section. This fact is particularly true when talking about critical information infrastructures, such as telecommunications, IT hardware, and IT software.

Stakeholders, strategic partners, and suppliers need to be made part of the organization, so that they will have just as much at stake as the organization does in ensuring adherence to security policies, enforcement of security controls, and consistent implementation of security procedures throughout the federation of IT infrastructures. To begin, identify which stakeholders, strategic partners, and suppliers qualify as definite insiders, pseudo-insiders, pseudo-outsiders, and definite outsiders. Assign security roles and responsibilities, and accountability and competence requirements accordingly. Require stakeholders, strategic partners, and suppliers to participate in security training and awareness activities, contingency and disaster recovery planning and preparedness, and security incident reporting and handling. There is a need to foster an understanding that "we are all in this together" so that each party is equally concerned about protecting the security and privacy of IT and information assets. Stakeholders, strategic partners, and suppliers must be given complete details about what level of performance is expected of them in regard to security roles and responsibilities. Business partners cannot be expected to comply if they have not been adequately informed. This information should be provided prior to contract negotiations. That way, business partners can prepare adequate cost estimates and have appropriate staff on board when a contract starts.

Often, when first presented with the idea, there is extreme reluctance for business partners to share information about security incidents. Sometimes, subcontractors can be convinced to share security incident information with the prime contractor but not with other subcontractors. There is a fear that the information will be misused and put them at a competitive disadvantage. This perception can be overcome in a variety of ways. An executive security coordination committee can be established for the purpose of coordinating security policies, procedures, and controls. Make the committee responsible for deciding what security information is and is not shared, how the information is shared and with whom, how the information will be protected to ensure its confidentiality, how long the information should be retained, and how the information should be destroyed when it is no longer needed. Once these issues are worked out to everyone's satisfaction, any objections to sharing should dissipate. To further reassure business partners, include clauses in everyone's contracts that (1) reinforce the decisions of the executive security coordination committee, and (2) provide for liability claims and other fines should security incident information be mishandled. There is too much potential benefit for all parties involved to not find a workable framework for sharing security incident information.

Many of the security and privacy regulations discussed in Chapter 3 mandate legal incentives, in terms of accountability, liability, and fines, to ensure a high degree of motivation and cooperation. In fact, most of the regulations mandate that the exact same security and privacy requirements be passed on to all third parties through contractual means. The end result is that business partners will be looking out for the prime organization's best interests because it is in their best interest to do so. There are immediate financial considerations (fines, penalties, rejected invoices) as well as their reputation to be concerned about when seeking future business with the same or other organizations. Business partners should also be encouraged to use their initiative to come up with better security policies, procedures, and controls; financial incentives can be used to stimulate creativity.

Do not cast the net too narrow when identifying stakeholders, strategic partners, and suppliers that could impact operational security. For example, consider suppliers of leased office equipment such as printers, scanners, fax machines, and photocopiers. Today, all of this equipment is digital. Every document ever copied, printed, scanned, or faxed is stored on the device's hard drive, until it is deliberately overwritten or erased. Has the organization ever taken the time to analyze who has access to these hard drives, either manually or across the network?[268] Who has access to these hard drives when maintenance is being performed on-site or off-site?[268] What happens to the hard drives when the lease is up — does the equipment, including the hard drive, just get rolled out the door?[268] Assuming that most of this information is company proprietary, and not public, it behooves an organization to insert security clauses into the contract with the equipment supplier. First, require hard drives to be sanitized at the end of the lease; spell out who performs the sanitization, where the sanitization is performed, and who witnesses and verifies the sanitization.[268] Second, include an option to buy back the hard drives at the end of the lease.[268] Third, include an option to have the hard drive destroyed at the end of the lease. For all three options, be sure to spell out strict chain-of-custody rules.

The following metrics can be used to measure the resilience of stakeholder, strategic partner, and supplier relationships as they relate to an organization's operational security.

Percentage (%) of strategic partner and other third-party relationships for which security policies, procedures, and controls are included in contracts with these parties[105].   2.4.14.1

Percentage (%) of known security vulnerabilities that are related to third-party relationships, by severity and security engineering domain.[105]   2.4.14.2

Percentage (%) of critical and essential assets for which access by third-party personnel is not allowed[105]:   2.4.14.3

    a. Percentage (%) of critical and essential assets for which electronic connection by third-party systems is not allowed[105]

Percentage (%) of third-party personnel with current asset access privileges whose privileges have been reviewed by a designated authority this reporting period to verify their continued need for access, by asset criticality and sensitivity.[105]   2.4.14.4

Percentage (%) of security incidents this reporting period and the last 12 months that involved third-party personnel, by incident severity and security engineering domain.[105]   2.4.14.5

Percentage (%) of third-party agreements that include proof of independent verification of security policies, procedures, and controls.[105]   2.4.14.6

Percentage (%) of third-party relationships that have been reviewed for compliance with security policies, procedures, and controls this quarter.[105]

2.4.14.7

Percentage (%) of out-of-compliance third-party review findings that have been corrected since the last review, by severity.[105]   2.4.14.8

Percentage (%) of contracts and other agreements with third parties that:

2.4.14.9

    a. Are consistent with security and privacy regulations
    b. Require sharing of security incident information
    c. Require third parties to participate in security awareness and training activities and contingency and disaster recovery exercises
    d. Include fines and other penalties when security policies, procedures, and controls are not adhered to or enforced

Operational Security Metrics Reports

We have just explored a total of 179 metrics that measure the resilience of operational security controls. The metrics are organized by the eight steps in the security engineering life cycle and the six ongoing risk management activities. An organization will use different metrics at different points in time to measure the resilience of their operational security controls. While the resilience of operational security controls is measured continuously, the particular metrics evaluated at any given time will depend on the GQM: what goal the organization is trying to accomplish, and the questions being asked to measure progress toward achieving or sustaining that goal. An organization may be exploring a single issue in depth, such as the resilience of its approach to vulnerability assessments. Measurements may be made locally, regionally, or enterprisewide, depending on the definition of the measurement boundaries for that GQM. An organization may be investigating a cross-cutting issue that involves the interactions between various components of the ongoing risk management activities or among the security engineering life-cycle activities and the ongoing risk management activities. Or, an organization may be required to measure the resilience of a particular operational security control to demonstrate compliance with security and privacy regulations, such as those discussed in Chapter 3.

The metrics report template presented earlier in Table 4.8 is also used for operational security metrics reports. Let us walk through a sample operational security metrics report to see the type of information that can be conveyed. The metrics in the report are selected and evaluated in response to the following GQM:

> **Goal:** Ensure adequate stakeholder participation and buy-in during all security engineering life-cycle activities.
>
> **Question$_x$:** How involved are stakeholders in the seven security engineering life-cycle activities?

Table 4.16 is a sample operational security metrics report that evaluates a cross-cutting issue — the extent of stakeholder involvement in security engineering life-cycle activities. At the start of a new project, there is often a lot of enthusiasm, particularly on the part of end users. As the project and schedule winds on, enthusiasm usually wanes, especially in those who are not directly involved in the development or acquisition process. A concerted effort is needed to keep all stakeholders involved throughout the project, and not just at the beginning. The less stakeholders are involved, the more likely the project is to fail or be rejected by end users. The sample metrics report shown in Table 4.16 tells a familiar story: stakeholder participation is dropping off as the project progresses. This situation should set off alarm bells for senior management. Why did the stakeholders quit participating? Were they not invited to participate after the security requirements were finalized? Were their views ignored and as a result they decided there was no point in coming? Was information presented in a format they could not understand? Or, did they give up hope that the new system would meet their needs? Using metrics like the ones shown in Table 4.16 can highlight this problem early, when there is still time to do something about it.

4.6 Summary

The security solutions an organization deploys — whether physical, personnel, IT, or operational security — are or should be in response to specific threats. Countermeasures are or should be proportional to the likelihood of a specific threat or combination of threats being instantiated and the worst-case consequences, should this occur. Nearly all the standards and regulations discussed in Chapter 3 state the requirement to deploy security controls that are commensurate with risk. There are standardized methods by which to assess risk. However, unless the resilience of the security controls is measured, there is

Table 4.16   Resilience Metric Report: Operational Security

Report Date: 7 March 2006

Security Domain(s): Operational Security

Sub-element(s): Security Engineering Life-Cycle Activities

Focus: Stakeholder Involvement

Measurement Boundary: enterprisewide   **Prediction or Actual Value:** Actual value

Time Interval: previous 12 months

Metric		Target Value	Observed Value	Interpretation
ID	*Definition*	*Value*	*Value*	*Interpretation*
2.4.1.1	Percentage (%) of stakeholder organizations actively involved during concept formulation	100%	100%	Green
2.4.1.3	By IT asset criticality, number and percentage of the following items that were (1) produced during concept formulation, and (2) agreed to by all stakeholders: a. Clear concise statement of need. b. Description of the functions that will and will not be performed. c. Updated IT asset inventory. d. Preliminary risk assessment, including criticality and sensitivity ratings. e. Proposed operational profile and duty cycle. f. List of potential users. g. Internal and external interfaces, connectivity, and dependencies. h. Constraints for the operational environment	100%	80%	Yellow
2.4.2.5	Number and percentage of stakeholder groups that: a. Participated during security requirements and analysis. b. Approved the final security requirements	100%	65%	Yellow
2.4.3.6.b	Percentage (%) of security architecture and design that have been agreed to by all stakeholders	100%	65%	Yellow

Table 4.16 Resilience Metric Report: Operational Security (continued)

Metric		*Target Value*	*Observed Value*	*Interpretation*
ID	*Definition*			
2.4.4.6.b	Percentage (%) of the as-built product or system that has been agreed to by all stakeholders	100%	50%	Red
2.4.5.6.b	Percentage (%) of ST&E, C&A, and IV&V activities and results that were approved and agreed to by all stakeholders	100%	50%	Red
2.4.5.10	Percentage (%) facility management staff, operations and maintenance staff, and end users that have been notified of the deployment schedule	100%	50%	Red
2.4.6.4	Extent to which a clear division of roles and responsibilities during delivery, installation, and deployment are defined (0 — not at all, 10 — completely, max. 70 points): a. Who is responsible for performing each activity. b. When each activity is to be performed. c. Who is responsible for verifying that each activity is complete and has been performed correctly. d. Dependencies between activities. e. Go/no-go milestones. f. Who is informed of progress and problems and the level of detail provided	70 points	45 points	Yellow
2.4.8.1	Percentage (%) of facility management staff, operations and maintenance staff, end users, and business partners who have been notified that the system is being decommissioned and the schedule for doing so	100%	65%	Red
Summary Red = 0 points Yellow = 5 points Green = 10 points		**Total Possible** 90 points	**Actual Score** 30 points or 33% **Overall Rating** Red	

no factual basis on which to make the claim that the security controls are indeed commensurate with risk. Likewise, it is not possible to determine the return on investment (ROI) in physical, personnel, IT, and operational security controls unless their resilience has been measured against the risk — hence the need for measuring the resilience of security controls and their ability to prevent, preempt, delay, mitigate, and contain these attacks.

Resilience is the capability of an IT infrastructure, including physical, personnel, IT, and operational security controls, to maintain essential services and protect critical assets while preempting and repelling attacks and minimizing the extent of corruption and compromise. Resilience is not a Boolean or yes/no function: a system or network is or is not secure. Rather, security is a continuum. That is why metrics are needed to determine where the organization falls on this continuous scale. Resilience does not imply that something is free from vulnerabilities. Rather, resilience emphasizes how well vulnerabilities are managed and attempts to exploit them are thwarted. By the same token, a person's character is not measured when everything is rosy and going his way. Instead, strength of character is measured by how well a person responds to the challenges, hurdles, and upsets that life throws his way. The parallels in telecommunications engineering are error detection and correction protocols. The parallel in software engineering is error handling routines. Resilience can be measured for a single mechanism, a cluster of mechanisms, a system, network, or the enterprise security architecture. Resilience can be measured for physical, personnel, IT, and operational security controls, individually or in any combination. Resilience metrics highlight how strong or weak a given security control is. This information is compared against the operational risk to determine acceptability or the need for further work and resources. Often, it is useful to compare the resilience of different types of security controls. Perhaps it is cheaper and just as or more effective to mitigate a given vulnerability with an operational security control than an IT security control, or with a physical security control than an operational security control, etc. These comparisons can be quite enlightening and cost-effective.

Physical security is perhaps the best known of the four types of security controls. People can easily grasp the concept of physical security, especially when talking about the physical security of their persons and their property. Not long ago, some people were questioning the value of physical security in the advent of the global information grid. Today, those views are in the minority. Current events throughout the world have reminded us all of the importance of physical security. Physical security is a key component of contingency and disaster recovery planning and preparedness, as well as day-to-day operations. The underlying goal of physical security is to protect assets from physical threats, such as theft, tampering, disruption, destruction, and misappropriation. The physical threats from which assets need protection can be accidental or intentional, natural, man-made, or a combination of both. Physical threats can occur as the result of specific action or inaction. Physical security controls include tools, techniques, devices, and operational procedures to prevent unauthorized access, damage, and interference to an organization's premises and information.[28]

Physical security controls seek to protect against loss and damage. The notion of loss includes the total cost of the loss and the total cost of the impact of the loss, both short term and long term. The purpose of physical security controls is to protect assets. People, of course, are any organization's chief asset. Few would dispute that the intrinsic value of human life is far above that of any other asset. Some assets are more important than others, and hence require more robust protection; this aspect is referred to as asset criticality. Asset criticality may change over time and depends on one's perspective and role. That is why it is crucial to (1) have all stakeholders involved in determining asset criticality, and (2) reassess asset criticality on a regular basis.

Physical security is one of four security domains, the other three being personnel security, IT security, and operational security. Is physical security the most important security domain? No. Is physical security the least important security domain? No. None of the four security domains are more important or less important than the others. All four security domains are equally essential to achieving, sustaining, and assessing enterprisewide security. This is true because there are many interdependencies between the four security domains. While physical security is closely intertwined with the other three security domains, its first cousin is physical safety. Physical safety and physical security are not synonymous, but they do seek to accomplish many of the same goals. Both physical safety and physical security seek to prevent, eliminate, and mitigate natural and man-made hazards, regardless of whether they are accidental or intentional in origin. Many of the same analysis, design, and verification tools are used by physical safety and security engineers.

In terms of physical security, resilience means that the IT infrastructure is able to withstand (prevent, preempt, mitigate, delay, and contain) physical security attacks. The IT infrastructure can keep rolling or bounce back and not miss a beat despite a physical security attack, regardless of the type, timing, time interval, and duration of the attack. Resilience is not a Boolean function, such that a physical security is or is not resilient. Rather, resilience is a continuum and there are different levels of intensity or resilience — hence the need for resilience metrics. The resilience of physical security controls should be correlated to the likelihood and severity of specific physical security threats. Natural physical threats such as hurricanes, earthquakes, etc. cannot be eliminated or prevented. As a result, it is necessary to plan and prepare for the worst-case likelihood and severity scenario. That is, the resilience of physical security controls should be proportional to the risk of a physical security threat being instantiated. If physical security threats are deployed that provide a higher degree of resilience than the assessed risk warrants, you have wasted limited security funds. On the other hand, if physical security controls are deployed that provide a lower degree of resilience than the assessed risk, you have under-spent and created a vulnerability and a weak link that most likely will be exploited. Similar to other security domains, physical security controls seek to minimize the opportunity to execute a successful attack, increase the expertise required to carry out a successful attack, and restrict the availability of the resources needed to initiate a successful attack or make them cost prohibitive. The key to neutralizing the opportunity, expertise, and resources part of the attack equation is to deploy physical security controls with the appropriate level of resilience. The resilience is just far enough over a certain threshold to make the attack too difficult, take too long, or cost too much. Physical security parameters fall into three categories:

1. Facility protection
2. Asset protection
3. Mission protection

In simplest terms, an organization protects its facilities in an effort to safeguard assets and thereby ensure the ability to perform its mission. Conversely, for an organization to reliably achieve its mission, it must safeguard its assets by protecting the facilities that house them. Think of this as a three-layered onion. The core is the organization's mission. The middle ring is composed of the organization's assets that are needed to perform the mission, some of which are more important or essential than others. The outer layer consists of the facilities that contain the organization's assets.

Personnel security is a variety of ongoing measures that are undertaken to reduce the likelihood and severity of accidental and intentional alteration, destruction, misappropriation, misuse, misconfiguration, unauthorized distribution, and unavailability of an organization's logical and physical assets, as the result of action or inaction by insiders and known outsiders, such as business partners. Personnel security measures are an attempt to minimize the risk of an organization incurring damage to or loss of its assets by people who routinely have approval to access them. Damage or loss can be accidental or intentional and the result of action or inaction. Someone can accidentally or intentionally crash a system. A file cabinet or desktop system can be accidentally or intentionally left open. A system administrator can "forget" to perform backups or update virus signatures. Damage can be very visible (such as deleted files or corrupted applications) or very subtle (such as slight changes to data or system configurations that do not generate any error messages and go undetected for a period of time). Personnel security attempts to determine whether people who have logical and physical access rights to develop, operate, use, and maintain an organization's assets are likely to abuse or misuse these privileges for personal motives or gain or act irresponsibly, such that damage or loss occurs. The people in question include permanent and temporary employees, contractors, consultants, vendors, service personnel, and a host of other business partners who have regular access to an organization's assets.

Personnel security is all about finding and acknowledging human weaknesses. Human beings are not perfect and never will be. People can be careless, inattentive, in a hurry, preoccupied, or in a bad mood; they can also be deliberately deceitful or destructive or just lose control. It is essential to design and implement personnel security measures that acknowledge this fact. Personnel security is a delicate matter due to the long-term consequences to the individual and the organization, and the fact that this area is more of a soft science than physical, IT, or operational security — not to mention the possibility of lawsuits for wrongful action on part of the organization. Personnel security also raises a multitude of privacy issues that must be dealt with in an ethical, legal, fair, and consistent manner. It is reasonably easy to weed out the psychopaths and those with a long criminal history who would jump at the chance to do damage their first day on a new job. It is not so easy to identify who, among the vast majority of the populace that are honest, ethical, and law abiding, might sometime in the future do damage should the world situation or their personal situation, attitudes, or beliefs change. That is why an organization needs a variety of different ongoing personnel security measures.

Personnel security is composed of five elements:

1. Accountability
2. Background investigations
3. Competence
4. Separation of duties
5. Workforce analysis

The first three categories focus on one individual at a time, while the last two categories look across the workforce as a whole. An effective personnel security program requires a combination of controls in all five areas. Given the dynamic nature of personnel security, these controls must be monitored on an ongoing basis. At times it may be appropriate to probe into the details of one of these areas. On other occasions it may be preferable to take a composite view across the entire personnel security program. The quantity and specific types of metrics used in these situations will depend on the Goal being measured and the Questions being investigated in order to measure progress toward achieving or sustaining that Goal.

The third security engineering domain is IT security. The high-tech industry has been wandering in the wilderness for years when it comes to IT security metrics. Some false prophets have declared that return on investment (ROI) metrics represent the true manifestation of IT security metrics. Other equally misguided oracles have latched onto statistics emanating from IDS logs as the divine truth. A third group seeks an epiphany from monolithic high-level process metrics, while the remainder await divine revelation from the latest and greatest whiz-bang gizmo their anointed salesman guided them (like sheep) to buy. Jelen describes this situation quite aptly[169]:

> *You have to know what "it" is before you can measure it!*

The problem is that many people, in all types of organizations and at all levels within an organization, have a vague, distorted, incomplete, fragmented, or microscopic understanding of IT security. Compounding the problem is the fact that most of these people are unaware of their knowledge gap, due to the barrage of misinformation from the general media and over-zealous salesmen — and hence, the difficulty the industry has had in developing useful IT security metrics.

To overcome this situation, a clear, complete, and concise definition of IT security is needed: IT security is the inherent technical features and functions that collectively contribute to an IT infrastructure achieving and sustaining confidentiality, integrity, availability, accountability, authenticity and reliability. Notice that this definition does not mention anything about firewalls, IDSs, or encryption. Rather, the definition refers to "…features and functions that collectively…." IT security is not about individual products. There is no one single product (or even two products) that will magically deliver IT security. The crux is for an IT infrastructure as a whole to be secure, not individual products. Consequently, the emphasis is on a combination of different complementary security features and functions that, working together, will achieve and sustain a specified level of confidentiality, integrity, availability, accountability, authenticity, and reliability under normal and abnormal conditions. The real measure of IT security is under abnormal conditions. That is why the selection, implementation, and configuration of security features should correspond to worst-case scenarios, not some idyllic notion of normal operations that never occurs. Worst-case scenarios determine the specific level of confidentiality, integrity, availability, accountability, authenticity, and reliability that is needed.

Notice also that the definition does not include the phrases "network security," "computer security," "database security," etc. On the contrary, IT security encompasses the totality of an IT infrastructure. If any aspect of the security of the IT infrastructure is neglected or shortchanged (i.e., operating system, e-mail, application, LAN, WAN, etc.), it will not be possible to achieve or sustain any level of IT security. The weakest link will be quickly compromised and used as an entry point for attacking the remaining infrastructure, and the domino principle will take over. Hence, the emphasis is on a combination of different complementary security features and functions working together. A complete set of security features and functions is needed that mitigates all types of risk at all layers of the protocol stack. Duplication and gaps in security features and functions need to be eliminated. The exact set of security features and functions needed is unique to each organization, based on its particular IT infrastructure, the criticality of its mission and operations, the sensitivity of its assets, their risk exposure, and regulatory requirements, if applicable. The selection, implementation, and configuration of security features and functions should not be a case of chasing after the Joneses. Make no mistake: this is one area where it is essential to set your own style and do some serious custom tailoring.

Conceptually, IT security is composed of two systems: (1) an IT security control system and (2) an IT security protection system. The IT security control system provides ongoing security functions during normal operations. These functions arbitrate access to and interaction with system assets on a regular basis. The corollary to this is the IT security protection system which protects system assets from and during abnormal operations. The IT security protection system is responsible for stepping in and taking proactive, preventive, and, if need be, reactive measures whenever anomalous operating conditions are suspected or confirmed. As technology moves closer and closer toward self-healing and autonomic responses, the relative importance of the IT security protection system increases.

There are nine components of an IT security control system, each of which contributes to providing security functionality during normal operations:

1. Logical access control
2. Data authentication, non-repudiation
3. Encryption, cryptographic support
4. Flow control (operational and data)
5. Identification and authentication
6. Maintainability, supportability
7. Privacy
8. Residual information protection
9. Security management, credential management, rules management

There are seven components of an IT security protection system, each of which contributes to protecting IT and information assets from and during abnormal operations:

1. Audit trail, alarm generation
2. Availability (redundancy, diversity, fault tolerance, block recovery, dynamic reconfiguration, rollback, self-healing)
3. Error, exception, and incident handling
4. Fail safe, fail secure, graceful degradation, degraded mode operations
5. Integrity (hardware, software, network, active data, stored data, system)
6. Domain separation (partitioning, information hiding, security kernels, encapsulation)
7. Resource management (resource allocation, service priority, capacity management)

Metrics are defined to ascertain where on the resilience scale a particular implementation and configuration of an IT security feature or function falls. Keep in mind that a low resilience rating is not necessarily bad, while a high resilience rating is not necessarily good. The objective is to achieve and sustain a resilience rating that is proportional to operational risk, so that assets are neither over- nor under-protected. IT security resilience metrics can be used in several ways — for example, to evaluate COTS products prior to purchase, to identify vulnerabilities in legacy systems, and to determine whether a new system is sufficiently robust and ready to deploy. A total of 229 metrics were presented that measure the resilience of IT security controls. The metrics are organized by the nine components of an IT security control system and the seven components of an IT security protection system. An organization will use different metrics at different points in time to measure the resilience of their IT security controls. While the resilience of IT security controls is measured continuously, the particular metrics evaluated at any given time will depend on the GQM: what goal the organization is trying to accomplish, and the question or questions being asked to measure progress toward achieving or sustaining that goal. An organization may be exploring a single issue in depth, such as the resilience of their logical access controls. Measurements may be made locally, regionally, or enterprisewide, depending on the definition of the measurement boundaries for that GQM. An organization may be investigating a cross-cutting issue that involves the interactions between various components of the IT security control and protection systems. The resilience of the IT security control system or IT security protection system as a whole may need to be measured. Or, an organization may be required to measure the resilience of a particular IT security control in order to demonstrate compliance with security and privacy regulations, like those discussed in Chapter 3.

The fourth security engineering domain is operational security. Operational security is perhaps the least well understood of the four security engineering domains. As a result, operational security is often ignored, neglected, or, at best, given lip service. A poor operational security program can undo an excellent IT security program. Hence, the lack of understanding surrounding operational security is extremely problematic. Mention the term "operational security" and the few people who have heard of it think you are talking about the security of a military campaign or intelligence operation. This is not the first technical term to have a dual identity.

Operational security is an essential part of security engineering because it represents the interaction between people and technology. Physical security focuses on protecting physical entities (facilities, assets, people) from natural and man-made hazards. Personnel security takes a deeper look at the people who might be given access to these facilities and assets, in particular in regard to their accountability and competence. IT security zeroes in on the inherent security features and functions of technology. In contrast, operational security represents the nexus of people and technology. Achieving an effective operational security program can be quite a challenge, because people are any organization's greatest security liability; but it is well worth the effort.

Operational security refers to the implementation of standard operational security procedures that define the nature and frequency of the interaction between users, systems, and system resources, the purpose of which is to (1) achieve and sustain a known secure system state at all times, and (2) prevent accidental or intentional theft, release, destruction, alteration, misuse, or sabotage of system resources.[156] Operational security defines how, when, under what circumstances, and why people in different roles interact with IT assets. These interactions are documented in formal procedures that are reviewed, reaffirmed, and updated on a regular basis, or following a major technology upgrade or change. Here we see a link between operational security and the accountability principle of personnel security. Employees and pseudo-insiders are held accountable for adhering to standardized operational security procedures. Contrary to a common misconception, operational security does not begin during the operations and maintenance phase, but rather long before then.

The resilience of operational security is measured according to the thoroughness, completeness, and robustness of an operational security activity. An organization may have all the required operational security procedures in place to pass an audit, but are they any good? Do the procedures have any depth, or do they merely skim the surface and mouth empty platitudes? Does anyone know about the procedures? Are they routinely followed and enforced? Are the procedures effective in preventing, preempting, and repelling cyber security attacks, while minimizing the extent of corruption and compromise? What kind of story do the results from performing operational security activities tell?

At a conceptual level, operational security is comprised of two different categories of activities: (1) security engineering life-cycle activities, and (2) ongoing security risk management activities. Security engineering life-cycle activities begin during concept formulation and carry on through system decommissioning. These security engineering life-cycle activities are applicable regardless of which system engineering life-cycle model is followed. Likewise, these activities are applicable regardless of whether the system is constructed entirely of COTS products, entirely of custom-developed components, or a combination of both. The exact nature of how these tasks are executed varies, depending on the COTS/custom equation, but they are still performed. In addition, there are ongoing security risk management activities that are performed repeatedly throughout the life of a system. The features and functions of IT security control and protection systems are specified and built during the security engineering life-cycle activities. The resilience of the features and functions of IT security control and protection systems is assessed and ensured by the ongoing security risk management activities.

Both the security engineering life-cycle activities and the ongoing risk management activities comprise several components. There are eight security engineering life-cycle activities; each represents a different step in specifying, building, and deploying a secure system:

1. Concept formulation
2. Security requirements analysis and specification
3. Security architecture and design
4. Development and implementation
5. Security test and evaluation (ST&E), certification and accreditation (C&A), independent validation and verification (IV&V)
6. Delivery, installation, and deployment
7. Operations and maintenance
8. Decommissioning (transition, sanitization, reuse, destruction)

There are six ongoing security risk management activities; each focuses on a different aspect of achieving and sustaining a known secure system state:

1. Vulnerability assessment
2. Security policy management
3. Security audits and reviews

4. Security impact analysis, privacy impact analysis, configuration management, patch management
5. Security awareness and training, guidance documents
6. Stakeholder, strategic partner, supplier relationships

A total of 179 metrics were presented that measure the resilience of operational security controls. The metrics are organized by the eight steps in the security engineering life cycle and the six ongoing risk management activities. Operational security metrics can be used in several ways; for example, to evaluate the thoroughness and completeness of information security requirements, to evaluate the coverage and results from security test and evaluation (ST&E), to determine whether security impact analysis is being performed and the results taken into account before implementing a change or upgrade, and to determine the extent to which security requirements have been passed on to business partners.

4.7 Discussion Problems

1. How is resilience evaluated?
2. When should resilience metrics be collected and analyzed?
3. Explain the relationship between resilience and OMER.
4. What type of threats do physical security controls address?
5. Give examples of tangible and intangible assets.
6. Explain the interaction and dependencies among facility protection, asset protection, and mission protection.
7. Describe the similarities, differences, and dependencies between logical and physical security perimeters. Which is more important?
8. Describe the similarities, differences, and dependencies between access control policies and security perimeters. Which is more important?
9. Describe the similarities and differences in planning and preparing for natural and man-made hazards. Which is more difficult?
10. What is a loss event profile used for? When it is prepared?
11. Compare asset sensitivity, criticality, and value. When are these assessments made?
12. Why is asset disposal and reuse part of physical security?
13. What role do third parties play in mission protection?
14. Why does a comprehensive personnel security program need to encompass more than background investigations?
15. Why are people an organization's greatest security liability?
16. Why do insiders continue to account for ~80 percent of total security incidents year after year?
17. Why do personnel security measures need to be ongoing?
18. Personnel safety makes extensive use of human factors engineering. How can these principles be applied to personnel security?
19. Why do security policies, procedures, and standards have to be tied to specific assets and job functions?
20. Explain the relationship between sanctions and accountability.

21. How is accountability enforced?
22. Which group needs more robust accountability requirements: (a) definite insiders, (b) pseudo insiders, (c) pseudo outsiders, or (d) definite outsiders? Why?
23. What does competence have to do with personnel security?
24. Explain the relationship between job rotation and separation of duties.
25. When should workforce analysis be performed and by whom?
26. Explain the interaction among the different components of the IT security control system. Explain the interaction among the different components of the IT security protection system.
27. Cite examples of metrics that measure the positive resilience of an IT security control or protection system function. Cite examples of metrics that measure the negative resilience of an IT security control or protection system function.
28. Explain why it is necessary to measure both positive and negative resilience.
29. Explain the interaction among the security engineering life-cycle activities. Explain the interaction among the ongoing risk management activities and the security engineering life cycle.
30. Give examples of how ongoing risk management activities apply to all four security engineering domains.
31. Develop a sample metrics report that evaluates the resilience of vulnerability analysis as applied to all four security engineering domains.
32. If you had to use only one metric from the ST&E, C&A, and IV&V category, which one would it be and why?
33. Should more metrics be used earlier or later in the security engineering life cycle? Why?

Chapter 5

Measuring Return on Investment (ROI) in Physical, Personnel, IT, and Operational Security Controls

By using metrics, program managers and system owners can isolate problems, justify investment requests, and target investments specifically to the areas in need of improvement. By using metrics to target security investments, organizations can get the best value from available resources.[57]

—NIST SP 800-55

5.1 Introduction

This chapter presents a new comprehensive security ROI model that:

- Is appropriate for all four types of security controls (physical, personnel, IT, and operational)
- Can be used at any point in the security engineering life cycle
- Can be used to evaluate individual security controls or collections of security controls
- Acknowledges different asset values and different threat environments
- Builds upon the foundation already established for compliance and resilience metrics

If the IT industry has been wandering in the desert for years when it comes to IT security resilience metrics, it has been meandering in a fog for an equivalent amount of time concerning security ROI (return on investment) metrics. A few feeble attempts have been made to dispel the haze, but they proved a temporary mirage. Historically, security ROI metrics, like security metrics in general, have been considered "too hard." The old paradigm was that "you had to implement security and it had to be as good as possible."[121] A tolerable percentage of the IT budget was allocated to security — like the magic 4 percent number discussed in Chapter 2. The goal was to achieve what was technically possible.[220] That paradigm may have made some sense in the decades prior to distributed or globally interconnected systems and networks, a time when few organizations beyond the defense, intelligence, and financial communities were concerned about security. But it does not make any sense today, and a new paradigm is needed where security funds are spent to achieve what is economically optimal.[220] Tenants in the corporate suite have a right to expect that a business case be made for security expenditures, just like any other major expenditure. Why should any organization spend millions of dollars on anything without a solid cost justification? Security costs, like any other costs, should be justified. Executives have a right to ask some hard questions about why $5 million is needed for security and not $2 million or $10 million. They also have a right to know what specific benefit the organization will receive for that $5 million investment. The Chief Security Officer (CSO) and security engineering staff need to be prepared with concrete answers in the form of *bona fide* security ROI metrics. More funding does not equate to better security, for the same reason that more funding in education does not result in higher student test scores. That is why security ROI metrics are needed to help an organization choose the most economical security solution from among the set of technically acceptable solutions.

Security ROI analysis is an attempt to perform an actuarial-like risk analysis of the economic value of information and IT assets, the probability of a loss due to a security incident, and the economic consequences. The goal of security ROI analysis is to maximize the benefits of a fixed investment in security controls given limited security engineering funds.[144] Investments in security controls generally do not generate revenue; rather, they prevent losses.[144] Hence, a different approach to security ROI analysis is needed. A few security ROI models have been proposed. These models are overly simplistic and attempt to evaluate a security program as a whole without first providing a methodology to evaluate the individual security components that comprise the security program and are applied to mitigate specific risks. (It is difficult to summarize the details if the details are unknown.) These models lack the level of granularity necessary to provide real insight into the costs and benefits, strengths, and weaknesses of the organization's security engineering program as a whole or individual security controls. These models do not identify or consider the primitives that comprise the major cost elements or from where they derived. Most likely, this situation will lead to inconsistent use of these models and invalid results. Furthermore, these models do not take into account the fact that different parts of an organization have different threat and operational environments and different types and values of assets.

5.2 Security ROI Model

So what is a return on investment, and how is this concept applied to security engineering? In simplest terms, ROI implies that a measurable benefit will accrue as a result of expending funds for a specific purpose. Assume that a one-year certificate of deposit is purchased with a fixed annual 4.5 percent interest rate. At the end of the 12-month term, the gross ROI would be 4.5 percent. The net ROI would be 4.5 percent minus any federal, state, and county or city income taxes. If the financial institution is insured by the Federal Deposit Insurance Corporation (FDIC) in the United States or the equivalent organization elsewhere and the account balance is less than $100,000, the risk is virtually nil. In this situation, the ROI is guaranteed; in most cases, an ROI is not guaranteed. Assume instead that the funds were invested in the stock market, where the future ROI may be predicted but in reality is unknown. If the stock does well, an investor might earn 10 percent or more. Or, the stock value may stay flat or even decrease. This scenario illustrates the fact that an ROI can be positive, negative, or zero. Because stocks are not purchased for a fixed period of time, the ROI is variable and only actualized on the exact date and time of sale. Unlike an investment with a fixed ROI, there is risk associated with a variable ROI; the potential earnings are usually higher, but so are the potential losses. The gross ROI is calculated by comparing the proceeds from the sale to the initial investment. The net ROI is calculated by comparing the proceeds from the sale, minus account administration fees and federal, state, county, and city income taxes.

Both of these examples illustrate a passive ROI — the investor does little more than purchase the investment. In contrast, a combination of direct and indirect costs are associated with an active ROI. Suppose instead that an investment was made in paintings. The direct costs would include the cost of the paintings and the sales tax. The indirect costs would include the cost to ship the paintings to their new location, the cost of an appraisal to establish the real market value and authenticity, the cost of insurance premiums, the cost of physical security controls to prevent theft, the cost of environmental controls to prevent deterioration, especially in older paintings, and display costs such as special lighting and perhaps a new frame or easel. The direct costs are one-time costs, while the indirect costs are a mixture of one-time and recurring costs. If the investor sold the paintings ten years later, the gross ROI would be:

$$\text{Gross ROI} = (\text{Sale price} + \text{Sales commission}) -$$
$$(\text{Direct costs} + \text{One-time indirect costs}$$
$$+ (10 \times \text{Annual recurring indirect costs}))$$

Of course, this sum represents the tangible ROI. Many investments, such as art, have an intangible ROI as well. If the paintings were purchased for a private estate, the intangible ROI would include the pleasure derived from owning the paintings and the perceived increase in the value of the property in which they were displayed. If the paintings were purchased for a non-profit museum, the intangible ROI would include the positive publicity, an enhanced reputation, increased attendance, benefit to the community, such as visiting school groups, and increased donations from members and art patrons.

In summary, an ROI can be fixed or variable. Unlike a fixed ROI, a variable ROI has risk associated with it and as a result can be positive, negative, or zero. An ROI can accrue from the active or passive involvement of the investor. A passive ROI only requires direct expenditures, while an active ROI requires a combination of direct and indirect expenditures. Direct expenditures represent one-time up-front costs. In contrast, indirect expenditures represent a mixture of one-time and recurring costs for as long as the item is owned. Most active ROIs can be expressed in terms of quantitative tangible benefits and qualitative intangible benefits. Finally, it is important to distinguish between the gross ROI and the net ROI. In the world of security engineering, an active ROI is pursued that involves direct and indirect expenditures and yields tangible and intangible benefits. The ROI for security controls is variable because unless the funds are spent on the appropriate types of security controls and for the specific level of resilience needed in a given operational environment, the ROI can be negative or zero. (This aspect is explored further later in this chapter.)

A variety of parameters must be measured and analyzed to determine the ROI in security controls. Similar to resilience, there is no one simple calculation that answers all the security ROI questions; rather, a series of metrics is evaluated and aggregated. Some of the primitives are actual measurements; other primitives are estimates. Security ROI metrics can and should be used throughout the security engineering life cycle. In the beginning, security ROI metrics can be used to guide IT capital investments and perform cost-benefit comparisons between products prior to purchase. Once deployed, security ROI metrics can be used to monitor actual benefits. As these benefits decrease over time, security ROI metrics can help flag devices that are becoming obsolete and are good candidates for technology refresh, because at some point in time the ROI will drop from being positive to being zero or even negative. Most likely, the level of protection being provided will drop as well, causing a vulnerability to resurface. Many of the same metrics can be reused throughout the security engineering life cycle. This process allows the primitives and hence the results, to be fine-tuned along the way.

ROI is measured in a variety of ways across different industries, from wholesale manufacturing to retail merchandising to financial services, as well as in the non-profit and public sectors. That is because a *return* on investment does not always equate to profit. Rather, the return can take several other forms, such as increased operational efficiency, cost avoidance, cost savings, and loss prevention. Figure 5.1 presents a taxonomy of parameters that are part of the equation when calculating security ROI. These parameters, which are discussed below, fall into eight categories:

1. Problem identification and characterization
2. Total cost of the security feature, function, or control
3. Depreciation period
4. Tangible benefits

<u>**Problem Identification and Characterization**</u>
- Specific risk being mitigated
  - Severity and likelihood
  - Scope of potential impact
- Assets being protected
  - Type and quantity
  - Location
  - Remaining useful life span
  - Asset criticality
  - Asset value
  - Level of resilience needed in security control

<u>**Total Cost of Security Feature, Function, or Control**</u>
- One-time direct costs: purchase price, tax, shipping
- One-time indirect costs: installation, training
- Annual recurring indirect costs: I/O devices, cables, connectors, licenses, telecommunications support, spare parts, disks, HVAC, electricity, floor space, racks, operations and maintenance labor

<u>**Depreciation Period (months)**</u>
- Minimum, maximum, and most likely useful life span

<u>**Tangible Benefits (worst case, best case)**</u>
- Total cost of losses prevented
- Regulatory and contractual fines avoided
- Liability lawsuits avoided
- Increased operational efficiency

<u>**Intangible Benefits (worst case, best case)**</u>
- Impact on OMER of would-be attackers
- Customer confidence
- Investor confidence
- Business partner confidence
- Employee morale

<u>**Payback Period**</u>
- Minimum, maximum, and most likely

<u>**Comparative Analysis**</u>
- To cost of doing nothing
- To cost of alternate approaches

<u>**Assumptions**</u>
- IT infrastructure
- Operational profile and duty cycle
- Operational environment
- Threat environment
- Resilience levels
- Others

Figure 5.1   Taxonomy of security ROI parameters.

5. Intangible benefits
6. Payback period
7. Comparative analysis
8. Assumptions

Problem Identification and Characterization

The first step is to identify and characterize the specific security problem that is being solved. In particular, what specific risk is this security feature, function, or control supposed to mitigate? Here we see (again) the absolute necessity of robust ongoing risk management activities, spearheaded by regular and thorough vulnerability assessments. If the security feature, function, or control is being purchased simply because it is the latest security fad, an omniscient salesman divined that your organization "needs" to buy the device, or the device will look impressive when the corporate executives come by for their next tour, there is no point in trying to calculate the ROI because it is zero under benign conditions or perhaps even negative under not so benign conditions. Security solutions must be deployed in response to specific security problems if they are to provide any measurable benefit or ROI. That is why the first step in calculating the ROI of a security feature, function, or control is to identify and characterize the specific security problem being solved.

Several pieces of information are involved in identifying the specific risk. First, the nature of the risk is identified. What exactly could go wrong? Is data being corrupted, compromised, stolen, or destroyed? Are system resources being damaged, made unavailable, or misappropriated? Is private personal or business information being exposed? Or does everything *appear* to be operating normally when in fact subtle unauthorized changes have been made to the system or network configurations? Remember that real hackers "leave no trace." Next, the severity of the consequences, should things go wrong, is clarified, using the standard severity categories defined in Chapter 2. As a general rule, the worst-case scenario is used for risk management purposes. In some instances there may be a considerable spread between the best possible outcome and the worst-case scenario, and a most likely severity can be assigned with a high degree of certainty. That practice is acceptable as long as it is noted under the assumptions. If a most likely severity cannot be determined with any degree of certainty, it is wise to stick with the worst case. The likelihood of the vulnerability being exploited is also identified, using the standard likelihood categories defined in Chapter 2. Careful consideration should be given to the likelihood determination because it is often underestimated. Likelihood determinations also frequently fail to consider that two or three minor anomalous events may occur simultaneously or in rapid succession, thus triggering a more serious event. Hence, likelihood determinations should not just examine isolated events or isolated sequences of events, but rather the "big picture." There is another twist that must be taken into account when characterizing severity and likelihood. That is the fact that severity and likelihood are not (usually) constants. Instead, the severity and likelihood of a specific risk tend to change over time as the IT infrastructure evolves, the operational environment becomes more complex, the operational profile and duty cycle expand, and the threat environment emerges. As a result, severity and likelihood may increase or decrease from one point in time to the next, and the changes are not always in the same direction. This is an important factor to remember when calculating ROI over the life span of a device.

The scope of the potential impact, should the threat be instantiated and the vulnerability exploited, is also characterized. That is, to what extent is the IT infrastructure affected? A single server, desktop, or LAN? All the desktops, servers, and networks in a single facility? An entire facility, campus, or region? A single application system and the data associated with it? All application systems and data? Active data that is stored online? Archived data that is stored offline? The entire enterprise? Just as it is important to establish appropriate measurement boundaries for metrics, it is essential to correctly identify the scope of the potential impact of each specific risk. Conversely, if the scope of the impact is ill-defined, it is difficult to have any confidence that the risk is really understood.

Another aspect to clarify is the extent of risk mitigation provided by the security feature, function, or control. That is, is this particular feature, function, or control responsible for mitigating the entire risk by itself? Generally, a combination of physical, personnel, IT, and operational security controls is employed to mitigate a specific risk. More than one device can be employed as part of a particular IT security control. As a result, when calculating security ROI, it is important to clarify what portion of the risk is being mitigated by the security feature, function, or control. That means that credit for mitigation activities must be apportioned among all the security controls that contribute directly to mitigating the risk. Why is this important? Because security ROI metrics will be invalid and misleading if, when multiple controls are involved in mitigating a risk, each takes 100 percent credit for mitigation. Consider the following situation. Assume the risk of sensitive data being misappropriated by insiders within one facility is mitigated by a combination of physical security controls, personnel security controls, logical access controls, encryption, audit trails, and alarms. If each of these five security controls takes 100 percent credit for mitigating the risk, the end result would be 500 percent risk mitigation, which is nonsense. Instead, the 100 percent risk mitigation should be allocated among the five different security controls, keeping in mind that risks are rarely if ever 100 percent mitigated. Perhaps an even distribution is appropriate, wherein each control takes credit for 20 percent risk mitigation. Or, perhaps an uneven distribution is more accurate; for example:

- 15 percent physical security controls
- 10 percent personnel security controls
- 35 percent logical access controls
- 30 percent encryption
- 10 percent audit trails and alarms

As a corollary to the scope of the impact, the assets being protected are identified. Specifically, which assets will the particular security feature, function, or control protect from this risk? Identify the type and quantity of assets being protected. In addition, identify the geographic location of the assets and their logical position in the IT infrastructure. This information should be as detailed and specific as possible. Furthermore, this information should be consistent with the asset inventory. Cross referencing security ROI metrics to the asset inventory serves three purposes: (1) it verifies that the assets are real (and not a figment of someone's imagination who is three degrees removed from the physical IT architecture) and legitimate components, not some renegade devices installed by a division prone to freelancing; (2) it highlights which assets are and are not adequately protected by a specific security feature, function, or control; and (3) it provides a secondary verification of the accuracy, completeness, and currency of the IT asset inventory. This is why, not only are the assets identified, but also the level of resilience needed in the device(s) protecting them.

Asset criticality and asset value are revisited when calculating security ROI. Remember from the discussion in Chapter 4 that the value of an asset does not equate to its unit cost or price. Instead of purchase price, asset value reflects the degree of debilitating impact that the organization as a whole would experience by the incapacity or destruction of that asset.[45] That is, there is a direct correlation between asset value and the severity of the consequences of the loss of that asset. To illustrate, what impact would be felt across different or nested security perimeters if that asset were compromised, corrupted, or stolen? What assets are essential to maintain normal operations or a minimum operational capability?[45] What assets are essential to ensure the health and safety of the occupants?[45] What are the primary services or outputs generated at each facility, and how essential is this asset to their production? Are there any required inputs from external organizations? What happens if those external assets are lost or unavailable?

To determine the true value of an asset, follow the process illustrated in Table 5.1. List the assets as identified in the asset inventory in the first column. Asset importance is then derived as a function of asset criticality and sensitivity. Criticality reflects how critical a given asset is to achieving an organization's mission. There are three standard categories of asset criticality: (1) critical, (2) essential, and (3) routine. Critical assets are those systems, functions, services, or information that, if lost, would prevent an organization from achieving its mission or business goals. The loss of essential assets would reduce the ability of an organization to achieve its mission, but not prevent it altogether. In contrast, the loss of a routine asset might be a nuisance or require some temporary workarounds; however, it would not significantly degrade the ability of an organization to achieve its mission. There is not a "none" category for criticality, for the simple reason that if the criticality is none, there is no reason for the asset to exist; hence, it represents waste. Determine the appropriate criticality for each asset and enter the weighting factor from Part II of the table in column 2.

Sensitivity reflects the relative degree of confidentiality and privacy protection a given asset needs. Most organizations have many sensitive assets, information or otherwise. Corporate R&D, marketing strategies, expansion plans, and prototypes of new products can all be considered sensitive, as is information that by law requires privacy protections. The location, contents, and activities conducted in certain facilities may also be sensitive. Sensitivity ratings are assigned to assets based on the potential adverse effect on organizational operations, reputation, financial status, other assets, or individuals resulting from the compromise of that asset. Ascertain the appropriate sensitivity rating for each asset and enter the weighting factor from Part II of the table in column 3.

Next, the impact of the loss of each asset is examined, in terms of the severity of the loss, the scope of the loss, and the duration of the loss. In this

Table 5.1   Asset Value Determination Worksheet

I. Asset Value Ranking

Asset ID	Asset Importance		Impact of Asset Loss			Asset Value Ranking[a]
	Criticality	Sensitivity	Loss Severity	Scope of Loss	Loss Duration	
Asset 1						
Asset 2						
Asset 3						
Asset x						

[a] Minimum value 17, maximum value 200.

II. Weighting Factors

Criticality	Sensitivity	Loss Severity	Scope of Loss	Loss Duration
60 — critical 30 — essential 15 — routine	20 — high 10 — moderate 5 — low 0 — none	60 — catastrophic 30 — moderate 15 — minor 7 — marginal 0 — none	40 — beyond single enterprise (critical infrastructure) 32 — enterprisewide 24 — region-wide 20 — campus-wide 16 — facility-wide 4 — single work area 2 — single device	20 — +1 month 15 — 1 to 4 weeks 10 — 1 to 6 days 8 — 1 to 23 hours 4 — 1 to 59 min 0 — <1 min

case, severity represents the worst-case consequences of the loss. There are four standard categories of severity; they are defined in terms of property loss, financial loss, death, injury, illness, and environmental damage. Catastrophic consequences result in loss, death, permanent total disability, property loss (including information assets) exceeding $1M, or irreversible severe environmental damage. Critical consequences result in loss, permanent partial disability, injuries, or occupational illness that may result in hospitalization of at least three personnel, property loss (including information assets) exceeding $200K but less than $1M, or reversible environmental damage. Marginal consequences result in loss, injury or occupational illness resulting in a lost workday, property loss (including information assets) exceeding $10K but less than $200K, or mitigable environmental damage. Insignificant consequences result in loss, injury or illness not resulting in a lost workday, property loss (including information assets) exceeding $2K but less than $10K, or minimal environmental damage. Determine the severity of the loss of each asset and enter the weighting factor from Part II of the table in column 4.

The scope of the loss of an asset also affects the impact. There is quite a broad spectrum for the scope of a loss, from a single device to a facility, region, or the entire enterprise. In some instances, the impact may even be felt way beyond the primary organization. The impact on business partners, stakeholders, customers, and the community at large must be factored in. The weighting factor for the scope of loss is entered in column 5.

The third aspect of the impact of losing an asset is the duration of the loss, which can range from minutes to days, weeks, or more. Here, there are many alternate scenarios for an organization to consider. Perhaps a catastrophic loss of a minute or less is easier to tolerate than a sustained minor loss that goes on for more than a month. The duration should reflect the total time required to remedy the loss and return operations to normal, locally and enterprisewide. Select the appropriate duration weighting factor and enter it in column 6.

Then the weighting factors for each asset are totaled by row. The asset value ranking can range from a minimum of 17 to a maximum of 200. Asset values have a direct impact on security ROI for several reasons. Asset value rankings highlight which assets need the most resilient security controls and robust protection. Very high asset value rankings may also indicate the need for spares, hot standbys, alternate suppliers, diverse paths, and other factors related to ensuring availability and eliminating single points of failure. One way to group assets by their relative value is shown below:

Qualitative Label	Asset Value (From Table 5.1)
Ultra high	164–200
High	128–163
Medium	92–127
Low	55–91
Little to none	17–54

It is often difficult to assign values to information assets. In physical terms, information may be little more than a piece of paper or some electronic bits stored on a server. However, the value of this information to an organization and its economic well-being may be considerable. As a result, be sure to take this value into account when performing ROI analysis for security controls that protect information assets. Also keep in mind that the value of information changes over time. Peltier has identified several parameters to consider when determining the value of information assets[199]:

- The cost of producing the information
- The value of the information on the open market
- The cost of reproducing the information if it is lost, damaged, or destroyed
- The benefit of the information in meeting the organization's mission and goals
- Repercussions to the organization if the information is not readily available when needed
- Advantages to a competitor if they can use, change, or destroy the information
- The cost to the organization if the information were subject to unauthorized release, destruction, or alteration
- The loss of public confidence in the organization if the information is not handled correctly
- The loss of credibility and embarrassment to the organization if the security of the information is compromised

A final point to clarify is the remaining useful life span of the assets being protected. ROI calculations frequently talk about the useful life span of the security control being purchased, but they neglect to consider the remaining useful life span of the assets being protected. This is a serious and potentially expensive oversight. For example, assume the data being protected has a useful life span of three months. Then by law the data must be archived for seven years offline. The security ROI calculation for the security controls that protect the online data must reflect the fact that the risk exposure interval is three months. Likewise, the security ROI calculations for the security controls that protect the archived data must reflect the fact that the risk exposure interval is seven years. The same principle applies to security controls that protect IT assets such as servers, routers, and desktops. But, you say, these assets will be replaced during a technology refresh cycle and the new assets will need to same protection. Yes and no. The retired assets will be replaced, but by newer and perhaps different, more advanced or consolidated equipment. As a result, the threat environment will be different — meaning that (1) a new vulnerability assessment is needed, (2) the asset inventory needs to be updated, (3) the effectiveness and resilience of the security architecture need to be reevaluated, and (4) the security ROI calculations for this particular combination of risk, assets, and security controls need to be redone. At this point in time, the security controls would be old while the assets would be new. Most likely, the existing security controls will need to be augmented, which will upset the original security ROI calculation.

Total Cost of Security Feature, Function, or Control

The second category of parameters evaluated to calculate the security ROI is the total cost of the security feature, function, or control that contributes to mitigating the risk identified in Part I. And, the emphasis is on the *total* cost. The total cost for any security feature, function, or control includes a combination of direct and indirect, one-time, and recurring costs. When talking about an IT security control, the direct costs include the purchase price of the device, any sales or use tax, and the shipping or delivery cost. These are one-time costs that occur up-front early in the life cycle. Too often these are the only costs considered, when in fact there are many more costs involved in owning and operating a security device throughout its useful life. This is where the indirect costs come into play and they are not insignificant. In fact, in some cases the indirect costs far exceed the direct costs. The situation can be analogous to home ownership. Over the period of a typical 30-year mortgage, the purchase price is surpassed by the total costs associated with interest payments, property taxes, maintenance and upkeep, landscaping and yard work, public utilities, not to mention furnishing the house and redecorating every so often or the capital gains tax paid when the property is sold.

A mixture of one-time and recurring indirect costs is associated with most security controls. The one-time indirect costs include items such as the cost of installing the device and the cost of training end users and operations and maintenance staff about the correct operation and use of the device. There are a variety of recurring indirect costs associated with any security control. The exact list depends on the particular security control. In general, the cost of the following items is involved:

- I/O devices, cables, and connectors that interface with the device
- Hardware and software licenses, subscriptions for emergency patches, upgrades, and on-call support
- Telecommunications to connect the device to the IT infrastructure
- Spare parts, disks, and other expendables necessary to operate the device or retrieve information from it
- Environmental support for the device, such as electricity and special HVAC, if necessary
- The floor and rack space the device occupies (real estate is not free!)
- Labor to operate and maintain the device

Depreciation Period

The third category of parameters evaluated to calculate security ROI concerns the depreciation period. Depreciation is defined as:

> **Depreciation:** (1) decline in value of a capitalized asset, a form of capital recovery applicable to a property value with two or more years useful life span, in which an appropriate portion of the asset's value is periodically charged to current operations; (2) the loss of value because of obsolescence or due to attrition.[311]

Today, most security controls have a short useful life span, due to rapid advances in technology, evolving operational environments, and ever-changing threat environments. At the time of purchase an assumption may be made, based on the best information available, about how long a device can be used. In reality, this assumption may prove to have been optimistic and the useful life span of the device considerably less than estimated. For this reason, the depreciation period is estimated for three different parameters: the minimum, maximum, and most likely useful life span. The intent is to arrive at a more realistic estimate. First, the minimum useful life span of the device is estimated. For many IT security controls, this number might range anywhere from 12 to 18 months. These numbers may come as a shock to many organizations that are accustomed to replacing desktop computers on a five-year basis and telecommunications equipment on a 10- to 15-year basis. For physical or personnel security controls, the time frame would likely be much longer. Next, the maximum useful life span of the security control is estimated. For IT security controls, this number is usually somewhere between three and five years. Often, product vendors can work with an organization to help determine the estimated minimum and maximum useful life span. To compensate for the fact that the above estimates tend to be optimistic, a third time frame is estimated as well — the most likely useful life span. The most likely useful life span is derived using the following formula:

$$
\text{Most likely useful life span (months)} = [(\text{Minimum useful life span} \times 2) +
$$
$$
(\text{Minimum useful life span} \times 0.75) +
$$
$$
\text{Maximum useful life span} +
$$
$$
(\text{Maximum useful life span} \times 0.75)]/5
$$

The annual recurring indirect costs are multiplied by the most likely useful life span to determine the total recurring indirect costs:

$$
\text{Total recurring indirect costs} = \text{Annual recurring indirect costs} \times
$$
$$
(\text{Most likely useful life span}/12)
$$

Tangible Benefits

The fourth category of parameters examined to calculate security ROI is the tangible benefits derived from implementing the security feature, function, or control. Tangible in this context simply means that the benefits can be easily measured and translated into financial terms. Again, because these are estimates, two scenarios are examined: (1) the worst case and (2) the best case. The exact list of tangible benefits depends on the organization's mission, the specific security control, operational environment, IT infrastructure, threat environment, etc. Many tangible benefits are unique to a given situation. This is particularly true when talking about the public and non-profit sectors. There are also significant differences in the tangible benefits among the four different types of security controls. However, there are some elements that are common to calculating tangible benefits in all situations. These include the total cost of the losses prevented, regulatory fines avoided, liability lawsuits avoided, and increased operational efficiency resulting from implementing the security feature, function, or control.

To begin, an organization must identify the specific types of losses that will be experienced if the security feature, function, or control is not deployed. This information derives from the vulnerability assessment, in particular the information captured for the Problem Identification and Characterization. That is, what specific losses will occur if the vulnerability is exploited and the threat instantiated? The types of losses correlate directly to the severity of the consequences. There may be several different types of losses associated with a single risk. The total cost of loss should reflect them all, scaled of course to reflect both the worst-case and the best-case scenarios. Some examples include loss of worker productivity during downtime, lost business opportunities, inability to submit bills or collect revenue, loss of sensitive information about new products or marketing strategies, losses from the shutdown of manufacturing equipment or utilities, losses from the unavailability of transportation or telecommunications equipment, decreased profit margins due to a delay in completing a business transaction, such as placing an order, etc.

The total cost of loss reflects: (1) assets that will be damaged and hence unusable for a period of time, but are repairable, and assets that will be totally destroyed or stolen and unrecoverable; (2) losses associated with the inability to achieve the organization's mission due to these losses, and (3) other related costs.[116] For example, what is the impact on the rest of the organization if this facility or function is lost? How readily can the function performed or the products produced at this facility be restored at this facility or replaced at another facility? The cost of loss normally includes items such as permanent replacement costs, the cost of temporary substitute workspace, equipment, or personnel, the cost impact on the rest of the organization, lost income, (re)training, and other related expenses.[116] The cost of loss can be expressed as[116]:

$$K = (C_p + C_t + C_r + C_l) - (I - a) \qquad\qquad 2.1.2.10$$

where
K = Total cost of loss
C_p = Cost of permanent replacements (facilities, equipment, supplies, and personnel)
C_t = Cost of temporary replacements (facilities, equipment, supplies, and personnel)
C_r = Total cost of direct and indirect related costs (restoral, recovery, retraining, delays)
C_l = Lost income cost (current and future)
I   = Insurance or indemnity
a   = Allocable insurance premium

Of course, to have any meaning, K should be calculated for a specified time frame. The loss is bounded by a specific time interval, which is referred to as the loss duration. In general, there is a combination of immediate loss, short-term loss, and long-term loss durations.

Concomitant with the losses prevented are the fines avoided by deploying the security feature, function, or control. As discussed in Chapter 3, most regulated industries face rather stiff fines for security incidents that result in the loss, corruption, or compromise of sensitive information, particularly private personal information. These fines are likely to increase in the future as the legal systems around the world gain a better understanding of the fact that these losses are preventable. Likewise, most business contracts include rather stiff fines for failing to meet product delivery dates or provide specified services. A case in point is the telecommunications industry. Tariffs are based on a guarantee to provide a specified level of service (bandwidth, throughput, latency, availability, etc.). These terms are stipulated in service level agreements (SLAs). A significant credit reverts to the customer or a fine is incurred whenever the carrier does not meet the terms of the SLA. Similar situations exist in other industries. State regulatory authorities often impose similar penalties, particularly on public utilities. As a result, a notable tangible benefit accrues when a security feature, function, or control allows an organization to avoid such fines.

The avoidance of liability lawsuits is another area of potential intangible benefits. All the standards and regulations discussed in Chapter 3 require organizations to exercise due care and due diligence when implementing security controls to protect information, IT assets, and the services they provide. It is important to understand these two terms in the context of security engineering.

> **Due care:** *Black's Law Dictionary*® — just, proper, and sufficient care, so far as the circumstances demand; the absence of negligence. That degree of care that a reasonable person can be expected to exercise to avoid harm, reasonably foreseeable if such care is not taken.

> **Due diligence:** *Black's Law Dictionary*® — such a measure of prudence, activity, or assiduity, as is properly to be expected from, and ordinarily exercised by, a reasonable and prudent person under the particular circumstances; not measured by any absolute standard, but depending on the relative facts of the special case.

Due care and due diligence imply that (1) the set of security controls employed are appropriate and sufficient for the inherent risk of a given situation, the sensitivity of the information, and the criticality of the assets; (2) robust ongoing risk management activities are in place to identify, prevent, and preempt foreseeable security incidents; and (3) all staff are competent to perform their assigned security duties and are accountable for doing so. Due care and due diligence represent the opposite of negligence.

> **Negligence**: *Black's Law Dictionary*® — failure to use such care as a reasonably prudent and careful person would use under similar circumstances; the doing of some act which a person of ordinary prudence would not have done under similar circumstances or failure to do what

> a person of ordinary prudence would have done under similar circum-
> stances; conduct that falls below the norm for the protection of others
> against unreasonable risk of harm. It is characterized by inadvertence,
> thoughtlessness, inattention, recklessness, etc.

That is, cutting corners, cutting security staff, having an inadequate security
budget, not adhering to security best practices or standards, not having the
right mix of junior and senior staff, doing favors for end users and business
partners rather than following security policies, and throwing your hands up
in the air and crying that you are helpless every time a new virus or worm
comes out just does not cut it. Why? Because the absence of due care and
due diligence — or conversely, the presence of negligence — leaves an
organization open to liability lawsuits. In addition to the fines imposed by
regulatory authorities, the individuals and organizations impacted by the
security incident have the option to sue the negligent party. Consequently, a
significant tangible benefit accrues when a security feature, function, or control
allows an organization to avoid such lawsuits, especially class action lawsuits.

Case law is rapidly expanding in the area of cyber security and cyber crime
and is expected to continue to do so in the future.[121] That is why E-insurance
has been offered since 1999 to provide some degree of indemnity to organizations that suffer losses due to[220]:

- Unauthorized access and use of IT resources
- Denial of service and other service disruptions
- Passive attacks such as viruses and worms
- In-house errors of omission and errors of commission

Of course, organizations must meet rather strict criteria to qualify for this
insurance. In essence, they must meet the due care and due diligence test.
The organization's approach to security risk management is evaluated, along
with its security policies, procedures, and practices, the turnover rate of key
staff, and its customers' perception of the importance of security to the
organization.[220]

Another area of tangible benefits is often overlooked — increased operational efficiency.[181] The process of developing a security architecture, defining
security policies, procedures, and practices, analyzing vulnerabilities and
threats, selecting security controls, and enforcing configuration management,
in addition to enhancing an organization's overall security program produces
fringe benefits. Standardization and taking a top-down enterprisewide view
to security, rather than isolated stovepipe fiefdoms, naturally creates opportunities for increased operational efficiencies. Duplication of effort and equipment, waste, and inefficient and unnecessary processes and equipment are
all exposed, along with opportunities to combine, consolidate, and streamline
operations. @Stake Labs identified one example of increased operational
efficiency just by looking at servers. This study concluded that server efficiency
was increased by an average of 3 percent simply by disabling unused and
unnecessary scripts.[109] This result was possible because the CPU spent less

time querying unused processes and larger runtime slices were allocated to productive processes.[109] In addition, labor costs were reduced because less time was spent patching unnecessary services.[109] A 3 percent increase in server efficiency and the concurrent labor savings enterprisewide are not small peanuts. This tangible benefit accrues from one simple security practice: disabling unused and unnecessary scripts. There are plenty of other similar opportunities out there. The CSO and security engineering staff just have to keep their eyes open when setting up, executing, and evaluating the security program. While it is unlikely security engineering will ever turn into a profit-making center, there is no reason to ignore or discount the cost savings that result from the operational efficiencies gained by introducing security features, functions, or controls.

Intangible Benefits

The fifth category of parameters examined to calculate security ROI is the intangible benefits derived from implementing the security feature, function, or control. In this context, intangible means that the benefits cannot be measured and translated into financial terms with mathematical certainty. Again, estimates are developed for two different scenarios: (1) the worst case and (2) the best case. Similar to tangible benefits, the exact list of intangible benefits depends on the organization's mission, the specific security control, operational environment, IT infrastructure, threat environment, etc. Many intangible benefits are unique to a given situation. This is particularly true when talking about the public and non-profit sectors. There are also significant differences in the intangible benefits among the four different types of security controls. The unique items must be determined on a case-by-case basis by each organization. However, there are some common elements when calculating intangible benefits in all situations. These include the impact of the security feature, function, or control on the OMER of would-be attackers, the increased confidence of customers, investors, and business partners, and improved employee morale.

First and foremost is the impact of the security feature, function, or control on the OMER of would-be attackers. Some might be inclined to count the OMER impact as a tangible benefit. The OMER impact is a significant item. However, the measurements generally fall on qualitative nominal or ordinal scales rather than quantitative interval or ratio scales. As a result, it is more appropriate to consider the OMER impact as an intangible benefit.

The fist item to evaluate as part of the OMER impact is *opportunity*. What is the effect of the security control on the opportunity for an attacker to exploit a vulnerability? A logical approach is to compare the opportunity before and after the security control is introduced. To be credible, the measurement of opportunity before deploying a security control must be consistent with the likelihood assigned to the risk of the threat being instantiated. Likelihood implies that the opportunity to exploit a vulnerability exists and will be taken advantage of. To illustrate, it is not credible to rate likelihood as frequent and opportunity as remote, or vice versa, for the same situation. Rather, likelihood and opportunity ratings must be consistent.

Recall from the discussion in Chapter 2 that likelihood can be expressed in qualitative or quantitative terms — hence the ability to match opportunity ratings. The six standard levels of likelihood are*:

1. **Incredible:** unlikely to occur in the life of an item, with a probability of occurrence less than 10^{-7}
2. **Improbable:** so unlikely, it can be assumed occurrence may not be experienced, with a probability of occurrence less than 10^{-6}
3. **Remote:** unlikely, but possible to occur in the life of an item, with a probability of occurrence of less than 10^{-3} but greater than 10^{-6}
4. **Occasional:** likely to occur sometime in the life of an item, with a probability of occurrence of less than 10^{-2} but greater than 10^{-3}
5. **Probable:** will occur several times in the life of an item, with a probability of occurrence of less than 10^{-1} but greater than 10^{-2}
6. **Frequent:** likely to occur often in the life of an item, with a probability of occurrence greater than 10^{-1}

The delta between the before and after measurements of opportunity represents the intangible benefit from deploying the security control. For example, assume the opportunity before a security control is introduced is rated frequent, and the opportunity after a security control is introduced is rated remote. Then the intangible benefit from implementing the security control is a reduction in the opportunity to exploit the vulnerability by at least three orders of magnitude. This is impressive, especially considering the fact that it is rare, if not impossible, to be able to reduce opportunity to zero.

As discussed in Chapter 4, none of the four types of security controls have any impact on *motive*. Other techniques and approaches can impact the motive of an attacker in a positive or negative way, but they are beyond the scope of this book. Hence, motive is not evaluated as part of the OMER impact on intangible benefits.

The second item evaluated as part of the OMER impact is *expertise*. How does the introduction of the security control impact the expertise required to exploit the vulnerability? Let us face it, some security controls are so simplistic and superficial that a fourth grader can bypass them. This kind of security control might allow an organization to check off a box that, yes, it does have access control (or whatever type of control is being talked about), but the deterrence factor, and hence ROI, are zero. To be effective and provide appropriate resilience, a security control should, as part of risk mitigation, increase the level of expertise required to exploit the vulnerability or bypass the security control. The goal is to make it too difficult or take too long for the would-be attacker to bother with — they will move on to another target. As part of the vulnerability assessment process, an organization should decide

---

* Adapted from MIL-STD 882D, "Mishap Risk Management," U.S. Department of Defense Standard Practice, October 1998.

who is most likely to initiate attacks against the organization's assets and their skill level: script kiddies, bored college students, insiders with detailed knowledge and access privileges, organized crime, industrial espionage, or state-sponsored cyber terrorists? If an organization's likely adversaries are industrial spies or state-sponsored cyber terrorists and the level of expertise required to defeat or bypass the security control is that of a script kiddy, the security control will be ineffective and the ROI will be zero or negative.

There are five generally recognized levels of expertise required to bypass or defeat security controls[45]:

1. **None:** most any adult can figure out how easily
2. **Low:** basic technical knowledge is required that is available from open sources
3. **Medium:** detailed technical knowledge is required that can be obtained through study at a technical or undergraduate school or open scientific and technical literature
4. **High:** advanced technical knowledge is required that can be obtained only through specialized training and access to rare scientific or unclassified literature
5. **Ultra high:** very advanced technical knowledge is required that can be obtained only through very specialized training, a graduate degree, or access to controlled sensitive or classified information

To determine the intangible benefit, a comparison is made between the level of expertise required to exploit a vulnerability before and after the security control is implemented. Then this information is correlated to the level of expertise expected of the would-be attackers. To be effective, the level of expertise required after a security control has been implemented should be higher than that expected of would-be attackers. To illustrate, assume that without the security control the level of expertise required is "low," while the level of expertise of the would-be attackers is "medium." That means that after the security control is deployed, the level of expertise required must be raised to "high" for any benefit to accrue. If not, the ROI is zero or negative and the security control will be ineffective.

The third item evaluated as part of the OMER impact is resources. How does the implementation of the security control alter the extent of resources required to exploit the vulnerability? As part of the mitigation strategy, implementation of the security control should increase the type and quantity of resources required to exploit the vulnerability and defeat or bypass the security control. The intent is to make the exploit too expensive or too resource intensive for would-be attackers. Again, an organization should have a good idea of who its likely attackers are in order to determine what resources are (or are not) easy for them to obtain. The goal is to make the type and quantity of resources needed beyond the reach of the would-be attackers, without overcompensating. The exact spread of resources required depends on the organization's mission, the operational environment, the IT infrastructure, the threat environment, etc., and must be determined on a case-by-case basis. A spread might look something like this:

- **None:** one person, no special equipment, and $2K or less is required.
- **Low:** two to three people, no special equipment, and $2 to 10K is required.
- **Medium:** four to seven people, limited special equipment, and $11 to 50K is required.
- **High:** eight to fifteen people, special equipment, and $51 to 250K is required.
- **Ultra high:** sixteen or more people, extensive special equipment, and more than $250K is required.

Another factor to consider is the time interval in which the resources are needed. That is, are the people and equipment needed part-time for a week or less or for a sustained 24/7 effort over several months?

A comparison is made between the resources required for a successful exploit before and after the security control is implemented in order to assess the benefit. Then this information is compared to the resources expected to be at the disposal of the would-be attackers. For example, assume that prior to implementing the security control, no special resources were required. One person with a laptop computer could successfully exploit the vulnerability in a matter of days. After the security control is implemented, a high level of resources is required to successfully exploit the vulnerability: several people with specialized equipment working for an extended period of time. That would represent an increase of three orders of magnitude in the resources required. Does that represent an intangible benefit? It depends on the level of resources the would-be attackers are expected to have. If they are only expected to have low to medium resources, then the ROI is positive and there is an intangible benefit. However, if the would-be attackers are expected to have access to ultra high resources, there is no intangible benefit and the ROI is zero or negative.

Ideally, implementation of the security control should result in resource requirements that are one order of magnitude higher than that the would-be attackers are expected to have. If the resource requirements are lower than that of the would-be attackers, there is no intangible benefit. If the resource requirements are two orders of magnitude higher than that of the would-be attackers, the vulnerability may be mitigated and there is an intangible benefit, but the ROI is not what it should be because the organization has overcompensated. What happens if the resource requirements after the security control is implemented equal that of the would-be attackers? This is a likely outcome when dealing with the high and ultra high resource requirement levels and sophisticated attackers. If the resource levels for the security control and the would-be attackers match, and that for the security control cannot reasonably be increased, the organization should first acknowledge that fact head-on and not go into a state of denial or hide behind a cloud of buzzwords. Second, the organization should compensate for this fact by further decreasing the opportunity to exploit the vulnerability, increasing the expertise required to exploit the vulnerability, and employing other complementary security controls in tandem with this one to reduce the overall likelihood of exploitation.

As just discussed, implementation of a particular security control impacts the opportunity, expertise, and resources required to exploit a vulnerability. Which is more important — opportunity, expertise, or resources — when evaluating intangible benefits and ROI? Logic would dictate that the order of importance is consistent with the sequence of these items in the acronym OMER. If there is little to no opportunity to exploit a vulnerability, the expertise and resources required are not as important. Expertise is more difficult to come by than resources; hence expertise is more important than resources. Consequently, the relative weighting of the OMER impact on ROI can be represented as:

OMER impact = (Opportunity × 4) + (Expertise × 2) + Resources

Another category of intangible benefits is the potential for a security control to increase the confidence of customers, investors, and business partners. Cyber crime tends to make the front page of the newspaper these days, especially identity theft; and the bigger the heist, the more exposure the crime gets in the media. In some industries, cyber crime is hushed up to prevent mass panic. Ever wonder why ATM fees and credit card interest rates are so high? Basically, people who pay their bills on time are making up for the losses due to fraud and other delinquent behavior. Retail and other businesses are not protected by the same cone of silence, and the negative publicity can be extremely damaging in both the short term and the long term. Negative publicity, whether it is accurate or not, takes on a life of its own and is very difficult to recover from. For customers, investors, and business partners to have confidence in a security control, it must be real and not some feel-good fluff or a phony facade. A robust, legitimate, and necessary security control that is implemented wisely and operated efficiently and effectively can go a long way toward increasing the confidence of customers, investors, and business partners. In contrast, a phony security facade, especially one that is exposed in the media, can be extremely damaging to an organization's reputation.

Customers today are aware of the need for their business transactions and other personal information to be processed and stored securely. Customers may not understand the intricacies of elliptic curve encryption; at the same time, they do not want to be left hanging in the digital breeze because of carelessness by a retailer or healthcare provider. After all, it is this carelessness, or *negligence* as it is called in legal terms, that makes cyber crime possible. Organizations suffer direct financial loss as the result of some types of cyber crime. Other types of cyber crime, such as identity theft, cause individuals to experience direct financial loss and other hardships. And, as the saying goes, a happy customer tells one or two people, while an unhappy customer tells ten people. Only in this instance, we are not talking about one unhappy customer. Cyber crime is not concerned about stealing one person's sensitive personal or financial information, but rather stealing thousands of people's information at one time. That means there will be thousands of unhappy customers, each complaining to at least ten other people. Unhappy customers can be very vocal and drive many other customers away. So, in addition to the regulatory fines and liability lawsuits discussed earlier, organizations also face lost revenue streams as a result of inadequate security controls. Fines and penalties are one-time events, while customers and the revenue they generate may be lost permanently. While occasionally they forget, non-profit organizations and government agencies do have customers. In this instance, customers are the beneficiaries of the services provided by the non-profit or government agency. These customers can be just as vocal, if not more so, when they are unhappy. Does the Veterans Administration identity theft fiasco ring a bell?

If customers do not have confidence in an organization's security practices, they are unlikely to do or continue to do business with that organization. All it takes is one negative incident and a multi-year business relationship can come to a screeching halt. The perception is that the organization is not serious about security and, by extension, does not care about its customers. Some organizations have come to realize that fact, while other organizations still have a lot to learn, as the following examples illustrate.

Case Study 1. A co-worker purchased concert tickets over the telephone through a ticketing service using a debit card. Four months later, an erroneous ticket charge appeared on her bank statement. She called the bank and the bank called the ticket agency. The ticket agency representative concocted a story that they "thought" she would enjoy this concert too. Problem number one: she never ordered or received any tickets. Problem number two: the ticket agency retained her debit card information months after the valid transaction was complete although there was no legitimate reason to do so. Problem number three: the bank processed the transaction without authorization or confirmation from the customer. The end result: my co-worker closed all her accounts with that bank and took her business elsewhere. Neither she, nor anyone she talked to, have purchased any tickets through that ticket agency since. The bank could not understand how she could close her account over "such a small thing," having been a loyal customer for 30 years. Loyalty is a two-way street. If the bank could carelessly deduct $150 for erroneous tickets one day, what is to prevent them from erroneously deducting $1500 the next? Debit cards do not have any of the protections that credit cards possess. The customer had no confidence that there were any protections in place to prevent the same situation from happening again and ended the business relationship.

Case Study 2. I opened a certificate of deposit (CD) at a bank. A week later I received a letter in the mail from the bank's out-of-state headquarters telling me my user ID for online and telephone banking. I immediately wrote back to them, explaining that I had declined the online and telephone banking option when the CD was opened. What is the point of online banking for a CD? The interest rate does not change. The end date does not change and the bank automatically sends you a letter when it is time to renew the CD. I instructed them to disable the online and telephone banking options. After dead silence for a month, I sent the letter a second time. In response, I received a form letter stating that the online and telephone banking options are automatically created any time a new account is opened, apparently regardless of whether or not the customer wants it. Also, they informed me that if I did not want online or telephone banking, I just should not use it (what a stroke of brilliance!), but no they were not going to disable these options. Just because a customer does not use online or telephone banking does not mean that hackers will not try to access their accounts. Problem number one: the letter containing my unwanted user ID was not sealed. Problem number two: the address my user ID was mailed to was incorrect. Problem number three: the bank was totally unconcerned that I never received the PIN. They probably mailed that to the wrong address too. Very convenient for the recipient because they already had the user ID! This exchange took place with the bank's headquarters staff. If was obvious that they had no understanding of cyber security, cyber crime, identity theft, or the internal controls required by the Sarbanes-Oxley Act. And if headquarters staff does not have this understanding, neither does the IT staff, or personnel working in branch offices. I closed the CD immediately, despite the penalty, because I had no confidence in the bank's security practices. In fact, I would say that the odds are 10 to 1 that this institution will be in the news within 12 months for a major security break-in (unless it is so bad that the news is hushed up).

Case Study 3. A neighbor did not receive two consecutive biweekly statements in the mail from a major financial institution. The statement was for an umbrella account with a balance greater than $100K. For obvious reasons, my neighbor was alarmed and tried to report it. The local office could not do anything about it because the statements are mailed from Philadelphia. He was told to call an 800-number in Minneapolis. The first customer service representative did not take the call seriously. My neighbor was told to "just wait a few more days; the mail is probably slow this time of year." He called back again and tried to explain that he was concerned about fraudulent activity taking place in his account. Perhaps someone had changed the account address and the next step would be to change the contents of the account and where the proceeds were deposited. The customer service representative could have cared less and referred him back to the local office. The local office declined — all they do is sell investments — only the 800-number could handle problems. He called the 800-number three or four more times, working his way up the line of supervisors. All were totally oblivious to the fact that something might have gone wrong. He asked the last person to please just check to see if there had been any unusual account activity. She first asked what he meant by "unusual account activity" and then proceeded to tell him she could not do that unless he gave her, over an unsecure line to an 800 call center, his social security number, date of birth, place of birth, account numbers, dates the accounts were opened, expected balances, date of last transaction, blood type, Rh factor, and DNA sample. Because, she said, she needed that information to make sure he was not an imposter! But that is the exact set of information an imposter needs to precipitate identity theft and other cyber crime. All someone would have to do is: (1) tap the 800-numbers of the major financial institutions, and (2) capture the personal account information requested by the customer service representatives, and they are all set to clean out customer accounts — and not one at a time — for the low price of a telephone tap. My neighbor hung up the phone in disbelief, drove down to the local office, and closed his account on the spot. Again, the organization was clueless about operational security. The customer had no confidence in the organization's security practices and took his business elsewhere. As for the missing statements ... they never appeared.

The moral to the story is that business is built on confidence and trust. Cheap prices and fads are a temporary infatuation. If customers lack confidence in an organization, they take their business elsewhere. When that happens, an organization's revenue shrinks. If revenue shrinks enough, the organization ceases to exist. Consequently, physical, personnel, IT, and operational security controls that enhance customer confidence represent a major intangible benefit. (Keep in mind that customer confidence may be intangible, but revenue lost as a result of a lack of customer confidence will be quite tangible.)

Investors are also part of the confidence equation. In this context, the term "investors" is used rather broadly, to include any source that contributes funding to the organization. In the private sector, that would include publicly traded investments, such as stocks, as well as private investments, venture capital, etc. For non-profit organizations, the term "investors" would include donors and organizations that award grants and endowments. For government agencies, the term "investors" would apply to legislative bodies that allocate funding, as well as investors who buy municipal, state, and federal bonds. This diverse group of "investors" will release or withhold funding (in part) based on their confidence in an organization's security controls. This is only logical. Why would a savvy investor commit funds to an organization that is about to be (or worse, has already been) hit with stiff regulatory fines or a class action liability lawsuit for a major security breach that was caused by a lack of appropriate security controls? Why would a savvy investor buy stock in a nationwide retail business when surveys tell them that customer perception is that the business does not care about protecting the security and privacy of customer information? Why would bonds be approved for sale by a county that was caught selling voter registration information or a state that was caught selling driver's license information, in violation of privacy laws and regulations, and now faces major litigation? Why would Wall Street be excited about bonds for a major healthcare provider that has flunked one HIPAA audit after another and an employee was caught selling the protected health information of 20,000 patients, the scandal making the front pages of the newspapers? Investors, particularly large investment firms, do their homework. When they see red flags that raise doubts about the security practices of an organization, practices that could lead to lost revenue, fines, and liability lawsuits, their investment capital flows elsewhere. As a result, physical, personnel, IT, and operational security controls that increase investor confidence represent a significant intangible benefit.

Business partners are the third part of the confidence equation. Business partners monitor the same things customers and investors monitor, although they may be more discreet about it. Business partners do not want to be associated with a firm that makes the news for a cavalier attitude toward security. They fear the boomerang from the "guilt by association" phenomenon — it is bad for business. Occasionally, liability lawsuits, like compost, roll downhill. The accounting firms and financial institutions on the periphery of Enron's house of cards got caught in the eddy too; some of them no longer exist. Business partners are concerned for a second reason, which often outweighs the first. That is the interconnectedness of their IT infrastructure with the organization in question. It is one thing to be concerned about how well another organization protects its information and IT assets; it is a whole other ball-game to be concerned about how well that same organization is protecting your data. If an organization's security practices are sloppy or non-existent, that same careless attitude will be extended to their business partner's information and IT assets. Sharing passwords with temporary employees who are here today and gone tomorrow will be OK. Not logging out at the end of a shift will be all right. Of course, it takes too long to have each employee log in and log out; in addition, accountability should be avoided at all costs because then the "we are so helpless" excuse can be used when something goes wrong (which, with this attitude, undoubtedly will). Backups, background investigations, encryption, virus scanning, and firewalls are all too much trouble. Why hire competent seasoned security professionals when other people can be hired for half the price? That would cut into the profit margin.

If a business partner lacks confidence in an organization's security practices, four different things can happen, all of which will have a negative impact on the organization's bottom line. It is important to remember that non-profit organizations and government agencies also have business partners. In this instance, a business partner can be another non-profit or government agency or a supplier. A business partner might restrict or withhold certain access rights and connectivity to protect its own systems, networks, and data from contamination or compromise. A business partner might purposely make it more difficult, cumbersome, or time consuming to exchange information in an attempt to create an extra degree of separation between its IT infrastructure and that of the organization. A business partner might insist on very expensive contractual penalty clauses for security breaches. It is always a good idea to include such clauses in contracts to make sure all parties get the message that security practices are to be taken seriously. However, when one party has doubts about the resilience of the other party's security practices, the contractual penalties will most likely escalate tenfold. Finally, a business partner might simply take its business elsewhere and avoid the risk of doing business with the organization altogether. Depending on the business partner's perception of the risk, that may be the easiest, most cost-effective, and most practical option. Business partners, like customers and investors, do have a variety of choices from which to choose. In some industrial sectors, adherence to specific security standards, such as the Payment Card Industry Data Security Standard (PCI DSS) or the North American Electric Reliability Council (NERC) security standards discussed in Chapter 3, is mandatory. Failure to comply can leave an organization completely cut off from would-be business partners. Again, physical, personnel, IT, and operational security controls that increase the confidence of business partners represent a significant intangible benefit.

Employee morale is a final area of intangible benefits. Employees want to work for a company that is on the up-and-up. Employees want to feel that they are part of a professional operation that is well organized and well run. This is particularly true for the IT and security engineering staff. Like customers, investors, and business partners, employees want to be associated with a winner, and not some shoddy, poorly run, fly-by-night operation. If they are working for a winner, they feel like there is a good opportunity to grow and advance with the organization and that they will acquire good credentials to put on their resume. As a result, morale goes up, employees are more productive and conscientious, and turnover is low. On the other hand, employees who work for a shoddy, poorly run, fly-by-night operation tend to have low morale, low productivity, and a high turnover rate.

The IT and security engineering staff are in the best position to know whether robust security practices are being followed and enforced. They are usually the best source for suggestions on how to enhance security policies and procedures. When the IT and security engineering staff become aware of deficiencies in security policies, procedures, and standards or the lax enforcement of them, they will become unwilling or fearful of making suggestions to improve the program. When it becomes apparent that corporate executives do not take security seriously (regardless of applicable regulations), the IT and security engineering staff will become either very frustrated or fearful of over-achieving and making waves. Even more damaging, they may fear that they are being set up as the fall guy for when something does go wrong. As a result, employee morale is low, productivity is low, and turnover is high. This historical knowledge of the organization's IT infrastructure, subtle nuances, and vulnerabilities walks out the door every 9 to 12 months. Consequently, deploying and consistently enforcing robust security controls has a major impact on employee morale, which translates directly into an intangible benefit.

Payback Period

The sixth part of a security ROI analysis is the evaluation of the payback period. The payback period is different from the depreciation period discussed previously. The depreciation period reflects the estimated useful life span of a security control. In contrast, the payback period represents the calendar time needed for the related profit or savings in operational costs to equal the amount of the investment.[311] Simply put, the payback period is an estimate of when the ROI will become positive. The payback period marks the magic transition from breaking even to realizing a positive tangible and intangible ROI. Two security controls may have the same estimated positive ROI over their useful life span. However, the payback period for one security control may be much shorter than for the other security control. When choosing between security controls, organizations need to decide whether the cumulative ROI or the payback period is more important.

The payback period is a projection about future events — the extent to which tangible and intangible benefits will be realized over time. The projection makes assumptions, which are documented in Part VIII of the security ROI analysis, about which items in the operational environment, IT infrastructure, operational profile, duty cycle, threat environment, etc. will remain constant and which will change. To increase the accuracy of the payback period projection, three different estimates are prepared: the minimum, maximum, and most likely payback period. The minimum represents the most optimistic estimate. Should everything go as planned, the payback period will occur quickly. Given that life in general and technology in particular are usually not so predictable, a pessimistic estimate is also needed. The maximum payback period estimate acknowledges that things in the world of technology do not always go as planned, especially because a number of facts are not under the organization's control. The maximum payback period estimate attempts to build in a buffer time-wise to account for the unforeseen. Reality usually lies somewhere between the optimistic and pessimistic estimates. As a result, a most likely payback period is also estimated, using the following formula:

Most likely payback period (months) = [(Minimum payback period × 1.25) +
Minimum payback period +
(Maximum payback period × 0.75) +
(Maximum payback period × 2)]/5

Comparative Analysis

A comparative analysis is the seventh part of a security ROI analysis. The security ROI analysis of a security control demonstrates that not only is the control technically beneficial, but also that it is economically beneficial. Similar to any technical problem, there is always more than one possible security solution. The technical analysis indicates which solutions are technically viable and perhaps rank-orders the solutions in terms of the best technical solution. The security ROI analysis complements the technical analysis by determining which of the technically viable solutions are also economically viable and rank-orders them. That way, an organization can select the solution that best meets its technical and economic needs, given the fact that security budgets are rarely unlimited. One area where security ROI metrics can shine is by showing that loss is preventable.[198] The estimated cost of a loss and the cost of recovery are compared to the cost of security controls. In essence, the cost of doing nothing, or allowing the vulnerability to remain, is compared to the cost of preventing or correcting the weakness.[136, 153, 197] As a result, the comparative analysis generally takes two forms:

1. A comparison to the cost of doing nothing
2. A comparison to the cost of alternate approaches

First, the cost of the security control and its tangible and intangible benefits are compared to the cost and consequences of doing nothing. That is, what are the cost and consequences of leaving the vulnerability "as is" or unmitigated? This is an important question to ask because, contrary to popular myth, not every vulnerability needs to be mitigated in order for IT and information assets to be secure. More needs to be known about a vulnerability than just its existence before funds are spent on mitigation, in particular the likelihood, severity, and accessibility of the vulnerability.

If the likelihood of the vulnerability being exploited is extremely low, such that it is rated incredible or improbable, it may not make any sense to invest in mitigation. At that low level of likelihood, most likely a technology refresh cycle will occur before the vulnerability is (or is estimated to be) exploited. As a result, the threat environment will have changed and a new vulnerability assessment is needed. If the severity of the consequences, should the vulnerability be exploited, is extremely low, such as an insignificant rating, it may not make sense to invest in mitigation. At that low level of severity, the total cost of the security control is likely to far outweigh the tangible and intangible benefits. The simple fact is that there are not too many security controls whose total cost over their entire useful life span is less than $10K. The accessibility of the vulnerability also needs careful scrutiny. As discussed in Chapter 4, vulnerabilities can be directly exposed, indirectly exposed, or inaccessible. It does not make any sense to expend funds to mitigate an inaccessible vulnerability. Indirectly exposed vulnerabilities should be evaluated on a case-by-case basis. In some cases it will make sense to invest in security controls; in other cases it will not. Directly exposed vulnerabilities, on the other hand, will almost always present an opportunity for a positive security ROI. Another factor that must be evaluated is the value and criticality of the assets being protected. The investment in mitigation should be proportional to asset value and criticality. It does not make sense to spend $500K to mitigate a vulnerability for a routine asset that can be purchased for $5K.

In summary, the cost of doing nothing reflects the total cost of the worst-case losses that might be experienced if a vulnerability is not mitigated. This includes the cost of regulatory fines, liability lawsuits, lost customer, investor, and business partner confidence, and other tangible and intangible losses over the time frame the vulnerability is allowed to remain unmitigated. In some instances, it may make sense not to mitigate a vulnerability in the short term because a better security control will be available in the near future or a planned enhancement to the IT infrastructure or operational procedures will eliminate the vulnerability. In essence, the organization decides to assume the risk in the short term. In other instances, it may make sense not to mitigate the vulnerability in the long term either. In this situation, the total cost of the projected losses, during the time frame the vulnerability is allowed to remain unmitigated, is less (usually considerably less) than the total cost of the security control, even factoring in the tangible and intangible benefits. If the security control were deployed in this situation, the ROI would be zero or negative.

In the second comparison, the total cost of a security control, taking tangible and intangible benefits into account, is compared to the total cost of technically viable alternate security controls. Alternate security controls present different sets of technical pros and cons; they also present different sets of economic pros and cons. One security solution might be technically superior but cost ten times what the organization can afford. Another security solution might come in second place technically, but it is affordable. Or perhaps two security solutions receive the same technical rating but there is a 60 percent cost difference over the useful life span of the devices. That is why a thorough security ROI analysis must be performed, in addition to the technical evaluation, to ensure that the organization acquires the best overall security solution that meets its needs.

Assumptions

Assumptions are the eighth and final part of a security ROI analysis. When determining the security ROI and analyzing the total cost, depreciation period, tangible benefits, intangible benefits, and payback period, certain assumptions are made. These assumptions should be documented as part of the ROI analysis because they form the basis on which various decisions and estimates were made. These assumptions should become part of the security ROI record so that anyone reviewing the security ROI analysis, in the present or in the future, is aware of and understands the assumptions on which the security ROI analysis is based. Documenting the assumptions provides an open forum for validating the assumptions and helps to ensure that the assumptions are accurate and complete. This minimizes the likelihood that some detail has been overlooked, and prevents one person or group from operating on their own set of undocumented assumptions, while another person or group operates on a different set of undocumented assumptions. The assumptions should be dated to reflect the time period in which they were created and considered accurate. As the security ROI analysis is updated, the assumptions should also be revisited. Any changes needed should be made and a new date recorded. Keeping a historical record of the assumptions associated with a security ROI analysis provides a useful tool downstream when analyzing how security ROI analyses can be improved. The more mathematically inclined may want to perform a sensitivity analysis or assign a confidence level to various assumptions.

Assumptions can be associated with any of the other seven parts of the security ROI analysis. They can be related to any aspect of the security control being evaluated, the IT infrastructure in which the security control will be deployed, the operational environment, the operational profile, the duty cycle, etc. Assumptions can be made related to pricing structures or the premises on which tangible and intangible benefits were calculated. Each set of assumptions is unique to each situation and the items being evaluated. However, one area of assumptions — resilience levels — should be addressed in all security ROI analyses. Part I of the security ROI analysis, problem identification and characterization, states the level of resilience needed in the security control. The assumptions that were made to determine and justify that resilience level should be thoroughly documented. Assumptions about what will happen if the security control deployed has a lower resilience level than that required should also be thoroughly documented. Sometimes, commercial products are not available at the necessary resilience level or they are available but are cost prohibitive. In either case, additional compensating measures must be taken that impact the security ROI. There is a direct correlation between the resilience of a security control and the expertise and resources required by a would-be attacker. The higher the resilience level, the higher the level of expertise and resources required to defeat or bypass a security control. So while the cost of a security control increases with the resilience level, so do the tangible and intangible benefits.

5.3 Security ROI Primitives, Metrics, and Reports

We have just reviewed the individual components of the basic security ROI model. As shown, there are a variety of different parameters, tangible and intangible, quantitative and qualitative, that must be evaluated to calculate security ROI. There is no simple e = mc² formula for security ROI, although some such models have been proposed, as discussed in Section 5.1. Instead, a series of primitives, metrics, and aggregate metrics must be collected, analyzed, and merged to determine the security ROI of a security control or combination of security controls. Accordingly, this section explains how to convert the basic security ROI model discussed in Section 5.2 into primitives, metrics, and aggregate metrics. In addition, this section illustrates how to combine the metrics into a report format. A distinction has been made between worksheets that are used to collect primitives and reports that are used to communicate metrics. The worksheets are set up so that they can easily be plugged into spreadsheets.

Part I — Problem Identification and Characterization

Table 5.2 presents the worksheet for Part I of security ROI analysis — Problem Identification and Characterization. The information collected in Part I establishes the context for the remainder of the analysis. A limited amount of information is captured in text format; the remainder is converted into numeric format for use as primitives. First, the specific risk being mitigated is identified. The risk identification number, risk name, and description are taken from the vulnerability assessment. Cross-referencing the vulnerability analysis and the security ROI analysis increases the integrity and confidence in both analyses. For example, if this risk is not part of the vulnerability assessment, is it real? If not, why spend limited funds to mitigate a phantom risk? Or, is the vulnerability assessment incomplete or out of date? If so, the vulnerability assessment should be corrected. Next, the severity of the consequences, should the threat be instantiated, is captured using the standard severity categories defined in Chapter 2. Point values are assigned to each of the five severity categories. Severity is evaluated for both the short term and the long term. While often overlooked, most security incidents have an immediate impact, and then there is a long-term impact. These two scenarios may have very different severities.

Table 5.2 Security ROI Worksheet, Part I — Problem Identification and Characterization

Part I — Problem Identification and Characterization

1. Specific risk being mitigated

Risk ID #	Risk Name	Description

2. Severity of the consequences: catastrophic — 60, moderate — 30, minor — 15, marginal — 7, none — 0

Outcome	Short-term	Long-term
Worst case:		
Best case:		
Most likely:		

3. Likelihood of the threat being instantiated and the vulnerability exploited: frequent: 60, probable: 40, occasional: 27, remote: 18, improbable: 9, incredible: 0

Time Frame	Likelihood
Within 3 months	
Within 3 to 6 months	
Within 6 to 12 months	
Within 13 to 24 months	
Within 25 to 48 months	

4. Scope of the impact (select the highest applicable rating):_____

Beyond a single enterprise or organization, critical infrastructure	40
Enterprisewide, the corporate WAN or intranet, all application systems and data	32
Region-wide, a single application system and the data associated with it, archived data	24
Campus-wide	20
Facility-wide, all desktops, servers, and networks in a facility	16
Single work area	4
Single device, server, desktop, or LAN	2

5. Allocation of risk mitigation

Extent of risk mitigation provided by this security feature, function, or control (0–100%)	

Table 5.2   Security ROI Worksheet, Part I — Problem Identification and Characterization (continued)

6. *Assets being protected*	
Asset ID #	
Asset ID name	
Asset type	
Quantity	
Geographical location	
Logical location	
Asset value (from Table 5.1)	
Resilience level needed in security feature, function, or control: ultra high — 60, high — 40, medium — 20, low — 10, none — 0	
Remaining useful life span (years)	

The likelihood of the threat being instantiated and the vulnerability exploited is captured using the standard likelihood categories defined in Chapter 2. Point values are assigned to each of the six likelihood categories. Likelihood is examined across different time frames. This distinction is an important part of security ROI analysis. To illustrate, assume that the useful life span of a security control is four years. The security ROI analysis would be very different for threat A, which has a likelihood of once every three months, versus threat B, which has a likelihood of once every five years. The scope of the impact of a security incident varies dramatically, depending on the type and source of the attack. Individual components may be affected here and there. A single facility or region may be down. The complete thread of an application system and its data may be impacted. An entire region may be limited to degraded mode operations. The entire enterprisewide IT infrastructure — all systems, networks, and data — may be compromised. Or, the scope may involve multiple organizations or part of the nation's critical infrastructure. The differences in scope are profound and are reflected in the worksheet by different point values.

These first four items characterize the risk and its consequences to the organization. Beginning with the fifth item, the focus shifts to the role of the security feature, function, or control. A major point to clarify is the extent to which this security feature, function, or control mitigates this specific risk. This is the risk mitigation allocation step. There are two factors to keep in mind when performing risk mitigation allocation. First, generally a combination of security controls, versus a single control, is employed to mitigate a specific risk. Second, 100 percent risk mitigation is rarely achieved. To address the first item, it may make more sense to perform security ROI analysis on a combination of security controls rather than a single control.

Finally, the assets that will be protected by the security feature, function, or control are identified. The asset identification number, name, type, and quantity are pulled from the asset inventory. Cross-referencing the security ROI analysis and the asset inventory increases the integrity and the confidence in both analyses because inconsistencies will be identified and corrected. The geographical or physical location of the asset is captured, as well as the logical location of the asset within the IT infrastructure. This information helps clarify the scope of the impact; it is also used to determine where, within the security architecture, the security control should be deployed to obtain the maximum benefit. To adequately protect this asset, the resilience level needed in the security feature, function, or control is also specified. The resilience level is determined as a function of the severity of the consequences, likelihood of exploitation, scope of impact, asset value, and expertise and resources of would-be attackers, using the following formula:

Resilience level needed = Worst-Case severity + Annual likelihood +
(Scope of impact × 2) + (Asset value × 2) +
Expertise of would-be attackers +
Resources of would-be attackers

(Asset value is calculated using Table 5.1 as discussed previously. The expertise and resources of would-be attackers are discussed as part of Table 5.5, which follows.) This value is then aligned with the following key to identify the resilience level needed:

Resilience Level	
Ultra high	565–720
High	409–564
Medium	253–408
Low	97–252
None	0–96

The final item captured is the remaining useful life span of the assets being protected. This information is recorded in years.

These nine items are repeated for each type of asset being protected by the security feature, function, or control. A security control rarely protects a single asset. If there is a difference in the resilience levels needed for this combination of assets, the highest individual rating is used to determine the overall resilience level needed. That is, the overall resilience level needed can be higher, but not lower, than any individual rating. If the spread between the highest and lowest resilience levels needed is considerable, it may make sense to partition the security architecture differently.

Part II — Total Cost of Security Feature, Function, or Control, and Part III — Depreciation Period

Table 5.3 presents the worksheet for Parts II and III of a security ROI analysis — Total Cost of a Security Feature, Function, or Control and the Depreciation

Table 5.3   Security ROI Worksheet, Parts II and III — Total Cost of Security Feature, Function, or Control and Depreciation Period

Part II — Total cost of security feature, function, or control	
1. One-time direct costs	
Purchase price	
Tax	
Shipping	
Other	
Subtotal	
2. One-time indirect costs	
Installation	
Training	
Other	
Subtotal	
3. Annual recurring indirect costs	
I/O devices, cables, connectors	
Licenses, vendor support	
Telecommunications support	
Spare parts	
Disks, paper, toner, other expendables	
HVAC, electricity	
Floor space	
Racks	
Operations and maintenance labor	
Other	
Subtotal	
4. Total recurring indirect costs	
= Annual recurring indirect costs × (Most likely useful life span/12)	
5. Total	
= One-time direct costs + One-time indirect costs + Total recurring indirect costs	

Table 5.3   Security ROI Worksheet, Parts II and III — Total Cost of Security Feature, Function, or Control and Depreciation Period (continued)

Part III — Depreciation period (months)	
*6. Minimum useful life span:*_____	
*7. Maximum useful life span:*_____	
8. Most likely useful life span:	
= [(Minimum useful life span × 2) + (Minimum useful life span × 0.75) + Maximum useful life span + (Maximum useful life span × 0.75)]/5	

Period. The total cost of a security feature, function, or control is composed of three major cost components: (1) one-time direct costs, (2) one-time indirect costs, and (3) recurring indirect costs. The first section of Table 5.3 captures the one-time direct costs. These are the costs that are incurred up-front when a security control is initially acquired. Items such as the purchase price, sales, use, or value-added tax, and shipping or delivery charges form the one-time direct costs. After the new security control is received, but prior to full deployment, a combination of one-time indirect costs are incurred. These include items such as installation costs (vendor and in-house) and training for end users and operations and maintenance staff. These costs are recorded in the second section of Table 5.3. After deployment there are a series of annual recurring indirect costs associated with owning and operating the security control throughout its useful life span. Recurring indirect costs include items such as I/O devices, cables, and connectors needed to operate the device, licenses and vendor support, telecommunications, spare parts that are kept on-site, expendables such as disks, paper and toner, electricity, and of course, the labor costs for the operations and maintenance staff.

The total recurring indirect costs cannot be computed until the depreciation period is determined. So we need to shift to Part III of Table 5.3. The depreciation period is expressed in months because most security controls have a very short useful life span. A minimum and maximum useful life span are estimated, with input from vendors — after all, they know the planned evolution of the product line. Then, the most likely useful life span is calculated using the formula given in Part III of Table 5.3.

The total recurring indirect costs can be calculated two ways:

(1) = Annual recurring indirect costs × (Most likely useful life span/12)
(2) = Annual recurring indirect costs × (Maximum useful life span/12)

Organizations that tend to have frequent technology upgrade cycles should use the most likely useful life span. Organizations that always find themselves behind the technology upgrade curve and short on security funds may be more comfortable using the maximum useful life span. Once an organization decides which approach is best for them, the total recurring indirect costs are calculated and recorded in Section 4 of Table 5.3.

The final step is to calculate the total cost of the security control. This total represents the sum of the one-time direct costs, the one-time indirect costs, and the total recurring indirect costs. This value is recorded in Section 5 of Table 5.3.

Part IV — Tangible Benefits

Table 5.4 presents a worksheet for Part IV of a security ROI analysis — Tangible Benefits. Tangible benefits are composed of three major cost components: (1) the total cost of the losses prevented, (2) fines avoided, and (3) liability lawsuits avoided. Tangible benefits emphasize the preventive aspect of security controls by chaining together all the events and losses prevented.

The total cost of losses prevented captures the loss elements the organization would experience if the security control were not implemented. Three main categories of loss elements are evaluated: losses related to asset damage, losses related to the inability to perform the organization's mission, and other related costs. This is often referred to as the operational cost of failure.[194]

Asset damage can take three forms; usually an organization will experience a combination of all three following a security incident. Some assets will be temporarily damaged, but can be recovered in less than 24 hours. In this case, the cost of asset damage is limited to restoral and recovery costs, such as labor and replacement parts. In other instances, an asset may be damaged to the point where it is not useable; however, it can be recovered. The recovery period takes longer than 24 hours, so a temporary replacement or workaround is needed. The cost of asset damage would include the labor and replacement parts to restore the original unit, as well as the costs associated with the temporary replacement or workaround. The worst scenario is when an asset is totally destroyed or stolen. This is a common situation when sensitive data is the target of cyber crime. Stolen data cannot be retrieved. Data that is completely corrupted is not recoverable; the data will have to be regenerated from backups. As a result, the cost of asset damage includes the value of the assets that were stolen or destroyed, the cost of replacing the assets, and the labor involved. The cost of asset damage for all three scenarios is recorded in Section 1 of Table 5.4. The projected losses, for both best-case and worst-case scenarios are captured, along with the time interval or duration in which the loss is experienced. Redundant or diverse equipment may be in place for high criticality assets. If the specific risk being evaluated is expected to damage the redundant or diverse equipment too, those costs should also be reflected.

The losses experienced as a result of an organization not being able to perform its mission are evaluated next. There are a variety of factors to consider. An immediate impact is lost worker productivity. If the IT infrastructure or parts of it are down, most employees will not be able to perform their job or at least all of it. Long lunches, chatting in the hallway, or leaving early will become the order of the day. Following suit are lost business opportunities. If the IT infrastructure (or part of it) is down, customers and business partners may not be able to reach an organization. Customers will most likely just go to another source. Business partners may wait a little longer, but eventually they have their own deadlines to meet and will end up going elsewhere too.

Asset damage may cause an organization to be transitioned to degraded mode operations — in which case some types of transactions will not be allowed, while those that are allowed will take longer. Delays in completing business transactions can also be a source of losses. Perhaps a proposal was due at noon, but the organization was unable to submit it until 3:30 p.m. Most likely, the proposal will be rejected. Perhaps as a result of degraded mode operations there is a delay in submitting or receiving an order. A delay in submitting an order could result in higher prices. A delay in receiving an order could result in an unhappy customer (best case) or the order being canceled (worst case). Similarly, invoices are late or cannot be submitted; nor can revenue be collected electronically. The loss of sensitive information may result in lost market share or loss of a competitive advantage. These and other situations, caused by an organization's inability to perform its mission, all translate into lost income. Again, the losses are projected for both a best-case and a worst-case scenario and recorded in Section 2 of Table 5.4. The loss duration corresponds to that of the asset damage that caused the loss.

An organization can experience other losses as a result of the asset damage caused by a security incident. For example, if one facility, system, or network is shut down, there will be a ripple effect on the rest of the organization and the losses will compound. This ripple effect is analogous to the ripple effect that airlines experience when one major airport has a weather delay. Soon other airports are also in a delay situation. The longer the delay at the original airport, the more airports are impacted by the delay and the longer the delay experienced. End users and operations and maintenance staff may need to be retrained in response to the temporary or permanent replacement assets. Perhaps something has changed in the command sequence or user interface. If the asset damage is significant and recovery and restoral times are expected to be lengthy, the organization may need to switch to its backup site. Unless the backup site is fully staffed and fully operational, there are considerable costs involved in activating it — for starters, transportation costs to get all the staff there. Other losses will be incurred as well, losses that are directly tied to an organization's mission. Best-case and worst-case losses are captured, along with the loss duration.

If an organization has cyber security insurance or another form of indemnity that covers these situations, the losses may be offset by the insurance payment, minus the allocable portion of the insurance premium. If not, it might be time for the organization to reconsider its standing on this issue. Then, all of the loss elements are summed to determine the total cost of the losses prevented under both best-case and worst-case scenarios.

The second category of tangible benefits is the fines that an organization avoids by employing the security control. Fines can be imposed by regulatory agencies operating at the municipal, state, federal, and international levels for failure to comply with security and privacy provisions, such as those discussed in Chapter 3. Sometimes the fines are a fixed amount. Other times the fines are proportional to the amount of damage caused. Major fines make the news and generate negative publicity, which impacts the confidence of customers, investors, and business partners in the organization's security and privacy

Table 5.4   Security ROI Worksheet, Part IV: Tangible Benefits

Part IV: Tangible Benefits		
1. Total cost of losses prevented		
Loss Element	*Best-Case Duration[a]/Loss*	*Worst-Case Duration[a]/Loss*
a. Asset Damage:		
Assets damaged, but recoverable		
Unusable assets, recoverable but temporary replacements needed		
Unrecoverable assets, permanent replacements needed (assets totally destroyed or stolen)		
b. Inability to Perform Organization's Mission:		
Lost worker productivity		
Lost business opportunities		
Losses due to delays in completing business transactions		
Inability to submit invoices or collect revenue		
Loss or compromise of sensitive information		
Losses due to shutdown of telecommunications, application, or process control systems		
Lost income		
Other		
c. Other Related Costs:		
Concomitant losses experienced by other parts of the organization		
Retraining		
Cost of activating backup site		
Other		
d. Offsets:		
Insurance or indemnity payment, minus cost of allocable insurance premium	( )	( )
e. Subtotal		

[a] Need to define loss duration period.

Table 5.4   Security ROI Worksheet, Part IV: Tangible Benefits (continued)

2. Fines avoided		
Source of Fine	*Best-Case Time Interval[a]/Fines*	*Worst-Case Time Interval[a]/Fines*
a. Regulatory Fines:		
Municipal		
State		
National		
International		
b. Cost to Restore License(s) Revoked by the Fines:		
c. Contractual Fines:		
Contract A		
Contract B		
Contract C		
d. Subtotal		

[a] Need to define time frame the fine applies to, especially in the case of recurring fines.

3. Liability lawsuits avoided				
	Best Case		*Worst Case*	
Litigants	*Settlement Amount[a]*	*Legal and Court Costs[a]*	*Settlement Amount[a]*	*Legal and Court Costs[a]*
Litigant 1				
Litigant 2				
Litigant 3				
Subtotal				

[a] Litigation usually takes several years. However, the settlement, legal, and court costs (or loss) are applied to the year that the loss event took place.

4. Increased operational efficiency		
Savings in operational costs, including labor, from increased operational efficiency as a result of deploying the security control		
5. Total		
Total tangible benefits for the loss duration period	*Best Case*	*Worst Case*
= Total cost of losses prevented, fines avoided, and liability lawsuits avoided + Savings from increased operational efficiency		

controls. This aspect is explored in relation to Table 5.5. In some instances, the fact that an organization has been fined can also result in certain business licenses being revoked. The lack of a license can impede the ability of an organization to participate in certain business activities, resulting in a loss of revenue until the license is restored. Fines may have other conditions associated with them as well, such as a requirement to have an independent security audit annually for the next x years. These conditions equate to increased costs. The scope of the loss from regulatory fines is rather broad and includes costs such as the amount of the fines, the additional costs incurred as a result of conditions attached to the fine (or settlement to avoid the fine), costs related to restoring a business license that was revoked as part of the fine, and revenue lost due to the fine or revoked business license. These costs are recorded in Section 2 of Table 5.4 for both best-case and worst-case scenarios. Some organizations are subject to multiple regulations, such as the HIPAA and Sarbanes-Oxley Act. If adequate planning and analysis are performed, the organization may be able to deploy a single security control, such as accountability, and satisfy requirements of more than one regulation. If so, Table 5.4 should account for the fines avoided under all applicable regulations. Contracts also include fines for security violations, the loss, compromise or corruption of data, and unavailable IT services. These fines should also be recorded. A loss duration period should be defined for each of the fines, because some fines are one-time events while others recur on a regular basis until the deficiency is corrected. Finally, all the fines are summed to highlight the total cost of the fines avoided by implementing the security control.

The third category of tangible benefits is the liability lawsuits that are avoided. Failure to exercise due diligence and due care in regard to security and privacy controls can lead to a liability lawsuit. Rarely is only one person involved. Instead, usually thousands are affected by a single security incident. So, the liability lawsuits being avoided are expensive class action lawsuits. Consider the following example. A Fortune 500 organization decides not to deploy a security control that has a total life-cycle cost of $250,000 because it is "too expensive" (not because it does not have technical merit). The foreseeable result is a security breach that results in the theft of sensitive personal and financial information of 25,000 individuals. The regulatory authorities determine that the organization was negligent and fines them. The next day a major law firm files a class action lawsuit seeking $6000 in compensatory damages per individual ($6000 being the average cost to recover from identity theft) and $9000 in punitive damages per individual because the organization was negligent and should have known better. The lawsuit costs the organization:

$$\frac{\begin{array}{l} 25{,}000 \ \text{individuals} \\ \times \ (\$6000 + \$9000) \ \text{compensatory and punitive damages} \end{array}}{\$375{,}000{,}000 \ \text{settlement}}$$

In addition, legal fees and courts costs, which are not insignificant, are added to the settlement. It will be difficult for the organization to wiggle out of the lawsuit because the regulatory authorities found them negligent. Maybe that $250,000 security control is not so expensive after all....

The costs of potential liability lawsuits — including the settlement, legal fees, and court costs — are recorded in Section 3 of Table 5.4.

In summary, the total tangible benefits from deploying a security control equals the sum of the total losses prevented, total fines avoided, total liability lawsuits avoided, and increased operational efficiency over a uniform loss duration period. This information is recorded in Section 5 of Table 5.4.

Part V — Intangible Benefits

Table 5.5 presents a worksheet for Part V of a security ROI analysis — Intangible Benefits. Intangible benefits consist of five major cost components: the impact on the OMER of would-be attackers, customer confidence, investor confidence, business partner confidence, and employee morale.

The purpose of deploying security controls is to make the OMER such that it is impractical, infeasible, and too expensive for a would-be attacker to successfully exploit a given vulnerability. As a result, the impact a security control has on the OMER of a would-be attacker is a significant intangible benefit. The resilience metrics in Chapter 4 provide the input necessary for the OMER impact analysis.

Opportunity is evaluated first. That is, to what extent does the security control reduce the opportunity for a would-be attacker to exploit a vulnerability? Opportunity is assessed before and after the security control is deployed to determine its benefit. Opportunity correlates to likelihood; hence, the same standard six categories defined for likelihood in Chapter 2 are used for opportunity. Likelihood registers the notion that a would-be attacker is likely to try an exploit and is successful, while opportunity registers the notion that the opportunity exists for a would-be attacker to initiate an exploit and because of that the would-be attacker is likely to try the exploit. In essence, opportunity is a prerequisite for likelihood. The difference between the "before" opportunity and the "after" opportunity, expressed in orders of magnitude, represents the benefit derived from the security control. To achieve any benefit, the "after" opportunity must be at least one order of magnitude less than the "before" opportunity. To contribute to effective mitigation of the specific risk, the "after" opportunity must be one order of magnitude less than the annual likelihood recorded in Section 3 of Table 5.2. The delta between likelihood and "after" opportunity is referred to as the degree of positive (or negative) compensation, or the security margin.

Expertise is evaluated next using the five standard categories shown in Table 5.5. The first step is to determine who the most likely would-be attackers are and their level of expertise. Then the expertise required before the security control is deployed is assessed. Following that, the expertise required after the security control is deployed is assessed. The difference between the "before" expertise and the "after" expertise represents the benefit derived from the security control. To contribute to effective mitigation of this specific risk,

Table 5.5   Security ROI Worksheet — Part V: Intangible Benefits

1. Impact on OMER of would-be attackers	
a. Opportunity: frequent – 0, probable – 9, occasional – 18, remote – 27, improbable – 40, incredible – 60	
Opportunity before deploying security control	
Opportunity after deploying security control	
Annual likelihood from Table 5.2	
Degree of positive (or negative) compensation	
b. Expertise: ultra high – 60, high – 30, medium – 15, low – 7, none – 0	
Most likely would-be attackers	
Expertise of most likely would-be attackers	
Expertise required before deploying security control	
Expertise required after deploying security control	
Degree of positive (or negative) compensation	
Impact if expertise required after deployment is same or less than that of would-be attackers	
c. Resources: ultra high – 60, high – 30, medium – 15, low – 7, none – 0	
Most likely would-be attackers	
Resources available to would-be attackers	
Resources required before deploying security control	
Resources required after deploying security control	
Duration that resources are needed	
Degree of positive (or negative) compensation	
Impact if resources required after deployment are same or less than that of would-be attackers	
d. Summary of OMER impact (minimum – 0, maximum – 420)	
= ((Opportunity after × 4) + (Expertise after × 2) + (Resources after))/ ((Opportunity before × 4) + (Expertise before × 2) + (Resources before))	
= ((Opportunity after × 4) + (Expertise after × 2) + (Resources after))/ ((Opportunity before × 4) + (Expertise of most likely would-be attackers × 2) + (Resources of most likely would-be attackers))	
2. Customer confidence: high – 25, medium – 16, low – 8, none – 0	
a. Customer confidence in organization's security controls and practices	
b. Customer confidence in organization's privacy controls and practices	
c. Customer confidence that organization is serious about security	

Table 5.5   Security ROI Worksheet — Part V: Intangible Benefits (continued)

d. Customer confidence that organization is concerned about customer privacy	
e. Estimated revenue lost in the past 12 months due to lack of customer confidence (accounts closed, deposits withdrawn early, lost purchases, etc.)	
f. Percentage (%) of total income or revenue, from last annual report, that originates from customers	
g. Revenue protected by customer confidence in security and privacy controls = (((a + b + c + d)/100) × f)	
h. Revenue at risk of loss due to lack of customer confidence = ((100 − (a + b + c + d)/100) × f	
3. Investor confidence: high − 25, medium − 16, low − 8, none − 0	
a. Investor confidence in organization's security controls and practices	
b. Investor confidence in organization's privacy controls and practices	
c. Investor confidence that organization is serious about security	
d. Investor confidence that organization is concerned about privacy	
e. Estimated revenue lost in the past 12 months due to lack of investor confidence (capital withheld, withdrawn funds, premature sales of investments, etc.)	
f. Percentage (%) of total income or revenue, from last annual report, that originates from investors	
g. Revenue protected by investor confidence in security and privacy controls = (((a + b + c + d)/100) × f)	
h. Revenue at risk of loss due to lack of investor confidence = ((100 − (a + b + c + d)/100) × f	
4. Business partners confidence: high − 25, medium − 16, low − 8, none − 0	
a. Business partner confidence in organization's security controls and practices	
b. Business partner confidence in organization's privacy controls and practices	
c. Business partner confidence that organization is serious about security	
d. Business partner confidence that organization is concerned about privacy	
e. Estimated revenue lost in the past 12 months due to lack of business partner confidence (contracts canceled, cost of establishing new contracts and suppliers, increased cost of business services, etc.)	
f. Percentage (%) of total income or revenue, from last annual report, that originates from business partners	

Table 5.5   Security ROI Worksheet — Part V: Intangible Benefits (continued)

g. Revenue protected by business partner confidence in security and privacy controls = (((a + b + c + d)/100) × f)	
h. Revenue at risk of loss due to lack of business partner confidence = ((100 − (a + b + c + d)/100) x f	
5. Employee morale: high − 20, medium − 15, low − 7, none − 0	
a. Employee confidence in organization's security controls and practices	
b. Employee confidence in organization's privacy controls and practices	
c. Employee confidence that senior executives are serious about security	
d. Employee confidence that senior executives are serious about protecting the privacy of sensitive personal and financial information	
e. Employee confidence that senior executives welcome suggestions about how to improve the organization's security and privacy controls and practices	
f. Total number of IT and security engineering staff	
g. Average salary of IT and security engineering staff	

h. Annual turnover rate of IT and security engineering staff:
   Very high: 70–100%
   High: 40–69%
   Medium: 16–39%
   Low: 0–15%	

i. Cost of turnover = (f × h) × [(g × 10%) + ((g + (g × 10%)) × (h + 100%))]	
j. Overall employee confidence level = 100 − (a + b + c + d + e)/100	
k. Productivity loss due to lack of confidence in security and privacy controls = (a + b + c + d + e)/100	
6. Summary of intangible benefits related to confidence	
= (Revenue at risk of loss due to customer lack of confidence in security and privacy controls) + (Revenue at risk due to investor lack of confidence in security and privacy controls) + (Revenue at risk of loss due to business partner lack of confidence in security and privacy controls) + (Cost of turnover) + (Productivity loss)	

the "after" expertise must be one order of magnitude higher than that the most likely would-be attackers possess. The delta between the level of expertise of the most likely would-be attackers and the "after" expertise represents the degree of positive (or negative) compensation. There may be overriding technical or financial reasons that prevent an organization from raising the expertise requirement higher than that of the most likely would-be attackers. If so, the impact of that situation should be documented, along with recommendations for other compensating measures that can be taken instead.

The final part of the OMER impact is the resources that must be available to would-be attackers for them to initiate a successful exploit. The most likely would-be attackers and the resources they are expected to have at their disposal are identified first. Resource requirements are expressed in terms of the five standard categories shown in Table 5.5. Resource requirements are assessed before and after the security control is deployed. In addition, the time interval or duration that the resources are needed is recorded. Sometimes it is more difficult to obtain resources for an extended period of time; other times it is more difficult to have everything needed available all at once. Again, the difference between the "before" and "after" resource requirements represents the benefit derived from the security control. To achieve any benefit, the "after" resource requirements must be one order of magnitude higher than the "before" resource requirements. To contribute to effective mitigation of this specific risk, the "after" resource requirements must be one order of magnitude higher than that of the most likely would-be attackers. The delta between the resource requirements of the most likely would-be attackers and the "after" resource requirements represents the degree of positive (or negative) compensation. Again, there may be overriding technical or financial reasons that prevent an organization from raising the resource requirements higher than that of the most likely would-be attackers. If so, the impact of that situation should be documented, along with recommendations for other compensating measures that can be taken instead.

Now all the pieces are put together to determine the overall impact the security control has on the OMER of would-be attackers. The overall impact is examined in two ways. First, the net benefit of the security control is examined by comparing the before and after status, using the formula in Section 1 of Table 5.5. Second, the net effectiveness of the security control in deterring the most likely would-be attackers is assessed. Both numbers are important, as the following example illustrates:

	Before	*After*	*Most Likely Would-Be Attackers*
Opportunity	36 — probable	108 — remote	36 — probable
Expertise	14 — low	120 — ultra high	60 — high
Resources	7 — low	30 — high	15 — medium
Total	**57**	**258**	**111**

The net benefit of the security control is 452 percent, while the net increase in difficulty for the would-be attackers is 232 percent. The numbers show that the security control has increased the difficulty of exploitation fourfold overall. However, there is only a twofold increase in the difficulty of exploitation by the most likely would-be attackers. There is no point in getting hung up about whether the net benefit or net increase in difficulty is 252 percent or 237 percent or 269 percent — we are only looking for orders of magnitude.

The next three sections of Table 5.5 assess confidence, specifically the level of confidence customers, investors, and business partners have in an organization's security and privacy controls and practices. Confidence is the foundation of all business transactions. Customers should have confidence in an organization's security and privacy controls or they will not use online shopping sites, credit cards, or debit cards. Investors should have confidence in an organization's security and privacy controls before they will believe any financial reports and invest their capital. Business partners should have confidence in an organization's security and privacy controls in order to be convinced that their sensitive information and IT assets will not be compromised. If customers, investors, and business partners do not have confidence in an organization's security and privacy controls, they will not interact with it and the organization will soon cease to exist.

Confidence can be measured through surveys, preferably independent surveys conducted by third parties, and by monitoring certain behaviors. The intent is to find out what customers, investors, and business partners think about the organization's security and privacy controls and how it is affecting their business transactions with that organization. A similar process is used to evaluate customer, investor, and business partner confidence, as shown in Sections 2 through 4 of Table 5.5. The thrust is to determine (1) the current level of confidence and (2) how the security control can be used to enhance this perception and correct any existing concerns. During this process, confidence is translated into an intangible benefit.

First, four areas of confidence are rated:

1. Confidence in the organization's security controls
2. Confidence in the organization's privacy controls
3. Confidence that the organization is serious about security
4. Confidence that the organization is serious about protecting the privacy of sensitive personal and financial information

Each of the four areas are weighted equally, with a maximum score of 25. A perfect overall score would then equate to 100, or a 100 percent confidence level. Next, the total revenue lost in the past 12 months due to a lack of confidence in the organization's security and privacy controls is estimated. This would include accounts that were closed abruptly, investments and deposits that were withdrawn early, a rapid decline in purchases, especially online purchases, and other sudden changes in behavior. It is acknowledged that security and privacy may not have been the only reasons behind these decisions, but they may have been the penultimate reason. Surveys and follow-up telephone calls, correspondence, and other investigations may be necessary to ferret out the real reasons behind these actions.

After that cheery news, we examine the organization's annual report to determine the percentage of total income or revenue that originates from each group: customers, investors, and business partners. It is useful to look at both the percentage and the actual dollar amount. The formula shown in item g of Sections 2, 3, and 4 is used to calculate the percentage of this revenue or income that is reasonably safe because of confidence in the organization's security and privacy controls. More importantly, item h in Sections 2, 3, and 4 highlights the percentage of revenue or income that is at risk due to a lack of confidence. A comparison between item e (estimated annual revenue or income lost due to a lack of confidence in the organization's security and privacy controls) and item h (revenue or income at risk of loss due to lack of confidence in the organization's security and privacy controls) can be helpful in detecting trends. Again, a lack of confidence in security and privacy controls may not be the only factor contributing to a loss of revenue, but it is likely to be the proverbial straw that breaks the camel's back. Why? Because a lack of security is more of an emotional issue and more likely to cause panic than lower prices or more color choices. Hence, the proposed security control has the potential to help prevent the loss of this revenue.

The fifth cost component of intangible benefits is employee morale. Sometimes organizations forget to look inside their own walls when calculating security ROI. This discussion explains why that is not a wise practice. This discussion pertains primarily to the IT and security engineering staff; however, there is a ripple effect among the general employee population. While there are many facets to employee morale, the security ROI analysis focuses on employees' confidence in the organization's security and privacy controls and practices. This assessment is similar to the process used to assess the confidence of customers, investors, and business partners, except that in this case the perception of insiders is being captured. Five areas of employee morale are examined:

1. Employee confidence in the organization's security controls
2. Employee confidence in the organization's privacy controls
3. Employee confidence that senior executives are serious about security
4. Employee confidence that senior executives are serious about protecting the privacy of sensitive personal and financial information
5. Employee confidence that senior executives welcome suggestions about how to improve the organization's security and privacy controls and practices

Each of the five items are weighted equally and has a maximum score of 20. A perfect score overall would equate to 100. Particular attention should be paid to the score for item e, because if employees are hesitant to make suggestions on how to improve security and privacy controls, soon the score in the other four areas will fall, as will the resilience of the IT infrastructure. This information can be collected through anonymous mail-in surveys, online surveys, focus groups, and other forums. It is essential that, whatever format is used, employees feel comfortable in saying what they really think without fear of retribution.

Next, the number of employees who perform IT and security engineering functions on a half-time or more basis is recorded in item f. The average salary of this group of employees is recorded in item g. Then the annual turnover rate of the IT and security engineering staff is recorded in item h. This information should be readily available from the personnel department.

These primitives can be used to evaluate how employee confidence (or lack of confidence) in security and privacy controls and practices is influencing two items that impact the security ROI: (1) the turnover rate for the IT and security engineering staff, and (2) the productivity of the IT and security engineering staff. Again, there is not a one-to-one correlation. However, confidence in security and privacy controls and practices can be a major driver in both the turnover rate and productivity of the IT and security engineering staff.

The turnover rate is captured as an absolute percentage and as a qualitative label. Then the cost of the turnover is calculated using the formula in item i. Consider the following example:

f = 1000 employees in the IT and security engineering staff
g = $100,000, their average salary
h = 40 percent annual turnover
i = Cost of turnover
   = (1000 × .40) × [(100,000 × 0.10) + ((100,000 + (100,000 × 0.10)) × (0.40 + 1.00))]
   = 400 × [(10,000 + ((100,000 + (10,000)) × (1.40))]
   = 67,200,000

That is, it costs $168,000, or a loss of $68,000 per employee, to replace an employee who was making an average of $100,000 by the time recruitment costs, lost productivity, overtime to compensate for the vacancy, training and ramp-up costs, and an average 10 percent salary increase are factored in. Employees' lack of confidence in security and privacy controls and practices contributes to the organization paying $27,200,000 more per year because of turnover. In most cases, it would be cheaper to address the exiting employees' security concerns.

The productivity rate is captured using the formula shown in item h. Then the potential productivity loss due to employees' lack of confidence in the organization's security and privacy controls is calculated using the formula in item k. Consider the following example:

a = 20 = Employee confidence in security controls
b = 15 = Employee confidence in privacy controls
c = 20 = Employee confidence that senior executives are serious about security
d = 15 = Employee confidence that senior executives are serious about protecting
           the privacy of sensitive personal and financial information
e = 15 = Employee confidence that senior executives welcome suggestions about
           how to improve security and privacy controls and practices

That means that the productivity of the IT and security engineering staff is 85 percent of the maximum it could be, if they had complete confidence in the organization's security and privacy controls and practices. That is, there is a 15 percent potential productivity loss because of a slight lack of confidence in the organization's security and privacy controls on the part of the IT and security engineering staff. Consequently, enhanced security controls represent an opportunity to improve productivity.

Part VI — Payback Period

Table 5.6 presents a worksheet for Part VI of a security ROI analysis — Payback Period. The payback period represents the calendar time needed for the related profit or savings in operational costs to equal the amount of the investment.[311] The evaluation of the payback period in Part VI makes use of primitives that were collected earlier in Tables 5.3, 5.4, and 5.5. Because the payback period is a projection, three different scenarios are evaluated: the minimum, maximum, and most likely payback period. The payback period is calculated using the formula shown in item e for Sections 1 and 2 of Table 5.6. The most likely payback period is an input for Part VII of a security ROI analysis, which is discussed under Table 5.7. The following example illustrates how the payback period is calculated.

Minimum Payback Period
- a. 175 = One-time direct costs + One-time indirect costs
- b. 50 = Annual recurring indirect costs
- c. 75 = Annual best-case tangible benefits
- d. 60 = Annual best-case intangible benefits
- e. Payback period = (a)/((c + d) − b) = 1.5 years

Maximum Payback Period
- a. 175 = One-time direct costs + One-time indirect costs
- b. 50 = Annual recurring indirect costs
- c. 50 = Annual worst-case tangible benefits
- d. 40 = Annual worst-case intangible benefits
- e. Payback period = (a)/((c + d) − b) = 3.1 years

Most Likely Payback Period
= ((1.5 × 1.25) + 1.5 + (3.1 × .75) + (3.1 × 2))/5
= 2.4 years

Part VII — Comparative Analysis

Table 5.7 presents a worksheet for Part VII of a security ROI analysis — Comparative Analysis. The comparative analysis is composed of two major cost components: (1) a comparison to the cost of doing nothing and (2) a comparison to the cost of alternate approaches. The purpose of the comparative analysis is to determine which of the technically acceptable security solutions is the best solution economically. The comparative analysis looks at both best-case and worst-case scenarios. For the most part, the comparative analysis makes use of primitives that were collected in previous worksheets.

To start, the severity and likelihood from Table 5.2 are recorded in items a and b. The accessibility of the vulnerability is also captured. Accessibility has a direct impact on the opportunity of would-be attackers and, hence, security ROI. Accessibility is an important consideration should an organization determine that doing nothing is the preferable approach. Next, the total cost of the security feature, function, or control and the most likely useful life span

Table 5.6   Security ROI Worksheet — Part VI: Payback Period

1. Minimum payback period	
a. One-time direct costs + One-time indirect costs (from Table 5.3)	
b. Annual recurring indirect costs (from Table 5.3)	
c. Annual best-case tangible benefits (from Table 5.4)	
d. Annual best-case intangible benefits (from Table 5.5)	
e. Payback period = (One-time direct costs + One-time indirect costs)/((Annual best-case tangible benefits + Annual best-case intangible benefits) – Annual recurring indirect costs)[311] = (a)/((c + d) - b)[311]	
2. Maximum payback period	
a. One-time direct costs + One-time indirect costs (from Table 5.3)	
b. Annual recurring indirect costs (from Table 5.3)	
c. Annual worst-case tangible benefits (from Table 5.4)	
d. Annual worst-case intangible benefits (from Table 5.5)	
e. Payback period = (One-time direct costs + One-time indirect costs)/((Annual worst-case tangible benefits + Annual worst-case intangible benefits) – Annual recurring indirect costs)[311] = (a)/((c + d) − b)[311]	
3. Most likely payback period	
= [(Minimum payback period × 1.25) + Minimum payback period + (Maximum payback period × 0.75) + (Maximum payback period × 2)]/5	

Table 5.7   Security ROI Worksheet — Part VII: Comparative Analysis

	Best Case	Worst Case
1. To the cost of doing nothing		
a. Severity of consequences from Table 5.2		
b. Likelihood of vulnerability being exploited within 12 months from Table 5.2		
c. Accessibility of the vulnerability		
d. Total cost of security feature, function, or control from Table 5.3		
e. Most likely useful life span from Table 5.3		
f. Total annual tangible benefits from Table 5.4		
g. Total annual intangible benefits from Table 5.5		

Table 5.7 Security ROI Worksheet — Part VII: Comparative Analysis (continued)

h. Cost of doing nothing = ((Annual tangible benefits + Annual intangible benefits) x (Most likely useful life span/12))[a] = (f + g) × (e/12)		
i. Benefit of deploying security control = ((Annual tangible benefits + Annual intangible benefits) × (Most likely useful life span/12)) − Total cost of security feature, function, or control = ((f + g) × (e/12)) − d = h − d		

[a] Substitute time frame the vulnerability is allowed to remain open, if vulnerability will be mitigated prior to end of useful life span of the security control.

2. To the cost of alternate approaches	Option A		Option B		Option C	
	Best Case	*Worst Case*	*Best Case*	*Worst Case*	*Best Case*	*Worst Case*
a. Total cost of security feature, function, or control from Table 5.3						
b. Total annual tangible benefits from Table 5.4						
c. Total annual intangible benefits from Table 5.5						
d. Most likely useful life span from Table 5.3						
e. Most likely payback period from Table 5.6						
f. Net benefit of security control = ((Annual tangible benefits + Annual intangible benefits) × (Most likely useful life span/12)) − Total cost of security feature, function, or control = ((b + c) × (d//12)) − a						

are pulled from Table 5.3. Likewise, the total tangible and intangible benefits are captured from Tables 5.4 and 5.5, respectively.

Using this information, the cost of doing nothing can be calculated using the formula shown in item h. In essence, the cost of doing nothing represents a loss of the tangible and intangible benefits over the life span of the security control. The asset damage, losses due to an inability to perform the organization's mission, and other losses, such as fines and liability lawsuits, will not be prevented due to the absence of the security control. The OMER of would-be attackers will not be restricted and the confidence of customers, investors, and business partners will not be enhanced. An organization should be aware of these facts before making a decision to assume the risk.

Note that the formula in item h makes use of the most likely useful life span. The assumption is that the vulnerability will remain unmitigated through what would have been the useful life span of the security control. If, however, the vulnerability will only be allowed to remain open for a short period of time, that time frame should be used in the calculation instead of the most likely useful life span.

Finally, the cost of doing nothing is compared to the cost of implementing the security control. The total cost of the security feature, function, or control is subtracted from the total tangible and intangible benefits over the life span of the security control, as shown in item i. If the result is a positive number, the benefits from implementing the security control outweigh its cost. If the result is a negative number, the cost of the security control is higher than the cost of doing nothing. The following example illustrates this process:

d = $125,000 = Total cost of security control
e = 48 months = Most likely useful life span
f = $75,000 = Annual tangible benefits
g = $50,000 = Annual intangible benefits
h = $500,000 = Cost of doing nothing
i = $375,000 = Benefit from deploying the security control

That is, the organization will have $375,000 more in its pocket at the end of the four-year period (e) if it deploys the security control than it will if it does nothing.

A similar process is followed in Section 2 of Table 5.7 to compare the cost of alternate security solutions. The total cost of each security solution is captured in item a. The annual tangible and intangible benefits from each approach are recorded next, as is the most likely useful life span. Unlike the comparison to the cost of doing nothing, the payback period is captured for each alternative. The payback period may be an important consideration for organizations that want to see a quick return. Then the net benefit of each security control is calculated using the formula in item f. In essence, the total tangible and intangible benefits of the security control over its useful life span are compared to the total cost of owning and operating the security control over its useful life span. A positive result indicates a net benefit from implementing the security control. A negative result indicates that the security control costs more than the benefits it provides. At this point, an organization can compare the payback period and net benefit of the alternate security approaches to determine which best meets its needs.

Part VIII — Assumptions

Table 5.8 presents a worksheet for Part VIII of a security ROI analysis — Assumptions. Part VIII is not used in the security ROI calculations unless a sensitivity analysis is performed. Instead, Part VIII forms an important part of a security ROI analysis by completing the historical record and documenting

Table 5.8 Security ROI Worksheet — Part VIII: Assumptions

1. IT Infrastructure (as of date: _____)

Assumption	*Part of ROI Analysis Impacted*	*Confidence Level in Assumption (high, medium, low, none)*	*Effect on ROI Analysis if Assumption Is Wrong*	*Events or Changes that Could Invalidate the Assumption*
Assumption 1				
Assumption 2				
Assumption N				

2. Operational Environment (as of date: _____)

Assumption	*Part of ROI Analysis Impacted*	*Confidence Level in Assumption (high, medium, low, none)*	*Effect on ROI Analysis if Assumption Is Wrong*	*Events or Changes that Could Invalidate the Assumption*
Assumption 1				
Assumption 2				
Assumption N				

3. Operational Profile and Duty Cycle (as of date: _____)

Assumption	*Part of ROI Analysis Impacted*	*Confidence Level in Assumption (high, medium, low, none)*	*Effect on ROI Analysis if Assumption Is Wrong*	*Events or Changes that Could Invalidate the Assumption*
Assumption 1				
Assumption 2				
Assumption N				

4. Resilience Levels (as of date: _____)

Assumption	*Part of ROI Analysis Impacted*	*Confidence Level in Assumption (high, medium, low, none)*	*Effect on ROI Analysis if Assumption Is Wrong*	*Events or Changes that Could Invalidate the Assumption*
Assumption 1				
Assumption 2				
Assumption N				

Table 5.8   Security ROI Worksheet — Part VIII: Assumptions (continued)

5. Pricing Structures *(as of date: _____)*				
Assumption	*Part of ROI Analysis Impacted*	*Confidence Level in Assumption (high, medium, low, none)*	*Effect on ROI Analysis if Assumption Is Wrong*	*Events or Changes that Could Invalidate the Assumption*
Assumption 1				
Assumption 2				
Assumption N				

6. Other				
Assumption	*Part of ROI Analysis Impacted*	*Confidence Level in Assumption (high, medium, low, none)*	*Effect on ROI Analysis if Assumption Is Wrong*	*Events or Changes that Could Invalidate the Assumption*
Assumption 1				
Assumption 2				
Assumption N				

the assumptions upon which various decisions and estimates were made. Table 5.8 lists five categories of assumptions related to security ROI analysis: assumptions related to the IT infrastructure, operational environment, operational profile, duty cycle, and pricing structure. There may be several other categories of assumptions, depending on the situation being evaluated.

Five classes of information should be captured about each assumption. First, of course, is the assumption itself. State the assumption as clearly and completely as possible. Next, indicate what part of the security ROI analysis this assumption relates to: the worksheet or Part, the Section, and item(s). Make the reference as detailed as possible in order to provide complete traceability. Then the level of confidence in the assumption is recorded as high, medium, low, or none. Sometimes a project team finds itself in the position of having to make an assumption when there are not a lot of concrete facts to go on. It is best to be honest and say that the team did the best it could under the circumstances, but the level of confidence in the assumption is low. There are no instances in the world of security engineering when painting an overly rosy picture is a good idea. Continuing with the honesty and openness theme, the fourth category of information captured is an indication of how the security ROI analysis would be affected if the assumption turns out to be wrong. Sometimes assumptions are correct. Sometimes assumptions are almost right. Other times, assumptions are totally wrong. What happens to the security ROI analysis in the third case? Is the security ROI analysis off by 5 percent, 50 percent, or 500 percent? What needs to be recalculated? The fifth category of information lists events or changes that could invalidate an otherwise perfectly good assumption. In the unpredictable world we live in, things do not always happen as planned. Budgets are slashed in half. At the same time, the end-user population and traffic volume doubles. A product that was supposed to be available in March is not released until November. The interface to the security control now requires a different protocol. This is the place to capture dependencies on external events and dependencies between assumptions. After this information is complete, it is a good idea to revisit the confidence level. The next challenge is keeping the assumptions current.

Security ROI analysis is a bottom-up exercise. After collecting the primitives and generating the preceding eight worksheets, security ROI reports can be generated. Conversely, security ROI reports cannot be generated, at least not accurate ones, until after the primitives defined above have been collected and analyzed through the preceding eight worksheets. Many earlier attempts at security ROI analysis got off track because they prematurely jumped into defining metrics without taking the time to consider or analyze: (1) what the pertinent primitives are, and (2) where the primitives are derived from.

To keep the security ROI report straightforward, three items that are usually part of cost analyses have been purposely omitted. It was determined that these three items, while complicating the calculations, did not add any real value to the thrust of the analysis — determining which of the technically feasible security solutions is best economically. (It is assumed that the security ROI analysis is preceded by a technical evaluation of alternate security solutions using the resilience metrics in Chapter 4.) Hence, no distinction is made between equity capital and borrowed capital. The analysis reflects a before-tax analysis, not an after-tax analysis. And the time value of money has been ignored. It is common practice in life-cycle cost models to add a percentage increase per year to compensate for inflation, the consumer price index, etc. However, because the same percentage would be added to the annual recurring costs and the annual recurring benefits, there is no point in going through this exercise.

Several ROI models are commonly used when decisions are based solely on profit motives, such as the internal rate of return (IRR), external rate of return (ERR), and explicit reinvestment rate of return (ERRR). When profit is not a primary motive and a combination of tangible and intangible benefits accrue, a cost-benefit analysis is more appropriate.[311] That is, what is the equivalence between the worth of the anticipated benefits and the estimated costs?[311] Often, the benefits accrue to end users, customers, taxpayers, and others, not necessarily the organization that purchased the security control. However, as shown in the analysis of intangible benefits, when benefits that third parties expect do not accrue, the organization may experience losses.

Because security ROI analysis relies on estimates for the total cost of the security feature, function, or control, tangible benefits, intangible benefits, and depreciation period, it is best to use more than one analytical method.[311] That is the same reason that most worksheets capture a best case and a worst case, or a minimum, maximum, and most likely value. We are not looking for an exact measure of security ROI, but rather a range. That is why security ROI is calculated using three different calculations for both best-case and worst-case scenarios. In addition, the payback period is analyzed.

The three standard security ROI calculations are shown below. In essence, they compare benefits to costs. All three calculations yield a ratio of benefits to costs. All three will be illustrated using the following primitives, which were used earlier under the discussion of Part VII, the comparison to the cost of doing nothing.

a = $75,000 = Annual tangible benefits
b = $50,000 = Annual intangible benefits
c = $15,000 = Annual recurring costs
d = $40,000 = One-time direct costs
e = $25,000 = One-time indirect costs
f = 48 months = Most likely useful life span

Ratio 1 = [((Annual tangible benefits + Annual intangible benefits) × Most likely useful life span) − ((One-time direct costs + One-time indirect costs) + (Annual recurring indirect costs × Most likely useful life span))]/ ((One-time direct costs + One-time indirect costs) + (Annual recurring indirect costs × Most likely useful life span))
    = [((a + b) × f) − ((d + e) + (c × f))]/((d + e) + (c × f))
    = 375/125
    = 3.0 with intangible benefits
    = 1.4 without intangible benefits
    = 2.2 average

Ratio 2 = (Annual tangible benefits + Annual intangible benefits)/[((One-time direct costs + One-time indirect costs)/Most likely useful life span) + Annual recurring costs]
    = (a + b)/[((d + e)/f) + c]
    = (75,000 + 50,000)/[((40,000 + 25,000)/4) + 15,000]
    = 125,000/31,250
    = 4.0 with intangible benefits
    = 2.4 without intangible benefits
    = 3.2 average

Ratio 3 = ((Annual tangible benefits + Annual intangible benefits) − Annual recurring costs)/((One-time direct costs + One time indirect costs)/ Most likely useful life span)
    = ((a + b) − c)/((d + e)/f)
    = ((75,000 + 50,000) − 15,000)/((40,000 + 25,000)/4)
    = 110,000/16,250
    = 6.76 with intangible benefits
    = 3.69 without intangible benefits
    = 5.22 average

The goal in all three cases is to demonstrate that the security solution is acceptable because the ratio of benefits to costs is greater than 1.0.[311] The ratio is calculated twice, including and excluding the intangible benefits. Then the two ratios are averaged. This step is performed because the estimate for intangible benefits is softer than that for tangible benefits. Again, we are not looking for exact measurements. Ratios 1 and 2 tend to be closer to the mark and are good for rank ordering alternatives. Remember that the calculations should be repeated using both best-case and worst-case tangible and intangible benefits. In addition, sometimes it is useful to repeat the calculations for minimum and maximum useful life spans as well.

A one-page summary report is then created for senior executives and other decision makers. The intent is to put everything they need to know in order to make a decision on one page, and use the worksheets as backup data.

Table 5.9 illustrates the format of a security ROI analysis summary report, continuing the previous example. The report captures the incremental and cumulative benefit of a security control over its useful life span. The first column lists the years of the security control's life span. In this example, the most likely useful life span is shown. It may be useful to show also the minimum and maximum useful life spans. If the actual useful life span turns out to be longer than the most likely useful life span, more benefits will accrue. If the actual useful life span is closer to the minimum useful life span, less benefits will accrue. The second column records the initial investment, which is the sum of the one-time direct costs and the one-time indirect costs. Normally this investment occurs during the first year. The third column records the annual tangible benefits that are estimated to accrue throughout the life of the security control. Be sure to indicate whether these are the best-case or worst-case tangible benefits. The fourth column records the annual intangible benefits that are estimated to accrue throughout the life of the security control. Again, be sure to indicate whether the estimate is for the best case or worst case. The same scenario should be used for both tangible and intangible benefits. The fifth column records the annual recurring indirect costs. Then the incremental benefit and cumulative benefit are calculated with and without the intangible benefits. Additional summary information is captured on the bottom of the report, such as the payback period and the three cost-benefit ratios. This information can also be presented graphically as shown in Figure 5.2.

An important part of security ROI analysis is examining the impact of the security control on the OMER of the most likely would-be attackers. Often it is easier to communicate this information graphically. As shown in Figure 5.3, four scenarios are evaluated. Graph 1.a. compares the opportunity to exploit a vulnerability before and after the security control is implemented to highlight the net benefit. Graph 1.b. compares the expertise required to exploit a vulnerability before and after the security control is implemented to highlight the net benefit. This information is also compared to the expertise of the most likely would-be attackers to discern the increased difficulty of vulnerability exploitation. Graph 1.c. compares the resources required to exploit a vulnerability before and after the security control is implemented to highlight the net benefit. A comparison is also made to the level of resources the most likely would-be attackers are expected to have at their disposal. Graph 1.d. summarizes the impact the security control has on the OMER of would-be attackers. The overall impact is assessed with and without the security control implemented. All the information for these graphs comes from Section 1 of Table 5.5. The OMER impact is compared to the resilience level needed, as

Table 5.9   Security ROI Analysis Summary Report

Year End	Initial Investment (d + e)	Annual Tangible Benefits (a)	Annual Intangible Benefits (b)	Annual Recurring Costs (c)	Incremental Benefit with Intangible Benefits (a + b + c + d + e)	Incremental Benefit without Intangible Benefits (a + c + d + e)	Cumulative Benefit with Intangible Benefits	Cumulative Benefit without Intangible Benefits
1	$(65,000)	$75,000	$50,000	$(15,000)	$45,000	$(5,000)	$45,000	$(5,000)
2		$75,000	$50,000	$(15,000)	$110,000	$60,000	$155,000	$55,000
3		$75,000	$50,000	$(15,000)	$110,000	$60,000	$265,000	$115,000
4[a]		$75,000	$50,000	$(15,000)	$110,000	$60,000	$375,000	$175,000
5		$75,000	$50,000	$(15,000)	$110,000	$60,000	$485,000	$235,000
Payback Period					7 months	13 months		
Benefit-Cost Ratios			Average					
(1)			2.2		3.0	1.4		
(2)			3.2		4.0	2.4		
(3)			5.2		6.76	3.69		

[a] Most likely useful life span 48 months.

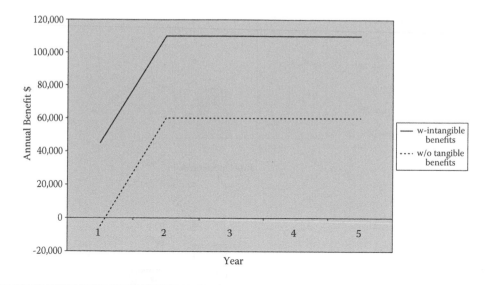

Figure 5.2   Security ROI analysis summary.

specified in Table 5.2. The summary OMER impact should correspond to the level of resilience needed. If an ultra high resilience level is needed, the score for the summary OMER impact should also be ultra high. As part of the comparative analysis, it is useful to compare the OMER graphs of alternate approaches to highlight which approach restricts the OMER of would-be attackers the most and then relate this to the total life-cycle costs. The following scales can be used to correlate the resilience level needed and the summary OMER impact:

	OMER Impact	Resilience Level Needed
Ultra high	336–420	565–720
High	252–365	409–564
Medium	168–251	253–408
Low	84–167	97–252
None	0–83	0–96

The security ROI model presented in Section 5.2 and the primitives, worksheets, metrics reports, and graphs discussed in this section are applicable to all four types of security controls. There are, however, certain considerations to keep in mind.

The risk mitigation allocation, item 5 in Table 5.2, is an important consideration when calculating security ROI. Be sure to clarify the extent to which each security control, or collection of security controls, mitigates the specified risk. The total risk mitigation allocation from all security controls assigned to mitigate a specific risk cannot exceed 100 percent. The total tangible and intangible benefits should then be scaled to represent the percent mitigation. That is, if the risk mitigation allocation of a given security control equals 75

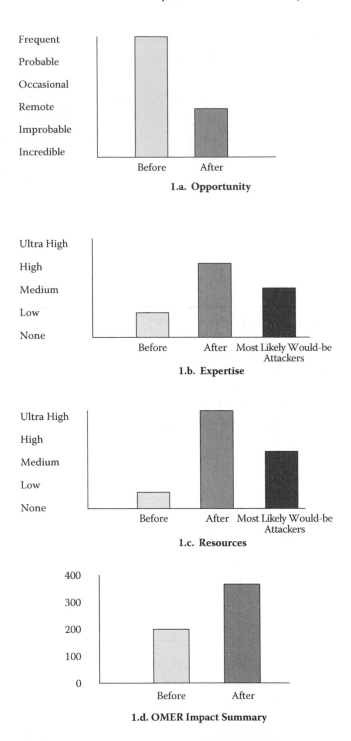

Figure 5.3   Security ROI analysis: OMER impact.

percent, then only 75 percent of the credit for the tangible and intangible benefits can be claimed. Other security controls that provide the remaining 25 percent risk mitigation claim credit for the remaining 25 percent of the tangible and intangible benefits.

Many physical security controls have a longer life than the IT and information assets they were originally acquired to protect. That raises questions as to whether or not the physical security control can be adapted to other uses, changing threat environments, and more sophisticated attacks in the future. Or, does the physical security control become obsolete and throw-away? Will the new assets require different and more advanced physical security controls? Perhaps the old physical security control can be augmented more cheaply than it can be replaced in order to meet the protection needs of the new assets. These questions need to be considered when evaluating the ROI of long-life physical security controls. Consider the following example. A physical security control has a useful life span of 15 years. The assets the physical security control is designed to protect have a useful life span of five years and are not being replaced. As a result, the physical security control will become throw-away at the end of the five-year period unless some unforeseen future use is found. Therefore, the security ROI calculation must use a five-year useful life span for the physical security control, not 15 years.

Another consideration is common to both physical and personnel security controls: allocation of the benefits of a physical or personnel security control across multiple assets. For example, physical security controls are purchased for the exterior of a building. Most buildings house a variety of different assets, each with a different asset value and useful life span. The costs and benefits of the exterior physical security controls should be allocated accordingly. The same principle applies to personnel security controls.

Pay particular attention when estimating the useful life span of personnel security controls. Changes in an organization's mission, the economic situation, the political situation, etc. can invalidate the estimated useful life span of personnel security controls quite abruptly. Accountability measures may need to be adapted to a new situation. Background investigations may need to be redone due to a change in trust level or trust type. Competence requirements and the separation of duties strategy may need to be redone due to a change in the organization's mission. Any changes in the above four items will have a ripple effect on workforce analysis. The actual useful life span of personnel security controls tends to be much shorter than originally estimated.

The security ROI analysis for IT security controls should take into account the interaction between: (1) the IT security control system and the IT security protection system, and (2) IT security controls and operational security controls. Because of this interaction, it may make more sense to evaluate a collection of security controls rather than individual security controls. Also, it is important to ensure that the OMER impact from Section 1 of Table 5.5 is consistent with the level of resilience needed, as specified in Section 6 of Table 5.2. Inconsistencies in these two items can result in a negative ROI.

The useful life span of operational security controls can also be tricky to calculate. The duration of a security engineering life-cycle activity or an ongoing risk management activity may only be a few months. However, that is not the value that should be used as the useful life span. The duration of an operational security control is used to calculate its cost. However, the useful life span of an operational security control represents the time interval that the results or outcome of that activity are valid. To illustrate, the length of time a vulnerability analysis is valid, the length of time a security impact analysis is valid, the length of time a security policy is in effect, the length of time security awareness and training materials are accurate and current, and the length of time security audits and reviews are accurate, complete, and current are all examples of the useful life span of operational security controls. Be sure not to confuse the validity period of an operational security control with laziness on the part of the organization. Just because an organization only does vulnerability assessments once every five years does not mean that the vulnerability assessment is valid for five years.

5.4 Summary

This chapter presented a new comprehensive security ROI model that:

- Is appropriate for all four types of security controls
- Can be used at any point in the security engineering life cycle
- Can be used to evaluate individual security controls or collections of security controls
- Acknowledges different asset values and different threat environments
- Builds upon the foundation already established for compliance and resilience metrics

In simplest terms, ROI implies that a measurable benefit will accrue as a result of expending funds for a specific purpose. A return on investment (ROI) can be fixed or variable. Unlike a fixed ROI, a variable ROI has risk associated with it and, as a result, can be positive, negative, or zero. An ROI can accrue from the active or passive involvement of the investor. A passive ROI only requires direct expenditures, while an active ROI requires a combination of direct and indirect expenditures. Direct expenditures represent one-time up-front costs. In contrast, indirect expenditures represent a mixture of one-time and recurring costs for as long as the item is owned. Most active ROIs can be expressed in terms of quantitative tangible benefits and qualitative intangible benefits. Finally, it is important to distinguish between the gross ROI and the net ROI. In the world of security engineering, an active ROI is pursued that involves direct and indirect expenditures and yields tangible and intangible benefits. The ROI for security controls is variable because unless the funds are spent on the appropriate types of security controls and for the specific level of resilience needed in a given operational environment, the ROI can be negative or zero. Security ROI metrics can and should be used throughout the security engineering life cycle. In the beginning, security ROI metrics can be used to guide IT capital investments and perform cost-benefit comparisons between products prior to purchase. Once deployed, security ROI metrics can be used to monitor actual benefits. As these benefits decrease over time, security ROI metrics can help flag devices that are becoming obsolete and are good candidates for technology refresh.

A variety of parameters must be measured and analyzed to determine the ROI in security controls. Similar to resilience, there is no one simple calculation that answers all the security ROI questions; rather, a series of metrics are evaluated and aggregated. Some of the primitives are actual measurements; other primitives are estimates. These parameters fall into eight categories:

1. Problem identification and characterization
2. Total cost of the security feature, function, or control
3. Depreciation period
4. Tangible benefits
5. Intangible benefits
6. Payback period
7. Comparative analysis
8. Assumptions

The first step is to identify and characterize the specific security problem that is being solved. In particular, what specific risk is this security feature, function, or control supposed to mitigate? Security solutions must be deployed in response to specific security problems if they are to provide any measurable benefit or ROI. Several pieces of information are involved in identifying the specific risk, such as the nature of the risk, the severity of the consequences should things go wrong, the likelihood of the vulnerability being exploited, and the scope of the impact. Another aspect to clarify is the extent of risk mitigation provided by the security feature, function, or control. Generally, a combination of physical, personnel, IT, and operational security controls are employed to mitigate a specific risk. As a corollary to the scope of the impact, the assets being protected are identified. This information should be consistent with the asset inventory. Asset criticality and asset value are revisited when calculating security ROI. Remember from the discussion in Chapter 4 that the value of an asset does not equate to its unit cost or price. Instead, there is a direct correlation between asset value and the severity of the consequences of the loss of that asset. A final point to clarify is the remaining useful life span of the assets being protected. ROI calculations frequently talk about the useful life span of the security control being purchased, but they neglect to consider the remaining useful life span of the assets being protected. This is a serious and potentially expensive oversight.

The second category of parameters evaluated to calculate the security ROI is the total cost of the security feature, function, or control that contributes to mitigating the risk identified in Part I. And, the emphasis is on the *total* cost. The total cost for any security feature, function, or control includes a combination of direct and indirect, one-time and recurring costs. Too often, only the purchase price is considered, when in fact there are many more costs involved in owning and operating a security device throughout its useful life.

The third category of parameters evaluated to calculate security ROI concerns the depreciation period. The depreciation period is estimated for three different parameters: the minimum, maximum, and most likely useful life span.

The fourth category of parameters examined to calculate security ROI is the tangible benefits derived from implementing the security feature, function, or control. Tangible in this context simply means that the benefits can be easily measured and translated into financial terms. Again, because these are estimates, two scenarios are examined: (1) the worst case and (2) the best case. The exact list of tangible benefits depends on the organization's mission, the specific security control, operational environment, IT infrastructure, threat environment, etc. Many tangible benefits are unique to a given situation. However, there are some elements that are common to calculating tangible benefits for all situations. These include the total cost of the losses prevented, regulatory fines avoided, liability lawsuits avoided, and increased operational efficiency resulting from implementing the security feature, function, or control.

The fifth category of parameters examined to calculate security ROI is the intangible benefits derived from implementing the security feature, function, or control. In this context, intangible means that the benefits cannot be measured and translated into financial terms with mathematical certainty. Again, estimates are developed for two different scenarios: (1) the worst case and (2) the best case. Similar to tangible benefits, the exact list of intangible benefits depends on the organization's mission, the specific security control, operational environment, IT infrastructure, threat environment, etc. However, there are some common elements when calculating intangible benefits for all situations. These include the impact of the security feature, function, or control on the OMER of would-be attackers; the increased confidence of customers, investors, and business partners in an organization's security and privacy controls; and improved employee morale.

The payback period represents the calendar time needed for the related profit or savings in operational costs to equal the amount of the investment.[311] Simply put, the payback period is an estimate of when the ROI will become positive. Two security controls can have the same estimated positive ROI over their useful life span. However, the payback period for one security control may be much shorter than that for the other security control.

Like any technical problem, there is always more than one possible security solution. The technical analysis indicates which solutions are technically viable and perhaps rank orders the solutions in terms of the best technical solution. The security ROI analysis complements the technical analysis by determining which of the technically viable solutions are also economically viable and rank orders them. The estimated cost of a loss and the cost of recovery are compared to the cost of security controls. In addition, the cost of doing nothing, or allowing the vulnerability to remain, is compared to the cost of preventing or correcting the weakness.[136, 153, 197] As a result, the security ROI comparative analysis generally takes two forms:

1. A comparison to the cost of doing nothing
2. A comparison to the cost of alternate approaches

The cost of doing nothing reflects the total cost of the worst-case losses that might be experienced if a vulnerability is not mitigated.

Assumptions are the eighth and final part of a security ROI analysis. When determining the security ROI and analyzing the total cost, depreciation period, tangible benefits, intangible benefits, and payback period, certain assumptions are made. These assumptions should be documented as part of the ROI analysis because they form the basis on which various decisions and estimates were made. Assumptions can be associated with any of the other seven parts of the security ROI analysis. Assumptions can be related to any aspect of the security control being evaluated, the IT infrastructure in which the security control will be deployed, the operational environment, the operational profile, the duty cycle, etc. Assumptions can be made related to pricing structures or the premises on which tangible and intangible benefits were calculated.

There are a variety of different parameters, tangible and intangible, quantitative and qualitative, that must be evaluated to calculate security ROI. There is no simple $e = mc^2$ formula for security ROI, although some such models have been proposed, as discussed in Section 5.1. Instead, a series of primitives, metrics, and aggregate metrics should be collected, analyzed, and merged to determine the security ROI of a security control or combination of security controls. Accordingly, the security ROI model discussed in Section 5.2 has been converted into primitives, metrics, and aggregate metrics. Examples are given of how to combine the metrics into a report format. A distinction has been made between worksheets that are used to collect primitives and reports that are used to communicate metrics. The worksheets are set up so that they can easily be plugged into spreadsheets.

5.5 Discussion Problems

1. Why is it necessary to identify the specific security problem being solved as the first step of ROI analysis?
2. What is meant by risk mitigation allocation? How important is it?
3. How do resilience levels affect security ROI analysis?
4. Explain the differences and similarities between payback period and depreciation period.
5. What role do assumptions play in ROI analysis?
6. What is the purpose of comparing the cost of a security feature, function, or control with the cost of doing nothing? What happens if this step is skipped?
7. What is the purpose of comparing the cost of a security feature, function, or control to alternate approaches? What happens if this step is skipped?
8. Why does security ROI analysis include worst-case and best-case, minimum, maximum, and most likely values?
9. Explain the difference between tangible and intangible benefits. Which is more important?
10. What role does the purchase price of a security control play in security ROI analysis?
11. Explain the relationship between (a) scope of impact and loss duration, (b) risk mitigation allocation and resilience level, and (c) depreciation period and total cost of a security feature, function, or control.

12. What role does the most likely would-be attacker play in security ROI analysis?
13. Why is it necessary to know the duration that resources are required?
14. What happens if the expertise required is the same or less than that of the most likely would-be attackers? What can an organization do in this situation?
15. Describe the relationship between security controls and (a) investors, (b) employee productivity, and (c) staff turnover.

Annex A

Glossary of Terms, Acronyms, and Abbreviations

The discipline of security metrics, not to mention security engineering, is replete with acronyms and terminology. This annex defines these acronyms and terms as they are used in this book. Standardized definitions have been used wherever possible. When more than one standardized definition exists, multiple definitions are provided. (See integrity, threat, and vulnerability as examples.) When the legal and technical definitions of a term differ, both are provided. The legal definitions are reprinted from *Black's Law Dictionary*®*, H. Black, J. Nolan, and J. Nolan-Haley, 6th edition, 1991, with permission of Thomson West. The legal definitions are applicable to the legal system of the United States. Definitions commonly used by the SANS Institute in courses and conferences are labeled "SANS."

Acceptable risk: A concern that is acceptable to responsible management, due to the cost and magnitude of implementing countermeasures.[49]

Access: The ability or the means necessary to read, write, modify, or communicate data/information or otherwise use any system resource.[80]

Accountability: The security goal that generates the requirement for actions of an entity to be traced uniquely to that entity. This supports non-repudiation, deterrence, fault isolation, intrusion detection and prevention, and after-action record and legal action.[14, 50]

Accreditation: The official management decision given by a senior agency official to authorize operation of an information system and to explicitly accept the

---

* Black, H., Nolan, J., and Nolan-Haley, J., *Black's Law Dictionary*®, 6th edition, West Publishing Company, 1991.

risk to agency operations (including mission, functions, image, or reputation), agency assets, or individuals, based on the implementation of an agreed-upon set of security controls.[51]

Accreditation boundary: All components/devices of an information system to be accredited. Separately accredited components generally are not included within the boundary.[51, 100] (synonym: security perimeter)

Actionable: Subject to or affording ground for an action or suit at law. (*Webster's Dictionary*)

Accuracy: (1) The difference between the data and the actual value.[137] (2) The degree of agreement of individual or average measurements with an accepted reference value or level.[204]

Achieved availability: Observed availability once a system has reached a steady state operationally. Often expressed as[197]

$$A_A = MTBMA/(MTBMA + MMT)$$

where:

MTBMA = Mean time between maintenance actions, both preventive and corrective

MMT = Mean maintenance action time

((Number of corrective maintenance actions per 1000 hours × MTTR for corrective maintenance) +

(Number of preventive maintenance actions per 1000 hours MTTR for preventive maintenance))/

(Number of corrective maintenance actions +

Number of preventive maintenance actions)

Also referred to as final availability.

Adequate security: Security is commensurate with the risk and magnitude of the harm resulting from the loss, misuse, or unauthorized access to or modification of information. This includes assuring that systems and applications used by the agency operate effectively and provide appropriate confidentiality, integrity, and availability, through the use of cost-effective management, personnel, operational, and technical controls.[101]

Administrative safeguards: Administrative actions, policies, and procedures to manage the selection, development, implementation, and maintenance of security measures to protect electronic health information and to manage the conduct of the covered entity's workforce in relation to protecting that information.[81]

ALARP: As low as reasonably practical; a method of correlating the likelihood of a hazard and the severity of its consequences to determine risk exposure acceptability or the need for further risk reduction.[156]

API: Advance passenger information; personal information about passengers that is required to be sent by carriers to destination government authorities before arrival.

Asset: Something of importance or value and can include one or more of the following types of elements: (a) human — the human aspect of an asset includes both the employees to be protected and the personnel who may present an insider threat, (b) physical — the physical aspect may include both tangible property and the intangible (e.g., information).[98]

Asset value: Degree of debilitating impact that would be caused by the incapacity or destruction of an asset.[45]

Assumption of risk: *Black's Law Dictionary*® — A plaintiff may not recover for an injury to which he assents; that is, that a person may not recover for an injury received when he voluntarily exposes himself to a known and appreciated danger. The requirements for the defense … are that: (1) the plaintiff has knowledge of facts constituting a dangerous condition, (2) he knows that the condition is dangerous, (3) he appreciates the nature or extent of the danger, and (4) he voluntarily exposes himself to the danger. Secondary assumption of risk occurs when an individual voluntarily encounters known, appreciated risk without an intended manifestation by that individual that he consents to relieve another of his duty.

Assurance: (1) Measure of confidence that the security features, practices, procedures, and architecture of an information system accurately mediates and enforces the security policy.[100] (2) Grounds for confidence that the other four security goals (integrity, availability, confidentiality, and accountability) have been adequately met by a specific implementation. "Adequately met" includes: (a) functionality that performs correctly, (b) sufficient protection against unintentional errors by users or software, and (c) sufficient resistance to intentional penetration or bypass.[50]

Attack: Attempt to gain unauthorized access to an information system's services, resources, or information, or the attempt to compromise an information system's integrity, availability, or confidentiality.[100]

Attack potential: Perceived potential for success of an attack, should an attack be launched, expressed in terms of an attacker's expertise, resources, and motivation.[19]

Attribute: A feature or property of an entity.[137] (*See:* Internal attribute and external attribute.)

Audit: Independent review and examination of records and activities to assess the adequacy of system controls, to ensure compliance with established policies and operational procedures, and to recommend necessary changes in controls, policies, or procedures.[100]

Audit trail: Chronological record of system activities to enable the reconstruction and examination of the sequence of events and/or changes in an event.[100]

Authentication: (1) A function for establishing the validity of a claimed identity of a user, device, or another entity in an information or communications system.[71] (2) Corroboration that a person is the one claimed.[80]

Automated security monitoring: Use of automated procedures to ensure security controls are not circumvented or the use of these tools to track actions taken by subjects suspected of misusing the information system.[100]

Availability: (1) The security goal that generates the requirement for protection against: (a) intentional or accidental attempts to perform unauthorized deletion of data or otherwise cause a denial of service or data, and (b) unauthorized use of system resources.[50] (2) The property that data, information, and information systems and communications networks are accessible and usable upon demand by an authorized person.[80] (3) The ability of an item (under combined aspects of its reliability, maintainability, and maintenance support) to perform its required function at a stated instant of time or over a stated period of time.[197] Often expressed as[153]:

$$A_1 = MTBF/(MTBF + MTTR)$$

See also: Demand mode operation, Continuous mode operation, Inherent availability, Operational availability, and Achieved availability.

C&A: (Security) certification and accreditation.

CAC: Cyber access control.[161]

Cascading: Downward flow of information through a range of security levels greater than the accreditation range of a system network or component.[100]

Case study: A research technique where you identify key factors that may affect the outcome of an activity and then document the activity, its inputs, constraints, resources, and outputs.[137]

CBP: Continuity of business processes.[161]

CCF: Common cause failure.

Certification: (1) Comprehensive evaluation of the technical and nontechnical security safeguards of an information system to support the accreditation process that establishes the extent to which a particular design and implementation meets a set of specified security requirements.[100] (2) The process of verifying the correctness of a statement or claim and issuing a certificate as to its correctness.[48] (3) A comprehensive assessment of the management, operational, and technical security controls in an information system, made in support of security accreditation, to determine the extent to which the controls are implemented correctly, operating as intended, and producing the desired outcome with respect to meeting the security requirements for the system.[51]

Certification package: Product of the certification effort documenting the detailed results of the certification activities.[100]

CFR: Code of Federal Regulations.

CIIP: Critical information infrastructure protection.

CI/KR: Critical infrastructure/key resource.[98]

CISWG: Corporate Information Security Working Group.

CIO: Chief Information Officer.

CIP: Critical infrastructure protection.

CISO: Chief Information Security Officer.

CMF: Common mode failure.

CMM: Capability Maturity Model.

CMVP: Cryptographic module validation program; a program to independently validate and certify compliance with FIPS cryptographic standards; currently, CMVP labs are accredited in the United States and Canada, and other countries will be added soon.

COBIT: Control objectives for information and related technologies, issued by IT Governance Institute.

Common cause failure: Failure of multiple independent system components occurring from a single cause that is common to all of them.

Common mode failure: Failure of multiple independent system components that fail in an identical mode.

Community risk: Probability that a particular vulnerability will be exploited within an interacting population and adversely impact some members of that population.[100]

Computer security: Measures and controls that ensure confidentiality, integrity, and availability of information system assets including hardware, software, firmware, and information being processed, stored, and communicated.[100]

Computer security contingency: An event with the potential to disrupt computer operations, thereby disrupting critical mission and business functions, for example, a power outage, hardware failure, fire, or storm. If the event is very destructive, it is often called a disaster.[60]

Computer trespasser: A person who accesses a protected computer without authorization and thus has no reasonable expectation of privacy in any communication transmitted to, through, or from the protected computer.[104]

Confidentiality: (1) The security goal that generates the requirement for protection from intentional or accidental attempts to perform unauthorized data reads. Confidentiality covers data in storage, during processing, and in transit.[50] (2) The property that data or information is not made available or disclosed to unauthorized individuals, entities, or processes. [71, 80]

Conformance testing: A process established by NIST within its responsibilities of developing, promulgating, and supporting FIPS for testing specific characteristics of components, products, and services, as well as people and organizations for compliance with a FIPS.[48]

Consistency: Data should be consistent from one measuring device or person to another, without large differences in value; i.e., the data values are repeatable.[137]

Contamination: Type of incident involving the introduction of data of one security classification or security category into data of a lower security classification or different security category.[100]

Continuous mode operation: Systems or subsystems that are operational continuously, 24 hours a day, 7 days a week.

Controller: (1) Natural or legal person, public authority, agency, or any other body which alone or jointly with others determines the purposes and means of the processing of personal data; where the purposes and means of processing are determined by national or community laws and regulations, the controller or specific criteria for his nomination may be designated by national or Community law.[65] (2) A party who, according to domestic law, is competent to decide about the contents and use of personal data regardless of whether or not such data are collected, stored, processed, or disseminated by that party or by an agent on its behalf.[64]

Correctness: The data were collected according to the exact rules defined in the metric.[137]

COSO Guidelines: Committee of the Sponsoring Organizations of the Treadway Commission, enterprise risk management framework issued by the American Institute of Certified Public Accountants.

Countermeasure: (1) Action, device, procedure, technique, or other measure that reduces the vulnerability of an information system.[51, 100] (2) Synonymous with security controls and safeguards.[60]

Critical asset: Those facilities, systems, and equipment which, if destroyed, damaged, degraded, or otherwise rendered unavailable, would affect the reliability or operability of the bulk electric system.[31–38]

Critical cyber asset: Those cyber assets essential to the reliable operation of critical assets.[31–38]

Critical infrastructure: (1) Those physical and cyber-based systems essential to the minimum operations of the economy and government.[100] (2) Systems and assets, whether physical or virtual, so vital to the United States that the incapacity or destruction of such systems and assets would have a debilitating impact on security, national economic security, national public health or safety, or any combination of those matters.[98, 104]

Criticality: The relative importance of an asset to performing or achieving an organization's mission.

Cryptography: The discipline which embodies principles, means, and methods for the transformation of data in order to hide its information content, establish its authenticity, prevent its undetected modification, prevent its repudiation, or prevent its unauthorized use.[71]

Cryptographic key: A parameter used with a cryptographic algorithm to transform, validate, authenticate, encrypt, or decrypt data.[71]

Cryptographic methods: Cryptographic techniques, services, systems, products, and key management systems.[71]

CSO: Chief Security Officer.

Cyber assets: Those programmable electronic devices and communication networks including hardware, software, and data associated with bulk electric system assets.[31-38]

Cyber security incident: Any malicious act or suspicious event that: (a) compromises, or was an attempt to compromise, the electronic or physical security perimeter of a critical cyber asset, or (b) disrupts or was an attempt to disrupt the operation of a critical cyber asset.[31-38]

Damage: (1) *Black's Law Dictionary*® — Loss, injury, or deterioration caused by the negligence, design, or accident of one person to another, in respect of the latter's person or property; the harm, detriment, or loss sustained by reason of an injury. (2) Any impairment to the integrity or availability of data, a program, a system, or information.[104]

Dangling threat: Set of properties about the external environment for which there is no corresponding vulnerability and therefore no implied risk.[100]

Dangling vulnerability: Set of properties about the internal environment for which there is no corresponding vulnerability and therefore no implied risk.[100]

Data: (1) Representations of information or concepts, in any form.[62] (2) The representation of information in a manner suitable for the communication, interpretation, storage, or processing.[71]

Data subject: An individual who is the subject of personal data.[64]

Decertification: Revocation of the certification of an information system item or equipment for cause.[100]

Decryption: The inverse function of encryption.[71]

Defect: (1) *Black's Law Dictionary*® — Deficiency, imperfection, insufficiency, the absence of something necessary for completeness or perfection; a deficiency in something essential to the proper use or the purpose for which a thing is to be used; a manufacturing flaw, a design defect, or inadequate warning. (2) A product anomaly. Examples include such things as: (a) omissions and imperfections found during early lifecycle phases; and (b) faults contained in software sufficiently mature for test or operation.[8, 9]

Defense-in-depth: (1) Information assurance strategy integrating people, technology, and operations capabilities to establish variable barriers across multiple layers and dimensions of networks.[100] (2) The approach of using multiple layers of security to guard against failure of a single security component [SANS].

Demand mode operation: Systems or subsystems that are used periodically on-demand; for example a computer-controlled braking system in a car.

Dependent variable: A factor whose value is affected by changes in one or more independent variables.[137]

DHS: Department of Homeland Security.

Direct metric value: A numerical target for a factor to be met in the final system. For example, MTBF is a direct metric of final system reliability.[12]

Disclosure: (1) Unauthorized or premature accidental release of proprietary, classified, company confidential, personal, or otherwise sensitive information.[199] (2) Release, transfer, provision of, access to, or divulging in any other means information outside the entity holding the information.[80]

Diversity: Using multiple different means to perform a required function or solve the same problem. Diversity can be implemented in hardware and software.[156]

Due care: (1) Due care ensures that a minimal level of protection is in place in accordance with the best practice in the industry [SANS]. (2) Managers and their organizations have a duty to provide for information security to ensure that the type of control, the cost of control, and the deployment of control are appropriate for the system being managed.[50] (3) *Black's Law Dictionary®* — Just, proper, and sufficient care, so far as the circumstances demand; the absence of negligence. That degree of care that a reasonable person can be expected to exercise to avoid harm, reasonably foreseeable if such care is not taken.

Due diligence: (1) Due diligence is the requirement that organizations must develop and deploy a protection plan to prevent fraud, abuse, and additionally deploy a means to detect them if they occur [SANS] (2) *Black's Law Dictionary®* — Such a measure of prudence, activity, or assiduity, as is properly to be expected from, and ordinarily exercised by, a reasonable and prudent person under the particular circumstances; not measured by any absolute standard, but depending on the relative facts of the special case.

E-Gov: Public Law 107-347 passed by the 107th Congress and signed into law by the President in December 2002 recognized the importance of information security to the economic and national security interests of the United States. Title III of the E-Government Act is FISMA.

EAL: Evaluation assurance level.

EBS: Employment background screening.[161]

Electronic security perimeter: The logical border surrounding the network or group of sub-networks (the "secure network") to which the Critical Cyber Assets are connected, and for which access is controlled.[31–38]

Encryption: The transformation of data by the use of cryptography to produce unintelligible data (encrypted data) to ensure its confidentiality.[71]

Entity: An object or an event in the real world.[137]

EOP: Executive Office of the President.

EPHI: Electronic protected health information.

Error: The difference between a computed, observed, or measured value or condition and the true specified, or theoretically correct value or condition.[8–12]

Error of commission: An error that results from making a mistake or doing something wrong.[156]

Error of omission: An error that results from something that was not done.[156]

EU: European Union.

Evaluation assurance level: (1) Set of assurance requirements that represent a point on the Common Criteria predefined assurance scale.[100]

Event: (1) Occurrence, not yet assessed, that may affect the performance of an information system.[100] (2) An event is an observable occurrence in a system or network [SANS].

Exposure: A threat action whereby sensitive data is directly released to an unauthorized entity [SANS].

External attribute: Attributes that can be measured only with respect to how the product, process, or resource is important in a given environment, not the entity itself.[137, 138] Examples of external attributes include usability, integrity, efficiency, testability, portability, maintainability, reliability, interoperability, throughput, and capacity.

FAA: U.S. Federal Aviation Administration.

Fail safe/fail secure: Automatic protection of programs or processing systems when a hardware or software failure is detected.[100]

Fail soft: Selective termination of affected nonessential processing when a hardware or software failure is determined to be imminent.[100] Also referred to as degraded-mode operations or fail operational.

Failure: Failing or inability of a system, entity, or component to perform its required functions, according to specified performance criteria, due to one or more fault conditions. Three categories of failure are commonly recognized: (1) incipient failures are failures that are about to occur; (2) hard failures are failures that result in a complete shutdown of a system; and (3) soft failures are failures that result in a transition to degraded-mode operations or a fail operational status. [8–12, 197]

Failure access: Type of incident in which unauthorized access to data results from a hardware or software failure.[100]

Failure control: Methodology used to detect imminent hardware or software failure and provide fail safe or fail soft recovery.[100]

Failure mechanism: Root cause of a failure. This points the way to a corrective action necessary for developing a new control or modifying an existing control.[120]

Failure mode: The way a device or process fails to perform its intended function.[120]

Failure rate: For a stated period in the life of an item, the ratio of the total number of failures in a sample to the cumulative observed time on that sample. The observed failure rate is to be associated with particular and stated time intervals in the life of an item and under stated conditions.[197]

Fault: A defect that results in an incorrect step, process, data value, or mode/state.[156]

Fault tolerance: To provide service complying with the specification despite faults.[203]

Federal Information Processing Standards: A standard for adoption and use by federal departments and agencies (in the United States) that has been developed within the Information Technology Laboratory and published by NIST, a part of the U.S. Department of Commerce. A FIPS covers some topic in information technology to achieve a common level of quality or some level of interoperability.[48]

FERC: Federal Energy Regulatory Commission.

FIPS: Federal information processing standard.

FISMA: Federal Information Security Management Act.

Flaw: Error of commission, omission, or oversight in an information system that may allow protection mechanisms to be bypassed.[100]

Flaw hypothesis methodology: System analysis and penetration technique in which the specification and documentation for an information system are analyzed to produce a list of hypothetical flaws. This list is prioritized on the basis of the estimated probability that a flaw exists and the ease of exploiting it, and on the extent of control or compromise it would provide. The prioritized list is used to perform penetration testing of a system.[100]

FMEA: Failure mode effects analysis.

FMECA: Failure mode effects criticality analysis.

Formal development methodology: Software development strategy that proves security design specifications.[100]

Formal experiment: A rigorous controlled investigation of an activity, where key factors are identified and manipulated to document their effects on the outcome.[137]

Formal proof: Complete and convincing mathematical argument presenting the full logical justification for each proof step and for the truth of a theorem or set of theorems.[100]

Formal security policy model: Mathematically precise statement of a security policy. Such a model must define a secure state, an initial state, and how the model represents changes in state. The model must be shown to be secure by proving the initial state is secure and all possible subsequent states remain secure.[100]

Formal top-level specification: Top-level specification written in a formal mathematical language to allow theorems, showing the correspondence of the system specification to its formal requirements, to be hypothesized and formally proven.[100]

Formal verification: (1) Process of using formal proofs to demonstrate the consistency between formal specification of a system and formal security policy model (design verification) or between formal specification and its high-level program implementation (implementation verification).[100]

FOUO: For Official Use Only; an information asset sensitivity label used in the United States.

FRACAS: Failure reporting and corrective action system, commonly used by safety and reliability engineers. Compare with POA&M.

FTA: Fault tree analysis.

FTC: Federal Trade Commission.

GLB: Gramm-Leach-Bliley Act.

GQM: Goal question metric; a paradigm developed by V. Basili for identifying meaningful metrics.

Graduated security: A security system that provides several levels (e.g., low, moderate, high) of protection based on threats, risks, available technology, support services, time, human concerns, and economics.[48]

Hardening: The process of identifying and fixing vulnerabilities in a system [SANS].

Health information: Any information, whether oral or recorded form or medium, that (a) is created or received by a healthcare provider, health plan, public health authority, employer, life insurer, school or university, or healthcare clearinghouse; and (b) relates to the past, present, or future physical or mental health or condition of an individual, the provision of healthcare to an individual, or the past, present, or future payment for the provision of health care to an individual.[80]

HECA: Hardware error confinement area.[203]

HIAA: Health Insurance Association of America.

HIPAA: Health Insurance Portability and Accountability Act.

HSPD: Homeland Security Presidential Directive.

Hypothesis: Tentative theory or supposition that you think explains the behavior you want to explore.[137]

IAM: Infosec assessment methodology (NSA).

IEC: International Electrotechnical Commission.

IEEE: Institute for Electrical and Electronic Engineers.

IIA: Institute of Internal Auditors.

Incident — security: (1a) Assessed occurrence having actual or potentially adverse effects on an information system; (1b) occurrence that potentially jeopardizes the security of COMSEC material or the secure electrical transmission of national security information or information governed by 10 U.S.C. Section 2315.[100] (2) An adverse network event in an information system or network or the threat of the occurrence of such an event [SANS]. (3) Attempted or successful unauthorized access, use, disclosure, modification, or destruction of information or interference with system operations in an information system.[80]

Incident handling: An action plan for dealing with intrusions, cyber-theft, denial of service, fire, floods, and other security-related events. It is comprised of a six-step process: preparation, identification, containment, eradication, recovery, and lessons learned [SANS].

Independent variable: A factor that can characterize your project and influence your evaluation results; they can be manipulated to affect the outcome.[137] Synonym of state variable. Antonym of dependent variable.

Information manager: A person or body that (a) processes, stores, or destroys personal health information for a trustee, or (b) provides information management or information technology services to a trustee.[61]

Information security: Protecting information and information systems from unauthorized access, use, disclosure, disruption, modification, or destruction in order to provide: (a) integrity, which means guarding against improper information modification or destruction, and includes ensuring information non-repudiation and authenticity; (b) confidentiality, which means preserving authorized restrictions on access and disclosure, including means for protecting personal privacy and proprietary information; and (c) availability, which means ensuring timely and reliable access to and use of information.[68]

Information system security manager: Individual responsible for a program, organization, system, or enclave's information assurance.[100]

Information system security officer: Individual responsible to the ISSM for ensuring the appropriate operational information assurance posture is maintained for a system, program, or enclave.[100]

Inherent availability: Estimated availability, while a system or subsystem is still in the development phase. Often expressed as[197]:

$$A_1 = MTBF/(MTBF = MTTR)$$

Also referred to as potential availability.

Integrity — data: (1) The state that exists when data is the same as the source information and has not been exposed to accidental or malicious addition, deletion, alteration, or destruction.[156] (2) The property that data or information has not been modified or altered in an unauthorized manner.[71, 80, 81] (3) The need to ensure that information has not been changed accidentally or deliberately, and that it is accurate and complete [SANS].

Integrity — safety: Probability of a safety-related system satisfactorily performing the required safety functions under all stated conditions within a stated period of time. Safety integrity relates to the performance of safety-related systems carrying out the specified safety requirements.[5]

Integrity — security: (1) A security goal that generates the requirement for protection against either intentional or accidental attempts to violate data integrity (the property that data has when it has not been altered in an unauthorized manner) or system integrity (the quality that a system has when it performs its intended function in an unimpaired manner, free from unauthorized manipulation).[50] (2) Quality of an information system reflecting the logical correctness and reliability of the operating system; the logical completeness of the hardware and software implementing the protection mechanisms; and the consistency of the data structures and occurrence of the stored data.[100] (3) guarding against improper information modification or destruction, and including ensuring information non-repudiation and authenticity.[51]

Interim approval: Temporary authorization granted by a Designated Approval Authority for an information system to process information based on preliminary results of a security evaluation of the system.[100] Generally, the interim approval is contingent upon taking remedial action to mitigate cited deficiencies.

Internal attribute: Those attributes that can be measured purely in terms of the product, process, or resource itself, separate from its behavior.[137, 138] Examples of internal attributes include: functionality, modularity, redundancy, diversity, syntactic correctness, and structuredness of control and data flows.

Interoperability: For cryptographic methods means the technical ability of multiple cryptographic methods to function together.[71]

Interval scale: Indicates exact differences between measurement points.[174]

Intrusion: (1) Unauthorized act of bypassing the security mechanisms of a system.[100] (2) Intentional operational fault.[112]

Intrusion tolerance: The capability to deal with residual security vulnerabilities by continuing to provide service after a penetration; the damage caused by an intruder is contained and possibly automatically repaired. It is preferable to continue system operation with possibly degraded characteristics, as opposed to completely withdrawing the system and the service it provides.[112]

ISO: International Organization for Standardization.

ISSM: Information system security manager.

ISSO: Information system security officer.

IT-related risk: The net mission impact considering (a) the probability that a particular threat-source will exercise (accidentally trigger or intentionally exploit) a particular information system vulnerability and (b) the resulting impact if this should occur. IT-related risks arise from legal liability or mission loss due to:

- Unauthorized (malicious or accidental) disclosure, modification, or destruction of information
- Unintentional errors and omissions
- IT disruptions due to natural or man-made disasters
- Failure to exercise due care and diligence in the implementation and operation of the IT system[50]

IT security: Inherent technical features and functions that collectively contribute to an IT infrastructure achieving and sustaining confidentiality, integrity, availability, accountability, authenticity, and reliability.

Key assets: Individual targets whose destruction could cause large-scale injury, death, or destruction of property, and/or profoundly damage national prestige and confidence (a subset of key resources).[98]

Key holder: An individual or entity in possession or control of cryptographic keys. A key holder is not necessarily a user of the key.[71]

Key management system: A system for generation, storage, distribution, revocation, deletion, archiving, certification, or application of cryptographic keys.[71]

Key resources: Publicly or privately controlled resources essential to the minimal operations of the economy and government.[98]

Lawful access: Access by third party individuals or entities, including governments, to plaintext, or cryptographic keys, of encrypted data, in accordance with law.[71]

Level of concern: Rating assigned to an information system indicating the extent to which protection measures, techniques, and procedures must be applied. High, medium, and basic are identified levels of concern. A separate level of concern is assigned to each information system for confidentiality, integrity, and availability.[100]

Level of protection: Extent to which protective measures, techniques, and procedures must be applied to information systems and networks based on risk, threat, vulnerability, system interconnectivity considerations, and information assurance needs. Levels of protection are: 1 — basic: information systems and networks requiring implementation of standard minimum security countermeasures; 2 — medium: information systems and networks requiring layering of additional safeguards above the standard minimum security countermeasures; and 3 — high: information systems and networks requiring the most stringent protection and rigorous security countermeasures.[100]

Liability: *Black's Law Dictionary®* — condition of being or potentially subject to an obligation; condition of being responsible for a possible or actual loss, penalty, evil, expense, or burden; condition that creates a duty to perform an act immediately or in the future, including almost every character of hazard or responsibility, absolute, contingent, or likely.

Likelihood: The qualitative or quantitative likelihood that a potential hazard will occur or a potential threat will be instantiated. Most international standards define six levels of likelihood (lowest to highest): incredible, improbable, remote, occasional, probable, and frequent.[156]

Loss: Any reasonable cost to any victim, including the cost of responding to an offense, conducting a damage assessment, and restoring the data, program, system or information to its condition prior to the offense, and any revenue lost, cost incurred, or other consequential damages incurred because of interruption of service.[104]

Maintain: Includes maintain, collect, use, or disseminate.[108]

Maintainability: The ability of an item, under stated conditions of use, to be retained in, or restored to, a state in which it can perform its required functions, when maintenance is performed under stated conditions and using prescribed procedures and resources.[197]

Maintenance — corrective: The actions performed, as a result of a failure, to restore an item to a specified condition.[197]

Maintenance — preventive: The actions performed in an attempt to retain an item in a specified condition by providing systematic inspection, detection, and prevention of incipient failures.[197]

Management control: The security controls (i.e., safeguards and countermeasures) applied to an information system that focuses on the management of risk and the management of the information security system. Actions that are performed primarily to support management decisions with regard to information system security.[51, 60]

Measure: (1) The number or symbol assigned to an entity by the measurement process in order to characterize an attribute.[137, 138] (2) A quantitative assessment of the degree to which a software product or process possesses a given attribute.[8, 9]

Measurement: (1) The process by which numbers or symbols are assigned to entities in the real world in such a way as to describe them according to clearly defined rules.[137, 138] (2) A process that is a repeated application of a test method using a measuring system.[204] (3) The comparison of a property of an object to a similar property of a standard reference. Measurements are effective when they are used either to orient decisions, to define corrective actions, or to get a better understanding of causal relationships between intended expectations and observed facts.[8, 9]

Metric: (1) A proposed measure or unit of measure.[138] (2) Tools designed to facilitate decision making and improve performance and accountability through collection, analysis, and reporting of relevant performance-related data.[57]

MNWF: Must not work function; an illegal function or operational state that the system must never be allowed to reach or system safety and/or security will be seriously compromised.

Mobility: Of cryptographic methods means the technical ability to function in multiple countries, information systems, and communications networks.[71]

MTBF: (For repairable items) mean time between failures. For a stated period in the life of an item, the ratio of the mean value of the length of time between consecutive failures, computed as the ratio of the cumulative observed time to the number of failures under stated conditions.[197] Often expressed as:

$$MTBF = \text{total time/number of failures}$$

MTBF is the reciprocal of the failure rate:

$$MTBF = 1/\text{Failure rate}$$

$$\text{Failure rate} = 1/MTBF$$

MTTF: (For non-repairable items) mean time to failure. For a stated period in the life of an item, the ratio of the cumulative time for a sample to the total number of failures in the sample during the period under stated conditions.[197]

MTTR: Mean time to repair. Total maintenance time divided by the total number of corrective maintenance actions during a given period of time.[197]

MWF: Must work function; a critical function that must function correctly for the system to remain in a known safe or secure state at all times.

NCUA: National Credit Union Administration.

Need-to-know: A method of isolating information assets based on an individual's need to have access to that asset, or even know of its existence, but no more, in order to perform his job; for example, a personnel officer needs access to sensitive personnel records and a marketing manager needs access to sensitive marketing information but not vice versa. The terms "need-to-know" and "least privilege" express the same idea. Need-to-know is generally applied to people, while least privilege is generally applied to IT processes.[156]

Negligence: *Black's Law Dictionary®* — Failure to use such care as a reasonably prudent and careful person would use under similar circumstances; the doing of some act which a person of ordinary prudence would not have done under similar circumstances or failure to do what a person of ordinary prudence would have done under similar circumstances; conduct that falls below the norm for the protection of others against unreasonable risk of harm. It is characterized by inadvertence, thoughtlessness, inattention, recklessness, etc.

NERC: North America Electric Reliability Council.

NISP: National Industrial Security Program.

NIST: National Institute of Standards and Technology.

Nominal scale: Classification into categories that are mutually exclusive and jointly exhaustive of all possible categories of an attribute. The names and sequence of the categories bear no assumptions about relationships between or among categories.[174]

Nonpublic personal information: Personally identifiable financial information — (i) provided by a consumer to a financial institution; (ii) resulting from any transaction with the consumer or any service performed for the consumer; or (iii) otherwise obtained by the financial institution.[75]

Non-Repudiation: A property achieved through cryptographic methods, which prevents an individual or entity from denying having performed a particular action related to data (such as mechanisms for non-rejection of authority (origin), for proof of obligation, intent, or commitment, or for proof of ownership).[71]

OECD: Organization for Economic Co-operation and Development.

OMER: Opportunity, motive, expertise, resources; a paradigm used to evaluate attack sources and methods.

Operational availability: Observed availability following initial system deployment. Often expressed as[197]:

$$A_O = MTBMA/(MTBMA + MDT)$$

where:
MTBMA = Mean time between maintenance actions
MDT   = Mean down time

Also referred to as actual availability.

Operational controls: The security controls (i.e., safeguards and countermeasures) applied to an information system that are primarily implemented and executed by people (as opposed to the information system).[51, 60]

Operational security: The implementation of standardized operational security procedures that define the nature and frequency of the interaction between users, systems, and system resources, the purpose of which is to: (1) achieve and sustain a known secure system state at all times; and (2) prevent accidental or intentional theft, destruction, alteration, or sabotage of system resources.[156]

OPSEC: Operations security.

Ordinal scale: Measurement operations through which the subjects can be arranged in order; however there is no information on the magnitude of the differences between elements.[174]

PCSCS: Process control systems cyber security.

Percentage: A proportion converted to terms of per hundred units.[174]

Personal data: Any information relating to an identified or identifiable natural person ("data subject"); an identifiable person is one who can be identified, directly or indirectly, in particular by reference to an identification number or to one or more factors specific to his physical, physiological, mental, economic, cultural, or social identity.[65, 69, 71]

Personal data filing system: Any structured set of personal data which is accessible according to specific criteria, whether centralized, decentralized, or dispersed on a functional or geographic basis.[65]

Personal information: Information about an identifiable individual, but does not include the name, title, or business address or telephone number of an employee of an organization.[62]

Personnel security: A variety of ongoing measures that are undertaken to reduce the likelihood and severity of accidental and intentional alteration, destruction, misappropriation, misuse, misconfiguration, and unavailability of an organization's logical and physical assets, as the result of action or inaction by insiders and known outsiders, like business partners.

PHI: Protected health information.

Physical safeguards: Physical measures, policies, and procedures to protect a covered entity's electronic information systems and related buildings and equipment from natural and environmental hazards, and unauthorized intrusion.[60, 80]

Physical security: Protection of hardware, software, and data against physical threats; to reduce or prevent disruptions to operations and services and loss of assets.[156]

Physical security perimeter: The physical border surrounding computer rooms, telecommunications rooms, operations centers, and other locations in which critical cyber assets are housed and for which access is controlled.[31–38]

PIPEDA: Personal Information Protection and Electronics Document Act.

PIV: Personal identity verification.

Plaintext: Intelligible data.[71]

Plan of action and milestones: A plan of action and milestones, also referred to as a corrective action plan, is a tool that identifies tasks that need to be accomplished. It details resources required to accomplish the elements of the plan, any milestones in meeting the task, and scheduled completion dates for the milestones. The purpose of the POA&M is to assist agencies in identifying, assessing, prioritizing, and monitoring the progress of corrective efforts for security weaknesses found in programs and systems.[103]

PNR: Passenger name record; part of the advance information carriers must send to the destination government authorities prior to arrival.

POA&M: Plan of action and milestones resulting from security certification and accreditation (C&A) activities. Compare with FRACAS.

Portability: Of cryptographic methods means the technical ability to be adapted and function in multiple systems.[71]

Precision: The degree of mutual agreement among individual measurements made under prescribed-like conditions, or simply, how well identically performed measurements agree with each other. This concept applies to a process or a set of measurements, not to a single measurement.[204]

Predictive metric value: A numerical target related to a factor to be met during system development. This is an intermediate requirement that is an early indicator of final system performance.[12]

Primitive: Data relating to the development or use of software that is used in developing measures of quantitative descriptions of software. Primitives are directly measurable or countable, or may be given a constant value or condition for a specific measure. Examples include error, fault, failure, time, time interval, date, and number of an item.[8, 9]

Privacy — breach of: *Black's Law Dictionary*® — knowingly and without lawful authority (a) intercepting, without consent of the sender or receiver, a message by telephone, telegraph, letter, or other means of private communications; (b) divulging, without consent of the sender or receiver, the existence or contents of such message if such person knows that the message was illegally intercepted, or if he illegally learned of the message in the course of employment with an agency transmitting it.

Privacy impact: An analysis of how information is handled: (a) to ensure handling conforms to applicable legal, regulatory, and policy requirements regarding privacy; (b) to determine the risks and effects of collecting, maintaining, and disseminating information in identifiable form in an electronic information system; and (c) to examine and evaluate protections and alternative processes for handling information to mitigate potential privacy risks.[52]

Privacy — invasion of: *Black's Law Dictionary*® — Unwarranted appropriation or exploitation of one's personality, publicizing one's private affairs with which public has no legitimate concern, or wrongful intrusion into one's private activities, in such a manner as to cause mental suffering, shame, or humiliation to person of ordinary sensibilities.

Privacy laws: *Black's Law Dictionary*® — Those federal and state statutes which prohibit an invasion of a person's right to be left alone (e.g., to not be photographed in private), and also restrict access to personal information (e.g., income tax returns, credit reports) and overhearing of private conversations (e.g., electronic surveillance).

Privacy — right of: *Black's Law Dictionary*® — Right to be left alone; right of a person to be free from unwarranted publicity; and right to live without unwarranted interference by the public in matters with which the public is not necessarily concerned. There are four general categories of tort actions related to invasion of privacy: (a) appropriation, (b) intrusion, (c) public disclosure of private facts, and (d) false light privacy.

Process: (1) Collection of related activities that are ordered or related over time.[137] (2) Any specific activity, set of activities, or time period within the manufacturing or development project.[138]

Process maturity assessment: An ongoing evaluation of an organization's capability to produce products of sufficient quality for user needs. Process maturity assessment includes product maturity assessment with the objective of process repair when necessary.[8, 9]

Processing of personal data: Any operation or set of operations which is performed upon personal data, whether or not by automatic means, such as collection, recording, organization, storage, adaptation or alteration, retrieval, consultation, use, disclosure by transmission, dissemination or otherwise making available, alignment or combination, blocking, erasure, or destruction.[65]

Processor: A natural or legal person, public authority, agency, or any other body which processes personal data on behalf of the controller.[65]

Product: Any artifacts, deliverables, or documents that result from a process activity. A product can be an output of one process activity and an input to another.[137, 138]

Product maturity assessment: A certification of product readiness for operation (including an estimation of support necessary for corrective maintenance).[8, 9]

Proportion: Result from dividing one quantity by another, where the numerator is part of the denominator; best used to describe multiple categories within one group.[174]

Protect and secure: Reducing the vulnerability of CI/KR to deter, mitigate, or neutralize terrorist attacks, i.e., the activities that identify CI/KR, assess vulnerabilities, prioritize CI/KR, and develop protective programs and measures.[98]

Protected health information: (1) Individually identifiable health information that is transmitted or maintained electronically or by using any other medium; excludes educational and employment records.[60] (2) Individually identifiable health information that is: (a) transmitted by electronic media, (b) maintained by electronic media, or (c) created, received, transmitted, or maintained in any other form or medium; excludes educational and employment records. [80]

Quality: The totality of features and characteristics of a product or service that bear on its ability to satisfy stated or implied needs.[13]

Random failure: Failures that result from physical degradation over time (i.e., the physics of failure) and variability introduced during the manufacturing process.[156]

Rate: Dynamic of change of the phenomena of interest, generally over time.[174]

Ratio: Result from dividing one quantity by another. The numerator and denominator are from two distinct populations and are mutually exclusive.[174]

Ratio scale: An interval scale on which an absolute or non-arbitrary zero point can be located.[174]

Recipient: Natural or legal person, public authority, agency, or any other body to whom data are disclosed, whether a third party or not; however, authorities which may receive data in the framework of a particular inquiry shall not be regarded as recipients.[65]

Record: (1) Includes any correspondence, memorandum, book, plan, map, drawing, diagram, pictorial or graphic work, photograph, film, microfilm, sound recording, videotape, machine-readable record, and any other documentary material, regardless of physical form or characteristics, and any copy of any of those things.[62] (2) Any item, collection, or grouping of information about an individual that is maintained by an agency, including, but not limited to, his education, financial transactions, medical history, and criminal or employment history and that contains his name, or the identifying number, symbol, of other identifying particular assigned to the individual, such as a finger or voice print or a photograph.[108]

Redundancy: Controlling failure by providing several identical functional units, monitoring the behavior of each to detect faults, and initiating a transition to a known safe/secure state if a discrepancy is detected.[7]

Reliability: (1) Of measurement data — consistency of a number of measurements taken using the same measurement method on the same measurement subject.[174] (2) Of a system or subsystem — ability of an item to perform a required function under stated conditions for a stated period of time.[13, 97, 156]

Reportable condition: A reportable condition exists when a security or management control weakness does not rise to the level of a significant deficiency, yet is still important enough to be reported to internal management. A security weakness not deemed to be a significant deficiency by agency management, yet affecting the efficiency and effectiveness of agency operations, may be considered a reportable condition.[103]

Residual risk: (1) Portion of risk remaining after security measures have been applied.[100] (2) The risk that remains after risk control measures have been employed. Before a system can be certified and accredited, a determination must be made about the acceptability of residual risk.[156]

Resilience: The capability of an IT infrastructure, including physical, personnel, IT, and operational security controls, to maintain essential services and protect critical assets while preempting and repelling attacks and minimizing the extent of corruption and compromise.

Resource: (1) Entities required as inputs to a process activity.[137] (2) Any item forming or providing input to a process.[138]

Risk: (1) Possibility that a particular threat will adversely impact an information system by exploiting a particular vulnerability.[100] (2) Product of the level of threat with the level of vulnerability; it establishes the likelihood of a successful attack [SANS]. (3) The level of impact on agency operations (including mission, functions, image, or reputation), agency assets, or individuals resulting from the operation of an information system given the potential impact of a threat and the probability of that threat occurring.[50, 51] (4) The possibility of harm or loss to any software, information, hardware, administrative, physical, communications, or personnel resource within an automated information system or activity.[49]

Risk analysis: (1) A series of analyses conducted to identify and determine the cause(s), consequences, likelihood, and severity of hazards. Note that a single hazard may have multiple causes.[156] (2) Examination of information to identify the risk to an information system.[100]

Risk assessment: (1) Process of analyzing threats to and vulnerabilities of an information system, and the potential impact resulting from the loss of information or capabilities of a system. This analysis is used as a basis for identifying appropriate and cost-effective security countermeasures.[100] (2) Process by which risks are identified and the impact of those risks determined [SANS]. (3) The process of identifying risks to agency operations (including mission, functions, image, or reputation), agency assets, or individuals by determining the probability of occurrence, the resulting impact, and additional security controls that would mitigate this impact. Part of risk management, synonymous with risk analysis, and incorporates threat and vulnerability analyses.[50, 51]

Risk control: Techniques that are employed to eliminate, reduce, or mitigate risk, such as inherent safe and secure (re)design techniques/features, alerts, warnings, operational procedures, instructions for use, training, and contingency plans.[156]

Risk management: (1) Systematic application of risk analysis and risk control management polices, procedures, and practices.[156] (2) The process of managing risks to agency operations (including mission, functions, image, or reputation), agency assets, or individuals resulting from the operation of an information system. It includes risk assessment; cost-benefit analysis; the selection, implementation, and assessment of security controls; and the formal authorization to operate the system. This process considers effectiveness, efficiency, and constraints due to laws, directives, policies, or regulations.[50, 51] (3) The ongoing process of assessing the risk to automated information system resources and information, as part of a risk-based approach used to determine adequate security for a system by analyzing the threats and vulnerabilities and selecting appropriate cost-effective controls that achieve and maintain an acceptable level of risk.[49]

Risk mitigation: The selection and implementation of security controls to reduce risk to a level acceptable to management, within applicable constraints.[60]

ROI: Return on investment.

ROSI: Return on security investment.

Routine use: With respect to the disclosure of a record, the use of such record for a purpose which is compatible with the purpose for which it was collected.[108]

Safeguard: (1a) Protection included to counteract a known or expected condition, (1b) incorporated countermeasure or set of countermeasures within a base release.[100] (2) Synonymous with security controls and countermeasures.[60] (3) Protective measures prescribed to meet the security requirements (i.e., confidentiality, integrity, and availability) specified for an information system. Safeguards may include security features, management constraints, personnel security, and security of physical structures, areas, and devices. Synonymous with security control and countermeasures.[51] (4) A practice, procedure, or mechanism that reduces risk.[14]

SCADA: Supervisory control and data acquisition.

SEC: Securities and Exchange Commission.

SECA: Software error confinement area.

Security category: The characterization of information or an information system based on an assessment of the potential impact that a loss of confidentiality, integrity, or availability of such information or information system would have on organizational operations, organizational assets, or individuals.[46]

Security controls: (1) The management, operational, and technical controls (safeguards or countermeasures) prescribed for an information system and the security controls in place or planned for meeting those requirements.[60] (2) The management, operational, and technical controls (i.e., safeguards or countermeasures) prescribed for an information system to protect the confidentiality, integrity, and availability of the system and its information.[46]

Security fault analysis: An assessment, adapted from safety engineering, performed on information system to determine the security properties of the appliance when a fault is encountered.

Security impact analysis: The analysis conducted by an agency official, often during the continuous monitoring phase of the security certification and accreditation process, to determine the extent to which changes to the information system have affected the security posture of the system.[51]

Security inspection: Examination of an information system to determine compliance with security policy, procedures, and practices.[100]

Security margin: Degree of positive (or negative) compensation a security control provides in relation to the OMER of the most likely would-be attackers.

Security perimeter: All components/devices of an information system to be accredited. Separately accredited components generally are not included within the boundary.[100] (Synonym is accreditation boundary.)

Security safeguards: Protective measures and controls prescribed to meet the security requirements specified for an information system. Safeguards may include security features, management constraints, personnel security, and security of physical structures, areas, and devices.[100]

Security test and evaluation: Examination and analysis of the safeguards required to protect an information system, as they have been applied in an operational environment, to determine the security posture of that system.[100]

Security testing: Process to determine that an information system protects data and maintains functionality as intended.[100]

Sensitive personal data: Personal information consisting of information as to[64]:
Racial or ethnic origin of the data subject
His political opinions
His religious beliefs of other beliefs of a similar nature
Whether he is a member of a trade union
His physical or mental health or condition
His sexual life
Commission or alleged commission by him of any offence
Any proceedings for any offence committed or alleged to have been committed by him, the disposal of such proceedings or the sentence of any court in such proceedings

Sensitivity: The relative degree of confidentiality and privacy protections needed for a given information asset to prevent unauthorized disclosure.

Separation of duties: The practice of dividing and distributing the steps in a process, procedure, or system function, among several individuals or user roles to prevent a single individual from subverting that process, procedure, or function; separating security critical functions, like the ability to create, issue, and revoke security credentials, among multiple different user roles to prevent an individual from misusing system privileges.

Severity: The severity of the worst-case consequences should a potential hazard occur. Most international standards define four levels of hazard severity (lowest to highest): insignificant, marginal, critical, and catastrophic.[156]

SFA: Security fault analysis.

SIA: Security impact analysis.

Significant deficiency: A weakness in an agency's overall information systems security program or management control structure, or within one or more information systems, that significantly restricts the capability of the agency to carry out its mission or compromises the security of its information, information systems, personnel, or other resources, operations, or assets.[103]

SIL: Safety integrity level; a level of how far safety is to be pursued in a given context, assessed by reference to an acceptable risk, based on the current values of society.[4]

Situational metrics: The appropriate collection of measures to control a project, given its characteristics.[138]

SPC: Statistical process control.

SPICE: Software Process Improvement and Capability Determination.

SSE-CMM®: System Security Engineering Capability Maturity Model.

SSI: Sensitive security information; a sensitivity label used for information assets in the United States.

ST&E: Security test and evaluation.

State variable: A factor that can characterize your project and influence your evaluation results; they can be manipulated to affect the outcome.[137] Synonym of independent variable. Antonym of dependent variable.

Statistical process control: A collection of techniques for use in the improvement of any process. It involves the systematic collection of data related to a process and graphical summaries of that data for visibility. These techniques include Pareto analysis, process analysis, cause and effect analysis, sampling, scatter diagrams, histograms, defect maps, and decision trees.[204]

Suitability: Character traits and past conduct that indicate fitness or eligibility for employment relative to the ability to carry out a job reliably with effectiveness and efficiency.[43]

Survey: A retrospective study of a situation to try to document relationships and outcomes.[137]

System integrity: Attribute of an information system when it performs its intended function in an unimpaired manner, free from deliberate or inadvertent unauthorized manipulation of the system.[100]

System of records: A group of any records under the control of any agency from which information is retrieved by the name of the individual or by some identifying number, symbol, or other identifying particular assigned to the individual.[108]

System survivability: The ability to continue to make resources available, despite adverse circumstances including hardware malfunction, accidental software errors, accidental and malicious intentional user activities, and environmental hazards such as dust, fire, flood, power outage, and EMC/EMI/RFI.[156]

Systematic failure: Failures that result from an error of omission, error of commission, or operational error in a life-cycle activity.[7]

Technical (controls or) safeguards: (1) The security controls (i.e., safeguards and countermeasures) applied to an information system that are primarily implemented and executed by the information system through mechanisms contained in the hardware, software, or firmware components of the system.[51, 60] (2) The technology and the policy and procedures for its use that protect electronic protected health information and control access to it.[80]

The data subject's consent: Any freely given and specific and informed indication of his wishes by which the data subject signifies his agreement to personal data relating to him being processed.[65]

Third party: Any natural or legal person, public authority, agency, or any other body other than the data subject, the controller, the processors, and the persons who, under the direct authority of the controller or processor, are authorized to process the data.[65]

Threat: (1) Any circumstance or event with the potential to adversely impact an information system through unauthorized access, destruction, disclosure, modification of data, and/or denial of service.[51, 100] (2) A potential for violation of security, which exists when there is a circumstance, capability, action, or event that could breach security and cause harm [SANS]. (3) The potential for a threat source to exercise (accidentally trigger or intentionally exploit) a specific vulnerability.[50]

Threat analysis: (1) Examination of information to identify the elements comprising a threat.[100] (2) Examination of threat sources against system vulnerabilities to determine the threats for a particular system in a particular operational environment.[50]

Threat assessment: (1) Formal description and evaluation of threats to an information system.[51, 100] (2) The identification of types of threats that an organization might be exposed to [SANS].

Threat model: A threat model is used to describe a given threat and the harm it could do to a system if it has a vulnerability [SANS].

Threat monitoring: Analysis, assessment, and review of audit trails and other information collected for the purpose of searching out system events that may constitute violations of system security.[100]

Threat source: Either (a) intent and method targeted at the intentional exploitation of a vulnerability, or (b) a situation and method that may accidentally trigger a vulnerability. Synonymous with threat agent.[50, 51]

Threat vector: The method a threat uses to get to the target [SANS].

TIR: Threat and incident reporting.[161]

TMR: Triple modular redundancy.

Trustworthiness: Security decision with respect to extended investigations to determine and confirm qualifications, and suitability to perform specific tasks and responsibilities.[48]

TTRS: Time to restore service.

Validity: Of data measurements — the measurement or metric really measures what we intend it to measure.[174]

Vulnerability: (1) Weakness in an information system, system security procedures, internal controls, or implementation that could be exploited or triggered by a threat source.[51, 100] (2) A flaw or weakness in a system's design, implementation, or operation and management that could be exploited to violate the system's security policy [SANS]. (3) A flaw or weakness in the design or implementation of an information system (including the security procedures and security controls associated with the system) that could be intentionally or unintentionally exploited to adversely affect an organization's operations or assets through a loss of confidentiality, integrity, or availability.[60] (4) A flaw or weakness in system security procedures, design, implementation, or internal controls that could be exercised (accidentally triggered or intentionally exploited) and result in a security breach or a violation of the system's security policy.[50]

Vulnerability analysis: Examination of information to identify the elements comprising a vulnerability.[100]

Vulnerability assessment: Formal description and evaluation of vulnerabilities of an information system.[51, 100]

Use: Sharing, employment, application, utilization, examination, or analysis of information within an entity that maintains such information.[80]

Weakness: Any and all IT security weaknesses pertaining to that system.[103]

Annex B

Additional Resources

This collection of additional resources lists the sources that were used during the development of this work and provides pointers to additional resources that may be of interest to the reader. It is organized in three parts: (1) standards, (2) policies, regulations, and other government documents, and (3) publications.

B.1 Standards

This section lists contemporary standards related to various aspects of security metrics. Given that most national and international standards are reaffirmed, updated, or withdrawn on a three- to five-year cycle, for implementation or assessment purposes, be sure to verify that you have the current approved version.

International

1. IEC 61508-1(1998-12), Functional Safety of Electrical/Electronic/Programmable Electronic Safety-Related Systems — Part 1: General Requirements.
2. IEC 61508-2(2000-5), Functional Safety of Electrical/Electronic/Programmable Electronic Safety-Related Systems — Part 2: Requirements for Electrical/Electronic/Programmable Electronic Safety-Related Systems.
3. IEC 61508-3(1998-12), Functional Safety of Electrical/Electronic/Programmable Electronic Safety-Related Systems — Part 3: Software Requirements.
4. IEC 61508-4(1998-12), Functional Safety of Electrical/Electronic/Programmable Electronic Safety-Related Systems — Part 4: Definitions and Abbreviations of Terms.
5. IEC 61508-5(1998-12), Functional Safety of Electrical/Electronic/Programmable Electronic Safety-Related Systems — Part 5: Examples of Methods for the Determination of Safety Integrity Levels.
6. IEC 61508-6(2000-4), Functional Safety of Electrical/Electronic/Programmable Electronic Safety-Related Systems — Part 6: Guidelines on the Application of Parts 2 and 3.

7. IEC 61508-7(2000-3), Functional Safety of Electrical/Electronic/Programmable Electronic Safety-Related Systems — Part 7: Overview of Techniques and Measures.
8. IEEE Std. 982.1-1988, Standard Dictionary of Measures to Produce Reliable Software.
9. IEEE Std. 982.2-1988, Guide for the Use of the Standard Dictionary of Measures to Produce Reliable Software.
10. IEEE Std. 1028-1997, Standard for Reviews and Audits.
11. IEEE Std. 1045-1992, Standard for Software Productivity Metrics.
12. IEEE Std. 1061-1998, Software Quality Metrics Methodology.
13. ISO 9000 Compendium — International Standards for Quality Management, 10th edition, 2000.
14. ISO/IEC TR 13335-1(1996-12-15) — Information Technology — Guidelines for the Management of IT Security — Part 1: Concepts and Models for IT Security.
15. ISO/IEC TR 13335-2(1997-12-15) — Information Technology — Guidelines for the Management of IT Security — Part 2: Managing and Planning IT Security.
16. ISO/IEC TR 13335-3(1998-06-15) — Information Technology — Guidelines for the Management of IT Security — Part 3: Techniques for the Management of IT security.
17. ISO/IEC TR 13335-4(2000-03-01) — Information Technology — Guidelines for the Management of IT Security — Part 4: Selection of Safeguards.
18. ISO/IEC TR 13335-5(2001-11-01) — Information Technology — Guidelines for the Management of IT Security — Part 5: Management Guidance on Network Security.
19. ISO/IEC 15408-1(1999-12-01), Information Technology — Security Techniques — Evaluation Criteria for IT Security — Part 1: Introduction and General Model.
20. ISO/IEC 15408-2(1999-12-01), Information Technology — Security Techniques — Evaluation Criteria for IT Security — Part 2: Security Functional Requirements.
21. ISO/IEC 15408-3(1999-12-01), Information Technology — Security Techniques — Evaluation Criteria for IT Security — Part 3: Security Assurance Requirements.
22. ISO/IEC PDTR 15446(2001-04), Information Technology — Security Techniques — Guide for the Production of Protection Profiles and Security Targets.
23. ISO/IEC 15504-1(2004) — Information Technology — Process Assessment — Part 1: Concepts and Vocabulary.
24. ISO/IEC 15504-2(2004) — Information Technology — Process Assessment — Part 2: Performing an Assessment.
25. ISO/IEC 15504-3(2004) — Information Technology — Process Assessment — Part 3: Guidance on Performing an Assessment.
26. ISO/IEC 15504-4(2004) — Information Technology — Process Assessment — Part 4: Guidance on Use for Process Improvement and Process Capability Determination.
27. ISO/IEC 15504-5(2005) — Information Technology — Process Assessment — Part 5: An Exemplar Process Assessment Model.
28. ISO/IEC 17799(2000-12-01) — Information Technology — Code of Practice for Information Security Management.
29. ISO/IEC 21827(2002-10-17), Information Technology — Systems Security Engineering — Capability Maturity Model (SSE-CMM®).
30. NERC Reliability Functional Model: Function Definitions and Responsible Entities, North America Electric Reliability Council, version 2, 10 February 2004.
31. Standard CIP-002-1 — Cyber Security — Critical Cyber Assets, North America Electric Reliability Council (NERC), April 2006.
32. Standard CIP-003-1 — Cyber Security — Security Management Controls, North America Electric Reliability Council (NERC), April 2006.
33. Standard CIP-004-1 — Cyber Security — Personnel and Training, North America Electric Reliability Council (NERC), April 2006.
34. Standard CIP-005-1 — Cyber Security — Electronic Security, North America Electric Reliability Council (NERC), April 2006.

35. Standard CIP-006-1 — Cyber Security — Physical Security, North America Electric Reliability Council (NERC), April 2006.
36. Standard CIP-007-1 — Cyber Security — System Security Management, North America Electric Reliability Council (NERC), April 2006.
37. Standard CIP-008-1 — Cyber Security — Incident Reporting and Response Planning, North America Electric Reliability Council (NERC), April 2006.
38. Standard CIP-009-1 — Cyber Security — Recovery Plans, North America Electric Reliability Council (NERC), April 2006.
39. Implementation Plan for Cyber Security Standards CIP-002-1 through CIP-009-1, North America Electric Reliability Council (NERC), April 2006.
40. SAE JA 1006: Software Support Concept, Society for Aerospace Engineering (SAE), June 1999.
41. SAE JA 1004: Software Supportability Program Standard, Society for Aerospace Engineering (SAE), July 1998.
42. SAE JA 1005, Software Supportability Program Implementation Guide, Society for Aerospace Engineering (SAE), (draft) March 2000.

United States

43. FAA Order 1370.89, Information Operation Conditions, 25 August 2003.
44. FAA Order 1600.1E, FAA Personnel Security Program, 25 July 2005.
45. FEMA 452, Risk Assessment: A How To Guide to Mitigate Potential Terrorist Attacks against Buildings, January 2005.
46. FIPS PUB 199 — Standards for Security Categorization of Federal Information and Information Systems, National Institute of Standards and Technology, December 2003.
47. FIPS PUB 200 — Security Controls for Federal Information Systems, National Institute of Standards and Technology, scheduled for December 2005; replaces SP 800-53, including Annexes 1 through 3.
48. FIPS PUB 201 — Personal Identity Verification (PIV) of Federal Employees and Contractors, National Institute of Standards and Technology, 25 February 2005.
48a SP 800-79 — Guidelines for the Certification and Accreditation of PIV Card Issuing Organizations, draft 1.1, National Institute of Standards and Technology, June 2005.
48b *Federal Identity Management Handbook,* public draft, U.S. General Services Administration, March 2005.
48c SP 800-76 — Biometric Data Specification for Personal Identity Verification (draft), National Institute of Standards and Technology, 24 January 2005.
48d SP 800-73 — Interfaces for Personal Identity Verification, National Institute of Standards and Technology, April 2005.
49. SP 800-18 — Guide for Developing Security Plans for Information Technology Systems, National Institute of Standards and Technology, December 1998.
50. SP 800-30 — Risk Management Guide for Information Technology Systems, National Institute of Standards and Technology, July 2002.
51. SP 800-37 — Guide for the Security Certification and Accreditation of Federal Information Systems, National Institute of Standards and Technology, May 2004.
52. SP 800-53 — Recommended Security Controls for Federal Information Systems, February 2005.
53. Annex 1 to SP 800-53 — Recommended Security Controls for Federal Information Systems: Minimum Security Controls, Low Baseline, February 2005.
54. Annex 2 to SP 800-53 — Recommended Security Controls for Federal Information Systems: Minimum Security Controls, Moderate Baseline, February 2005.

55. Annex 3 to SP 800-53 — Recommended Security Controls for Federal Information Systems: Minimum Security Controls, High Baseline, February 2005.
56. SP 800-53A — Guide for Assessing the Security Controls in Federal Information Systems, National Institute of Standards and Technology, Spring 2005.
57. SP 800-55 — Security Metrics Guide for Information Technology Systems, National Institute of Standards and Technology, July 2003.
57a. SP 800-80 — Guide for Developing Performance Metrics for Information Security (draft), National Institute of Standards and Technology, May 2006.
58. SP 800-60 — Volume I: Guide for Mapping Types of Information and Information Systems to Security Categories, National Institute of Standards and Technology, July 2004.
59. SP 800-60 — Volume II: Appendices to Guide for Mapping Types of Information and Information Systems to Security Categories, National Institute of Standards and Technology, July 2004.
60. SP 800-66 — An Introductory Resource Guide for Implementing the Health Insurance Portability and Accountability Act (HIPAA) Security Rule, National Institute of Standards and Technology (draft), May 2004.

B.2 Policies, Regulations, and Other Government Documents

This section lists contemporary laws and regulations related to security and privacy. Given that most local and national laws and regulations tend to be modified over time, for implementation or assessment purposes, be sure to verify that you have the current approved version.

International

61. The Personal Health Information Act, Statutes of Canada, 28 June 1997
62. Bill C-6: Personal Information Protection and Electronic Documents Act (PIPEDA), Statutes of Canada, 13 April 2000.
63. Basel II: The International Convergence of Capital Measurement and Capital Management: A Revised Framework, Basel Committee on Banking Supervision, June 2004.
64. Data Protection Act, 1998, Chapter 29, United Kingdom.
65. Directive 95/46/EC, The Data Protection Directive, European Parliament and of the Council, 24 October 1995.
66. High-Level Principles for the Cross-Border Implementation of the New Accord, Basel Committee on Banking Supervision, August 2003
66a. Principles for the Home-Host Recognition of AMA Operational Risk Capital, Basel Committee on Banking Supervision, January 2004.
67. Implementation of Basel II: Practical Considerations, Basel Committee on Banking Supervision, July 2004.
68. OECD Guidelines for the Security of Information Systems and Networks: Towards a Culture of Security, Organization for Economic Co-operation and Development, 25 July 2002.
68a. Implementation Plan for the OECD Guidelines for the Security of Information Systems and Networks: Towards a Culture of Security, Organization for Economic Co-operation and Development, 2 July 2003.
68b. Summary of Responses to the Survey on the Implementation of the OECD Guidelines for the Security of Information Systems and Networks: Towards a Culture of Security, Organization for Economic Co-operation and Development, 24 September 2004.

69. OECD Guidelines on the Protection of Privacy and Trans-Border Flows of Personal Data, 23 September 1980.

69a. Ministerial Declaration on the Protection of Privacy on Global Networks, Organization of Economic Co-operation and Development, Ottawa, 7–9 October 1998.

70. Background Material on Biometrics and Enhanced Network Systems for the Security of International Travel, Organization for Economic Co-operation and Development, 23 December 2004.

71. OECD Guidelines for Cryptography Policy, Organization for Economic Co-operation and Development, 1997.

71a. 1997 OECD Cryptography Guidelines: Recommendation of the Council, Organization for Economic Co-operation and Development, 27 March 1997.

71b. Report on Background and Issues of Cryptography Policy, Organization for Economic Co-operation and Development, 1997.

United States

72. E-Government Act, Public Law 107-347 — Title III — Federal Information Security Management Act, U.S. Congress, 17 December 2002.

72a. OMB Memo M-04-25, FY2004 Reporting Instructions for the Federal Information Security Management Act, 23 August 2004.

72b. OMB Memo from M. Forman, Certification and Accreditation — What an Agency Can Do Now, 3 July 2003.

72c. OMB Memo M-05-15, FY2005 Reporting Instructions for the Federal Information Security Management Act and Privacy Officer, 13 June 2005.

72d. OMB Memo M-06-20, FY2006 Reporting Instructions for the Federal Information Security Management Act and Agency Privacy Management, 17 July 2006.

72e. OMB Memo M-06-16, Protection of Sensitive Agency Information, 23 June 2006.

72f. OMB Memo M-06-19. Reporting Incidents Involving Personally Identifiable Information and Incorporating the Cost of Security in Agency Information Technology Investments, 12 July 2006.

73. GAO-04-354, Critical Infrastructure Protection: Challenges and Efforts to Secure Control Systems, Report to Congress, U.S. General Accounting Office, March 2004.

74. GAO-05-551, Information Security: Radio Frequency Identification Technology in the Federal Government, May 2005.

75. Gramm-Leach-Bliley Act, Public Law 106-102, Title V — Privacy, U.S. Congress, 12 November 1999.

75a. Gramm-Leach-Bliley Act, Department of the Treasury — Privacy of Consumer Financial Information; Final Rule, 12 CFR Parts 40, 216, 332, and 573, 1 June 2000.

75b. Gramm-Leach-Bliley Act, Federal Trade Commission — Privacy of Consumer Financial Information; Final Rule, 16 CFR Part 313, 24 May 2000.

75c. Gramm-Leach-Bliley Act, Securities and Exchange Commission — Privacy of Consumer Financial Information (Regulation S-P); Rules, 17 CFR Part 248, 29 July 2000.

75d. Gramm-Leach-Bliley Act, National Credit Union Administration — Privacy of Consumer Financial Information; Requirements for Insurance; Final Rule, 12 CFR Parts 716 and 741, 18 May 2000.

75e. Gramm-Leach-Bliley Act, Federal Trade Commission — Standards for Safeguarding Customer Information; Final Rule, 16 CFR Part 314, 23 May 2002.

75f. How to Comply with the Privacy of Consumer Information Rule of the Gramm-Leach-Bliley Act: A Guide for Small Business, Federal Trade Commission, July 2002.

76. Right to Financial Privacy Act of 1978, Public Law 95-630, as codified at 12 U.S.C. Chapter 35.

77. Privacy Protection Act of 1980, Public Law 96-440, as codified at 42 U.S.C. § 2000aa.

78. Electronic Communication Privacy Act of 1986, Public Law 99-508, as codified at 18 U.S.C. Chapter 121.

79. Computer Matching and Privacy Act of 1988, Public Law 100-503, as codified at 5 U.S.C. § 552a.

80. Health Insurance Portability and Accountability Act of 1996, Public Law 104-91, U.S. Congress, 21 August 1996.

81. Health Insurance Reform: Part II — Department of Health and Human Services — Security Standards; Final Rule, 45 CFR Parts 160, 162, 164, 20 February 2003.

82. Health Insurance Reform: Part V — Department of Health and Human Services — Standards for Privacy of Individually Identifiable Health Information; Final Rule, 45 CFR Parts 160 and 164, 14 August 2002.

83. Homeland Security Presidential Directive/HSPD-1: Organization and Operation of the Homeland Security Council, 29 October 2001.

84. Homeland Security Presidential Directive/HSPD-2: Combating Terrorism through Immigration Policies, 29 October 2001.

85. Homeland Security Presidential Directive/HSPD-3: Homeland Security Advisory System, March 2002.

86. Homeland Security Presidential Directive/HSPD-4: [unclassified version] National Strategy to Combat Weapons of Mass Destruction, December 2002.

87. Homeland Security Presidential Directive/HSPD-5: Management of Domestic Incidents, 28 February 2003.

88. Homeland Security Presidential Directive/HSPD-6: Integration and Use of Screening Information, 16 September 2003.

89. Homeland Security Presidential Directive/HSPD-7: Critical Infrastructure Identification, Prioritization, and Protection, 17 December 2003.

90. Homeland Security Presidential Directive/HSPD-8: National Preparedness, 17 December 2003.

91. Homeland Security Presidential Directive/HSPD-9: Defense of United States Agriculture and Food, 30 January 2004.

92. Homeland Security Presidential Directive/HSPD-10: Bio-defense for the 21st Century, 28 April 2004.

93. Homeland Security Presidential Directive/HSPD-11: Comprehensive Terrorist-Related Screening Procedures, 27 August 2004.

94. Homeland Security Presidential Directive/HSPD-12: Policy for a Common Identification Standard for Federal Employees and Contractors, 27 August 2004.

94a. OMB Memo M-06-18, Acquisition of Products and Services for Implementation of HSPD-12, 30 June 2006.

95. Video Privacy Protection Act of 1988, Public Law 100-618, as codified at 18 U.S.C. § 2710.

96. Corporate and Auditing Accountability, Responsibility, and Transparency Act, known as the Sarbanes-Oxley Act of 2002.

97. In Brief: The Financial Privacy Requirements of the Gramm-Leach-Bliley Act, Federal Trade Commission, February 2005.

98. Real ID Act of 2005, Public Law 109-13, as codified at 49 USC § 30301.

99. Interim National Infrastructure Protection Plan, Department of Homeland Security, February 2005.

100. National Information Assurance (IA) Glossary, Committee on National Security Systems (CNSS) Instruction 4009, May 2003.

101. OMB Circular No. A-130, Appendix III, Security of Federal Automated Information Resources, 26 March 2003.

102. Telemarketer Protection Act of 1991, Public Law 102-243, as codified at 47 U.S.C. § 227.

103. Letter from Representative Carolyn Maloney to Jo Anne Barnhart, Commissioner of the Social Security Administration, 27 May 2005.

104. USA Patriot Act of 2001, Public Law 107-56, U.S. Congress, 26 October 2001.

105. Report of the Best Practices and Metrics Teams, Corporate Information Security Working Group, Subcommittee on Technology, Information Policy, Intergovernmental Relations and the Census, Government Reform Committee, U.S. House of Representatives, 10 January 2005.

106. The National Plan for Research and Development in Support of Critical Infrastructure Protection, The Executive Office of the President, Office of Science and Technology Policy and The Department of Homeland Security, Science and Technology Directorate, 2005.

107. The National Strategy to Secure Cyberspace, Department of Homeland Security, February 2003.

108. The Privacy Act of 1974, Public Law 93-579, as codified at 5 U.S.C. § 552a (as Amended).

108a. OMB Memo M-05-08, Designation of Senior Agency Officials for Privacy, 11 February 2005.

B.3 Publications

109. @stake Labs, "Defined Security Creates Efficiencies," *Secure Business Quarterly,* Fourth Quarter 2001.

110. A Status Report of the Auditor General of Canada to the House of Commons, Office of the Auditor General of Canada, February 2005.

111. Akhir, T., Return on Security Investment, EI7010-Keamanan Sisten Lanjut, Semester III, Department Teknik Elektro — Institut Teknologi Bandung, 2004.

112. Ammann, P., Barnes, B., Jajodia, S., and Sibley, E. (Eds.), *Proceedings, Computer Security, Dependability, and Assurance: From Needs to Solutions,* IEEE Computer Society Press, 1998.

113. Armstrong, I., "Budgeting for Infosecurity: Are Funds Growing?" *SC Magazine,* April 2002.

114. Armstrong, I., "Failure Must Be Part of the Plan," *SC Magazine,* pp. 24–28, May 2005.

115. *Assessment Guide for U.S. Legislative, Regulatory, and Listing Exchange Requirements Affecting Internal Auditing,* The Institute of Internal Auditors (IIA) Research Foundation, 10 November 2004.

116. *Asset Protection and Security Management Handbook,* POA Publishing LLC, Auerbach Publications, 2003.

117. Bayuk, J.L., "Security Metrics," *Computer Security Journal,* Computer Security Institute, January 2001.

118. Beaver, K. and Herold, R., *The Practical Guide to HPAA Privacy and Security Compliance,* Auerbach Publications, 2003.

119. Beaver, K., *Healthcare Information Systems,* 2nd edition, Auerbach Publications, 2002.

120. Bieda, J., *Practical Product Assurance Management,* ASQ Quality Press, 1997.

121. Blakely, B., "An Imprecise but Necessary Calculation," *Secure Business Quarterly,* Fourth Quarter 2001.

122. Bolz, F., Dodonis, K.J., and Schultz, D.P., *The Counterterrorism Handbook: Tactics, Procedures, and Techniques,* 2nd edition, CRC Press, 2002.

123. Briney, A., "Doom or Boom? Fearing the Worst, Companies Are Diversifying Their Security Spending," *Information Security,* April 2004.

124. Brenner, B., "HIPAA Security Compliance Not Just an IT Problem," Search Security.com, 30 September 2004.

125. Buskin, A. and Schaen, S., *The Privacy Act of 1974: A Reference Manual for Compliance,* System Development Corporation, McLean, VA, 1975.

126. Caralli, R., *Managing for Enterprise Security,* Software Engineering Institute, Carnegie Mellon University, December 2004.

127. Chaula, J.A., Security Metrics and Public Key Infrastructure Interoperability Testing, Licentiate thesis, Department Computer and Systems Sciences, Stockholm University and Royal Institute of Technology, 12 December 2003.

128. Clafin, B., "Information Risk Management at 3Com," *Security Business Quarterly,* Fourth Quarter 2001.

129. "Compliance: Changing Our Approach to Data," *Connected,* Hewlett-Packard e-newsletter, July 2004.

130. DeBrino, R., "HIPAA Compliance: One Organization's Tale," *CIO Decisions,* p. 29, May 2005.

131. Dunn, L., Explicit Routing: The Fish at 4+yrs, Cisco, 2002.

132. Earthlink: Security from the Inside: A Dialogue with Lisa Ekman and Lisa Hoyt, *Secure Business Quarterly,* Fourth Quarter 2001.

133. Emam, K., Drouin, J., and Melo, W., *SPICE: The Theory and Practice of Software Process Improvement and Capability Determination,* IEEE Computer Society Press, 1998.

134. *Energy Security,* Breakwater Security Associates, February 2005

135. *Energy and Utility Security Standards,* Breakwater Security Associates, February 2005

136. Evans, N., High Risk, High Rewards, *Optimize,* TechWeb Business Technology Network, March 2002, Issue 5.

137. Fenton, N. and Pfleeger, S., *Software Metrics: A Rigorous and Practical Approach,* International Thomson Computer Press, 2nd edition, 1997.

138. Fenton, N., Whitty, R., and Iizuka, Y. (Eds.), *Software Quality Assurance and Measurement: A Worldwide Perspective,* International Thomson Computer Press, 1995.

139. Feudo, C., "Beyond A Security Metrics Paradigm," *Interactive Technologies 2004 Conference,* Society for Applied Learning Technology.

140. "FTC Enforces Gramm-Leach-Bliley Act's Safeguards Rule against Mortgage Companies," Federal Trade Commission Press Release, 16 November 2004.

141. Fuldner, G., Sensitive Information in Financial Services, for CS 457a course, Yale, 14 November 2003.

142. Foundstone Quantifies ROI of Proactive and Automated Vulnerability Management, foundstone.com, 6 February 2004.

143. Garigue, R. and Stefaniu, M., "Information Security Governance Reporting," *EDP Audit,* 76-15-11, Auerbach Publications, October 2003.

144. Geer, D.E., "Making Choices to Show ROI," *Secure Business Quarterly,* Fourth Quarter 2001.

145. Geer, D.E., Soo Hoo, K., and Jaquith, A., "Why the Future Belongs to the Quants," *Security and Privacy Magazine,* IEEE, July 2003, pp. 24–32.

146. Gerard, P., *Risk Based E-Business Testing,* Artech House, 2002.

147. Gilb, T., "Quantifying Security," *Proceedings of International Conference on Practical Software Quality and Testing,* May 2–6, 2005.

148. Gilb, T. and Graham, D., *Software Inspection,* Addison-Wesley, 1993.

149. Gilliam, D., Wolfe, T., Sherif, J., and Bishop, M., "Software Security Checklist for the Software Life Cycle," *Proceedings 12th IEEE International Workshop on Enabling Technologies: Infrastructure for Collaborative Enterprises,* 2003.

150. Gossels, J. and Noll, L.C., "HIPAA Compliance," System Experts Corporation, 2004.

151. Gray, G.L., *Changing Internal Audit Practices in the New Paradigm: The Sarbanes-Oxley Environment,* The Institute of Internal Auditors Research Foundation, 2004.

152. Hale, R., *The Chief Security Officer: A Guide to Protecting People, Facilities, and Information,* Auerbach Publications, 2004.

153. Hecht, H., *Systems Reliability and Failure Prevention,* Artech House, 2004.

154. Herrmann, D., "Common Criteria Cleared for Take Off at the U.S. Federal Aviation Administration," *Information Security Bulletin,* December 2004, pp. 379–388.

155. Herrmann, D., *Using the Common Criteria for IT Security Evaluation,* Auerbach Publications, 2003.

156. Herrmann, D., *A Practical Guide to Security Engineering and Information Assurance,* Auerbach Publications, 2002.

157. Herrmann, D. and Keith, S., "Application of Common Criteria to Telecom Services," *Computer Security Journal,* 17(2), 21–28, 2001.

158. Herrmann, D., *Software Safety and Reliability: Techniques, Approaches, and Standards of Key Industrial Sectors,* IEEE Computer Society Press, 1999.

159. Herrmann, D., "Sample Implementation of the Littlewood Holistic Model for Analyzing Software Safety and Reliability," *Proceedings of the Annual Reliability and Maintainability Symposium (RAMS'98),* IEEE, 1998.

160. Hollingworth, D, *Towards Threat, Attack, and Vulnerability Taxonomies,* Network Associates Laboratories, 2002.

161. INEEL/EXT-04-02428, rev. 0, "A Comparison of Electrical Sector Cyber Security Standards and Guidelines," Idaho National Engineering and Environmental Lab, 2 November 2004.

162. Information Security and Cyber Crime Update, *Cooley Godward LLP e-newsletter,* 3 October 2003.

163. Information Security Governance: A Call to Action, Corporate Governance Task Force Report, National Cyber Security Summit Task Force, April 2004.

164. Information Security under the Basel II Accord, ContinuityCentral.com, 30 January 2004.

165. Information Technology for Counter-terrorism: Immediate Actions and Future Possibilities, Computer Science and Telecommunications Board (CSTB), National Academies of Science, National Academies Press, 2003.

166. Jackson, W., "New Federal ID Standard Approved," *Government Computer News,* 25 February 2005.

167. Novak, R., Threat of the Auditors: The Sarbanes-Oxley Act Is a Danger to Growth, *The Washington Post,* p. A31, 7 April 2005.

168. Jaquith, A., The Security of Applications: Not All Are Created Equal, Research Report, @stake.com, February 2002.

169. Jelen, G., "SSE-CMM® Security Metrics," Profiles, Assurance and Metrics Committee, International Systems Security Engineering Association, presented at *NIST Workshop,* Washington, D.C., June 2000.

170. Johnson, A., "Cyber Security for the Bulk Electric System," *NERC Cyber Security Workshops,* January and March 2005.

171. Johnson, M., Passing the Audit, *CIO Decisions,* pp. 48–51, April 2005.

172. June, D.L., *Protection, Security, and Safeguards: Practical Approaches and Perspectives,* Auerbach Publications, 2000.

173. Kalvar, S.T., Focusing Measurements and Metrics on Security, CNET Networks, Inc., 2003.

174. Kan, S.H., *Metrics and Models in Software Quality Engineering,* Addison-Wesley, 1995.

175. Karofsky, E., "Executive Summary: Insight into Return on Security Investment," *Security Business Quarterly,* Fourth Quarter 2001.

176. Knight, M., Compliance Tops IT Priority List, AccountancyAge.com/news, 10 November 2004.

177. Krist, M.A., *Standard for Auditing Computer Applications,* Auerbach Publications, 1998.

178. Leo, R., *The HIPAA Program Reference Handbook,* Auerbach Publications, 2004.

179. Levandowki, T., Gramm-Leach-Bliley Act Privacy Requirements, Vice President and Assistant General Counsel, First Union Corporation/Educaid, 2002.

180. Levi, S.T. and Agrawala, A.K., *Fault Tolerant System Design,* McGraw-Hill, Inc., 1994.

181. Lindstrom, P. "Security: Measuring Up," *Information Security*, February 2005, pp. 48–55.

182. Lovejoy, K., "Know Your Customers Inside & Out: The Best Way to Work with the Patriot Act," *SC Magazine,* p. 78, May 2005.

183. Lineman, D.J., A Brief History of Regulatory Time, InformationShield.com, 2004.

184. Lyu, M. (Ed.), *Handbook of Software Reliability Engineering,* IEEE Computer Society Press, 1996.

185. MacKay, R. and Smith. M., "Bill C-13: An Act to Amend the Criminal Code, Capital Markets Fraud and Evidence Gathering," LS-469E, Legislative Summaries, Library of Parliament, Parliamentary Information and Research Service, 2004.

186. *Making the Nation Safer: The Role of Science and Technology in Countering Terrorism,* National Academies of Science, National Academies Press, 2002.

187. McCollum, T., "U.S. Working Group Reports on Security Metrics," *IT Audit*, Institute of Internal Auditors, Vol. 8, 1 February 2005.

188. McCollum, T., U.S. Working Group Issues Security Proposals, *IT Audit*, Institute of Internal Auditors, Vol. 7, 1 June 2004.

189. McConnel, P., A 'Standards-Based' Approach to Operational Risk Management under Basel II, ContinuityCentral.com, 14 January 2005.

190. McCracken, *A. Practical Guide to Business Continuity Assurance,* Artech House, 2004.

191. Hard Problem List, Infosec Research Council (IRC), November 2005.

192. Mimoso, M., Keeping the Data and Oil Flowing, *Information Security,* pp. 44–48, May 2005.

193. Miller, J., "Whose in Charge of Privacy Issues? Agencies Have until March 11 to Figure It Out," *Government Computer News,* GCN.com, 17 February 2005.

193a. Miller, J., "Is Your Agency Required to Have a Privacy Officer?," *Government Computer News,* GCN.com, 13 December 2004.

194. Mizzi, A., Return on Information Security Investment: Are You Spending Enough? Are You Spending Too Much?, Geocities.com/amz, January 2005.

195. Musa, J., Iannino, A., and Okumoto, K., *Software Reliability: Measurement, Prediction, Application,* McGraw-Hill, Inc., 1987.

196. Oblivion, B., "Secure Hardware Design," Black Hat Briefings, 26–27 July 2000.

197. O'Connor, P., *Practical Reliability Engineering,* 3rd edition, John Wiley & Sons, Ltd., 1991.

198. *Out-Think Shrink — What Every Retailer Should Know about Loss Prevention,* IntelliQ Ltd., 2004.

199. Peltier, T., *Information Security Risk Analysis,* Auerbach Publications, 2001.

200. Perin, M., "Utilities Face Deadline from NERC to Meet FERC Security Mandate," Energy Beat, *Houston Business Journal,* 10 January 2005.

201. Petco Settles FTC Charges, Federal Trade Commission Press Release, 17 November 2004.

202. Peterson, J.K., *Understanding Surveillance Technologies: Spy Devices, Their Origins, and Applications,* CRC Press, 2001.

203. Pullum, L., *Software Fault Tolerance: Techniques and Implementation,* Artech House, 2001.

204. Pyzdek, T. and Berger, R. (Eds.), *Quality Engineering Handbook,* Marcel Dekker, Inc. and ASQC Press, 1992.

205. Quainton, D., "We Must Learn to Love Compliance," *SC Magazine*, February 2005, pp. 28–31.

206. Radding, A., "Meeting the Challenges of Security Mandates," *CIO Decisions,* pp. 26–28, May 2005.

207. Rothke, B., "Sticking Plaster that Won't Stick: Why HIPAA Has Failed to Achieve the Same Level of Success as SOX," *SC Magazine,* pp. 45–46, May 2005.

208. Savage, M., "Will HIPAA Bite?," *SC Magazine,* pp. 40–42, May 2005.

209. Schulmeyer, G. and McManus, J. (Eds.), *Handbook of Software Quality Assurance,* 2nd edition, International Thomson Computer Press, 1996.

210. Schulmeyer, G. and McManus, J. (Eds.), *Total Quality Management for Software,* International Thomson Computer Press, 1996.

211. Sherwood, J., "SABSA® Security Architecture," Netigy Corporation, 2000

212. "Side-by-Side Comparison of Major Privacy Regulations and Laws Affecting Health Insurers," Health Insurance Association of America (HIAA), Department of Policy and Information, 23 October 2000.

213. Silverman, K., *Lightning Man: The Accursed Life of Samuel F.B. Morse,* Alfred A. Knopf, 2003.

214. Soo Hoo, K., *Metrics of Network Integrity,* Sygate Technologies, Inc., July 2004.

215. Soo Hoo, K., Sudbury, A., and Jaquith, A., "Tangible ROI through Secure Software Engineering," *Secure Business Quarterly,* Fourth Quarter 2001.

216. Stephenson, P., "S_TRAIS: A Method for Security Requirements Engineering Using a Standards-Based Network Security Reference Model," Netigy Corporation, 2001.

217. Sterneckert, A.B., *Critical Incident Management,* Auerbach Publications, 2003.

218. Summary of Sarbanes-Oxley Act of 2002, American Institute of Certified Public Accountants (AICPA), 2005.

219. Summers, C. and Weers, K., *Security Metrics Consortium Founded by Top CSOs/CISOs,* Shift Communications, 24 February 2004.

220. Thieme, R., "What Insurance Can — and Can't — Do for Security Risks," *Secure Business Quarterly,* Fourth Quarter 2001.

221. Thomas, D., Security Must Be Key Part of Outsourcing, AccountancyAge.com/features, 18 November 2004.

222. Tipton, H.F. and Krause, M., *Information Security Management Handbook,* 4th edition, Auerbach Publications, 2003.

223. Vaugn, R., Henning, R., and Siraj, A., "Information Assurance Measures and Metrics — State of Practice and Proposed Taxonomy," *Proceedings of the 36th Hawaii International Conference on System Sciences (HICSS-03),* IEEE Computer Society, 2003.

224. Utilities Face Deadline for Security Mandate, GreatRiverEnergy.com, February 2005.

225. Walsh, L. and Taylor, D., "Big Brother's Watchful Eyes," *Information Security,* pp. 34–42, May 2005.

226. Weinstock, C. and Rushby, J., *Dependable Computing for Critical Applications — 7,* IEEE Computer Society Press, 1999.

227. Wolstenholme, L.C., *Reliability Modeling: A Statistical Approach,* Chapman & Hall/CRC Press, 1999.

228. Wylder, J., *Strategic Information Security,* Auerbach Publications, 2003.

229. Kehaulani-Goo, S., "House Endorses Altering Security Alerts," *The Washington Post,* pp. A9, 19 May 2005.

230. Associated Press, "Expanded Patriot Act to Be Proposed," *The Washington Post,* pp. A8, 19 May 2005.

231. Mark, R., "Swindle: Somebody Has to Pay," *Information Security News,* internetnews.com, 17 May 2005.

232. USA Patriot Act Sunset, Electronic Privacy Information Center, epic.org, 19 May 2005.

233. Spotlight on Surveillance: Homeland Security ID Card Is Not So Secure, Electronic Privacy Information Center, epic.org, April 2005.

234. Letter to Senate Select Committee on Intelligence, American Booksellers Association, et al. (24 co-signers), 23 May 2005.

235. Letter to Senate Select Committee on Intelligence, Electronic Privacy Information Center, epic.org, 23 May 2005.

236. Spotlight on Surveillance: Transportation Agency's Plan to X-ray Travelers Should Be Stripped of Funding, Electronic Privacy Information Center, epic.org, June 2005.

237. "Backscatter" X-Ray Screening Technology, Electronic Privacy Information Center, epic.org, June 2005.

238. Rapiscan Secure 1000, Rapiscan Systems Product Brochure #9150068-1, undated.

239. Just Say "9/11" to Obtain Social Security Information, EPIC FOIA Notes #4, 26 April 2005, Electronic Privacy Information Center, epic.org.

240. Zeraga, M., The Right Way to Get SOX Compliant, *CIO Decisions,* June 2005, p. 60.

241. "Extreme Availability: NYSE's New IT Infrastructure Puts Hand-Held Wireless Terminals in Brokers' Hands," *Communications News,* June 2005, pp. 12–17.

242. Allard, Pierre-Paul, "Ensure Data Center Resiliency: Intelligent networks can lower costs and improve security and business continuity," *Communications News,* June 2005, pp. 40–43.

243. Patriot Second Act," *The Washington Post,* 13 June 2005, pp. A18.

244. Silverman, E., Reining in Risk Turns into Big Business: Sarbanes-Oxley Creates Winners, *The Washington Post,* 13 June 2005, pp. D1 and D9.

245. "Senate Panel Approves New FBI Powers for Patriot Act," *The Washington Post Express,* 8 June 2005, p. 3.

246. Miller, J., "OMB Releases FIMSA Guidance with Focus on Privacy," *Government Computer News,* gcn.com, 15 June 2005.

247. Krim, J. and Barbaro, M., "40 Million Credit Card Numbers Hacked: Data Breached at Processing Center," *The Washington Post,* 18 June 2005, pp. A1 and A10.

248. Lipowicz, A., "California to Revisit RFID Restrictions," *Government Computer News,* gcn.com, 24 June 2005.

249. Mosquera, M., "State Tells Lawmakers Biometrics Will Ensure Identity," *Government Computer News,* gcn.com, 23 June 2005.

250. Lancaster, J., "Outsourcing in India in Crisis over Scam: British Paper Alleges Security Breach," *The Washington Post,* 25 June 2005, p. A18.

251. Olsen, F., "OMB Modifies Security Reporting," *Federal Computer Week,* fcw.com, 20 June 2005.

252. Jackson, W., "Draft Guidelines Released for Certifying PIV Card Issuers," *Government Computer News,* gcn.com, 20 June 2005.

253. Dizard III, W.P., "GAO Study of RFID Technology, Policy Seen Flawed," *Government Computer News,* gcn.com, 31 May 2005

254. Lerner, E., "Biometric Identification," *The Industrial Physicist,* 6(1), 20–23, 2000.

255. Rendell, A., "Security, Privacy, and Fraud Research," *Safety Systems,* 9(2), 13–15, 2000.

256. Jones, B. and Deane, D., "Between Friends: Don't Extend Trust Too Far," *SC Magazine,* February 2005, pp. 39–40.

257. Sterlicchi, J., "Stop That Fraud: Fingerprints Will Secure Texas Systems," *SC Magazine,* February 2005, p. 42.

258. Armstrong, I., "Would You Show This Card to Mom," *SC Magazine,* March 2005, p. 15.

259. www.soxonline.com.

260. Rasch, M., "Sarbanes-Oxley for IT Security," securityfocus.com, 3 May 2005.

261. IT Control Objectives for Sarbanes-Oxley, IT Governance Institute, April 2004.

262. Jackson, W., "New FISMA Standard Advances toward Finalization," *Government Computer News,* gcn.com, 19 July 2005.

263. Starkman, D., "Enron Fraud Pacts Set Records: CIBC Deal Brings Total to $7 Billion," *The Washington Post,* 3 August 2005, pp. D1–D2.

264. Cullinane, D., "Law is Nothing without Enforcement," *SC Magazine,* August 2005, p. 20.

265. Mix, S., Securing the Electric Grid — NERC CIP Standards, *Infragard 2005 National Conference,* 8–11 August 2005, Washington, D.C.

266. Payment Card Industry Data Security Standard, Visa U.S.A., Inc., December 2004.

267. Mont, M.C., Bramhall, P., and Chan, K.N., "Management and Enforcement of Privacy Obligations in Enterprises," *Information Security Bulletin,* September 2005, pp. 245–258.

268. Monchuk, J., Alberta Privacy Office: Hi-Tech Fax Machines a Security Risk, cnews.canoe.ca., 20 March 2005.

269. Lotem, A. and Moiseles, M., Using Attack Simulation and Risk Models for Automated Vulnerability Management, *Information Security Bulletin,* March 2005, pp. 45–54.

270. Denning, D., *Information Warfare and Security,* Addison-Wesley, 1999.

271. Rozenblit, M., *Security for Telecommunications Network Management,* IEEE, 1999.

272. Gollmann, D., *Computer Security,* John Wiley & Sons, 1999.

273. Rubin, A. and Geer, Jr., D., "A Survey of Web Security," *Computer,* 31(9), pp. 34–43, 1998.

274. Feghi, J., Feghi, J., and Williams, P., Digital Certificates: Applied Internet Security, Addison-Wesley, 1998.

275. Martin, J., *Design and Strategy for Distributed Data Processing,* Prentice-Hall, 1981.

276. Schneier, B., *Applied Cryptography: Protocols, Algorithms, and Source Code in C,* 2nd edition, John Wiley & Sons, 1995.

277. Tung, B., *Kerberos: A Network Authentication System,* Addison-Wesley, 1999.

278. Pankanti, S., Bolle, R., and Jain, A., "Biometrics: the Future of Identification," *Computer,* 33(2), 46–49, 2000.

279. Chadwick, D., "Smart Cards Aren't Always the Smart Choice," *Computer,* 32(12), 142–143, 1999.

280. Garber, L., "News Briefs: Companies Join Forces for Smart Card Standard," *Computer,* 31(11), 19–20, 1998.

281. Tilton, C., "An Emerging Biometric API Standard," *Computer,* 33(2), 130–132, 2000.

282. Frischoltz, T. and Dickmann, U., "Bio ID: A Multimodal Biometric Identification System," *Computer,* 33(2), 64–69, 2000.

283. Lerner, E., "Biometric Identification," *The Industrial Physicist,* 6(1), 20–23, 2000.

284. Hankins, M., "Trusted Gate Closes on Thin-Client Computer Network Security Holes," *SIGNAL,* December 1999, pp. 67–69.

285. Storey, N., Safety-Critical Computer Systems, Addison-Wesley, 1996.

286. Levenson, N., *Safeware: System Safety and Computers,* Addison-Wesley, 1995.

287. Jajoda, S., Ammann, P., and McCollum, C., "Surviving Information Warfare Attacks," *Computer,* 32(4), pp. 57–63, 1999.

288. Sander, T. and Tschudin, C., Toward Mobile Cryptography, *IEEE Symposium on Security and Privacy,* 1998, pp. 215–224.

289. Lindquist, U. and Jonssen, E., "A Map of Security Risks Associated with using COTS," *Computer,* 31(6), 60–66, 1998.

290. Ritter, T., "Cryptography: Is Staying with the Herd Really Best?," *Computer,* 32(8), 94–95, 1999.

291. Cheswick, W. and Bellovin, S., *Firewalls and Internet Security, Repelling the Wiley Hacker,* Addison-Wesley, 1994.

292. Tarman, T., Hutchinson, R., Pierson, L., Sholander, P., and Witzke, E., "Algorithm-Agile Encryption in ATM Networks," *Computer,* 31(9), 57–64, 1998.

293. Garber, L., "Melissa Virus Creates a New Type of Threat," *Computer,* 32(6), 16–19, 1999.

294. Morris, D., *Introduction to Communication Command and Control Systems,* Pergamon Press, 1977.

295. Wang, H., Lee, M., and Wang, C., "Consumer Privacy Concerns about Internet Marketing," *Communications of the ACM,* 41(3), 63–70, 1998.

296. Blackburn, N., "Can You Keep a Secret?," *The Jerusalem Post,* September 10, 1999, pp. 28–29.

297. Rindfleisch, T., "Privacy, Information Technology and Health Care," *Communications of the ACM,* 40(8), 92–100, 1997.

298. McDermid, J., *Issues in the Development of Safety-Critical Systems, Safety Critical Systems,* Chapman & Hall, 1993, pp. 16–42.

299. Deutertre, B. and Stavridou, V., A Model of Noninterference for Integrating Mixed Criticality Software Components, Weinstock, C. and Rushby, J. (Eds.), *Dependable Computing for Critical Applications 7,* IEEE, pp. 301–316, 1999.

300. Fraser, T., Badger, L., and Feldman, M., Hardening COTS Software with Generic Software Wrappers, *IEEE Symposium on Security and Privacy,* 1999.

301. Ybarra, M., "Resurging Business Challenges Hotel IT," *CIO Decisions,* January 2006, pp. 26–28.

302. Arbaugh, W., Davin, J., Farber, D., and Smith, J., "Security for Virtual Private Intranets," *Computer,* 31(9), 48–56, 1998.

303. Neumann, P., *Computer Related Risks,* Addison-Wesley, 1995.

304. Brewer, D., *Applying Security Techniques to Achieving Safety, Directions in Safety-Critical Systems,* Springer-Verlag, 1993, pp. 246–256.

305. Coe, E., "Maryland Unclear on New Driver's License Law: Real ID Act Will Mean Extra Time when Trying to Renew, Obtain Card," *Cumberland Times-News,* 5 December 2005, pp. 1A, 9A.

306. Powell, S.M., "Secret Court Modified Wiretap Requests: Intervention May Have Led Bush to Bypass Panel," *Seattle Post-Intelligencer,* 24 December 2005.

307. *System Safety Analysis Handbook,* 2nd edition, System Safety Society, July 1997.

308. Billings, C.W., *Grace Hopper: Navy Admiral and Computer Pioneer,* Enslow Publishers, 1989.

309. Kellman, L., House Renews USA Patriot Act; Bush to Sign, ABCnews.go.com, 8 March 2006.

310. Babington, C., Congress Votes to Renew Patriot Act, With Changes, *The Washington Post,* pp. A3, 8 March 2006

311. DeGarmo, E.P., Sullivan, W.G., and Canada, J.R., *Engineering Economy,* 7th edition, Macmillan Publishing Company, 1984.

312. Herrmann, D., Security and Privacy Metrics, invited presentation to *Federal Information Assurance Conference (FIAC),* Washington, D.C., October 2005.

Index

C

California, ban on public agency RFID tags, 302
Candidate metrics
    refining, 64, 65–66
    tailoring, 62–63
Capability Maturity Model (CMM), 45, 53, 117, 118, 756
Capacity loading, 598
Capacity management, 573, 576
    and service priority, 575
Card Systems Solutions Inc., security violations, 353
Cascade encryption, 503, 756
Case law, for cyber security, 702
Catastrophic consequences, 696
Cause consequence analysis, 598
Cell phone tracking, 5
Certificate revocation lists (CRLs), 513
Certification and accreditation (C&A), 618–619, 683, 756
    and competency, 458
    FISMA metrics, 286
    misuse of sacred numbers, 56–57
    for software engineers, 117
    specifying during concept formulation phase, 591
Certification and accreditation (C&A) boundaries, 40
Certification package, 756
Certifications, overreliance for competency requirements, 457
Chain of custody rules, 37–38
Change control, 657
    and configuration control, 659–660
    NERC standards, 320
    and system/security failures, 656
Change impact analysis, 598
Change requests, 659, 660
Chat rooms, clandestine surveillance of, 328
Chemical agents, 388
    likelihood worksheet, 394
    threat scenario, 390
Chief executive officer (CEO), hierarchical view, 49
Chief Information Officer (CIO), 756
    FISMA responsibilities, 282
Chief Information Security Officer (CISO), 756
Chief Privacy Officer, FISMA mandated, 287
Chief security officer (CSO), 688, 758
    hierarchical view, 49
ChoicePoint, Inc., 6
Cipher block chaining (CBC), 501
Cipher feedback (CFB), 501
Cipher modes of operation, 498, 501
CitiBank, India outsourcing scandal, 162
Citizenship, workforce analysis of, 470, 472

Civil rights, 335
    complaints of Patriot Act abuses, 341
    Patriot Act potential violations, 330
    public concerns about violations of, 334
Clean desk/clean screen policy, 416
Clear, complete, concise, correct, consistent, verifiable, 595, 599, 608, 610, 618, 645
Clipper chip wars, 218
CNACI background investigations, 447
Code of Federal Regulations (CFR), 157, 756
    CFR 314, 159
Cold stand-by, 85
Cold War, 329
Collateral damage, 385, 386, 387
Collection limitation principle, 524
    cross-comparison of international privacy regulations, 277
    in OECD Privacy Guidelines, 2, 215
Commercial off the shelf (COTS) software, 552, latent defects in603
    delivery, installation, and development, 624–625
    downfall of generic design, 628
    dynamic analysis of, 618–619
    integrating from multiple vendors, 608
    mismatch to operational environment, 609
    NERC measurement of integrity, 320
    prevalence of errors in, 554
    security policy software, 645
    security problems with, 103
    security requirements for, 595
    simplifying security architecture and design step with, 603
    specifying during concept formulation phase, 591
    untrusted status of, 570
Commissioner, in U.K. Data Protection Act, 244
Committee on National Security Systems (CNSS), 8
Commodities and Futures Traders Commission, 157
Common cause failures (CCFs), 85
    minimizing with information hiding, 105
Common Criteria evaluation assurance levels (EALs), 100
Common Identification Standard for Federal Employees and Contractors, 298–300
Common mode failure (CMF), 756
Common sense, use in metrics program design, 59
Communications and IT systems, metrics, 418–421
Community risk, 68, 756
Comparative analysis, 691, 749, 750
    in security ROI model, 713–715
    security ROI primitives/metrics/reports for, 735–738

Printed and bound by CPI Group (UK) Ltd, Croydon, CR0 4YY

17/10/2024

01775700-0008